CONFETTI ICE-CREAM
TOWER CAKES
PG. 158

LADIES' HOME
JOURNAL.®

Recipes
2000

Ladies' Home Journal® Books
Des Moines, Iowa

Ladies' Home Journal® Books
An Imprint of Meredith® Books

LADIES' HOME JOURNAL®

Recipes 2000

Project Editor: Kristi M. Fuller

Contributing Project Editor: Winifred Moranville

Contributing Editors: Sarah P. Basso,
   Spectrum Communication Services,
   Kelly Staikopoulos, Joyce Trollope

Art Director: Richard Michels

Graphic Designer: Kimberly B. Zarley

Copy Chief: Catherine Hamrick

Copy and Production Editor: Terri Fredrickson

Copy Editor: Kim Catanzarite

Proofreaders: Marcia Gilmer,
   Gretchen Kauffman, Susan J. Kling

Electronic Production Coordinator:
   Paula Forest

Editorial and Design Assistants: Judy Bailey,
   Mary Lee Gavin, Karen Schirm

Production Director: Douglas M. Johnston

Book Production Managers: Pam Kvitne,
   Marjorie J. Schenkelberg

MEREDITH® BOOKS

Editor in Chief: James D. Blume

Design Director: Matt Strelecki

Managing Editor: Gregory H. Kayko

Executive Food Editor: Jennifer Dorland Darling

Vice President, General Manager:
   Jamie L. Martin

LADIES' HOME JOURNAL®
MAGAZINE

Editor in Chief: Myrna Blyth

Food Editor: Jan Hazard

Associate Food Editor: Carol Prager

Assistant Editor: Jane Yagoda-Goodman

Recipe Testers: Cynthia DePersio,
   Sarah Reynolds, Michele Peters

Consumer Marketing Director: Beth von Linden

MEREDITH PUBLISHING GROUP

President, Publishing Group:
   Christopher M. Little

Vice President, Finance & Administration:
   Max Runciman

MEREDITH CORPORATION

Chairman and Chief Executive Officer:
   William T. Kerr

Chairman of the Executive Committee:
   E. T. Meredith III

COVER PHOTOGRAPH:

Chocolate-Caramel Cheesecake
(see recipe, page 270)
Photographer: Alan Richardson

TOMATO GALETTE
PG. 104

All of us at Meredith® Books are dedicated to providing you with the information and ideas you need to create delicious foods. We welcome your comments and suggestions. Write to us at: Meredith® Books, Food Editorial Department, 1716 Locust St., Des Moines, IA 50309-3023.

If you would like to order additional copies of this book, call 1-800-439-4119.

GRILLED TUNA
SALAD
PG. 94

Table of Contents

MELON
MEDLEY
PG. 217

ITALIAN HERO
CALZONES
PG. 72

Recipes
2000

Welcome back to the LHJ kitchen

MYRNA BLYTH

JAN HAZARD

Sharing is one our favorite words. We are proud to share with you our second annual cookbook filled with over 350 recipes from the Ladies' Home Journal® Kitchen.

Our triple-tested recipes assure you success even the first time you try them—and they have been created to suit your needs whether you're seeking a quick weeknight meal or a yummy dessert for a relaxing weekend treat.

We also gladly share our cooking tips, entertaining ideas and simple techniques. As an added bonus, many of the recipes have do-ahead instructions to help all of us cope with the demands of our busy lives.

The recipes have been created with you in mind to make in *your* kitchen. Here's to another year of great eating! See you in the kitchen.

Myrna Blyth • *Editor-in-Chief*

Jan Hazard • *Food Editor*

Recipes 2000

CAESAR SALAD
PG. 36

great
beginnings

CRAB ON CORNMEAL
PANCAKES
PG. 30

Start fresh with a first course sparked by colorful fruits and vegetables, aromatic herbs and outstanding cheeses. Whether it's cocktails under the stars or nibbles for the big game, our flavors from around the globe make every gathering out of this world.

finger foods free your guests

TUSCAN-STYLE
BRUSCHETTA
PG. 22

DEVILED EGGS AND
CUCUMBER CUPS
PG. 9
ARTICHOKE AND
TOMATO EMPANADAS
PG. 34
OLIVE AND CHEESE
PLATTER WITH SAGE
PG. 20

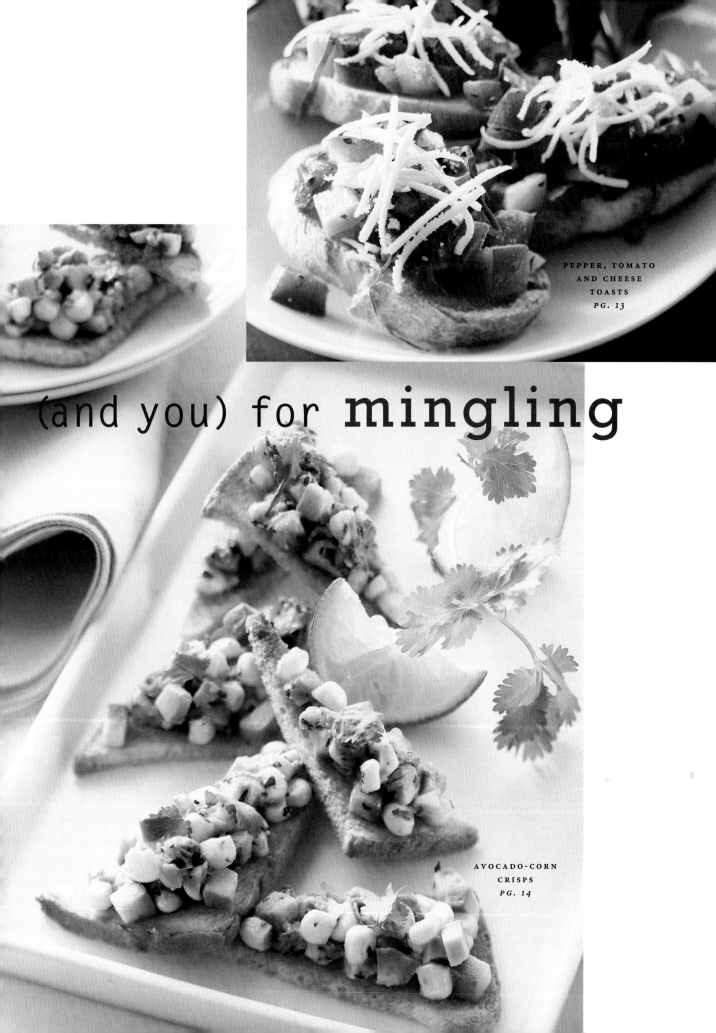

PEPPER, TOMATO
AND CHEESE
TOASTS
PG. 13

(and you) for mingling

AVOCADO-CORN
CRISPS
PG. 14

all's well that starts well

BLACKENED
SHRIMP WITH
TOMATO
MAYONNAISE
PG. 28

SPICE
TWISTS
PG. 21

deviled eggs and cucumber cups *EASY*

These make-ahead stuffed eggs and cucumbers couldn't be easier. Guests will love the contrast of creamy-rich deviled egg filling piped into the cool and crunchy cucumber cups. See our tip above for a simple way to pipe in the filling. Pictured on page 6.

Total prep time: 30 minutes

- 1 **dozen large hard-cooked eggs, peeled**
- ¼ **cup finely chopped celery ribs with leaves**
- 2 **tablespoons finely chopped cornichons or sour pickles**
- 2 **tablespoons mayonnaise**
- 2 **tablespoons sour cream**
- 2 **teaspoons Dijon mustard**
- ¾ **teaspoon salt**
- ½ **teaspoon hot red pepper sauce**
- 1 **large English (seedless) cucumber**
- 2 **tablespoons finely chopped onion**
- 1 **tablespoon snipped fresh chives and ¾ teaspoon poppy seeds or black mustard seeds, for garnish (optional)**

1. Cut a small piece from the pointed end of each hard-cooked egg. Cut a third off the rounded end of egg. Carefully remove yolk, reserving egg white pieces. Arrange egg cups on a large jelly-roll pan lined with foil. Coarsely chop yolks and egg white pieces; transfer to a large bowl.

2. Add celery, pickles, mayonnaise, sour cream, mustard, salt and pepper sauce to egg mixture,

stirring until combined. *(Can be made ahead. Cover filling and egg cups with plastic wrap and refrigerate overnight.)*

3. Remove 1-inch-wide strips lengthwise down cucumber using a vegetable peeler. Cut cucumber crosswise into ¾-inch pieces. Using the tip of a small spoon or melon baller, remove cucumber flesh from each cucumber piece, being careful not to cut through the other side. Finely chop cucumber flesh; drain on paper towels. Transfer to bowl with egg filling. Rinse onion in a small strainer under cold water; drain. Transfer to bowl with egg filling. Makes 1¾ cups.

4. Transfer cucumber cups to jelly-roll pan with egg cups. Fill a plastic storage bag with filling and pipe into egg whites and cucumber cups. Arrange egg and cucumber cups on a large serving plate. Sprinkle tops with chives and poppy seeds, if desired. Makes 12 egg and 18 cucumber cups.

Per egg cup: 50 calories, 3 g total fat, 1 g saturated fat, 86 mg cholesterol, 146 mg sodium, 1 g carbohydrates, 5 g protein, 14 mg calcium, 0 g fiber
Per cucumber cup: 38 calories, 3 g total fat, 1 g saturated fat, 86 mg cholesterol, 91 mg sodium, 1 g carbohydrates, 1 g protein, 12 mg calcium, 0 g fiber

roquefort-walnut dip *EASY*

The base for this dip is a piquant, somewhat salty cheese paired with the slightly tart taste of mayonnaise and sour cream. Walnuts add an unexpected flavor note.

Total prep time: 10 minutes

- 1 **cup chopped walnuts, toasted**
- 1 **cup crumbled Roquefort cheese**
- ¾ **cup mayonnaise**
- ½ **cup sour cream**
  Assorted fresh vegetables (optional)

Combine nuts, Roquefort, mayonnaise and sour cream in a medium bowl; mix until blended. Serve with assorted vegetables, if desired. Makes 2½ cups.

Per tablespoon: 65 calories, 6.5 g total fat, 1.5 g saturated fat, 6 mg cholesterol, 76 mg sodium, 1 g carbohydrates, 1 g protein, 25 mg calcium, 0 g fiber

pesto origins and creations

What did we ever do without pesto? While traditionally a sauce for pasta, these days pesto is used to flavor sandwiches, soups, grilled meats, dips and, well, just about everything except dessert! Here's more about this versatile ingredient:

WHAT'S IN A NAME: The word "pesto" derives from the Italian word "pestato," which means to crush with mortar and pestle. This probably describes the way the garlic, basil and nuts in this recipe were combined before the days of food processors and blenders.

THE REAL THING: Originally, the predominant herb in pesto was fresh basil, but today's boundary-slashing versions may include other herbs or greens, such as cilantro, mint—and, as in Arugula Pesto Dip (below)—parsley and arugula. Garlic, basil, nuts, Parmesan cheese and olive oil remain some of the pesto's hallmark ingredients.

arugula pesto dip EASY

Wonderful, peppery arugula takes the place of basil in this pesto recipe. Thoroughly dry the leaves before pureeing in a blender.

Total prep time: 30 minutes

- 1½ **cups fresh parsley leaves**
- 1 **cup (2 oz.) arugula leaves**
- ½ **cup olive oil**
- ⅓ **cup pine nuts, toasted**
- ¼ **cup freshly grated Parmesan cheese**
- 2 **tablespoons fresh lemon juice**
- ¼ **teaspoon salt**
  Assorted fresh vegetables (such as endive, radishes, asparagus, yellow bell pepper and carrots) (optional)

Combine all ingredients in a blender, except assorted vegetables; puree until smooth, scraping down sides with rubber spatula. *(Can be made ahead. Transfer to an airtight container. Refrigerate up to 3 days. Bring to room temperature before serving.)* Serve with assorted vegetables, if desired. Makes 1 cup.

Per tablespoon: 85 calories, 8.5 g total fat, 1.5 g saturated fat, 1 mg cholesterol, 67 mg sodium, 1 g carbohydrates, 2 g protein, 35 mg calcium, 1 g fiber

grilled eggplant dip LOW FAT EASY

Garlic-studded eggplants give this dip its tantalizing fusion of flavors, but it's the grilling that bumps it up a notch. One of the secrets is those delicious, brown blisters that come from roasting eggplant over an outdoor fire, adding a smoky flavor. The other is cooking the garlic until it becomes sweet, mellow and buttery soft.

Prep time: 20 minutes • Grilling time: 35 to 45 minutes

- 2 **medium eggplants (1¼ lbs. each)**
- 2 **cloves garlic, very thinly sliced**
- 1 **medium tomato**
- ¼ **cup chopped fresh flat-leaf parsley**
- 3 **tablespoons extra-virgin olive oil**
- 1 **teaspoon fresh lemon juice**
- ¾ **teaspoon salt**
- ¼ **teaspoon freshly ground pepper**
- ¼ **cup chopped walnuts, toasted**
  Assorted fresh vegetables (optional)
  Toasted French bread or pita bread (optional)

1. Heat grill. Cut slits all over eggplant with a small knife and insert garlic slices into slits. Grill eggplant over medium-hot heat, turning occasionally, 35 to 45 minutes, until charred and beginning to collapse. Grill tomato, turning occasionally, 3 to 5 minutes, until beginning to char.

2. Let eggplant and tomato stand until cool enough to handle. Remove skin and stems from eggplant; discard. Cut eggplant in half lengthwise and remove as many seeds as possible; discard. Chop eggplant and transfer to a medium bowl. Remove skin and seeds from tomato; discard. Coarsely chop tomato and add to bowl.

3. Stir in parsley, oil, lemon juice, salt and pepper. *(Can be made ahead. Cover and refrigerate up to 8 hours.)* Stir in walnuts just before serving. Serve with fresh vegetables and toasted bread, if desired. Makes 2 cups.

Per tablespoon: 25 calories, 1 g total fat, 0 g saturated fat, 0 mg cholesterol, 53 mg sodium, 3 g carbohydrates, 1 g protein, 5 mg calcium, 1 g fiber

nacho cheese dip EASY

Everyone loves nachos and dip, especially the hostess! This recipe is a breeze, calling for just a handful of ingredients and taking less than a half hour to prepare. Serve with purple tortilla chips and orange bell peppers for a vibrant color contrast on your table. We gave this dip a spider web design for Halloween, but feel free to pipe on any seasonally inspired decoration.

Total prep and cooking time: 25 minutes
Microwave used

- 1 **package (8 oz.) pasteurized process cheese spread (Velveeta), cut into cubes**
- 1 **can (10 oz.) diced tomatoes and green chiles**
- 1 **cup shredded Monterey Jack cheese**
- 1 **cup shredded mild Cheddar cheese**
- 1 **teaspoon cumin**
- 2 **tablespoons tapenade (black olive paste)**
- 1 **teaspoon water**
  Purple tortilla chips, orange bell pepper wedges or carrot sticks (optional)

1. Combine cheese spread, diced tomatoes and green chiles, Monterey Jack cheese, Cheddar cheese and cumin in a microwaveproof bowl. Microwave on HIGH 4 to 5 minutes, stirring once, until melted and smooth. Pour into a serving bowl.

2. Meanwhile, combine tapenade and water in a small resealable plastic storage bag; knead to mix. Cut a tiny hole in one corner and pipe a spider web design on top of dip. Serve warm with chips, bell pepper wedges or carrot sticks. Makes 2¼ cups.

Per tablespoon: 50 calories, 4 g total fat, 2 g saturated fat, 12 mg cholesterol, 193 mg sodium, 1 g carbohydrates, 3 g protein, 82 mg calcium, 0 g fiber

snapper hash

Your guests will savor this elegant appetizer made with fresh cilantro, garlic, green onions, jalapeño and cherry tomatoes. Make it a day ahead to let the flavors mellow.

Prep time: 20 minutes plus cooling
Cooking time: 10 minutes

- 2 **medium (12 oz.) skinned snapper fillets**
- ¼ **cup packed fresh cilantro leaves**
- 2 **green onions**
- 2 **large cloves garlic**
- 1 **jalapeño chile, stem removed, chopped with seeds (see tip, page 15)**
- 4 **tablespoons butter, divided (no substitutes)**
- 1 **teaspoon cumin**
- ⅛ **teaspoon cinnamon**
  Pinch ground cloves
- ½ **teaspoon salt**
- ¼ **cup chopped cherry tomatoes**
  Tortilla chips (optional)

1. With tweezers, remove small bones from fillets. Arrange fish and ½ cup water in a 10-inch skillet (top of fish will not be covered with water). Bring water to simmer. Reduce heat to medium-low, cover and cook 1 minute. Turn fish, cover and cook 1 minute more. Remove from heat; let stand 3 minutes. Uncover and cool fish in poaching liquid. With a slotted spoon, transfer fish to a bowl; reserve liquid. Break fish into flakes, remove bones.

2. Finely chop cilantro, green onions, garlic and jalapeño. Melt 3 tablespoons of the butter in a large nonstick skillet. Add cumin, cinnamon and cloves; remove from heat and stir 30 seconds. Add cilantro mixture and salt; return to heat and cook 1 minute, until bright green and aromatic. Add fish.

3. Melt remaining 1 tablespoon butter in another large skillet over medium-high heat; add tomatoes. Bring to boil and cook 1 minute. Remove from heat. Gently fold in fish-cilantro mixture and reserved poaching liquid. Return to heat and cook 1 minute more. Spoon into a medium bowl. Serve warm or at room temperature with tortilla chips, if desired. Makes 2 cups.

Per tablespoon: 26 calories, 1.5 g total fat, 1 g saturated fat, 8 mg cholesterol, 60 mg sodium, 0 g carbohydrates, 2 g protein, 6 mg calcium, 0 g fiber

potted shrimp

A pâté-like shrimp spread usually calls for a good amount of butter. Not our version—we used just a dab, letting jalapeño, cumin and oregano pump up the flavor instead.

Prep time: 20 minutes • Cooking time: 4 to 5 minutes

- **1 tablespoon butter or margarine**
- **1 large jalapeño chile, seeded and minced (see tip, page 15)**
- **2 teaspoons minced garlic**
- **1 pound large shrimp, peeled and deveined**
- **¾ teaspoon salt**
- **¼ teaspoon cumin seed**
- **¼ teaspoon dried oregano**
- **3 tablespoons mayonnaise**
  Assorted crackers (optional)

1. Melt butter in a large nonstick skillet over medium heat. Add jalapeño and garlic and cook 30 to 40 seconds, until fragrant and beginning to color. Add shrimp and cook, 1 minute per side. Add salt, cumin and oregano; cook, stirring, 1 minute more, until shrimp turn pink and are opaque.

2. Transfer to food processor; pulse until finely chopped. Transfer to a bowl; stir in mayonnaise. Pack into serving bowl. *(Can be made ahead. Cover surface directly with plastic wrap. Refrigerate up to 24 hours. Let stand at room temperature 1½ hours before serving.)* Serve with crackers. Makes 2 cups.

Per tablespoon: 25 calories, 1.5 g total fat, 0.5 g saturated fat, 19 mg cholesterol, 83 mg sodium, 0 g carbohydrates, 2 g protein, 7 mg calcium, 0 g fiber

sesame-white bean dip

Tahini (a sesame paste available at many supermarkets, gourmet shops and health food stores) lends this dip a Middle Eastern flavor. A little tahini goes a long way, so if you have any extra it can be stored in the refrigerator.

Total prep time: 10 minutes

- **1 can (19 oz.) white kidney or cannellini beans, drained and rinsed**
- **¼ cup tahini (sesame paste)**
- **3 tablespoons fresh lemon juice**
- **¼ teaspoon salt**
- **¼ teaspoon freshly ground pepper**
- **¼ cup olive oil**
- **¼ cup chopped green onions**
- **1 tablespoon sesame seeds, toasted**
  Garlic Pita Chips (see recipe, below) (optional)
  Assorted fresh vegetables (optional)

1. Combine beans, tahini, lemon juice, salt and pepper in a food processor. With machine on, add oil through feed tube in a steady stream and process 30 seconds, until smooth.

2. Transfer to a serving bowl and stir in green onions. *(Can be made ahead. Cover and refrigerate up to 24 hours.)* Sprinkle with sesame seeds. Serve with Garlic Pita Chips and assorted vegetables, if desired. Makes 2 cups.

Per tablespoon: 40 calories, 3 g total fat, 0 g saturated fat, 0 mg cholesterol, 40 mg sodium, 3 g carbohydrates, 1 g protein, 11 mg calcium, 1 g fiber

garlic pita chips

These fragrant toasts are a perfect match for our Sesame-White Bean Dip, left, or our Grilled Eggplant Dip, page 10.

Prep time: 10 minutes • Baking time: 10 minutes

- **¼ cup butter or margarine**
- **1½ teaspoons minced garlic**
- **¼ teaspoon freshly ground pepper**
- **4 (5- to 6-inch) white or whole wheat pita breads, split**

Heat oven to 400°F. Melt butter over low heat with garlic and pepper in a small saucepan. Lightly brush butter mixture onto cut side of pita halves. Cut each half into 6 wedges and place buttered side up on a large cookie sheet. Bake 10 minutes, until toasted. *(Can be made ahead. Wrap well and store at room temperature up to 2 days.)* Makes 48 chips.

Per chip: 25 calories, 1 g total fat, 0.5 g saturated fat, 3 mg cholesterol, 40 mg sodium, 3 g carbohydrates, 1 g protein, 5 mg calcium, 0 g fiber

roasted tomato and basil salsa EASY

Roasting tomatoes brings out their intense sweet flavor. We paired them with garlic, olive oil and basil for this sublime salsa.

Prep time: 15 minutes • Baking time: 1 hour

1½ pounds plum tomatoes, quartered
10 large fresh basil leaves
3 large cloves garlic, lightly crushed
2 tablespoons olive oil
½ teaspoon salt
½ teaspoon freshly ground pepper
Rosemary Flatbread (see recipe, page 14) or foccacia (optional)

1. Heat oven to 325°F. Combine all ingredients except Rosemary Flatbread or foccacia in a large ovenproof skillet or 13×9-inch baking dish. Bake 1 hour, until tomatoes and garlic are very soft. Cool 10 minutes.

2. Coarsely chop tomato-garlic mixture. Transfer to a serving bowl. *(Can be made ahead. Cover and refrigerate overnight. Bring to room temperature before serving.)* Serve with Rosemary Flatbread or purchased foccacia, if desired. Makes 2 cups.

Per tablespoon: 15 calories, 1 g total fat, 0 g saturated fat, 0 mg cholesterol, 38 mg sodium, 1 g carbohydrates, 0 g protein, 2 mg calcium, 0 g fiber

pepper, tomato and cheese toasts EASY

Serve these juicy-ripe tomato, bell pepper and herb French bread toasts with fresh salad greens, grilled chicken or steak. Pictured on page 7.

Total prep and cooking time: 30 minutes

2 tablespoons plus 1 teaspoon olive oil, divided
½ teaspoon minced garlic
20 ½-inch slices French bread
1 cup fresh basil leaves
½ cup diced yellow bell pepper
2 medium ripe tomatoes, diced (about 2 cups)
1 tablespoon chopped fresh mint
¼ teaspoon salt
¼ teaspoon freshly ground pepper
⅓ cup shredded ricotta salata or crumbled feta cheese

1. Heat oven to 375°F. Combine 2 tablespoons of the oil and the garlic in a cup, brush on 1 side of each bread slice. Place oil side up in a single layer on a large cookie sheet. Bake 12 minutes, until toasted. Set aside.

2. Stack basil leaves, roll up and slice crosswise into thin shreds.

3. Heat the remaining 1 teaspoon oil in a large skillet over medium-high heat. Add bell pepper and cook about 2 minutes, until lightly charred. Remove skillet from heat. Stir in basil, tomatoes, mint, salt and pepper. Divide tomato mixture onto toasts; sprinkle with cheese. Makes 20 toasts.

Per toast: 95 calories, 3 g total fat, 0.5 g saturated fat, 2 mg cholesterol, 221 mg sodium, 14 g carbohydrates, 3 g protein, 26 mg calcium, 1 g fiber

---

test kitchen tip
crudités with class

A spread of appetizers would hardly be complete without a tray of artfully arranged crudités for color and crunch. To serve the pick of the crop at its best, remember:

If you prepare crudités in advance, refresh the cut vegetables in ice water before storing. Drain well, then seal them in resealable plastic bags each lined with a paper towel to absorb the excess moisture.

For parties and gatherings, crudités can be arranged on serving platters up to two hours in advance. Cover them with damp paper towels and mist occasionally to remoisten.

avocado-corn crisps

This avocado and sweet corn appetizer is seasoned with lime and cilantro. Mashing half of the avocado helps the mixture cling to the toasted crisps. Look for medium-ripe avocados for this recipe. Pictured on page 7.

Total prep and cooking time: 30 minutes

4	teaspoons olive oil, divided
¾	teaspoon cumin, divided
8	very thin slices firm white bread (such as Pepperidge Farm)
¾	cup fresh corn kernels (about 2 small ears)
1	tablespoon minced shallot
1	medium ripe avocado, finely diced
1	tablespoon minced fresh cilantro
1	tablespoon fresh lime juice
½	teaspoon salt
¼	teaspoon freshly ground pepper

1. Heat oven to 350°F. Combine 3 teaspoons of the oil and the ¼ teaspoon of the cumin in a cup; lightly brush on 1 side of each bread slice. (It will be a very light coating.) Stack bread slices and cut diagonally into 4 triangles. Place oil side up in a single layer on a large cookie sheet. Bake 12 minutes, until toasted. Set aside.

2. Heat the remaining ½ teaspoon cumin in a large skillet over low heat 2 minutes, until toasted. Scrape into a bowl. Heat the remaining 1 teaspoon oil in a skillet over medium heat. Add corn and shallot and cook 2 minutes, until heated through. Add to bowl with toasted cumin.

3. Mash ¼ cup of diced avocado on a plate using a fork. Stir mashed avocado into corn mixture with the remaining avocado, the cilantro, lime juice, salt and pepper. Divide and spoon mixture onto toast triangles. Makes 32 crisps.

Per crisp: 30 calories, 1.5 g total fat, 0 g saturated fat, 0 mg cholesterol, 58 mg sodium, 3 g carbohydrates, 1 g protein, 5 mg calcium, 0 g fiber

rosemary flatbread

Never baked bread before? Then try your hand at this basic recipe. All you'll need is a bowl and a spoon to mix the ingredients! We recommend serving it sliced and toasted with the fabulous Roasted Tomato and Basil Salsa, page 13, or the Arugula Pesto Dip, page 10, but it's equally tasty served with a wedge of cheese or a tossed salad.

Prep time: 30 minutes plus rising and standing
Baking time: 20 to 25 minutes

	Pinch sugar
½	cup warm water (105°F. to 115°F.)
1	package active dry yeast
1	cup water, at room temperature
3	tablespoons olive oil, divided
3½	to 4 cups all-purpose flour, divided
2	teaspoons salt
2	teaspoons chopped fresh rosemary or 1 teaspoon dried rosemary
½	teaspoon freshly ground pepper
	Fresh rosemary sprigs (optional)

1. Dissolve sugar in warm water in a large bowl. Sprinkle top of mixture with yeast and let stand 5 to 10 minutes, until yeast is bubbly. Stir in room temperature water, 2 tablespoons of the oil, 1 cup of the flour, the salt, rosemary and pepper until smooth. Stir in remaining flour, until a smooth dough forms and pulls away from side of bowl.

2. On a lightly floured surface, knead dough 8 to 10 minutes, until smooth and elastic. Gather dough into a ball. Place dough in a large greased bowl, turning to grease top. Cover with plastic wrap and let rise in a warm, draft-free place until doubled in bulk, 1 to 1½ hours.

3. Punch down dough; let rest 10 minutes. Transfer dough to a jelly-roll pan and gently stretch into a small rectangle. Let dough stand 10 to 15 minutes until pliable enough to stretch to edges of pan. Cover pan with plastic wrap and let dough stand 15 minutes more.

4. Meanwhile, adjust oven rack to lowest position. Heat oven to 450°F. Uncover dough and brush top with remaining 1 tablespoon oil. Bake 20 to 25 minutes, until golden. Cool flatbread in pan on wire rack 5 minutes; unmold and cool completely on wire rack. *(Can be made ahead. Wrap well and freeze up to 1 week. Thaw 2 hours at room temperature.)*

5. Cut bread into quarters. Cut each quarter into 1-inch slices. Lightly toast slices. Garnish with rosemary sprigs, if desired. Makes 28 slices.

Per slice: 80 calories, 2 g total fat, 0 g saturated fat, 0 mg cholesterol, 167 mg sodium, 13 g carbohydrates, 2 g protein, 3 mg calcium, 1 g fiber

spicy pork tenderloin with lime mayonnaise

For easy entertaining on a budget, here's a great alternative to beef tenderloin. Think of it when you're putting together a more hearty appetizer buffet.

Prep time: 15 minutes plus chilling
Roasting time: 20 to 25 minutes

DRY MARINADE:
- 1 tablespoon minced garlic
- 2 teaspoons paprika
- 1 teaspoon salt
- 1 teaspoon dried oregano
- 1 teaspoon cumin
- ½ teaspoon ground red pepper
- ½ teaspoon freshly ground pepper

- 2 pork tenderloins (1½ lbs. total)

LIME MAYONNAISE:
- 1 cup mayonnaise
- 1 teaspoon grated lime peel
- 2 tablespoons fresh lime juice

- 2 loaves (1 lb. each) French bread, thinly sliced
  Lime wedges and cilantro, for garnish (optional)

1. *Make dry marinade:* Combine marinade ingredients in a small bowl. Rub all over pork. Wrap pork with plastic wrap and marinate in refrigerator overnight.

2. Let pork stand at room temperature 30 minutes. Heat oven to 425°F.

3. Unwrap pork; place in a roasting pan and roast 20 to 25 minutes, until a meat thermometer inserted in thickest part of tenderloin reaches 155°F. Cool to room temperature. *(Can be made ahead. Cover and refrigerate up to 24 hours. Remove from refrigerator 30 minutes before serving.)*

4. *Make lime mayonnaise:* Combine mayonnaise, lime peel and juice in a small bowl. *(Can be made ahead. Cover and refrigerate up to 24 hours.)*

5. To serve, cut pork into very thin slices and serve on French bread with Lime Mayonnaise. Garnish with lime wedges and cilantro, if desired. Makes about 80 appetizers.

Per appetizer with ½ teaspoon mayonnaise and 1 slice bread: 63 calories, 3 g total fat, 0 g saturated fat, 7 mg cholesterol, 113 mg sodium, 7 g carbohydrates, 3 g protein, 11 mg calcium, 0 g fiber

test kitchen tip

handling chile peppers

Cooking with chile peppers requires extra precautions:

HANDLING: Because all chile peppers contain volatile oils that can burn your skin and eyes, avoid direct contact with them as much as possible. When working with chile peppers, wear plastic or rubber gloves. If your bare hands do touch the chile peppers, wash your hands well with soap and water.

COOKING: As chile peppers cook, they release fumes that can irritate your breathing passages and cause coughing. Avoid breathing these fumes by switching on exhaust fans and opening windows.

the asian pantry

Look for the following Asian ingredients in spice aisles or ethnic sections of supermarkets and in Asian specialty stores.

ASIAN CHILE SAUCE: A thin, orange-red sauce that combines chiles with sugar, salt, oil and vinegar. Often used as a condiment, it ranges from mild heat to fiery hot.

ASIAN FISH SAUCE: (nam pla; nuoc nam) A fermented extract of anchovies. This deliciously salty condiment adds a special richness to savory dishes like stir-fries, curries and dipping sauces.

ASIAN SESAME OIL: Golden brown oil extracted from crushed sesame seeds. With an intense, toasted nutty flavor, only a small amount is needed to enrich stir-fries or cold noodle salads. Can be combined with other oils.

CHINESE FIVE-SPICE POWDER: A spice blend usually made from equal parts star anise, cloves, cinnamon, fennel seeds and sichuan peppercorns. It is widely used in Asian marinades, sauces and barbecued meats.

CILANTRO: [(sih-LAHN-troh) coriander, Chinese parsley] A zesty, earthy-limy herb. Use chopped leaves and tender stems, or whole leaves, in marinades and curries or as a garnish.

COCONUT MILK: A creamy, slightly sweet liquid processed from shredded coconut and water. It is an essential ingredient in Southeast Asian curries, soups and desserts. Store in refrigerator 1 to 2 days after opening. Freeze up to 2 months.

sesame-soy meatballs

Serve these fragrant beef meatballs on skewers with chunks of fresh pineapple and papaya.

Prep time: 30 minutes plus chilling
Grilling time: 10 to 12 minutes

1	pound lean ground beef
⅓	cup minced green onions
¼	cup chopped onion
3	tablespoons soy sauce
2	tablespoons sesame seeds, toasted
1	tablespoon sugar
1	tablespoon vegetable oil
20	(4- to 5-inch) wooden skewers
	Pineapple or papaya, cut into 1-inch chunks

1. Mix ground beef, green onions, onion, soy sauce, sesame seeds, sugar and oil in a medium bowl. Shape meat mixture into 1-inch balls. Transfer meatballs to a jelly-roll pan; cover and refrigerate 1 hour.

2. Meanwhile, soak skewers in a shallow bowl of water 30 minutes; drain. Heat grill or broiler. Thread 2 meatballs on each skewer. Grill over medium heat 5 to 6 minutes per side, until meat is no longer pink and cooked through. Serve with pineapple or papaya chunks. Makes 20 appetizers.

Per appetizer: 60 calories, 4 g total fat, 1 g saturated fat, 4 mg cholesterol, 167 mg sodium, 1 g carbohydrates, 4 g protein, 14 mg calcium, 0 g fiber

thai dumplings

These savory dumplings are served with a delightfully unique sweet-and-sour dipping sauce.

Prep time: 1½ hours • Cooking time: 15 minutes per batch

DIPPING SAUCE:

1	cup water
½	cup sugar
½	cup distilled vinegar
¼	cup golden raisins
1	tablespoon minced garlic
1½	teaspoons grated fresh ginger

1 teaspoon ground red pepper

½ teaspoon salt

FILLING:

½ pound medium shrimp, peeled, deveined
    and finely chopped

½ pound lean ground pork

¼ cup minced green onions

2 tablespoons chopped fresh cilantro

1 tablespoon minced jalapeño chile
    (see tip, page 15)

1 large egg white

1 teaspoon salt

1 teaspoon minced garlic

½ teaspoon freshly ground pepper

20 egg roll wrappers*

40 fresh cilantro leaves

1. *Make dipping sauce:* Combine all of the dipping sauce ingredients in a saucepan. Bring to boil; simmer 20 minutes. Puree in a blender.

2. *Make filling:* Combine all of the ingredients for the filling in a medium bowl until blended.

3. Cut 40 circles from egg roll wrappers with a 3-inch round biscuit cutter. Keep wrappers and circles covered with plastic wrap. Place 1 heaping teaspoon of filling in center of each circle; top with 1 cilantro leaf. Bring wrapper up around filling, pleating wrapper firmly, but leaving top open for some filling to show. Gently flatten bottoms of dumplings so they stand upright. Place each dumpling on a 3-inch square of waxed paper.

4. Place wire rack or greased bamboo steamer basket in wok or 10-inch skillet. Add enough water to reach just below rack. Place dumplings on waxed paper, open sides up, ½ inch apart on rack. (Cover and chill extra dumplings.) Bring water to boil. Cover; steam 15 minutes for each batch, adding more boiling water if necessary. Serve warm with Dipping Sauce. Makes 40 dumplings.

*Note: Can be found in the refrigerated section of supermarkets or in Asian specialty stores.

Per dumpling with 1 teaspoon sauce: 70 calories, 2 g total fat, 0.5 g saturated fat, 12 mg cholesterol, 163 mg sodium, 11 g carbohydrates, 3 g protein, 7 mg calcium, 1 g fiber

the asian pantry continued

More Asian specialty ingredients to be found in ethnic sections or spice aisles of supermarkets and in Asian specialty stores:

DRIED SHRIMP PASTE: Cooking mellows the salty shrimp taste of this incredibly pungent paste and gives curries an authentic, rich flavor. Available in cellophane-wrapped blocks, plastic tubs or glass jars. Keep sealed in a heavy-duty plastic bag.

FRESH GINGER: A tan, knobby root with a crisp, fiery sweet flavor. Adds a fresh zing to savory foods. Slice, mince or crush its yellowish interior. Choose firm roots.

GALANGAL: (guh-LANG-guhl, or guh-LANG-ga; Thai ginger) Related to ginger, galangal is preferred in Southeast Asian cooking for its clean, slightly lemony taste. Can be sliced or crushed before adding to recipes. Look for its pinkish opaque skin and firm white flesh.

KAFFIR LIME LEAVES: (ka-FEAR) Glossy dark-green leaves. Just one will add a citrusy-floral aroma and a wonderful zest to your curries. Discard whole kaffir leaves before serving; however, if they're shredded, leave them in. Refrigerate fresh leaves 5 to 7 days; substitute dried leaves, if desired.

LEMONGRASS: Firm, pale-green stalks that resemble green onions. Adds a fragrant, lemony essence to dishes. Cut off green top and slice white, tender core for marinades, sauces, soups and spice mixtures.

SICHUAN PEPPERCORNS: (SEHCH-wahn) The citrusy-spicy aroma and sharp distinct taste of these small, flower-shaped berries is wonderful added to dry marinades for meats. This spice is available ground or whole, and it's often sold in cellophane bags.

salad rolls

These tasty, never-fried morsels make refreshing starters.

Total prep time: 1 hour

- **2** ounces rice vermicelli noodles*
- **2** cups bean sprouts
- **1** cup shredded carrots
- **½** cup fresh cilantro leaves
- **½** cup fresh mint leaves
- **24** (8- to 8½-inch) round rice paper wrappers*
- **8** leaves Boston lettuce, torn into thirds
- **24** medium shrimp, cooked, peeled, deveined and halved lengthwise

DIPPING SAUCE:

- **½** cup water
- **2** tablespoons sugar
- **2** tablespoons rice wine vinegar
- **2** tablespoons Asian fish sauce (see tips, pages 16 and 17)
- **1** tablespoon finely shredded carrot

1. Bring a large saucepan of water to boil. Add vermicelli and cook 1 to 2 minutes, just until tender. Rinse under cold water; drain well. Toss vermicelli with bean sprouts, carrots, cilantro and mint leaves in a large bowl until combined. Quickly dip each rice paper in a shallow bowl of hot water 3 to 4 seconds, until just softened. (Keep remaining wrappers covered.) Shake off excess water and place on a clean, cotton dish towel.

2. Place 1 wrapper in front of you on towel. Place a piece of lettuce in center of rice paper and top with ¼ cup vermicelli mixture. Fold bottom third of wrapper tightly over filling; fold in 2 sides of wrapper to form an envelope. Place 2 shrimp halves, cut side up and back to back, on flap of envelope and roll up tightly. Transfer to a serving plate and cover with a clean, damp towel. Repeat with remaining wrappers, lettuce, vermicelli mixture and shrimp. *(Can be made ahead. Cover with a damp towel and refrigerate up to 6 hours.)*

3. *Make dipping sauce:* Combine water and sugar in a small saucepan. Bring to boil, stirring, until sugar dissolves. Remove from heat; stir in vinegar, Asian fish sauce and carrot. Serve with Salad Rolls. Makes 24 rolls.

Note: Can be found in the ethnic sections of supermarkets or in Asian speciality stores.

Per 2 rolls with 1 tablespoon sauce: 60 calories, 1 g total fat, 0 g saturated fat, 31 mg cholesterol, 36 mg sodium, 7 g carbohydrates, 5 g protein, 1 mg calcium, 17 g fiber

beef and chicken saté with peanut sauce EASY

The spice is right—this intriguing Asian blend makes a worldly marinade for chicken breast and beef sirloin.

Prep time: 30 minutes plus marinating
Cooking time: 2 to 4 minutes per batch

- **30** (6- to 8-inch) wooden skewers
- **½** pound boneless, skinless chicken breast halves (1 large)
- **½** pound beef sirloin steak (1 inch thick)

MARINADE:

- **2** tablespoons olive oil
- **1** teaspoon coriander
- **½** teaspoon salt
- **½** teaspoon cumin
- **½** teaspoon curry powder

PEANUT SAUCE:

- **1** tablespoon olive oil
- **2** teaspoons minced garlic
- **2** teaspoons grated fresh ginger
- **¼** teaspoon red pepper flakes
- **½** cup unsweetened coconut milk
- **¼** cup crunchy peanut butter
- **¼** cup water
- **2** tablespoons soy sauce
- **1** tablespoon fresh lime juice
- **1** tablespoon firmly packed brown sugar

1. Soak skewers in a shallow bowl of water 30 minutes; drain. Meanwhile, slice chicken diagonally into 4½×¼-inch strips. Cut steak across the grain into 4×¼-inch strips.

2. *Make marinade:* Combine oil, coriander, salt, cumin and curry powder in a bowl. Transfer half of the mixture to another bowl. Add chicken to 1 bowl and steak to the other; toss each to coat. Marinate chicken and steak at room temperature 15 minutes.

3. ■ *Make peanut sauce:* Heat oil in a medium skillet over low heat. Add garlic, ginger and red pepper flakes and cook 1 minute, until fragrant. Add remaining peanut sauce ingredients; bring to boil, stirring until smooth. Simmer 3 minutes, to blend flavors. Transfer sauce to a small bowl.

4. ■ Drain skewers. Thread 1 piece each of chicken and steak on each skewer. Heat a grill pan or heavy skillet over medium-high heat until very hot. Grill skewers in batches, 1 to 2 minutes per side, until chicken is cooked through and steak is medium-rare. Transfer skewers to a platter and serve with Peanut Sauce. Makes about 15 skewers.

Per skewer: 110 calories, 7.5 g total fat, 2.5 g saturated fat, 17 mg cholesterol, 237 mg sodium, 3 g carbohydrates, 8 g protein, 9 mg calcium, 1 g fiber

fried spring rolls with spicy dipping sauce

The spicy dipping sauce really kicks up these chicken rolls.

Prep time: 45 minutes • Cooking time: 20 minutes

DIPPING SAUCE:
- 3 tablespoons Asian fish sauce (see tips, pages 16 and 17)
- 2 small jalapeño chiles, seeded and minced (see tip, page 15)
- 2 tablespoons chopped fresh cilantro
- 2 tablespoons fresh lime juice
- 2 tablespoons lite soy sauce
- 1½ teaspoons sugar

FILLING:
- 1 boneless skinless chicken thigh (4 to 5 oz.)
- ½ teaspoon minced garlic
- 1 teaspoon peanut or vegetable oil
- ¼ pound shiitake or white mushrooms, stems removed and thinly sliced
- 1 tablespoon dry sherry
- 1 tablespoon lite soy sauce
- ¼ teaspoon sugar
- ⅛ teaspoon red pepper flakes
- 3 ounces snow peas, cut into thin slices
- 3 tablespoons minced yellow bell pepper

- 2 tablespoons thinly sliced green onion
- 2 tablespoons flour
- 4 teaspoons water

  ■

- 24 wonton wrappers*
- 3 tablespoons peanut or vegetable oil, divided

1. ■ *Make dipping sauce:* Combine all of the dipping sauce ingredients in a small bowl. Set aside.

2. ■ *Make filling:* Chop chicken; toss with garlic and ¼ teaspoon salt on a cutting board.

3. ■ Heat a large nonstick skillet 2 minutes, until hot over high heat. Add chicken, breaking pieces apart with a spoon, and cook 1½ to 2 minutes, just until no longer pink. Transfer to a medium bowl.

4. ■ Add oil and mushrooms to same skillet. Cook 3 minutes, stirring, until lightly browned and tender. Add sherry, soy sauce, sugar and red pepper flakes; allow mixture to bubble 5 seconds. Transfer mixture to bowl with chicken; cool. Stir in snow peas, bell pepper and green onion. Wipe out skillet.

5. ■ Stir flour and water together to form a flour paste in a cup. Arrange 4 wonton wrappers 1 inch apart on a work surface. (Keep remaining wrappers covered with a clean kitchen towel.) Spoon 1 level tablespoon of filling toward 1 corner of each wrapper; lift corner with filling up over filling to center of square. Moisten edges with flour paste; fold in sides, leaving opposite corner open like an envelope flap. Roll up into a 2-inch long roll. Set aside on a sheet of waxed paper. Repeat with 3 more wonton wrappers. Then repeat process with remaining wrappers and filling, making 4 at a time.

6. ■ Heat oven to 200°F. Line a cookie sheet with paper towels. Heat 1 tablespoon oil in same skillet over medium heat. Add 8 spring rolls and cook, turning occasionally, 3 minutes, until browned on all sides. Drain on paper towels and keep warm in oven. Repeat process with remaining oil and spring rolls. Transfer to large serving plate. Serve warm with Dipping Sauce. Makes 24 rolls.

*Note: Can be found in the refrigerated section of supermarkets or in Asian specialty stores.

Per roll with 1 teaspoon dipping sauce: 59 calories, 2 g total fat, 0 g saturated fat, 5 mg cholesterol, 316 mg sodium, 7 g carbohydrates, 2 g protein, 9 mg calcium, 0 g fiber

olive and cheese platter with sage

For such a small fruit, olives pack a whole lot of flavor on their own, but when given a good soak with compatible partners—such as the fresh sage, red pepper flakes and olive oil in this recipe—they take on even more culinary intrigue. The ricotta salata served alongside the olives adds a pleasant textural contrast. Offer slices of Rosemary Flatbread, page 14, or a purchased foccacia, with the platter. Pictured on page 6.

Total prep time: 10 minutes

- ¼ **cup extra-virgin olive oil**
- 8 **large fresh sage leaves, very thinly sliced**
- ⅛ **teaspoon red pepper flakes**
- 1¼ **pounds assorted olives (about 3 cups)**
- ½ **pound ricotta salata or feta cheese, at room temperature**
  Fresh thyme sprig, for garnish (optional)

1. Heat oil in a small saucepan over medium-low heat. Add sage and red pepper flakes. Cook, stirring, 1 minute (sage will sizzle and darken).

2. Combine half of the oil-sage mixture and the olives in a medium bowl. *(Can be made ahead. Cover olives; transfer remaining sage and oil to a cup, cover and refrigerate both overnight. Bring to room temperature before serving.)*

3. Arrange cheese on a large serving platter; spoon remaining oil-sage mixture over cheese. Serve with olives and garnish with thyme sprig, if desired. Makes 8 servings.

Per serving: 230 calories, 21.5 g total fat, 6 g saturated fat, 25 mg cholesterol, 1,340 mg sodium, 6 g carbohydrates, 4 g protein, 165 mg calcium, 2 g fiber

sweet italian peppers with garlic crumbs

If you're not familiar with Italian sweet peppers—also called Italian frying peppers, Italianelles or cubanels—it's high time to give them a try! The seeds of these tender, pale-green peppers lend a distinctively sweet taste. Serve them as part of an overall antipasto platter with Italian meats and cheeses, imported olives and thick slices of Italian bread.

Prep time: 10 minutes • Roasting time: 15 to 18 minutes

- 2 **pounds sweet Italian peppers**
- 4 **tablespoons olive oil, divided**
- 1 **teaspoon salt**
- 4 **to 5 slices firm white bread (such as Pepperidge Farm), cut up**
- 1 **tablespoon finely chopped garlic**
- ¼ **teaspoon dried oregano**
- ¼ **cup water**

1. Heat oven to 425°F. Adjust oven racks in upper and lower third of oven.

2. Toss peppers with 2 tablespoons of the oil and the salt on 2 large jelly-roll pans or jelly-roll pan and the bottom of broiler pan. Roast peppers 15 to 18 minutes, turning once halfway through.

3. Meanwhile, pulse bread in food processor until crumbs form. Heat remaining 2 tablespoons oil in a large skillet over medium heat. Add garlic and cook 30 seconds. Add bread crumbs and oregano. Cook, stirring, 8 to 9 minutes, until crumbs are toasted and golden. Cool. *(Can be made ahead. Transfer crumbs to an airtight container and store at room temperature up to 2 days.)*

4. Transfer peppers to a large bowl. Add water and half of the crumbs; toss. Transfer to a serving platter; sprinkle with remaining crumbs. Makes 8 servings.

Per serving: 130 calories, 7.5 g total fat, 1 g saturated fat, 0 mg cholesterol, 379 mg sodium, 14 g carbohydrates, 2 g protein, 29 mg calcium, 2 g fiber

spice twists

Foolproof prepared puff pastry is seasoned with sesame and cumin seeds or Cheddar cheese. Pictured on page 8.

Total prep and cooking time: 30 minutes

- **1 large egg yolk**
- **1 teaspoon water**
- **1 package (17.3 oz.) prepared frozen puff pastry sheets, thawed according to package directions**
- **1 tablespoon white sesame seeds**
- **1 tablespoon black sesame seeds**
- **1 teaspoon salt**
- **1 teaspoon cumin seeds, crushed**

1. Heat oven to 400°F. Beat yolk with water in a cup. On a lightly floured board, roll each sheet of pastry into a 12×16-inch rectangle. Brush pastry rectangles with half of the yolk mixture. Sprinkle each evenly with sesame seeds, salt and cumin seeds. Roll each top lightly with rolling pin; let stand 5 minutes until no longer sticky.

2. Turn sheets over, seed side down, and brush each top with the remaining yolk mixture. Fold each rectangle in half crosswise; roll into a 10×16-inch rectangle. Cut along the 10-inch side into ¾-inch strips. Twist strips; arrange 1-inch apart on an ungreased cookie sheet. Bake, 1 sheet at a time, 10 minutes, until twists are golden. Repeat. Makes about 2 dozen.

Per spice twist: 120 calories, 8.5 g total fat, 1 g saturated fat, 9 mg cholesterol, 148 mg sodium, 9 g carbohydrates, 2 g protein, 11 mg calcium, 0 g fiber

Cheese Twists Variation: Substitute 1 cup coarsely shredded Cheddar cheese for the sesame seeds and cumin seeds and omit salt.

black bean salsa in phyllo cups

Here's another super-easy appetizer that takes just a short time to prepare. Vitamin-rich mangoes, fully ripened and finely diced, help sweeten the salsa. If you need to speed up the ripening process, store mangoes in a small paper bag. Loosely close the bag and store at room temperature.

Total prep and baking time: 28 minutes

- **1 can (15½ oz.) black beans, drained and rinsed**
- **2 tablespoons fresh lime juice**
- **1 chipotle chile in adobo*, minced (see tip, page 15)**
- **½ cup finely diced ripe mango**
- **¼ cup finely diced tomato**
- **2 tablespoons chopped fresh cilantro**
- **1 green onion, thinly sliced**
- **½ teaspoon salt**
- **2 boxes (2 oz. each) frozen mini phyllo pastry shells****

1. Heat oven to 350°F. Coarsely mash ½ cup of the beans, the lime juice and chipotle chile in a medium bowl. Stir in remaining beans, mango, tomato, cilantro, green onion and salt.

2. Arrange phyllo shells on a large cookie sheet. Divide and fill with bean mixture, using about 1 tablespoon for each phyllo shell.

3. Bake 8 minutes, until warm. Serve immediately. Makes 30 appetizers.

**Note:* Can be found in the ethnic sections of supermarkets or in Latino speciality stores.

***Note:* Can be found in the freezer section of supermarkets.

Per appetizer: 39 calories, 1 g total fat, 0 g saturated fat, 0 mg cholesterol, 89 mg sodium, 5 g carbohydrates, 1 g protein, 6 mg calcium, 1 g fiber

mexican meatballs

Fiery chipotle chiles provide the kick in these mini meatballs made with both ground beef and pork. Friends and family will make more than one trip to this tasty tray, and they'll most likely ask for your recipe, too.

Prep time: 45 minutes plus chilling
Cooking time: 45 minutes

6	cloves garlic, divided
1½	teaspoons salt, divided
½	cup masa harina*
¼	cup warm water
1	pound lean ground pork
1	pound lean ground beef
1	large egg
½	teaspoon freshly ground pepper
2	cans (28 oz. each) tomatoes in juice, drained
1	cup water
3	chipotle chiles in adobo*, drained (see tip, page 15)
¼	cup vegetable oil
½	cup chopped onion
1	chicken bouillon cube
1	teaspoon cumin
	Fresh parsley or cilantro, for garnish (optional)

1. Mash 4 cloves of the garlic with ½ teaspoon of the salt into a garlic paste. Combine masa harina with warm water in a large bowl. Add ground pork, beef, egg, garlic-salt paste, remaining 1 teaspoon of salt and the pepper; mix well. Shape meat mixture into 1-inch balls.

2. Puree tomatoes with remaining 2 cloves garlic in a blender until smooth; press mixture through a sieve into a small bowl. Puree chipotle chiles and 1 cup water in a blender; strain through sieve into another small bowl.

3. Heat oil in a large Dutch oven over medium heat. Add onion and cook, stirring frequently, 2 minutes. Add tomato puree; cook, covered, 5 minutes. Stir in bouillon cube and cumin; cook 2 minutes more. Gradually add chile puree, tasting for desired spiciness after each addition.

4. Add meatballs and bring to boil. Cook, covered, 3 minutes. Reduce heat and simmer 30 minutes, turning meatballs, until meat is no longer pink. Cool. Cover and refrigerate overnight. *(Can be made ahead. Cover and refrigerate up to 3 days or freeze up to 1 month.)*

5. Reheat over medium heat, stirring gently, about 30 minutes, until heated through. Transfer to a serving bowl and garnish with parsley or cilantro, if desired. Makes 84 appetizer meatballs.

*Note: Can be found in the ethnic sections of supermarkets or in Latino speciality stores.

Per meatball: 45 calories, 3 g total fat, 1 g saturated fat, 11 mg cholesterol, 160 mg sodium, 2 g carbohydrates, 3 g protein, 9 mg calcium, 0 g fiber

tuscan-style bruschetta

Smoked ham, peppery greens and white bean salad on "bruschetta" (broo-SKEH-tah) (grilled garlic bread) is a cool idea for a warm summer night. Pictured on page 6.

Total prep and cooking time: 30 minutes

1	can (15 oz.) cannellini or white kidney beans, drained and rinsed
¼	cup diced red onion
2	tablespoons extra-virgin olive oil, divided
½	teaspoon grated lemon peel
1	tablespoon fresh lemon juice
¼	teaspoon minced garlic
⅛	teaspoon salt
⅛	teaspoon freshly ground pepper
4	½-inch large slices sourdough bread
¼	pound thinly sliced prosciutto or smoked ham
8	large arugula leaves

1. Heat a grill pan or heavy skillet over medium heat.

2. Combine beans, onion, 1 tablespoon of the oil, the lemon peel, lemon juice, garlic, salt and pepper in a bowl.

3. Grill bread slices 2 to 3 minutes per side, until toasted. Place on plates. Drizzle with the remaining 1 tablespoon oil. Divide and top each slice with prosciutto, arugula and bean mixture. Makes 4 servings.

Per serving: 275 calories, 12.5 g total fat, 2 g saturated fat, 23 mg cholesterol, 885 mg sodium, 27 g carbohydrates, 16 g protein, 58 mg calcium, 5 g fiber

smoked turkey quesadilla EASY

Just say yes! Offer these enticing quesadillas at your next gathering, and that's what your guests will undoubtedly say. These are made especially memorable with a pepper-Jack and Cheddar cheese filling and a fresh mango dip. When selecting a mango, look for yellow, unblemished skin with a red blush. And feel free to substitute cooked shredded chicken or turkey for the smoked turkey, if preferred.

Prep time: 30 minutes plus standing
Baking time: 10 to 12 minutes

MANGO DIP:
- 1 ripe mango, peeled, seeded and cut into chunks
- ⅓ cup sour cream or plain low-fat yogurt
- 2 tablespoons fresh lime juice
- ½ teaspoon salt
- ⅛ teaspoon ground red pepper

- 2 tablespoons olive oil, divided
- 1 medium red onion, thinly sliced
- ½ teaspoon cumin
- 1 cup shredded pepper-Jack or Monterey Jack cheese
- 1 cup shredded Cheddar cheese
- 1 piece (8 oz.) smoked turkey, cut into thin strips (about 2 cups)
- ⅓ cup prepared barbecue sauce
- 8 (6- to 8-inch) flour tortillas
- ¼ cup chopped fresh cilantro

1. *Make mango dip:* Process all mango dip ingredients in a food processor or blender until smooth. Transfer to a small bowl.

2. Heat oven to 425°F. Heat 1 tablespoon of the oil in a large nonstick skillet over medium heat. Add onion and cook 10 minutes, until softened and browned, stirring occasionally. Stir in cumin. Remove from heat.

3. Combine cheeses in a small bowl. Combine turkey and barbecue sauce in another bowl. Lay 4 tortillas on a flat work surface. Sprinkle with half of the cheeses. Cover with the turkey mixture, onions, cilantro and the remaining cheeses. Top with 4 remaining tortillas, pressing firmly.

4. Brush a large cookie sheet with 1½ teaspoons oil. Transfer quesadillas to prepared sheet; brush top of quesadillas with remaining 1½ teaspoons oil. Bake 10 to 12 minutes, until lightly browned.

5. Transfer to a cutting board and let stand 5 minutes. Cut each quesadilla into 6 wedges and serve immediately with Mango Dip. Makes 24 wedges.

Per wedge: 108 calories, 6 g total fat, 3 g saturated fat, 16 mg cholesterol, 287 mg sodium, 9 g carbohydrates, 5 g protein, 88 mg calcium, 1 g fiber

m e n u

tex-mex appetizer spread

BLACK BEAN SALSA IN PHYLLO CUPS
page 21

SMOKED TURKEY QUESADILLA
left

NACHO CHEESE DIP
page 11

MARGARITAS

mixed mushroom pizzas

Fans of fresh mushrooms—the more the merrier in this recipe—will devour these scrumptious two-cheese pizzas. Found in specialty markets, white truffle oil is a bit pricey, but the exceptional flavor is well worth it!

Prep time: 40 minutes plus rising and standing
Cooking and baking time: 23 to 26 minutes

DOUGH:
- 1   teaspoon active dry yeast
- ²⁄₃   cup warm water (105°F. to 115°F.)
- 2   cups all-purpose flour
- 1   teaspoon salt

TOPPING:
- 1   medium portobella mushroom (4 to 5 oz.)
- ¾   pound assorted exotic mushrooms (such as shiitake, chanterelle, cremini or oyster mushrooms), stemmed and thickly sliced
- 1   tablespoon olive oil
- ¼   teaspoon salt
- ¼   teaspoon freshly ground pepper
- 1   teaspoon minced garlic
- ¾   cup diced Italian Fontina cheese
- 3   tablespoons freshly grated Parmesan cheese
- 1   tablespoon snipped fresh chives
- 1   tablespoon white truffle oil (optional)

1. *Make dough:* Sprinkle yeast over warm water in a cup; let stand 5 minutes, until yeast is bubbly.

2. Meanwhile, pulse together flour and salt in a food processor to combine. With machine on, pour yeast mixture through feed tube; process 1 minute, until mixture forms a ball. (If mixture doesn't form a ball, add water 1 teaspoon at a time). Process dough 45 seconds more to knead.

3. Place dough in a greased bowl, turning to grease top. Cover bowl with plastic wrap and let dough rise in a warm, draft-free place until doubled in bulk, about 1½ hours.

4. Divide dough in half. On a lightly floured surface, shape each piece into a smooth ball. Cover balls with plastic wrap; let stand 30 minutes at room temperature.

5. *Make topping:* Meanwhile, remove and discard stem from portobella mushroom. Turn mushroom top side down and gently scrape away dark gill with a knife or side of a spoon; discard gill. Cut mushroom cap in half, stack halves and cut crosswise into ¼-inch slices. Combine portobella with assorted mushrooms in a bowl.

6. Heat a 12-inch skillet over medium-high heat. Add olive oil and swirl to coat. Add mushroom mixture, salt and pepper and cook 4 to 5 minutes, until mushrooms are lightly browned and any liquid evaporates. Stir in garlic and cook 1 minute more. Transfer mushrooms to a plate. Set aside.

7. Meanwhile, adjust oven rack to lowest position. Heat oven to 450°F. Grease 2 large cookie sheets. On a lightly floured surface with a floured rolling pin, roll each piece into a 16×5-inch rectangle. Place 1 rectangle on each prepared cookie sheet.

8. Sprinkle rectangles with Fontina cheese, top with mushroom mixture, then sprinkle with Parmesan. Bake 15 to 20 minutes, rotating pans halfway through, until crusts are golden brown. Transfer pizzas to a cutting board and sprinkle with chives. Drizzle with truffle oil, if desired. Cut each pizza crosswise into 12 alternating wedges. Makes 24 wedges.

Per wedge: 68 calories, 2 g total fat, 1 g saturated fat, 6 mg cholesterol, 173 mg sodium, 8 g carbohydrates, 3 g protein, 39 mg calcium, 1 g fiber

smoked salmon pizza

This first course pizza is pure indulgence! Don't skimp on the toppings. Using tangy crème fraîche and premium smoked salmon makes all the difference in taste.

Prep time: 15 minutes plus rising
Baking time: 8 to 10 minutes

DOUGH:
- 3   to 3¼ cups all-purpose flour, divided
- 1   package active dry yeast
- ¾   to 1 cup hot water (120°F. to 130°F.)
- 3   tablespoons olive oil, divided
- 1   tablespoon honey

1½ teaspoons salt, divided

¼ teaspoon freshly ground pepper

TOPPING:

½ cup crème fraîche (see tip, page 26) or sour cream

8 ounces thinly sliced smoked salmon

2 teaspoons minced fresh chives

8 lemon wedges

1. *Make dough:* Combine 3 cups of the flour and the yeast in a large mixing bowl. Add hot water, 2 tablespoons of the oil, the honey and 1 teaspoon of the salt and beat at high speed until dough forms a ball.

2. Knead dough on a lightly floured surface 5 minutes, until smooth and elastic, using as much of the remaining ¼ cup flour as necessary. Place dough in a greased bowl, turning to grease top. Cover bowl with a clean kitchen towel and let rise in a warm, draft-free place 30 minutes.

3. Divide dough into quarters and roll each piece into a tight ball. Place balls on a lightly greased cookie sheet. Cover with a damp towel and refrigerate at least 1 hour or overnight.

4. Adjust oven rack on lowest position. Heat oven to 500°F. Lightly grease 2 cookie sheets.

5. Remove dough from refrigerator and roll each piece of dough into an 8-inch circle. Place 2 circles on each prepared cookie sheet. Brush circles with remaining tablespoon of olive oil and lightly sprinkle tops with the remaining ½ teaspoon salt and the pepper.

6. Bake 8 to 10 minutes, rotating cookie sheets halfway through, until crusts are golden brown.

7. Place each pizza on a serving plate. Spread 2 tablespoons of crème fraîche over each. Divide smoked salmon between pizzas, covering evenly. Sprinkle tops with minced chives. Cut each pizza into 4 wedges and serve immediately. Serve each piece with a lemon wedge. Makes 8 servings.

Per serving: 290 calories, 9.5 g total fat, 3 g saturated fat, 13 mg cholesterol, 507 mg sodium, 40 g carbohydrates, 11 g protein, 25 mg calcium, 2 g fiber

greek pizza

Tortillas topped with creamy Fontina cheese and cherry tomatoes provide the base for these no-fuss "pizzas." The Greek influence? Rich kalamata olives and feta cheese, tossed with fresh spinach, cucumbers and a touch of olive oil for Hellenic heaven.

Prep time: 20 minutes
Baking time: 10 minutes

4 (6- to 8-inch) flour tortillas

1 tablespoon plus 1 teaspoon olive oil, divided

1 teaspoon minced garlic

¼ teaspoon dried oregano

½ cup shredded Fontina cheese

1 cup grape tomatoes or cherry tomatoes, halved

½ cup finely shredded fresh spinach

¼ cup peeled, seeded, finely diced cucumber

¼ cup pitted kalamata olives, thinly sliced

3 tablespoons crumbled feta cheese

1 green onion, thinly sliced

1 teaspoon red wine vinegar

⅛ teaspoon salt

⅛ teaspoon freshly ground pepper

1. Heat oven to 450°F. Arrange tortillas on a large cookie sheet. Combine 1 tablespoon of the oil, the garlic and oregano in a small bowl; brush on tortillas. Divide and sprinkle tortillas with Fontina, then top with tomatoes, cut sides up. Bake 10 minutes, until tortillas are browned and crisp.

2. Meanwhile, toss spinach, cucumber, olives, feta cheese, green onion, vinegar, salt, pepper and remaining 1 teaspoon oil in a medium bowl.

3. Remove pizzas from oven. Divide spinach mixture on hot pizzas. Cut each pizza into 6 wedges and serve immediately. Makes 24 wedges.

Per wedge: 43 calories, 2 g total fat, 1 g saturated fat, 4 mg cholesterol, 90 mg sodium, 4 g carbohydrates, 1 g protein, 30 mg calcium, 0 g fiber

crème fraîche

Made from whipping cream and a bacterial culture, crème fraîche has a sharp, tangy flavor that's somewhat similar to sour cream, but more mild. Look for it in specialty food stores or make your own from scratch. Here's how:

Combine ½ cup whipping cream and ½ cup dairy sour cream. Cover and let stand at room temperature for 2 to 5 hours, until it thickens. Refrigerate for up to 1 week.

In addition to using crème fraîche in recipes like Smoked Salmon Pizza, page 24, it also makes a rich yet refreshing dessert when spooned over fresh, in-season fruit.

leek pizza

Serve little bites of this sophisticated leek, prosciutto, and goat cheese pizza as an appetizer, and your guests will never be able to look at an ordinary onion, Canadian bacon and mozzarella pizza quite the same way.

Prep time: 40 minutes • Baking time: 20 minutes

- 1   **bunch leeks (1¼ lbs.)**
- 3   **tablespoons extra-virgin olive oil**
- 2   **cloves garlic, thinly sliced**
- ⅛   **teaspoon red pepper flakes**
- 1   **piece (2 oz.) prosciutto, diced**
      Pinch of salt
- 1   **tablespoon yellow cornmeal**
- ¼   **teaspoon freshly ground pepper**
- 1   **pound prepared pizza dough***
- 2   **ounces goat cheese, crumbled (½ cup)**

1. Adjust oven rack to lowest position. Heat oven to 450°F.

2. Trim roots from leeks; remove any outer withered leaves. Cut off dark green tops to where dark green begins to pale. Halve leeks lengthwise stopping at the root end. Rinse leeks under cold running water to remove any grit; slice into ½-inch

slices and transfer to a bowl of cold water. Let stand 10 minutes. Transfer leeks with a slotted spoon to paper towels and drain.

3. Heat oil, sliced garlic and red pepper flakes in a small skillet over medium-low heat 3 to 5 minutes, just until garlic softens. Transfer to small bowl.

4. Heat 1 tablespoon of the garlic oil over medium-low heat in a large skillet. Add prosciutto; cook 3 to 5 minutes, until prosciutto begins to brown on edges. Increase heat to medium, add leeks and cook 5 to 7 minutes more, until leeks soften and begin to lightly color. Stir in salt; remove from heat.

5. Sprinkle cornmeal and black pepper on a large cookie sheet. Divide pizza dough in half. On a lightly floured surface, shape dough into two 6-inch circles. Transfer circles to prepared cookie sheet. Spoon remaining garlic oil and sliced garlic evenly on both pieces of dough. Divide and sprinkle leek mixture and cheese over tops. Bake pizzas 20 minutes, until crusts are golden brown. Serve immediately. Makes 6 wedges.

*Note: Look for fresh or frozen pizza dough at a neighborhood bakery, pizza parlor or supermarket.

Per wedge: 320 calories, 13.5 g total fat, 3.5 g saturated fat, 15 mg cholesterol, 992 mg sodium, 41 g carbohydrates, 12 g protein, 68 mg calcium, 3 g fiber

devils on horseback

This hot hors d'oeuvre graced the pages of Ladies' Home Journal *during the 1920s. We decided these tasty morsels, a classic combination of sweet and salty, were ready for a comeback.*

Prep time: 20 minutes • Broiling time: 3 to 4 minutes

- 2   **dozen pitted prunes**
- ¼   **cup chopped stuffed green olives**
- 12   **slices bacon, halved**

1. Heat broiler. Cut a slit lengthwise in each prune; spoon ½ teaspoon of chopped olives into each cavity. Wrap prunes in bacon and secure with wooden toothpicks.

2. Arrange on a broiler pan and broil 3 to 4 minutes, turning halfway through, until bacon is crisp. Serve hot. Makes 24 appetizers.

Per appetizer: 40 calories, 2 g total fat, 1 g saturated fat, 3 mg cholesterol, 85 mg sodium, 5 g carbohydrates, 1 g protein, 5 mg calcium, 1 g fiber

fried mozzarella with anchovy dip

Mini grilled cheese sandwiches for the sophisticate!

Prep time: 25 minutes • Cooking time: 2 minutes per batch

ANCHOVY DIP:
- 2 tablespoons butter or margarine
- 1 can (2 oz.) flat anchovies, drained and chopped
- 1 teaspoon minced garlic
- 1 tablespoon capers, drained and chopped
- 1 tablespoon chopped fresh parsley

SANDWICHES:
- 6 tablespoons butter or margarine, softened
- 2 tablespoons chopped fresh parsley
- ½ teaspoon grated lemon peel
- 20 very thin slices firm white bread (such as Pepperidge Farm), crusts trimmed
- 1 pound mozzarella cheese, very thinly sliced
  Lemon wedges (optional)

1. *Make anchovy dip:* Melt butter in a small skillet over low heat. Add anchovies, garlic, capers and parsley. Cook until heated through; set aside. Makes ⅓ cup.

2. *Make sandwiches:* Combine butter, parsley and lemon peel in a small bowl. Spread mixture evenly over 1 side of bread slices. Arrange mozzarella on unbuttered sides of 10 slices of bread; top with remaining slices, buttered side out.

3. Heat a large nonstick skillet over medium heat. Cook sandwiches in batches about 1 minute per side, until golden brown. Transfer sandwiches to a cutting board and cut diagonally into 4 triangles. *(Can be made ahead. Cool sandwiches; transfer to*

cookie sheets. Cover with plastic wrap and refrigerate up to 24 hours. Uncover and reheat in a 350°F. oven 4 to 5 minutes.) Transfer sandwiches to a serving plate. Serve with warm Anchovy Dip and lemon wedges, if desired. Makes 40 appetizers.

Per appetizer: 80 calories, 5 g total fat, 3 g saturated fat, 16 mg cholesterol, 161 mg sodium, 5 g carbohydrates, 3 g protein, 91 mg calcium, 0 g fiber

oysters rockefeller

This classic appetizer was created in 1899 by Jules Alciatore of Antoine's, in New Orleans. And though we're pretty sure he used watercress, our version uses spinach because we love its flavor and texture.

Prep time: 25 minutes • Cooking time: 11 minutes

- 2 pounds fresh spinach, stems removed
- ⅓ cup butter, melted, divided (no substitutes)
- 1 tablespoon fresh lemon juice
- 1 tablespoon anise-flavored liqueur
- ¼ teaspoon salt
- ¼ teaspoon ground red pepper
- 24 shucked oysters on the half shell
- ⅓ cup plain dry bread crumbs
- 4 slices bacon, cooked and crumbled

1. Heat oven to 475°F. Wash spinach thoroughly and drain. Place spinach in a large skillet; cover and cook over medium heat, stirring occasionally, about 3 minutes, until wilted. Drain in a colander. When cool enough to handle, squeeze dry with paper towels and coarsely chop. Combine spinach, 4 tablespoons of the melted butter, the lemon juice, liqueur, salt and red pepper in a medium bowl.

2. Arrange oysters on the half shell on 2 jelly-roll pans. Spoon about 1 tablespoon spinach mixture on each oyster. Combine bread crumbs and remaining butter in a small bowl. Sprinkle about ½ teaspoon crumb mixture evenly on each oyster. Top each with a little crumbled bacon. Bake 8 minutes, until golden and oysters are cooked through. Makes 6 servings.

Per serving: 210 calories, 14 g total fat, 7 g saturated fat, 62 mg cholesterol, 461 mg sodium, 11 g carbohydrates, 9 g protein, 130 mg calcium, 16 g fiber

luscious lime shrimp LOW FAT EASY

For a quick and easy appetizer, try this fragrant cilantro and citrus shrimp served on cucumber slices.

Prep time: 35 minutes plus standing
Broiling time: 3 minutes

DRESSING:

- 3 tablespoons fresh lime juice
- 1 green onion, chopped
- 2 tablespoons chopped fresh cilantro
- 1 teaspoon minced jalapeño chile (see tip, page 15)
- 1 teaspoon olive oil
- ½ teaspoon minced garlic
- ⅛ teaspoon salt

- 20 large shrimp (about 1 lb.), peeled and deveined
- 1 tablespoon minced red bell pepper
- 20 cucumber slices

1. *Make dressing:* Stir together lime juice, green onion, cilantro, jalapeño, oil, garlic and salt in a medium bowl. Toss shrimp with 2 tablespoons of the dressing in another medium bowl.

2. Cover and marinate shrimp in the refrigerator 30 minutes. Set remaining dressing aside.

3. Heat broiler. Broil shrimp 3 inches from heat 1½ minutes per side, or until shrimp turn pink and are opaque.

4. Immediately toss hot shrimp with remaining dressing and the bell pepper; cool slightly and refrigerate 15 minutes. Arrange shrimp on cucumber slices. Makes 20 appetizers.

Per appetizer: 25 calories, 1 g total fat, 0 g saturated fat, 28 mg cholesterol, 41 mg sodium, 1 g carbohydrates, 4 g protein, 12 mg calcium, 0 g fiber

blackened shrimp with tomato mayonnaise EASY

Just a touch of saffron lends fabulous flavor to the Cajun seasoning used here. Wait to crush the threads just before you're ready to use them. Leftover saffron can be stored in an airtight container in a cool, dark place for up to six months. Pictured on page 8.

Total prep and cooking time: 23 to 24 minutes
Microwave used

TOMATO MAYONNAISE:

- Large pinch saffron threads (about ¼ teaspoon), crumbled
- 1 tablespoon hot water (120°F. to 130°F.)
- ½ cup mayonnaise
- 2 tablespoons tomato paste
- 1 tablespoon fresh lemon juice
- 1 small clove garlic, crushed through a press

- 3 tablespoons butter or margarine
- 3 tablespoons Cajun seasoning
- 1 pound large shrimp, peeled, deveined, tails left on

1. *Make tomato mayonnaise:* Crumble saffron into a small bowl. Add hot water; let stand 2 minutes. Whisk in mayonnaise, tomato paste, lemon juice and garlic until blended. Transfer to a small serving bowl; refrigerate while cooking shrimp.

2. Place butter in a microwaveproof pie plate; microwave on HIGH 1 minute, until melted. Spread Cajun seasoning on a piece of waxed paper. Dip 1 side of shrimp in butter and then into Cajun seasoning.

3. Heat a 10-inch cast-iron skillet over medium-high heat until hot. Add half of the shrimp to hot skillet, seasoned side down. Cook 2 minutes; turn. Cook 1 to 2 minutes more, until shrimp turn pink and are opaque. Arrange on a serving platter. Repeat with remaining shrimp. Serve warm with Tomato Mayonnaise. Makes 8 servings.

Per serving: 270 calories, 21.5 g total fat, 6 g saturated fat, 119 mg cholesterol, 1,561 mg sodium, 5 g carbohydrates, 13 g protein, 40 mg calcium, 0 g fiber

gravlax

This dish must be prepared at least three days in advance. The salmon "cooks" in the refrigerator with the help of a curing rub made of salt, sugar, dill and gin.

Total prep time: 20 minutes plus marinating

- 2 **same-size pieces salmon fillets with skin (about 2½ lbs.)**
- ¼ **cup kosher salt**
- ¼ **cup sugar**
- 2 **tablespoons ground white pepper**
- 1 **tablespoon crushed juniper berries**
- 1 **large bunch fresh dill, trimmed**
- 3 **tablespoons gin**

MUSTARD-DILL SAUCE:

- 1½ **teaspoons dry mustard**
- 1 **tablespoon gin**
- 1 **cup mayonnaise**
- ¼ **cup chopped fresh dill**
- 2 **tablespoons Dijon mustard**
- 1 **tablespoon fresh lemon juice**
  Small fresh dill sprigs, for garnish (optional)
  Toast triangles (optional)

1. Rinse salmon under cold running water; pat dry. Stir together salt, sugar, pepper and juniper berries in a small bowl. Rub a generous amount of salt mixture into skin of 1 piece of salmon.

2. Place salmon, skin side down, in a shallow glass or ceramic dish. Sprinkle with some more of the salt mixture, then top with dill and sprinkle with gin.

3. Top with second piece of salmon, skin side up. Rub skin with remaining salt mixture. Cover with plastic wrap. Weigh down with a cutting board that fits just inside the dish, topped with several heavy fruit or vegetable cans. Cover and refrigerate at least 72 hours or up to 1 week, turning every 12 hours and spooning marinade liquid over fish.

4. *Make mustard-dill sauce:* Dissolve dry mustard in gin in a small bowl. Let stand 30 minutes. Stir in mayonnaise, chopped dill, Dijon mustard and lemon juice. *(Can be made ahead. Cover and refrigerate up to 24 hours.)*

5. To serve, remove salmon from marinade. Scrape away dill and spices; pat dry. Place salmon skin side down on a cutting board and cut diagonally into thin slices; remove and discard skin. Arrange slices on a serving platter and garnish with dill sprigs, if desired. Serve with Mustard-Dill Sauce and toast triangles, if desired. Makes 12 servings.

Per serving: 380 calories, 21 g total fat, 3 g saturated fat, 63 mg cholesterol, 733 mg sodium, 2 g carbohydrates, 19 g protein, 36 mg calcium, 0 g fiber

---

test kitchen tip
shrimp savvy

Follow these tips to get the most out of this ever-popular catch of the day:

CHOOSE shrimp that are moist and firm, with translucent flesh and a fresh smell. Avoid shrimp that have an ammonia odor and blackened edge spots on the shells.

STORE frozen shrimp for up to three months. Remember to keep the shrimp tightly wrapped (first in plastic wrap and then foil) to prevent freezer burn. When ready to use, thaw shrimp overnight in the refrigerator. Or, place the sealed package of frozen shrimp in a bowl of cold water and change water every 10 minutes, until shrimp is defrosted. Rinse shrimp under cold running water, drain well, transfer to a layer of several paper towels and pat dry.

WHAT'S WHAT: While some restaurants and fish markets use the terms shrimp, prawns and scampi interchangeably, there is a difference. Shrimp come in a variety of sizes, from miniature and small to jumbo and colossal. Prawns are similar to jumbo and colossal shrimp, but are actually a different species. Because of their large size and sweet, lobster-like flavor, prawns are often served stuffed. In America, "scampi" refers to a dish of shrimp sautéed in garlic butter; however, the term is used in the Mediterranean areas to denote the tail of a small lobster.

choosing crab

Dining on chilled cracked crab, delicious Crab on Cornmeal Pancakes, below, or hot crab cakes— these are but a few of the delights of a crab lover. Many varieties of crab exist. The ones you are mostly like to see in seafood markets include:

BLUE CRABS: Named for their blue claws, they are the major type of crab marketed from the Atlantic coast. They are known for their tender meat and are sold in the hard-shell and soft-shell stages. We feel that blue crabs make the best crab cakes.

DUNGENESS CRABS: Larger in size than the blue crab, these West Coast favorites have a rich and distinctive flavor. They generally are sold as whole cooked crab.

KING CRAB: From Alaska, king crabs are large, averaging 10 pounds. Their legs are filled with long pieces of red-flecked, white meat.

crab on cornmeal pancakes

Crab salad with creamy lime dressing spooned over warm cornmeal cakes is a perfect starter for your next elegant sit-down party. Pictured on page 5.

Prep time: 35 minutes plus rising
Cooking time: 10 minutes • Microwave used

PANCAKES:

- 1 teaspoon active dry yeast
- 2 tablespoons warm water (105°F. to 115°F.)
- 1¼ cups all-purpose flour
- ¾ cup cornmeal
- ¼ teaspoon sugar
- ¼ teaspoon salt
- ¾ cup warm milk (105°F. to 115°F.)
- ½ cup warm buttermilk (105°F. to 115°F.)
- 2 large eggs yolks
- 2 tablespoons butter or margarine
- ½ teaspoon cumin seed, crushed
- 3 large egg whites
  Vegetable cooking spray

CRAB TOPPING:

- ⅓ cup mayonnaise
- ⅓ cup finely diced yellow bell pepper
- 2 tablespoons finely diced sweet onion
- ¼ teaspoon grated lime peel
- 2 tablespoons fresh lime juice
- ½ teaspoon salt
- ¼ teaspoon ground red pepper
- 1 pound lump or jumbo crabmeat, picked over

1. *Make pancakes:* Sprinkle yeast over water in a cup; let stand 5 minutes, until yeast is bubbly. Whisk together flour, cornmeal, sugar and salt in a bowl. Whisk together milk, buttermilk, egg yolks and yeast mixture in another bowl. Gradually beat milk mixture into flour mixture with a spoon. Cover and let stand in a warm, draft-free place until batter is bubbly, 45 to 60 minutes.

2. Combine butter and cumin seed in a microwaveproof cup. Microwave on HIGH 30 to 40 seconds, until melted.

3. Beat egg whites in large mixer bowl, just to stiff peaks. Fold beaten whites into yeast mixture; fold in butter mixture.

4. Coat a 12-inch nonstick skillet with cooking spray; heat over medium-high heat. Drop batter by tablespoonfuls onto skillet, spreading with back of spoon to form 2-inch circles. Cook 30 to 40 seconds, until golden. Turn and cook 30 to 35 seconds more. Transfer pancakes to wire rack. Repeat with remaining batter. *(Can be made ahead. Cool. Wrap well and freeze up to 1 week. To reheat, thaw pancakes at room temperature 2 hours. Wrap in foil; reheat in 350°F. oven 10 minutes.)*

5. *Make crab topping:* Combine all crab topping ingredients except crab in a bowl, stirring to mix well. Gently fold in crab. *(Can be made ahead. Cover and refrigerate topping up to 2 hours.)* To assemble, spoon about 1 tablespoon topping onto each pancake. Arrange on a tray. Makes 42 pancakes.

Per pancake: 60 calories, 3 g total fat, 0.5 g saturated fat, 24 mg cholesterol, 96 mg sodium, 5 g carbohydrates, 3 g protein, 23 mg calcium, 0 g fiber

shrimp and potatoes with caper sauce

Shrimp and red potatoes boiled with allspice make an impressive spread over fresh salad greens drizzled with a creamy caper dressing. It's important to use a premium quality mayonnaise—not salad dressing—in this plated first course.

Prep time: 15 minutes • Cooking time: 14 minutes

- 4 small red potatoes (about ¾ lb.)
- 1 teaspoon salt
- ½ teaspoon whole allspice
- 1 pound medium shrimp, peeled, deveined, tails left on

CAPER DRESSING:

- 3 tablespoons milk
- 3 tablespoons mayonnaise
- 4 teaspoons capers, drained
- 1 teaspoon white wine vinegar
- ¾ teaspoon Dijon mustard
- ¼ teaspoon Worcestershire sauce
  Pinch sugar
  Pinch salt

- 2 cups mesclun greens

1. Bring potatoes, enough water to cover by 1 inch, salt and allspice to boil in a 3-quart saucepan. Reduce heat slightly and simmer 13 minutes, until potatoes are just tender. Add shrimp and cook 1 minute more, until shrimp turn pink and are opaque (do not wait for second boil); drain in colander. Discard allspice.

2. *Make caper dressing:* Meanwhile, whisk caper dressing ingredients in a small bowl.

3. Divide greens onto 4 serving plates and drizzle 1 tablespoon dressing over each. Slice warm potatoes. Divide and arrange potato slices and shrimp on greens. Drizzle with remaining dressing. Makes 4 servings.

Per serving: 270 calories, 11 g total fat, 2 g saturated fat, 179 mg cholesterol, 513 mg sodium, 16 g carbohydrates, 26 g protein, 104 mg calcium, 2 g fiber

asian sesame tuna skewers

No fuss required. A simple marinade consisting of soy sauce, brown sugar, garlic and freshly grated ginger is all you need to make fresh tuna truly memorable.

Prep time: 20 minutes plus marinating
Cooking time: 1 to 2 minutes per batch

MARINADE:

- ½ cup lite soy sauce
- ¼ cup firmly packed brown sugar
- 1 tablespoon minced garlic
- 2 teaspoons grated fresh ginger

- 1 tuna steak (1 lb.), cut into ¾-inch cubes
- 1 tablespoon Asian sesame oil
- 2 tablespoons white sesame seeds
- 2 tablespoons black sesame seeds*
  Wooden skewers or long toothpicks
  Lite soy sauce, pickled ginger, wasabi paste*, for garnish (optional)

1. *Make marinade:* Combine all marinade ingredients in a large resealable plastic storage bag. Seal bag and knead until all ingredients are thoroughly mixed. Add tuna and reseal bag. Marinate in the refrigerator 1 hour.

2. Drain tuna and pat dry; transfer to a large bowl and toss with sesame oil until coated. Spread white and black sesame seeds separately on 2 sheets of waxed paper. Dip 1 side of each piece of tuna in white, then black seeds; transfer to a cookie sheet.

3. Heat a large nonstick skillet over high heat until hot. Add half of tuna to skillet and spread out to a single layer. Cook 1 to 2 minutes, until seared on outside, but still translucent in center, turning once. Remove to a plate. Repeat with remaining tuna.

4. Thread 2 pieces of tuna on each skewer. Serve with soy sauce. Garnish with pickled ginger and wasabi paste, if desired. Makes about 30 skewers.

*Note: Can be found in the ethnic section of supermarkets or Asian specialty stores.

Per skewer: 36 calories, 2 g total fat, 1 g saturated fat, 19 mg cholesterol, 63 mg sodium, 4 g carbohydrates, 2 g protein, 19 mg calcium, 0 g fiber

blini with sour cream

In Russia and Poland, these small, thin buckwheat pancakes are often garnished with smoked salmon, caviar or cheese and served with sour cream as hors d'oeuvres.

Prep time: 20 minutes plus rising
Cooking time: 1½ minutes per batch

BLINI:

2   **large egg whites, at room temperature 20 to 30 minutes**
1   **cup milk**
    Pinch sugar
½   **cup warm water (105°F. to 115°F.)**
1   **teaspoon active dry yeast**
1   **cup buckwheat flour**
¾   **cup all-purpose flour**
2   **teaspoons sugar**
½   **teaspoon salt**
¼   **cup sour cream**
1   **large egg yolk**
1   **tablespoon butter or margarine, melted**

    Vegetable cooking spray
1   **cup plus 2 tablespoons sour cream**
1   **jar (4 oz.) caviar**

1. *Make blini:* Heat milk in a small saucepan until bubbles appear around edge of pan, cool slightly.

2. Dissolve sugar in warm water in a small bowl. Sprinkle top of mixture with yeast and let stand 5 to 10 minutes, until yeast is bubbly.

3. Combine flours, sugar and salt in a large bowl. Beat milk, sour cream, egg yolk and butter with a fork in a medium bowl; add yeast mixture. Stir milk mixture into flour mixture with a wooden spoon, just until combined and all ingredients are moistened. (Batter will be slightly lumpy.) Cover bowl with plastic wrap and let batter rise in a warm, draft-free place until doubled in bulk and bubbly, 30 to 40 minutes.

4. Beat whites in a small mixer bowl just to stiff peaks; gently fold into batter with a rubber spatula.

5. Lightly coat a large nonstick skillet with cooking spray; heat over medium heat 1 minute until a drop of water sizzles. Drop about 10 level tablespoons of batter onto skillet; gently spread each into 1¾-inch circles, if necessary. Cook blini 45 seconds, until bubbles appear on surface. Turn and cook 45 seconds more. Transfer with small spatula to a sheet of waxed paper. Cover with plastic wrap. Continue with remaining batter, greasing pan occasionally in between batches. *(Can be made ahead. Cool completely. Stack blini in a large resealable heavy-duty freezer-proof plastic storage bag; press out excess air, seal bag and refrigerate overnight. To reheat, remove blini from bag, wrap in foil and heat in a 350°F. oven 10 minutes.)*

6. Spoon 1 teaspoon sour cream on each blini and top with ¼ teaspoon caviar. Arrange on a platter and serve immediately. Makes about 54 appetizers.

Per blini: 36 calories, 2 g total fat, 1 g saturated fat, 19 mg cholesterol, 63 mg sodium, 4 g carbohydrates, 2 g protein, 19 mg calcium, 0 g fiber

roasted potatoes with caviar

This easy appetizer makes a fancy first course.

Prep time: 5 minutes • Roasting time: 25 minutes

2   **tablespoons butter or margarine, melted**
1   **pound small red potatoes, cut into ½-inch slices**
¼   **teaspoon salt**
¼   **teaspoon freshly ground pepper**
¼   **cup sour cream**
2   **tablespoons lumpfish or salmon caviar**

1. Heat oven to 400°F. Brush a jelly-roll pan with 1 teaspoon of the butter. Arrange potato slices on prepared pan. Brush potatoes with the remaining butter. Sprinkle with salt and pepper.

2. Bake 15 minutes. Turn potatoes and bake about 10 minutes more, until tender and golden. Transfer potatoes to a serving platter. Spread ½ teaspoon sour cream on each slice and top with ¼ teaspoon caviar. Makes about 24 appetizers.

Per appetizer: 30 calories, 2 g total fat, 1 g saturated fat, 11 mg cholesterol, 55 mg sodium, 4 g carbohydrates, 1 g protein, 8 mg calcium, 0 g fiber

potato latkes

Traditionally served at Hanukkah celebrations, these delicate potato pancakes are topped with applesauce and sour cream. For a dressier, party version try serving these golden fritters with sour cream, snipped chives or thinly sliced smoked salmon.

Prep time: 20 minutes • Cooking time: 5 minutes per batch

- **2 pounds all-purpose potatoes, peeled**
- **1 medium onion**
- **½ cup boiling water**
- **3 large eggs**
- **⅓ cup all-purpose flour**
- **1 teaspoon salt**
- **½ teaspoon baking powder**
- **¼ teaspoon freshly ground pepper**
- **1 cup vegetable oil, for frying**
- **Applesauce and sour cream (optional)**

1. Insert a shredding blade in a food processor. With machine on, add potatoes through feed tube and process to shred. Transfer 2 cups shredded potatoes to a bowl; set aside. With machine on, add onion through feed tube and process to shred. Replace shredding blade with a metal blade. Coarsely chop the remaining potatoes and onions in a work bowl 20 seconds.

2. Strain off liquid from work bowl; spoon potato-onion mixture into a large bowl. Pour boiling water over mixture and mix well. Beat in eggs, flour, salt, baking powder and pepper. Stir in reserved 2 cups shredded potatoes.

3. Heat oven to 200°F. Meanwhile, heat oil in a 10-inch skillet over medium-high heat (oil should be ½-inch deep in pan). Drop potato batter by the tablespoonful into hot oil, 4 or 5 at a time. Fry 2½ minutes each side, until golden brown. Remove latkes with a slotted spoon and drain on paper towels. Transfer latkes to a cookie sheet and keep warm in oven while cooking remaining potato batter. *(Can be made ahead. Cool to room temperature; cover and refrigerate up to 2 days. Reheat in 400°F. oven 5 to 10 minutes.)* Serve with applesauce and sour cream, if desired. Makes 40 pancakes.

Per pancake: 40 calories, 2 g total fat, 0 g saturated fat, 16 mg cholesterol, 69 mg sodium, 5 g carbohydrates, 1 g protein, 7 mg calcium, 0 g fiber

test kitchen tip

roasting red peppers

Though they're nothing new to Italians, Spaniards or the French, roasted red bell peppers are one of those up-and-coming ingredients that are making quite a splash in contemporary American cooking. Find them canned or in jars at most supermarkets. Or, roast your own at home:

HEAT broiler. Rinse 2 large red bell peppers; drain well on paper towels. Place peppers on a foil-lined cookie sheet.

BROIL 6 inches from heat 14 to 18 minutes, turning occasionally, until skins are bubbly and evenly charred.

IMMEDIATELY WRAP foil around peppers. Let stand 20 to 30 minutes, until peppers are cool enough to handle. Cut peppers lengthwise in half. Cut out stems, seeds and membranes and discard them.

REMOVE blistered skin from peppers using a sharp knife to gently and slowly pull it off in strips. Makes about 1 cup.

If you are in a pinch, use 1 jar (7oz.) roasted red peppers, drained, for 2 fresh bell peppers.

Use roasted peppers as part of an antipasto tray, alongside olives, marinated artichoke hearts and imported meats and cheeses. Or, serve chopped roasted red peppers, sprinkled with fresh herbs, atop toasted French or Italian bread slices for a colorful bruschetta.

artichoke and tomato empanadas

These savory turnovers feature easy-to-prepare frozen artichoke hearts. Good choices to serve alongside these empanadas include the Deviled Eggs and Cucumber Cups, page 9, and the Olive and Cheese Platter with Sage, page 20. Pictured on page 6.

Prep time: 45 minutes • Baking time: 22 to 28 minutes

PASTRY:

- 2 cups all-purpose flour
- 1 tablespoon sugar
- 1 teaspoon salt
- 6 tablespoons cold butter or margarine, cut up
- 3 tablespoons vegetable shortening
- 3 to 4 tablespoons cold water
- 1½ teaspoons white vinegar

FILLING:

- 1 tablespoon olive oil
- ½ cup finely chopped onion
- 2 teaspoons minced garlic
- 1 package (9 oz.) frozen artichoke hearts, cooked according to package directions
- 3 plum tomatoes, diced
- 2 teaspoons minced fresh thyme or ¼ teaspoon dried thyme
- ½ teaspoon salt
- ⅛ teaspoon freshly ground pepper
- ½ cup coarsely shredded Gruyère or Swiss cheese
- 2 tablespoons freshly grated Parmesan cheese
- 1 large egg yolk, lightly beaten

1. *Make pastry:* Pulse together flour, sugar and salt in food processor to combine. Add butter and shortening; pulse until butter is size of small peas. Combine 3 tablespoons cold water and vinegar in a cup. Add liquid through feed tube; pulse until dough just starts to come together. (Add remaining 1 tablespoon water, if necessary.)

2. Gather dough into a ball; gently press and form into a disk. Wrap in plastic wrap and refrigerate 30 minutes. (*Can be made ahead. Refrigerate up to 2 days.*)

3. *Make filling:* Heat oil in a large skillet over medium heat. Add onion and garlic and cook 3 minutes, just until softened. Increase heat to medium-high. Add artichoke hearts, tomatoes, thyme, salt and pepper and cook 2 to 5 minutes more, until tomatoes are softened and mixture is slightly golden. Set aside to cool.

4. Transfer filling to food processor; pulse until very finely chopped. Transfer to a medium bowl and stir in cheeses.

5. Heat oven to 375°F. Lightly grease 2 large jelly-roll pans or large cookie sheets.

6. Unwrap pastry. On a lightly floured surface, roll dough into a 14½-inch circle, ⅛ inch thick. With a 3-inch round biscuit cutter or top of a glass, cut out as many circles as possible, rerolling scraps and dipping the cutter into flour between cuts as needed to prevent sticking. Lightly reroll each into a 3½-inch circle.

7. Place 1 slightly mounded tablespoon of filling in center of each circle. Lightly moisten edge of circle with a little water. Gently fold 1 edge of circle over filling to make a semicircle. Using floured tines of a fork, press along edges to seal. Prick top of each empanada with the fork so steam can escape. Lightly brush each top with some egg yolk. Transfer to prepared cookie sheets.

8. Bake 22 to 28 minutes, rotating pans halfway through, until empanadas are golden brown. (*Can be made ahead. Cool completely. Freeze on cookie sheet until firm; transfer to a large resealable heavy-duty freezer-proof plastic storage bag and freeze up to 2 weeks. Reheat in 350°F. oven 10 to 15 minutes.*) Makes 24 appetizers.

Per empanada: 110 calories, 6.5 g total fat, 3 g saturated fat, 20 mg cholesterol, 198 mg sodium, 10 g carbohydrates, 2 g protein, 38 mg calcium, 1 g fiber

pepper-jack empanadas

These flaky phyllo triangles filled with three rich and creamy cheeses are voluptuous! Try them with guacamole.

Prep time: 1 hour • Baking time: 12 to 15 minutes

FILLING:

1	package (3 oz.) cream cheese, softened
1½	cups shredded pepper-Jack cheese
1	cup ricotta cheese
½	cup walnuts, toasted and ground
⅓	cup chopped fresh parsley
1	large egg, lightly beaten
6	to 8 drops hot red pepper sauce

20	sheets (18×14 inches) phyllo dough, divided
½	cup butter or margarine plus 2 tablespoons butter or margarine, melted

1. Heat oven to 375°F. Lightly grease 2 cookie sheets.

2. *Make filling:* Beat cream cheese in a medium bowl until smooth. Stir in pepper-Jack cheese, ricotta, walnuts, parsley, egg and pepper sauce until combined.

3. Place 1 phyllo sheet on a work surface (keep remaining phyllo covered with plastic wrap and a clean kitchen towel). Lightly brush phyllo sheet with melted butter. Top with a second phyllo sheet and brush with butter. With a sharp knife, cut layered sheets crosswise into 5 equal strips.

4. Place 1 rounded teaspoon cheese mixture on the end of each strip. Fold up corner around filling to form a triangle (flag-style). Transfer triangles, seam side down, to prepared cookie sheets and lightly brush tops with butter. Repeat with remaining phyllo, butter and filling. *(Can be made ahead. Freeze on cookie sheets. Transfer to resealable heavy-duty freezer-proof plastic storage bags and store up to 1 month.)*

5. Bake 12 to 15 minutes (20 to 25 minutes, if frozen), until lightly golden. Serve warm. Makes 50 appetizers.

Per appetizer: 75 calories, 6 g total fat, 3 g saturated fat, 17 mg cholesterol, 82 mg sodium, 4 g carbohydrates, 2 g protein, 39 mg calcium, 0 g fiber

mussels and mangoes

This mussel dish builds on a traditional seafood preparation with mango and coconut milk. Scotch bonnets are among the hottest of the chiles, so be sure to wear rubber gloves while handling and chopping them.

Prep time: 20 minutes • Cooking time: 12 minutes

2	tablespoons olive oil
¼	cup minced shallots
1	tablespoon minced garlic
20	large mussels (about 2 lbs.) scrubbed and debearded*
½	cup dry white wine
½	cup fresh corn kernels
½	cup diced red bell pepper
1	teaspoon cumin
1	teaspoon minced Scotch bonnet chile or 1 to 2 tablespoons minced jalapeño chile (see tip, page 15)
1	mango, peeled and finely diced
½	cup unsweetened coconut milk**
¼	teaspoon salt
1	tablespoon chopped fresh chervil or parsley

1. Heat oil in a large saucepan over medium-high heat. Add shallots and garlic and cook 2 minutes, until tender. Add mussels and cook 30 seconds. Add wine; cover and simmer 2 minutes.

2. Add corn, bell pepper, cumin and Scotch bonnet chile; cover and cook 2 minutes. Add mango and coconut milk; cover and cook 5 minutes more, until mussels open. (Discard any unopened and empty shells.) Season broth with salt and chervil. Arrange mussels in individual soup bowls with broth, mango and vegetables. Makes 4 servings.

*Note: To debeard mussels: Scrub the shells with a stiff brush under cold running water; then, with a small sharp knife, cut off the "beards" (small black tufts attached to shells).

**Note: Can be found in the ethnic sections of supermarkets or in Asian specialty stores.

Per serving: 265 calories, 10 g total fat, 7 g saturated fat, 18 mg cholesterol, 201 mg sodium, 21 g carbohydrates, 10 g protein, 89 mg calcium, 2 g fiber

hail caesar (cardini, that is)

One might think the Caesar salad was created in Rome, but believe it or not, it hails from Tijuana.

Legend has it that Alex Cardini, an Italian Air Force veteran, was visiting his brother, Caesar, in Caesar's south-of-the-border restaurant. A group from California came into the restaurant to celebrate the 4th of July, and Cardini set out to feed them. When he raided the kitchen, he found eggs, romaine lettuce, dry bread, Parmesan cheese, garlic, olive oil, lemon juice and pepper. He made croutons from the dry bread and combined them with the other ingredients. Anchovies weren't added until later, against Cardini's wishes.

caesar salad

Enjoy a favorite first-course salad—without sacrificing your waistline. In our slimmed-down version, the king of all salads loses some its fat, but none if its classic zesty taste, thanks to our blend of light mayonnaise, chicken broth, Dijon mustard and anchovies. Pictured on page 5.

Prep time: 20 minutes • Baking time: 5 to 8 minutes

4 ounces French bread, cubed
1 medium clove garlic, chopped
2 anchovy fillets
1 tablespoon light mayonnaise
1 tablespoon extra-virgin olive oil
2 tablespoons fresh lemon juice
1 tablespoon chicken broth
1/2 teaspoon Dijon mustard
1/4 teaspoon salt
1/8 teaspoon freshly ground pepper
1 head (1 1/4 lbs.) romaine lettuce, leaves torn
2 tablespoons shredded Parmesan cheese

1. Heat oven to 400°F. Spread bread cubes on cookie sheet. Bake 5 to 8 minutes, until toasted. Cool.

2. Mash garlic with a fork against the side of a large wooden bowl. Add anchovies and mash until a paste forms. Add mayonnaise and mash into anchovy paste. Whisk in oil, juice, broth, mustard, salt and pepper. (Dressing will be thin.) Add romaine and croutons to bowl; toss with dressing. Sprinkle with Parmesan and toss again. Makes 4 servings.

Per serving: 155 calories, 7 g total fat, 1.5 g saturated fat, 5 mg cholesterol, 513 mg sodium, 18 g carbohydrates, 6 g protein, 101 mg calcium, 2 g fiber

warm zucchini and feta salad

Guests will love the way the garlic-infused, mild and mellow zucchini contrasts with the peppery tones of the salad greens. A crumbling of feta adds extra flavor.

Prep time: 20 minutes • Cooking time: 5 to 10 minutes

2 tablespoons extra-virgin olive oil, divided
1 1/2 teaspoons very thinly sliced garlic
2 large zucchini, halved lengthwise and sliced
1/2 teaspoon minced fresh thyme
1/2 teaspoon salt, divided
1/8 teaspoon freshly ground pepper
1/4 teaspoon grated lemon peel
1 teaspoon fresh lemon juice
1 bunch (5 oz.) arugula, stems removed and coarsely chopped
1 bunch (2 oz.) radicchio, coarsely chopped
3/4 cup (4 oz.) crumbled feta cheese

1. Heat 1 tablespoon of the oil in a 12-inch nonstick skillet. Add garlic and cook, stirring, 30 seconds. Add zucchini; cook, stirring, 5 minutes. Add thyme, 1/4 teaspoon of the salt and the pepper; cook 1 minute more, until just tender.

2. Meanwhile, whisk remaining 1 tablespoon oil, lemon peel, juice and remaining 1/4 teaspoon salt in a large bowl. Add arugula and radicchio and toss. Transfer to a large serving platter; top with zucchini and sprinkle with feta. Makes 4 servings.

Per serving: 169 calories, 13 g total fat, 5 g saturated fat, 25 mg cholesterol, 475 mg sodium, 8 g carbohydrates, 7 g protein, 224 mg calcium, 2 g fiber

insalata di frutti di mare

The Italian "frutti di mare"—like its French equivalent, "fruits de mer"—literally means "fruits of the sea." Leave it to these food-loving cultures to come up with such a fanciful term for seafood! Our version of the classic Italian starter features shrimp, scallops, squid and mussels, but in Italy the kinds of fish may vary from region to region. Clams, crab, monkfish and oysters all work well.

Prep time: 35 minutes plus marinating and standing
Cooking time: 25 minutes

DRESSING:

- ¼ cup fresh lemon juice
- ½ teaspoon salt
- ¼ teaspoon minced garlic
- ⅛ teaspoon freshly ground pepper
- ¼ cup olive oil

SALAD:

- 2 cups water
- 1 carrot, cut up
- Half of 1 celery rib, peeled and cut into 2-inch pieces
- ½ small lemon, sliced
- 6 peppercorns
- 1 clove garlic, crushed through a press
- ½ pound medium shrimp, peeled and deveined
- ½ pound sea scallops, halved
- ½ pound cleaned squid (calamari), bodies sliced thin
- 1 pound small mussels, scrubbed and debearded (see note, page 35)
- 2 tablespoons chopped fresh parsley
- Lemon wedges, for garnish (optional)

1. *Make dressing:* Combine lemon juice, salt, garlic and pepper in a medium bowl. Slowly whisk in oil until blended; set aside.

2. *Make salad:* Combine water, carrot, celery, lemon, peppercorns and garlic in a medium saucepan. Bring to boil over high heat. Reduce heat to medium; add shrimp, cover and cook 2 minutes, until opaque. Transfer shrimp with a slotted spoon to a large bowl.

3. Return liquid to boil; add scallops and cook 2 minutes, until just cooked through. Transfer to bowl with shrimp.

4. Repeat with squid, cook 30 seconds. Transfer to bowl with shrimp and scallops. Return liquid to boil; add mussels, cover and cook 5 minutes, until mussels open. Transfer opened mussels to a plate. Cover and cook remaining mussels 1 minute more. (Discard any unopened mussels and empty shells.) Remove remaining mussels from shells; discard shells. Add to bowl with other seafood.

5. Add dressing to seafood, tossing to coat. Cover and marinate in the refrigerator 5 to 6 hours. *(Can be made ahead. Cover and refrigerate up to 8 hours.)*

6. To serve, let salad stand at room temperature 30 minutes. Stir in parsley and garnish with lemon wedges, if desired. Makes 6 servings.

Per serving: 210 calories, 11 g total fat, 2 g saturated fat, 154 mg cholesterol, 376 mg sodium, 6 g carbohydrates, 21 g protein, 60 mg calcium, 0 g fiber

---

test kitchen tip

selecting scallops

Whether your recipe calls for sea scallops or the smaller, sweeter bay scallop, remember:

CHOOSE sweet-smelling scallops that are firm and free of excess cloudy liquid. A strong sulfur odor indicates the scallops are spoiled. Scallops should be creamy pink, creamy white or tan—if they're completely white, it could mean they've been soaked in water to increase weight.

STORE fresh shucked scallops (the most common type on the market) in the refrigerator, covered with their own liquid, in a covered container for up to 2 days.

grapefruit and endive salad

Get a jump-start on the prep by sectioning the grapefruit. This can be done ahead and refrigerated, as can the slicing of the radishes. Belgian endive, however, cannot be cut ahead because it will turn brown. For optimum crunch, toss the salad just before serving.

Total prep time: 10 minutes

- **2 large grapefruit**
- **DRESSING:**
- **1 tablespoon white balsamic or white wine vinegar**
- **1 teaspoon minced shallot**
- **½ teaspoon salt**
- **¼ teaspoon sugar**
- **¼ teaspoon grated fresh ginger**
- **⅛ teaspoon freshly ground pepper**
- **3 tablespoons extra-virgin olive oil**
- ■
- **2 large heads Belgian endive (¾ lb.)**
- **1 large bunch (12 oz.) radishes, leaves removed, halved and sliced**

1. ■ Peel grapefruit with a small sharp knife. Place 1 of the grapefruit over a small bowl and cut into sections, reserving juice in bowl. Repeat with remaining grapefruit. Transfer sections with a slotted spoon to a large bowl.

2. ■ *Make dressing:* Whisk vinegar, shallot, salt, sugar, ginger and pepper into grapefruit juice. Gradually whisk in oil until thickened. Set aside.

3. ■ Carefully separate 12 large outer leaves from heads. Divide and arrange whole leaves among 4 serving plates. Remove cores and thinly slice remaining endive.

4. ■ Add sliced endive and radishes to grapefruit sections. Add dressing, tossing to coat. Divide and spoon mixture onto center of serving plates. Makes 4 servings.

Per serving: 160 calories, 10 g total fat, 1.5 g saturated fat, 0 mg cholesterol, 318 mg sodium, 16 g carbohydrates, 2 g protein, 14 mg calcium, 3 g fiber

leeks vinaigrette

Leeks get the noble treatment in this French classic appetizer, a great alternative to garden salad. The leeks simmer in broth and thyme, then are tossed with a light vinaigrette and garnished with chopped hard-cooked egg.

Prep time: 20 minutes • Cooking time: 35 to 45 minutes

- **2 bunches leeks (2 lbs.)**
- **3 teaspoons butter or margarine, softened, divided**
- **1 cup chicken broth**
- **2 sprigs fresh thyme**
- **VINAIGRETTE:**
- **2 anchovy fillets, finely chopped**
- **2 tablespoons red wine vinegar**
- **½ teaspoon fresh thyme leaves**
- **Pinch salt**
- **¼ cup olive oil**
- ■
- **1 large bunch (8 oz.) watercress, trimmed**
- **1 hard-cooked egg, peeled and finely chopped**
- **Freshly ground pepper**

1. ■ Heat oven to 350°F.

2. ■ Fill a large bowl with cold water. Trim roots from leeks; discard outer withered leaves. Cut off dark green tops to where dark green begins to pale. Trim root end. Halve leeks lengthwise, stopping at root end. Rinse leeks under cold running water to remove any grit. Place leeks in cold water; let stand 10 minutes. Transfer leeks with a slotted spoon to paper towels and drain; set aside.

3. ■ Brush 1½ teaspoons of butter on bottom and sides of a 9-inch square baking dish. Cut a piece of parchment slightly smaller than dish. Brush 1 side of parchment with remaining 1½ teaspoons butter. Arrange leeks in a single layer in prepared dish. Add broth and thyme sprigs. Place parchment buttered side down directly on top of leeks. Bake 35 to 45 minutes, until a toothpick easily pierces thickest part of each leek.

4. ■ *Make vinaigrette:* Meanwhile, whisk anchovies, vinegar, thyme leaves and salt in a medium bowl. Gradually whisk in oil until blended. Set aside.

5. Remove leeks with tongs, letting excess broth drip into baking dish. Transfer leeks to plate and let cool 15 minutes; discard broth.

6. Divide and arrange watercress on 4 plates. Place leeks on top; spoon vinaigrette over leeks. Sprinkle with chopped egg and pepper. Makes 4 servings.

Per serving: 245 calories, 18.5 g total fat, 4 g saturated fat, 62 mg cholesterol, 451 mg sodium, 16 g carbohydrates, 5 g protein, 198 mg calcium, 4 g fiber

patio salad with cilantro dressing (EASY)

As its name implies, this is a great warm-weather salad. A refreshing cilantro dressing, crisp greens and jicama strips make it cool and crunchy. Tip: To toast the pine nuts for the dressing, cook and stir in a skillet over medium heat 3 to 4 minutes.

Total prep time: 20 minutes

DRESSING:
- 1   cup fresh cilantro leaves
- 2   tablespoons pine nuts, lightly toasted
- ¼   cup extra-virgin olive oil
- 3   tablespoons freshly grated Parmesan cheese
- 2   tablespoons sherry vinegar
- 1   tablespoon fresh orange juice
- 1   teaspoon minced garlic
- ¾   teaspoon salt
- ¼   teaspoon freshly ground pepper

SALAD:
- 1   large head (1¾ lb.) romaine lettuce
- 1   medium head (1¼ lb.) iceberg lettuce
- 1   large (8 oz.) head radicchio
- ½   pound jicama, peeled and cut into thin strips (2 cups)

1. *Make dressing:* Combine cilantro and pine nuts in food processor; pulse until finely chopped. With machine running, add remaining dressing ingredients through feed tube and process until smooth. Makes ¾ cup. *(Can be made ahead. Transfer to a small bowl and cover top of dressing directly with a sheet of plastic wrap. Refrigerate up to 6 hours.)*

2. *Make salad:* Core lettuces and radicchio, tear leaves into 1-inch pieces and transfer to large bowl. Add dressing and jicama, gently tossing to coat. Makes 8 servings.

Per serving: 130 calories, 9.5 g total fat, 1.5 g saturated fat, 2 mg cholesterol, 282 mg sodium, 9 g carbohydrates, 5 g protein, 125 mg calcium, 4 g fiber

---

test kitchen tip

the real reggiano

A lot of Americans grew up getting their Parmesan cheese out of a can, but once you've tasted the original Parmesan cheese (called Parmigiano-Reggiano, which some food-lovers shorten simply to "Reggiano"), there's no going back! A little background and know-how for the connoisseur:

• Authentic Parmigiano-Reggiano hails from the Emilia-Romagna region in northern Italy. It is crafted from a tradition that dates back nearly 700 years.

• In the United States, Parmesan cheeses usually age 14 months, whereas the authentic Italian varieties usually age 2 years. In fact, wheels given the highest label are aged 4 years.

• A real Reggiano will have the words "Parmigiano-Reggiano" stenciled—in small dots—on the rind.

• Hallmark qualities of a real Reggiano include its granular texture and intense, snappy flavor.

• While the grated cheese finds its way into a variety of recipes, it's not for grating only! Serve shards of the cheese (it can't be sliced) alongside nuts and fruits, either as an appetizer or a light dessert.

wonton soup

This recipe makes enough wontons for two batches of soup. They freeze well, so you can enjoy them now and then again next week.

Prep time: 45 minutes plus marinating
Cooking time: 15 minutes

WONTONS:

- **1 pound ground chicken**
- **⅓ cup chopped canned water chestnuts**
- **2 tablespoons diced green onions**
- **1 tablespoon soy sauce**
- **2 teaspoons grated fresh ginger**
- **1 teaspoon rice vinegar**
- **1 teaspoon finely chopped garlic**
- **1 teaspoon Asian sesame oil**
- **½ teaspoon sugar**
- **1 package (14 oz.) wonton wrappers (about 60)**

- **4 cans (14½ oz. each) chicken broth**
- **½ teaspoon soy sauce**
- **1 cup chopped fresh spinach**
- **1 piece smoked ham (2 oz.), cut into thin strips**

1. *Make wontons:* Combine all wonton ingredients except wonton wrappers in a medium bowl. Cover; let stand at room temperature 15 minutes.

2. Line 2 jelly-roll pans with waxed paper. Place 1½ teaspoons filling in center of 1 wonton wrapper. Brush the edge of wrapper with water. Fold sides of wrapper together to form a triangle; lightly pinch edge and seal. Bring long ends over, overlapping slightly. Transfer to prepared pan and cover loosely with a sheet of waxed paper. Repeat process with remaining filling and wrappers, dividing the wontons between the 2 pans. Cover with plastic wrap and refrigerate 1 pan of wontons. *(Freeze remaining wontons 1 hour, or until firm. Transfer to a large resealable heavy-duty freezer-proof plastic storage bag and freeze up to 2 weeks.*)*

3. Meanwhile, bring a large pot of salted water to boil. Bring broth and soy sauce to boil in another large pot; reduce heat and simmer 10 minutes. When salted water comes to a boil, add a third of the refrigerated wontons. Cook, carefully stirring to prevent wontons from sticking on bottom,

1 to 2 minutes, until wontons begin to float. Using a slotted spoon, transfer wontons to simmering broth. Stir in spinach and ham. Repeat with remaining refrigerated wontons. Makes 6 servings.

*Note: To cook frozen wontons, prepare recipe for soup as directed, except cook wontons (do not defrost) in boiling water 2 to 4 minutes.

Per serving: 340 calories, 6 g total fat, 1.5 g saturated fat, 63 mg cholesterol, 1,947 mg sodium, 42 g carbohydrates, 27 g protein, 53 mg calcium, 2 g fiber

shrimp and miso soup

Sweet shrimp, nutty sesame oil, salty soy sauce, and the varying touches of spiciness from ginger, cilantro and red pepper flakes, give this Asian soup many layers of flavor.

Prep time: 20 minutes • Cooking time: 10 minutes

- **½ pound medium shrimp, peeled and deveined**
- **¼ teaspoon salt**
- **⅛ to ¼ teaspoon red pepper flakes**
- **1 teaspoon Asian sesame oil***
- **4 cups water**
- **½ pound shiitake mushrooms, stems removed and thinly sliced**
- **2 tablespoons soy sauce**
- **4 teaspoons miso paste***
- **1 teaspoon grated fresh ginger**
- **2 tablespoons chopped fresh cilantro**

Toss shrimp with salt and pepper flakes. Heat oil in a 3-quart saucepan over high heat; add shrimp, in a single layer, and cook 1 minute per side, until golden. Transfer to a bowl. Add water, mushrooms, soy sauce, miso and ginger to saucepan. Bring to simmer and cook 7 minutes, until mushrooms are tender. Add shrimp and cilantro; cook 1 minute more, until heated though. Serve immediately. Ladle into 4 serving bowls. Makes 4 servings.

*Note: Can be found in the ethnic section of supermarkets or Asian specialty stores.

Per serving: 119 calories, 2.5 g total fat, 0.5 g saturated fat, 86 mg cholesterol, 909 mg sodium, 10 g carbohydrates, 14 g protein, 41 mg calcium, 2 g fiber

TORTILLA-
CRUSTED
CHICKEN
PG. 49

daily
dinner
inspirations

Who has time to cook on weeknights? You do, thanks to new styles of fresh, fuss-free comfort food. Our crisp-coated chicken, creamy casseroles and delicious steaks, stews and fish dishes are full of good foods and great flavors sure to please everyone around your table.

ENCHILADA
CASSEROLE
PG. 58

VEGETARIAN
SKILLET CHILI
PG. 71

fresh takes on
the classics
make dinnertime

GOOD-FOR-YOU
MEATLOAF
PG. 56

WARM GERMAN
POTATO SALAD
PG. 76
LEMON BROCCOLI
PG. 79

GOOD FORTUNE
DINNER
PG. 61

SOUTHERN-STYLE
BARBECUE PORK CHOPS
PG. 60
CRISPY HASH BROWNS
PG. 78
LIMA BEANS
WITH RED PEPPER
PG. 63

both familiar—
and fun!

HOMESTYLE
BEEF AND
VEGETABLE STEW
PG. 59
GUILTLESS
MASHED
POTATOES
PG. 76
PEAS WITH RED
ONION
PG. 79

VIETNAMESE
LEMONGRASS
CHICKEN
PG. 54

meet the new
chicken and noodles

CHICKEN PAD
THAI
PG. 51

PAPPARDELLE
WITH ESCAROLE
PG. 63

INDONESIAN
CURRY
PG. 52

and other worldly takes
on suppertime favorites

JAPANESE
CHICKEN-NOODLE
BOWL
PG. 52

SKILLET STEAK
WITH
MUSHROOMS
AND ONION
PG. 57
SPICY
OVEN FRIES
PG. 76

kid food?

grown-up food?

CUCUMBER-
YOGURT
CHICKEN
PG. 49

PENNE WITH
RUSTIC
TOMATOES
PG. 68

CHICKEN
WITH HERB
RUB
PG. 49

THYME-GARLIC
BAKED POTATOES
PG. 79
ROAST PORK
WITH GARLIC AND
APPLES
PG. 60
SPINACH SAUTÉ
PG. 63

we've got everyone

covered

ITALIAN
HERO
CALZONE
PG. 72

for **easy** suppers, egg it on!

MUSHROOM
AND PEPPER
FRITTATA
PG. 67

EGG AND BLACK
BEAN BURRITOS
PG. 66

tortilla-crusted chicken *EASY*

A crunchy take on baked chicken. Pictured on page 41.

Total prep and cook time: 20 minutes

- 1 **cup crushed tortilla chips**
- ¾ **teaspoon salt**
- ½ **teaspoon dried oregano**
- ¼ **teaspoon cumin**
- ¼ **teaspoon freshly ground pepper**
- 1 **large egg**
- 4 **boneless, skinless chicken breast halves (6 to 7 oz. each)**
- 1 **tablespoon vegetable or corn oil**

1. Heat oven to 350°F. Combine chips, salt, oregano, cumin and pepper in a pie plate. Beat egg in a shallow bowl. Dip chicken in egg, then coat in crushed chip mixture.

2. Heat oil in a 12-inch nonstick ovenproof skillet over medium-high heat. Add chicken and cook 3 minutes per side, until brown. Transfer chicken in skillet to oven. Bake 8 to 9 minutes, until cooked through. Makes 4 servings.

Per serving: 360 calories, 12.5 g total fat, 2.5 g saturated fat, 160 mg cholesterol, 684 mg sodium, 14 g carbohydrates, 46 g protein, 64 mg calcium, 1 g fiber

cucumber-yogurt chicken *EASY*

The yogurt sauce comes together quickly! Pictured on page 46.

Total prep and cook time: 27 minutes

- 1 **cup peeled and diced English (seedless) cucumber**
- 1 **cup plain low-fat yogurt**
- ½ **cup finely diced radish**
- 2 **tablespoons mayonnaise**
- ¼ **teaspoon grated lemon peel**
- 1 **tablespoon fresh lemon juice**
- 1 **teaspoon salt, divided**
- ¼ **teaspoon minced garlic**
- ¼ **teaspoon hot red pepper sauce**
- 1 **tablespoon olive or vegetable oil**
- 4 **boneless, skinless chicken breast halves (6 to 7 oz. each)**
- ½ **teaspoon ground red pepper**

1. Heat oven to 350°F. Mix cucumber, yogurt, radish, mayonnaise, lemon peel, lemon juice, ½ teaspoon of the salt, the garlic and red pepper sauce in a small bowl. Cover; refrigerate yogurt sauce.

2. Heat oil in a 12-inch nonstick, ovenproof skillet over medium-high heat. Sprinkle chicken with the remaining ½ teaspoon salt and the ground red pepper and cook 3 minutes per side, until brown. Transfer chicken in skillet to oven. Bake 8 to 9 minutes, until cooked through. Serve with yogurt sauce. Serves 4.

Per serving: 330 calories, 12 g total fat, 2.5 g saturated fat, 114 mg cholesterol, 791 mg sodium, 6 g carbohydrates, 46 g protein, 136 mg calcium, 1 g fiber

chicken with herb rub *EASY*

Fennel and mint make a great combo. Pictured on page 47.

Total prep and cook time: 30 minutes

- ½ **cup fresh mint leaves, chopped**
- 2 **to 4 teaspoons fennel seeds, crushed**
- 2 **tablespoons sesame seeds**
- 2 **teaspoons dried thyme**
- 1 **teaspoon salt**
- ¼ **teaspoon freshly ground pepper**
- 4 **boneless, skinless chicken breast halves (6 to 7 oz. each)**
- 1 **tablespoon olive or vegetable oil**

1. Heat oven to 350°F. Combine all ingredients except chicken and oil in a small bowl. Rub herb mixture over both sides of chicken.

2. Heat oil in a 12-inch nonstick, ovenproof skillet over medium-high heat. Add chicken and cook 3 minutes per side, until brown. Transfer chicken in skillet to oven. Bake 8 to 9 minutes, until cooked through. Makes 4 servings.

Per serving: 275 calories, 8.5 g total fat, 1.5 g saturated fat, 107 mg cholesterol, 710 mg sodium, 4 g carbohydrates, 44 g protein, 130 mg calcium, 2 g fiber

chicken cacciatore

We add fresh and dried mushrooms to the sauce, so it's rich and flavorful without lengthy simmering.

Total prep and cook time: 30 minutes

- **1 package (.35 oz.) dried porcini mushrooms**
- **¼ cup boiling water**
- **1½ pounds boneless, skinless chicken thighs**
- **¾ teaspoon salt, divided**
- **¼ teaspoon freshly ground pepper**
- **1 tablespoon olive oil**
- **½ pound sliced mushrooms**
- **1 medium onion, chopped**
- **1 can (28 oz.) tomatoes in puree, chopped**
- **½ teaspoon dried oregano**

1. Rinse porcini well in a sieve under cold running water; transfer to a cup. Add boiling water; let stand 10 minutes. Chop porcini, reserving liquid.

2. Sprinkle chicken with ½ teaspoon of the salt and the pepper. Brown chicken 5 minutes in a 12-inch nonstick skillet; remove.

3. Heat oil in skillet. Add sliced mushrooms and onion and cook 3 minutes. Add the remaining ¼ teaspoon salt and cook until onion is golden.

4. Return chicken to skillet. Add porcini, reserved liquid, tomatoes and oregano. Bring to boil. Reduce heat and simmer 16 minutes, until chicken is cooked through. Makes 4 servings.

Per serving: 330 calories, 10.5 g total fat, 2 g saturated fat, 141 mg cholesterol, 902 mg sodium, 20 g carbohydrates, 38 g protein, 104 mg calcium, 3 g fiber

sweet-and-sour chicken

This Chinese staple has always been a popular takeout meal. Use a deep-fat thermometer to regulate the temperature of the hot cooking oil.

Prep time: 20 minutes plus marinating
Cooking time: 10 to 13 minutes

SAUCE:
- **½ cup pineapple juice**
- **½ cup rice vinegar**
- **5 tablespoons sugar**
- **2 tablespoons ketchup**
- **2 tablespoons lite soy sauce**
- **1 tablespoon water**
- **1 teaspoon cornstarch**

MARINADE:
- **¼ teaspoon salt**
- **1 pound boneless, skinless chicken thighs, cut into 1-inch pieces**
- **1 tablespoon lite soy sauce**
- **1 teaspoon cornstarch**
- **1 teaspoon dry sherry**
- **1 teaspoon Asian sesame oil (see tips, pages 16 and 17)**

BATTER:
- **½ cup cornstarch**
- **¼ cup all-purpose flour**
- **1 teaspoon baking powder**
- **1 teaspoon salt**
- **¼ teaspoon freshly ground pepper**
- **½ cup water**

- **2 cups peanut or vegetable oil**
  Green onion, for garnish (optional)
  Steamed broccoli (optional)

1. *Make sauce:* Combine all sauce ingredients except water and cornstarch in a small saucepan. Cook, stirring, over medium heat 3 minutes, until sugar dissolves. Stir water and cornstarch together in a cup until smooth. Add cornstarch mixture to saucepan and gently boil 1 minute more, stirring constantly. Remove from heat. Makes 1¼ cups. *(Can be made ahead. Cool. Refrigerate in airtight container up to 1 week.)*

2. *Make marinade:* Sprinkle salt over chicken. Combine soy sauce, cornstarch, sherry and sesame oil in a medium bowl. Add chicken, tossing to coat. Cover and marinate chicken in refrigerator 15 minutes; then marinate 15 minutes more at room temperature.

3. *Make batter:* Combine cornstarch, flour, baking powder, salt and pepper in a large bowl. Whisk in water until mixture is smooth. Add a third of the chicken to batter, stirring to coat. Remove chicken from batter with tongs, letting excess drip into bowl. Place chicken on a tray lined with waxed paper. Repeat with remaining chicken and batter.

4. Meanwhile, heat oven to 250°F. Line a jelly-roll pan with paper towels; set aside.

5. Heat oil in a large 2-inch-deep, heavy skillet over medium-high heat 5 to 8 minutes, until temperature reaches 375°F.

6. Add one-third of chicken, 9 to 10 pieces, to oil. Fry 2 to 3 minutes, until golden brown and cooked through, turning pieces occasionally with long-handled tongs to keep them separate so they cook evenly. Transfer pieces to prepared pan and keep warm in oven. Repeat with remaining chicken and batter. To serve, garnish chicken with green onions and serve with sauce and broccoli, if desired. Serves 4.

Per serving: 455 calories, 19 g total fat, 4 g saturated fat, 94 mg cholesterol, 1,487 mg sodium, 45 g carbohydrates, 24 g protein, 89 mg calcium, 1 g fiber

chicken pad thai

Meet Thailand's most famous noodle dish. Don't soak the rice noodles too long or they'll break when cooked. Pictured on page 44.

Prep time: 15 minutes • Cooking time: 13 to 15 minutes

½ **pound rice noodles (Vietnamese banh pho)***
TOPPING:
¼ **cup salted peanuts, finely chopped**
1 **tablespoon granulated sugar**
½ **teaspoon grated lime peel**
SAUCE:
2 **tablespoons firmly packed brown sugar**
2 **tablespoons fresh lime juice**

2 **tablespoons Asian fish sauce (see tips, pages 16 and 17)**
1½ **tablespoons rice vinegar**
1 **tablespoon Asian chile sauce (see tips, pages 16 and 17)**
1½ **teaspoons dried shrimp paste (see tips, pages 16 and 17) or mashed anchovy**

3 **tablespoons vegetable oil, divided**
¼ **cup chopped shallots**
1 **pound boneless, skinless chicken breasts, cut into 3-inch strips**
1 **tablespoon finely chopped garlic**
1 **large egg, lightly beaten**
1 **cup fresh bean sprouts**
⅓ **cup sliced green onions and 2 tablespoons chopped fresh cilantro, for garnish (optional)**

1. Place noodles in a large bowl. Add enough hot tap water to cover; let stand 10 to 15 minutes, until pliable, but not too soft. Drain well in a colander.

2. *Make topping:* Combine all topping ingredients in a cup. Set aside.

3. *Make sauce:* Combine all sauce ingredients in a small bowl, stirring until smooth. Set aside.

4. Heat 1 tablespoon of the oil in a 12-inch nonstick skillet over medium-high heat. Add shallots; cook 2 minutes, until softened and lightly browned. Add chicken and garlic. Cook, stirring, 6 minutes more, until chicken is browned and cooked through. Transfer mixture to a bowl. Set aside.

5. Add egg to same skillet and cook 30 seconds. Turn egg with a spatula and cook 30 to 60 seconds more, just until set. Remove and chop. Set aside.

6. Heat the remaining 2 tablespoons oil in same skillet 30 seconds over high heat. Add drained noodles and sprouts and stir-fry 2 minutes. Add sauce and chicken mixture. Cook 1 to 2 minutes more, until heated through. Divide among 4 serving plates. Divide and sprinkle with egg and topping. Garnish with green onions and cilantro, if desired. Makes 4 servings.

*Note: Can be found in ethnic sections of supermarkets or in Asian specialty stores.

Per serving: 565 calories, 18.5 g total fat, 3 g saturated fat, 120 mg cholesterol, 838 mg sodium, 68 g carbohydrates, 33 g protein, 49 mg calcium, 1 g fiber

japanese chicken-noodle bowl

Oodles of noodles, five-spice chicken and vegetables come together in this richly satisfying main-dish soup. Pictured on page 45.

Total prep and cooking time: 40 to 43 minutes

- ½ teaspoon Chinese five-spice powder (see tips, pages 16 and 17)
- ¼ teaspoon salt
- 2 boneless chicken breast halves, skin on (6 to 7 oz. each)
- 1 tablespoon vegetable or peanut oil
- 3 cans (14½ oz. each) chicken broth, divided
- 2 tablespoons miso paste*
- 1 teaspoon lite soy sauce
- 2 large cloves garlic, thinly sliced
- 1 tablespoon thinly sliced fresh ginger
- 1 carrot, cut into ½-inch slices
- 2 bunches baby bok choy, 1 bunch bok choy or ½ pound spinach, trimmed, cut into ½-inch-thick slices
- 4 ounces firm tofu, diced
- 8 ounces Soba noodles*, cooked according to package directions, then drained and rinsed under cold water

1. Heat oven to 325°F. Combine five-spice powder and salt in a cup; sprinkle over chicken.

2. Heat oil in a medium Dutch oven 1 minute over medium-high heat. Add chicken, skin side down, cover and cook 3 minutes per side, until golden brown. Transfer chicken to a small baking dish; discard drippings. Bake 12 to 15 minutes, until chicken is cooked through.

3. Meanwhile, combine ¼ cup of the broth, the miso paste and soy sauce in a small bowl. Heat the same Dutch oven over medium heat. Add garlic and ginger and cook 1 minute, stirring often. Stir in the remaining broth and the miso mixture until smooth; add carrot. Bring mixture to boil; cover and simmer 15 minutes.

4. Add bok choy and tofu. Cook, uncovered, 5 minutes more, until bok choy is just tender and tofu is heated through. (If using fresh spinach, cook 2 minutes.)

5. To serve, slice each breast diagonally into 6 pieces. Divide noodles among 4 bowls. Ladle soup over noodles and top with chicken pieces. Makes 4 servings.

*Note: Can be found in ethnic sections of supermarkets or in Asian specialty stores.

Per serving: 510 calories, 18.5 g total fat, 4 g saturated fat, 59 mg cholesterol, 1,968 mg sodium, 53 g carbohydrates, 37 g protein, 225 mg calcium, 9 g fiber

indonesian curry

The secrets to this chicken stew are curry paste, coconut milk and kaffir lime leaves. Pictured on page 45.

Prep time: 15 minutes plus marinating
Cooking time: 42 to 43 minutes

MARINADE:
- 1 tablespoon grated fresh ginger
- 1 teaspoon turmeric
- 1 teaspoon salt
- 1 teaspoon sugar

- 1 whole chicken (3½ to 4 lbs.), cut up
- 4 teaspoons vegetable oil, divided
- 2 medium onions, cut into very thin wedges
- 1 bay leaf

CURRY PASTE:
- 2 medium onions, coarsely chopped
- 2 large cloves garlic
- 2 tablespoons water
- 2 teaspoons Madras curry powder*
- 1½ teaspoons coriander
- ½ teaspoon cinnamon
- ½ teaspoon ground red pepper

- 1 can (13.5 oz.) unsweetened coconut milk*
- 1½ fresh kaffir lime leaves* or 1 teaspoon grated lime peel
- 1 tablespoon chopped fresh cilantro
  Hot cooked rice (optional)
  Sliced cilantro leaves, sliced green onion, chopped peanuts, sliced hot fresh chiles and soy sauce, for garnish (optional)

1. *Make marinade:* Combine all marinade ingredients in a large bowl; add chicken and toss to coat. Cover and marinate chicken in the refrigerator 1 hour. *(Can be made ahead. Refrigerate overnight.)*

2. Heat 2 teaspoons of the oil in a 2-inch-deep 12-inch, heavy skillet over medium-high heat. Add onions and bay leaf and cook 8 minutes, until onions are lightly browned. Transfer onions to a plate with slotted spoon. Set aside.

3. *Make curry paste:* Meanwhile, combine all curry paste ingredients in a blender; puree until smooth, scraping sides with rubber spatula, if necessary.

4. Heat the remaining 2 teaspoons of oil in same skillet over medium-high heat. Add curry paste and cook 4 to 5 minutes, until thickened, stirring often. Add chicken and coat with curry paste. Cover and simmer 10 minutes. Stir in coconut milk, reserved onions and lime leaves. Simmer, uncovered, 20 minutes more, until chicken is cooked through.

5. To serve, remove bay leaf and lime leaves; discard. Divide chicken and sauce among 4 serving plates. Sprinkle with chopped cilantro. Serve with rice and garnishes, if desired. Makes 4 to 6 servings.

Note: Can be found in ethnic sections of supermarkets or in Asian specialty stores.

Per serving: 745 calories, 55 g total fat, 25 g saturated fat, 174 mg cholesterol, 643 mg sodium, 17 g carbohydrates, 46 g protein, 81 mg calcium, 2 g fiber

asian noodles with steak EASY

Our noodles require less peanut butter (which is high in fat) than the take-out version, plus a bonus of crispy strips of lean, iron-rich top round steak. Freeze the steak while you gather the remaining ingredients so it will be easy to cut into match-size strips.

Prep time: 20 minutes • Cooking time: 20 minutes

- 3 tablespoons lite soy sauce, divided
- 3 tablespoons rice vinegar, divided
- 2 tablespoons molasses, divided
- 1 teaspoon vegetable oil
- ¾ teaspoon chili sauce, divided

- ½ pound beef top round steak, cut into ¼-inch matchstick strips
- ½ cup chunky or smooth peanut butter
- 2 tablespoons chopped fresh ginger, divided
- 2 large cloves garlic, pressed
- ⅓ cup plus ½ cup fat-free chicken broth, divided
- 12 oz. linguine fine or spaghettini
- 2 bunches (3 lbs.) bok choy, thinly sliced
- 1 bunch green onions, cut into ½-inch-thick diagonal pieces

1. Combine 1 tablespoon each of the soy sauce, vinegar and molasses, the oil and ¼ teaspoon of the chili sauce. Add beef. Cover and refrigerate.

2. Process peanut butter, the remaining 2 tablespoons each of the soy sauce and vinegar, 1 tablespoon each of the molasses and ginger, the garlic, ⅓ cup of the broth and the remaining ½ teaspoon chili sauce in a blender until smooth.

3. Start to cook pasta according to package directions. Combine bok choy, green onions, the remaining 1 tablespoon ginger and ½ cup of broth in a large skillet. Cook over medium-high heat 5 minutes, until vegetables are tender and liquid has evaporated. Transfer vegetables to a large bowl. Set aside.

4. Remove beef from marinade; discard marinade. Pat beef dry with paper towels. Heat a large nonstick skillet over medium-high heat 1 minute. Add beef and increase heat to high heat. Cook, stirring often, 3 to 5 minutes, until beef is well browned. Set aside.

5. Drain pasta; rinse briefly under lukewarm running water. Transfer pasta to a large bowl; add bok choy mixture and peanut sauce. Toss mixture until well combined.

6. To serve, divide pasta among 4 shallow serving bowls. Divide and sprinkle beef over the top. Makes 4 servings.

Per serving: 695 calories, 24 g total fat, 5.5 g saturated fat, 35 mg cholesterol, 1,068 mg sodium, 86 g carbohydrates, 38 g protein, 426 mg calcium, 8 g fiber

sources for Asian ingredients

Our delicious Asian-inspired recipes call for specialty ingredients such as lemongrass, fish sauce and Chinese five-spice powder, which may not be available at your local supermarket. Look for a nearby Asian food store, or the online and mail-order sources here:

ADRIANA'S CARAVAN: An international food source offering exotic spices and condiments by mail. Call 800-316-0820. You may also download a catalog from their website at *adrianascaravan.com.*

MING.COM: This website is great because it offers exclusively Asian ingredients and is a breeze to navigate. You also may call 888-888-2418 or e-mail *ming.com.*

TEMPLEOFTHAI.COM: Another site that's comprehensive and easy to use. Phone (toll-free) 877-449-0554 or e-mail *CustomerService@templeofthai.com.*

IMPORTFOOD.COM: Offers a wide variety of products. Accepts credit cards only. Call 1-425-392-7516 or e-mail *info@importfood.com* for more information.

For descriptions of Asian ingredients and their uses, see tips on pages 16 and 17.

vietnamese lemongrass chicken EASY

Cut off the green tops of the lemongrass for the marinade; reserve for flavoring soups and stews. Pictured on page 44.

Prep time: 15 minutes plus marinating
Baking time: 30 minutes

MARINADE:
- ¼ pound lemongrass (3 to 4 stalks) (see tips, pages 16 and 17)
- 1 large shallot, finely chopped
- ½ teaspoon grated lime peel
- 2 tablespoons fresh lime juice
- 2 tablespoons Asian fish sauce (see tips, pages 16 and 17)
- 1 tablespoon peeled and finely chopped galangal (see tips, pages 16 and 17) or fresh ginger
- 1½ teaspoons sugar
- ½ teaspoon red pepper flakes

- 8 chicken thighs (2½ to 3 lbs.)
  Rice and steamed Chinese green beans (optional)

1. *Make marinade:* Remove tough outer peel from stalks of lemongrass (about 2 or 3 layers). Finely chop white part of stalks; transfer to a large bowl. Add remaining marinade ingredients. Mash mixture together with a wooden spoon to combine.

2. Add chicken and rub mixture all over to coat. Cover and marinate in the refrigerator 1 hour. *(Can be made ahead. Refrigerate overnight.)*

3. Heat oven to 450°F. Line a broiler pan bottom with foil. Adjust oven rack to upper level.

4. Transfer chicken to prepared pan. Roast 10 minutes. Reduce oven temperature to 425°F. Roast 20 minutes more, until chicken is cooked through. Serve with rice and green beans, if desired. Makes 4 servings.

*Note: Can be found in ethnic sections of supermarkets or in Asian specialty stores.

Per serving: 555 calories, 33 g total fat, 9 g saturated fat, 191 mg cholesterol, 472 mg sodium, 8 g carbohydrates, 53 g protein, 37 mg calcium, 0 g fiber

chicken, barley and squash stew

This one-pot wonder features quick-cooking barley, boneless, skinless chicken thighs and vitamin-rich winter squash. Look for convenient precut squash and sliced mushrooms in the produce aisle at the supermarket.

Prep time: 15 minutes • Cooking time: 16 to 17 minutes

- 1¼ to 1½ pounds boneless, skinless chicken thighs, cubed
- 2 large cloves garlic, pressed
- 1 teaspoon salt, divided
- ¼ teaspoon freshly ground pepper
- 3 teaspoons olive oil, divided
- 1 package (16 oz.) sliced mushrooms
- 1 large onion, diced
- ⅓ cup white wine
- 3 cans (14½ oz. each) chicken broth
- 1 package (16 oz.) peeled cut-up squash, cut into 1-inch cubes, or 1 squash (1½ lb.), peeled, seeded and cubed
- 1 box (11 oz.) quick-cooking barley
- 1 bay leaf
- ⅛ teaspoon cinnamon
- Sliced green onions, for garnish (optional)

1. ▪ Toss chicken with garlic, ½ teaspoon of the salt and the pepper in a bowl. Set aside.

2. ▪ Heat 1 teaspoon of the oil in a 4-quart heavy Dutch oven over high heat. Add chicken and cook, stirring often, 3 to 4 minutes, until browned. Transfer to another bowl.

3. ▪ Heat the remaining 2 teaspoons of oil in the Dutch oven. Add mushrooms and onion and cook 3 minutes, until softened. Stir in wine. Bring to boil. Add broth, squash, barley, bay leaf, remaining ½ teaspoon salt, the cinnamon and browned chicken. Return mixture to boil. Reduce heat; cover and simmer 10 minutes, until barley and squash are tender and chicken is cooked through; remove bay leaf. Garnish with green onions, if desired. Serves 6.

Per serving: 425 calories, 9 g total fat, 2 g saturated fat, 86 mg cholesterol, 1,362 mg sodium, 54 g carbohydrates, 31 g protein, 62 mg calcium, 8 g fiber

chicken with pineapple-kiwi salsa

If you're a kiwi fan, you'll love the salsa served with these chicken cutlets. The refreshing salsa assembly includes kiwi, pineapple, fresh lime juice, cilantro, ginger and, for a little kick, jalapeño chile. You can also try the salsa with grilled pork chops or fish.

Prep time: 25 minutes • Baking time: 8 to 9 minutes

- ½ teaspoon salt
- ⅛ teaspoon freshly ground pepper
- 4 boneless, skinless chicken cutlets (6 to 7 oz. each)
- 1 tablespoon olive oil

SALSA:
- 2 tablespoons chopped red onion
- 1 tablespoon finely chopped fresh cilantro
- 3 kiwis, peeled and diced (1¼ cups)
- 1 can (14 oz.) pineapple chunks in juice, diced, juice reserved
- 2 tablespoons fresh lime juice
- 1 teaspoon chopped jalapeño chile (see tip, page 15)
- ¼ teaspoon salt
- ¼ teaspoon grated fresh ginger

1. ▪ Heat oven to 350°F. Sprinkle salt and pepper evenly over chicken.

2. ▪ Heat oil in a large nonstick skillet over medium-high heat. Add chicken and cook 3 minutes per side, until browned. Transfer chicken to a jelly-roll pan or cookie sheet.

3. ▪ Bake the chicken 8 to 9 minutes, until cooked through.

4. ▪ *Make salsa:* Rinse onion under hot running water in fine sieve for 20 seconds; drain. Combine onion and all of the remaining ingredients for salsa in a medium bowl. Serve with chicken. Makes 4 servings.

Per serving: 335 calories, 6 g total fat, 1 g saturated fat, 107 mg cholesterol, 535 mg sodium, 25 g carbohydrates, 44 g protein, 59 mg calcium, 3 g fiber

summer fiesta

MEXICAN BEEF ROLL-UPS
below

WATERMELON SALAD
page 114

DULCE DE LECHE ICE CREAM

mexican beef roll-ups *EASY*

We help a little lean ground beef go a long way by mixing it with corn and rice and rolling it up in spicy low-fat tortillas.

Prep time: 20 minutes • Cooking time: 20 minutes

- ½ **cup rice**
- 1 **can (16 oz.) whole tomatoes in puree, tomatoes chopped**
- 1 **whole chipotle chile in adobo, chopped, plus 1 teaspoon adobo sauce (see tip, page 15)**
- 2 **tablespoons water**
- 1 **tablespoon olive oil**
- 1½ **cups chopped onions**
- 1 **large green bell pepper, diced**
- 2 **large cloves garlic, pressed**
- ½ **pound lean ground beef**
- ½ **teaspoon salt**
- ½ **teaspoon cumin**
- 1 **cup frozen corn, thawed**

SPICED TORTILLAS:

- 1 **tablespoon olive oil**
- ¾ **teaspoon cumin**
- ¼ **teaspoon paprika**
- 8 **(7-inch) low-fat flour tortillas**

- 1½ **cups shredded lettuce**
- ½ **cup (2 oz.) coarsely shredded pepper-Jack cheese**
- ¼ **cup reduced-fat sour cream (optional)**

1. Cook rice according to package directions.

2. Meanwhile, bring tomatoes in puree, chipotle chile, adobo sauce and water to boil in a medium saucepan. Reduce heat; simmer 10 minutes.

3. Heat 1 tablespoon oil in a large skillet over medium-high heat. Add onions and bell pepper; cook 4 minutes, until lightly browned. Add garlic and cook 1 minute more. Add beef, salt and cumin and cook, breaking up beef with a spoon, 2 to 3 minutes, until no longer pink. Stir in tomato-chipotle sauce and corn. Bring to boil. Reduce heat; simmer 3 to 4 minutes.

4. *Make spiced tortillas:* Meanwhile, heat oven to 350°F. Combine oil, cumin and paprika in a cup. Brush 1 side of the tortillas with spice oil. Wrap tortillas in foil and bake 10 minutes, until heated through.

5. To serve, on each of 4 serving plates, arrange 2 of the spiced tortillas. Divide and fill each tortilla with lettuce, meat mixture, rice and cheese. Serve with sour cream, if desired. Makes 4 servings.

Per serving: 600 calories, 25 g total fat, 8 g saturated fat, 58 mg cholesterol, 1,015 mg sodium, 80 g carbohydrates, 23 g protein, 314 mg calcium, 11 g fiber

good-for-you meatloaf *EASY*

Making a moist meatloaf using very lean beef has always been a challenge, but with the addition of a few inventive elements—chopped portobellas, onions and prunes—we came up with a winner. Pictured on page 42.

Prep time: 20 minutes
Baking time: 55 to 60 minutes

- **Vegetable cooking spray**
- 1 **tablespoon olive oil**
- 1 **medium onion, chopped (1 cup)**
- 1 **package (6 oz.) sliced portobella mushrooms, chopped**
- 4 **pitted prunes, chopped**
- 1 **large egg**
- ¾ **pound lean ground beef**
- ¾ **pound lean ground veal**
- ⅔ **cup fresh bread crumbs (2 slices)**

3 tablespoons finely chopped carrot
2 teaspoons coarse grain mustard
1 teaspoon salt
1 teaspoon minced garlic
¼ teaspoon freshly ground pepper

1. Heat oven to 375°F. Line a 13×9-inch baking pan with foil; lightly coat foil with vegetable cooking spray.

2. Heat oil in a 12-inch skillet over high heat. Add onion and mushrooms and cook, stirring occasionally, 6 to 7 minutes, until mushroom liquid has evaporated and mushrooms are browned. Cool.

3. Meanwhile, puree prunes with egg in a blender or food processor until almost smooth.

4. Lightly toss together onion mixture with egg mixture and the remaining ingredients in a large bowl. Transfer meat mixture to center of prepared pan; shape into a 9×4-inch loaf.

5. Cover top with another sheet of foil and bake 30 minutes. Uncover and bake 25 to 30 minutes more, until instant-read thermometer inserted into center of meatloaf registers 160°F. Let meatloaf stand in pan 5 minutes.

6. To serve, remove meatloaf from pan using a large spatula and transfer to a serving platter. Makes 4 servings.

Per serving: 400 calories, 20 g total fat, 6 g saturated fat, 176 mg cholesterol, 819 mg sodium, 18 g carbohydrates, 37 g protein, 73 mg calcium, 3 g fiber

skillet steak with mushrooms and onion EASY

Love teriyaki steak? Then you'll love our tasty top sirloin with sherry, sweet onion, shiitake mushrooms, garlic and fresh ginger. Pictured on page 46.

Prep time: 20 minutes plus standing
Cooking time: 25 minutes

1 tablespoon peanut or vegetable oil
1 medium sweet onion (such as Spanish or Vidalia), very thinly sliced
2 teaspoons minced garlic

1 teaspoon grated fresh ginger
1 pound shiitake mushrooms, sliced
3 tablespoons dry sherry, divided
⅔ cup chicken broth
¼ cup teriyaki sauce
½ teaspoon cornstarch
1 beef loin top sirloin steak, boneless (1½ lbs.), about 1 inch thick
1 teaspoon salt
½ teaspoon freshly ground pepper
    Spicy Oven Fries (recipe, page 76) and steamed green beans (optional)

1. Heat oven to 350°F.

2. Heat oil in a 12-inch nonstick, ovenproof skillet over medium-high heat. Add onion and cook 4 minutes, until softened and beginning to brown. Add garlic and ginger; cook 30 seconds, until fragrant. Add mushrooms and 1 tablespoon of the sherry. Cover and cook 3 minutes, until softened. Stir mushrooms and cook, uncovered, 5 minutes more, until mushrooms are lightly browned.

3. Meanwhile, whisk broth, teriyaki sauce, the remaining 2 tablespoons sherry and the cornstarch together in a small bowl. Add to mushroom mixture and bring to boil. Boil 30 seconds. Transfer mixture to a bowl. Cover and keep warm.

4. Wipe skillet with paper towels. Sprinkle steak with salt and pepper. Heat skillet 2 minutes over medium-high heat, until very hot. Add steak and cook 1½ minutes per side, until browned.

5. Transfer steak in skillet to oven. Bake steak 5 minutes. Remove skillet from oven, turn steak over and insert an instant-read thermometer at an angle into center of steak (temperature should register 125°F.). Transfer steak to a cutting board; let stand 5 minutes. (Temperature will increase to 130°F. to 135°F. for medium-rare.)

6. To serve, slice steak and transfer to 4 serving plates. Top with mushroom mixture. Serve with Spicy Oven Fries and steamed green beans, if desired. Makes 4 servings.

Per serving: 420 calories, 18 g total fat, 6 g saturated fat, 127 mg cholesterol, 1,549 mg sodium, 14 g carbohydrates, 46 g protein, 36 mg calcium, 2 g fiber

enchilada casserole

It may look like lasagna, but don't let that fool you. This south-of-the-border dinner features layers of corn tortillas (no need to boil noodles!), salsa-spiked tomato sauce (for extra zing), chiles, zucchini and cheese. It can be assembled a day before you bake it, so it's a perfect timesaving meal for family or friends. Pictured on page 41.

Prep time: 1 hour 10 minutes
Baking time: 50 minutes

- **4** poblano chiles (12 oz.), cut in half lengthwise, seeds and stems removed (see tip, page 15)
- **1** jalapeño chile, cut in half lengthwise, seeds and stem removed (see tip, page 15)
- **1** tablespoon olive oil
- **1** cup chopped onion
- **1** tablespoon chopped garlic
- **1** pound lean ground beef
- **½** teaspoon salt
- **½** teaspoon cumin
- **¼** teaspoon ground red pepper
- **¼** teaspoon cinnamon
- **½** pound feta cheese, rinsed and patted dry
- **2** cups shredded Monterey Jack cheese, divided
- **1** cup whole-milk ricotta cheese
- **2** tablespoons chopped fresh parsley
- **1** can (35 oz.) plum tomatoes in juice
- **1** jar (16 oz.) mild salsa
- **16** (6- to 8-inch) corn tortillas
- **1** zucchini, cut into ¼-inch-thick slices
  Tossed green salad (optional)

1. Heat broiler. Place poblano chiles, cut side down, on a foil-lined cookie sheet. Broil 3 inches from heat 10 to 15 minutes, turning occasionally, until skins are bubbly and evenly charred. Immediately transfer poblano chiles to a large resealable plastic storage bag and seal. Let stand 10 to 15 minutes, until chiles are cool enough to handle.

2. Remove blistered skin from poblano chiles using a small paring knife to gently and slowly pull it off in strips. Slice poblano chiles into thin strips; transfer to a small bowl. Chop jalapeño; transfer to a medium bowl. Set both aside.

3. Heat oven to 350°F.

4. Meanwhile, heat oil in a large skillet over medium heat. Add onion and garlic and cook 2 to 3 minutes, until onion is softened. Stir in ground beef, salt, cumin, red pepper and cinnamon, breaking up beef with the back of a spoon. Cook mixture 3 to 5 minutes more, until beef is no longer pink. Transfer to a small bowl.

5. Crumble feta cheese in bowl with chopped jalapeño. Stir in 1 cup of the Monterey Jack cheese, the ricotta cheese and parsley. Puree tomatoes and salsa in a blender or food processor. Set tomato sauce mixture and cheese mixture aside.

6. Spoon 1 cup of the tomato sauce mixture into bottom of a 13×9-inch baking dish. Arrange 6 tortillas on top of sauce, overlapping slightly to fit. Sprinkle half of the meat mixture on top of tortillas, then half of the poblano strips and zucchini slices.

7. Spread half of the cheese mixture on top of zucchini. Spoon 1 cup of the tomato sauce over cheese. Arrange 4 tortillas over top. Repeat process with remaining meat, poblanos, cheese, zucchini, 1 cup sauce and 6 tortillas. *(Can be made ahead. Cover and refrigerate casserole, remaining 1³/₄ cups tomato sauce and 1 cup Monterey Jack cheese separately overnight. Let casserole and sauce stand at room temperature 1 hour.)*

8. Spoon the remaining tomato sauce over top. Cover top loosely with foil. (Try to keep foil from touching tortillas.)

9. Bake 45 minutes (60 to 65 minutes, if casserole was refrigerated overnight), until tomato sauce is bubbly. Remove foil, sprinkle top with remaining 1 cup Monterey Jack cheese and bake 5 minutes more, until cheese melts. Cool casserole on wire rack 5 to 10 minutes before serving. Serve with tossed green salad, if desired. Makes 12 servings.

Per serving: 400 calories, 24.5 g total fat, 12 g saturated fat, 79 mg cholesterol, 899 mg sodium, 27 g carbohydrates, 19 g protein, 371 mg calcium, 3 g fiber

homestyle beef and vegetable stew

A satisfyingly slow-braised winter stew. Pictured on page 43.

Prep time: 25 minutes
Baking time: 2½ to 2¾ hours

- **1 tablespoon coarsely chopped garlic**
- **1 teaspoon salt**
- **½ teaspoon freshly ground pepper**
- **2½ pounds beef bottom round roast, cut into 1-inch cubes**
- **6 teaspoons olive or vegetable oil, divided**
- **2 cups chopped onions**
- **1 celery rib, chopped**
- **⅓ cup red wine**
- **1 bay leaf**
- **¼ teaspoon cinnamon**
- **1 pound carrots, diced**
- **2 medium (¾ lb.) turnips, peeled and diced**
- **1 can (14½ oz.) diced tomatoes in juice**
- **Guiltless Mashed Potatoes (recipe, page 76) and Peas with Red Onion (see tip, page 79) (optional)**

1. Heat oven to 325°F. Chop garlic again with salt. Press with side of knife to form a paste; mix in pepper. Rub surface of beef with garlic paste.

2. Heat 2 teaspoons of the oil in a Dutch oven over medium-high heat. Add half the beef and cook 3 to 4 minutes, until browned on all sides. Transfer to a bowl. Repeat with the remaining beef and 2 teaspoons of the oil.

3. Add onions, celery and the remaining 2 teaspoons oil to Dutch oven; cook 3 to 4 minutes, just until vegetables start to brown. Add wine, bay leaf and cinnamon. Bring to boil; boil 1 minute.

4. Add beef, carrots, turnips and tomatoes. Bring mixture back to boil. Cover and bake 2½ to 2¾ hours, until beef is tender. Remove bay leaf.

5. To serve, divide stew into 6 to 8 shallow serving bowls. Serve with Guiltless Mashed Potatoes and Peas with Red Onion, if desired. Serves 6 to 8.

Per serving: 380 calories, 21.5 g total fat, 7.5 g saturated fat, 90.8 mg cholesterol, 502 mg sodium, 15 g carbohydrates, 31 g protein, 62 mg calcium, 4 g fiber

grilled steak with chile sauce

Serve up this gutsy grilled steak glazed with roasted garlic and fiery chile sauce for an incredible meal.

Prep time: 20 minutes plus standing
Grilling time: 15 to 24 minutes

- **4 large cloves garlic, unpeeled**
- **2 chipotle chiles in adobo with 1 tablespoon adobo sauce (see tip, page 15)**
- **1 tablespoon fresh lime juice**
- **1 tablespoon honey**
- **2 teaspoons olive oil**
- **½ teaspoon salt**
- **1 beef top round steak (2 lbs.), 1¾ inches thick**
- **½ cup chicken broth**

1. Heat unpeeled garlic in a small, heavy skillet over medium heat. Cover and cook 5 minutes, turning cloves once. Uncover; cook 3 to 5 minutes more, turning occasionally, until skins are lightly charred and cloves can be easily pierced with a knife. Cool; peel.

2. Finely chop garlic and chiles; transfer mixture to a cup. Stir in adobo sauce, lime juice and honey.

3. Brush oil and sprinkle salt on each side of steak. Heat a 10-inch grill-pan skillet or cast-iron skillet 2 minutes over medium-high heat. Arrange steak in pan; spoon half of chile mixture over top. Grill steak 5 to 7 minutes, turn and spread remaining chile mixture on top of steak. Grill 5 to 7 minutes. Add broth to skillet; reduce heat to medium. Turn steak and grill 5 to 10 minutes more, until instant-read thermometer inserted in center of steak registers 135°F. for medium-rare.

4. Transfer steak to a cutting board; let stand 5 minutes. Thinly slice; serve with sauce. Makes 6 servings.

Per serving: 305 calories, 16 g total fat, 6 g saturated fat, 92 mg cholesterol, 411 mg sodium, 5 g carbohydrates, 33 g protein, 15 mg calcium, 0 g fiber

southern-style barbecue pork chops

These chops brown in an ovenproof skillet to seal in the juices, then are slathered in a fabulous barbecue sauce. Pictured on page 43.

Prep time: 10 minutes • Cooking time: 1 hour 15 minutes

BARBECUE SAUCE:

- 2 teaspoons olive oil
- ½ cup finely chopped onion
- 1 tablespoon chopped garlic
- 1 teaspoon cumin
- ¼ to ½ teaspoon ground red pepper
- 1 cup tomato sauce
- ¾ cup water
- ¼ cup ketchup
- 2 tablespoons packed brown sugar
- 2 tablespoons Worcestershire sauce
- 2 tablespoons cider vinegar

- 1 teaspoon salt
- 1 teaspoon cumin
- ½ teaspoon freshly ground pepper
- ⅛ teaspoon ground red pepper
- 2 teaspoons olive oil
- 4 pork loin rib chops (6 to 7 oz. each), 1-inch thick, excess fat trimmed

---

Crispy Hash Browns (recipe, page 78) and Lima Beans with Red Pepper (see tip, page 63) (optional)

1. *Make barbecue sauce:* Heat oil in a 3-quart saucepan over medium heat. Add onion and garlic; cook 3 to 5 minutes, until onion softens. Stir in cumin and red pepper; cook 3 minutes. Stir in the remaining barbecue sauce ingredients. Bring to boil. Reduce heat and simmer 1 hour, stirring occasionally. *(Can be made ahead. Cool. Store in airtight container up to 1 week. To reheat: Microwave sauce on HIGH 4 to 5 minutes.)*

2. Heat oven to 350°F.

3. Combine salt, cumin, black pepper and red pepper in a cup. Rub mixture on both sides of chops. Heat oil in a large nonstick, ovenproof skillet 2 minutes over medium-high heat. Add chops and cook 2 minutes per side. Spoon 2 tablespoons of the Barbecue Sauce on top of each chop.

4. Bake chops 8 to 10 minutes, until an instant-read thermometer inserted 1½ inches deep into side of each chop registers 155°F. Serve chops with additional Barbecue Sauce, Crispy Hash Browns and Lima Beans with Red Pepper, if desired. Makes 4 servings.

Per serving: 310 calories, 12 g total fat, 3 g saturated fat, 76 mg cholesterol, 1,285 mg sodium, 20 g carbohydrates, 30 g protein, 60 mg calcium, 2 g fiber

roast pork with garlic and apples (EASY)

The secret to our tender, juicy pork is to marinate it in a "brine"—a solution of water, sugar and seasonings. The recipe goes great with Thyme-Garlic Baked Potatoes, page 79, and Spinach Sauté, page 63. Pictured on page 47.

Prep time: 25 minutes plus marinating
Cooking time: 60 to 70 minutes • Microwave used

BRINE:

- 4 cups water, divided
- 1 apple, cut into 8 wedges
- ¼ cup kosher salt
- ¼ cup sugar
- 4 large cloves garlic, crushed
- 2 teaspoons whole black peppercorns
- 4 fresh sage leaves or 1 teaspoon dried sage

- 2½ pounds boneless, center-cut pork loin
- 2 tablespoons finely chopped garlic
- 2 tablespoons chopped fresh sage or 2 teaspoons dried sage
- 1 tablespoon olive oil
- 2 teaspoons cider vinegar
- ½ teaspoon freshly ground pepper
- ¼ teaspoon salt
- 2 apples, peeled, cored and cut into 8 wedges

1. *Make brine:* Microwave 2 cups of the water in a bowl on HIGH 3 minutes, until steaming. Add the remaining brine ingredients and stir until sugar has almost dissolved. Stir in the remaining 2 cups water. Cool to room temperature.

2. Pour brine into a large heavy-duty, resealable plastic storage bag. Add pork. Push out excess air from bag and seal. Marinate pork in the refrigerator 24 hours, turning the bag several times.

3. Combine garlic, sage, oil, vinegar, pepper and salt in a cup. Set aside.

4. Heat oven to 350°F.

5. Drain pork in a colander; discard brine and solids. Rinse pork under cold running water. Pat dry with paper towels. Rub surface of pork with garlic mixture.

6. Spread apple wedges in an 11×7-inch baking dish. Place pork on top of apples in dish. Roast pork and apples 60 to 70 minutes, until an instant-read thermometer inserted in center of pork registers 155°F.

7. Transfer pork to a serving plate; cover loosely with foil. Remove apples from baking dish, coarsely chop and transfer to a bowl. Skim fat from drippings in pan. Stir drippings into apples. Serve pork with apples. Makes 6 servings.

Per serving: 410 calories, 23.5 g total fat, 8.5 g saturated fat, 116 mg cholesterol, 431 mg sodium, 9 g carbohydrates, 38 g protein, 54 mg calcium, 1 g fiber

good fortune dinner (EASY)

Southerners say that eating "Hoppin' John" on New Year's Day brings luck. But this stew is so tasty, your family will feel lucky digging into it anytime! Pictured on page 43.

Total prep and cook time: 30 minutes

- 1½ **pounds boneless center-cut pork loin, cut into 1-inch cubes**
- ½ **teaspoon salt**
- ¼ **teaspoon freshly ground pepper**
- 1 **tablespoon olive oil**
- 1 **large clove garlic, minced**

- 3½ **cups chicken broth**
- 1 **pound kale, stems trimmed and coarsely chopped**
- 2 **cups refrigerated cut-up, ready-to-use golden potatoes**
- 1 **box (10 oz.) frozen black-eyed peas, thawed**

Sprinkle pork with salt and pepper. Heat oil in a 2-inch deep 12-inch skillet. Add pork and cook, turning pieces, 3 minutes, until browned. Add garlic and cook 30 seconds more. Transfer to a bowl. Add broth, kale, potatoes and peas to skillet; bring to boil. Cover and simmer 15 minutes. Stir in pork and cook 2 to 3 minutes more, until cooked through. Makes 4 servings.

Per serving: 600 calories, 28 g total fat, 9 g saturated fat, 119 mg cholesterol, 1,582 mg sodium, 39 g carbohydrates, 48 g protein, 157 mg calcium, 6 g fiber

---

test kitchen tip
positively pork

Whether you sauté, braise, grill, broil or roast your pork, here are a few tips to get the ultimate result on your dinner plate:

COOK IT RIGHT: Fresh pork loin is now leaner than ever. That's why it's important to resist the tendency to overcook pork loin and tenderloin. Doing so completely dries out the meat. These cuts should be cooked to an internal temperature of 155°F. (Upon standing, the meat will increase to 160°F.) The juices should run clear when the meat is pierced with a fork. This will yield the utmost flavor and tenderness and ensure that the meat is cooked according to safety standards.

STORE IT SAFE AND SOUND: Before cooking, store fresh pork, wrapped in the package in which it was purchased, in the refrigerator 3 to 5 days (ground pork for 1 to 2 days). Pork chops can be frozen 4 to 6 months, ground pork 3 to 4 months, and roasts 4 to 12 months. If freezing the pork in its original package longer than 2 months, overwrap the packages with airtight heavy-duty foil, plastic wrap, or freezer paper.

pork tenderloin with quinoa and greens

Enjoy a hearty roast pork supper that's ready in minutes instead of hours! Lean pork tenderloin is comparable in fat and calories to boneless, skinless chicken breast.

Prep time: 15 minutes • Cooking time: 25 minutes

- **2 tablespoons Indian curry paste***
- **2 pork tenderloins (about 1¾ lbs. total), each cut crosswise in half**
- **2 cans (14½ oz each) chicken broth, divided**
- **1 cup quinoa, rinsed and drained****
- **1 bag (16 oz.) fresh chopped kale**
- **2 large cloves garlic, pressed**
- **1 tablespoon olive oil**
- **Low-fat yogurt (optional)**
- **Fresh parsley, for garnish (optional)**

1. Rub curry paste on all sides of each piece of pork. Arrange on a jelly-roll pan and refrigerate.

2. Heat oven to 425°F.

3. Bring 1 can of the broth to boil in a medium saucepan. Stir in quinoa. Reduce heat; cover and simmer 15 minutes, until liquid is absorbed and quinoa is tender. Remove from heat; let stand, covered, 5 minutes.

4. Roast pork 10 minutes. Turn and roast pork 8 to 10 minutes more, or until an instant-read thermometer inserted in center of each piece of pork reaches 155°F. (The end sections of the tenderloin may cook faster, so remove if necessary). Transfer pork to a cutting board; let stand 5 minutes.

5. Meanwhile, bring kale and the remaining 1 can of broth to boil in a medium saucepan. Add garlic and oil. Reduce heat; simmer, stirring often, 20 minutes, until kale is tender. Transfer kale mixture to a large serving bowl. Fluff quinoa with a fork. Stir quinoa into kale mixture.

6. To serve, thinly slice pork and divide among 4 serving plates. Serve with quinoa and kale

mixture. Serve with yogurt and garnish with parsley, if desired. Makes 4 servings.

*Note: Can be found in ethnic food sections of supermarkets or in Asian specialty stores.

**Note: Can be found in supermarkets or health food and specialty stores.

Per serving: 570 calories, 21 g total fat, 4.5 g saturated fat, 119 mg cholesterol, 1,320 mg sodium, 43 g carbohydrates, 53 g protein, 205 mg calcium, 9 g fiber

pork and white bean stew

If making dinner always seems to cause a "pan jam" on your stovetop, it's time to pull out your favorite pot and make this stew. Fresh ginger, soy sauce, Asian chili sauce and slow cooking result in a wonderfully rich flavor. We use dried beans because they retain their texture and shape better than canned.

Prep time: 20 minutes plus standing
Baking time: 1 hour 45 minutes

- **4 teaspoons olive oil, divided**
- **2½ pounds pork butt (pork leg, rump portion, boneless), cut into ¾-inch pieces, excess fat removed**
- **1 teaspoon salt**
- **1 tablespoon chopped garlic**
- **2 teaspoons grated fresh ginger**
- **1 pound dry navy beans, soaked according to package directions, then drained**
- **2 cans (14½ oz. each) chicken broth**
- **1 cup finely chopped green bell pepper**
- **1 cup water**
- **2 tablespoons lite soy sauce**
- **1 tablespoon ketchup**
- **2 teaspoons Asian chili sauce (see tips, pages 16 and 17)**
- **Crusty bread (optional)**

1. Heat oven to 350°F.

2. Heat 2 teaspoons of the oil in a Dutch oven over high heat. Add pork and cook 2 minutes. Sprinkle with salt, turn pieces and cook 2 minutes, until browned. Stir in garlic and ginger; cook 1 minute more. Stir in all of the remaining ingredients except bread. Bring to boil; cover and transfer to oven.

3. Bake 1 hour and 45 minutes, until pork and beans are very tender. Serve with crusty bread, if desired. Makes 8 servings.

Per serving: 425 calories, 11.5 g total fat, 3.5 g saturated fat, 96 mg cholesterol, 1,007 mg sodium, 37 g carbohydrates, 43 g protein, 102 mg calcium, 6 g fiber

pappardelle with escarole

Here's a recipe that's not only tasty, but also surprisingly time efficient as well. While you're waiting for the pasta water to boil, the bacon is crisped. Then while the pasta is cooking, the rest of the meal is prepared—pork, escarole (good-for-you greens), chicken broth and garlic—all in the same skillet the bacon was cooked in. Pictured on page 44.

Total prep and cooking time: 30 minutes

- **2 slices bacon**
- **1 package (8 oz.) pappardelle or wide egg noodles, cooked according to package directions**
- **¾ pound boneless pork chop, cut into ¾-inch cubes**
- **1 tablespoon chopped garlic**
- **1 teaspoon salt, divided**
- **1¼ pounds escarole, cored and chopped**
- **1 can (14½ oz.) chicken broth**
- **¼ teaspoon freshly ground pepper**

1. Heat water for pasta.

2. Meanwhile, cook bacon in a 2-inch-deep 12-inch skillet over medium-high heat, just until crisp. Transfer bacon with a slotted spoon to paper towels; drain.

3. Start to cook pasta. Add pork, garlic and ¼ teaspoon of the salt to same skillet. Cook over high heat 2 to 3 minutes, until pork is browned. Add escarole, broth, the remaining ¾ teaspoon salt and the pepper; bring to boil. Reduce heat to medium and simmer 3 minutes more.

4. Drain pasta. Toss hot pasta in a large bowl with pork mixture; crumble bacon over top. Makes 4 servings.

Per serving: 480 calories, 19 g total fat, 6.5 g saturated fat, 61 mg cholesterol, 1,366 mg sodium, 48 g carbohydrates, 27 g protein, 96 mg calcium, 4 g fiber

test kitchen tip

great sides

Two great green ways to round out dinner:

spinach sauté

Pictured on page 47.

Heat 1 tablespoon olive oil in a Dutch oven. Add ¼ cup chopped shallots; cook 2 minutes. Add 2 bags (10 to 12 oz. each) fresh spinach, cover and cook 3 to 4 minutes, stirring, until spinach wilts. Stir in 1½ teaspoons balsamic vinegar, ¼ teaspoon salt and ⅛ teaspoon freshly ground pepper. Makes 4 servings.

Per serving: 70 calories, 4 g total fat, 0.5 g saturated fat, 0 mg cholesterol, 268 mg sodium, 7 g carbohydrates, 5 g protein, 158 mg calcium, 4 g fiber

lima beans with red pepper

Pictured on page 43.

Microwave 1 bag (16 oz.) frozen lima beans according to package directions; drain well. Heat 1 tablespoon olive oil in a skillet. Add ½ cup chopped onion and cook 5 minutes. Stir in ½ cup diced red bell pepper and cook 6 minutes. Stir in 2 teaspoons chopped garlic; cook until fragrant. Add lima beans and ½ cup chicken broth. Cook until lima beans are heated through, 3 to 5 minutes more. Stir in ¼ teaspoon freshly ground pepper. Serves 4.

Per serving: 170 calories, 4 g total fat, 0.5 g saturated fat, 0 mg cholesterol, 195 mg sodium, 26 g carbohydrates, 8 g protein, 36 mg calcium, 7 g fiber

crispy catfish

Looking for a new way to do fish? Our cornmeal and red pepper coated fillets are served up with a creamy blue cheese yogurt sauce that cools things down in a decidedly delicious fashion.

Prep time: 15 minutes plus chilling
Cooking time: 12 minutes

BLUE CHEESE SAUCE:

- 1 container (8 oz.) low-fat plain yogurt
- 3 tablespoons crumbled blue cheese
- 2 tablespoons mayonnaise
- ¼ teaspoon minced garlic
- ½ cup peeled and diced English (seedless) cucumber

COATING:

- ½ cup cornmeal
- ½ teaspoon salt
- ½ teaspoon ground red pepper

- 4 catfish fillets (1½ to 2 lbs. total)
- 1 large egg, lightly beaten
- 2 tablespoons butter or margarine, divided
- 1 teaspoon vegetable oil
- 1 tablespoon hot red pepper sauce
  Celery sticks (optional)

1. *Make blue cheese sauce:* Line a sieve with a paper towel or coffee filter; set over a bowl. Spoon yogurt into sieve; cover and refrigerate 1 hour to drain. Combine drained yogurt and remaining ingredients for blue cheese sauce in a medium bowl. Cover and refrigerate 15 minutes.

2. *Make coating:* Combine cornmeal, salt and ground red pepper in a 9-inch pie plate. Dip each fillet in egg, then into coating, shaking off excess.

3. Heat 1 tablespoon of the butter and the oil in a large nonstick skillet over medium-high heat. Fry fish 3 to 4 minutes per side, until golden brown and cooked through. Transfer to 4 serving plates.

4. Melt the remaining 1 tablespoon butter in same skillet over low heat; remove from heat and stir in pepper sauce. Divide butter mixture and drizzle over fish, scraping pan with a rubber spatula. Serve immediately with Blue Cheese Sauce and celery sticks, if desired. Makes 4 servings.

Per serving: 535 calories, 33.5 g total fat, 9.5 g saturated fat, 154 mg cholesterol, 684 mg sodium, 16 g carbohydrates, 41 mg protein, 107 mg calcium, 1 g fiber

zesty citrus catfish

Reel in some catfish if you're bargain hunting for dinner tonight. Our version has a light lemon-lime marinade which perfectly complements the mild, slightly sweet flavor of the fish.

Prep time: 15 minutes • **Cooking time:** 20 minutes

- 4 catfish fillets (1½ lbs.), cut into 8 pieces
- 2 tablespoons plus 2 teaspoons olive oil, divided
- 1 tablespoon grated lemon peel
- 1 tablespoon grated lime peel
- 2 tablespoons fresh lemon juice
- 2 tablespoons fresh lime juice
- 2 cups chopped onions
- 1 small jalapeño, sliced into ¼-inch rings (see tip, page 15)
- ½ teaspoon salt
- ½ teaspoon cumin
- 1 bag (10 oz.) fresh spinach
  Lemon wedges, for garnish (optional)

1. Combine catfish, 2 tablespoons of the oil, the lemon and lime peel and juices in a large glass baking dish. Cover and refrigerate.

2. Heat the remaining 2 teaspoons oil in a 12-inch nonstick skillet over medium heat. Add onions, jalapeño, salt and cumin. Cook 8 to 10 minutes, until onions soften. Stir in spinach and cook 3 to 4 minutes, just until spinach wilts. Transfer onion mixture to a bowl; cover and keep warm.

3. Heat same skillet over medium-high heat 1 minute. Remove fish from marinade, letting excess drip into dish; discard marinade. Cook fish 4 minutes, until well browned. Turn fish and cook 3 to 4 minutes more, just until fish is cooked through.

4. To serve, divide fish and onion mixture among 4 serving plates. Garnish with lemon wedges, if desired. Makes 4 servings.

Per serving: 175 calories, 10 g total fat, 1.5 g saturated fat,
19 mg cholesterol, 367 mg sodium, 10 g carbohydrates,
12 g protein, 92 mg calcium, 3 g fiber

salmon teriyaki

*Grilled salmon steaks and asparagus make an elegant pair
as well as a very simple supper. Some of the teriyaki
dressing is brushed on the salmon while grilling; the rest is
set aside to drizzle over the fish for a finishing touch.*

Prep time: 15 minutes • Grilling time: 10 to 12 minutes

TERIYAKI DRESSING:

- 3 tablespoons teriyaki sauce
- 2 tablespoons orange juice
- 1 tablespoon brown sugar
- 2 teaspoons chopped garlic
- ¼ teaspoon salt

- 1½ pounds asparagus, trimmed
- 1 tablespoon olive oil
- ¾ teaspoon salt, divided
- ¼ teaspoon freshly ground pepper, divided
- 4 salmon steaks, ½-inch thick (6 to 7 oz. each)
- 1 cup rice, cooked according to package directions

1. Oil and heat grill.

2. *Make teriyaki dressing:* Combine all ingredients
for teriyaki dressing in a cup, stirring until sugar is
dissolved. Transfer 2 tablespoons to another cup.

3. Toss asparagus with oil, ¼ teaspoon of the salt
and ⅛ teaspoon of the pepper in a shallow dish.
Grill asparagus over medium-high heat, turning
as spears brown, 10 to 12 minutes, until tender.
Set aside.

4. Meanwhile, sprinkle salmon with the remaining
½ teaspoon of salt and ⅛ teaspoon pepper. Grill
over medium-high heat 4 to 5 minutes per side,
until cooked through, brushing with reserved
2 tablespoons teriyaki dressing. Remove salmon to
serving plates; drizzle salmon with remaining
dressing. Serve with asparagus and rice. Serves 4.

Per serving: 555 calories, 21.5 g total fat, 4 g saturated fat,
96 mg cholesterol, 1,199 mg sodium, 49 g carbohydrates,
41 g protein, 73 mg calcium, 2 g fiber

lentil and bean bowl

*Lentils are a great and inexpensive source of calcium and
iron. Combine them with a can of high-fiber black beans,
chickpeas, tomatoes and spices, and you've got a speedy
chili-style supper. Substitute vegetable broth for the
chicken if you want a vegetarian meal.*

Prep time: 10 minutes • Cooking time: 25 to 27 minutes

- 1 tablespoon olive oil
- 1 cup chopped onions
- 2 large cloves garlic, pressed
- 2 cans (14½ oz. each) chicken or vegetable broth
- 3 tablespoons white wine
- 1½ cups brown lentils
- ¼ teaspoon allspice
- 1 can (16 oz.) black beans, drained and rinsed
- 1 can (16 oz.) chickpeas, drained and rinsed
- 1 cup canned whole tomatoes in puree, chopped
- ½ cup water
- 2 tablespoons chopped fresh cilantro
  Fresh cilantro sprigs, for garnish (optional)

1. Heat oil in a Dutch oven over medium-high
heat. Add onions and cook, covered, 2 minutes,
until lightly browned. Add garlic and cook, covered,
1 minute more.

2. Add broth and wine. Bring to boil. Stir in lentils
and allspice. Reduce heat to medium; simmer,
uncovered, 15 minutes. Add beans, chickpeas,
tomatoes and water. Cook 6 to 10 minutes more.

3. To serve, ladle into 4 serving bowls. Sprinkle
with cilantro and garnish with cilantro sprigs, if
desired. Makes 4 servings.

Per serving: 480 calories, 8 g total fat, 1 g saturated fat,
0 mg cholesterol, 1,284 mg sodium, 71 g carbohydrates,
31 g protein, 115 mg calcium, 15 g fiber

eggs for easy suppers

They're not just for breakfast or brunch anymore. Because eggs keep well, they're usually on hand and make for a super-easy way to get supper on the table. Kids love eggs, too, so when they demand dinner on-the-double, remember eggs for a fast fix. The microwave scrambles eggs even faster than a stovetop (and you don't have to dirty a pan!). And don't forget omelets; they're a fantastically fast—and delicious—way to fold in vegetables you'd like to use. All of the above are terrific, of course, served with basic toast or salad. Here are more serve-along ideas:

PAIR fresh melon and prosciutto (after all, no one says it has to be served as an appetizer) with an omelet or frittata.

SERVE broccoli or spinach with any egg dish.

HARD COOK eggs and toss with cooked bacon, shallots, mushrooms, greens and oil and vinegar for a quick spinach salad.

OFFER soft-cooked eggs with a side of our Crispy Hash Browns (recipe, page 78).

SLICE a pita pocket in half. Place cut side up and arrange avocado and hard-cooked egg slices (or scrambled eggs) over each half. Then sprinkle crumbled Gorgonzola over the top and heat in 350°F. oven, until pita is slightly toasted and cheese is melted.

HAVE LEFTOVER STEAK? Slice and serve over buttered, garlicked and toasted English muffins with poached eggs.

MICROWAVE new potatoes to serve with an omelet, frittata or scrambled eggs.

egg and black bean burritos

Here's a fabulous dinner that's wrapped up in a jiffy. Cooked eggs with melted Cheddar are topped with black beans, salsa and fresh cilantro. This mixture is used to fill flour tortillas, which are then tucked, rolled and sliced. Serve with additional salsa and avocado and a tossed salad, if desired. Pictured on page 48.

Total prep and cooking time: 17 to 19 minutes

- 1 **can (16 oz.) black beans, rinsed and drained well**
- 1 **cup prepared salsa**
- 1 **tablespoon chopped fresh cilantro or parsley**
- 8 **large eggs**
- ¼ **cup water**
- ½ **teaspoon salt**
- 2 **tablespoons vegetable oil**
- 1 **cup shredded Cheddar cheese**
- 4 **(6- to 8-inch) flour tortillas, warmed**
  Sliced avocado (optional)

1. Combine beans, salsa and cilantro in a bowl. Whisk together eggs, water and salt in another bowl. Set aside.

2. Heat broiler. Heat oil in a 12-inch nonstick, ovenproof skillet over medium heat. Add eggs; cover and cook 3 minutes. Lift edge of eggs to allow uncooked egg to run under; cook 1 to 2 minutes more, until almost set. Sprinkle with cheese; transfer skillet to broiler. Broil 1 to 2 minutes, until cheese is melted. Cut into quarters.

3. For each burrito, place one-quarter of the egg in a tortilla. Top with a generous ⅓ cup of the bean mixture. Fold in sides and roll up; cut in half. Serve with avocado and more salsa, if desired. Makes 4 servings.

Per serving: 530 calories, 29.5 g total fat, 10.5 g saturated fat, 455 mg cholesterol, 1,382 mg sodium, 37 g carbohydrates, 27 g protein, 322 mg calcium, 5 g fiber

mushroom and pepper frittata

Frittatas are great morning, noon or night; and here, sautéed onion, bell pepper and shiitake mushrooms fill them with great tastes in every bite. For best results, once you add the egg mixture to the pan, make sure the heat is on medium-low. Pictured on page 48.

Total prep and baking time: 30 minutes

- **2 tablespoons oil, divided**
- **1 medium onion, chopped**
- **1 red bell pepper, chopped**
- **½ pound sliced shiitake mushrooms**
- **8 large eggs**
- **1 cup grated Asiago cheese, divided**
- **¼ cup water**
- **¼ teaspoon salt**
- **¼ teaspoon freshly ground pepper**
- **¼ cup fresh basil leaves, sliced into thin strips**

1. Heat 1 tablespoon of the oil in a large nonstick, ovenproof skillet. Cook onion and bell pepper 2 to 3 minutes. Add mushrooms; cover and cook 1 minute. Stir and cook 2 minutes more. Transfer to a bowl.

2. Heat broiler. Whisk eggs, ¾ cup of the cheese, the water, salt and pepper in a bowl. Heat the remaining 1 tablespoon oil in skillet. Add egg mixture and basil and cook 1 minute; reduce heat to medium-low. Sprinkle mushrooms over eggs. Cover and cook 5 to 6 minutes more, until just the edge is puffed.

3. Sprinkle the remaining ¼ cup cheese over top; broil 1 minute. Makes 4 servings.

Per serving: 365 calories, 25 g total fat, 10 g saturated fat, 445 mg cholesterol, 591 mg sodium, 9 g carbohydrates, 23 g protein, 308 mg calcium, 2 g fiber

scrambled eggs with feta and dill

In a hurry? There's nothing faster or easier than eggs, and this version, with Canadian bacon, feta cheese and fresh dill, makes a savory and satisfying supper. Also try it for your next Sunday brunch. Crisp slices of country-bread toast and a fresh fruit salad round out the meal.

Total prep and baking time: 17 to 19 minutes

- **1 teaspoon vegetable oil**
- **8 pieces pre-sliced Canadian bacon**
- **8 large eggs**
- **¼ cup water**
- **1 tablespoon snipped fresh dill or**
  - **¼ teaspoon dried dill plus**
  - **1 teaspoon chopped fresh parsley**
- **⅛ teaspoon freshly ground pepper**
- **1 cup crumbled feta cheese**
- **1 tablespoon butter or margarine**
- **Toasted bread slices (optional)**

1. Heat oil in a 12-inch nonstick skillet over medium-high heat; add bacon and cook 1 to 2 minutes per side, until lightly browned. Transfer to a plate; cover and keep warm. Wipe skillet with a paper towel.

2. Whisk eggs, water, dill and pepper in a bowl. Add feta; mix well.

3. Melt butter in same skillet over medium heat, swirling to coat bottom. Pour in egg mixture and cook 2 minutes, until eggs start to set. Occasionally turn eggs with a spatula and continue to cook 4 to 5 minutes more, until eggs are just set. Serve with bacon and toast, if desired. Makes 4 servings.

Per serving: 410 calories, 27 g total fat, 12 g saturated fat, 505 mg cholesterol, 1,732 mg sodium, 4 g carbohydrates, 35 g protein, 223 mg calcium, 0 g fiber

penne with rustic tomatoes *EASY*

Almost everyone has a tried-and-true recipe for pasta with tomato sauce—here's a tantalizing twist on the theme. Chopped anchovies and capers team up with olives, kicking up the flavor. Fresh thyme is the perfect complement. Pictured on page 46.

Total prep and cooking time: 25 minutes

- 4   tablespoons olive oil, divided
- 1   medium onion, chopped
- 1   can (2 oz.) rolled anchovies and capers, chopped
- 1   tablespoon chopped garlic
- 1   can (35 oz.) whole tomatoes in juice
- 1   pound penne or ziti, cooked according to package directions
- ½   cup pitted olives, coarsely chopped
- 1   teaspoon chopped fresh thyme or ½ teaspoon dried thyme
- ¼   teaspoon freshly ground pepper

1. Heat water for pasta.

2. Meanwhile, heat 3 tablespoons of the oil in a 12-inch skillet over medium-high heat. Add onion; cook 3 minutes, stirring occasionally, until softened. Add anchovies and capers and garlic; cook 1 to 2 minutes more. Add tomatoes, breaking them up with a spoon. Bring to boil; boil 5 minutes.

3. Start to cook pasta. Add olives, thyme and pepper to sauce. Simmer 10 minutes more.

4. Drain pasta. Return to pot and toss hot pasta with 2 cups of the sauce. Transfer pasta to a bowl. Top with the remaining sauce and 1 tablespoon oil; toss again. Makes 4 servings.

Per serving: 685 calories, 21.5 g total fat, 3 g saturated fat, 6 mg cholesterol, 1,518 mg sodium, 102 g carbohydrates, 21 g protein, 126 mg calcium, 5 g fiber

orzo and mushroom risotto *EASY*

This hearty dish mimics the traditional Italian risotto, but we substitute orzo pasta for short-grain rice. Like the classic, it's delectably creamy, and the Italian herb-seasoned chicken broth is a terrific flavor-booster.

Prep time: 20 minutes • Cooking time: 20 minutes

- 2¾   cups Swanson Seasoned Chicken Broth with Italian Herbs
- 2¼   cups water
- ½   pound boneless, skinless chicken thighs, cut into ½-inch pieces
- ¼   teaspoon salt
- ¼   teaspoon freshly ground pepper
- 2   tablespoons olive oil, divided
- ½   pound sliced shiitake mushrooms
- ½   pound sliced white mushrooms
- ½   pound orzo pasta
- ¼   cup freshly grated Parmesan cheese

1. Bring broth and water to simmer in a saucepan.

2. Sprinkle chicken with salt and pepper. Heat 1 tablespoon of the oil in a 12-inch nonstick skillet over high heat. Add chicken and cook 1½ minutes per side, until browned and cooked through. Transfer with slotted spoon to a bowl.

3. Add the remaining 1 tablespoon oil to skillet. Add mushrooms; cover and cook 2 minutes, until softened. Add orzo and cook 1 minute more, until lightly toasted.

4. Set 1 cup of the hot broth aside in a glass measure. Gradually add remaining broth to pasta, 1 cup at a time, every 2 to 3 minutes, stirring occasionally (mixture will be soupy). Add chicken and reserved 1 cup broth and cook 2 to 4 minutes more, until thickened. Stir in Parmesan. Makes 4 servings.

Per serving: 410 calories, 12.5 g total fat, 3 g saturated fat, 54 mg cholesterol, 965 mg sodium, 50 g carbohydrates, 24 g protein, 117 mg calcium, 3 g fiber

fisherman's chowder LOW FAT

Peel and devein the shrimp and dice the celery, carrots and shallots in the morning; they will be all ready and waiting in the refrigerator when you get home. Diced potato makes this a hearty chowder, and for a really hungry bunch, serve with crusty bread to sop up every last drop.

Prep time: 25 minutes • Cooking time: 34 to 37 minutes

- ½ **pound medium shrimp**
- 1 **cup white wine**
- ¾ **cup water**
- 1 **bay leaf**
- 1 **teaspoon olive oil**
- 1 **cup diced celery**
- ½ **cup diced carrot**
- ½ **cup diced shallots (3 oz.)**
- 2 **bottles (8 oz. each) clam juice**
- ½ **pound all-purpose potatoes, peeled and cut into ½-inch cubes**
- ¾ **teaspoon salt**
- ½ **teaspoon chopped fresh thyme or ¼ teaspoon dried thyme**
- ¼ **teaspoon freshly ground pepper**
- 1 **pound cod or scrod fillet, cut into 1-inch chunks**
- **Sprigs fresh thyme, for garnish (optional)**

1. Peel and devein shrimp; reserve shells. Transfer shrimp to a small bowl; cover and refrigerate. Bring shells, wine, water and bay leaf to boil in a medium saucepan. Reduce heat to medium-low and simmer mixture 10 minutes.

2. Line a sieve with a double layer of cheesecloth; place over a 1-quart glass measure. Strain shrimp broth through sieve; discard shells and bay leaf. Add enough water to equal 4 cups of liquid. Set aside.

3. Meanwhile, heat oil in a Dutch oven over medium-high heat. Add celery, carrot and shallots. Cover and cook 5 minutes, until tender, stirring occasionally. Stir in the reserved broth mixture, clam juice, potatoes, salt, thyme and pepper.

4. Cover and simmer broth and vegetables over medium-low heat 20 minutes, until potatoes are fork-tender.

5. Add cod and reserved shrimp. Simmer 4 to 7 minutes more, just until cod is cooked through and shrimp turns pink. Ladle chowder into 4 serving bowls. Garnish with thyme sprigs, if desired. Makes 4 servings.

Per serving: 220 calories, 3 g total fat, 0.5 g saturated fat, 125 mg cholesterol, 868 mg sodium, 15 g carbohydrates, 33 g protein, 95 mg calcium, 5 g fiber

test kitchen tip
kid favorites

Lots of kids love to help in the kitchen, and it can actually be a successful venture when parents go about it in an organized fashion. Here are a few kid-friendly ideas:

TACOS are fun for children to make (they can be as creative—or picky—as they want). Just fill several small bowls with a variety of ingredients: cooked ground beef, chicken, turkey or pork; chopped fresh tomatoes; shredded cheese and lettuce; salsa; etc. Check the ethnic section of your supermarket for a wide assortment of taco shells, salsas and condiments.

MINI PIZZAS are an easy, sure-fire hit with kids. Purchase a prepared crust and divide it into portions, or use English Muffins. Have at the ready: a bowl of prepared tomato sauce, shredded cheese and cut-up raw and/or cooked vegetables and cooked meats (pepperoni, meatballs, chicken or turkey, sausage, etc.). Remember, you need to supervise or take over the baking part of this project.

FAJITAS are yet another type of food that leaves the selection of ingredients up to the individual. Put out a plate of warmed tortillas as well as bowls of sautéed onions, sweet bell peppers, guacamole, sour cream and yellow rice, as well as the cooked meat of your choice.

zesty meatball noodle soup EASY

Cheese-rich mini-meatballs star in this hearty dynamite meal in a bowl featuring fettuccine, zucchini and tomatoes with green chiles. Serve with Italian bread for irresistibly delicious dipping!

Total prep and cooking time: 30 minutes

    2 cans (14½ oz. each) chicken broth
    1 can (10 oz.) diced tomatoes with green chiles
       (see tip, page 71)
 1½ teaspoons minced garlic, divided
    1 teaspoon cumin
   ½ pound lean ground beef
    1 cup shredded Monterey Jack cheese, divided
   ⅛ teaspoon salt
   ⅛ teaspoon freshly ground pepper
 4½ ounces fresh fettuccine, cut into 2-inch
       lengths
    1 large zucchini, diced

1. Combine broth, tomatoes, 1 teaspoon of the garlic and the cumin in a pot. Cover; bring to boil. Reduce heat; simmer 5 minutes.

2. Combine the remaining ½ teaspoon garlic, the beef, ½ cup of the cheese, the salt and pepper in a medium bowl; mix well. Shape meat mixture into ¾-inch meatballs.

3. Add meatballs to broth mixture. Cover and simmer 4 minutes. Add fettuccine and zucchini; bring to boil. Simmer 2 minutes more, until fettuccine and zucchini are tender and the meatballs are no longer pink and cooked through. Serve with the remaining ½ cup of cheese. Makes 4 servings.

Per serving: 400 calories, 22.5 g total fat, 10.5 g saturated fat, 96 mg cholesterol, 1,362 mg sodium, 23 g carbohydrates, 23 g protein, 285 mg calcium, 2 g fiber

curried chicken noodle soup EASY

The aromatic Asian flavors in this soup serve up a welcome change from traditional chicken noodle.

Total prep and cooking time: 30 minutes

    3 cans (14½ oz. each) chicken broth
    1 medium sweet potato, peeled and chopped
    1 to 2 tablespoons green or red Thai curry
       paste*
    1 package (5 oz.) Japanese curly dried wheat-
       flour noodles* or capellini
    1 medium tomato, diced
    2 boneless, skinless chicken breast halves
       (6 to 7 oz. each), sliced crosswise ¼-inch
       thick
   ½ teaspoon salt
    1 cup unsweetened coconut milk*
    1 cup fresh cilantro leaves

1. Combine broth, potato and curry paste in a pot. Bring to boil. Reduce heat; cover and simmer 5 minutes.

2. Add noodles and tomato to broth mixture. Return to boil. Reduce heat; cover and simmer, stirring occasionally, 2 minutes.

3. Meanwhile, sprinkle chicken strips with salt. Add chicken to broth mixture and simmer 2 to 3 minutes more, until cooked through. Stir in coconut milk and heat through. Sprinkle with cilantro. Makes 6 servings.

*Note: Can be found in ethnic sections of supermarkets or in Asian specialty stores.

Per serving: 295 calories, 12 g total fat, 8 g saturated fat, 30 mg cholesterol, 1,440 mg sodium, 29 g carbohydrates, 18 g protein, 29 mg calcium, 2 g fiber

winter vegetable soup LOW FAT EASY

Here's a weeknight soup that tastes like you were in the kitchen all day. Creamy butternut squash and carrots make a tasty pair, along with sautéed onion and kielbasa. Tiny tubetti pasta is added at the end with red kidney beans and Swiss chard to round out the meal.

Total prep and cooking time: 35 minutes

- ½   **pound kielbasa, sliced**
- 1   **medium onion, chopped**
- 3   **cans (14½ oz. each) chicken broth**
- 3   **cups water**
- 1   **pound butternut squash, peeled and cubed**
- ½   **pound carrots, sliced**
- ½   **teaspoon salt**
- ¼   **teaspoon freshly ground pepper**
- 1½ **cups tubetti or tubettini pasta**
- 1   **can (15 to 16 oz.) red kidney beans, drained and rinsed**
- ½   **pound Swiss chard, trimmed and chopped**

1. Cook kielbasa and onion in a pot over medium-high heat 5 minutes. Add broth, water, squash, carrots, salt and pepper. Bring to boil. Reduce heat; cover and simmer 10 to 15 minutes, just until vegetables are tender.

2. Stir in pasta and beans. Return to boil; cover and boil gently 6 minutes, stirring often.

3. Stir in Swiss chard. Reduce heat; simmer, uncovered, 2 to 3 minutes more, until chard is tender. Makes 6 servings.

Per serving: 350 calories, 12 g total fat, 4 g saturated fat, 28 mg cholesterol, 1,598 mg sodium, 48 g carbohydrates, 15 g protein, 125 mg calcium, 7 g fiber

---

test kitchen tip

tex-mex convenience

Canned diced tomatoes with green chiles are a quick way to add zest to Tex-Mex recipes. RO-TEL Diced Tomatoes with Green Chiles are available in most supermarkets, or from Secrets to Cooking Tex Mex: 877-243-8839; www.texmex.net.

vegetarian skillet chili EASY

A speedy one-skillet meal of good-for-you sweet potato, zucchini and black beans heats up every bite. Have no fear though—it's not too hot to handle—just a touch of heat comes from chili powder as well as the green chiles found in the canned tomatoes. Pictured on page 42.

Total prep and cook time: 30 minutes

- 2   **tablespoons olive oil**
- 1   **cup chopped onions**
- 2   **teaspoons chili powder**
- 1   **teaspoon cumin**
- 2   **cans (10 oz. each) diced tomatoes and green chiles (see tip, above)**
- 1   **large sweet potato (8 oz.), peeled and diced**
- 2   **cans (16 to 19 oz. each) black beans, drained and rinsed**
- 1   **large zucchini (12 oz.), diced**

1. Heat oil in a 12-inch skillet. Cook onions until lightly browned. Stir in chili powder and cumin; cook 1 minute.

2. Add tomatoes and green chiles and potato; bring to boil. Reduce heat; cover and simmer 6 minutes, until potato is partially cooked. Add beans and zucchini; cook just until zucchini is tender and beans are heated through. Makes 4 servings.

Per serving: 300 calories, 9 g total fat, 1 g saturated fat, 0 mg cholesterol, 1,020 mg sodium, 44 g carbohydrates, 12 g protein, 116 mg calcium, 12 g fiber

chicken-tapenade pizza EASY

It's so easy. Start with a purchased crust, bake and then spread with prepared tapenade (a paste made from ripe olives, olive oil and lemon juice). Top with fresh spring greens and pan-grilled chicken.

Prep time: 15 minutes • Baking time: 8 to 10 minutes

- **1** **(12-inch) prepared pizza crust**
- **12** **ounces boneless, skinless chicken breasts**
- **¾** **teaspoon salt, divided**
- **½** **plus ⅛ teaspoon freshly ground pepper, divided**
- **3** **tablespoons olive oil, divided**
- **1** **tablespoon balsamic vinegar**
- **5** **cups mesclun salad greens or 1 bag (5 oz.) spring salad mix**
- **⅓** **cup tapenade (black olive paste)***

1. Heat oven to 450°F. Bake crust 8 to 10 minutes.

2. Meanwhile, sprinkle both sides of chicken with ½ teaspoon of the salt and ½ teaspoon of the pepper.

3. Heat 1 tablespoon of the oil in a large grill pan or cast-iron skillet over medium-high heat. Add chicken and cook 5 to 6 minutes each side, until browned and cooked through. Wrap in foil and set aside.

4. Combine the remaining 2 tablespoons oil, the vinegar, and the remaining ¼ teaspoon salt and ⅛ teaspoon pepper in a medium bowl. Toss with greens.

5. Spread hot crust with tapenade, leaving a 1-inch border. Top with greens. Thinly slice chicken and arrange on greens. Makes 4 servings.

**Note:* Can be found in condiment section of supermarkets.

Per serving: 550 calories, 23 g total fat, 3.5 g saturated fat, 55 mg cholesterol, 1,593 mg sodium, 52 g carbohydrates, 34 g protein, 145 mg calcium, 2 g fiber

italian hero calzone EASY

The kids will give you kudos when you serve these tasty pizza-with-the-works-inspired calzones. Rolled out pizza dough pieces are packed with olives, fresh tomatoes and mozzarella cheese (of course), made meaty with smoked turkey and salami, then brushed with olive oil and baked. To cut prep work when suppertime rolls around, have olives and tomatoes chopped and ready to go. Pictured on page 47.

Prep time: 50 minutes • Baking time: 15 to 18 minutes

- **2** **tablespoons cornmeal**
- **½** **cup chopped black olives**
- **⅓** **cup chopped fresh tomatoes**
- **1** **teaspoon plus 2 tablespoons olive oil, divided**
- **1** **pound prepared pizza dough***
- **8** **ounces sliced smoked turkey**
- **1** **package (8 oz.) shredded mozzarella cheese**
- **3** **ounces sliced salami**

1. Adjust oven rack to lowest position. Heat oven to 425°F.

2. Sprinkle cornmeal on a large cookie sheet. Combine olives, tomatoes and 1 teaspoon of the oil in a bowl. Set both aside.

3. Divide dough into 4 equal pieces. On a lightly floured surface, shape dough into four 7-inch circles. Place one quarter of turkey in bottom half of 1 circle, leaving a ½-inch border. Top turkey with one quarter of cheese, olive mixture and salami. Fold top half of circle over filling to make a semicircle. Fold edge over and flute. Transfer calzone to prepared sheet. Refrigerate. Repeat process with remaining dough and filling.

4. Brush top of each calzone with the remaining 2 tablespoons oil. Bake 15 to 18 minutes, until golden brown. Makes 4 servings.

**Note:* Look for fresh or frozen pizza dough at a neighborhood bakery, pizza parlor or supermarket.

Per serving: 725 calories, 35 g total fat, 12 g saturated fat, 90 mg cholesterol, 2,086 mg sodium, 63 g carbohydrates, 38 g protein, 314 mg calcium, 2 g fiber

sloppy joe calzone (EASY)

Sloppy Joes are an all-time favorite for kids, and calzones are downright fun—so what could be a better combination? Store-bought marinara sauce and ground beef team up with onion, celery and garlic for a sloppy yet oh-so-satisfying filling. Freshly grated Parmesan cheese tops it off. Tip for double duty: Freeze the remaining 2 cups of filling and use as a delicious topping for pasta at another meal.

Prep time: 40 minutes plus cooling
Baking time: 15 to 20 minutes

- **2**   **tablespoons cornmeal**
- **1**   **teaspoon plus 2 tablespoons olive oil, divided**
- **½**   **cup finely chopped onion**
- **¼**   **cup finely chopped celery**
- **1**   **tablespoon chopped garlic**
- **¼**   **teaspoon salt**
- **1**   **pound lean ground beef**
- **1**   **jar (24 oz.) prepared marinara sauce**
- **½**   **small carrot, finely chopped**
- **1**   **pound prepared pizza dough***
- **¼**   **cup freshly grated Parmesan cheese, divided**

1. Adjust oven rack to lowest position. Heat oven to 425°F. Sprinkle cornmeal on a large cookie sheet. Set aside.

2. Heat 1 teaspoon of the oil in a large skillet over medium heat. Add onion, celery, garlic and salt. Cook, stirring, 3 minutes, until vegetables soften. Stir in ground beef, breaking up with the back of the spoon. Cook 3 to 5 minutes, until beef is no longer pink. Add marinara sauce and carrot, stirring until combined. Reduce heat to medium-low; simmer 15 minutes. Transfer to a large bowl; cool 15 to 20 minutes, until room temperature. Makes 4 cups.

3. Divide dough into 4 equal pieces. On a lightly floured surface, shape dough into four 7-inch circles. Spread ½ cup of the meat filling in bottom half of dough circle, leaving a ½-inch border. Sprinkle with 1 tablespoon of the Parmesan. Fold top half of circle over filling to make a semicircle. Fold edge over and flute. Transfer calzone to prepared sheet. Refrigerate. Repeat process with remaining dough and 1½ cups filling. *(For another batch of calzones or a pasta topper: Freeze remaining 2 cups filling in a microwaveproof bowl for up to 2 weeks. To reheat: Microwave on HIGH 5 to 6 minutes.)* Brush top of each calzone with the remaining 2 tablespoons oil. Bake 15 to 20 minutes, until golden brown. Makes 4 servings.

*Note: Look for fresh or frozen pizza dough at a neighborhood bakery, pizza parlor or supermarket.

Per serving: 840 calories, 43 g total fat, 12.5 g saturated fat, 90 mg cholesterol, 2,171 mg sodium, 78 g carbohydrates, 36 g protein, 137 mg calcium, 5 g fiber

barbecued-pork sandwiches (EASY)

Here's serious barbecue, Southern style. The pork is slow-roasted until it's fork-tender and then piled on a soft roll that soaks up the savory juices.

Prep time: 20 minutes • Baking time: 1 hour 30 minutes

- **1½**   **pounds boneless pork roast**
- **½**   **teaspoon salt**
- **¼**   **teaspoon freshly ground pepper**
- **1**   **jar (18 or 19 oz.) barbecue sauce**
- **4**   **soft hamburger rolls**
-   **Coleslaw (optional)**

1. Heat oven to 325°F.

2. Sprinkle pork with salt and pepper. Heat a Dutch oven 1 minute over medium-high heat. Brown pork on all sides, about 4 minutes per side.

3. Add barbecue sauce to Dutch oven; cover and bake 1½ hours, until pork is fork-tender.

4. Transfer pork to cutting board. Shred into thin pieces. Return to Dutch oven and cook 5 minutes more over medium heat.

5. To serve, place rolls on serving plates. Divide pork mixture and spoon onto each roll. Serve with coleslaw, if desired. Makes 4 servings.

Per serving: 640 calories, 33.5 g total fat, 10.5 g saturated fat, 121 mg cholesterol, 1,745 mg sodium, 45 g carbohydrates, 37 g protein, 88 mg calcium, 1 g fiber

side ways for sandwiches

Serving a hearty sandwich that calls for just a little nibble on the side? Or perhaps a lighter one beckoning a more substantial side dish? Any way you slice it, a sandwich can always use an alluring accompaniment to complete the meal. Here are some quick fixes:

CREATE an enticingly easy antipasto-style salad: Combine canned artichoke hearts, pepperoncini, black olives and fresh red and yellow cherry tomatoes. Toss with extra-virgin olive oil.

SERVE baked beans. It's a great item to team with warm sandwiches.

BOIL red potatoes, drizzle with extra-virgin olive oil and sprinkle with salt, pepper and a touch of rosemary.

SPEAR chunks of fresh fruit onto wooden skewers for colorful kabobs.

SAUTÉ the tried-and-true trio of sweet bell peppers, onions and your favorite mushrooms.

SLICE garden-fresh tomatoes, topped with a touch of extra-virgin olive oil, a pinch of sugar, salt, pepper and a little chopped fresh basil.

CHECK health food stores for multi-grain snacks and other lower-fat, lower-salt alternatives to potato chips.

golden onion and swiss burgers EASY

Love the classic "Patty Melt" on rye? We use a super-sweet onion for the topping and add sliced beefsteak tomatoes.

Total prep and cooking time: 30 minutes

- **2 tablespoons butter, divided**
- **1 large sweet onion (such as Spanish or Vidalia), very thinly sliced**
-    **Salt**
- **1 pound lean ground beef or ground turkey**
- **1 cup shredded Swiss cheese**
- **1 tablespoon Dijon mustard**
- **1 teaspoon salt**
- **½ teaspoon freshly ground pepper**
- **½ teaspoon chopped fresh thyme**
- **8 slices rye bread**
- **1 large beefsteak tomato, sliced**

1. Heat 1 tablespoon of the butter in a 12-inch nonstick pan over medium heat. Add onion and cook 18 to 20 minutes, until browned and very tender, stirring occasionally. Add a pinch of salt.

2. Toss beef with cheese, mustard, salt, pepper and thyme; shape into four ½-inch-thick patties.

3. Heat a grill pan or cast-iron skillet. Grill patties 5 to 6 minutes per side, until an instant-read thermometer inserted into side of burger registers 160°F. for medium (165°F. for turkey).

4. Heat a large nonstick skillet over medium heat. Spread the remaining 1 tablespoon butter evenly over 1 side of bread slices. Place 2 slices, buttered side down, in skillet and cook about 1 minute, until toasted. Spread onion topping on untoasted side of bread; add tomato and burger. Top each with another bread slice, butter side out. Turn and toast other side. Repeat with remaining bread slices, onion, tomato and burgers. Makes 4 servings.

Per serving: 585 calories, 30.5 g total fat, 15 g saturated fat, 112 mg cholesterol, 718 mg sodium, 41 g carbohydrates, 35 g protein, 352 mg calcium, 6 g fiber

southwest burgers EASY

Thick 'n' juicy cilantro burgers, topped with roasted poblano chiles, salsa and Monterey Jack cheese, are a surefire crowd-pleaser.

Total prep and cooking time: 30 minutes

3	large poblano chiles (see tip, page 15)
1¼	pounds lean ground beef or ground turkey
¼	cup chopped fresh cilantro
2	tablespoons coarsely grated onion
1	teaspoon salt
½	teaspoon freshly ground pepper
¼	pound Monterey Jack cheese, sliced
	Salsa or ketchup (optional)
4	kaiser rolls, toasted

1. Heat broiler. Place chiles on a foil-lined cookie sheet. Broil 3 inches from heat 10 to 15 minutes, turning occasionally, until skins are bubbly and evenly charred. Immediately transfer chiles to a large resealable plastic storage bag and seal. Let stand 10 to 15 minutes, until chiles are cool enough to handle. Remove skins from chiles, seed and cut into strips.

2. Meanwhile, toss beef with cilantro, onion, salt and pepper; shape into four ½-inch-thick patties.

3. Heat grill pan or cast-iron skillet. Grill patties 5 to 6 minutes per side, until an instant-read thermometer inserted into side of burger registers 160°F. for medium (165°F. for turkey).

4. Top each burger with cheese; remove from heat. Cover pan and let stand 1 minute, until cheese is melted.

5. To serve, place burgers, chile strips and salsa, if desired, on bottom half of rolls; add top half of rolls. Makes 4 servings.

Per serving: 580 calories, 30 g total fat, 12.5 g saturated fat, 118 mg cholesterol, 1,129 mg sodium, 39 g carbohydrates, 39 g protein, 295 mg calcium, 2 g fiber

beef and zucchini burgers EASY

Diced zucchini juices up the burgers and adds crunch to the zesty mayo topping.

Total prep and cooking time: 30 minutes

SAUCE:

3	tablespoons mayonnaise
3	tablespoons prepared salsa
½	teaspoon Worcestershire sauce
⅛	teaspoon freshly ground pepper
2	teaspoons olive oil
1	medium onion, finely diced
1	zucchini, finely diced
1¼	pounds ground beef or ground turkey
2	teaspoons Worcestershire sauce
1	teaspoon salt
½	teaspoon freshly ground pepper
4	(5 to 6-inch) white or whole wheat pita breads, warmed

1. *Make sauce:* Combine all ingredients for sauce in a small bowl. Set aside.

2. Heat oil in a nonstick skillet. Add onion and half of the zucchini. Cook 3 to 4 minutes, until tender. Cool.

3. Toss ground beef with zucchini mixture, Worcestershire, salt and pepper. Shape into four ½-inch-thick patties.

4. Heat a grill pan or cast-iron skillet. Grill patties 5 to 6 minutes per side, until an instant-read thermometer inserted into side of burger registers 160°F. for medium (165°F. for turkey).

5. Place burgers, sauce and remaining chopped zucchini inside pitas. Makes 4 servings.

Per serving: 560 calories, 30 g total fat, 9 g saturated fat, 94 mg cholesterol, 1,156 mg sodium, 40 g carbohydrates, 32 g protein, 81 mg calcium, 2 g fiber

warm german potato salad LOW FAT EASY

We substitute broth for most of the oil and use plenty of mustard and shallots in the dressing. Pictured on page 42.

Prep time: 15 minutes • Cooking time: 18 to 20 minutes
Microwave used

DRESSING:

- **1 slice bacon**
- **3 tablespoons minced shallots**
- **1 tablespoon olive oil**
- **⅓ cup chicken broth**
- **2 tablespoons white wine vinegar**
- **2 tablespoons coarse grain mustard**
- **½ teaspoon salt**
- **¼ teaspoon sugar**
- **Pinch ground red pepper**
  - ■
- **2 pounds red potatoes, scrubbed and cut into 1-inch chunks**
- **1 tablespoon salt**

1. ■ *Make dressing:* Cook bacon in a skillet until crisp. With slotted spoon, transfer to a paper towel. Cool; crumble and set aside.

2. ■ Add shallots and oil to skillet. Cook 1½ to 2 minutes, until shallots are lightly browned. Transfer shallot-oil mixture to a microwaveproof cup, scraping with rubber spatula. With fork, whisk in chicken broth, vinegar, mustard, salt, sugar and ground red pepper. *(Can be made ahead. Cover and let dressing stand at room temperature up to 4 hours.)*

3. ■ Bring potatoes, salt and enough cold water to cover potatoes by 2 inches to boil in a large saucepan. Reduce heat; cover and simmer 18 to 20 minutes, until potatoes are fork-tender. Drain in colander; let stand 5 minutes.

4. ■ Transfer potatoes to a serving bowl. Microwave dressing on HIGH 1 minute, until heated through. Pour dressing over potatoes and toss gently with a spatula. Sprinkle bacon over top. Makes 6 servings.

Per serving: 175 calories, 5 g total fat, 1 g saturated fat, 3 mg cholesterol, 541 mg sodium, 28 g carbohydrates, 3 g protein, 2 mg calcium, 3 g fiber

guiltless mashed potatoes LOW FAT EASY

We boiled red potatoes with fresh rosemary, then mashed them with low-fat milk and chicken broth for spuds so tasty no one will miss the pat of butter. Pictured on page 43.

Prep time: 15 minutes • Cooking time: 18 to 20 minutes
Microwave used

- **2 pounds red potatoes, peeled**
- **1 sprig fresh rosemary**
- **¼ cup chicken broth**
- **¼ cup low-fat (1%) milk**
- **1 teaspoon salt**
- **¼ teaspoon freshly ground pepper**

1. ■ Bring potatoes, rosemary sprig and enough cold water to cover potatoes by 2 inches to boil in a large saucepan. Reduce heat; cover and simmer 18 to 20 minutes, until potatoes are fork-tender.

2. ■ Drain potatoes; discard rosemary. Microwave broth and milk in a microwaveproof cup on HIGH 1 minute, until hot. Return potatoes to saucepan and cook 2 minutes over low heat to dry.

3. ■ Coarsely mash potatoes with a potato masher or large wooden spoon. Stir in broth mixture, salt and pepper until combined and heated through. Makes 6 servings.

Per serving: 115 calories, 0.5 g total fat, 0 g saturated fat, 0 mg cholesterol, 446 mg sodium, 25 g carbohydrates, 3 g protein, 13 mg calcium, 2 g fiber

spicy oven fries EASY

These chunky potato wedges, made crisp with a touch of olive oil, are perfect with steak. Pictured on page 46.

Prep time: 15 minutes • Baking time: 24 to 28 minutes

- **6 teaspoons olive oil, divided**
- **1 teaspoon onion powder**
- **1 teaspoon turmeric**
- **¾ teaspoon salt**
- **¼ teaspoon white pepper**
- **1½ pounds russet potatoes or baking potatoes**

1. Adjust oven racks in upper and lower third of oven. Heat oven to 425°F. Lightly brush 2 large cookie sheets with 2 teaspoons of the oil.

2. Combine onion powder, turmeric, salt and pepper in a cup.

3. Scrub potatoes; quarter lengthwise and cut each quarter into 4 long wedges. Blot dry with paper towels. Toss potatoes with the remaining 4 teaspoons oil in a large bowl. Sprinkle with half of the seasoning mixture, turning potatoes gently with rubber spatula. Toss potatoes again with remaining seasoning mixture until coated on all sides.

4. Divide and spread potatoes evenly on prepared baking sheets. Bake 24 to 28 minutes, switching pans halfway through, until potatoes are golden and crisp. Makes 4 servings.

Per serving: 200 calories, 7 g total fat, 1 g saturated fat, 0 mg cholesterol, 450 mg sodium, 31 g carbohydrates, 3 g protein, 4 mg calcium, 3 g fiber

french fries

These tasty fries rival those at your favorite steakhouse!

Prep time: 15 minutes plus chilling
Cooking time: 4 to 7 minutes per batch

  2 **pounds russet or baking potatoes, scrubbed**
  1 **(24-oz.) bottle peanut oil***
     Kosher salt

1. Cut each potato lengthwise into ¼-inch slices. Stack 3 slices, then cut into ¼-inch-wide sticks. Transfer potato sticks to a large bowl; add enough cold water to cover. Repeat. Refrigerate potatoes 2 hours. *(Can be refrigerated 8 hours.)*

2. Drain potatoes; transfer to a large jelly-roll pan lined with paper towels. Blot potatoes until dry.

3. Heat oil in a medium Dutch oven or deep fryer over medium heat to 325°F. Line another large jelly-roll pan with paper towels. Place one-fourth of the potatoes in a frying basket or fine-meshed sieve. Cook 2 to 4 minutes, until potatoes are tender and edges are slightly crisp, turning occasionally. (Potatoes should not be browned.) Drain on prepared pan. Repeat with remaining potatoes.

4. Heat oil over medium heat about 5 minutes, until temperature reaches 375°F. Heat oven to 300°F. Re-fry one fourth of potatoes 2 to 3 minutes, until crisp and golden. Transfer french fries to a cookie sheet lined with paper towels and keep warm in oven while refrying remaining potatoes. To serve, sprinkle french fries with salt. Serve immediately. Makes 4 servings.

*Note: Oil can be used again for frying. Cool completely and strain through a double thickness of cheesecloth. Cover and store at room temperature.

Per serving: 340 calories, 18.5 g total fat, 3 g saturated fat, 0 mg cholesterol, 293 mg sodium, 41 g carbohydrates, 4 g protein, 2 mg calcium, 4 g fiber

---

test kitchen tip

the right spud for the job

When a recipe specifies a variety of potato, it's best not to substitute with any old spud. Some potatoes work better than others in certain recipes. Here's a potato primer:

FOR BAKING, choose russets (sometimes called Idaho potatoes) or long white potatoes (sometimes called white rose potatoes).

BOILING POTATOES include round white and round red potatoes, Yukon gold potatoes, and All-Blue Potatoes (an heirloom variety that's celebrating a revival in markets).

FOR FRENCH FRIES, the russet's the choice.

FOR POTATO SALADS, choose a variety that keeps its shape when cooked, including those classified as "waxy," such as long whites and round reds. New potatoes also hold their shape well. The term "new potatoes" does not refer to a particular variety of potato. Rather, they're a young, small potato of any variety and are available in spring and early summer. To add color to the salad, use yellow potatoes, such as Yukon gold or Yellow Finn.

golden potato gratin EASY

A potato "gratin" usually means butter, heavy cream and cheese, but not this time. We use rich-tasting Yukon gold potatoes instead of all-purpose potatoes and replace the cream with chicken broth.

Prep time: 15 minutes plus standing
Baking time: 55 to 60 minutes

- **3** teaspoons butter, softened and divided
- **1** large clove garlic
- **1⅓** cups chicken broth
- **½** teaspoon salt
- **⅛** teaspoon freshly ground pepper
- **2** pounds Yukon gold potatoes, peeled and cut into ¼-inch-thick slices
- **½** cup shredded Gruyère or Swiss cheese
- **¼** cup finely shredded Parmesan cheese
- **1** tablespoon snipped fresh chives

1. Heat oven to 400°F. Grease a 2-quart shallow baking dish with 1 teaspoon of the butter. Set aside.

2. Smash garlic with side of knife. Bring broth, garlic, salt and pepper to boil in a small saucepan. Remove from heat and let stand 10 minutes.

3. Arrange half of the potatoes in overlapping slices to cover bottom of prepared dish. Remove garlic from broth; discard garlic. Pour half of the broth over potatoes. Sprinkle with half of the cheeses. Repeat with remaining potatoes, broth and cheeses. Sprinkle top with chives. Dot with the remaining 2 teaspoons butter.

4. Cover dish with foil and bake 40 minutes. Uncover; bake potatoes 15 to 20 minutes more, until top is golden and potatoes are tender when pierced with a knife. Makes 6 servings.

Per serving: 198 calories, 7.5 g total fat, 4 g saturated fat, 19 mg cholesterol, 558 mg sodium, 25 g carbohydrates, 8 g protein, 154 mg calcium, 2 g fiber

crispy hash browns LOW FAT EASY

Your family will love these tasty hash brown potatoes (and will never guess they're low in fat!). Pictured on page 43.

Prep time: 20 minutes • Cooking time: 35 to 38 minutes

- **2** tablespoons olive oil, divided
- **1** cup chopped onions
- **½** cup finely chopped green bell pepper
- **½** cup chopped celery
- **1** bay leaf
- **¾** teaspoon salt
- **½** teaspoon paprika
- **¼** teaspoon freshly ground pepper
- **1¼** cups chicken broth
- **3** russet potatoes (1½ lbs.), peeled and diced
- **1** sweet potato (½ lb.), peeled and diced

1. Heat 1 tablespoon of the oil 1 minute over medium heat in a large nonstick skillet. Add onion and cook 3 minutes, until softened. Stir in bell pepper, celery, bay leaf, salt, paprika and pepper. Cook 5 minutes, until vegetables soften. Discard bay leaf. Transfer vegetables to a small bowl; set aside.

2. Bring broth and potatoes to boil in same skillet over medium heat. Cover and simmer potatoes 17 to 20 minutes, until tender and most of the liquid has evaporated. Uncover skillet; stir in reserved vegetables. Add the remaining 1 tablespoon oil. Cook 10 minutes more, stirring often to prevent sticking, until potatoes are golden brown. Makes 4 to 6 servings.

Per serving: 210 calories, 6.5 g total fat, 1 g saturated fat, 0 mg cholesterol, 631 mg sodium, 34 g carbohydrates, 4 g protein, 22 mg calcium, 4 g fiber

thyme-garlic baked potatoes

Slit the top of each potato, tuck in thyme sprigs and garlic, and you have a new twist on an old favorite. Pictured on page 47.

Prep time: 15 minutes • Baking time: 50 to 55 minutes
Microwave used

- **2 teaspoons butter or margarine**
- **2 teaspoons olive oil**
- **3 slices garlic**
- **4 large baking potatoes (8 oz. each), scrubbed**
- **12 3-inch sprigs fresh thyme**
- **½ teaspoon salt**
- **¼ teaspoon freshly ground pepper**

1. Heat oven to 450°F.

2. Combine butter, oil and garlic in a microwaveproof cup; cover with plastic wrap. Microwave on MEDIUM-HIGH 1 minute, until butter melts. Let stand, covered, 5 minutes; remove garlic and discard.

3. Arrange 1 of the potatoes, flat side down, on a work surface. With a small, sharp knife, make 4 crosswise cuts into top of each potato about two-thirds of the way through, being careful not to cut all the way through.

4. Cut 3 of the sprigs of thyme into ½-inch pieces. With the tip of the knife, divide and tuck pieces into each slit. Repeat process with the remaining potatoes and thyme pieces.

5. Transfer potatoes to a jelly-roll pan. Drizzle cut sides of potatoes with melted butter mixture. Sprinkle with salt and pepper. Bake 50 to 55 minutes, until tender when pierced with a knife. Makes 4 servings.

Per serving: 220 calories, 4.5 g total fat, 1.5 g saturated fat, 5 mg cholesterol, 323 mg sodium, 42 g carbohydrates, 5 g protein, 28 mg calcium, 4 g fiber

---

test kitchen tip
more great sides

Choose from these speedy side dishes to serve alongside any weeknight meat-and-potato dinner:

lemon broccoli

Pictured on page 42.

Place steamer basket in a saucepan. Add enough water to reach just under the basket. Arrange 1 bag (16 oz.) fresh broccoli florets in basket; cover and bring water to boil. Cook broccoli 3 to 4 minutes, until just tender. Microwave 1 tablespoon olive oil and ¼ teaspoon minced garlic in a microwaveproof bowl on HIGH 40 to 60 seconds, until garlic is fragrant. Stir in ¼ teaspoon lemon peel, 1 tablespoon fresh lemon juice, ½ teaspoon salt and ⅛ teaspoon pepper. Add broccoli and toss. Makes 6 servings.

Per serving: 40 calories, 2 g total fat, 0.5 g saturated fat, 0 mg cholesterol, 213 mg sodium, 4 g carbohydrates, 2 g protein, 41 mg calcium, 2 g fiber

peas with red onion

Pictured on page 43.

Heat 1 teaspoon each olive oil and butter in a saucepan. Add ¼ cup chopped red onion and cook 2 minutes. Add 2 cups frozen peas, 2 tablespoons water, ⅛ teaspoon each salt and pepper. Cover and cook vegetables 3 to 4 minutes, until hot. Stir. Makes 4 servings.

Per serving: 80 calories, 2.5 g total fat, 1 g saturated fat, 3 mg cholesterol, 165 mg sodium, 11 g carbohydrates, 4 g protein, 9 mg calcium, 3 g fiber

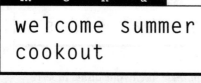

new classic potato salad

Always the perfect summer picnic fare—ours cooks up quick and tasty with dill pickles and pan-roasted corn.

Total prep and cooking time: 30 minutes

- 1 **bag (1½ lb.) refrigerated, ready-to-cook red potatoes**
- ¼ **cup mayonnaise**
- ¼ **cup chopped kosher dill pickles**
- 2 **tablespoons finely chopped shallot**
- 1 **tablespoon white wine vinegar**
- ½ **teaspoon sugar**
- ½ **teaspoon salt**
- 1 **teaspoon olive oil**
- 1 **cup frozen whole-kernel corn, partially thawed**

1. Cook potatoes according to package directions. Drain in a colander under cool running water, 30 seconds. Set aside.

2. Meanwhile, combine mayonnaise, pickles, shallot, vinegar, sugar and salt in a large bowl. Set aside.

3. Heat oil in a large nonstick skillet over high heat. Add corn and cook, stirring occasionally, 1 to 2 minutes, until corn starts to pop and lightly brown in spots.

4. Transfer corn to bowl with mayonnaise mixture. With a rubber spatula, gently stir in warm, drained potatoes to combine. Makes 4 servings.

Per serving: 265 calories, 12.5 g total fat, 2 g saturated fat, 8 mg cholesterol, 494 mg sodium, 41 g carbohydrates, 6 g protein, 30 mg calcium, 4 g fiber

walnut and blue-cheese potato salad

Toasted walnuts and tangy cheese give this favorite a sophisticated update. No need to make a separate dressing—simply toss the blue cheese with the warm spuds to soften, making a wonderfully creamy sensation.

Total prep and cooking time: 30 minutes

- ⅓ **cup chopped walnuts**
- 1 **bag (1½ lb.) refrigerated, ready-to-cook home fries potatoes**
- 2 **cups water**
- 2 **tablespoons olive oil**
- 2 **tablespoons mayonnaise**
- 2 **tablespoons snipped fresh chives**
- 4 **teaspoons cider vinegar**
- ¼ **teaspoon salt**
- ⅛ **teaspoon sugar**
- ¼ **cup crumbled Maytag or Danish blue cheese**

1. Heat oven to 325°F. Bake walnuts 6 to 8 minutes, until toasted. Cool. Set aside.

2. Meanwhile, combine potatoes and water in a saucepan. Bring to boil. Cook potatoes 4 to 5 minutes. Drain in a colander. Set aside.

3. Whisk together oil, mayonnaise, chives, vinegar, salt and sugar in a large bowl. With a rubber spatula, gently stir in walnuts, drained potatoes, and cheese to combine. Serve warm. Makes 4 servings.

Per serving: 320 calories, 20.5 g total fat, 4 g saturated fat, 10 mg cholesterol, 301 mg sodium, 33 g carbohydrates, 8 g protein, 80 mg calcium, 4 g fiber

SHRIMP AND
ASPARAGUS ON
LINGUINE
PG. 98

market fresh and fabulous

TARRAGON
CHICKEN SALAD
PG. 89

Whether your veggies come from the supermarket across town or the farm stand across the street, whether you like them seasoned to the taste of home or spiced to transport you across the globe, here's a bushel basketful of ways to enjoy them fresh every day.

CLASSIC
COBB SALAD
PG. 89

satisfy
your appetite

SHRIMP AND RICE
NOODLE SALAD
PG. 92

GRILLED
TUNA SALAD
PG. 94

for freshness

HAM AND
LENTIL SALAD
PG. 91

Market Fresh and Fabulous **83**

enliven
everyday meals...

PASTA WITH
SAUSAGE AND
PESTO
PG. 96

LEFT:
VEGETABLE
CLAM
CHOWDER
PG. 100

RIGHT:
SUMMER
VEGETABLE
BOUILLABAISSE
PG. 101

SAUSAGE AND
PEPPER HERO
PG. 96

...with **tomatoes**
potatoes, peppers

and more

TOMATO
GALETTE
PG. 104

these days, the salad bowl is more **interesting** than ever!

ZESTY FISH FILLETS ON
GREENS
PG. 95

DEVILLED EGG SALAD ON
SPINACH
PG. 103

GREEN BEANS WITH
BEETS AND CUCUMBERS
PG. 115

YELLOW BELL PEPPER
SOUP
PG. 118

(same goes
for the
soup bowl)

increase the
market value
of your meals

GRILLED
VEGETABLE
RISOTTO
PG. 102

SAUSAGE WITH
WHITE BEANS
PG. 97

classic cobb salad [EASY]

Hollywood's Brown Derby Restaurant made this all-star salad famous. Every bite boasts a pleasing combination of chopped chicken and egg, avocado, crisp lettuce and crispy bacon, creamy herb dressing and tangy Roquefort cheese. Pictured on page 82.

Prep time: 20 minutes • Cooking time: 15 minutes

- **2 boneless, skinless chicken breast halves (6 to 7 oz. each)**
- **2 teaspoons fresh lime juice**
- **¼ teaspoon salt**
- **⅛ teaspoon freshly ground pepper**
- **2 teaspoons olive oil**
- **4 slices thick-cut bacon**

DRESSING:
- **1 cup mayonnaise**
- **⅓ cup chopped fresh flat-leaf parsley**
- **¼ cup chopped fresh chives**
- **2 anchovy fillets, finely chopped**
- **2 tablespoons water**
- **2 tablespoons white wine vinegar**
- **2 teaspoons fresh lime juice**
- **Pinch sugar**
■
- **1 large head iceberg lettuce, chopped**
- **2 hard-cooked eggs, peeled and finely chopped**
- **1 ripe avocado, diced**
- **1 cup (4 oz.) crumbled Roquefort cheese or blue cheese**

1. Toss chicken with lime juice, salt and pepper. Heat oil in a large nonstick skillet 1 minute over medium-high heat. Add chicken. Cover and cook 6 to 7 minutes, until golden brown. Turn chicken; cover and cook 6 to 7 minutes more, until chicken is cooked through. Wrap chicken in a large piece of foil and seal. Cool 20 minutes, then dice.

2. Meanwhile, cook bacon in same skillet over medium heat 7 to 8 minutes, just until crisp. Transfer bacon with a slotted spoon to paper towels; drain.

3. *Make dressing:* Whisk together all of the dressing ingredients in a small bowl until smooth.

4. Arrange lettuce on a large platter. Then arrange chicken, eggs, avocado, cheese and bacon in rows over top. Serve with dressing. Makes 4 servings.

Per serving: 840 calories, 73 g total fat, 17 g saturated fat, 222 mg cholesterol, 1,228 mg sodium, 15 g carbohydrates, 35 g protein, 394 mg calcium, 4 g fiber

tarragon chicken salad [EASY]

Tarragon adds a subtle licorice flavor to the mayonnaise dressing. The yellow squash, carrot and celery provide a delightful crunch. Tip: Keep things cool in your kitchen—use rotisserie chicken from the supermarket. Pictured on page 81.

Total prep time: 30 minutes

DRESSING:
- **½ cup mayonnaise**
- **3 tablespoons white balsamic vinegar or white wine vinegar**
- **½ teaspoon salt**
- **½ teaspoon sugar**
- **½ teaspoon freshly ground pepper**
■
- **2 cups chopped cooked chicken**
- **½ cup finely chopped red onion**
- **½ cup chopped yellow summer squash**
- **⅓ cup chopped carrot**
- **⅓ cup chopped celery ribs with leaves**
- **1 tablespoon fresh tarragon leaves, chopped or 1 teaspoon dried tarragon with 1 tablespoon chopped fresh parsley**
- **1 package (5 oz.) spring salad mix (mesclun)**
- **Toasted French bread (optional)**

1. *Make dressing:* Whisk together all of the dressing ingredients in a small bowl until smooth. Set aside.

2. Combine chicken, red onion, squash, carrot, celery and tarragon in a large bowl. Add dressing; stir until well coated. Divide salad mix and chicken mixture among 4 serving plates. Serve with toast, if desired. Makes 4 servings.

Per serving: 360 calories, 27 g total fat, 4.5 g saturated fat, 79 mg cholesterol, 529 mg sodium, 7 g carbohydrates, 22 g protein, 54 mg calcium, 1 g fiber

warm turkey, nectarine and watercress salad

A refreshing ensemble of sweet nectarines, crisp jicama, peppery watercress and an orange-lime dressing jazzes up quick-to-cook turkey cutlets. When selecting watercress, look for crisp, bright-colored leaves.

Prep time: 15 minutes • Cooking time: 8 minutes

CITRUS DRESSING:

- ¼ cup fresh orange juice
- 3 tablespoons white wine vinegar
- 2 tablespoons fresh lime juice
- 2 tablespoons finely chopped shallots
- 1 tablespoon extra-virgin olive oil
- 1 tablespoon honey
- 1 teaspoon salt

- 2 large ripe nectarines or plums, sliced
- 2 cups thin jicama strips

- 1 teaspoon coriander
- ¾ teaspoon salt
- ¼ teaspoon sugar
- ¼ teaspoon freshly ground pepper
- 1½ pounds turkey cutlets
- 2 teaspoons vegetable oil, divided

- ¾ pound watercress, trimmed

1. *Make citrus dressing:* Combine all of the ingredients for the citrus dressing in a large bowl. Stir in nectarines and jicama. Set aside.

2. Combine coriander, salt, sugar and pepper in a cup. Arrange turkey cutlets flat on a piece of waxed paper. Sprinkle top side with coriander mixture.

3. Heat 1 teaspoon of the oil in a large skillet over medium-high heat. Add half of the cutlets. Cook 2 minutes per side, until lightly browned and cooked through. Transfer to a large plate; cover and keep warm. Repeat process with the remaining 1 teaspoon oil and cutlets.

4. To serve, toss watercress with nectarine and jicama mixture. Divide turkey cutlets among 4 serving plates. Top each with a quarter of the nectarine-watercress salad. Makes 4 servings.

Per serving: 345 calories, 7.5 g total fat, 1 g saturated fat, 106 mg cholesterol, 1,138 mg sodium, 25 g carbohydrates, 45 g protein, 129 mg calcium, 6 g fiber

corn and orzo salad with lamb kebabs

Fresh cranberry beans, corn kernels and diced carrot get dressed to the nines with a zesty lemon, cilantro and white wine vinaigrette. The dressing—which also coats the lamb kebabs—may be made and refrigerated up to 2 hours ahead. The extra time allows the red onion flavor to permeate the dressing.

Prep time: 15 minutes • Cooking time: 29 to 30 minutes

- 4 (8-inch) wooden skewers
- ½ pound shelled fresh cranberry beans
- 1 teaspoon salt
- ½ cup orzo pasta
- 6 ears fresh corn, kernels cut from cobs
- ⅔ cup diced carrot

DRESSING:

- ¼ cup olive oil
- 2 tablespoons chopped fresh cilantro
- 2 tablespoons fresh lemon juice
- 1 tablespoon white wine vinegar
- 1¼ teaspoons cumin
- ½ teaspoon salt
- ¼ teaspoon paprika
- ¼ cup thinly sliced red onion

- 1¼ pounds leg of lamb or beef top sirloin, cut into 1-inch cubes
- ¼ teaspoon salt
- ¼ teaspoon freshly ground pepper
- 2 bunches (6 oz.) arugula, trimmed

1. Soak skewers in a shallow bowl of water 30 minutes. Drain; set aside.

2. ■ Meanwhile, bring cranberry beans and enough cold water to cover to boil in a large saucepan. Reduce heat and simmer 15 minutes. Add the 1 teaspoon salt. Cook 10 minutes more, until beans are tender. Drain; set aside.

3. ■ Meanwhile, cook orzo according to package directions, except add corn and carrot during the last 1 minute of cooking time. Drain mixture in a colander; rinse under cool running water 30 seconds. Set aside.

4. ■ *Make dressing:* Whisk together all of the ingredients for the dressing except onion slices in a large bowl. Transfer 2 tablespoons of the dressing to a cup. Stir onion slices into dressing in the bowl.

5. ■ Oil and heat a grill pan or heavy skillet. Divide and thread lamb on skewers. Brush with reserved 2 tablespoons of the dressing and sprinkle with the 1/4 teaspoon salt and the pepper. Grill lamb kebabs 4 to 5 minutes, until lamb is medium-rare, turning as meat browns.

6. ■ Toss arugula with 1 tablespoon of the dressing (including some onion slices) in a medium bowl. Stir cranberry beans and orzo-corn mixture into the remaining dressing in large bowl. Divide among 4 serving plates. Top each serving with arugula. Serve with a lamb kebab. Makes 4 servings.

Per serving: 720 calories, 33.5 g total fat, 9.5 g saturated fat, 98 mg cholesterol, 831 mg sodium, 66 g carbohydrates, 43 g protein, 116 mg calcium, 9 g fiber

ham and lentil salad EASY

Lentils fit right in with lean smoked ham, red onion and a light citrus dressing. For a special treat, seek out tiny, flavorful French "Le Puy" lentils, which retain their shape well when cooked. Brown lentils will also work. Pictured on page 83.

Prep time: 25 minutes • Cooking time: 6 to 10 minutes

- 3/4 **cup French green lentils or brown lentils**
- 1/2 **cup finely diced carrot**
- 1/2 **cup finely diced celery**
- 1/4 **teaspoon grated orange peel**
- 2 **tablespoons fresh orange juice**
- 1/4 **teaspoon grated lemon peel**
- 1 **tablespoon fresh lemon juice**
- 1 **tablespoon olive oil**
- 2 **teaspoons white wine vinegar**
- 1/8 **teaspoon freshly ground pepper**
■

- 1 **piece (12 oz.) smoked ham, about 1/2 inch thick or 1 package (13 oz.) Aidell's fully cooked New Mexico Brand Smoked Turkey and Chicken Sausage with Fire-Roasted Red Peppers**

DRESSING:
- 1/2 **cup thinly sliced red onion**
- 2 **tablespoons fresh orange juice**
- 1/4 **teaspoon lemon peel**
- 1 **tablespoon fresh lemon juice**
- 2 **teaspoons white wine vinegar**
- 1 **teaspoon olive oil**
- 1/4 **teaspoon salt**
- 1/8 **teaspoon freshly ground pepper**
■

- 1 **head (8 oz.) frisée or chicory lettuce, torn into bite-size pieces**

1. ■ Bring a medium saucepan filled two-thirds full with salted water to boil. Add lentils and cook 11 minutes (14 minutes for brown lentils). Add carrot and celery. Cook 1 minute more, until lentils are tender but not mushy. Drain lentil mixture in a colander. Cool lentils 15 minutes, stirring once. Toss lentil mixture with orange peel and juice, lemon peel and juice, oil, vinegar, 1/2 teaspoon *salt* and the pepper in a medium bowl. Set aside.

2. ■ Meanwhile, heat grill or grill pan over medium heat. Grill ham 6 to 10 minutes, turning once halfway through, until evenly browned. (Or, grill sausage according to package directions.)

3. ■ *Make dressing:* Rinse red onion in a sieve under cold running water; drain. Combine onion and all of the ingredients for the dressing in a large bowl.

4. ■ Toss dressing with frisée. Transfer frisée mixture to a large platter. Top with lentil mixture. Slice ham or sausages and arrange on top of lentil salad. Makes 4 servings.

Per serving: 310 calories, 9.5 g total fat, 2 g saturated fat, 40 mg cholesterol, 1,697 mg sodium, 30 g carbohydrates, 28 g protein, 100 mg calcium, 6 g fiber

steak salad with mango salsa (EASY)

The flank steak is rubbed with a fiery Thai curry paste, lime juice, fresh mint and ginger. The cool-as-a-cucumber mango salsa with crisp jicama deliciously tames the heat.

Prep time: 30 minutes plus marinating
Grilling time: 14 minutes

MARINADE:

- 1 to 2 tablespoons green curry paste*
- 1 tablespoon finely chopped shallot
- 2 teaspoons fresh lime juice
- 2 teaspoons chopped fresh mint
- 1 teaspoon grated fresh ginger
- ½ teaspoon salt

- 1 (1½ lbs.) beef flank or top round steak

SALSA:

- 1 ripe mango, peeled and diced
- 1 small jicama, peeled and diced
- ½ cup peeled, seeded and sliced cucumber
- 1 tablespoon fresh lime juice
- 2 teaspoons chopped fresh mint
- ¼ teaspoon salt
- 2 teaspoons sugar

- 1 tablespoon olive oil
- 1 large bunch watercress, trimmed (6 cups)
- ½ cup fresh cilantro leaves
  Lime wedges, for garnish (optional)

1. *Make marinade:* Stir together the curry paste (1 to 1½ tablespoons for flank or 2 tablespoons for top round), shallot, lime juice, mint, ginger and salt in a small bowl until smooth.

2. Rub marinade over both sides of steak. Let steak marinate at room temperature up to 30 minutes.

3. *Make salsa:* Meanwhile, combine all of ingredients for salsa in a medium bowl. Set aside.

4. Heat a grill pan or heavy skillet. Brush oil on both sides of steak. Grill 7 minutes per side, until an instant-read thermometer inserted in thickest side of steak reaches 135°F. for medium-rare.

Transfer steak to a cutting board; let stand 5 minutes. Thinly slice steak across the grain.

5. Divide watercress and cilantro leaves among 4 large plates. Divide and arrange beef slices over greens, then top with mango salsa. Garnish with lime wedges, if desired. Makes 4 servings.

*Note: Can be found in ethnic sections of supermarkets or in Asian specialty stores.

Per serving: 420 calories, 21 g total fat, 7 g saturated fat, 85 mg cholesterol, 785 mg sodium, 23 g carbohydrates, 35 g protein, 97 mg calcium, 7 g fiber

shrimp and rice noodle salad (LOW FAT) (EASY)

Light, refreshing chilled Asian noodle dishes are the newest rave in cold pasta salads. Rice noodles, shrimp and celery are tossed with sparkling soy-lime dressing. Pictured on page 82.

Prep time: 20 minutes • Cooking time: 7 to 8 minutes

DRESSING:

- 1 teaspoon grated lime peel
- 5 tablespoons fresh lime juice
- 2 tablespoons minced shallots
- 2 tablespoons rice wine vinegar
- 2 tablespoons peanut or vegetable oil
- 1 tablespoon lite soy sauce
- 2 teaspoons grated fresh ginger
- 2 teaspoons minced red Thai chiles* (see tip, page 15) or ¼ teaspoon red pepper flakes
- 1½ teaspoons sugar
- 1¼ teaspoons salt

- 2 bunches (1 lb.) Broccolini or 1 bunch broccoli, cut into florets
- 1 pound large shrimp, peeled and deveined
- 2 large celery ribs, peeled and cut into ½-inch diagonal slices (1 cup)
- 1 package (8 oz.) rice noodles* or linguine

1. *Make dressing:* Whisk together all of the ingredients for dressing in a large bowl. Makes ⅔ cup. Set aside.

2. Place a steamer basket in a Dutch oven. Add enough water to reach just below basket. Place Broccolini in basket; cover and bring to boil. Reduce heat and steam 5 to 6 minutes, until tender. Rinse briefly under cold running water; drain well. Toss Broccolini with 2 tablespoons of the dressing in a bowl. Set aside.

3. Meanwhile, bring a stockpot filled two-thirds full with water to boil. Add shrimp and cook 1 minute. Add celery and cook 1 minute more. Transfer shrimp and celery with a slotted spoon to a colander, reserving water in pot. Rinse shrimp and celery under cold running water until cool; drain well. Transfer to a small bowl.

4. Return water to boil. Add noodles and cook according to package directions. Transfer noodles to a colander. Rinse noodles under cold running water until cool; drain well.

5. Toss shrimp and celery with the remaining dressing in bowl. Add noodles; gently toss to coat. Serve with Broccolini. Makes 4 servings.

Note: Can be found in produce or ethnic sections of supermarkets or in Asian specialty stores.

Per serving: 420 calories, 8.5 g total fat, 1.5 g saturated fat, 140 mg cholesterol, 1,173 mg sodium, 63 g carbohydrates, 24 g protein, 149 mg calcium, 2 g fiber

mizuma with grilled eggplant and shrimp

You'll find eggplants of many sizes and colors at the farmers' market, and any variety is suitable for grilling in this delightful salad. Available in spring and summer, mizuma (mih-ZOO-mah) is a feathery green that originated in Japan. If it's unavailable, you can substitute watercress in this recipe.

Prep time: 15 minutes • Cooking time: 15 minutes
Microwave used

1	**large red bell pepper**
	Pinch salt

DRESSING:

3	**tablespoons olive oil**
1	**tablespoon finely chopped garlic**
2	**tablespoons fresh lemon juice**
1	**tablespoon red wine vinegar**
¾	**teaspoon salt**
¼	**teaspoon freshly ground pepper**

1	**pound peeled and deveined medium shrimp**
1	**pound eggplant (Italian, American or White), cut into ½-inch slices (8 slices total)**
4	**cups mizuma or 1 bunch watercress, trimmed**
1	**cup fresh mint leaves**
½	**red bell pepper, cut into thin strips, for garnish (optional)**

1. Heat broiler. Cut bell pepper lengthwise in half; cut out stems, seeds and membranes. Place, cut-side down, on a foil-lined broiler pan. Broil 6 inches from heat, 8 to 10 minutes, turning occasionally, until evenly charred. Immediately wrap in foil; let stand until cool enough to handle. Remove blistered skin from peppers. Transfer pepper halves to a blender; puree with the pinch of salt.

2. Meanwhile, bring a large saucepan two-thirds filled with water to a boil.

3. *Make dressing:* Meanwhile, combine oil and garlic in a microwaveproof measuring cup. Microwave on HIGH 40 to 60 seconds, until fragrant. Whisk in the remaining ingredients for the dressing. Set aside.

4. Add shrimp to boiling water; cook 1½ minutes (do not wait for second boil), until shrimp turn pink and are opaque. Drain in a colander; rinse briefly under cool running water.

5. Heat and oil a large grill pan or heavy skillet over medium-high heat 2 minutes. Brush eggplant with 2 tablespoons of the dressing. Grill about 5 minutes each side, just until tender.

6. Toss shrimp, mizuma and mint in a large bowl with the remaining dressing. Arrange 2 eggplant slices on each of 4 serving plates. Divide and top with shrimp salad and red pepper sauce. Garnish with bell pepper strips, if desired. Makes 4 servings.

Per serving: 260 calories, 12.5 g total fat, 2 g saturated fat, 173 mg cholesterol, 627 mg sodium, 12 g carbohydrates, 26 g protein, 166 mg calcium, 3 g fiber

summer seafood salad with corn and basil

When it's time to give the seafood-and-butter combo a vacation, try this refreshing salad of the season's best—lobster, corn, zucchini, tomatoes and fresh basil.

Prep time: 40 to 45 minutes
Cooking time: 4 minutes

- **4 ears fresh corn, shucked**
- **2 cups finely diced zucchini**
- **1 lobster (1¼ lbs.), cooked and shelled, or 6 ounces cooked lobster or crab sticks**
- **½ pound shrimp, cooked and peeled**

DRESSING:

- **2 tablespoons fresh lemon juice**
- **2 tablespoons extra-virgin olive oil plus extra for drizzling**
- **½ teaspoon salt**
- **½ teaspoon freshly ground pepper**
- ■
- **½ cup thinly sliced fresh basil leaves, divided**
- **1 cup finely diced tomato**
  Lettuce leaves

1. ■ Bring a large pot of lightly salted water to boil. Carefully place ears into boiling water. Return water to boil. Cook corn 1 to 2 minutes. With tongs or a slotted spoon, transfer corn to a colander and drain; reserve water. When cool enough to handle; cut kernels from cobs (see note, at right).

2. ■ Meanwhile, return water to boil, add zucchini and cook 2 minutes. Pour into a colander and rinse under cold water; drain. Chop lobster coarsely; cut shrimp in half.

3. ■ *Make dressing:* Whisk together all of the ingredients for the dressing in a large bowl. Toss 1½ tablespoons of the dressing with lobster, shrimp and 2 tablespoons of the basil.

4. ■ Add tomato, corn, zucchini and the remaining basil to dressing in bowl; toss to coat. Arrange tomato mixture on a lettuce-lined platter. Top with seafood. Drizzle with oil, if desired. Serves 4.

*Note: To cut corn off cob, remove husks and silk from an ear of corn. Cut off top and bottom ends of cob. Stand one ear of corn on its end on a cutting board, holding ear near top. With a large knife parallel to cob, cut kernels off with a sawing motion.

Per serving: 245 calories, 9 g total fat, 1 g saturated fat, 109 mg cholesterol, 512 mg sodium, 23 g carbohydrates, 22 g protein, 69 mg calcium, 4 g fiber

grilled tuna salad

Our modern version of the French Salade Niçoise pairs grilled fresh tuna with garden-fresh green beans, golden potatoes, beets and fresh basil. Pictured on page 83.

Prep time: 30 minutes plus marinating
Cooking time: 1 hour 15 minutes

- **1 bunch fresh beets with leaves (1¼ to 1½ lbs.) (reserve beet leaves, or substitute baby spinach or romaine, optional)**
- **1 anchovy fillet, finely chopped**
- **2 tablespoons olive oil**
- **2 teaspoons coarse-grain or Dijon mustard**
- **2 tuna steaks (1 to 1¼ lbs.), cut 1 inch thick**
- **½ pound red or Yukon gold potatoes, peeled and quartered**
- **¾ pound green or wax beans, trimmed**

DRESSING:

- **3 anchovy fillets, finely chopped**
- **3 tablespoons white wine vinegar**
- **2 tablespoons fresh lemon juice**
- **2 teaspoons finely chopped shallot**
- **5 tablespoons olive oil**
- **¼ cup thinly sliced fresh basil leaves**
- ■
- **⅓ cup Moroccan dry-cured olives**

1. ■ Heat oven to 425°F.

2. ■ Trim beets; reserve leaves, if desired. (If using beet leaves; rinse and drain. If desired, substitute spinach or romaine for beet leaves.) Tightly wrap beets in a large sheet of foil. Roast 60 to 75 minutes, until fork-tender. Unwrap and cool completely. Peel beets with a small paring knife; dice. Transfer to a small bowl. (*Can be made ahead. Wrap in plastic wrap and refrigerate up to 3 days.*)

3. Combine anchovy, oil and mustard in a small bowl. Spread mixture over both sides of tuna steaks. Cover and marinate in the refrigerator 30 minutes.

4. Heat and oil grill. Grill tuna over medium-hot heat 4 minutes; gently turn. Grill 3 to 4 minutes more, until cooked through but still pink in the center. Transfer tuna to a platter and cool.

5. Place a steamer basket in a Dutch oven. Add enough water to reach just below basket. Place potatoes in basket; cover pan and bring to boil. Reduce heat slightly and steam 15 minutes, until potatoes are fork-tender. Transfer potatoes with a slotted spoon to a medium bowl. Add beans to steamer basket; steam 5 minutes, just until tender-crisp. Transfer beans to bowl with potatoes.

6. *Make dressing:* Whisk together all of the ingredients for dressing, except oil and basil, in a small bowl. Slowly whisk in oil until blended. Stir in basil.

7. Break tuna into large pieces in a medium bowl; gently toss with 2 tablespoons of the dressing. Toss potatoes and green beans with 2 tablespoons of the dressing in a bowl. Add olives to bowl with beets; gently toss with 1 tablespoon of the dressing.

8. To serve, arrange potatoes and beans, beets, olives and, if desired, beet greens on each of 4 large serving plates. Arrange tuna pieces on top. Divide and drizzle the remaining dressing over salads. Makes 4 servings.

Per serving: 545 calories, 34 g total fat, 5 g saturated fat, 46 mg cholesterol, 758 mg sodium, 28 g carbohydrates, 33 g protein, 127 mg calcium, 3 g fiber

zesty fish fillets on greens

Arctic char fillet has a flavor and texture that is described as a cross between trout and salmon. Pictured on page 86.

Prep time: 25 minutes plus chilling
Baking time: 12 to 13 minutes

DRESSING:

- 3 tablespoons fresh lemon juice
- 2 tablespoons packed chopped fresh cilantro
- 1 tablespoon olive oil
- 2 teaspoons finely chopped garlic
- 1 teaspoon salt
  ▪

  Vegetable cooking spray
- 1½ pounds Arctic char or trout fillets, skin on
- ⅛ teaspoon salt
- ⅛ teaspoon freshly ground pepper
- 1 medium (8 oz.) ripe tomato, diced
- 1 tablespoon white wine vinegar
- 1 tablespoon olive oil
- 2 bunches (4 to 5 oz. each) arugula, trimmed
- 1 small head romaine lettuce, torn into bite-size pieces
- 3 tablespoons pine nuts (pignoli), toasted

1. *Make dressing:* Combine all of the ingredients for dressing in a large bowl. Makes about ¼ cup. Set aside.

2. Heat oven to 325°F. Lightly coat a 13×9-inch baking dish with vegetable cooking spray.

3. Arrange fish in prepared dish; sprinkle with salt and pepper. Bake 12 to 13 minutes, until center of fish flakes easily. Immediately spoon 2½ tablespoons of the dressing over fish. Cool 10 minutes. Cover fish lightly with foil; refrigerate at least 1 hour.

4. Add tomato, vinegar and oil to the remaining 2 tablespoons dressing. Cover; refrigerate 1 hour.

5. Add arugula and romaine to tomato mixture and toss to coat. Remove skin from fish; break into large pieces. Arrange fish pieces on top of salad; sprinkle with nuts. Makes 4 to 6 servings.

Per serving: 295 calories, 17 g total fat, 2.5 g saturated fat, 71 mg cholesterol, 609 mg sodium, 7 g carbohydrates, 29 g protein, 142 mg calcium, 3 g fiber

pasta with sausage and pesto

What to do with the big bundle of fresh basil you just picked up from the farmers' market or snipped from your own herb garden? Make a palate-pleasing pesto with pine nuts, garlic and Parmesan cheese. Then toss it with tasty chicken sausage and dainty orecchiette pasta, and that's our final answer! Pictured on page 84.

Total prep and cooking time: 30 minutes

- **1   pound orecchiette or shell pasta**
- **PESTO:**
- **2   cups fresh basil leaves**
- **¼   cup pine nuts, toasted**
- **¼   cup freshly grated Parmesan cheese**
- **1   clove garlic**
- **¼   teaspoon freshly ground pepper**
- **⅛   teaspoon salt**
- **½   cup plus 1 teaspoon olive oil, divided**
  Grated peel and juice of ½ lemon

- **1   package (13 oz.) fully cooked or ready-to-serve chicken sausage links, diced**

1. Start to cook pasta according to the package directions.

2. *Make pesto:* Meanwhile, process basil, pine nuts, Parmesan, garlic, pepper and salt in a food processor or blender until almost smooth. With machine running, slowly add ½ cup of the oil through feed tube and process until smooth. Transfer pesto to a bowl; stir in lemon peel and juice. Set aside.

3. Heat the remaining 1 teaspoon of oil in a large nonstick skillet over medium-high heat. Add sausage. Cook 5 minutes, until edges brown, stirring often.

4. Drain pasta. Toss hot pasta in a large serving bowl with sausage and pesto. Serve immediately. Makes 4 servings.

Per serving: 920 calories, 44 g total fat, 8 g saturated fat, 78 mg cholesterol, 826 mg sodium, 89 g carbohydrates, 43 g protein, 215 mg calcium, 5 g fiber

sausage and pepper hero

This satisfying supper sandwich can be on your table in half an hour. Fresh sweet bell peppers (pick up an assortment for a colorful mix) are skillet-cooked with onions, red-wine vinegar and garlic and seasoned with oregano and salt. Fresh turkey sausage is available in most supermarkets. Use a mix of both spicy hot and sweet sausage for best results. Pictured on page 85.

Total prep and cooking time: 30 minutes

- **1½ pounds fresh turkey sausages**
- **5   tablespoons olive oil, divided**
- **4   green, red or yellow bell peppers, cut into 1-inch strips**
- **1   medium onion, chopped**
- **3   tablespoons red wine vinegar, divided**
- **2   cloves garlic, crushed**
- **1   tablespoon plus 1 teaspoon chopped fresh oregano, divided**
- **½   teaspoon salt**
- **4   hero rolls or 8 slices Tuscan-style bread, toasted**

1. Heat a grill pan or heavy skillet. Brush sausages with 1 tablespoon of the oil. Cover and cook 5 minutes per side, turning as links brown. Reduce heat and cook 3 minutes more, until cooked through and an instant-read thermometer inserted 1½ inches deep into end of links registers 165°F. Transfer sausages to a large plate. Cover and keep warm.

2. Meanwhile, heat 1 tablespoon of the oil in a large skillet over medium heat. Add bell peppers. Cover and cook 5 to 8 minutes, until softened. Stir in onion, 1 tablespoon of the vinegar, garlic, 1 teaspoon of the oregano and salt. Cover and cook 5 minutes more, until vegetables are golden brown.

3. Combine the remaining 3 tablespoons of oil, the 2 tablespoons of vinegar and the 1 tablespoon of oregano in a cup. Brush 1 side of each roll with oil-vinegar mixture. Divide and fill rolls with sausages and pepper mixture. Makes 4 servings.

Per serving: 640 calories, 37.5 g total fat, 8 g saturated fat, 91 mg cholesterol, 769 mg sodium, 45 g carbohydrates, 35 g protein, 113 mg calcium, 4 g fiber

sausages with white beans EASY

If you've never cooked with fresh sage leaves, this recipe is the perfect place to start. Some of the sage is chopped and cooked, adding its distinctive flavor to the white beans and sausage. The rest is sautéed until crisp for a lovely aromatic garnish. Pictured on page 88.

Total prep and cooking time: 30 minutes

1½	pounds or 8 fresh pork sausages
3	tablespoons olive oil, divided
15	fresh sage leaves
½	cup chopped onion
1½	tablespoons chopped garlic
2	cans (19 oz. each) cannellini beans, drained and rinsed
¾	cup chicken broth
1	medium tomato, chopped
¼	teaspoon salt

1. Heat oven to 425°F.

2. Arrange sausages on a jelly-roll pan; drizzle with 1 tablespoon of the oil. Bake sausages 10 minutes; turn. Bake 8 to 10 minutes more, until cooked through and an instant-read thermometer inserted 1½ inches deep into end of links registers 160°F.

3. Meanwhile, heat the remaining 2 tablespoons of oil in a large skillet over medium heat. Add 5 of the sage leaves. Cook 3 to 4 minutes, until leaves begin to crisp. Transfer with tongs to paper towels.

4. Add onion and garlic to same skillet. Cook 5 minutes, until onion is softened.

5. Chop the remaining 10 sage leaves. Add chopped sage, beans, broth, tomato and salt to onion mixture. Simmer 10 minutes.

6. Slice sausages. Transfer bean mixture to a serving bowl. Arrange sausage slices and fried sage leaves on top. Makes 4 servings.

Per serving: 510 calories, 27 g total fat, 9 g saturated fat, 67 mg cholesterol, 1,117 mg sodium, 36 g carbohydrates, 31 g protein, 100 mg calcium, 12 g fiber

---

test kitchen tip
speciality sausages

With the variety of sausages available in the marketplace, it's easy to explore creative new ways to take advantage of their culinary versatility. Here's a small sampling of what's out there, with serving suggestions:

ANDOUILLE: A peppery and smoked Cajun sausage made with pork and tripe, chitterlings, pepper and sometimes wine, onions, and spices. Serve grilled or in gumbos, stews or mixed with red beans.

BRATWURST: Smooth veal and pork sausage of German origin seasoned with an array of spices. Serve hot with rice or vegetables or with sautéed onion for a hearty sandwich.

CHORIZO: A Spanish (and Latin-American) spicy hot pork sausage made with cayenne (or another hot pepper), red bell pepper and sometimes garlic. Serve it with pasta; in casseroles, soups or stews; or on pizza.

ITALIAN: Pork sausage flavored with garlic and fennel seed. Hot and sweet varieties. Serve with pasta or mix sweet and hot Italian sausage with ground beef for zesty meatballs. Enjoy on pizza, too.

KIELBASA: Smoked pork sausage, sometimes with beef added. Serve hot with sauerkraut or add to potato casseroles.

METTWURST: German pork sausage seasoned with salt, coriander and white pepper. It's cured and smoked. Great on bread or crackers with cheese and mustard.

MORTADELLA: Smoked ground beef and pork sausage with pork fat and garlic. Serve with a variety of cheeses or add it to sandwiches.

shrimp and asparagus on linguine EASY

Fresh asparagus, most often served on the side, can also star as a meal's main highlight. Here shrimp is quickly cooked and combined with lemon juice, chicken broth and sautéed shallots, while the asparagus is simply added to the pasta water during the last 2 minutes of cooking time. A dish that's truly fresh, fast and fabulous. Pictured on page 81.

Total prep and cooking time: 29 minutes

- 1 pound shelled and deveined shrimp
- ¾ teaspoon salt, divided
- ¼ teaspoon freshly ground pepper
- 3 tablespoons butter or margarine, divided
- 12 ounces thin linguine
- 2 lemons
- ⅓ cup chopped shallots
- 1 can (14½ oz.) chicken broth
- 1 bunch (1 lb.) asparagus, trimmed and sliced
- 2 tablespoons snipped fresh chives

1. Heat water for pasta.

2. Toss shrimp with ½ teaspoon of the salt and the pepper. Melt 1 tablespoon of the butter in a 12-inch skillet over high heat. Cook shrimp 1 minute per side; transfer to a bowl.

3. Start to cook pasta. Grate enough peel from lemons to equal 1 teaspoon; squeeze ¼ cup juice.

4. Melt the remaining 2 tablespoons butter in a skillet. Add shallots; cook until golden. Add broth, lemon juice and the remaining ¼ teaspoon salt. Bring to boil and boil 2 minutes. Add shrimp and remove from heat. Add asparagus to pasta during last 2 minutes of cooking; drain.

5. To serve, toss asparagus-pasta mixture in bowl with shrimp mixture, lemon peel and chives. Serve immediately. Makes 4 servings.

Per serving: 560 calories, 13 g total fat, 6 g saturated fat, 196 mg cholesterol, 1,430 mg sodium, 72 g carbohydrates, 38 g protein, 106 mg calcium, 3 g fiber

fettuccine with grilled summer vegetables LOW FAT EASY

Everything's coming up veggies—so why not take advantage? Grill a basketful of the freshest and toss with fettuccine or your favorite pasta.

Prep time: 30 minutes • Cooking time: 29 minutes

- 4 large cloves garlic, skewered, unpeeled
- 2 medium green bell peppers, quartered
- 1 medium red bell pepper, quartered
- 1 eggplant (1½ lbs.), cut into ½-inch lengthwise slices
- 1 large red onion, cut into ½-inch slices
- 2 large zucchini (1 lb.), cut into ½-inch lengthwise slices
- 8 large plum tomatoes, halved lengthwise
- 4 tablespoons olive oil, divided
- 2 teaspoons salt, divided
- ½ teaspoon chopped fresh thyme
- ⅓ cup chopped fresh basil
- ½ teaspoon freshly ground pepper
- 1 pound fettuccine, cooked according to package directions

1. Heat grill. Brush garlic, bell peppers, eggplant, onion, zucchini and tomatoes with 2 tablespoons of the oil. Sprinkle with 1 teaspoon of the salt.

2. Grill vegetables over medium-hot heat until vegetables are tender, turning occasionally (garlic 10 to 20 minutes, bell peppers 12 to 15 minutes, eggplant 10 to 12 minutes, onion 8 to 12 minutes, zucchini and tomatoes 5 to 10 minutes).

3. Remove garlic from skin. Combine with the remaining 2 tablespoons oil, 1 teaspoon of salt and the thyme in a small bowl; mash with fork. Set aside. Cool and peel bell peppers. Cut bell peppers and remaining grilled vegetables into bite-size pieces. Toss all the vegetables in a large serving bowl with basil, pepper and mashed garlic mixture. Toss with hot pasta. Makes 6 servings.

Per serving: 550 calories, 11 g total fat, 1.5 g saturated fat, 0 mg cholesterol, 794 mg sodium, 77 g carbohydrates, 14 g protein, 56 mg calcium, 8 g fiber

rigatoni with vegetables

A cheesy pasta bursting with flavor sounds too good to be on a diet menu! But this rigatoni with roasted vegetables and low-fat cheese is light enough to fit in.

Prep time: 45 minutes • Baking time: 20 to 25 minutes

Vegetable cooking spray
2 **teaspoons garlic-flavored olive oil**
1 **eggplant (about 1 lb.), peeled and cubed**
2 **medium zucchini, cubed**
1 **package (10 oz.) mushrooms, diced**
1 **medium onion, diced**
½ **teaspoon salt**
¼ **teaspoon freshly ground pepper**
2 **cups prepared marinara sauce, divided**
½ **pound rigatoni, cooked according to package directions**
¼ **cup freshly grated Parmesan cheese**
1 **cup shredded reduced-fat mozzarella cheese**
Fresh rosemary sprigs, for garnish (optional)

1. Heat oven to 450°F. Lightly coat 2 jelly-roll pans with vegetable cooking spray. Drizzle oil over eggplant, zucchini, mushrooms and onion in a large bowl; toss. Arrange vegetables on both prepared pans. Sprinkle with salt and pepper. Roast 30 minutes, until vegetables are tender.

2. Reduce oven temperature to 400°F. Spread ½ cup of the marinara sauce over bottom of a 13×9-inch baking dish.

3. Combine pasta, vegetables, 1 cup of the marinara sauce and Parmesan in a large bowl. Spoon mixture into prepared dish. Spread the remaining ½ cup of the marinara sauce over top. Sprinkle with mozzarella cheese. Bake 20 to 25 minutes, until bubbly. Garnish with rosemary, if desired. Makes 6 servings.

Per serving: 297 calories, 8 g total fat, 2.5 g saturated fat, 12 mg cholesterol, 710 mg sodium, 45 g carbohydrates, 15 g protein, 222 mg calcium, 5 g fiber

south-of-the-border pasta

Rippled-edge radiatore catches the tangy lime-avocado dressing in this refreshing room-temperature dish. Peppers provide crunch and pepper-Jack cheese lends a dose of heat.

Prep time: 30 minutes • Cooking time: 9 to 11 minutes

1 **box (12 or 14 oz.) radiatore, cooked according to package directions**
DRESSING:
4 **medium assorted bell peppers (red, green and/or yellow), chopped**
¼ **cup finely chopped fresh cilantro**
1 **teaspoon grated lime peel**
5 **tablespoons fresh lime juice**
3 **tablespoons finely chopped red onion**
3 **tablespoons vegetable oil**
2 **teaspoons white wine vinegar**
1½ **teaspoons salt**
¾ **teaspoon cumin**
½ **teaspoon sugar**

1 **tablespoon fresh lime juice**
⅛ **teaspoon sugar**
⅛ **teaspoon salt**
⅛ **teaspoon freshly ground pepper**
2 **ripe avocados, cut into ¾-inch chunks**
8 **ounces pepper-Jack cheese, diced**
Flour tortillas (optional)
Fresh cilantro, for garnish (optional)

1. Rinse hot pasta under cold running water in a large colander until cool; drain well. Set aside.

2. *Make dressing:* Combine all of the ingredients for the dressing in a large serving bowl.

3. Combine lime juice, sugar, salt and pepper in a small bowl; add avocado and toss gently to coat. Toss cooled pasta with dressing, avocado mixture and cheese. Divide among 6 serving bowls. Serve with tortillas and garnish with fresh cilantro, if desired. Makes 6 servings.

Per serving: 519 calories, 27 g total fat, 9.5 g saturated fat, 33 mg cholesterol, 841 mg sodium, 54 g carbohydrates, 18 g protein, 309 mg calcium, 6 g fiber

choosing clams

When buying live clams, look for moist shells without cracks and chips. Select clam shells that are tightly shut. If the shell is open slightly, tap it lightly. If it doesn't close up, that means the clam is dead and should be thrown away. It's best to purchase clams the day of cooking. Here are two varieties:

LITTLENECK CLAMS are used in our delicious clam chowder recipe (below). They are the smallest, sweetest and most tender of the East Coast hard-shell clams.

CHERRYSTONE CLAMS may substitute if your local seafood market doesn't have the littlenecks. They're slightly larger than the littleneck clams.

vegetable clam chowder LOW FAT EASY

Here's a slimmed-down clam chowder that we highly recommend for fans of this old favorite to try on for size. It comes without the heavy cream notorious in many chowders, and instead packs lots of flavor. Laden with chopped fresh vegetables, potatoes and littleneck clams, the chowder is finished with a colorful and aromatic herb garnish made with oregano, parsley, lemon and cherry tomatoes. Pictured on page 84.

Prep time: 15 minutes • Cooking time: 26 to 31 minutes

- 2 **tablespoons butter or margarine**
- 1 **large onion, chopped**
- ¾ **cup diced carrot**
- ½ **cup diced celery**
- 1 **large green bell pepper, chopped**
- 1 **pound chopped fresh ripe tomatoes (2 cups)**
- 1 **can (14½ oz.) chicken broth**
- 1 **bottle (8 oz.) clam juice**
- ½ **pound small golden (Yellow Finn) or red potatoes (French Fingerling), cut into chunks**

- 2 **dozen fresh littleneck clams or 1½ dozen fresh cherrystone clams, rinsed and scrubbed (see note, below)**

HERB GARNISH:
- 2 **tablespoons packed fresh oregano leaves**
- 2 **tablespoons packed fresh flat-leaf parsley leaves**
- 1 **medium clove garlic**
- ½ **teaspoon grated lemon peel**
- ¼ **teaspoon freshly ground pepper**
- ½ **cup diced yellow cherry or grape tomatoes**
- ½ **cup diced red cherry or grape tomatoes**

1. Melt butter in a large saucepan over medium-high heat. Add onion, carrot and celery; cover and cook 4 minutes. Add bell pepper. Cook 4 minutes, just until tender. Add tomatoes. Cover and cook 3 minutes. Stir in chicken broth, clam juice and potatoes. Bring to boil. Reduce heat to medium; cover and cook 15 to 20 minutes more, until potatoes are tender.

2. Meanwhile, cover and cook clams in a Dutch oven or stockpot over high heat 7 to 8 minutes, until shells open.

3. *Make herb garnish:* Finely chop all of the ingredients for herb garnish on a cutting board. Set aside.

4. Uncover clams. When cool enough to handle, remove clams from shells, reserving juice, and chop coarsely. (Discard shells and any unopened clams.) Stir chopped clams, reserved clam juice and pepper into hot chowder; remove from heat.

5. To serve, ladle chowder into 4 soup bowls. Top each with diced tomatoes. Sprinkle with Herb Garnish. Makes 4 servings.

Note: To prepare live clams or mussels for cooking, scrub them under cold running water. Combine 4 quarts water and ⅓ cup salt in a large pot. Add clams or mussels and soak 15 minutes. Drain and rinse; discard water. Place in the refrigerator for 30 minutes.

Per serving: 250 calories, 8 g total fat, 4 g saturated fat, 44 mg cholesterol, 715 mg sodium, 30 g carbohydrates, 15 g protein, 100 mg calcium, 5 g fiber

summer vegetable bouillabaisse

Bouillabaisse—a seafood stew that originated in Provence—is a wonderful way to enjoy an assortment of fish and shellfish. This version highlights monkfish, sea scallops and mussels. Also, the key to the most tender seafood is to never go beyond a gentle simmer when cooking in a broth. Pictured on page 84.

Prep time: 35 minutes • Cooking time: 20 to 24 minutes

- ¾ **pound small fresh tomatillos, husked, rinsed and halved**
- 1 **tablespoon olive oil**
- 2 **yellow bell peppers, diced**
- 2 **green bell peppers, diced**
- 1 **large onion, chopped**
- ½ **cup chopped shallots**
- 1½ **cups white wine**
- 1 **bottle (8 oz.) clam juice**
- 2 **pounds monkfish, cut into 1½-inch chunks**
- 1 **pound sea scallops**
- 3 **ears fresh corn, shucked and cut crosswise into 1½-inch chunks**
- 1 **bag (2 lbs.) mussels, scrubbed and debearded (see note, page 147)**
- 1 **pound peeled and deveined shrimp**

CHILI AÏOLI:
- ⅓ **cup mayonnaise**
- 1½ **teaspoons Asian chili garlic sauce***

CILANTRO GREMOLATA:
- ¾ **cup fresh cilantro leaves**
- 1 **large clove garlic**
- ½ **teaspoon salt**
- 1 **tablespoon fresh lime juice**

- 6 **1-inch slices French bread, toasted**

1. Heat broiler. Line a broiler pan with foil. Place tomatillos, cut side down, on prepared pan. Broil 5 to 6 minutes. Cover with foil; set aside.

2. Heat oil in a large stockpot over medium-high heat. Add bell peppers, onion and shallots. Cover and cook 4 to 5 minutes, until vegetables are just softened. Add wine and bring to boil. Boil 2 minutes. Add clam juice and bring to simmer. Stir monkfish and scallops into broth mixture. Cover

and simmer 6 minutes. Stir in corn; cover and cook 2 to 3 minutes more, just until corn is tender.

3. Meanwhile, arrange mussels in a large deep skillet. Cover and cook over high heat 4 minutes, until shells begin to open. Add shrimp on top of mussels; cover and cook 1 minute, until shells open. (Discard any unopened mussels.) Push shrimp down into mussel broth; cover skillet and remove from heat. Let stand 5 to 6 minutes.

4. *Make chili aïoli:* Combine mayonnaise and chili garlic sauce in a small bowl. Makes ⅓ cup.

5. *Make cilantro gremolata:* Chop cilantro, garlic and salt on a cutting board. Transfer to a cup; stir in lime juice.

6. To serve, combine monkfish mixture, tomatillos, mussels, shrimp and any juice from mussels in a very large serving bowl. Spread toasted bread with Chili Aïoli. Sprinkle bouillabaisse with Cilantro Gremolata and serve with toasts. Makes 6 servings.

*Note: Can be found in ethnic sections of supermarkets or in Asian specialty stores.

Per serving: 700 calories, 20 g total fat, 2.5 g saturated fat, 197 mg cholesterol, 1,060 mg sodium, 56 g carbohydrates, 64 g protein, 158 mg calcium, 5 g fiber

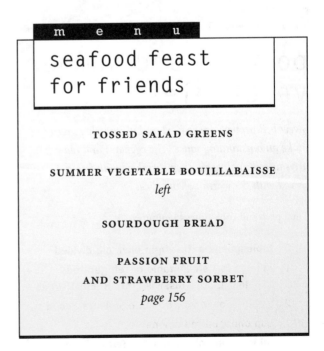

m　e　n　u

seafood feast for friends

TOSSED SALAD GREENS

SUMMER VEGETABLE BOUILLABAISSE
left

SOURDOUGH BREAD

PASSION FRUIT AND STRAWBERRY SORBET
page 156

pondering polenta

What is polenta? A true Italian staple, it's actually a "mush," or porridge, made by boiling a mixture of cornmeal or farina and water:

IF YOU HAVE NEVER COOKED with prepared polenta (shelf-stable or refrigerated), the first thing to know, aside from its great flavor and texture, is that it's a busy cook's dream. Preparing polenta from scratch isn't difficult, but it's nice to have a quick option.

WE SKILLET-COOK polenta slices in the recipe below. It takes just a few minutes and is then combined with eggplant, sweet bell peppers and feta cheese. Polenta can also be sliced, fried and tossed with Parmesan cheese or other flavorful cheeses. Or enjoy prepared polenta to sop up tomato sauce, gravy or the juices of any entrée.

WHERE TO LOOK. Prepared polenta can be found in the refrigerated produce sections or near the dairy sections of supermarkets.

---

polenta and summer vegetables

Sweet bell peppers are roasted and ultimately pureed to make an outstanding sauce. The eggplant and red onion are sautéed in olive oil, then sprinkled with feta cheese and served with the warm polenta slices.

Total prep and cook time: 45 minutes

- 3 tablespoons extra-virgin olive oil, divided
- 1 tube (1 lb.) shelf-stable or refrigerated polenta, cut crosswise into 8 equal slices
- 2 small (6 oz. each) Italian eggplants, diced
- 1 cup chopped red onions
- 2 tablespoons chopped fresh flat-leaf parsley
- 2 teaspoons balsamic vinegar
- ½ teaspoon salt, divided
- ¼ teaspoon freshly ground pepper

- 3 red bell peppers, halved and roasted (see tip, page 33)
- ½ cup crumbled feta cheese

1. Heat oven to 300°F.

2. Heat 1 tablespoon of the oil in a large nonstick skillet over medium-high heat. Add polenta slices and cook polenta 2 to 3 minutes per side, until golden brown. Transfer to a cookie sheet; keep warm in oven. Repeat with the remaining polenta.

3. Wipe out skillet. Heat 1 tablespoon of the oil over medium heat. Add eggplant and cook, stirring often, 8 to 10 minutes, until tender and golden brown. Transfer to a large bowl. Heat the remaining 1 tablespoon oil in same skillet over medium-high heat. Add red onions and cook, stirring often, 5 minutes, until lightly charred. Stir red onions, parsley, vinegar, ¼ teaspoon of the salt and the pepper into bowl with eggplant.

4. Puree bell peppers in blender with the remaining ¼ teaspoon salt. Divide bell pepper sauce and eggplant mixture among 4 serving plates. Add 2 polenta slices to each. Sprinkle with feta. Makes 4 side-dish servings.

Per serving: 290 calories, 14 g total fat, 3.5 g saturated fat, 12 mg cholesterol, 893 mg sodium, 37 g carbohydrates, 7 g protein, 94 mg calcium, 8 g fiber

---

grilled vegetable risotto

The vegetables are combined with a luscious risotto made with rich cheese. If you can find it, splurge for Italian Fontina—it makes a difference. Pictured on page 88.

Prep time: 25 minutes • Cooking time: 28 to 32 minutes

- 2 leeks (9 oz.), white part only
- 1 medium yellow tomato (8 oz.), cut into 1-inch slices
- 1 small radicchio (5 oz.), cut into 1-inch wedges
- 1 zucchini (5 oz.), cut into ½-inch slices
- 4 tablespoons extra-virgin olive oil, divided
- 4 cans (14½ oz. each) chicken broth
- 2 cups arborio or medium-grain rice
- 1 tablespoon chopped garlic
- 2 fresh thyme sprigs or ½ teaspoon dried thyme

½ teaspoon salt
½ cup white wine
¼ pound Fontina cheese, cut into small pieces

1. Slice leeks lengthwise, keeping root end intact. Rinse well to remove any dirt clinging to inner leaves. Brush both sides of leeks, tomato slices, radicchio wedges and zucchini slices with 3 tablespoons of the oil.

2. Oil and heat a large grill pan or heavy skillet. Grill leeks and radicchio 3 to 5 minutes each side, until tender and lightly charred. (Radicchio will brown.) Transfer vegetables to a cutting board.

3. Grill tomato and zucchini 2 to 3 minutes each side, until tender and lightly charred. Transfer vegetables to a cutting board. Coarsely chop all of the vegetables, reserving juices.

4. Meanwhile, bring broth to a simmer in a medium saucepan. Heat the remaining 1 tablespoon oil in a Dutch oven over medium heat. Stir in rice, garlic, thyme sprigs and salt. Cook 2 minutes, until garlic is fragrant and grains are glistening. Add wine and cook 1 to 2 minutes, until liquid is absorbed.

5. Set 1 cup of the hot broth aside in a glass measure. Add the remaining broth to rice, 1 cup at a time, stirring constantly, 20 minutes, until liquid is absorbed. (Add ½ cup water to rice, if necessary.)

6. Remove thyme sprigs; discard. Stir in grilled vegetables and the reserved 1 cup broth. Add cheese, stirring until melted. Makes 6 servings.

Per serving: 415 calories, 18 g total fat, 5.5 g saturated fat, 22 mg cholesterol, 1,527 mg sodium, 52 g carbohydrates, 12 g protein, 132 mg calcium, 5 g fiber

deviled egg salad on spinach

Here's a new combo based on two great classics—stuffed deviled eggs and spinach salad. Pictured on page 86.

Prep time: 30 minutes • Cooking time: 10 minutes

6 large eggs
2 medium (¾ lb.) all-purpose potatoes, peeled and cut into chunks

¼ cup mayonnaise
2 tablespoons snipped fresh chives
¼ teaspoon grated lemon peel
4 teaspoons fresh lemon juice
1 tablespoon coarse-grain mustard
1 teaspoon salt, divided
½ teaspoon freshly ground pepper, divided
½ cup crumbled feta cheese
3 teaspoons olive oil, divided
2 teaspoons balsamic vinegar, divided
2 large (8 oz. each) beefsteak tomatoes, sliced
1 bunch (12 oz.) or bag (10 oz.) fresh spinach, trimmed and rinsed

1. Place eggs in a single layer in a 3-quart saucepan with enough cold water to cover by 1 inch. Bring to boil; cover. Remove from heat and let stand 20 minutes; drain. Fill pan with cold water and let stand 10 minutes more; drain. Peel and chop eggs. Set aside.

2. Meanwhile, bring potatoes and enough cold water to cover in a saucepan to boil. Cook potatoes 10 minutes, until tender. Drain and coarsely chop. Set aside.

3. Combine mayonnaise, chives, lemon peel and juice, mustard, ½ teaspoon of the salt and ¼ teaspoon of the pepper in a large bowl. Gently fold in eggs, potatoes and feta. (*Can be made ahead. Cover and refrigerate up to 2 hours.*)

4. Combine 1 teaspoon of the oil, 1 teaspoon of the vinegar, ¼ teaspoon of the salt and ⅛ teaspoon pepper in a 9-inch glass pie plate. Add tomato slices, turning to coat.

5. Whisk the remaining 2 teaspoons oil, 1 teaspoon vinegar, ¼ teaspoon salt and ⅛ teaspoon pepper in a large bowl. Add spinach and toss.

6. To serve, arrange tomato slices in a single layer on a serving platter. Top with spinach, then egg mixture. Makes 6 servings.

Per serving: 250 calories, 17.5 g total fat, 4.5 g saturated fat, 228 mg cholesterol, 699 mg sodium, 14 g carbohydrates, 11 g protein, 130 mg calcium, 3 g fiber

test kitchen tip
heirloom tomatoes

In the case of heirloom tomatoes, what you see is not necessarily representative of what you get. Heirloom tomatoes—those grown from an open pollinated seed—may not be as perfect in shape as the uniformly round supermarket variety, but their superb flavor and intriguing colors make them truly special.

THE SPECTACULAR COLORS of heirlooms are a treat for the eyes. They range in color from pink to purple, to striped red, green and yellow to orange. Their attention-getting appearance makes them a satisfying addition to your summer meals.

LOOK FOR HEIRLOOM TOMATOES at farmers' markets or specialty produce stores. Sizes vary from pea size to vine-bending jumbo. Traditional heirloom varieties come in all sorts of odd shapes and asymmetries.

WHEN PURCHASING tomatoes, look for unblemished skin and a pleasant aroma. Store at room temperature, rather than in the refrigerator, for best flavor and texture. If they need some ripening, place them in a brown paper bag at room temperature. Setting them in the sun may cause them to become mushy.

tomato galette

Heirloom tomatoes star in this recipe. Pictured on page 85.

Prep time: 40 minutes • Baking time: 30 minutes

PASTRY:
- 1 cup all-purpose flour
- 3 tablespoons cornmeal
- ¼ teaspoon salt
- 5 tablespoons cold butter or margarine, cut into small pieces
- 2 tablespoons sour cream
- 2 tablespoons cold water

- ⅓ cup freshly shredded Parmesan cheese
- ¾ cup shredded Fontina or Swiss cheese
- ½ cup crumbled goat cheese
- 4 small ripe heirloom tomatoes, cut into ¼-inch slices
- ½ cup lightly packed fresh basil leaves
- 1 tablespoon olive oil
- ⅛ teaspoon freshly ground pepper

1. *Make pastry:* Process flour, cornmeal and salt in a food processor until blended. Add butter and pulse until mixture is the texture of meal, but with some small pieces of butter remaining. Combine sour cream and water in a cup. Drizzle over flour mixture. Pulse just until pastry holds together; shape into a disk. Wrap and refrigerate 1 hour. (*Can be made ahead. Refrigerate up to 2 days.*)

2. Heat oven to 400°F. On a lightly floured surface with a floured rolling pin, roll pastry to a 14-inch circle. Drape pastry over rolling pin and carefully unroll onto a large cookie sheet.

3. Sprinkle Parmesan over pastry, leaving a 1½-inch border along edge. Top with Fontina and goat cheeses. Arrange tomato slices and basil leaves on top. Drizzle with oil; sprinkle with pepper. Fold edge of pastry up onto filling, pleating where necessary. Bake 30 minutes, until crust is brown. Cool on cookie sheet 10 minutes. Loosen crust with a thin spatula; slide onto a wire rack. Serve warm or at room temperature. Make 8 servings.

Per serving: 255 calories, 17 g total fat, 9.5 g saturated fat, 43 mg cholesterol, 342 mg sodium, 18 g carbohydrates, 9 g protein, 9 mg calcium, 2 g fiber

squash muffaletta

We took the New Orleans muffaletta (muhf-fuh-LEHT-tuh) and made it vegetarian by substituting roasted slices of yellow squash and zucchini for the salami and ham.

Prep time: 30 minutes • Cooking time: 25 minutes

- 3 tablespoons olive oil, divided
- ½ cup chopped sweet onion
- 1 celery rib, peeled and chopped
- 2 large cloves garlic, minced

⅛ teaspoon red pepper flakes

1 tablespoon red wine vinegar

¼ cup roasted red bell pepper, chopped

¼ cup pimento-stuffed green olives, chopped

¼ cup kalamata olives, pitted and chopped

1 tablespoon chopped fresh oregano

2 pounds summer squash

¼ teaspoon salt

¼ teaspoon freshly ground pepper

1 small bunch arugula, trimmed

1 large baguette, split lengthwise

¼ pound thinly sliced provolone cheese

1. Heat 2 tablespoons of the oil over medium-low heat in a large nonstick skillet. Add onion and celery. Cook, stirring often, 10 minutes, until softened. Add garlic and red pepper flakes; cook 1 minute more. Stir in vinegar and remove skillet from heat. Stir in roasted pepper, olives and oregano. Set aside.

2. Divide oven into thirds with 2 racks. Heat oven to 425°F. Cut squash lengthwise into ¼-inch slices. Arrange on 2 large cookie sheets. Brush lightly with the remaining 1 tablespoon oil; sprinkle with salt and pepper. Roast 12 to 15 minutes, until tender, rotating cookie sheets once during roasting.

3. Arrange arugula on bottom half of bread. Top with squash, cheese and onion-olive mixture. Top with remaining half of bread. Press top and slice with a serrated knife. Makes 6 servings.

Per serving: 325 calories, 16 g total fat, 4 g saturated fat, 76 mg cholesterol, 362 mg sodium, 60 g carbohydrates, 14 g protein, 60 mg calcium, 2 g fiber

chicken with spinach and potatoes

Here's an ideal way to enjoy fresh spinach and creamy-textured Yukon gold potatoes. Cooked chicken thighs round out the meal, but it's the fresh produce that shines.

Prep time: 20 minutes • Cooking time: 23 to 26 minutes

1 pound boneless, skinless chicken thighs, cut into 1-inch pieces

¾ teaspoon turmeric, divided

½ teaspoon salt, divided

¼ teaspoon freshly ground pepper

2 tablespoons olive oil, divided

½ cup chopped onion

1 tablespoon chopped garlic

1 tablespoon chopped fresh ginger

1 tablespoon chopped jalapeño chile, (see tip, page 15)

2 cardamom pods, lightly crushed

1 teaspoon cumin

1½ pounds Yukon gold potatoes, cut into 1-inch pieces

1 cup chicken broth

2 large bunches fresh spinach, stems removed, leaves coarsely chopped

Hot cooked rice and plain yogurt (optional)

1. Coat chicken with ¼ teaspoon of the turmeric, ¼ teaspoon of the salt and the pepper in a shallow bowl.

2. Heat 1 tablespoon of the oil in a 2-inch-deep 12-inch skillet over medium-high heat. Add chicken and cook 1½ minutes per side, until well browned. Transfer to a small bowl.

3. Reduce heat to medium; add the remaining 1 tablespoon of oil to same skillet. Stir in onion, garlic, ginger, jalapeño, cardamom, cumin, the remaining ½ teaspoon turmeric and the remaining ¼ teaspoon salt. Cook 3 minutes, until onion is golden, stirring often.

4. Stir in potatoes, coating with spices. Add broth and bring mixture to boil. Cover and simmer 12 to 15 minutes, until potatoes are tender.

5. Uncover and stir in chicken and spinach, adding spinach in small batches. Cook 5 minutes more, until chicken is cooked through and spinach is just tender, stirring often. Serve with rice and yogurt, if desired. Makes 4 servings.

Per serving: 380 calories, 12.5 g total fat, 2 g saturated fat, 94 mg cholesterol, 740 mg sodium, 38 g carbohydrates, 29 g protein, 129 mg calcium, 6 g fiber

pasta with cauliflower

Yes—cauliflower! It's probably one of the most unappreciated vegetables around. Here it's boiled until tender and later simmered in a skillet with pine nuts, currants, tomato paste, sautéed anchovies and red onion.

Prep time: 25 minutes • Cooking time: 35 minutes

1½	cups coarse fresh bread crumbs
⅓	cup freshly grated Pecorino Romano or Parmesan cheese
4	tablespoons olive oil, divided
1½	cups chopped red onions
4	anchovies, chopped
1	head (1¾ to 2 lbs.) cauliflower, trimmed
12	ounces perciatelli or bucatini pasta
¼	cup pine nuts (pignoli)
¼	cup dried currants
2	tablespoons sun-dried tomato paste or tomato paste
½	teaspoon freshly ground pepper
¼	teaspoon salt
	Pinch saffron threads
2	tablespoons chopped fresh flat-leaf parsley

1. Heat oven to 350°F. Combine bread crumbs, cheese and 1 tablespoon of the oil in a bowl. Spread in a jelly-roll pan. Bake 8 to 10 minutes, stirring once, until bread is toasted. Transfer to a plate.

2. Bring a large pot of water to boil. Meanwhile, heat the remaining 3 tablespoons oil in a 12-inch nonstick skillet. Add onions and cook 10 minutes, until softened and beginning to brown. Stir in anchovies; cook 1 minute more. Remove from heat.

3. Break or cut cauliflower into small florets. Salt boiling water and add cauliflower. Cook about 4 minutes, until tender. With a slotted spoon, transfer cauliflower to a bowl. Set aside 1 cup of the cooking water. Return remaining water in pot to boil. Add pasta and cook according to package directions.

4. Meanwhile, stir cauliflower, the reserved 1 cup cooking water, the pine nuts, currants, tomato paste, pepper, salt and saffron together in skillet with onions. Bring to boil. Reduce heat and simmer 5 minutes, stirring to break up cauliflower.

5. Drain pasta; transfer to a large serving bowl. Add cauliflower mixture and toss. Sprinkle with crumb mixture and parsley. Makes 6 servings.

Per serving: 450 calories, 16 g total fat, 3 g saturated fat, 7 mg cholesterol, 415 mg sodium, 62 g carbohydrates, 17 g protein, 149 mg calcium, 7 g fiber

risotto alla primavera LOW FAT

Gathering the freshest vegetables on the market is essential when preparing risotto alla primavera ("spring style" in Italian). Our version calls for asparagus, onion, peas and watercress.

Prep time: 25 minutes • Cooking time: 40 to 45 minutes

3	cans (14½ oz. each) vegetable broth plus enough water to equal 6 cups
1	pound asparagus, cut into 1-inch pieces
1	tablespoon extra-virgin olive oil
1	cup finely chopped onions
1	teaspoon minced garlic
2	cups arborio or medium-grain rice
½	teaspoon salt
½	teaspoon dried thyme
½	teaspoon freshly ground pepper
1	cup white wine
1	cup fresh or frozen peas
1	large bunch (6 oz.) watercress, chopped
½	cup freshly grated Parmesan cheese
2	tablespoons chopped fresh parsley, divided

1. Bring broth and water to boil in a medium saucepan. Reduce heat and add asparagus. Simmer 5 minutes, just until tender-crisp. With a slotted spoon, remove asparagus to a plate; reserve broth.

2. Heat oil in Dutch oven over medium heat. Add onions and garlic; cook 3 minutes. Stir in rice, salt, thyme and pepper. Cook 1 minute, stirring, until grains are glistening. Add wine; cook about 2 minutes, until liquid is absorbed.

3. Set ½ cup of the broth aside; return the remaining broth to simmer. Gradually add remaining broth to rice, ½ cup at a time, stirring constantly, until liquid is absorbed, 25 to 30 minutes.

4. Stir in the reserved ½ cup broth, asparagus, peas and watercress. Remove from heat. Stir in Parmesan and 1 tablespoon of the parsley.

5. Spoon risotto into 6 serving bowls; sprinkle tops with the remaining 1 tablespoon parsley. Serve immediately. Makes 6 servings.

Per serving: 310 calories, 6 g total fat, 2 g saturated fat, 7 mg cholesterol, 1,374 mg sodium, 47 g carbohydrates, 13 g protein, 176 mg calcium, 3 g fiber

potato and green bean salad 🄴🄰🅂🅈

This delicious combination gets extra flavor from fresh basil and pitted kalamata olives.

Total prep and cooking time: 30 minutes

- 1 **bag (1½ lb.) refrigerated ready-to-cook golden potatoes**
- 1 **pound green beans, trimmed and cut into 1-inch pieces**
- 2 **teaspoons salt, divided**
- 2 **tablespoons olive oil**
- 2 **tablespoons red wine vinegar**
- 1 **teaspoon minced garlic**
- ⅛ **teaspoon freshly ground pepper**
- 2 **tablespoons finely chopped kalamata olives**
- 2 **tablespoons thinly sliced, packed fresh basil leaves**

1. Cook potatoes according to package directions. Drain in a colander under cool running water 30 seconds. Set aside.

2. Meanwhile, bring a large saucepan filled two-thirds with water to boil. Add green beans and 1½ teaspoons of the salt. Cook 5 to 6 minutes, until just tender. Drain in a colander under cool running water 30 seconds.

3. Whisk oil, vinegar, garlic, the remaining ½ teaspoon salt and the pepper in a large bowl. Add warm, drained potatoes, green beans, olives and basil. Toss gently with a rubber spatula to combine. Makes 6 servings.

Per serving: 150 calories, 5.5 g total fat, 0.5 g saturated fat, 0 mg cholesterol, 441 mg sodium, 26 g carbohydrates, 4 g protein, 45 mg calcium, 4 g fiber

---

test kitchen tip

keeping nutrients in fresh vegetables

Vegetables are loaded with vitamins, minerals and fiber; however, the processes of preparing and cooking vegetables break down these nutrients. Fortunately, there are some steps we can take to get the most from the garden's bounty:

SELECT THE BEST: Purchase vegetables with a bright, healthy-looking appearance. Avoid veggies with insect or other damage.

AVOID EXPOSURE: Elements such as heat, air, light and water hasten the loss of nutrients. When possible, keep fresh vegetables whole until the time you include them in a recipe.

MINIMIZE CHOPPING: The more surface area exposed, the more nutrients likely to be lost. Use larger pieces when possible.

COOK IT RIGHT: Cooking vegetables actually helps release minerals and phytochemicals, making these easier for your body to absorb. However, when vegetables are overcooked, these nutrients can be lost. To strike the right balance, cook fresh or frozen vegetables in a small amount of water just until tender-crisp. (The exception to this rule are potatoes and other root vegetables that are cooked until they become tender.)

hearty vegetables with basil mashed potatoes EASY

Here is a hearty way to celebrate fresh produce. Enjoy a satisfying meatless meal brimming with mushrooms, bell peppers, green onions and a heart-healthy bundle of spinach.

Prep time: 30 minutes • Cooking time: 30 to 35 minutes

BASIL MASHED POTATOES:

- 1 **pound russet potatoes, peeled and quartered**
- ¾ **teaspoon salt, divided**
- ⅓ **cup heavy or whipping cream**
- ⅓ **cup milk**
- 2 **tablespoons butter or margarine**
- ⅛ **teaspoon freshly ground pepper**
- ¼ **cup thinly sliced fresh basil leaves**

- ½ **teaspoon salt**
- ¼ **teaspoon freshly ground pepper**
- 4 **large (14 oz. total) portobella mushroom caps**
- 3 **tablespoons olive oil, divided**
- 1 **red bell pepper, cut into ½-inch strips**
- 1 **yellow bell pepper, cut into ½-inch strips**
- 1 **bunch green onions, cut into 1-inch pieces**
- 1 **tablespoon chopped garlic**
- 1 **bunch fresh spinach or 1 bag (10 oz.) fresh spinach, trimmed and rinsed**

1. *Make basil mashed potatoes:* Bring potatoes, ½ teaspoon of the salt and enough cold water to cover by 2 inches to boil in a large saucepan. Reduce heat and simmer 18 to 20 minutes, until potatoes are fork-tender. Drain. Return potatoes to saucepan and cook over low heat 2 minutes more to dry. Coarsely mash potatoes with a potato masher or a large wooden spoon. Stir in cream, milk, butter, the remaining ¼ teaspoon of the salt and the pepper. Mash mixture until well combined and heat through. Stir in basil. Cover and keep warm.

2. Heat oven to 425°F. Line a cookie sheet with foil. Combine the ½ teaspoon salt and the ¼ teaspoon pepper in a cup. Brush both sides of mushrooms with 2 tablespoons of the oil. Sprinkle with salt and pepper. Bake mushrooms 20 minutes, turning once halfway through, until tender.

3. Heat the remaining 1 tablespoon oil in a large skillet over medium-high heat. Add bell peppers and cook, stirring, 5 minutes. Stir in green onions and cook 3 to 5 minutes, until softened. Reduce heat to medium-low; add garlic. Cover and cook vegetables, stirring occasionally, 10 minutes more, until golden brown. Transfer vegetables to a large plate. Add spinach to same skillet and cook, uncovered, over medium-high heat 2 minutes, just until wilted. Transfer spinach to plate with vegetables. Serve with Basil Mashed Potatoes. Makes 4 servings.

Per serving: 450 calories, 24.5 g total fat, 10 g saturated fat, 45 mg cholesterol, 1,016 mg sodium, 51 g carbohydrates, 10 g protein, 136 mg calcium, 8 g fiber

oven-roasted tomato sauce EASY

You can use either red plum tomatoes or the lesser-known yellow variety. Either way, this garlicky sauce tastes great with grilled vegetables, meats, poultry or fish.

Prep time: 10 minutes • Baking time: 45 minutes

- 3 **pounds plum tomatoes, halved**
- ½ **cup extra-virgin olive oil**
- 3 **cloves garlic**
- 10 **fresh basil leaves**
- ¼ **teaspoon salt**

Heat oven to 425°F. Combine all of the ingredients except salt in a nonreactive roasting pan or a

13×9-inch baking dish. Bake 45 minutes, until tomatoes are very soft. Cool 20 minutes. Peel and discard skins. Coarsely chop tomatoes, garlic and basil; reserve juice. Transfer tomato mixture and juice to a large bowl; stir in salt. (*Can be made ahead. Transfer to an airtight container and refrigerate up to 3 days.*) Makes 1 quart.

Per ¼ cup: 80 calories, 7 g total fat, 1 g saturated fat, 0 mg cholesterol, 44 mg sodium, 4 g carbohydrates, 1 g protein, 6 mg calcium, 1 g fiber

grilled eggplant with smoked mozzarella

Thinly sliced basil is topped with eggplant, tomatoes and smoked mozzarella. Serve with grilled meat or chicken.

Prep time: 15 minutes • Grilling time: 8 to 10 minutes

- 2 cups fresh basil leaves, thinly sliced
- ½ pound smoked mozzarella, diced
- 1 large tomato, seeded and diced
- 4 tablespoons extra-virgin olive oil, divided
- 3 tablespoons white balsamic or white wine vinegar, divided
- ¼ teaspoon salt
- ¼ teaspoon freshly ground pepper
- 1 eggplant (1 lb.), cut into ½-inch slices

1. Heat grill. Remove 1 tablespoon of the sliced basil to a medium bowl. Stir in mozzarella, tomato, 1 tablespoon of the oil and 1 tablespoon of the vinegar. Arrange the remaining basil on a serving platter. Set both aside.

2. Whisk the remaining 3 tablespoons oil, the 2 tablespoons vinegar, salt and pepper in a small bowl. Brush 1 side of the eggplant slices with oil mixture. Arrange eggplant on grill, oiled side down. Brush tops with the remaining oil mixture. Grill slices over medium heat 4 to 5 minutes per side, until softened and lightly charred. Arrange eggplant on top of basil. Spoon mozzarella-tomato mixture on top of eggplant. Makes 5 servings.

Per serving: 285 calories, 23 g total fat, 9 g saturated fat, 48 mg cholesterol, 332 mg sodium, 11 g carbohydrates, 12 g protein, 328 mg calcium, 3 g fiber

quinoa with broccoli rabe

The slightly nutty flavor of quinoa blends perfectly with pungent broccoli rabe and garlic.

Prep time: 15 minutes • Cooking time: 25 to 30 minutes

- 1 cup quinoa
- 1 can (14½ oz.) chicken broth plus enough water to equal 2 cups
- 2 tablespoons extra-virgin olive oil
- ½ cup chopped onion
- 1 teaspoon chopped garlic
- 1 large bunch broccoli rabe (1¼ lbs.), trimmed and chopped
- ¼ teaspoon salt
- ¼ teaspoon red pepper flakes

1. Heat quinoa, stirring, in a nonstick skillet over medium-low heat 5 minutes, until toasted. Bring broth and water to boil in a medium saucepan. Stir in quinoa. Reduce heat to medium-low; cover and simmer 12 to 15 minutes, until liquid is absorbed and quinoa is tender. Fluff with fork and transfer to a large bowl; cover and keep warm.

2. Heat oil in a large skillet over medium-high heat. Add onion and garlic. Cook 3 minutes. Stir in broccoli rabe, salt and red pepper flakes. Cook 5 to 7 minutes more, until broccoli rabe is tender. Stir vegetables into quinoa. Serve warm or at room temperature. Makes 5 servings.

Per serving: 220 calories, 8 g total fat, 1 g saturated fat, 0 mg cholesterol, 410 mg sodium, 30 g carbohydrates, 9 g protein, 73 mg calcium, 5 g fiber

test kitchen tip
keen for quinoa

Tiny bead-shape quinoa is ivory in color and has a delicate mellow flavor comparable to couscous. Indigenous to South America, quinoa was regularly consumed by the ancient Incas. It has the highest protein content of any grain and it's rich in iron. Quinoa is available in most supermarkets and most health food and specialty stores.

menu

italian-style dinner

CHICKEN CACCIATORE
page 50

OVEN-BAKED BROCCOLI
below

ITALIAN BREAD

GELATO

ITALIAN ESPRESSO

oven-baked broccoli EASY

A great, versatile vegetable preparation, vibrant with fresh broccoli. Thinly sliced leeks make a lovely addition to this wholesome side.

Prep time: 5 minutes • Baking time: 20 to 22 minutes

- 2 **tablespoons olive oil**
- 4 **cups broccoli florets**
- 1 **cup thinly sliced leeks**
- ¼ **cup water**
- ½ **teaspoon salt**
- ¼ **teaspoon freshly ground pepper**

1. Heat oven to 450°F. Add oil to a 2-quart shallow glass baking dish. Heat dish in the oven for 2 minutes. Add broccoli. Stir to coat with oil. Cover top with foil. Bake 15 minutes.

2. Stir in leeks, water, salt and pepper to broccoli. Top dish with foil. Bake 5 to 7 minutes more, until broccoli is tender. Makes 4 servings.

Per serving: 95 calories, 6 g total fat, 1 g saturated fat, 0 mg cholesterol, 280 mg sodium, 8 g carbohydrates, 4 g protein, 63 mg calcium, 3 g fiber

fried cauliflower with lemon mayonnaise

Just-squeezed lemon juice, grated lemon peel and chopped parsley lend their refreshing qualities to the mayonnaise—a perfect partner for the cauliflower. If you've never before fried cauliflower, the outstanding flavor and texture will be a welcome surprise.

Prep time: 25 minutes • Cooking time: 15 minutes

LEMON MAYONNAISE:
- ½ **cup mayonnaise**
- 1 **teaspoon grated lemon peel**
- 2 **tablespoons fresh lemon juice**
- 1 **tablespoon chopped fresh parsley**
- ½ **teaspoon salt**
- ⅛ **teaspoon freshly ground black pepper**
  Large pinch ground red pepper

- 1½ **quarts vegetable oil**
- 1 **small head (1¼ lbs.) cauliflower, trimmed**
- ½ **cup all-purpose flour**
- ½ **cup freshly grated Parmesan cheese**
- ½ **cup water**
- 1 **large egg**
- ¼ **teaspoon salt**

1. *Make lemon mayonnaise:* Combine all of the ingredients for the lemon mayonnaise in a small bowl. Cover and refrigerate. Makes ½ cup. (*Can be made ahead. Refrigerate up to 24 hours.*)

2. Heat oven to 200°F. Line a jelly-roll pan with paper towels. Set aside.

3. Heat vegetable oil in a heavy 3-quart saucepan over medium heat until it registers 365°F. on a deep-fat thermometer.

4. Meanwhile, separate cauliflower into small, bite-size pieces. Whisk together flour, cheese, water, egg and salt in a large bowl until smooth. Add cauliflower and stir to coat.

5. Carefully add cauliflower, 5 or 6 pieces at a time, to hot oil and fry 1½ to 2 minutes, until browned. With a slotted spoon, transfer cauliflower to prepared sheet. Keep cauliflower warm in oven. Repeat with the remaining cauliflower pieces (making sure to adjust heat to maintain 365°F). Serve immediately with Lemon Mayonnaise. Makes 8 servings.

Per serving: 235 calories, 20 g total fat, 4 g saturated fat, 40 mg cholesterol, 443 mg sodium, 8 g carbohydrates, 6 g protein, 108 mg calcium, 2 g fiber

cauliflower gratin EASY

Here we transform a head of cauliflower into serious comfort food. Heavy cream, Fontina and Parmesan cheeses create a creamy-rich gratin.

Prep time: 30 minutes • Cooking time: 1 hour 5 minutes

1 large (2½ lbs.) head cauliflower
TOMATO SAUCE:
1 tablespoon olive oil
⅓ cup finely chopped onion
2 large cloves garlic, minced
⅛ to ¼ teaspoon red pepper flakes
1 can (14½ oz.) diced tomatoes
½ teaspoon salt
⅛ teaspoon freshly ground pepper
½ cup heavy or whipping cream

1 cup shredded Fontina cheese
¾ cup coarse fresh bread crumbs
⅓ cup freshly grated Parmesan cheese

1. Trim leaves from cauliflower. Remove core, leaving enough of the head of cauliflower so it remains intact. Bring 1 inch water to boil in a Dutch oven. Carefully add cauliflower, stem side down. Cover and cook 8 to 10 minutes, until knife inserted in bottom comes out easily. Set cauliflower into a colander; drain under cold running water until cool. Drain well; pat dry with paper towels.

2. *Make tomato sauce:* Heat oil in a 10-inch skillet over medium-low heat. Add onion and cook 6 minutes, until golden. Add garlic and red pepper flakes. Cook 1 minute. Stir in tomatoes, salt and pepper. Bring to boil. Reduce heat and simmer

15 minutes. Stir in cream and simmer for 2 minutes more.

3. Heat oven to 400°F. Cut cauliflower into ¾-inch slices. Spread Tomato Sauce into the bottom of a 2-quart shallow baking dish. Arrange overlapping slices of cauliflower over sauce.

4. Combine Fontina cheese, bread crumbs and Parmesan cheese in a bowl. Sprinkle over cauliflower. Bake 30 minutes, until top is brown and sauce is bubbly around the edges. Makes 8 servings.

Per serving: 200 calories, 14 g total fat, 8 g saturated fat, 43 mg cholesterol, 511 mg sodium, 10 g carbohydrates, 10 g protein, 213 mg calcium, 4 g fiber

minted vegetable medley LOW FAT EASY

April through June is peak season for sugarsnap peas, which are wonderfully sweet in this three-vegetable medley. No need to shell the peas—whole sugar snaps are absolutely delicious.

Prep time: 25 minutes • Cooking time: 13 to 15 minutes

1 tablespoon butter or margarine
1 pound carrots, cut into 2×¼-inch matchsticks
2 yellow bell peppers, cut into 1-inch squares
½ teaspoon salt
⅛ teaspoon freshly ground pepper
6 cups water
1 pound sugarsnap peas or green beans, trimmed
¼ cup chopped fresh mint

1. Melt butter in a large skillet over medium heat. Add carrots, bell peppers, salt and pepper. Cook 8 to 9 minutes, until vegetables are tender.

2. Meanwhile, bring water to boil in a large saucepan. Add peas; cook 5 to 6 minutes, until just tender-crisp. Drain.

3. To serve, toss carrot mixture, peas and mint in a medium bowl. Makes 6 servings.

Per serving: 100 calories, 2 g total fat, 1 g saturated fat, 5 mg cholesterol, 308 mg sodium, 18 g carbohydrates, 4 g protein, 44 mg calcium, 5 g fiber

it's a toss-up

These days, many farmers' markets and produce aisles brim with a bountiful bevy of fresh greens, each with their own distinct texture and flavor nuances. To make the most of your salad bowl, you'll want to toss the salad with an appropriate dressing or vinaigrette for the type of green you're using. For example, a mild green leaf may call for a pungent or rich creamy dressing, while flavorful greens beckon a toned-down dressing or vinaigrette. Here are ideas for mixing and matching:

ARUGULA (also called rocket, rucola): Nutty, peppery, from mild to bitter. Pair with Boston Bibb and add grilled portobella mushrooms, Gorgonzola cheese and a basic vinaigrette.

CHICORY: Prickly leaves, crunchy with semi-mild flavor. Toss with cooked smoky bacon, sautéed shallots, and an olive oil and red-wine vinaigrette.

GREEN LEAF LETTUCE: Loosely packed with soft ends, crisp center and faintly sweet flavor. Match with shredded radicchio, red onion, avocado, Gorgonzola and a light vinaigrette.

MESCLUN GREENS: A mix of young greens that can include arugula, chervil, frisée, dandelion and oak leaf, with flavors ranging from bitter to sweet. Try with grated Parmesan cheese, peppers and oil and vinegar.

RED LEAF LETTUCE: Soft leaves with red color at ends. Mild, slightly buttery flavor. Pair with green leaf lettuce, scallions and radishes with a balsamic vinaigrette.

SPINACH: Buttery with slightly bitter flavor. Combine with iceberg lettuce and yellow or red cherry tomatoes. Serve with a creamy Italian or ranch dressing.

WATERCRESS: Tender with a peppery snap. Mix with romaine lettuce, diced pears and a mild vinaigrette.

warm spinach and frisée salad with sweet onion

Sweet onion-lovers take note. To get the maximum helping of onion slices without overwhelming the greens, half is plunged in boiling water to remove any bitterness; the other half is lightly cooked.

Total prep time: 25 minutes

- **6** cups water
- **3** tablespoons plus 1 teaspoon white wine vinegar
- **1** large (12 oz.) sweet onion, thinly sliced

DRESSING:
- **4** ounces pancetta (Italian bacon) or 5 thick-cut bacon slices, diced
- **4** ounces shiitake or white mushrooms, sliced
- **¼** teaspoon salt
- **⅛** teaspoon freshly ground pepper
- **2** tablespoons olive oil

- **1** bag (10 oz.) fresh spinach, trimmed
- **1** head (4 oz.) frisée or chicory lettuce

1. Bring 6 cups water to boil in a medium saucepan. Remove from heat; stir in 1 teaspoon of the vinegar. Add half of the onion slices. Let mixture stand 1 minute. With a slotted spoon, remove onions. Drain on paper towels.

2. *Make dressing:* Heat a large nonstick skillet 1 minute over medium heat. Add pancetta and cook until crisp. Stir in the remaining onion and mushrooms. Cook until vegetables are softened. Stir in the remaining 3 tablespoons vinegar, salt and pepper. Remove from heat; stir in olive oil.

3. To serve, toss spinach, frisée and onion in a large serving bowl. Drizzle with warm dressing; toss to coat. Makes 4 servings.

Per serving: 215 calories, 15 g total fat, 5 g saturated fat, 11 mg cholesterol, 404 mg sodium, 8 g carbohydrates, 6 g protein, 110 mg calcium, 4 g fiber

roasted green onions

EASY

Here's a creative change of pace for using green onions, also known as scallions or spring onions. They are placed on a jelly-roll pan, tossed with salt, pepper and olive oil and roasted for 15 minutes. Select green onions no smaller than a one-half inch in diameter so they won't overcook. Note: This serves 8 people; cut the recipe in half if you're feeding a smaller group.

Prep time: 15 minutes • Roasting time: 15 minutes

- **4** **bunches (about 24) medium-size green onions, trimmed to 10 inches**
- **2** **teaspoons olive or vegetable oil**
- **½** **teaspoon salt**
- **¼** **teaspoon freshly ground pepper**

Heat oven to 375°F. Toss onions, oil, salt and pepper on a jelly-roll pan. Arrange in a single layer. Roast 15 minutes, until onions are tender. Makes 8 servings.

Per serving: 25 calories, 1 g total fat, 0 g saturated fat, 0 mg cholesterol, 153 mg sodium, 3 g carbohydrates, 1 g protein, 33 mg calcium, 1 g fiber

grilled artichokes and asparagus

Fresh artichokes and asparagus are brushed with olive oil, lemon juice and garlic, then grilled until tender-crisp. The length of grilling time for the asparagus depends on the thickness of the spears.

Prep time: 25 minutes plus standing
Grilling time: 10 to 18 minutes

- **8** **cups water**
- **6** **medium (10 to 12 oz. each) artichokes**

MARINADE:
- **½** **cup extra-virgin olive oil**
- **½** **cup fresh lemon juice**
- **1** **tablespoon minced garlic**
- **¾** **teaspoon salt**
- **¼** **teaspoon freshly ground pepper**

- **2** **pounds asparagus, trimmed**
- **Lemon wedges, for garnish (optional)**

1. Bring water to boil in a large saucepan. Line a large jelly-roll pan with paper towels.

2. Meanwhile, with a large sharp knife, cut one-quarter to one-third off top of artichokes; trim stems to 1 inch. Bend back tough outer petals until they snap off near base. Continue to snap off petals until a layer of tender yellow petals is exposed; discard outer petals. Using a small sharp knife, peel outer dark-green layer from base and stem. Cut artichokes into quarters. Remove purple and pink leaves and fuzzy centers.

3. Place 3 of the artichokes in boiling water; reduce heat and simmer 5 minutes, until bases of artichokes are almost tender when pierced with a fork. With a slotted spoon, transfer artichokes to paper towels; drain. Repeat process with remaining artichokes.

4. *Make marinade:* Whisk together all of the ingredients for the marinade in a large bowl. Add warm artichokes; toss gently to coat with marinade. Let stand 1 hour.

5. Generously oil and heat grill. With tongs, transfer artichokes to grill; reserve marinade. Grill over medium heat, 4 to 5 inches from heat source, 3 to 4 minutes. Lightly brush with some of the reserved marinade. Turn artichokes and grill 3 to 4 minutes more, until lightly charred. Transfer to a serving platter; cover and keep warm.

6. Discard paper towels; arrange asparagus on jelly-roll pan and lightly brush all sides with some of remaining marinade. With tongs, transfer asparagus to grill. Grill asparagus over medium heat 2 to 5 minutes each side, until lightly charred and tender. Transfer to platter with artichokes.

7. To serve, drizzle the remaining marinade over top of vegetables. Serve with lemon wedges, if desired. (*Can be made ahead. Cool. Cover with plastic wrap and refrigerate overnight. Let stand at room temperature 30 minutes before serving.*) Makes 8 to 10 servings.

Per serving: 170 calories, 12.5 g total fat, 2 g saturated fat, 0 mg cholesterol, 263 mg sodium, 13 g carbohydrates, 5 g protein, 59 mg calcium, 14 g fiber

garden tomato salad EASY

For a truly striking salad, use as many colors and shapes of tomatoes as you can find. A shallot-mint vinaigrette complements the flavor of ripe summer tomatoes.

Total prep time: 20 minutes

- ⅓ cup extra-virgin olive oil
- ¼ cup chopped fresh mint
- 1 shallot, minced (3 tablespoons)
- 3 tablespoons Japanese rice vinegar
- ½ teaspoon salt
- ⅛ teaspoon freshly ground pepper
- 3 pounds ripe heirloom tomatoes, sliced
- 1 cup small cherry tomatoes or grape tomatoes

1. Combine oil, mint, shallot, vinegar, salt and pepper in a jar with a tight-fitting lid. Cover with lid; shake until combined.

2. Arrange sliced tomatoes on a platter. Shake dressing again; drizzle over tomatoes. Sprinkle with cherry tomatoes. Makes 6 to 8 servings.

Per serving: 190 calories, 18 g total fat, 2 g saturated fat, 0 mg cholesterol, 189 mg sodium, 11 g carbohydrates, 2 g protein, 18 mg calcium, 2 g fiber

watermelon salad LOW FAT EASY

No question—watermelon is always great straight—but when you want to stir things up a bit, try this. In addition to watermelon, this marvelous melange includes watercress, fresh lemon juice, olive oil, a hint of red pepper and onion. Tip: When shopping for the watermelon, look for seedless varieties.

Total prep time: 20 minutes plus standing

- 1 small red onion, thinly sliced
- 3 tablespoons red wine vinegar
- 1 tablespoon sugar

DRESSING:

- 2 tablespoons fresh lemon juice
- 2 tablespoons olive oil
- 1 teaspoon sugar
- ¼ teaspoon salt
- ¼ teaspoon freshly ground pepper
- Pinch ground red pepper

- 3 cups cubed, seeded watermelon
- 1 large bunch (5 oz.) watercress, trimmed (about 3 cups)

1. Thoroughly rinse onion in a colander under cold running water; drain. Stir vinegar and sugar together in a small bowl, until sugar dissolves. Add onion; toss to coat. Let stand 30 minutes, stirring occasionally.

2. *Make dressing:* Whisk together all of the ingredients for the dressing in a large bowl.

3. Drain onion and add to dressing in bowl. Add watermelon and watercress; toss gently to coat. Serve immediately. Makes 6 servings.

Per serving: 90 calories, 5 g total fat, 0.5 g saturated fat, 0 mg cholesterol, 108 mg sodium, 11 g carbohydrates, 1 g protein, 39 mg calcium, 1 g fiber

grilled summer squash with salsa EASY

Topped with a lemony, slightly spicy salsa, this is one zingy way to serve summer squash. Look for squash of different sizes and shapes at local farmers' markets.

Prep time: 25 minutes plus standing
Cooking time: 6 minutes

- 2½ pounds summer squash
- 1 large ripe plum tomato, diced
- ⅓ cup diced red onion
- 4 tablespoons extra-virgin olive oil, divided
- 1 jalapeño chile, seeded and minced (see tip, page 15)
- ½ teaspoon grated lemon peel
- 1 tablespoon fresh lemon juice
- ½ teaspoon salt, divided
- ½ teaspoon freshly ground pepper, divided
- 1 clove garlic, crushed through a press

1. Dice enough of the squash to measure 1 cup. Combine squash, tomato, onion, 2 tablespoons of

the oil, the jalapeño, lemon peel and juice,
¼ teaspoon of the salt and ¼ teaspoon of the
pepper in a small bowl. Stir to combine and let
stand 1 hour; stir occasionally.

2. Heat grill. Cut the remaining squash lengthwise
into ½-inch slices. Stir together the remaining
2 tablespoons oil, ¼ teaspoon salt, ¼ teaspoon
pepper and the garlic in a cup. Brush oil mixture on
1 side of each squash slice. Grill over medium heat
3 or 4 minutes each side, turning once, until tender.
Arrange squash slices on a serving platter and
spoon salsa over mixture. Makes 6 servings.

Per serving: 120 calories, 9.5 g total fat, 1.5 g saturated fat,
0 mg cholesterol, 200 mg sodium, 9 g carbohydrates, 2 g protein,
44 mg calcium, 4 g fiber

green beans with beets and cucumbers LOW FAT EASY

*Here's a terrific trio you may have overlooked until now.
Vegetable tips: Don't overcook the beets; they will get soft
and lose flavor. Use the most tender green and yellow wax
beans. Pictured on page 87.*

Prep time: 20 minutes • Cooking time: 20 to 25 minutes

- 1 **bunch beets (1 pound), trimmed, peeled and quartered**
- ½ **teaspoon fennel seeds**
- 5 **whole black peppercorns**
- 1 **small cucumber, peeled, seeded and diced**
- 2 **tablespoons white wine vinegar**
- 1 **tablespoon chopped shallot**
- ¾ **teaspoon salt, divided**
- 2 **tablespoons olive oil**
- ¼ **cup thinly sliced fresh basil leaves**
- 1 **pound green and yellow wax beans, trimmed**

1. Bring beets, fennel seeds, peppercorns and
enough cold water to cover by 2 inches to boil in
a medium saucepan. Reduce heat and simmer
15 to 20 minutes, just until beets are tender. Drain.
Cool slightly and dice. Transfer beets to a large
bowl; stir in cucumber.

2. Meanwhile, whisk together vinegar, shallot
and ¼ teaspoon of the salt in a small bowl. Slowly
whisk in oil. Stir in basil. Drizzle over beets and
cucumbers; toss gently to coat.

3. Bring a medium saucepan filled halfway
with water to boil. Add beans and the remaining
½ teaspoon salt. Cook 5 minutes, just until
beans are tender-crisp. Drain; transfer beans to a
large serving platter. Spoon beets and cucumbers
over beans. Makes 6 servings.

Per serving: 90 calories, 4.5 g total fat, 1 g saturated fat,
0 mg cholesterol, 335 mg sodium, 12 g carbohydrates,
2 g protein, 46 mg calcium, 2 g fiber

summer vegetable salad LOW FAT EASY

*This salad of sweet bell peppers, jicama and celery, tossed
with a light sweet-sour rice wine vinaigrette, is pure
pleasure. Fresh chives are readily available at
supermarkets; but if you can't find them, substitute
finely diced green onions.*

Total prep time: 20 minutes

VINAIGRETTE:
- 3 **tablespoons snipped fresh chives**
- 3 **tablespoons rice wine vinegar**
- 1 **tablespoon olive oil**
- 1 **teaspoon salt**
- ¾ **teaspoon sugar**

- 4 **large celery ribs, peeled and sliced**
- 2 **yellow bell peppers, cut into 1-inch pieces**
- 1 **jicama (1 lb.), peeled and cut into ¼-inch strips**

1. *Make vinaigrette:* Combine all of the ingredients
for the vinaigrette in a large bowl.

2. Add celery, bell peppers and jicama to
vinaigrette in bowl; toss to coat. (*Can be made
ahead. Refrigerate overnight in airtight container.*)
Makes 8 servings.

Per serving: 45 calories, 2 g total fat, 0 g saturated fat,
0 mg cholesterol, 316 mg sodium, 7 g carbohydrates, 1 g protein,
19 mg calcium, 3 g fiber

corn on the cob

An old favorite with a slightly new twist. We provide the basic corn on the cob recipe, plus three flavored butters to slather over the summer-fresh ears.

Prep time: 10 minutes
Cooking time: 30 seconds to 1 minute

> **8** ears fresh corn
> Herb, Poblano Chile or Tequila and Lime Butter, see recipes, below and right (optional)

1. Bring a large pot of unsalted water to boil. Remove all but the inner 2 layers of husk, leaving the silk.

2. Carefully place 4 ears in boiling water. Return water to boil. Boil no longer than 30 seconds to 1 minute. Using tongs or a slotted spoon, transfer corn to a colander; drain. Return water to boil. Repeat with remaining corn.

3. To serve, pull back husks to base of each ear and remove silks. (Use the base of the corn as a handle, if desired.) Makes 8 servings.

Per serving: 75 calories, 1 g total fat, 0 g saturated fat, 0 mg cholesterol, 14 mg sodium, 17 g carbohydrates, 3 g protein, 2 mg calcium, 2 g fiber

herb butter

This is also perfect served with grilled fresh vegetables. Or spread it between slices of French bread, then heat.

Total prep time: 5 minutes plus chilling

> ½ **cup butter, softened (no substitutes)**
> 2 **tablespoons chopped fresh basil**
> 1 **tablespoon chopped fresh thyme leaves**
> 1 **teaspoon grated lemon peel**

With a rubber spatula, beat butter, basil, thyme and lemon peel in a small bowl until well combined. Transfer butter to a sheet of plastic wrap or waxed paper. Roll into an 8-inch log and refrigerate overnight. To serve, cut log crosswise into eight 1-inch slices. Makes 8 slices.

Per slice: 110 calories, 12 g total fat, 7.5 g saturated fat, 33 mg cholesterol, 124 mg sodium, 0 g carbohydrates, 0 g protein, 6 mg calcium, 0 g fiber

poblano chile butter

Sure it's tasty on corn, but why stop there? Give your grilled lamb or pork chops, chicken or thick and juicy T-bone steaks a flavor flair.

Prep time: 10 minutes plus standing and chilling
Broiling time: 10 to 12 minutes

> **1** poblano chile (4 oz.), sliced in half lengthwise, seeds and stems removed (see tip, page 15)
> ½ **cup butter, softened (no substitutes)**

1. Heat broiler. Line a broiler pan with foil. Arrange chile, cut side down, on foil. Broil 3 to 4 inches from heat, 10 to 12 minutes, until skins are evenly charred. Wrap in foil; cool. Peel and remove blistered skin from chile; discard. Finely chop chile.

2. With a rubber spatula, beat chile and butter in a bowl until well combined. Transfer butter to a sheet of plastic wrap or waxed paper. Roll into an 8-inch log and refrigerate overnight. To serve, cut log crosswise into eight 1-inch slices. Makes 8 slices.

Per slice: 115 calories, 12 g total fat, 7.5 g saturated fat, 33 mg cholesterol, 125 mg sodium, 2 g carbohydrates, 1 g protein, 8 mg calcium, 0 g fiber

tequila and lime butter

Want a super-easy-to-make sauce for the next time you grill succulent shrimp or fish? Serve this "butter with an attitude." It's sassy and assertive, with a touch of sophistication thrown in!

Total prep and cooking time: 10 minutes plus chilling

> ¼ **cup tequila**
> **Peel of 1 lime**
> ½ **cup butter, softened (no substitutes)**

1. Bring tequila and lime peel to boil in a small saucepan over medium-high heat. Reduce heat and simmer 3 to 4 minutes, until tequila just evaporates. Transfer peel to a cutting board; cool and finely chop.

2. With a rubber spatula, beat peel and butter in a bowl until well combined. Transfer butter to a sheet of plastic wrap or waxed paper. Roll into an 8-inch log and refrigerate overnight. To serve, cut log crosswise into eight 1-inch slices. Makes 8 slices.

Per slice: 120 calories, 12 g total fat, 7.5 g saturated fat, 33 mg cholesterol, 124 mg sodium, 0 g carbohydrates, 0 g protein, 4 mg calcium, 0 g fiber

corn and roasted garlic custard

For the freshest savory pudding ever, we use both whole and pureed corn kernels with roasted garlic, thyme and creamy goat cheese in our summer custard.

Prep time: 40 minutes • Baking time: 65 to 75 minutes

4	cloves garlic
8	ears fresh corn, kernels cut from cobs
1½	cups heavy or whipping cream, divided
4	large eggs
1	tablespoon flour
1	log goat cheese (4 oz.), crumbled
1	teaspoon fresh thyme leaves, chopped, or ¼ teaspoon dried thyme
½	teaspoon salt
¼	teaspoon freshly ground pepper

1. Heat oven to 350°F. Generously butter a 1½-quart baking dish. (Dish should be 2½ inches deep.) Place dish in a roasting pan with at least 1-inch of space between the edge of the baking dish and the roasting pan. Set aside.

2. Wrap garlic in foil. Bake 20 minutes, until cloves are very soft and center is tender when tested with a toothpick. Cool slightly. Gently squeeze garlic from cloves; discard peels. Coarsely chop garlic.

3. Puree half of the corn and ¼ cup of the cream in a blender. Transfer corn mixture to a large sieve set over a large bowl. With the back of spoon, press corn mixture to extract as much liquid as possible (measure 1 cup); discard corn hulls (skins).

4. Whisk the remaining 1¼ cups cream, the eggs and flour into corn mixture. Stir in the remaining corn kernels, the garlic, goat cheese, thyme, salt and

pepper. Pour corn mixture into dish. Pour boiling water into roasting pan around baking dish to a depth of 1 inch. Bake 65 to 75 minutes, until custard is just set in center and top is golden brown. Carefully remove custard from water bath. Cool on wire rack 15 minutes. Makes 8 servings.

Per serving: 310 calories, 24 g total fat, 14 g saturated fat, 179 mg cholesterol, 278 mg sodium, 18 g carbohydrates, 10 g protein, 83 mg calcium, 3 g fiber

---

test kitchen tip

five-a-day

When the National Cancer Institute and the Produce for Better Health Foundation teamed up to launch the "5-A-Day" campaign, the goal was simple: to get Americans to eat at least five servings of fruits and vegetables a day. It sounds like a lot, but the number is deceiving because a serving is much smaller than you might think.

WHAT'S WHAT A serving can come from fresh, canned, frozen or dried fruits and vegetables. The key to 5-A-Day is variety.

DAILY SERVING Examples of one serving:
1 medium-size apple, orange or banana
¾ cup (6 oz.) 100% fruit or vegetable juice
½ cup cooked or canned vegetable or fruit
1 cup salad greens
½ cup dry peas or beans
¼ cup dried fruit

DEVELOP A ROUTINE Have staple fruits and veggies on hand, and when buying fresh, take advantage of what's in season. There's always an abundance of goodness to choose from—so there's no excuse for not getting in 5-A-Day.

WHAT'S IN IT FOR YOU According to the Produce for Better Health Foundation, research shows that consuming five or more servings of fruits and vegetables a day may reduce the risk of certain types of cancer, heart disease and other illnesses.

yellow bell pepper soup

Sweet yellow bell peppers are sautéed with onion and shallot, and seasoned with ginger, coriander and delicate white pepper. Then it's pureed. Tip: crème fraîche stirs into swirls best when it's not too cold, so remove it from the refrigerator as you begin the recipe. Pictured on page 87.

Prep time: 15 minutes plus chilling
Cooking time: 17 minutes

- 1 tablespoon butter or margarine
- 3 large yellow bell peppers, seeded and cut into 1½-inch pieces
- ½ cup chopped onion
- 1 tablespoon minced shallot
- ½ teaspoon grated fresh ginger
- ¼ teaspoon coriander
- ⅛ teaspoon white pepper
- 1 can (14½ oz.) chicken broth
- 2 tablespoons crème fraîche, divided
  Fresh chives and thinly sliced yellow and red bell peppers, for garnish (optional)

1. Melt butter in a 3-quart saucepan over medium heat. Add bell peppers, onion and shallot. Cover and cook 5 minutes. Stir in ginger, coriander and pepper. Cover and cook 3 minutes more. Add broth; bring to boil. Reduce heat, cover and simmer 8 minutes.

2. Set a medium bowl in a larger bowl filled with enough ice and water to come halfway up side of a smaller bowl.

3. Using a slotted spoon, transfer pepper solids (leave broth in pot) into a blender container. Blend on low until smooth. Add broth and 1 tablespoon of the crème fraîche. Blend on high speed until very smooth. Pour mixture through a sieve into the chilled bowl. Let stand 10 minutes, until cool, stirring occasionally.

4. Ladle soup into 4 serving bowls. Divide the remaining 1 tablespoon of crème fraîche; swirl into soup. Garnish with chives and yellow and red bell peppers, if desired. Makes 4 servings.

Per serving: 75 calories, 5 g total fat, 3 g saturated fat, 11 mg cholesterol, 380 mg sodium, 6 g carbohydrates, 1.5 g protein, 23 mg calcium, 1 g fiber

carrot and sweet potato soup with apples

This carrot soup gets its delicate flavor from the diced apple and citrus peel sprinkled over each serving.

Prep time: 25 minutes
Cooking time: 25 to 30 minutes

- 3 tablespoons butter or margarine, divided
- 1 medium onion, chopped
- 1½ pounds carrots, sliced
- 2 Golden Delicious apples
- 3 cans (14½ oz. each) chicken broth
- 2 medium sweet potatoes, peeled and diced
- 1 cup water
- 2 bay leaves
- ⅛ teaspoon allspice
- 2 teaspoons grated orange peel
- ¼ cup fresh orange juice

1. Melt 2 tablespoons of the butter in a large Dutch oven over medium heat. Add onion and cook 2 minutes, until softened. Stir in carrots and cook 3 minutes.

2. Peel and dice 1 apple. Stir in the peeled and diced apple, the broth, sweet potatoes, water, bay leaves and allspice. Bring mixture to boil. Reduce heat, cover and simmer 20 to 25 minutes, until vegetables are tender.

3. Meanwhile, finely dice the remaining apple. Melt the remaining 1 tablespoon butter in a small skillet over medium heat. Add apple and cook, stirring often, 5 minutes, until softened. Stir in orange peel; remove from heat. Set aside.

4. Remove bay leaves from soup; discard. Transfer one-third of the mixture to a blender container and puree. Transfer to a large bowl. Repeat process with remaining mixture.

5. Return soup to the Dutch oven. Stir in orange juice; simmer 5 minutes, until heated through. Ladle soup into 6 serving bowls. Divide and top each with apple mixture. Makes 6 servings.

Per serving: 224 calories, 8 g total fat, 4 g saturated fat, 16 mg cholesterol, 755 mg sodium, 33 g carbohydrates, 6 g protein, 56 mg calcium, 6 g fiber

sweetened butternut squash

LOW FAT *EASY*

This recipe should turn your kids into squash fans fast! Small pieces of butternut squash cook in a saucepan with garlic and chicken broth, but the magic takes place during the last few minutes of cooking time when the squash is sweetened with applesauce. While squash is available year-round, it's best from early fall to winter.

Prep time: 10 minutes • Cooking time: 25 minutes

- **1 tablespoon olive oil**
- **2 teaspoons chopped garlic**
- **2½ pounds butternut squash, peeled and cut into 1-inch chunks (about 5 cups)**
- **¼ to ½ cup chicken broth**
- **1 teaspoon salt**
- **¼ teaspoon freshly ground pepper**
- **¼ cup applesauce**

Heat oil in a 2-quart saucepan for 1 minute over medium-high heat. Add garlic and cook 30 seconds. Stir in squash, chicken broth, salt and pepper. Reduce heat to medium, cover and cook 20 minutes, until squash is tender. Stir in applesauce and cook 2 to 3 minutes more. Makes 4 to 6 servings.

Per serving: 125 calories, 3 g total fat, 0.5 g saturated fat, 0 mg cholesterol, 526 mg sodium, 25 g carbohydrates, 2 g protein, 95 mg calcium, 4 g fiber

italian white beans

EASY

This savory bean casserole with fresh sage is wonderful with any summer menu. To trim cooking time, use the quick-soak method on the bean package.

Prep time: 15 minutes plus soaking
Baking time: 65 minutes

- **1 pound dried great Northern beans, rinsed**
- **4 tablespoons extra-virgin olive oil, divided**
- **¾ cup finely chopped onion**
- **½ cup finely chopped celery**
- **¼ cup finely chopped carrot**
- **1 tablespoon finely chopped garlic**
- **2 cans (14½ oz. each) chicken broth**
- **2 tablespoons thinly sliced fresh sage leaves or 2 teaspoons dried sage**
- **¾ teaspoon salt**

1. Soak beans according to package directions; drain. Set aside.

2. Heat oven to 350°F. Heat 3 tablespoons of the oil in a heavy, ovenproof Dutch oven over medium heat. Add onion, celery, carrot and garlic. Cook until vegetables are tender. Stir in beans, broth and sage. Bring to boil. Transfer beans in Dutch oven to oven.

3. Cover and bake 55 minutes, until beans are tender. Stir in salt. Bake, uncovered, 10 minutes more. (*Can be made ahead. Refrigerate overnight in airtight container. Bring to room temperature before serving.*) Stir in the remaining 1 tablespoon oil. Makes 8 servings.

Per serving: 275 calories, 8.5 g total fat, 1.5 g saturated fat, 0 mg cholesterol, 672 mg sodium, 38 g carbohydrates, 13 g protein, 111 mg calcium, 23 g fiber

---

m e n u

autumn harvest dinner

CARROT AND SWEET POTATO SOUP WITH APPLES
page 118

PAN-GRILLED PEPPER STEAK
page 134

BRUSSELS SPROUTS WITH PANCETTA AND PARMESAN
page 120

GINGER RICE
page 150

BOSTON CREAM PIE
page 240

pancetta

A highly flavorful Italian bacon cured with salt, spices and garlic, pancetta is made from the same cut of pork as bacon. Unlike bacon, however, it is not smoked.

Pancetta comes rolled up, shaped like a log, and is primarily used in sauces, soups and, of course, Italian dishes such as pasta. If not available in the supermarket, pancetta can be found in butcher shops and specialty food stores. Keep it well wrapped in the refrigerator up to 3 weeks, or in a heavy-duty plastic storage bag in the freezer for up to 6 months.

brussels sprouts with pancetta and parmesan EASY

Give Brussels sprouts another chance. They're absolutely amazing here—skillet-cooked with pancetta, garlic, chicken broth, cream and Parmesan cheese.

Prep time: 20 minutes • Cooking time: 11 to 15 minutes

- 2 ounces sliced pancetta (Italian bacon) or 3 slices bacon, diced
- 1 clove garlic, minced
- 2 containers (10 oz. each) fresh Brussels sprouts, trimmed and cut into ¼-inch lengthwise slices
- ¾ cup chicken broth
- ⅛ teaspoon salt
- ⅛ teaspoon freshly ground pepper
- ¼ cup heavy or whipping cream
- ¼ cup freshly shredded Parmesan cheese

1. Cook pancetta in a 12-inch nonstick skillet over medium heat 6 to 8 minutes, until crisp (6 minutes for bacon). With a slotted spoon, transfer to a plate.

2. Add garlic to drippings in skillet and cook and stir 1 minute, until golden. Add Brussels sprouts,

broth, salt and pepper. Bring to boil. Reduce heat to medium-high; cook 5 to 7 minutes, until Brussels sprouts are just tender-crisp.

3. Stir in cream and cook 1 minute more. Remove skillet from heat. Stir in pancetta and Parmesan. Makes 6 servings.

Per serving: 115 calories, 7 g total fat, 3.5 g saturated fat, 20 mg cholesterol, 329 mg sodium, 9 g carbohydrates, 6 g protein, 105 mg calcium, 4 g fiber

winter vegetable combo LOW FAT EASY

Packed with fresh butternut squash, Brussels sprouts and mushrooms, this dish makes a terrific meatless meal served with rice and tossed salad greens. Or serve it as a healthy side with broiled chicken breasts.

Prep time: 15 minutes • Cooking time: 10 to12 minutes

- 2 tablespoons butter or margarine
- 2 containers (10 oz. each) fresh Brussels sprouts, trimmed and halved
- ¼ pound cremini or white mushrooms, quartered
- ¼ pound peeled butternut squash, cut into ½-inch cubes (about 1 cup)
- 2 shallots, sliced
- 1 Granny Smith apple, peeled, cored and diced
- ½ cup chicken broth
- ½ cup apple cider
- 2 teaspoons chopped fresh sage or ½ teaspoon dried sage
- ½ teaspoon salt
- ⅛ teaspoon freshly ground pepper

Melt butter in a 12-inch skillet over medium-high heat. Add Brussels sprouts, mushrooms, squash and shallots. Cook 5 to 6 minutes, stirring frequently, until brown. Stir in apple, broth, cider, sage, salt and pepper. Cook 5 to 6 minutes more, until vegetables are tender. Makes 6 servings.

Per serving: 122 calories, 5 g total fat, 3 g saturated fat, 11 mg cholesterol, 327 mg sodium, 18 g carbohydrates, 5 g protein, 57 mg calcium, 5 g fiber

CHILI-COATED
PORK
TENDERLOIN
PG. 143

gathering for good times

PORCINI RACK OF
LAMB
PG. 140
CREAMY CHIVE
POTATO CAKES
PG. 150
FRENCH BEANS IN
SHALLOT BUTTER
PG. 151

From ringing in the New Year with rack of lamb to watching the game with a bowl o' red, if there's fun to be had, great food is part of the plan. Whatever the occasion, plan your menu here and count on a great time.

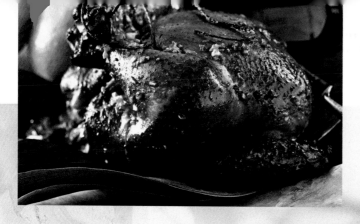

TEA-ROASTED
CHICKEN
PG. 130

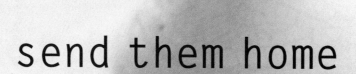

SPICED FRUIT
COMPOTE
PG. 155

send them home full...

BARBECUED
GLAZED HAM
PG. 144

HONEY-PEANUT
CHEESECAKE
PG. 156

TEXAS-STYLE
CHILI
PG. 139

of food and fun!

here's what to eat when you wear your little black dress

STRIPED BASS
AND RISOTTO
IN SPICE BROTH
PG. 145

PAN-GRILLED
PEPPER STEAK
PG. 134

LENTIL AND
ORZO SALAD
PG. 153

or your favorite
flannel shirt

BBQ BEEF
BRISKET
PG. 138

open-air
dining

MARINATED
GRILLED STEAK
PG. 135
FRESH SUGAR
SNAPS AND
ASPARAGUS
PG. 151
COUSCOUS
SALAD
PG. 154

GIANT LIME
SUGAR COOKIES
PG. 158
STRAWBERRY-RHUBARB
CRUMBLE
PG. 157

makes setting the scene a breeze

our ice cream is very social

CONFETTI
ICE-CREAM
TOWER CAKES
PG. 158

ICE CREAM
SANDWICHES
PG. 160

fava bean dip

This delicious spread is best served with toast or pita triangles and/or a variety of crackers. The season for fresh fava beans is brief—usually only from April through June. If you can't find them, frozen baby lima beans work, too.

Prep time: 30 minutes • Cooking time: 30 to 35 minutes

- **3** pounds fresh fava beans or 1 pound frozen baby lima beans, thawed*
- Extra-virgin olive oil (about ¾ cup)
- **2** cloves garlic, finely chopped
- **¼** teaspoon salt
- **¼** bay leaf
- **1** sprig fresh thyme
- **1** small sprig fresh rosemary
- **⅛** teaspoon freshly ground pepper
- **½** to 1 teaspoon fresh lemon juice

1. Bring a stockpot filled two-thirds with water to boil. Fill a large bowl with ice water. Meanwhile, remove fava beans from pods and discard pods. Add beans to boiling water and cook 1 minute. Drain beans in a colander, then immediately transfer to ice water until cold. Drain beans. Skin beans by piercing outer skin of bean with a thumbnail and with a slight squeeze of thumb and forefinger, pop out bright green bean inside.

2. Heat ½ cup of the oil over medium-low heat in a large non-aluminum skillet. Add beans, 2 tablespoons water, garlic, salt, bay leaf, thyme and rosemary. Cook beans at a slow simmer, stirring frequently for 25 to 30 minutes, until very tender. Add 1 to 2 tablespoons more water if necessary to prevent sticking. Discard bay leaf and herb sprigs from skillet; transfer mixture to a food processor. Puree beans until smooth, and with machine running, drizzle in 1 to 4 tablespoons of the remaining oil, the pepper, lemon juice and 2 to 3 tablespoons water, 1 tablespoon at a time, through feed tube, until the mixture is smooth and thick, but not stiff. Makes 1¾ cups

*Note: For frozen lima beans, prepare recipe as directed, except cook beans in boiling water 4 minutes; drain, add to ice water and drain again.

Per tablespoon: 75 calories, 6 g total fat, 1 g saturated fat, 0 mg cholesterol, 28 mg sodium, 4 g carbohydrates, 1 g protein, 5 mg calcium, 1 g fiber

scallop seviche

A classic Latin American appetizer, "seviche" (seh-VEE-che) is raw fish marinated in citrus juice (usually lime). The acid in the lime juice "cooks" the fish until firm and opaque. It's important to use only the freshest sea scallops for optimal results. This salsa-style appetizer is a super starter for outdoor gatherings.

Total prep time: 35 minutes plus chilling

- **½** pound sea scallops
- **1** cup fresh lime juice
- **1** navel orange
- **½** cup finely diced tomato
- **½** avocado, peeled, pitted and finely diced
- **¼** cup finely diced yellow bell pepper
- **1** jalapeño chile, seeded and minced (see tip, page 15)
- **2** tablespoons finely diced red onion
- **2** tablespoons chopped fresh cilantro
- **1** tablespoon olive oil
- **½** teaspoon salt
- **¼** teaspoon sugar
- Tortilla chips (optional)

1. Remove muscle from side of scallops; rinse and pat dry. Cut scallops into ¼-inch dice; combine with lime juice in a small bowl. Cover and refrigerate 5 hours, stirring occasionally, until scallops are opaque and "cooked through" by the lime juice.

2. With a small, sharp paring knife, remove peel and white pith from orange. To section, hold fruit in one hand over a bowl to catch the juice. Slice along one membrane to the center. Repeat on the other side of the section. Remove remaining sections this way. Cut sections into small pieces; transfer to bowl with orange juice.

3. Drain scallops; discard lime juice. Rinse scallops and pat dry. Add scallops, tomato, avocado, bell pepper, jalapeño, onion, cilantro, oil, salt and sugar to bowl with orange. Stir to combine. Serve with tortilla chips, if desired. Makes 6 servings.

Per serving: 80 calories, 4 g total fat, 0.5 g saturated fat, 12 mg cholesterol, 359 mg sodium, 5 g carbohydrates, 7 g protein, 19 mg calcium, 1 g fiber

tea-roasted chicken

Smoking the bird over a mixture of green tea leaves, rice and sugar before roasting it results in an ultra-moist chicken with crisp, mahogany skin. Save time the day of your party by marinating the chicken the night before and refrigerating it overnight. Pictured on page 122.

Prep time: 30 minutes plus marinating and standing
Cooking time: 50 to 59 minutes

- **2 teaspoons kosher salt**
- **1 teaspoon Sichuan peppercorns, crushed (see tips, pages 16 and 17)**
- **1 whole small chicken (about 2¾ lbs.)**
- **½ cup loose green tea leaves**
- **½ cup sugar**
- **½ cup uncooked white rice**
- **2 tablespoons soy sauce**
- **2 tablespoons rice vinegar**
- **1 tablespoon chopped shallots**
- **1 tablespoon peanut or vegetable oil**
- **Pinch sugar**

1. Combine salt and peppercorns in a cup; rub mixture over entire chicken. Cover and marinate in the refrigerator 1 hour. *(Can be made ahead. Refrigerate overnight.)* Remove chicken and let stand at room temperature 30 minutes.

2. Meanwhile, line a large, heavy-bottomed Dutch oven with 2 layers of heavy-duty foil, leaving a 2-inch overhang. Spread tea leaves, ½ cup sugar and rice on bottom of Dutch oven. Arrange a small wire rack over tea mixture. Fit 4 wooden chopsticks in a tic-tac-toe pattern over rack, breaking them if necessary to fit in the pan. Place chicken on top of chopsticks. (The chopsticks keep the chicken from sitting directly on the tea mixture and help air circulate in the Dutch oven.)

3. Cover top of Dutch oven with another sheet of foil, then a heavy lid. Cook tea mixture over high heat until smoke begins to form, 10 to 14 minutes. Reduce heat to medium and cook 10 minutes more. Remove from heat; let chicken stand covered 10 minutes. (This allows the smoke to penetrate the chicken.) Uncover and carefully transfer chicken to a roasting pan.

4. Meanwhile, heat oven to 375°F. Whisk together soy sauce, vinegar, shallots, oil and pinch sugar in a bowl. Brush half of the soy mixture on chicken. Roast chicken 15 minutes; brush with remaining soy mixture. Roast 15 to 20 minutes more, or until an instant-read thermometer inserted in thigh registers 180°F. Let stand 5 minutes before slicing. Makes 4 servings.

Per serving: 365 calories, 22 g total fat, 6 g saturated fat, 121 mg cholesterol, 1,390 mg sodium, 1 g carbohydrates, 38 g protein, 28 mg calcium, 0 g fiber

barbecued beer chicken

If you're serving a larger crowd, stretch the menu by grilling an assortment of hot or sweet Italian sausages over the hot coals after the chicken is done. This not only allows you to feed more guests, it also rounds out the meal by adding a variety of savory flavors. Pictured on page 127.

Prep time: 20 minutes plus standing
Grilling time: 60 to 70 minutes

- **2 cups hickory or apple wood chips**
- **4 cans (12 oz. each) beer**

SPICE RUB:
- **3 tablespoons paprika**
- **2 tablespoons onion powder**
- **1 tablespoon cumin**
- **1 tablespoon salt**
- **¾ teaspoon ground red pepper**
- **1½ teaspoons white pepper**
- **1½ teaspoons sugar**

- **3 whole small chickens (3 to 3¼ lbs. each), rinsed and patted dry**
- **Grilled hot or sweet Italian sausages (optional)**

1. Combine wood chips and 1 can of beer in a small foil pan. Let stand 1 hour.

2. *Make spice rub:* Meanwhile, combine all spice rub ingredients in a small bowl. Divide and sprinkle 1 tablespoon of the rub into the cavity of each chicken. Sprinkle remaining rub evenly over surface of chickens. *(Can be made ahead. Place each chicken in a large plastic storage bag, seal and refrigerate overnight.)* Rinse exterior of 3 beer cans; open cans and stand on a work surface with chicken. Punch 2 additional holes in the top of each can. Holding each chicken upright, place it over the can so that the can goes into main cavity. Pull chicken legs forward to form a sort of tripod, allowing the chicken to sit upright over can.

3. Prepare grill for indirect grilling. *For gas:* Drain wood chips; place chips in a small foil pan in front left-hand corner of the grill. Add $\frac{1}{2}$ cup water. Place a large disposable foil pan in center of bottom grate. Add 2 cups water. Replace top cooking grate. Close lid and heat burners on medium, 10 to 15 minutes. To grill, adjust burner controls. Be sure to position chickens in center of grill and turn off heat source directly under the chicken. (For a triple-burner grill, turn off center burner.) Cover and grill 60 to 70 minutes (reduce heat if necessary to maintain heat at 350°F.), until an instant-read thermometer inserted in thigh registers 180°F. *For charcoal briquettes:* Open all vents. Build two equal piles of briquettes (30 to 50 total, depending on the size of the grill) opposite each other on bottom grate near the grate's edge. Ignite and burn briquettes 25 to 30 minutes, until coals are covered with a light coating of gray ash. *(If one side seems hotter than the other, use long-handled tongs to rearrange coals.)* Place a disposable foil drip pan in center of bottom grate. Add 2 cups water. Replace top cooking grate. Transfer chickens to center of grill over drip pan. Drain wood chips and add 1 cup chips to top of each pile of hot briquettes. Cover and grill 60 to 70 minutes, until an instant-read thermometer inserted in thigh registers 180°F.

4. Carefully remove chickens and cans from grill. Insert a large fork into the neck of each chicken and lift the chickens, holding each can with an oven mitt to remove from chicken. Transfer to platter. Serve with grilled Italian sausages, if desired. Makes 8 servings.

Per serving: 585 calories, 32.5 g total fat, 9 g saturated fat, 207 mg cholesterol, 1,068 mg sodium, 5 g carbohydrates, 65 g protein, 55 mg calcium, 0 g fiber

chicken picante

"Picante" is a Spanish term meaning spicy hot. In this recipe, we call for prepared (store-bought) picante sauce to cut down on prep time. Once the chicken cutlets are skillet-cooked, all you need to do is stir up the chopped shallot and garlic, add the curry, picante sauce plus broth, and presto—you're good to go. This is the right dish for a casual get-together with close friends or family. Double the recipe if you're serving more than four, or if you just want to enjoy leftovers.

Prep time: 25 minutes • Baking time: 8 to 9 minutes

- ½ teaspoon salt
- ⅛ teaspoon freshly ground pepper
- 4 boneless, skinless chicken cutlets (6 to 7 oz. each)
- 1 tablespoon plus 1 teaspoon olive oil, divided
- ¼ cup finely chopped shallots
- 2 teaspoons finely chopped garlic
- 1 teaspoon curry powder
- 1 tablespoon prepared picante sauce
- 1 cup chicken broth
- 1 teaspoon finely chopped fresh parsley

1. Heat oven to 350°F. Sprinkle salt and pepper evenly over chicken.

2. Heat 1 tablespoon of the oil in a large nonstick skillet over medium-high heat; add chicken and brown 3 minutes per side. Transfer chicken to a jelly-roll pan or cookie sheet; bake 8 to 9 minutes until an instant-read thermometer inserted into thickest part of breast registers 170°F.

3. Meanwhile, heat the remaining 1 teaspoon oil over medium-high heat in same skillet. Add shallots and garlic; cook 1 minute, stirring. Add curry and cook 10 to 20 seconds. Add picante sauce and broth; bring to boil and cook 1 to 2 minutes more, until slightly reduced. Pour over chicken and sprinkle with parsley. Makes 4 servings.

Per serving: 265 calories, 7 g total fat, 1.5 g saturated fat, 107 mg cholesterol, 670 mg sodium, 4 g carbohydrates, 44 g protein, 33 mg calcium, 0 g fiber

chicken with red and yellow cherry tomatoes

Fresh tarragon and colorful cherry tomatoes pair up for this simply delicious chicken fix, perfect for a casual or last-minute gathering.

Prep time: 25 minutes • Baking time: 8 to 9 minutes

- ½ teaspoon salt
- ⅛ teaspoon freshly ground pepper
- 4 boneless, skinless chicken cutlets (6 to 7 oz. each)
- 1 tablespoon olive oil

TOMATO TOPPING:
- 1 tablespoon butter or margarine
- ½ pint red cherry tomatoes
- ½ pint yellow cherry tomatoes
- 2 tablespoons water
- 1 tablespoon white wine vinegar
- 1 tablespoon plus 2 teaspoons chopped fresh tarragon or 1 tablespoon plus 2 teaspoons chopped fresh parsley and ½ teaspoon dried tarragon, divided
- ¼ teaspoon salt
- ⅛ teaspoon freshly ground pepper

1. Heat oven to 350°F. Sprinkle salt and pepper evenly over chicken. Heat oil in a large nonstick skillet over medium-high heat; add chicken and brown 3 minutes per side. Transfer chicken to a jelly-roll pan or cookie sheet; bake 8 to 9 minutes, until an instant-read thermometer inserted into thickest part of breast registers 170°F.

2. *Make tomato topping:* Meanwhile, melt butter with tomatoes over medium-high heat. Add water, vinegar, 1 tablespoon of the tarragon (or 1 tablespoon of the parsley and dried tarragon), salt and pepper; cook 3 to 4 minutes, stirring occasionally, until tomatoes begin to break open. Pour tomato topping over chicken and sprinkle with the remaining 2 teaspoons tarragon or parsley. Makes 4 servings.

Per serving: 280 calories, 9 g total fat, 3 g saturated fat, 115 mg cholesterol, 573 mg sodium, 5 g carbohydrates, 43 g protein, 29 mg calcium, 1 g fiber

stuffed turkey breast

Easy, impressive company fare doesn't have to be a budget or fat buster if you serve this festive turkey breast. It's stuffed with creamy polenta and greens, and served with plenty of rich-tasting mushroom gravy.

Prep time: 40 minutes
Baking time: 1 hour 15 to 25 minutes
Microwave used

1	**whole boneless turkey breast with skin (5 to 5½ lbs.)**
1	**large bunch (1½ lb.) escarole, leaves separated**
1	**tablespoon olive oil**
1	**medium onion, chopped**
2	**cans (14½ oz. each) chicken broth, divided**
1	**teaspoon chopped fresh rosemary or ½ teaspoon dried rosemary**
¾	**teaspoon salt, divided**
½	**teaspoon freshly ground pepper, divided**
¾	**cup instant polenta**
¼	**cup (.3 oz.) dried mushrooms, rinsed well**
	Fresh rosemary sprigs, for garnish (optional)

1. Arrange turkey skin side down on a cutting board. Cut down center of breast to make two turkey breast halves; remove the cartilage in the middle.

2. Lift up tenderloin from each breast half, then holding knife parallel to meat, cut along thicker portion to open meat like a book (it should be an even thickness). Repeat with other breast half.

3. Pile escarole with any water that clings to the leaves in a 12-inch skillet. Add ¼ cup water; cover and cook over medium-high heat 3 to 5 minutes, stirring once halfway through cooking until tender. Drain in a colander. When cool enough to handle, squeeze dry between paper towels.

4. Meanwhile, for polenta mixture, heat oil in a 3-quart saucepan over medium-high heat; add onion and cook 4 minutes, stirring occasionally until golden. Add 1 can of the broth, the rosemary, ¼ teaspoon each of the salt and pepper; bring to boil. Gradually whisk in polenta and cook, stirring, 4 to 5 minutes until thick. Remove from heat and cool slightly, 10 minutes.

5. Heat oven to 350°F. Set aside half of the escarole. Arrange remaining escarole leaves in a single layer over each turkey-breast half. Divide and spread polenta over escarole (it may not cover completely, but that's okay). Top with remaining escarole over polenta mixture on each turkey-breast half. Starting at one long side, roll up each breast-half, jelly-roll fashion, to enclose filling. Tie with string at 1½-inch intervals. Tuck ends under and use skewers or toothpicks to secure.

6. Place turkey on bottom of a broiler pan. Combine remaining ½ teaspoon salt and ¼ teaspoon pepper in a cup; sprinkle seasonings over tops of turkey rolls. Roast 1 hour 15 to 25 minutes until a meat thermometer inserted into thickest part reaches 170°F. Transfer turkey to a cutting board; let stand 10 minutes.

7. Combine remaining 1 can of broth, dried mushrooms and any turkey drippings in a saucepan. Bring mixture to boil; reduce heat and simmer 10 minutes. Remove mushrooms with a slotted spoon; chop finely and set aside. Strain sauce through a strainer lined with a double thickness of cheesecloth into a 2-cup glass measure or a small microwaveproof bowl. Add mushrooms and microwave sauce on HIGH 1 to 2 minutes, until hot.

8. Discard string and skewers and cut turkey into ½-inch-thick slices. Garnish with rosemary, if desired, and serve with sauce. Makes 12 servings.

Per serving: 380 calories, 14 g total fat, 3.5 g saturated fat, 116 mg cholesterol, 556 mg sodium, 17 g carbohydrates, 42 g protein, 60 mg calcium, 3 g fiber

grilled caribbean skewers

Chunks of turkey, beef or lamb all taste great soaked in this marinade, so it's easy to mix and match the meats, if you like. Creating a varied assortment of kebabs also gives your guests a savory selection to choose from. Tip: Prepare the salsa and marinate the meat the night before so that you'll have less to do come party time.

Prep time: 15 minutes plus marinating
Grilling time: 10 to 16 minutes

MARINADE:

- ½ cup brandy
- 2 tablespoons olive oil
- 2 tablespoons brown sugar
- 1 tablespoon fresh lime juice
- 1 tablespoon chopped fresh mint
- 1 tablespoon minced garlic
- 1 teaspoon grated fresh ginger
- 1 teaspoon salt
- ½ teaspoon freshly ground pepper
  ▪
- ½ (3 lbs.) turkey breast, boned, skinned and cut into 1½-inch cubes, or 2 pounds trimmed boneless beef (sirloin, top round or chuck) or boneless leg of lamb, cut into 1½-inch cubes

PINEAPPLE-MINT SALSA:

- 1 tablespoon vegetable oil
- 3 tablespoons minced shallots
- 1 can (20 oz.) crushed pineapple in juice, drained
- ¼ cup sugar
- ¼ teaspoon salt
- ¼ cup brandy
- 1 tablespoon fresh mint leaves
  ▪
  Lemon wedges and fresh mint sprigs, for garnish (optional)

1. *Make marinade:* Combine all marinade ingredients in a glass measure; pour into a resealable heavy-duty plastic storage bag. Add turkey, beef or lamb; seal bag and press bag against meat to coat meat with marinade. Marinate in the refrigerator 3 hours. *(Can be made ahead. Refrigerate up to 24 hours.)*

2. *Make pineapple-mint salsa:* Meanwhile, heat oil in a small saucepan over medium heat. Add shallots and cook 1 minute, until softened. Add pineapple, sugar and salt; bring to boil. Boil 2 minutes, stirring occasionally. Add brandy; cook 30 seconds. Remove from heat; cool completely. Chop mint and stir into salsa. *(Can be made ahead. Refrigerate in airtight container overnight.)* Makes 2 cups.

3. Heat grill. Skewer 4 to 5 pieces of the turkey or meat on each of 8 metal skewers. Grill over medium-high heat, 12 to 16 minutes for turkey until cooked through, or 10 to 12 minutes for medium-rare beef or lamb. Serve with pineapple-mint salsa. Garnish with lemon wedges and mint sprigs, if desired. Makes 8 servings.

Per serving with turkey and 1 tablespoon salsa: 195 calories, 3 g total fat, 0.5 g saturated fat, 83 mg cholesterol, 230 mg sodium, 7 g carbohydrates, 33 g protein, 20 mg calcium, 0 g fiber
Per serving with beef and 1 tablespoon salsa: 205 calories, 8.5 g total fat, 2.5 g saturated fat, 76 mg cholesterol, 220 mg sodium, 7 g carbohydrates, 26 g protein, 16 mg calcium, 0 g fiber
Per serving with lamb and 1 tablespoon salsa: 210 calories, 9 g total fat, 2.5 g saturated fat, 76 mg cholesterol, 222 mg sodium, 7 g carbohydrates, 24 g protein, 14 mg calcium, 0 g fiber

pan-grilled pepper steak

For quick company fare, grilled flank steak always does the trick—and this juicy beauty needs little adornment. It couldn't be simpler, calling for just a jar of mixed whole peppercorns (black, green, red and white). Partner it with the Roasted Vegetable Salad (see recipe, page 152), drizzling some of the dressing over the steak, if you like. Pictured on page 124.

Prep time: 5 minutes • Grilling time: 10 to 14 minutes

- 1 tablespoon mixed whole peppercorns or black peppercorns, crushed
- ¾ teaspoon salt
- 1½ pounds beef flank steak

1. Oil a large grill pan or heavy skillet; heat over high heat until smoking, 5 minutes.

2. Combine peppercorns and salt; rub over both sides of steak. Grill steak 5 to 7 minutes per side for medium-rare. Makes 4 to 6 servings.

Per serving: 230 calories, 12.5 g total fat, 5.5 g saturated fat, 68 mg cholesterol, 430 mg sodium, 1 g carbohydrates, 27 g protein, 13 mg calcium, 0 g fiber

marinated grilled steak (EASY)

Here's an all-time favorite crowd pleaser: quality top-round steak marinated in chopped garlic, olive oil, balsamic and sherry vinegars, salt, pepper and freshly sliced basil. Marinate the steak overnight, if desired, and serve it with grilled corn on the cob and fresh-from-the-garden sliced tomatoes or potato and macaroni salad. For yet another cookout idea, see the menu at right. Pictured on page 126.

Prep time: 15 minutes plus marinating and standing
Grilling time: 14 to 17 minutes

- **5 large cloves garlic, chopped**
- **3 tablespoons olive oil**
- **2 tablespoons balsamic vinegar**
- **2 tablespoons sherry vinegar**
- **¾ teaspoon salt**
- **½ teaspoon freshly ground pepper**
- **½ cup thinly sliced fresh basil leaves**
- **1 (2-lb.) beef top round steak (about 1½ inches thick)**
- **Fresh parsley sprigs, for garnish (optional)**

1. Combine all ingredients except steak and parsley garnish in a shallow baking dish. Add steak and turn several times. Cover and marinate in the refrigerator 30 minutes. *(Can be made ahead. Refrigerate, turning meat occasionally, overnight.)*

2. Heat grill. Turn steak and let stand at room temperature 30 minutes.

3. Remove steak from marinade, letting excess marinade and garlic drip back into pan. (Do not discard marinade.) Grill steak over medium heat 6 minutes, turn and brush with some of marinade and pieces of garlic. Grill 5 minutes. Turn steak again and grill 3 to 6 minutes more, until an

instant-read thermometer registers 135°F. when inserted in center of steak for medium-rare. Transfer steak to a cutting board and let stand 5 minutes before slicing. (Temperature of meat should rise upon standing.) Garnish with parsley sprigs, if desired. Makes 8 servings.

Per serving: 230 calories, 13 g total fat, 3.5 g saturated fat, 69 mg cholesterol, 268 mg sodium, 1 g carbohydrates, 25 g protein, 19 mg calcium, 0 g fiber

---

m e n u

late-summer cookout

ROASTED TOMATO AND BASIL SALSA
page 13

FOCACCIA

ARUGULA PESTO DIP WITH CRUDITÉS
page 12

POTTED SHRIMP
page 12

MARINATED GRILLED STEAK
left

FRESH SUGAR SNAPS AND ASPARAGUS
page 151

COUSCOUS SALAD
page 154

LEMONADE FRUIT SALAD
page 160

ICE CREAM SANDWICHES
page 160

grilled steak and shrimp kebabs with vegetables and green sauce

This surf-and-turf special is accompanied by an array of colorful vegetables, roasted potatoes and grilled bread. The steak, shrimp and veggies are skewered for easy grilling and served with a zesty fresh herb-shallot sauce. Assemble the skewers a day ahead, and use the food processor to whip up the green sauce in seconds.

Prep time: 1 hour plus standing
Grilling time: 30 to 35 minutes

GREEN SAUCE:

3	ounces shallots, cut up (²⁄₃ cup)
¼	cup white wine vinegar
1	cup fresh parsley leaves
2	jars (3 oz. each) capers, drained
1	can (2 oz.) flat anchovy fillets, drained
2	teaspoons fresh thyme leaves or ½ teaspoon dried thyme
1	teaspoon salt
1	teaspoon freshly ground pepper
²⁄₃	cup extra-virgin olive oil

3	pounds small red potatoes, scrubbed
½	teaspoon plus ⅓ cup extra-virgin olive oil
1¼	teaspoons salt, divided
3	pounds boneless beef sirloin, cut into 1½-inch cubes
1½	pounds medium shrimp, peeled and deveined
2	pints cherry tomatoes
16	large white mushrooms
4	medium zucchini, cut diagonally into ½-inch slices
½	teaspoon freshly ground pepper
1	teaspoon fresh thyme leaves or ¼ teaspoon dried thyme
1	loaf focaccia bread, sliced

1. *Make green sauce:* Chop shallots in a food processor; transfer to a small bowl and stir in vinegar. Process remaining sauce ingredients, except oil, until finely chopped. Add to shallot mixture. Stir in oil. *(Can be made ahead. Cover and refrigerate up to 24 hours.)* Makes 2 cups.

2. Soak 3 dozen 12-inch wooden skewers in water to cover 1 hour.

3. Meanwhile, heat oven to 400°F. Combine potatoes, the ½ teaspoon oil and ¼ teaspoon of the salt in a 13×9-inch baking pan. Cover with foil and bake 40 to 60 minutes, until potatoes are tender when pierced with a fork. Cool. *(Can be made ahead. Cover and refrigerate up to 8 hours. Remove from refrigerator 30 minutes before grilling.)*

4. Heat grill. Loosely thread beef on 9 to 10 skewers. Loosely thread shrimp on 10 more skewers. Thread tomatoes, mushrooms and zucchini slices on remaining skewers, using only one type of vegetable per skewer.

5. Combine remaining ⅓ cup oil, 1 teaspoon of the salt, the pepper and thyme in a small bowl. Brush over beef, shrimp and vegetables.

6. Arrange potatoes around edge of grill. Meanwhile, grill mushrooms and zucchini over medium-hot heat until browned and cooked through, 5 to 7 minutes per side. Transfer to a serving platter. Grill tomatoes just until charred, 1 to 2 minutes; add to platter.

7. Grill shrimp 3 minutes per side until firm and opaque. Grill beef 5 minutes per side for medium-rare. Transfer shrimp and beef to platter; cover and keep warm.

8. Grill focaccia until lightly browned and crisped on both sides, 1 to 2 minutes. Place on serving platter with grilled vegetables, potatoes, beef and shrimp. Serve with green sauce. Makes 8 servings.

Per serving: 770 calories, 36.5 g total fat, 8 g saturated fat, 164 mg cholesterol, 1,563 mg sodium, 67 g carbohydrates, 45 g protein, 160 mg calcium, 8 g fiber

beef tenderloin with chipotle and cilantro sauces

Elegant and easy to carve, tenderloin of beef is a great cut for entertaining. This succulent roast is rubbed with a zesty spice mixture of dried chile, cumin and oregano and served with two equally luscious cream sauces—one red, one green.

Prep time: 15 minutes
Cooking time: 45 to 50 minutes plus standing

CHILE RUB:
- 2   tablespoons cumin seeds
- 1   ancho chile* (¾ oz.), seeded and chopped (see tip, page 15)
- 1   tablespoon freshly ground pepper
- 1   tablespoon salt
- 2   tablespoons dried oregano
- ▪
- 1   tablespoon vegetable oil
- 1   beef tenderloin (5 lbs.), trimmed and tied
       Chipotle and Cilantro Sauces (recipes right)

1. ▪ *Make chile rub:* Toast cumin seeds in a small skillet over medium heat, stirring occasionally, until fragrant, 2 to 3 minutes. Grind with remaining spices to a fine powder in a blender.

2. ▪ Heat oven to 450°F. Rub oil over tenderloin, then coat with chile rub. Roast tenderloin in a shallow roasting pan 45 to 50 minutes, until meat thermometer inserted in center registers 145°F. for medium. Cover and let stand 10 minutes before slicing. Serve with chipotle and cilantro sauces. Makes 10 servings.

*Note: Can be found in ethnic sections of supermarkets or in Spanish or Latino specialty stores.

Per 3 oz. serving without sauce: 220 calories, 12 g total fat, 4 g saturated fat, 75 mg cholesterol, 528 mg sodium, 2 g carbohydrates, 25 g protein, 43 mg calcium, 1 g fiber

chipotle and cilantro sauces EASY

Easy-to-prepare Mexican crema is the base for these festive sauces—perfect with the beef tenderloin recipe at left.

Total prep time: 20 minutes plus standing

MEXICAN CREMA:
- 3   cups heavy or whipping cream
- 3   tablespoons buttermilk
- ▪
- 2   canned chipotle chiles in adobo, seeded and minced* (see tip, page 15)
- 2   large bunches (5 oz.) fresh cilantro, stems removed and leaves chopped
- ½   teaspoon salt

1. ▪ *Make Mexican crema:* Combine cream and buttermilk in a glass pitcher; stir to blend. Cover and let stand at room temperature overnight to thicken. *(Can be made ahead. Cover and refrigerate up to 1 week.)*

2. ▪ *Make chipotle sauce:* Puree chipotle in food processor. Add ½ cup of the crema and process just until blended. Transfer to a small bowl; stir in 1 cup of the crema. Makes 1½ cups.

3. ▪ *Make cilantro sauce:* Puree cilantro in a food processor. Add ½ cup of the crema and the ½ teaspoon salt and process just until blended. Transfer to a small bowl; stir in 1 cup of the crema. Makes 2 cups. *(Can be made ahead. Cover and refrigerate sauces up to 3 days.)*

*Note: Can be found in ethnic sections of supermarkets or in Spanish or Latino specialty stores.

Per 2 tablespoons chipotle sauce: 105 calories, 11 g total fat, 7 g saturated fat, 41 mg cholesterol, 39 mg sodium, 1 g carbohydrates, 1 g protein, 23 mg calcium, 0 g fiber
Per 2 tablespoons cilantro sauce: 80 calories, 8.5 g total fat, 5 g saturated fat, 31 mg cholesterol, 87 mg sodium, 1 g carbohydrates, 1 g protein, 22 mg calcium, 0 g fiber

bbq beef brisket

This impressive barbecue brisket is a great dish to serve company, and it won't bust your budget. The meat is baked, refrigerated overnight and heated on the grill. Pictured on page 125.

Prep time: 25 minutes plus chilling
Cooking time: 3 hours 45 to 50 minutes
Microwave used

- ¼ cup firmly packed brown sugar
- 2 tablespoons cider vinegar
- 1 tablespoon chopped garlic
- 1 tablespoon coriander
- 1 tablespoon ginger
- 1 teaspoon salt
- 1 teaspoon Dijon mustard
- ½ teaspoon freshly ground pepper
- 1 beef brisket (5½ to 6 lbs.), flat half, boneless
- 1 pound onions, cut into ½-inch-thick wedges
- 1 can (32 oz.) tomatoes in juice, drained and chopped
- ½ bunch fresh thyme sprigs or 1 teaspoon dried thyme, divided
- 1 3-inch strip orange peel
- ¼ cup ketchup
- 1 chipotle chile in adobo, plus 1 tablespoon adobo sauce* (see tip, page 15)
- 1 tablespoon soy sauce
  Fresh thyme sprigs, for garnish (optional)
  Cooked carrots (optional)

1. *Make brisket:* Heat oven to 350°F. Combine brown sugar and next 7 ingredients in a small bowl; rub mixture over both sides of beef.

2. Arrange onions, tomatoes, half of the thyme sprigs (or ½ teaspoon of the dried thyme, if using) and orange peel on bottom of roasting pan. Arrange beef on top. Place remaining thyme sprigs or dried thyme on top of beef.

3. Cover pan tightly with foil. Bake until tender, about 3 hours. Carefully remove foil. Cool in pan about 15 minutes. Discard thyme sprigs and orange peel. Wrap brisket in foil. Transfer drippings and vegetables to an airtight container. Refrigerate both overnight. *(Can be made ahead. Refrigerate up to 2 days.)*

4. Prepare grill for indirect grilling. *For gas:* Place a large disposable foil pan in center of bottom grate. Replace top cooking grate. Close lid and heat burners on high (500°F. to 550°F.) 10 to 15 minutes. To grill, adjust burner controls. Be sure to position brisket in center of grill and turn off heat source directly under the beef. *(For triple-burner grill, turn off center burner.)* Reduce heat to low on remaining burners. *For charcoal briquettes:* Open all vents. Build two equal piles of briquettes (16 to 30 total, depending on the size of the grill) opposite each other on bottom grate near the grate's edge. Ignite and burn briquettes 25 to 30 minutes, until coals are covered with a light coating of gray ash. *(If one side seems hotter than the other, use long-handled tongs to rearrange coals.)* Place a disposable foil drip pan in center of bottom grate. Position top cooking grate with handles over coals so that additional coals can be added through side openings.

5. Meanwhile, discard any fat from the brisket and drippings. Let brisket stand at room temperature 30 minutes. Puree drippings and vegetables, ketchup, chipotle chile, adobo sauce and soy sauce in a blender (makes 3½ to 4 cups). Set aside 1 cup of sauce in a small bowl for basting. Transfer remaining sauce to a medium microwaveproof bowl and refrigerate.

6. Place brisket in center of grill over drip pan. Cover and grill 20 minutes. Brush top of brisket with ½ cup of the reserved sauce for basting. Close lid and grill 5 to 7 minutes. Turn meat. Brush top with all of remaining reserved sauce. Close lid and grill 20 to 25 minutes more, until meat is very tender and heated through.

7. Transfer brisket to a cutting board and let stand 5 minutes. Microwave refrigerated sauce on HIGH 45 seconds, or until hot. Thinly slice meat across the grain. Transfer to a serving platter. Serve with sauce and garnish with thyme sprigs and carrots, if desired. Makes 10 to 12 servings.

Note: Can be found in ethnic sections of supermarkets or in Spanish or Latino specialty stores.

Per serving: 640 calories, 52.5 g total fat, 20.5 g saturated fat, 156 mg cholesterol, 580 mg sodium, 13 g carbohydrates, 40 g protein, 46 mg calcium, 1 g fiber

texas-style chili 🍽️ EASY

Friends and family devour ever-popular chili—so why not serve a batch at the next ball game? Pictured on page 123.

Prep time: 40 minutes plus standing
Cooking time: 2 hours 20 to 50 minutes

DRIED CHILE PASTE:

4	to 5 dried ancho or 10 to 12 pasilla chiles (see tip, page 15)
4	large cloves garlic, unpeeled
½	teaspoon dried oregano
½	teaspoon salt
¼	teaspoon cumin
¼	teaspoon freshly ground pepper
¾	cup chicken broth

1¼	teaspoons salt
½	teaspoon freshly ground pepper
1	4-pound boneless beef chuck eye roast, trimmed and cubed
6	teaspoons vegetable oil, divided
2	medium onions, chopped
1	green bell pepper, diced
1	can (14¼ oz.) diced tomatoes
	Sour cream, tortillas and beans (optional)

1. *Make dried chile paste:* Heat a large skillet over medium heat. Toast chiles 2 to 3 minutes, turning once, until fragrant. Cut chiles in half; discard seeds and stems. Combine chiles with hot water to cover in a bowl. Let stand 20 minutes, until softened. Toast garlic in skillet over medium heat, turning, until skin is blackened on all sides, 15 minutes. Remove skins and discard. Drain chiles. Puree chiles, garlic, oregano, salt, cumin, pepper, and chicken broth in a blender. *(Can be made ahead. Cover and refrigerate up to 2 weeks.)* Makes 1 cup.

2. Combine salt and pepper in a large bowl. Add cubed beef and toss to coat. Heat 2 teaspoons of the oil in a large Dutch oven. Add one-third of the beef and cook 4 to 5 minutes, until browned. Transfer to another bowl. Repeat process two more times, adding 2 teaspoons of the oil for each batch.

3. Add onions to drippings in skillet and cook 5 minutes, until softened. Stir in the dried chile

paste, bell pepper, tomatoes and beef. Bring to boil. Reduce heat; cover and simmer 1½ to 2 hours, until beef is tender. Serve with sour cream, tortillas and beans, if desired. Makes 6 to 8 servings.

Per serving: 400 calories, 21 g total fat, 6 g saturated fat, 130 mg cholesterol, 944 mg sodium, 13 g carbohydrates, 41 g protein, 66 mg calcium, 4 g fiber

---

test kitchen tip

fresh and dried chiles

Here's a rundown of some of the fresh and dried chile varieties available:

FRESH CHILES: *Anaheim,* a.k.a. the California or long green chile, has a green vegetable flavor (best roasted); it's one of the milder chiles. The *Güero,* a.k.a. Hungarian wax, yellow or banana chile, has a slightly sweet, intense waxy taste. *Habanero* peppers (also available dried) have a tropical, citrusy flavor and are used in salsas and as pickled chiles; they are the hottest of all. *Jalapeño* chiles have a green vegetable flavor with heat; they're used in salsas, stews and sauces. *Poblano* peppers are often mislabeled as pasilla chiles; they have a bell-pepperish flavor (though never consumed raw) and are smoky when roasted. *Serrano* chiles have a crisp, pronounced flavor and are one of the hotter peppers; mainly used in salsas; and are pickled and roasted for sauces.

DRIED CHILES: *Ancho* chiles (often mislabeled as a pasilla) are dried poblanos with a sweet, rich, earthy and fruity flavor; they're used in sauces and moles. *Chipotle* chiles (dried, smoked jalapeños), a.k.a. chile ahumado or chile meco, have a smoky sweet flavor and are available canned in adobo sauce. *Guajillo,* a.k.a. Mirasol, has a spicy, tangy, slightly smoky flavor; one of the hotter chiles. *New Mexico Red,* a.k.a. chile colorado and dried California chile, have an earthy flavor. *Pasilla,* a.k.a. chile negro, has a complex flavor with berry and herbaceous tones.

porcini rack of lamb

No matter how you slice it (and whether you choose racks of lamb or venison, or a beef tenderloin), this is an elegant and quite decadent dish suitable for your next sit-down dinner party. A coating of dried porcini (pohr-CHEE-nee) mushrooms lends an intense, woodsy flavor to whichever meat you decide upon. Pictured on page 121.

Prep time: 30 minutes • Baking time: 45 to 65 minutes
Microwave used

PORT SAUCE:

- 3 large (4 oz.) unpeeled shallots
- 1½ teaspoons olive oil
- 1¼ cups port wine
- 3 tablespoons butter or margarine, divided
- 2 teaspoons very thinly sliced garlic
- 3 tablespoons flour
- 1 can (14½ oz.) chicken broth
- ¼ cup prepared duck and veal demi-glace*
- 1 teaspoon soy sauce
- ¾ teaspoon salt
- ⅛ teaspoon freshly ground pepper

- 3 packages (.35 oz. each) dried porcini mushrooms
- 1½ teaspoons salt
- 1½ teaspoons freshly ground pepper
- 3 racks of lamb (1¼ to 1¾ lbs. each rack) or 2 racks of venison* (1¾ to 2¼ lbs. each rack), trimmed, or 1 (3½ lbs.) center cut beef tenderloin (see instructions right)

1. *Make port sauce:* Heat oven to 425°F. Toss shallots with oil in a small baking dish. Roast 30 minutes, until tender; cool. Peel and cut away root and stem of each shallot.

2. Meanwhile, microwave port in a 2-cup glass measure on HIGH, 8 to 9 minutes, until reduced to ⅔ cup. Melt 1 tablespoon of the butter in a small saucepan; add garlic and cook 1 minute. Stir in flour and cook 1 minute more, until light golden. Gradually whisk in port, broth, demi-glace, soy sauce, salt and pepper.

3. Stir shallots into port mixture; bring to boil, stirring constantly. Simmer sauce 2 minutes; strain through a fine sieve into a 2-cup measure and discard shallots. *(Can be made ahead. Cool. Cover and refrigerate overnight.)*

4. Process porcini, salt and pepper in batches in a spice grinder or food processor to a powder. *(Can be made ahead. Store in container overnight.)*

5. Arrange oven rack in upper third of oven. Increase oven temperature to 475°F. Sprinkle porcini powder onto all meaty sides of lamb (or venison, if using). Arrange racks on a broiler pan meaty side up and roast 15 to 22 minutes, until instant-read thermometer inserted in center of lamb reaches 130°F. for medium-rare. (For venison, roast 22 to 25 minutes. Thermometer should reach 145°F. to 155°F. for medium.)

6. Transfer racks to a cutting board. Cover loosely and let stand 10 minutes.

7. Meanwhile, microwave port sauce on HIGH until hot, 1½ to 2 minutes. Cut up remaining 2 tablespoons butter and whisk into hot sauce. To carve racks, cut slices between rib bones. Serve with port sauce. Makes 8 servings.

For beef tenderloin: Arrange oven rack in center of oven; heat oven to 425°F. Process *only 1 package (.35 oz.) dried porcini mushrooms, 1 teaspoon salt* and ¾ *teaspoon pepper* to a powder. Rub over all sides of beef. Roast tenderloin 35 minutes, until an instant-read thermometer inserted into center of beef registers between 120°F. and 125°F. Cover tenderloin tightly with foil and let stand 10 minutes before carving. (Temperature will rise to 135°F. to 138°F. for medium-rare.)

Note: Duck and veal demi-glace and racks of venison may be purchased from D'Artagnan, 800-327-8246, or at specialty food stores.

Per serving (lamb): 450 calories, 34 g total fat, 15 g saturated fat, 104 mg cholesterol, 1,073 mg sodium, 12 g carbohydrates, 22 g protein, 34 mg calcium, 1 g fiber
Per serving (venison): 380 calories, 11 g total fat, 5 g saturated fat, 202 mg cholesterol, 1,095 mg sodium, 12 g carbohydrates, 54 g protein, 25 mg calcium, 1 g fiber
Per serving (beef tenderloin): 580 calories, 42.5 g total fat, 17.5 g saturated fat, 136 mg cholesterol, 940 mg sodium, 11 g carbohydrates, 36 g protein, 25 mg calcium, 1 g fiber

test kitchen tip

new year's eve dinner planner

2 WEEKS AHEAD:
- Order meat (lamb, venison or beef).

1 WEEK AHEAD:
- Make and freeze pancakes.
- Purchase nonperishable food.

3 DAYS AHEAD:
- Assemble and freeze Ice-Cream Tower Cakes (except for meringue and Three Sauces).

1 DAY AHEAD:
- Purchase perishable food.
- Prepare port sauce; refrigerate.
- Make porcini powder for meat.
- Make Creamy Chive Potato Cakes; refrigerate. Prepare beans; refrigerate.
- Make meringue and pipe on cakes; freeze.
- Make mango sauce; refrigerate.

4 HOURS BEFORE SERVING:
- Make kiwi and strawberry sauces; refrigerate.

2 HOURS BEFORE SERVING:
- Make crab topping; chill. Thaw pancakes.
- Broil meringue; unmold cakes and freeze.

90 MINUTES BEFORE SERVING:
- Heat cornmeal pancakes; keep oven on.
- Rub meat with porcini powder.

45 MINUTES BEFORE SERVING:
- Begin to roast beef tenderloin, if using.
- Cook shallots for beans

30 MINUTES BEFORE SERVING:
- Begin to roast lamb or venison, if using.
- Heat potato cakes.

JUST BEFORE SERVING:
- Assemble crab on pancakes; carve meat; reheat beans; reheat port sauce.

carolina country pork ribs

For a backyard spring or summer bash, barbecued ribs can't be beat. While they share certain qualities, barbecue sauces from different regions within the Carolinas have their own special distinctions. This one, from western North Carolina, is a typical blend of vinegar, sugar and ground red pepper, with the not-so-ordinary addition of ketchup.

Prep time: 25 minutes plus marinating
Grilling time: 2½ to 3 hours
Microwave used

MARINADE:

- 1   **cup cider vinegar**
- 2   **teaspoons dry mustard**
- ½   **cup water**
- 1   **tablespoon red pepper flakes**
- 1   **tablespoon minced garlic**
- 1   **tablespoon sugar**
- 2   **teaspoons salt**

- 1   **teaspoon freshly ground pepper**
- 1   **teaspoon dried thyme**
  ■
- 6   **pounds pork shoulder country-style ribs**

BARBECUE SAUCE:

- 1   **teaspoon vegetable oil**
- ½   **cup finely chopped onion**
- 1   **tablespoon minced garlic**
- 1   **cup cider vinegar**
- 1   **cup ketchup**
- ¼   **cup sugar**
- 2   **tablespoons fresh lemon juice**
- 1   **tablespoon Worcestershire Sauce**
- 1   **teaspoon ground red pepper**
- 1   **teaspoon salt**
- ½   **teaspoon freshly ground pepper**

1. *Make marinade:* Whisk vinegar and mustard in a small bowl until smooth. Whisk in remaining marinade ingredients.

2. Line a large disposable foil pan with plastic wrap. Add ribs and marinade, turning several times to coat. Cover and marinate the ribs in the refrigerator overnight.

3. *Make barbecue sauce:* Heat oil in a saucepan over medium heat. Add onion and garlic and cook until softened, 5 minutes. Stir in remaining barbecue sauce ingredients and bring to boil; reduce heat and simmer 30 minutes, stirring occasionally. Transfer to a microwaveproof bowl; cool. *(Can be made ahead. Cover and refrigerate overnight.)*

4. Remove ribs from pan. Transfer marinade to a bowl; discard plastic wrap. Set pan aside to use as a drip pan.

5. Prepare grill for indirect grilling. *For gas:* Place a large disposable foil drip pan in center of bottom grate. Add 2 cups hot water to pan. Replace top cooking grate. Close lid and heat burners on High (500°F. to 550°F.) 10 to 15 minutes. To grill, adjust burner controls. Be sure to position ribs in center of grill and turn off heat source directly under ribs. *(For triple-burner grill, turn center burner off.)* For *charcoal briquettes:* Open all vents. Build two equal piles of briquettes (16 to 30 total, depending on the size of the grill) opposite each other on bottom grate near the grate's edge. Ignite and burn briquettes 25 to 30 minutes until coals are covered with a light coating of gray ash. *(If one side seems hotter than the other, use long-handled tongs to rearrange coals.)* Place a disposable foil drip pan in center of bottom grate. Add 2 cups hot water to pan. Position top cooking grate with handles over coals so that additional coals can be added through side openings.

6. Arrange ribs in rib rack and place in center of grill directly over drip pan. Cover and grill ribs over low fire (275°F. to 300°F.) 2½ to 3 hours, adding 5 to 9 briquettes to each side every 30 minutes (if using a charcoal grill) and basting ribs with marinade every 20 minutes until meat is tender. Microwave barbecue sauce on HIGH 2 to 2½ minutes until hot. Serve ribs with barbecue sauce. Makes 6 servings.

Per serving with barbecue sauce: 905 calories, 57 g total fat, 19 g saturated fat, 259 mg cholesterol, 1,925 mg sodium, 25 g carbohydrates, 66 g protein, 71 mg calcium, 1 g fiber

chili-coated pork tenderloin 🅴🅰🆂🆈

It's love at first bite! This spice-rubbed pork is so scrumptious to eat and simple to put together, don't be surprised if the company you serve requests the recipe. Tip: Spread the spices over a sheet of waxed paper and roll the tenderloins over them for a speedy cleanup. Pictured on page 121.

Prep time: 5 minutes plus standing
Baking time: 25 to 30 minutes

1½	**pounds pork tenderloin, rinsed and patted dry**
1	**tablespoon chili powder**
1	**teaspoon salt**
1	**teaspoon dried oregano**
½	**teaspoon freshly ground pepper**
½	**teaspoon cumin**
¼	**teaspoon ground red pepper**

1. Let pork stand at room temperature 30 minutes. Grease a metal 13×9-inch baking pan. Heat oven to 450°F.

2. Combine all the spices on a sheet of waxed paper. Roll tenderloins in the spices to coat; transfer to pan. Roast 25 to 30 minutes, until an instant-

read thermometer inserted into thickest part of the tenderloin reaches 155°F. Remove pork from oven and let stand 5 minutes. (Temperature of meat should rise upon standing.) Makes 4 to 6 servings.

Per serving: 185 calories, 6.5 g total fat, 2 g saturated fat, 81 mg cholesterol, 538 mg sodium, 1 g carbohydrates, 29 g protein, 18 mg calcium, 1 g fiber

---

test kitchen tip

60-minute weekend menu plan

Hosting a dinner party over the weekend can be easy—and actually fun—if you plan it right. Just have your menu mapped out and follow an organized game plan. Here's a delicious example:

UP TO 1 WEEK AHEAD:
- Prepare Honey-Peanut Cheesecake. Cover and place in freezer.

UP TO 3 DAYS AHEAD:
- Prepare Arugula Pesto Dip. Cover and refrigerate.

1 DAY AHEAD:
- Remove cheesecake from freezer and thaw in refrigerator overnight.

DAY OF PARTY:
- Prepare vegetables to serve with Arugula Pesto Dip; cover and refrigerate until ready to serve. (Note: Belgian endive should be prepared right before serving time.)
- Remove cheesecake from refrigerator 1 to 2 hours before serving.
- Heat oven. Coat pork with spices.
- Prepare squash. Cut broccoli and leeks.
- Roast pork.
- Roast broccoli in same oven as pork.
- Cook squash. Add leeks to broccoli.

m e n u

sunday barbecue, southern style

BARBECUED GLAZED HAM
below

SPICED FRUIT COMPOTE
page 155

HOMESTYLE MACARONI SALAD
page 152

ICE CREAM SANDWICHES
page 160

barbecued glazed ham EASY

For fabulous smoky sweet flavor, a bone-in ham is coated with chili powder, cumin, cinnamon and cloves, then slow-cooked on the grill and brushed with a fruity glaze. Though this is a choice dish for friends and family anytime of year, try it at your next Easter celebration for a tasty twist on the traditional. Pictured on page 122.

Prep time: 30 minutes plus standing
Grilling time: 1 hour 30 to 50 minutes

- **2 tablespoons sugar**
- **1 tablespoon chili powder**
- **1 tablespoon paprika**
- **1 teaspoon cumin**
- **½ teaspoon cinnamon**
- **¼ teaspoon ground cloves**
- **1 fully cooked (6 to 7 lb.) bone-in smoked ham, shank or butt portion**

GLAZE:
- **¼ cup damson plum or peach preserves**
- **2 tablespoons orange juice**

1. Prepare grill for indirect heat. *For gas:* Place a disposable foil drip pan in center of bottom grate. Replace top cooking grate. Close lid and heat burners on high (500°F. to 550°F.) 10 to 15 minutes. To grill, adjust burner controls. Be sure to position ham in center of grill and turn off heat source directly under the ham. (For a triple burner grill, turn off center burner.) *For charcoal briquettes:* Open all vents. Build two equal piles of briquettes (16 to 30 total, depending on the size of the grill) opposite each other on bottom grate near the grate's edge. Ignite and burn briquettes 25 to 30 minutes, until coals are covered with a light coating of gray ash. *(If one side seems hotter than the other, use long-handled tongs to rearrange coals.)* Place a disposable foil drip pan in center of bottom grate. Position top cooking grate with handles over coals so additional coals can be added through side openings.

2. Combine sugar, chili powder, paprika, cumin, cinnamon and cloves in a small bowl.

3. Score top and sides of ham with a knife in a crisscross pattern. Rub with spice mixture.

4. Place ham, scored side up, in center of grill over drip pan. Close lid and grill 45 minutes. (If you have a grill thermometer, it should register between 375°F. and 425°F. during barbecuing.) Turn ham over (if using charcoal, add 5 to 9 briquettes on each side). Grill 45 to 60 minutes more, until instant-read thermometer inserted in center of ham registers 140°F.

5. Combine preserves and orange juice in a cup; brush over ham. Cover and grill 5 minutes more. Let stand 15 minutes. Makes 8 to 12 servings.

Per serving: 195 calories, 8 g total fat, 2.5 g saturated fat, 50 mg cholesterol, 1,290 mg sodium, 11 g carbohydrates, 20 g protein, 21 mg calcium, 1 g fiber

striped bass and risotto in spice broth

Fish is always nice for a small gathering, and this skillet-cooked bass goes beyond that when paired with creamy-rich risotto. Better yet, we've simplified the risotto —it requires no stirring during cooking time. Pictured on page 124.

Total prep and cooking time: 1 hour
Microwave used

RISOTTO:

1	tablespoon vegetable oil
½	cup diced carrot
¼	cup finely chopped shallot
2	teaspoons finely chopped garlic
4½	cups chicken broth
2	bottles (8 oz. each) clam juice
½	cup white wine
2	tablespoons heavy or whipping cream
½ to 1	teaspoon Thai red curry paste*
2	cups arborio or medium-grain rice
½	teaspoon salt
½	teaspoon grated lime peel, divided

4	teaspoons coriander
1½	teaspoons salt
½	teaspoon freshly ground pepper
8	striped bass fillets with skin (6 oz. each)
3	teaspoons vegetable oil, divided
2	tablespoons fresh lime juice
2	tablespoons chopped fresh cilantro
	Sautéed greens (optional)

1. *Make risotto:* Heat 1 tablespoon oil in a 3-quart heavy-bottomed saucepan. Add carrot, shallot and garlic; cook until vegetables soften. Combine broth, clam juice and wine in a glass measure (or a large bowl). Pour or ladle 1½ cups of the broth mixture into a 2-cup glass measure. Add cream and curry paste; set aside. Add remaining 5½ cups broth mixture to vegetables. Bring to boil; stir in rice and salt. Reduce heat to medium; cover and cook 20 minutes, until liquid is absorbed and rice is tender with a slight bite. Add ¼ teaspoon lime peel.

2. Heat oven to 350°F. Combine coriander, salt and pepper in a cup. Sprinkle over the skinless side of fish fillets. Heat 1½ teaspoons of the oil in a 12-inch skillet over high heat. Add 4 fillets, skin side down. Immediately place the bottom of a 9-inch pie plate on the fish and weight with a heavy heatproof bowl or measuring cup. (This will prevent the fish from curling.) Cook 2 to 3 minutes, until skin is browned. Remove plate and weight. Transfer fish with spatula, skin side down, to bottom of a broiler pan. Repeat with remaining fish. Bake 5 to 6 minutes, until fish flakes easily with a fork in center of fillets. Sprinkle with the lime juice.

3. Microwave reserved 1½ cups broth-cream mixture on HIGH 2 to 4 minutes until very hot; stir to dissolve curry paste. Add remaining lime peel.

4. Divide risotto among 8 serving plates. Arrange fish, skin side up, on top; pour reserved hot broth around risotto. Sprinkle with cilantro. Serve with sautéed greens, if desired. Makes 8 servings.

*Note: Can be found in ethnic sections of supermarkets or in Asian specialty stores.

Per serving: 385 calories, 10 g total fat, 2.5 g saturated fat, 75 mg cholesterol, 1,449 mg sodium, 36 g carbohydrates, 36 g protein, 38 mg calcium, 3 g fiber

test kitchen tip
all about arborio

Arborio rice is an Italian grain and the key ingredient in the classic dish risotto. Why arborio? The short grain's extremely high-starch content gives the dish its renowned creaminess. This particular rice boasts the extraordinary talent of truly absorbing flavors (the reason it's so delectable in our Striped Bass and Risotto in Spice Broth recipe, left). Its kernel is short and fat, and it features a white dot at the center of the grain. Arborio rice is the preferred choice for risotto, but if it's not available at your market, substitute medium-grain rice.

how to eat lobster

Leery of lobsters? No more. Cracking a cooked whole lobster open and enjoying each morsel of meat isn't so difficult once you get the hang of it. Here's how to do it.

- Grab the body of the lobster firmly and separate the tailpiece from the body by arching the lobster back until it cracks.

- Holding the lobster tail, bend back its flippers until they crack; remove. With one hand, straighten out the tail. Using your other hand, insert a fork, pull the tail meat up and cut through the wide end. Carefully remove all of the meat.

- To remove the lobster claws, twist them until they pull off. Using lobster crackers, break open each claw and remove the lobster meat with a fork or your fingers. (For the smaller connecting joints, crack open with the lobster crackers and remove the meat with a cocktail fork.)

crab-stuffed lobster fra diavolo

Fra Diavolo means "brother of the devil" in Italian—in other words—spicy hot. An exceptional crab-fennel stuffing is the unexpected star of this dish. Sound extravagant? It's well worth the extra effort when you're entertaining cherished company. Tip: Make the tomato sauce a day or two ahead to cut down on day-of-cooking prep time. If you feel super-organized, stuff the lobsters up to 24 hours in advance of serving.

Prep time: 1 hour • Cooking time: about 1 hour

TOMATO SAUCE:
- 1 medium (10 oz.) fennel bulb
- 2 tablespoons olive oil
- ¾ cup minced shallots
- 1 tablespoon minced garlic
- 1 bottle (8 oz.) clam juice
- ⅓ cup white wine
- ½ to ¾ teaspoon red pepper flakes
- 3 cans (28 to 32 oz. each) whole tomatoes in juice, chopped
- ½ cup tomato paste
- 1 teaspoon salt
- ¼ teaspoon dried oregano
- 2 tablespoons chopped fresh parsley

CRAB-FENNEL STUFFING:
- 5 slices good-quality white bread
- 4 tablespoons olive oil, divided
- ½ cup chopped shallots
- ¼ teaspoon red pepper flakes
- 3 tablespoons chopped fresh parsley
- 2 tablespoons white wine
- ¾ teaspoon salt
- ¼ teaspoon dried oregano
- ½ pound fresh or refrigerated canned crabmeat, (lump, special white or back fin), in large shreds

- 8 frozen lobster tails (5 to 6 oz. each), thawed

MUSSELS:
- 2 tablespoons olive oil
- 1 cup chopped onions
- 4 pounds mussels, scrubbed and debearded (see note, opposite page)
- ⅓ cup white wine

- 1½ pounds linguine

1. ■ *Make tomato sauce:* Cut out the core of the fennel bulb; set aside. Chop enough of the fennel bulb to equal 1 cup; reserve for stuffing. Heat oil in a 4-quart saucepot over medium heat. Add shallots; cook 3 minutes until softened. Add garlic; cook, stirring, 1 minute. Add clam juice, wine and red pepper flakes; bring to boil and boil 1 minute. Add tomatoes and juice, tomato paste, salt, oregano and core from fennel. Bring to boil; reduce heat and cook at a low boil 25 minutes, stirring occasionally. Remove fennel core and discard. Stir in parsley. *(Can be made ahead. Store in airtight container in refrigerator up to 2 days. Reheat before using over pasta and mussels.)*

2. *Make crab-fennel stuffing:* Pulse bread in a food processor to coarse crumbs. Heat a large skillet over medium heat 1 minute. Add bread crumbs and toast, stirring frequently, 4 to 6 minutes until golden. Transfer to a large bowl. Add 2 tablespoons of the oil to skillet; add reserved 1 cup chopped fennel, shallots and red pepper flakes and cook 6 to 7 minutes until tender and lightly browned. Toss with bread crumbs, parsley, wine, remaining 2 tablespoons oil, salt and oregano until blended. Gently mix in crabmeat.

3. *Stuff lobster tails:* Arrange oven rack in top third of oven. Heat oven to 400°F. Turn tails on back and cut underside with kitchen shears lengthwise (it's okay to cut some of the flesh). Place a clean kitchen towel on tail and press down with palm to open slightly. Arrange ½ cup stuffing on cut side of each tail, pressing stuffing together to mound; transfer stuffed tails, stuffing side up, to a 13×9-inch broiler-proof baking dish. Spoon ¼ cup of the tomato sauce (can be cold) over each stuffed tail. *(Can be made ahead. Cover with plastic wrap and refrigerate up to 24 hours.)* Remove wrap and bake 20 minutes. Switch oven to broil and broil 5 to 8 minutes until bread crumbs are browned.

4. *Steam mussels:* Meanwhile, heat oil in a stockpot over medium-high heat; add onions and cook 4 to 5 minutes until lightly browned. Add mussels and wine. Cover and cook 6 minutes until mussels open. Transfer mussels with a slotted spoon to a large serving bowl. Cover and keep warm. Reserve liquid from mussels.

5. Cook linguine according to package directions during last 10 minutes of lobster baking time. Drain and transfer to a large serving bowl. Set aside ⅓ cup of the mussel liquid; add remaining mussel liquid to linguine and let stand 1 minute. Toss with 1 cup tomato sauce; top with 1½ cups more sauce.

6. *Arrange lobster platter:* Transfer lobster tails to a large serving platter; pour reserved ⅓ cup hot mussel liquid over tails. Pour 1 cup tomato sauce over top of mussels. Arrange some of the mussels around tails to garnish. Serve immediately with linguine. Makes 8 servings.

Per serving: 760 calories, 18 g total fat, 2.5 g saturated fat, 128 mg cholesterol, 1,657 mg sodium, 98 g carbohydrates, 47 g protein, 232 mg calcium, 12 g fiber

clambake in a pot

You don't have to hit the beach to have a true Maine clambake—just grab two large pots. The meal in itself is complete: Everyone gets a steaming package filled with all the fixings. If you want to stretch your dollar, cook three lobsters; then cut each in half to make six servings.

Prep time: 20 minutes • Cooking time: 20 minutes

- **2 pounds (18 to 24) assorted small potatoes (Yukon gold, red and purple)**
- **1 pound kielbasa, cut into 1-inch pieces**
- **6 (1¼ lbs. each) live lobsters**
- **6 small ears corn, husks removed and broken in half**
- **1 pound mussels, scrubbed and debearded***
- **2 pounds littleneck clams, scrubbed**
- **½ cup butter, melted (no substitutes)**
- **2 lemons, cut into wedges**

1. Cut twelve 30-inch-long strips of cheesecloth (purchase enough cheesecloth to equal 10 yards—about 6 packages). Arrange 2 strips of cheesecloth into a cross. In the center of the cheesecloth, stack 3 to 4 potatoes, 3 to 4 pieces of kielbasa, 1 lobster, 2 pieces of corn, 4 to 5 mussels and 6 to 8 clams. Bring ends of cloth to center to enclose all the ingredients completely; tie each with kitchen string. Repeat process with remaining cheesecloth, vegetables, sausage and seafood to make 6 packages.

2. Meanwhile, pour enough water to come up 1 inch in 2 large lobster, canning or pasta pots; bring to boil. Place 3 packages in each pot. Cover each pot and return water to rolling boil. Boil seafood packages 20 minutes.

3. With tongs, remove the seafood packages and transfer to 6 large serving bowls. Serve with some of the cooking broth, butter and lemon. Makes 6 servings.

*Note: To debeard mussels, scrub the shells with a stiff brush under cold running water; then with a small sharp knife, cut off the "beards" (small black tufts attached to shells).

Per serving: 730 calories, 38.5 g total fat, 17.5 g saturated fat, 196 mg cholesterol, 1,545 mg sodium, 49 g carbohydrates, 47 g protein, 132 mg calcium, 5 g fiber

pasta with scallops and corn

Seafood and pasta lovers will be satisfied when you serve savory scallops cooked in wine and clam juice with seasoned corn and fresh tarragon. If fresh corn is not available, it's fine to substitute frozen or canned. Serve with crusty bread on the side.

Prep time: 10 minutes • Cooking time: 12 minutes

- 1 tablespoon flour
- ½ teaspoon salt
- 1 pound sea scallops
- 4 teaspoons olive oil, divided
- ¼ cup thinly sliced shallots
- 3 ears corn, husked and kernels cut off cobs
  Pinch red pepper flakes
- ¼ cup white wine
- 1 bottle (8 oz.) clam juice
- 1 tablespoon chopped fresh tarragon or
  ½ teaspoon dried tarragon
- ¼ teaspoon salt
- 12 ounces fedilini or thin spaghetti, cooked according to package directions
- 2 tablespoons snipped fresh chives, for garnish (optional)

1. Combine flour and salt in a cup. Place scallops on a sheet of waxed paper; dust both sides with flour mixture. Set aside.

2. Heat 2 teaspoons of the oil in a 12-inch nonstick skillet over high heat. Add shallots, corn and pepper; cook 6 minutes until lightly browned. Transfer to a bowl.

3. Add remaining 2 teaspoons oil to skillet. Reduce heat to medium-high. Add scallops; cook 2 minutes per side until browned. Add wine; cook 30 seconds. Add clam juice, corn mixture, tarragon and salt; bring to boil and boil 1 minute.

4. Toss hot pasta with scallop and corn mixture in a large serving bowl. Sprinkle top with chives, if desired. Makes 4 servings.

Per serving: 560 calories, 10.5 g total fat, 1 g saturated fat, 36 mg cholesterol, 1,079 mg sodium, 82 g carbohydrates, 32 g protein, 51 mg calcium, 4 g fiber

grilled salmon with tomato-ginger relish

Impress your guests with a whole salmon fillet. You can conveniently purchase the fish in many supermarkets at affordable prices. Freshly grated ginger adds an unexpected touch of sweetness and heat to the red-and-yellow cherry tomato relish.

Prep time: 40 minutes
Grilling time: 13 to 20 minutes per salmon fillet

  Vegetable oil
- 2 whole salmon fillets (3 to 3½ lbs. each), with skin
- 1 tablespoon extra-virgin olive oil
- 1 teaspoon salt
- ½ teaspoon freshly ground pepper
- 3 tablespoons fresh thyme leaves

TOMATO-GINGER RELISH:
- 3 pints red and/or yellow cherry tomatoes, finely chopped (6 cups)
- 3 tablespoons white balsamic vinegar or white wine vinegar
- 1 tablespoon grated fresh ginger
- 1 teaspoon salt

  Lime wedges and fresh thyme sprigs, for garnish (optional)

1. Brush grill generously with vegetable oil; heat grill. Brush both sides of salmon fillets with olive oil. Sprinkle both sides of fillets with salt and pepper. Sprinkle fresh thyme leaves on skinned side of each fillet.

2. Grill one salmon fillet, skin side up, over medium heat, 4 to 5 inches from heat source, 8 to 10 minutes until lightly browned. Using two large metal spatulas, carefully turn salmon. Grill 5 to 10 minutes more until just cooked through. Transfer to a serving platter; cover and keep warm.

3. Clean grill; brush generously with vegetable oil. Repeat process with remaining salmon. (*Can be made ahead. Cool, cover with plastic wrap and refrigerate up to 6 hours. Let stand at room temperature 30 minutes before serving.*)

4. *Make tomato-ginger relish:* Combine tomatoes, vinegar, ginger and salt in a bowl. *(Can be made ahead. Cover and refrigerate overnight. Let stand at room temperature 30 minutes before serving.)*

5. Serve salmon with tomato-ginger relish at room temperature. Garnish with lime wedges and thyme sprigs, if desired. Makes 8 to 10 servings.

Per serving: 460 calories, 21 g total fat, 3 g saturated fat, 166 mg cholesterol, 629 mg sodium, 4 g carbohydrates, 61 g protein, 52 mg calcium, 1 g fiber

eggplant parmesan

Here's a tasty recipe that comes in handy when entertaining those who prefer meatless meals (though it's definitely hearty enough to satisfy the rest). Put together a basic tomato sauce with fresh basil and rosemary; then add breaded and baked eggplant, and mozzarella and Parmesan cheese. The result is melt-in-your-mouth comfort food at its best. Serve with a tossed green salad and crusty bread.

Prep time: 40 minutes • Baking time: 60 to 65 minutes

- **2** medium eggplants (2 lbs.), peeled and sliced crosswise ½ inch thick

TOMATO SAUCE:
- **1** tablespoon olive oil
- **1** cup chopped onions
- **1** tablespoon finely chopped garlic
- **¼** cup white wine
- **1** can (28 oz.) crushed tomatoes
- **½** cup water
- **2** tablespoons chopped fresh basil
- **1** teaspoon minced fresh thyme or ½ teaspoon dried thyme
- **1** teaspoon minced fresh rosemary or ½ teaspoon dried rosemary
- **½** teaspoon salt
- **¼** teaspoon freshly ground pepper

- **2** large egg whites
- **1** large egg
- **2** tablespoons water

- **1** tablespoon olive oil
- **½** teaspoon salt
- **¼** teaspoon freshly ground pepper
- **1¼** cups Italian dry bread crumbs
- **¼** pound shredded mozzarella cheese
- **1** cup freshly grated Parmesan cheese

1. Arrange eggplant slices between double layers of paper towels; set aside.

2. Meanwhile, arrange racks in upper and lower third of oven. Heat oven to 450°F.

3. *Make tomato sauce:* Heat oil in a large saucepan over medium heat; add onions and cook 3 to 4 minutes until tender. Add garlic and cook 1 minute. Add wine; bring to boil. Stir in remaining tomato sauce ingredients and bring to boil. Reduce heat to medium-low and simmer sauce 12 minutes.

4. Pat eggplant dry with paper towels. Whisk together egg whites, egg, water, oil, salt and pepper in a 9-inch pie plate. Spread bread crumbs into a shallow dish.

5. Lightly grease 2 large cookie sheets with vegetable shortening. Dip each eggplant slice into egg mixture, then coat each side in bread crumbs. Arrange slices on prepared sheets. Bake 12 minutes. Turn slices over. Bake 13 minutes more until golden and tender. Transfer eggplant to wire racks.

6. Transfer upper rack to middle of oven. Reduce oven temperature to 375°F.

7. Toss mozzarella and Parmesan in a medium bowl. Spread 1 cup of the tomato sauce in the bottom of a 13×9-inch baking dish. Arrange half of the eggplant slices in a single layer. Spread 1 cup of the sauce over eggplant; top with half the cheese. Repeat with remaining eggplant, sauce and cheese.

8. Cover dish with foil and bake eggplant 40 to 43 minutes until sauce is bubbly. Let stand 5 minutes before serving. Makes 6 servings.

Per serving: 380 calories, 15 g total fat, 6 g saturated fat, 59 mg cholesterol, 1,592 mg sodium, 40 g carbohydrates, 21 g protein, 414 mg calcium, 6 g fiber

ginger rice

Flavored with onions that have been cooked with freshly grated ginger and cumin, this rice is heavenly with barbecued spareribs, beef or fish.

Prep time: 10 minutes • Cooking time: 23 to 24 minutes

1	tablespoon olive oil
½	cup chopped onion
4	teaspoons grated fresh ginger
½	teaspoon cumin seeds
4	cups water
1	teaspoon salt
2	cups long-grain rice

1. Heat oil in a large saucepan over medium-low heat; add onion, ginger and cumin seeds. Cook until onion is softened, 3 to 4 minutes.

2. Add water and salt; bring to boil. Stir in rice; cover, reduce heat and simmer 20 minutes. Remove from heat; let stand, covered, 5 minutes. Fluff with a fork before serving. Makes 8 servings.

Per serving: 190 calories, 2 g total fat, 0.5 g saturated fat, 0 mg cholesterol, 278 mg sodium, 38 g carbohydrates, 3 g protein, 19 mg calcium, 1 g fiber

creamy chive potato cakes

Here's the ultimate side dish for the most elegant of entrées. Mashed and diced Yukon Gold potatoes, goat cheese and sour cream are shaped into cakes and baked until golden and crisp. Pictured on page 121.

Prep time: 1 hour 15 minutes plus chilling
Baking time: 36 to 38 minutes

2	pounds Yukon Gold potatoes, peeled
	Salt
4	ounces goat cheese (such as Montrachet), crumbled
3	tablespoons snipped fresh chives
2	tablespoons butter or margarine, melted
2	tablespoons sour cream
¼	teaspoon freshly ground pepper
6	teaspoons olive oil, divided

1. Line a 9-inch square pan with plastic wrap, allowing a 6-inch overhang of wrap over two sides of the pan.

2. Bring potatoes, 1 tablespoon salt and cold water to cover to a boil in a stockpot. Cook potatoes 30 to 35 minutes, until tender; drain. Cool slightly. Coarsely mash half the potatoes in a bowl. Dice the other half and add to the mashed potatoes. Fold in cheese, chives, butter, sour cream, ¾ teaspoon salt and the pepper. Spread potato mixture into prepared pan; fold overhang of plastic wrap to cover top. Refrigerate 3 hours, until firm.

3. Unmold chilled potatoes onto a cutting board; peel off plastic wrap. Spray a 2½-inch oval or round cookie cutter with vegetable cooking spray. Cut out 8 ovals of potato mixture. Press scraps together to form a ¾-inch-thick disk; cut out 4 more ovals. Repeat, making a total of 16 cakes.

4. Heat 2 teaspoons of the oil in 12-inch nonstick skillet over medium-high heat. Cook one-third of the potato cakes, 3 minutes per side, until deep golden. Drain on paper towels. Repeat process 2 more times; cool. Transfer cakes to a jelly-roll pan. *(Can be made ahead. Wrap jelly-roll pan and refrigerate up to 24 hours.)*

5. Heat oven to 375°F. Bake potatoes (unwrapped if refrigerated overnight) 18 to 20 minutes, until heated through. Makes 16 potato cakes.

Per potato cake: 105 calories, 6 g total fat, 3 g saturated fat, 10 mg cholesterol, 311 mg sodium, 10 g carbohydrates, 3 g protein, 22 mg calcium, 1 g fiber

roasted new potatoes

Substitute the red-skinned potatoes with yellow-fleshed Yukon Gold, if you prefer.

Prep time: 10 minutes • Baking time: 45 to 50 minutes

3	pounds small red potatoes, scrubbed and quartered
2	tablespoons melted butter or olive oil
½	teaspoon salt
⅛	teaspoon freshly ground pepper

Heat oven to 450°F. Toss potatoes, butter, salt and pepper in a jelly-roll pan; arrange potatoes in a single layer. Roast potatoes on bottom oven rack 45 to 50 minutes, until golden brown and tender. Makes 6 servings.

Per serving: 215 calories, 4 g total fat, 2 g saturated fat, 10 mg cholesterol, 239 mg sodium, 41 g carbohydrates, 4 g protein, 21 mg calcium, 4 g fiber

french beans in shallot butter

Delicate and thin haricot verts (ah-ree-koh VEHR), the French term for "green string beans," live up to their classy, sophisticated name when steamed and combined with sautéed shallots. Pictured on page 121.

Prep time: 20 minutes • Cooking time: 5 to 10 minutes

- **1 pound French beans (haricot verts) or 1½ pounds green beans*, trimmed**
- **1 tablespoon butter or margarine**
- **2 tablespoons minced shallots**
- **¼ teaspoon salt**
- **¼ teaspoon freshly ground pepper**

1. Place steamer basket in a large saucepan; add enough water to reach just under the basket. Add beans to basket; bring water to boil. Cover and steam beans 3 to 4 minutes, until tender-crisp. *(Can be made ahead. Immediately rinse beans under cold running water until cool. Wrap and refrigerate up to 24 hours. Return beans to room temperature.)*

2. Melt butter in a large skillet over medium-high heat; add shallots and cook 1 minute. Add beans, salt and pepper. Cook 1 to 2 minutes more, until heated through. Makes 8 servings.

*Note: If using green beans, prepare recipe as directed, except steam beans 5 to 7 minutes and increase butter to 2 tablespoons, shallots to ¼ cup and salt to ½ teaspoon.

Per serving: 55 calories, 3 g total fat, 2 g saturated fat, 8 mg cholesterol, 180 mg sodium, 7 g carbohydrates, 2 g protein, 35 mg calcium, 2 g fiber

fresh sugar snaps and asparagus

Looking for a simple side dish for your next patio party? The crisp, clean flavor of fresh sugar snaps and asparagus shines through in this elegant salad tossed with dill and mustard dressing. Pictured on page 126.

Prep time: 20 minutes
Cooking time: 3 to 5 minutes per batch

- **1 pound sugar snap peas, trimmed**
- **1½ pounds asparagus, trimmed**
- **1 tablespoon fresh lemon juice**
- **1 tablespoon white wine vinegar**
- **1 teaspoon Dijon mustard**
- **1 teaspoon sugar**
- **½ teaspoon salt**
- **¼ teaspoon freshly ground pepper**
- **¼ cup olive oil**
- **2 tablespoons finely chopped red onion**
- **2 teaspoons chopped fresh dill**

1. Bring a large saucepan three-quarters full of water to boil. Add sugar snap peas and cook until they turn bright green and are still crunchy, 3 minutes. Transfer sugar snaps with a slotted spoon to a bowl filled with iced water. (Reserve cooking water.) Return cooking water to boil; add asparagus and cook until tender but still crisp, 4 to 5 minutes. Transfer asparagus to bowl of iced water. Drain sugar snaps and asparagus; transfer to a pan lined with paper towels.

2. Cut asparagus into 2-inch diagonal pieces. Transfer asparagus and sugar snaps to a large serving bowl.

3. Whisk together lemon juice, vinegar, mustard, sugar, salt and pepper in a medium bowl. Slowly whisk in oil until well blended. *(Can be made ahead. Cover vegetables and dressing separately with plastic wrap and refrigerate overnight. Return dressing to room temperature before using.)* Rinse onion under cold running water; drain. Toss asparagus and sugar snaps with onion, dill and dressing. Serve immediately. Makes 6 cups.

Per serving: 101 calories, 7 g total fat, 1 g saturated fat, 0 mg cholesterol, 161 mg sodium, 7 g carbohydrates, 3 g protein, 41 mg calcium, 2 g fiber

no-fuss
friday fare

OLIVE AND CHEESE PLATTER
WITH SAGE
page 20

PAN-GRILLED PEPPER STEAK
page 134

ROASTED VEGETABLE SALAD
below

GARLIC BREAD
use your favorite recipe

GIANT LIME SUGAR COOKIES
page 158

roasted vegetable salad EASY

This recipe is so versatile it makes a wonderful partner for grilled steak or chicken. Try it with the steak on page 134.

Prep time: 10 minutes • Baking time: 45 minutes

- **2** pounds red onions, cut into chunks
- **1** pound rutabaga or turnips, cut into chunks
- **1½** pounds white, red or Yukon Gold potatoes, cut into 1½-inch chunks
- **1** pound carrots, cut into 2-inch pieces
- **2** teaspoons dried rosemary
- **8** fresh sage leaves, torn into pieces, or 1 teaspoon dried sage
- **2** tablespoons extra-virgin olive oil
- **1** teaspoon salt
- **¼** teaspoon freshly ground pepper
- **1** tablespoon minced garlic

DRESSING:

- **¼** cup extra-virgin olive oil
- **2** tablespoons fresh lemon juice

- **1** tablespoon thinly sliced fresh sage leaves or ¼ teaspoon dried sage
- **1** teaspoon dried rosemary chopped with 1 tablespoon chopped fresh parsley
- **⅛** teaspoon salt
- **⅛** teaspoon freshly ground pepper
  ▪
- **½** of a 6-oz. bag fresh baby spinach
  Grilled steak or chicken (optional)

1. Arrange oven racks in center and lower third of oven. Heat oven to 425°F.

2. Toss all ingredients except garlic, dressing and spinach in a large bowl. Divide between and spread on the bottom of a broiler pan and one jelly-roll pan. Roast vegetables 20 minutes; stir, then switch pans between racks. Roast vegetables 20 minutes. Sprinkle garlic over vegetables; roast vegetables 5 minutes more.

3. *Make dressing:* Whisk together all dressing ingredients in a bowl (makes ⅓ cup).

4. Toss vegetables with spinach and 2 tablespoons of the dressing in a large bowl. Drizzle steak or chicken with remaining dressing, if desired. Makes 4 to 6 servings.

Per serving: 405 calories, 17 g total fat, 2.5 g saturated fat, 0 mg cholesterol, 616 mg sodium, 60 g carbohydrates, 8 g protein, 158 mg calcium, 11 g fiber

homestyle macaroni salad EASY

Everyone at your next summer gathering will pile their plates high with this all-time favorite. We use cavatappi (double-twisted elbow macaroni) tossed with a tangy buttermilk-mayo dressing. Pictured on page 127.

Prep time: 35 minutes • Cooking time: 10 to 15 minutes

- **1** pound cavatappi or macaroni pasta
- **4** hard-cooked eggs, chopped
- **1** cup chopped celery
- **⅓** cup finely chopped red bell pepper
- **1** tablespoon minced jalapeño (optional) (see tip, page 15)
- **⅓** cup chopped red onion
- **½** cup buttermilk

½ cup mayonnaise

2½ tablespoons cider vinegar

3 tablespoons snipped fresh chives

1¼ teaspoons salt

¼ teaspoon ground red pepper

¼ teaspoon freshly ground pepper

1. Cook pasta according to package directions. Transfer pasta to a colander and rinse under cold water; drain.

2. Meanwhile, combine remaining ingredients in a large bowl until mixed. Add cooled pasta and toss to coat. *(Can be made ahead. Cover and refrigerate up to 24 hours. Let stand at room temperature 30 minutes before serving.)* Makes 14 cups.

Per cup: 210 calories, 8.5 g total fat, 1.5 g saturated fat, 66 mg cholesterol, 289 mg sodium, 26 g carbohydrates, 6 g protein, 30 mg calcium, 1 g fiber

lentil and orzo salad EASY

This sophisticated side dish features sometimes-hard-to-find French green lentils, but they're definitely worth seeking out. Smaller than the more common brown lentils, green lentils are great to use in salads because they remain whole and firm when cooked. Serve them at your next outdoor party with simple grilled meats. Tip: This recipe can be made up to 2 days ahead. Pictured on page 125.

Prep time: 20 minutes • Cooking time: 20 to 25 minutes

1 pound French green lentils, picked over and rinsed*

½ pound (1¼ cups) orzo pasta

1 cup finely chopped red onions

½ cup extra-virgin olive oil

6 tablespoons red wine vinegar

¼ cup chopped fresh parsley

1½ teaspoons salt

½ teaspoon freshly ground pepper

1. Bring lentils and 6 cups water to boil in a medium saucepan. Reduce heat to medium-low and simmer 20 to 25 minutes, until tender. Drain and set aside.

2. Meanwhile, cook orzo according to package directions; drain. Transfer to a large bowl.

3. Combine orzo, onions, oil, vinegar, parsley, salt and pepper in a bowl. Stir in lentils. Cool. *(Can be made ahead. Cover and refrigerate up to 2 days. Let stand at room temperature 1 hour before serving.)* Makes 8 to 10 servings.

*Note: Can be found in gourmet food sections of supermarkets or in specialty food stores.

Per serving: 355 calories, 13.5 g total fat, 2 g saturated fat, 0 mg cholesterol, 375 mg sodium, 45 g carbohydrates, 16 g protein, 37 mg calcium, 17 g fiber

---

test kitchen tip

no-fuss friday game plan

For best results when cooking for company, stick to a well thought-out plan even if the menu is easy. This way, you can enjoy the party, too. Here's how to proceed with the menu on the opposite page:

UP TO 1 MONTH AHEAD:

• Make Giant Lime Sugar Cookies; freeze.

DAY OF PARTY:

• Remove cookies from freezer.
• Prepare Olive and Cheese Platter with Sage.
• Heat oven for Roasted Vegetable Salad.
• Cut vegetables for Roasted Vegetable Salad; divide between pans and start to roast.
• Heat grill pan for steak. Make dressing for Roasted Vegetable Salad.
• Grill steak.
• Make garlic bread.
• Toss vegetables with dressing and spinach.
• Slice steak; drizzle with remaining dressing.

ravishing radicchio

Vibrant red-leafed radicchio—an Italian chicory—is most often featured in salads (see recipe below right), and also it can be sautéed, grilled or baked. Radicchio leaves have a slightly bitter flavor. While there are many varieties, the most commonly available are radicchio di Verona (burgundy-red leaves, white ribs) and radicchio di Treviso (pink to burgundy-red, tapered heads). Select radicchio heads that carry full-color, firmly crisp leaves with no hint of browning. It may be stored in the refrigerator in a plastic bag for up to 1 week.

2. Meanwhile, heat broiler. Line a broiler pan with foil. Place peppers, cut side down, on prepared pan. Broil until skins are evenly charred, 8 to 10 minutes. Wrap in foil; cool 20 minutes. Peel and discard skins. Dice peppers; toss with couscous.

3. Heat oil over low heat in a small skillet; add garlic and cook until garlic softens and becomes fragrant, 3 to 5 minutes. Remove from heat. Stir garlic and oil with parsley, vinegar, lemon peel and juice, remaining ½ teaspoon salt and pepper into couscous until well blended. (*Can be made ahead. Cover and refrigerate overnight. Let stand at room temperature 2 hours before serving.*) Makes 5 cups.

Note: Can be found in gourmet or ethnic food sections of supermarkets or in specialty food stores.

Per cup: 245 calories, 6 g total fat, 1 g saturated fat, 0 mg cholesterol, 475 mg sodium, 41 g carbohydrates, 7 g protein, 31 mg calcium, 2 g fiber

couscous salad

If you're ready to try something out of the ordinary, here's an exotic choice. Pictured on page 126.

Prep time: 20 minutes plus cooling
Cooking time: 10 to 12 minutes

- **4** cups water
- **1** teaspoon salt, divided
- **1** package (8.5 oz.) toasted Israeli (grande) couscous* or acini di pepe pasta
- **1** yellow bell pepper, halved
- **1** red bell pepper, halved
- **2** tablespoons olive oil
- **2** tablespoons thinly sliced garlic
- **½** cup fresh parsley leaves, chopped
- **1** tablespoon red wine vinegar
- **½** teaspoon grated lemon peel
- **1** teaspoon fresh lemon juice
- **½** teaspoon freshly ground pepper

1. Bring water and ½ teaspoon of the salt to boil in a medium saucepan. Add couscous. Cover and simmer until cooked through, but still firm to the bite, 10 to 12 minutes. (If using pasta, cook according to package directions.) Drain couscous; transfer to a large bowl.

romaine and radicchio salad

Here's a versatile eye- and palate-pleasing side salad that pairs nicely with just about any meat or pasta dish.

Total prep time: 15 minutes

- **1** large head romaine lettuce (1½ lbs.), torn into bite-size pieces
- **1** large head radicchio (¾ lb.), torn into bite-size pieces
- **¼** cup white wine vinegar
- **4** flat anchovy fillets, finely chopped
- **½** teaspoon freshly ground pepper
- **¼** teaspoon salt
- **6** tablespoons extra-virgin olive oil
- **1** cup (4 oz.) fresh Parmesan cheese shavings

1. Combine romaine and radicchio in a large bowl. (*Can be made ahead. Transfer lettuces to resealable plastic storage bag; seal. Refrigerate up to 24 hours.*)

2. Whisk vinegar, anchovies, pepper and salt in a bowl; gradually whisk in oil. (*Can be made ahead. Cover and refrigerate overnight.*) Toss lettuces with dressing, then gently toss with Parmesan shavings. Makes 8 to 10 servings.

spiced fruit compote EASY

To section oranges, peel and hold over a bowl to catch the juices. Cut down against inside membrane of one segment on both sides; release segment. Repeat with remaining segments; remove any seeds. Pictured on page 122.

Prep time: 25 minutes • Baking time: 30 minutes

- **4** **oranges, peeled and sectioned**
- **3** **tablespoons tequila**
- **4** **cups cubed pineapple**
- **3** **cups cubed fresh mango or 1 jar (26 oz.) mango in light syrup, drained and cubed**
- **¼** **cup sugar**
- **½** **teaspoon grated lime peel**
- **2** **tablespoons fresh lime juice**
- **½** **teaspoon chili powder**
- **½** **cinnamon stick**

Heat oven to 450°F. Combine oranges and tequila in a bowl; set aside. Combine remaining ingredients in 2½-quart baking dish. Cover and bake 25 minutes. Stir in oranges and tequila. Bake, uncovered, 5 minutes more. Makes 6 cups.

crème brûlée

The French "crème brûlée," which translates to "burnt cream," is a dessert classic. Sometimes restaurants use a propane torch to "burn" the sugar on top.

Prep time: 15 minutes plus chilling
Baking time: 30 to 35 minutes

- **2** **cups heavy or whipping cream**
- **1** **vanilla bean, split lengthwise in half**
- **4** **large egg yolks**
- **6** **tablespoons plus 6 teaspoons sugar**

1. Heat cream and vanilla bean in a small saucepan over medium heat until small bubbles form around edge of pan. Remove from heat; cover and let stand 10 minutes.

2. Meanwhile, whisk together egg yolks and 6 tablespoons of the sugar in a medium bowl until mixture is pale yellow.

3. Remove vanilla bean from cream. Scrape seeds from bean with a small paring knife or spoon and stir into cream. (Rinse and reserve vanilla bean for another use. Pat dry and place bean in a canister with confectioners' or granulated sugar.) Slowly whisk hot cream into yolk mixture, until well blended. Strain mixture though a fine sieve set over a 2-cup glass measure.

4. Heat oven to 350°F. Arrange six (6 oz. each) custard cups in a 13×9-inch baking pan. *(Be sure the cups you are using can be subjected to broiler temperatures; some cups should not be used under the broiler.)* Divide and pour custard evenly among cups. Place pan on middle rack of the oven. Pour enough hot water into pan to come halfway up sides of cups. Bake until custard is just set and jiggles slightly in center, 30 minutes. Transfer pan to a wire rack; cool custards 5 minutes. Remove custards from water bath and cool completely on rack, about 45 minutes. Cover each custard with plastic wrap and refrigerate 1 hour until cold. *(Can be made ahead; refrigerate up to 2 days.)*

5. Heat broiler. Blot tops of custards dry with paper towels. Sprinkle each custard with 1 teaspoon sugar. Fill the same baking pan with ice cubes. Place 3 custard cups in ice; broil custards 3 inches from heat 4 to 5 minutes until sugar melts and turns dark brown. Transfer custards to another large baking pan halfway filled with ice. Let stand 15 minutes. Remove custards from ice; transfer to refrigerator.

6. Refill the same baking pan with ice and repeat broiling the remaining custards. Ice as directed above; chill and refrigerate. Refrigerate custards up to 3 hours. Makes 6 servings.

passion fruit and strawberry sorbet   LOW FAT   EASY

Try this taste of tropical paradise. Passion fruit and strawberry sorbets are spread between layers of crushed macaroon cookies, then topped with fresh strawberries and raspberries. This light, refreshing dessert is just what your guests desire after a rich meal.

Prep time: 20 minutes plus freezing
Baking time: 7 to 8 minutes

- ½ **pound coconut macaroon cookies (about 11)**
- 2 **pints strawberry sorbet, divided**
- 1 **pint passion fruit sorbet**
- 1 **pint fresh strawberries, sliced**
- ½ **pint fresh raspberries**

1. Heat oven to 375°F. Place a 9-inch springform pan in the freezer 15 minutes. Process macaroons in a food processor, pulsing until crumbly. Spread crumbs on a jelly-roll pan; bake 7 to 8 minutes until golden. Cool. Sprinkle 1 cup of the crumbs on bottom of prepared springform pan. Set remaining crumbs aside.

2. Soften 1 pint of the strawberry sorbet in refrigerator 10 to 15 minutes. Immediately spread sorbet over crumbs in prepared pan. Sprinkle top with half of the reserved crumbs. Cover with plastic wrap and freeze until firm, about 2 hours.

3. Repeat process to soften passion fruit sorbet and spread over strawberry layer; sprinkle remaining crumbs on top. Cover; freeze until firm, 2 hours.

4. Repeat process to soften remaining pint of strawberry sorbet, and spread over passion fruit layer. Cover and freeze overnight. *(Can be made ahead up to 2 days.)*

5. Uncover dessert; run a thin knife along side of pan. Unmold ring and place dessert on a serving plate. Arrange strawberries and raspberries on top; refrigerate 10 to 15 minutes to soften dessert before serving. Makes 8 to 10 servings.

Per serving: 270 calories, 3 g total fat, 0 g saturated fat, 0 mg cholesterol, 27 mg sodium, 61 g carbohydrates, 3 g protein, 18 mg calcium, 3 g fiber

honey-peanut cheesecake   EASY

A great dinner-party dessert! Pictured on page 123.

Prep time: 20 minutes plus chilling
Baking time: 1 hour 40 minutes

CRUST:
- 1¼ **cups gingersnap cookie crumbs**
- ¼ **cup ground unsalted peanuts**
- 2 **tablespoons sugar**
- 5 **tablespoons butter or margarine, melted**

FILLING:
- 4 **packages (8 oz. each) cream cheese, at room temperature**
- 5 **large eggs, at room temperature 20 to 30 minutes**
- 1 **cup sugar**
- ¼ **cup honey**

1. *Make crust:* Heat oven to 350°F. Combine cookie crumbs, nuts and sugar in a bowl. Stir in butter until crumbs are evenly moistened. Press crumbs evenly over bottom of a 9-inch springform pan. Bake until edges just begin to brown, 10 minutes. Cool on a wire rack. Cover outside of pan with heavy-duty foil. Reduce oven temperature to 325°F.

2. *Make filling:* Beat cream cheese in a large mixer bowl on medium speed until light and fluffy, about 5 minutes. Add eggs, one at a time, beating well after each addition and scraping side of bowl until blended. Beat in sugar and honey, 2 minutes, until mixture is smooth. Scrape bottom and sides of bowl; beat 30 seconds more (mixture should be completely smooth). Pour filling onto cooled crust. Place pan in large roasting pan and fill with enough hot water to come halfway up side of springform pan. Bake 1 hour and 30 minutes, until cheesecake is just set (it will firm as it cools). Remove pan from water bath. Cool on wire rack to room temperature. Remove side of springform pan. *(Can be made ahead. Cover and freeze up to 1 week. Let thaw in refrigerator overnight. Bring to room temperature 1 hour before serving.)* Makes 12 servings.

Per serving: 510 calories, 36 g total fat, 20.5 g saturated fat, 185 mg cholesterol, 392 mg sodium, 38 g carbohydrates, 10 g protein, 85 mg calcium, 1 g fiber

strawberry-rhubarb crumble

Strawberries and rhubarb are a yummy combination, especially in this dessert, which makes a great choice for one of the first cookouts of the season. When shopping for rhubarb, purchase crisp, bright-red stalks, and discard any leaves before using. Pictured on page 126.

Prep time: 45 minutes plus standing
Baking time: 1 hour to 1 hour 30 minutes

TOPPING:

- ¾ **cup all-purpose flour**
- ⅔ **cup firmly packed brown sugar**
- ⅓ **cup chopped toasted almonds**
- ½ **cup butter or margarine, softened**

FILLING:

- 3 **pints fresh strawberries, hulled**
- 2 **pounds fresh rhubarb, cut into 1-inch pieces, or 7 cups frozen cut-up rhubarb***
- 1¼ **cups sugar**
- 3 **tablespoons instant tapioca**
- 2 **teaspoons grated orange peel**
- 2 **teaspoons fresh thyme leaves (optional)**

- **Whipped cream**

1. *Make topping:* Combine all topping ingredients in a bowl until mixture just begins to hold together and resembles coarse crumbs.

2. *Make filling:* Heat oven to 350°F. Halve small and quarter large strawberries; transfer to a large bowl. Stir in remaining filling ingredients; let stand 15 minutes.

3. Lightly butter a shallow 3-quart baking dish. Pour filling into dish. Sprinkle topping evenly over filling. Bake until filling is bubbly and topping is golden, 60 to 75 minutes. Cool on a wire rack 1 hour before serving. Serve with whipped cream. Makes 8 servings.

*Note: If using frozen rhubarb, prepare recipe as directed, *except* spread frozen rhubarb in a single layer on a cookie sheet; let stand 30 minutes. Increase tapioca to ¼ cup; combine in a bowl with strawberries, sugar, orange peel and thyme, if desired. Let stand 15 minutes. Stir in rhubarb. Increase baking time to 1¼ to 1½ hours.

Per serving: 440 calories, 15 g total fat, 7.5 g saturated fat, 31 mg cholesterol, 148 mg sodium, 76 g carbohydrates, 4 g protein, 151 mg calcium, 4 g fiber

---

test kitchen tip

cooking with fresh herbs

We call for a wide array of fresh herbs in many of our recipes—even in the dessert recipe, at left. Fresh herbs, such as parsley and cilantro, are available year-round in most supermarkets, and home herb gardens are simple to start and maintain. Here are some tips for using fresh herbs:

REFRIGERATE most fresh herbs, whole leaves intact and dry, in a resealable plastic storage bag. (If the herbs come with stems or roots, store them with the roots immersed in water and the leaves loosely covered with a plastic bag.) Store basil as directed above, except do not refrigerate.

CHOP HERBS just before you're about to use them, for maximum flavor. In no-cook sauces, herbs retain their delicate flavors and can be mixed in any time, but for skillet sauces, it's a good rule to add them toward the end of the cooking time.

SUBSTITUTE dried herbs if need be; but use restraint when measuring the amount, as their flavor is more potent. As a substitute, start with ¼ teaspoon of dried herbs and a few sprigs of chopped fresh parsley. (Our recipes consistently call for flat-leaf parsley as opposed to curly because it has more flavor.)

CREATE an herb brush. Simply tie kitchen string around the stem ends of assorted fresh herbs (rosemary, thyme, sage, oregano or marjoram). Dip the sprigs in olive oil or vinaigrette dressing and brush over chicken, beef or vegetables while grilling.

giant lime sugar cookies *EASY*

Crispy on the outside, slightly chewy on the inside, with a punch of lime in every bite. Pictured on page 126.

Prep time: 30 minutes plus chilling
Baking time: 12 to 15 minutes per batch

- 2 cups all-purpose flour
- ¼ cup yellow cornmeal
- 1 teaspoon baking soda
- ½ teaspoon cream of tartar
- ½ teaspoon salt
- 6 tablespoons butter, softened (no substitutes)
- 6 tablespoons cold vegetable shortening
  Sugar (about 1½ cups total)
- 2 tablespoons light corn syrup
- 1 large egg
- 1 teaspoon vanilla extract
- 3 tablespoons plus ½ teaspoon grated lime peel, divided (about 4 limes)

1. Whisk together flour, cornmeal, baking soda, cream of tartar and salt in a large bowl. Set aside.

2. Beat butter, shortening and 1 cup of the sugar in a large mixer bowl on medium-high speed until light and creamy, 2 to 3 minutes. Beat in corn syrup, then egg, until combined. Beat in vanilla and 3 tablespoons of the lime peel, scraping sides of bowl until blended. At low speed, beat in flour mixture just until combined. Cover and refrigerate dough 1 hour.

3. Heat oven to 350°F. Combine 2 tablespoons sugar and remaining ½ teaspoon lime peel in a small bowl until well combined. Set aside.

4. Spread remaining ⅓ cup sugar on a plate. Line 2 cookie sheets with foil. Fill a ¼-cup dry measuring cup with dough. Shape dough into a ball, then roll in sugar. Place on the prepared cookie sheet. With the bottom of a glass, gently press top of ball into a 2½-inch circle. Repeat with remaining dough and sugar, arranging 4 cookies on each cookie sheet. Bake cookies until edges begin to color, 12 to 15 minutes. Cool cookies on pan 5 minutes. Sprinkle warm cookies with lime-sugar mixture. Transfer cookies to wire racks and cool completely. *(Can be made ahead. Freeze in airtight container up to one month.)* Makes 12 cookies.

Per serving: 285 calories, 12.5 g total fat, 5.5 g saturated fat, 33 mg cholesterol, 270 mg sodium, 40 g carbohydrates, 3 g protein, 9 mg calcium, 1 g fiber

confetti ice-cream tower cakes

If you really want to wow the crowd, this festive confection is truly spectacular. Pictured on page 128.

Prep time: 1 hour plus freezing
Baking time: 15 minutes

CAKE:
- 1 cup cake flour (not self-rising)
- 1 teaspoon baking powder
- ¼ teaspoon salt
- ½ cup butter or margarine, softened
- ¾ cup sugar
- 2 large eggs
- 2 tablespoons heavy or whipping cream
- 1 teaspoon vanilla extract
- 1 teaspoon grated lemon peel
- 1 tablespoon fresh lemon juice

- 1 pint raspberry sorbet
- ½ cup chopped toasted almonds
- 1 pint premium vanilla ice cream
- 1 pint passion fruit or mango sorbet

MERINGUE:
- 6 large egg whites, at room temperature 20 to 30 minutes*
- 1 cup sugar

THREE SAUCES:
- 2 ripe mangoes, peeled and chopped
- ½ cup sugar, divided
- 2 tablespoons fresh lemon juice
- ½ vanilla bean, split
- 4 kiwis, peeled and cut up
- 1 bag (12 oz.) frozen strawberries, thawed

1. *Make cake:* Heat oven to 350°F. Line a 15½×10½×1-inch jelly-roll pan with foil, leaving a 1-inch overhang. Grease foil, then flour, tapping out excess. Whisk cake flour, baking powder and salt in bowl; set both aside.

2. Beat butter and sugar in a mixer bowl until light and fluffy. Beat in eggs, one at a time. Beat in cream, vanilla, lemon peel and juice, until well combined. At low speed, beat in flour mixture just until blended. Spread batter evenly into prepared pan. Bake cake until golden and toothpick comes out clean when inserted in center, 15 minutes. Cool on wire rack.

3. Using eight 2½×3-inch cake rings or eight empty fruit cans (8½ oz. each) with tops and bottoms removed (for whole cake variation, see right), cut out 15 circles of cake. Reserve scraps.

4. Refrigerate raspberry sorbet 15 minutes to soften. Line a large jelly-roll pan with waxed paper; arrange cake rings on pan. Fit 1 cake circle in bottom of each ring or can; spread ¼ cup of the raspberry sorbet on top of each circle. Divide and gently press almonds into sorbet. Place cakes in freezer. Refrigerate vanilla ice cream 15 minutes to soften. Spread ¼ cup of the softened ice cream on top of almonds. Return cakes to freezer. Refrigerate passion fruit sorbet 15 minutes to soften. Using scraps of cake, make one more cake circle; fit remaining circles on top of ice cream in each ring. Spread each cake layer with ¼ cup of the passion fruit sorbet. Cover cakes and freeze overnight. *(Can be made ahead. Freeze up to 3 days.)*

5. *Make meringue:* Combine egg whites and sugar in a large mixer bowl. Set mixer bowl over a saucepan halfway filled with simmering water. Whisk mixture until sugar dissolves. Remove mixer bowl from water and beat on medium-high speed, until stiff. Fill a large pastry bag, fitted with a ¾-inch star tip, with meringue. Unwrap cakes, then decoratively pipe meringue on top of each, piping as close to cake ring as possible. Freeze cakes 2 hours, until meringue has completely set. *(Can be made ahead. Cover cakes loosely; freeze overnight.)*

6. *Make three sauces:* Puree mangoes, 3 tablespoons sugar and lemon juice in a blender until smooth. Transfer sauce to a bowl. Scrape seeds from vanilla bean; stir into sauce. *(Can be made ahead. Cover and refrigerate mango sauce overnight.)* Puree kiwis and 3 tablespoons sugar, just until smooth. (Tip: The seeds from the kiwis can cause the sauce to become bitter if overprocessed.) Transfer sauce to a

bowl. Puree strawberries and 2 tablespoons sugar until smooth. Strain sauce through a fine sieve into a bowl. *(Can be made ahead. Cover and refrigerate kiwi and strawberry sauces 4 hours.)*

7. Heat broiler. Transfer 2 cakes to a cookie sheet; broil 8 inches from heat, just until meringue is golden, 10 to 20 seconds. Immediately return cakes to freezer; repeat with remaining 6 cakes, broiling 2 at a time. Remove cakes from rings by gently pushing from the bottom cake layer of each ring. *(Can be made ahead. Return cakes to freezer and freeze up to 2 hours.)*

8. Place one-fourth of each sauce in each of 3 small resealable plastic storage bags; cut a small hole in the corner of each bag. Arrange cakes on 8 dessert plates; decoratively pipe sauces around each cake. Serve with remaining sauces. Makes 8 servings.

Whole cake variation: Use an 8×3-inch springform pan and prepare recipe as directed, *except:* Peel off foil from cake. Detach the ring from an 8×3-inch springform pan. Using the bottom of the pan as a guide, cut out one 8-inch circle of cake from the rectangle, starting from one short side of the cake. Cut out another 8-inch circle (you will not get a complete circle, and that's okay). Reserve scraps. Reattach springform ring and place pan on a jelly-roll pan lined with waxed paper. Fit whole cake circle in bottom of springform pan. Spread softened raspberry sorbet on top of cake; sprinkle top with almonds. Freeze as directed. Spread top with softened vanilla ice cream. Freeze as directed. Using reserved scraps of cake, fit remaining circle and scraps on top of ice cream layer. Cover with softened passion fruit sorbet and freeze as directed. Decoratively pipe meringue on top of cake. Broil as directed.

*Note: If you are concerned about serving and eating partially cooked egg whites, substitute an equivalent amount of pasteurized egg whites (not meringue powder) for the fresh egg whites.

Per serving with 1 tablespoon of each sauce: 685 calories, 25 g total fat, 12.5 g saturated fat, 112 mg cholesterol, 337 mg sodium, 111 g carbohydrates, 9 g protein, 130 mg calcium, 2 g fiber

ice cream sandwiches

Everybody loves ice cream sandwiches—especially when they're fudgy brownie ice-cream treats like these. We combine strawberry and vanilla ice creams for a tasty treat that's also pretty. Pictured on page 128.

Prep time: 35 minutes plus freezing
Baking time: 12 to 13 minutes
Microwave used

- **8 tablespoons butter or margarine**
- **4 ounces unsweetened chocolate squares, broken in half**
- **1 cup granulated sugar**
- **½ teaspoon vanilla extract**
- **2 large eggs**
- **1 cup all-purpose flour**
- **¼ teaspoon baking powder**
- **Pinch salt**
- **1 pint premium vanilla ice cream**
- **2 pints premium strawberry, chocolate or dulce de leche ice cream**
- **Confectioners' sugar, for garnish (optional)**

1. Heat oven to 325°F. Line a 15½×10½×1-inch jelly-roll pan with foil; lightly grease foil.

2. Combine butter and chocolate in a medium microwaveproof bowl; microwave on HIGH 2 minutes. Let stand 5 minutes; stir until smooth. Stir in sugar and vanilla. Beat in eggs with a wooden spoon until blended, then beat in flour, baking powder and salt until well combined.

3. Spread batter evenly in prepared pan. Bake 12 to 13 minutes, until brownie is set in center. Cool completely on wire rack. Invert brownie onto a cookie sheet; peel off foil and freeze 30 minutes.

4. Meanwhile, soften vanilla ice cream in the refrigerator 15 minutes. Line the same jelly-roll pan with plastic wrap. Spread softened vanilla ice cream evenly over one-half of pan (it should be approximately 10½×7½ inches). Freeze 1 hour. Soften strawberry ice cream in refrigerator 15 minutes. Evenly spread over remaining half of pan next to vanilla ice cream. (The strawberry layer will be thicker than the vanilla, and that's okay.) Freeze 1 hour.

5. Remove ice cream and brownie from freezer. Invert ice cream evenly onto brownie; remove pan and press lightly on the top of the wrap to adhere. Peel off wrap. Cut brownie and ice cream rectangle in half crosswise (each half should be a different ice cream flavor). Invert one half, ice cream side down, onto other half to form a sandwich. Freeze 30 minutes. Cut rectangle into quarters; then cut each quarter in half to make 8 sandwiches. Transfer sandwiches to a jelly-roll pan. Cover top of pan with heavy-duty foil and freeze overnight. *(Can be made ahead. Freeze up to 2 days.)* Just before serving, sprinkle tops of ice cream sandwiches with confectioners' sugar, if desired. Makes 8 sandwiches.

Per serving: 620 calories, 39 g total fat, 23.5 g saturated fat, 152 mg cholesterol, 230 mg sodium, 66 g carbohydrates, 9 g protein, 161 mg calcium, 3 g fiber

lemonade fruit salad LOW FAT EASY

We tossed pineapple, grapes, cherries and mango all together in a light lemony sugar syrup, but feel free to use any fresh fruit available at your local market.

Prep time: 25 minutes · Cooking time: 1 to 2 minutes

- **½ cup water**
- **3 tablespoons sugar**
- **2 teaspoons grated lemon peel**
- **1 teaspoon grated orange peel**
- **1 tablespoon fresh lemon juice**
- **1 pineapple (4 lb.) peeled, cored and cut into ¾-inch pieces**
- **1½ pounds red seedless grapes**
- **1 pound fresh Bing cherries, pitted**
- **1 mango, peeled, pitted and diced**

1. Bring water and sugar to boil in a small saucepan; stir to dissolve sugar. Add lemon and orange peels; cool to room temperature.

2. Transfer syrup to a large bowl; stir in lemon juice and fruits. *(Can be made ahead. Cover and refrigerate up to 6 hours.)* Makes 12 cups.

Per serving: 90 calories, 0.5 g total fat, 0 g saturated fat, 0 mg cholesterol, 2 mg sodium, 23 g carbohydrates, 1 g protein, 12 mg calcium, 2 g fiber

MARY DOYLE'S IRISH
SODA BREAD
PG. 172

kitchen pros share their best

Secrets of the culinary trade are well guarded. So here's a gift: A collection of specialties from well-known restaurants, favorites of top chefs and cookbook authors, and the best-loved recipes of LHJ editors—including perfect recipes for lemon bars, French toast and other classics.

PANELA-RUM
CURED SMOKED
SALMON
PG. 185

GRILLED
SHRIMP WITH
CHIMICHURRI
SAUCE
PG. 184

consider

our

barbecue

experts

BARBECUED PULLED
PORK SANDWICH
PG. 186

THE PERFECT
BURGER
PG. 181

CHICKEN
UNDER A BRICK
PG. 188
GRILLED PORTOBELLA
MUSHROOM SALAD
PG. 189

your own personal
pit crew

BARBECUED
BEEF BRISKET
PG. 186

ITALIAN
SAUSAGES WITH
POLENTA
PG. 177

food
editors
are busy, too...

PASTA WITH
BOLOGNESE
SAUCE
PG. 182

CRISPY
CHICKEN
TENDERS
PG. 180

CHICKEN SOUP
WITH
MUSHROOMS AND
CAVATAPPI
PG. 173

here are their
fastest favorites

LINGUINE WITH
ARTICHOKES
PG. 182

Kitchen Pros Share Their Best **165**

CURRIED
VEGETABLE
STEW WITH
COUSCOUS
PG. 183

pull out these
recipes

CHOCOLATE
CUPS WITH RICH
CHOCOLATE
MOUSSE
PG. 198

BUTTERFLIED
LEG OF LAMB
WITH HERB CRUST
PG. 178

BOUILLABAISSE
PG. 196

and **pull out** all
the stops

THE PERFECT
CINNAMON
ROLLS
PG. 169

ahhh . . .
sweet perfection

THE PERFECT
BUTTERMILK
PANCAKES
PG. 171

the perfect cinnamon rolls

What is it that makes these rolls rise and shine above the rest? We start with a sweet dough enriched with milk, egg and butter, so it bakes up extra-tender and moist. Next, we add a hefty dose of cinnamon-sugar to the filling, plus more butter and plenty of toasted pecans. Finally, the cinnamon rolls are topped with a sweet drizzle of tangy orange-sugar glaze. Pictured on page 168.

Prep time: 1 hour plus rising • Baking time: 35 minutes

DOUGH:
- 2 cups milk
- ¾ cup granulated sugar
- 2 packages active dry yeast
- ½ cup warm water (105°F. to 115°F.)
- 2 large egg yolks
- 1 teaspoon salt
- 7¼ to 8¼ cups all-purpose flour
- ¾ cup butter or margarine, softened

CINNAMON SUGAR:
- ¾ cup granulated sugar
- ¾ cup firmly packed brown sugar
- 2 tablespoons cinnamon

- 8 tablespoons butter or margarine, melted, divided
- 1½ cups pecan halves, chopped

GLAZE:
- 2 cups confectioners' sugar
- 2 to 2½ tablespoons orange juice

1. *Make dough:* Combine milk and sugar in a small saucepan. Heat, stirring occasionally, over medium heat, until sugar is dissolved. Cool until mixture is lukewarm. Sprinkle yeast over warm water in a large bowl; let stand 5 minutes, until yeast is foamy.

2. With a wooden spoon, beat milk mixture, egg yolks and salt into dissolved yeast, until blended. Beat in 4 cups of the flour, then softened butter, until mixture is smooth. Gradually stir in another 3¼ cups flour until blended and mixture forms a soft dough.

3. Grease a large bowl. On lightly floured surface, knead dough until smooth and elastic, adding as much of the remaining 1 cup of flour as necessary,

8 to 10 minutes. Place dough in a prepared bowl, turning to grease top. Cover bowl with plastic wrap and let dough rise in warm, draft-free place until doubled in bulk, 1 hour.

4. *Make cinnamon sugar:* Stir together granulated and brown sugars and cinnamon in a bowl, breaking up any small brown sugar lumps with a spoon; set aside.

5. Brush two 13×9×2-inch baking pans with 2 tablespoons of the melted butter. Sprinkle the bottom of each with ¼ cup of the cinnamon sugar. Turn dough out onto a lightly floured surface; cut in half. Roll 1 piece of dough into a 16×12-inch rectangle. Brush top with 3 tablespoons of the butter. Sprinkle entire surface evenly with ¾ cup of the cinnamon sugar; top evenly with half of the pecans. Starting at one long end of the rectangle, roll up dough tightly to form a log. Pinch edges to seal. With a serrated knife, cut log crosswise with a sawing motion into twelve 1¼-inch slices. Arrange slices cut side up in 4 rows, 3 per row, in one prepared pan, with space between the rows. Punch down remaining piece of dough. Repeat process, rolling and cutting with remaining melted butter, cinnamon sugar and pecans. Arrange slices in remaining prepared pan. Cover pans and let rolls rise until almost doubled in bulk, about 45 minutes (rolls will touch on all sides).

6. Meanwhile, adjust oven racks in middle and upper third positions. Heat oven to 350°F.

7. Uncover rolls and bake 20 minutes. Switch pans between racks and bake rolls 15 minutes, until golden and the middle of the center roll is baked. Immediately invert each pan, turning rolls out onto wire racks. Cool 5 minutes; turn rolls right side up. *(Can be made ahead. Cool completely. Wrap in plastic wrap and place in large food storage bag. Freeze up to 2 weeks. Thaw completely. Uncover and reheat on cookie sheet in 350°F. oven 15 minutes, until warm in center.)*

8. *Make glaze:* Meanwhile, combine confectioners' sugar and orange juice in bowl, stirring until smooth. Drizzle warm rolls with glaze. Makes 24 rolls.

Per roll: 415 calories, 16 g total fat, 7 g saturated fat, 46 mg cholesterol, 209 mg sodium, 63 g carbohydrates, 6 g protein, 5 mg calcium, 2 g fiber

the perfect egg

Here are four foolproof ways to cook eggs. And remember, great egg dishes depend on eggs that are in top condition. Whatever method you choose, buy refrigerated eggs with clean, uncracked shells and always store them in their cartons in the refrigerator.

HARD-COOKED: Place 2 to 12 large eggs in a single layer in a saucepan. Add enough cold water to come 1 inch above the eggs. Bring to boil. Remove from heat. Cover; let stand 15 minutes. Run cold water over eggs or place in ice water until cool enough to handle; peel.

SCRAMBLED: Beat 3 large eggs, 3 tablespoons milk, ¼ teaspoon salt and pinch ground pepper in a small bowl. Melt 1 teaspoon butter or margarine in a medium nonstick skillet over medium heat until butter is bubbly. Pour in eggs. As eggs begin to set, stir slowly, forming large, soft curds. Cook just until no liquid egg remains, but they are still glossy and moist.

SUNNY-SIDE UP: Melt 1 teaspoon butter or margarine in a medium nonstick skillet over medium heat until butter is bubbly. Break 2 large eggs into skillet. Cook about 1 minute, until whites are set. Add 2 teaspoons water. Cover skillet and cook 2 to 3 minutes, until yolks begin to thicken but are not hard.

POACHED: Bring 2 inches of water in a medium skillet (or fill a medium saucepan halfway up with water) to boil. Reduce heat so water is just simmering. Break 2 large eggs into a measuring cup with a handle. Carefully slide eggs into simmering water, holding the lip of cup as close to water as possible. Cook 2 to 4 minutes, until whites are completely set and yolks begin to thicken but are not hard. Using a slotted spoon, remove eggs. Season to taste.

the perfect french toast

To create melt-in-your-mouth first-rate French toast, begin with thick slices of challah, a bread that's just right for soaking up the egg mixture. Every porous inch of it sponges up the batter. Then, fry the bread slices in butter for crispy edges and an incredibly moist middle. Last but not least, combine traditional maple syrup with a trio of juicy berries for an incredible finish. Now that's perfection.

Prep time: 15 minutes • Cooking time: 15 minutes

BERRY SYRUP:
- ⅓ **cup water**
- ⅓ **cup pure maple syrup**
- ¼ **cup sugar**
- ½ **cup sliced fresh strawberries**
- ½ **cup fresh raspberries**
- ½ **cup fresh blueberries**
- 2 **tablespoons butter or margarine**
- 1 **teaspoon fresh lemon juice**

- 1 **loaf (1 lb.) challah or unsliced loaf white bread**
- 3 **tablespoons sugar**
- ¼ **teaspoon cinnamon**
- ¾ **cup half-and-half cream**
- 4 **large eggs**
- 2 **tablespoons orange-flavored liqueur (such as Grand Marnier)**
- 1 **teaspoon vanilla extract**
- 4 **tablespoons butter or margarine, divided**
  Fresh berries, for garnish (optional)

1. *Make berry syrup:* Combine water, maple syrup, sugar, strawberries, raspberries and blueberries in a medium saucepan. Bring to boil. Reduce heat; simmer 10 minutes, until berries soften and start to burst. Transfer mixture to a food processor; process until smooth. Strain through a fine sieve set over a bowl, stirring to strain as much as possible; discard seeds. Return to same saucepan; add butter. Cook and stir over low heat until butter melts. Stir in lemon juice. Set aside. Makes 1⅓ cups.

2. Cut challah crosswise into eight 1-inch-thick slices; discard ends of bread. Combine sugar and cinnamon in a medium bowl. Stir in cream, eggs, orange liqueur and vanilla. Pour mixture into a large jelly-roll pan. Add bread slices to pan, squeezing slightly to fit. Turn slices over. Let stand 10 minutes, until all of the egg mixture is absorbed.

3. Meanwhile, heat oven to 250°F. Heat two large skillets over medium-low heat. Add 1 tablespoon butter to each skillet. When butter is sizzling, add 2 slices of the challah to each skillet. Cook 3 minutes each side, until golden brown. Transfer slices to a cookie sheet; keep warm in oven. Repeat with remaining butter and bread. Serve with berry syrup. Garnish with berries, if desired. Makes 4 servings.

Per serving: 810 calories, 34.5 g total fat, 17 g saturated fat, 334 mg cholesterol, 819 mg sodium, 104 g carbohydrates, 19 g protein, 209 mg calcium, 4 g fiber

the perfect buttermilk pancakes

If you've ever known pancake nirvana, you've just come home. Without a doubt, these feather-light cakes stack up to the absolute best. Whip up a batch in no time for breakfast or supper and taste for yourself. (See box, right, for our secrets to super pancakes.) Pictured on page 168.

Prep time: 10 minutes
Cooking time: 3 to 5 minutes per batch

- **2 cups all-purpose flour**
- **2 tablespoons sugar**
- **2 teaspoons baking powder**
- **¾ teaspoon baking soda**
- **½ teaspoon salt**
- **2 cups buttermilk**
- **⅓ cup milk**
- **2 large eggs**
- **¼ cup butter or margarine, melted**
  Butter, vegetable oil or shortening, for frying
  Pure maple syrup and butter (optional)

1. Heat oven to 200°F. Whisk together flour, sugar, baking powder, baking soda and salt in a large bowl. Whisk together buttermilk, milk, eggs and melted butter in a medium bowl.

2. Heat a large nonstick griddle according to the manufacturer's instructions. (Or, heat a 12-inch nonstick skillet over medium-high heat.) When griddle is hot, add buttermilk mixture to dry ingredients. With a wooden spoon, stir just until moistened (batter will be lumpy).

3. Reduce heat to medium. Lightly grease griddle with butter, oil or shortening. Use a ladle or a ¼-cup dry measuring cup to pour batter onto prepared griddle. Cook 2 to 3 minutes, until bubbles break all over the surface. Use a spatula to turn pancakes. Cook 1 to 2 minutes more, until golden brown. Repeat with remaining batter. Place pancakes, in a single layer, on a paper towel-lined cookie sheet. Keep warm in oven. Serve with maple syrup and additional butter, if desired. Makes about 14 pancakes.

Per pancake: 140 calories, 5.5 g total fat, 3 g saturated fat, 44 mg cholesterol, 302 mg sodium, 18 g carbohydrates, 4 g protein, 94 mg calcium, 0 g fiber

---

test kitchen tip

perfecting pancakes

What's the key to making the fluffiest, lightest and most tender pancakes? Here are a few simple dos and don'ts to remember:

DO USE BUTTERMILK: It adds flavor and makes fluffy pancakes. If you don't have buttermilk on hand, for each cup you need, add 1 tablespoon vinegar plus enough milk to make 1 cup. Let stand 5 minutes before using.

USE A LIGHT HAND: Beating the batter until it is completely smooth produces tough pancakes. Stir the batter only until the dry ingredients are moistened. It will be lumpy.

DO USE UP ALL THE BATTER: Place pancakes, in a single layer, on a paper towel-lined cookie sheet. Keep them warm in a 200°F. oven until the last batch is cooked. Then, serve when you're ready to sit down. This way you can enjoy them while they're hot.

mary doyle's irish soda bread

A favorite at the Corner Bakery in Pawling, New York, this delectable bread, scented with caraway seeds and sweetened with raisins, isn't just served on Saint Patrick's Day. In fact, it is so popular they bake it year-round. The recipe is named in honor of Mary Doyle, mother of the bakery's prior owner. Pictured on page 161.

Prep time: 10 minutes • Baking time: 1 hour

- 2¾ **cups plus ¼ cup all-purpose flour, divided**
- ⅓ **cup sugar**
- 1 **teaspoon baking powder**
- ½ **teaspoon baking soda**
- ¾ **teaspoon salt**
- ⅔ **cup raisins**
- 1 **tablespoon caraway seeds**
- 1 **cup buttermilk**
- 2 **large eggs**
  Butter and jam (optional)

1. Adjust oven rack to center of oven. Heat oven to 325°F. Line a cookie sheet with parchment paper.

2. Whisk together 2¾ cups of the flour, the sugar, baking powder, baking soda and salt in a large bowl. Stir in raisins and caraway seeds. Whisk together buttermilk and eggs in a medium bowl. Add buttermilk mixture to dry ingredients. With a wooden spoon, stir just until moistened (dough will be sticky).

3. Sprinkle the remaining ¼ cup flour onto a work surface. Turn dough onto floured surface. With lightly floured hands, knead 10 to 12 strokes (dough will be soft and slightly sticky). Pat dough into a 6-inch round. Place in center of prepared cookie sheet. With a sharp paring knife, make a ½-inch-deep X across top of loaf.

4. Bake about 1 hour, until a toothpick inserted in center comes out clean. With a large spatula, transfer loaf to wire rack; cool completely. To serve, slice with a serrated knife. Serve with butter and jam, if desired. Makes twenty ½-inch slices.

Per slice: 105 calories, 1 g total fat, 0 g saturated fat, 22 mg cholesterol, 163 mg sodium, 22 g carbohydrates, 3 g protein, 38 mg calcium, 1 g fiber

tortilla soup

Hops! Bistro and Brewery in La Jolla, California, opened seven years ago, and this traditional Mexican soup is one of their most-ordered items. The lively combination of lime, cilantro and avocado really takes off in a zesty broth filled with diced smoked chicken, corn and tomatoes. The crisp tortilla chips add a delightful crunch.

Total prep and cooking time: 45 minutes

- 1½ **teaspoons olive oil**
- ⅓ **cup diced red onion**
- 1 **large clove garlic, minced**
- 2 **tablespoons seeded and minced jalapeño chile (see tip, page 15)**
- 4 **cans (14½ oz. each) chicken broth**
- 4 **ounces fully-cooked smoked boneless, skinless chicken breast, diced**
- ½ **cup fresh corn kernels**
- ⅓ **cup diced fresh tomato**
- ¼ **cup packed fresh cilantro leaves**
- 4 **small lime wedges, squeezed**
- 1 **medium ripe avocado, diced**
- 8 **to 12 tortilla chips**

1. Heat oil in a medium Dutch oven. Add onion, garlic and jalapeño. Cook over medium heat until vegetables soften, 6 to 8 minutes.

2. Add chicken broth. Stir in chicken. Bring to boil. Reduce heat and simmer 30 minutes. Remove the Dutch oven from heat. Add corn kernels, tomato and cilantro.

3. To serve, divide soup among 4 serving bowls. Top each serving with 1 of the lime wedges, ¼ of the diced avocado and 2 to 3 of the tortilla chips, broken into pieces. Serve immediately. Makes 4 servings.

Per serving: 125 calories, 6 g total fat, 1.5 g saturated fat, 12 mg cholesterol, 2,025 mg sodium, 8 g carbohydrates, 9 g protein, 11 mg calcium, 1 g fiber

chicken soup with mushrooms and cavatappi LOW FAT EASY

Assistant food editor Jane Yagoda Goodman makes this satisfying bowl of goodness especially for her youngest son, Will. He loves soup so much that he eats it year-round. To enrich the soup, Jane simmers the bones from the chicken thighs in the canned broth. Pictured on page 165.

Total prep and cooking time: 1 hour

- 4 skinless chicken thighs (1¼ lbs.)
- 1 boneless, skinless chicken breast (6 to 7 oz.)
- ¼ teaspoon salt
- ⅛ teaspoon freshly ground pepper
- 2 teaspoons olive oil, divided
- 4 ounces shiitake mushrooms, diced
- 2 carrots, cut into ½-inch diagonal pieces
- ⅓ cup finely chopped onion
- 2 cloves garlic, peeled
- 1 4½-inch slice fresh ginger
- 1 bay leaf
- 3 cans (14½ oz. each) chicken broth
- 1½ cups cavatappi or elbow macaroni
- 1½ cups chopped kale or Swiss chard

1. With a small, sharp knife, cut chicken thighs along the bone, removing as much thigh meat as possible. Reserve bones. Cut thigh and breast meat into 1-inch pieces. Sprinkle with salt and pepper.

2. Heat 1 teaspoon of the oil in a large saucepan or a small Dutch oven. Cook thigh meat until golden brown. With a slotted spoon, transfer to a bowl.

3. Add remaining 1 teaspoon oil. Cook chicken breast until golden brown. Transfer to another bowl.

4. Add mushrooms to saucepan. Cook 5 minutes. Add mushrooms to chicken breast in bowl. Add carrots, onion, garlic, ginger and bay leaf to same saucepan. Cook 3 to 5 minutes, until vegetables soften. Add chicken broth, reserved thigh meat and bones. Bring to boil. Cover; reduce heat and simmer 15 minutes.

5. Remove garlic, mash cloves and return to broth. Add pasta and chicken-mushroom mixture. Stir in kale. Cover and simmer 5 to 8 minutes, until

chicken is cooked through. Discard bay leaf and bones. Makes 4 servings.

Per serving: 430 calories, 10 g total fat, 2 g saturated fat, 119 mg cholesterol, 1,610 mg sodium, 40 g carbohydrates, 42 g protein, 75 mg calcium, 3 g fiber

macaroni and cheese chowder EASY

We developed this one-dish meal—another one of our fast favorites—for those weeknight suppers when you feel like eating a hot and hearty bowl of homemade chowder, but don't want to spend much time in the kitchen.

Prep time: 10 minutes • Cooking time: 12 to 14 minutes
Microwave used

- 1 tablespoon butter or margarine
- ¼ pound smoked ham, diced
- 1 cup chopped onions
- 1 package (12 oz.) Stouffer's frozen macaroni and cheese
- 1 can (14½ oz.) chicken broth
- 1 can (14¾ oz.) creamed-style corn
- 1 cup milk
- ¼ teaspoon salt
- ¼ teaspoon freshly ground pepper
- ½ pound boneless, skinless chicken breast, diced
   Fresh chives, for garnish (optional)
   Crusty bread (optional)

1. Heat butter in large saucepan over medium heat. Add ham and onions. Cook 5 minutes, stirring occasionally, until onions are softened and ham is lightly browned. Meanwhile, microwave the frozen macaroni and cheese according to the package directions.

2. Add macaroni and cheese, broth, corn, milk, salt and pepper to ham mixture. Bring to boil. Stir in chicken; reduce heat. Cover and simmer 3 to 4 minutes, until chicken is cooked through. Garnish with fresh chives and serve with crusty bread, if desired. Makes 4 servings.

Per serving: 385 calories, 14.5 g total fat, 6.5 g saturated fat, 74 mg cholesterol, 1,756 mg sodium, 38 g carbohydrates, 28 g protein, 207 mg calcium, 3 g fiber

minestra

Here's a fast favorite—Italian style—from our Italian food expert, Cynthia DePersio. This robust stew is filled with lots of vegetables and flavored with just a few links of Italian sausage. For easy slicing, first partially freeze the links, then cook until browned.

Prep time: 25 minutes • Cooking time: 35 minutes

- 2½ pounds escarole or Swiss chard, coarsely chopped
- ¼ cup water
- 1 teaspoon olive oil
- ½ pound sweet or hot Italian sausage links, cut into ½-inch-thick slices
- 1 tablespoon chopped garlic
- 1 can (16 oz.) whole tomatoes in juice
- 1 can (15 or 19 oz.) cannellini beans, drained and rinsed
- 2 pounds all-purpose potatoes, peeled and cut into 1-inch chunks
- ¼ teaspoon red pepper flakes
- 4 ounces Asiago or provolone cheese, diced

1. Combine escarole and water in a large stockpot. Cover and cook over medium heat until volume is reduced by half. Drain in a colander, reserving ½ cup cooking liquid in a cup.

2. Heat oil in stockpot over medium-high heat; add sausage slices and cook, turning frequently, 4 minutes, until browned. Add garlic and cook 30 seconds. Stir in tomatoes with juice and beans, breaking up tomatoes with a spoon. Bring to boil. Cook 3 minutes.

3. Reduce heat to medium-low. Stir in escarole with reserved ½ cup cooking liquid, the potatoes and red pepper flakes. Cover and cook 20 minutes, until potatoes are tender.

4. Stir cheese into stew; remove from heat and let stand until cheese is partially melted, about 5 minutes. Ladle into 6 large serving bowls. Makes 6 servings.

Per serving: 405 calories, 17.5 g total fat, 8 g saturated fat, 46 mg cholesterol, 708 mg sodium, 44 g carbohydrates, 21 g protein, 309 mg calcium, 13 g fiber

spring vegetable salad

Mollie Katzen, cookbook author and host of her own television cooking series, specializes in vegetarian cuisine. This recipe, from her Still Life with Menu Cookbook, *boasts a host of fresh vegetables as well as minced dill and fresh lemon juice. The ideal vegetables for this salad are the thinnest, youngest, most tender you can find.*

Total prep time: 50 minutes plus chilling

- 3 quarts water
- 8 small red potatoes (1¼ lbs.), halved
- 2¼ teaspoons salt, divided
- 3 tablespoons extra-virgin olive oil
- 1 teaspoon minced garlic
- 1 small head cauliflower, cut into 1-inch pieces
- ½ pound green beans, trimmed
- ¼ pound baby carrots, peeled and trimmed
- ½ pound snow peas, trimmed
- ½ pound asparagus, trimmed and cut into 1½-inch pieces
- 1 medium yellow squash, cut into ¼-inch slices
- ¼ cup mayonnaise
- 2 tablespoons minced fresh dill or 1 tablespoon minced fresh tarragon
- ¼ teaspoon freshly ground pepper
- 2 tablespoons fresh lemon juice

1. Bring water, potatoes and 2 teaspoons of the salt to boil in a Dutch oven. Cover; reduce heat and simmer 15 minutes, just until tender.

2. Meanwhile, combine oil and garlic in a large bowl. With a slotted spoon, transfer potatoes to a colander; drain well. Reserve water in Dutch oven. Toss potatoes with oil and garlic.

3. Return water to boil. Add cauliflower, green beans and carrots. Cook 8 to 10 minutes, until vegetables are just tender. With a slotted spoon, transfer vegetables to a colander; rinse under cold running water. Drain well; toss with potatoes. Reserve water in Dutch oven.

4. Return water to boil. Add snow peas, asparagus and squash. Cook 5 minutes, just until tender. Transfer to a colander; rinse under cold running water. Drain; toss gently with other vegetables.

5. Combine mayonnaise, dill, pepper and the remaining ¼ teaspoon salt in a small bowl; stir into vegetables; toss to coat. Cover and refrigerate until cold. Stir in lemon juice. Makes 14 cups.

Per cup: 115 calories, 6 g total fat, 1 g saturated fat, 2 mg cholesterol, 44 mg sodium, 12 g carbohydrates, 3 g protein, 33 mg calcium, 3 g fiber

tossed greens with goat cheese phyllo packets

When she was looking for new ways to serve the fresh greens that she brings home weekly from her local farmers' market, test kitchen associate Michele Peters came up with this terrific starter. Flaky phyllo packets are stuffed with oozing warm cheese and mango chutney, and served over crisp, cool greens for a clever twist on the warm goat cheese salad.

Prep time: 20 minutes • Baking time: 10 minutes

BALSAMIC VINAIGRETTE:

2	tablespoons balsamic vinegar
1	tablespoon prepared mango chutney, chopped
1	teaspoon finely chopped shallot
¼	teaspoon salt
⅛	teaspoon freshly ground pepper
3	tablespoons extra-virgin olive oil

3	sheets (18×14 inches) phyllo dough, thawed
2	tablespoons butter or margarine, melted
1	log (5 oz.) goat cheese with herbs
2	tablespoons prepared mango chutney
10	ounces mesclun or spring salad mix
3	large heads (8 oz.) Belgian endive, leaves separated
1	ripe pear, peeled, cored and thinly sliced

1. *Make balsamic vinaigrette:* Whisk together vinegar, chutney, shallot, salt and pepper in a bowl. Slowly whisk in oil. Set aside.

2. Lightly brush 1 of the phyllo sheets with melted butter. Top with a second sheet and brush with butter. Top with the remaining sheet and brush with butter. With a sharp knife, cut the layered

sheets in half lengthwise, then cut into 3 equal crosswise pieces.

3. Slice cheese into 6 equal pieces. Place 1 cheese slice in the center of each phyllo square. Top each with 1 teaspoon chutney. Bring corners of phyllo up around filling to enclose the filling.

4. Heat oven to 350°F. Lightly spray cookie sheet with vegetable cooking spray. Arrange phyllo packets on prepared sheet. Bake 10 minutes, until lightly browned. Meanwhile, toss greens, endive and pear slices with balsamic vinaigrette in a large bowl; arrange on plates. Top each with 1 warm phyllo packet. Makes 6 servings.

Per serving: 270 calories, 18.5 g total fat, 8.5 g saturated fat, 30 mg cholesterol, 327 mg sodium, 20 g carbohydrates, 7 g protein, 111 mg calcium, 2 g fiber

test kitchen tip
phyllo know-how

Phyllo (also spelled "filo" or "fillo") is ultra-thin pastry dough used to create both sweet and savory dishes. The tissue-thin sheets are delicate, so keep the following hints in mind:

THAW FROZEN PHYLLO overnight in the refrigerator. Once thawed, keep phyllo refrigerated and tightly wrapped. It will keep for 3 days. Phyllo becomes brittle if refrozen.

TO PREVENT THE THAWED PHYLLO from becoming dry and brittle, unfold sheets and remove only as many as you need. Place the stack of phyllo sheets between pieces of plastic wrap. Remove them one at a time as needed. Another method is to cover phyllo with a sheet of waxed paper topped by a slightly damp kitchen towel. However, if the cloth touches the phyllo, it will make the sheets soggy and unusable.

LIGHTLY BRUSH PHYLLO DOUGH with the melted butter or oil according to recipe, being sure to brush it all the way to the edges. This prevents the clumping of layers and keeps them separated, yielding the flakiest results.

calzones

Featured in Mollie Katzen's Enchanted Broccoli Forest Cookbook, *this recipe is a dynamite dinner in a pocket. Choose from one of two fillings—zucchini or provolone.*

Prep time: 30 minutes plus rising
Baking time: 15 to 17 minutes

DOUGH:

1	cup warm water (105°F. to 115°F.)
2	teaspoons sugar or honey
1½	teaspoons active dry yeast
1½	cups all-purpose flour, divided
1	cup whole wheat flour
¼	cup cornmeal
3	tablespoons olive oil or melted butter
1½	teaspoons salt

ZUCCHINI FILLING:

2	tablespoons olive oil
2	cups minced onions
1	teaspoon salt
1	teaspoon dried oregano
3	medium zucchini, thinly sliced
1	tablespoon minced garlic
¼	teaspoon freshly ground pepper
⅛	teaspoon red pepper flakes
2	cups shredded mozzarella cheese

PROVOLONE FILLING:

3	tablespoons olive oil
1	teaspoon minced garlic
½	cup fresh bread crumbs
4	cups shredded provolone cheese, divided
4	plum tomatoes, sliced
	Freshly ground pepper

1. *Make dough:* Combine water, sugar and yeast in a large bowl; let stand 5 minutes, until creamy. With a wooden spoon, beat in 1¼ cups of the all-purpose flour, the whole wheat flour, cornmeal, oil and salt until a smooth dough forms and pulls away from side of bowl. On a lightly floured surface, knead dough 5 minutes, adding the remaining ¼ cup of all-purpose flour. Place dough in a greased bowl, turning to grease top. Cover; let rise in warm, draft-free place until doubled in bulk, 1 hour.

2. Meanwhile, make the desired filling (see recipes, right).

3. Adjust oven rack to lowest position. Heat oven to 425°F. Lightly grease 2 cookie sheets.

4. Divide dough into 8 equal pieces. On a lightly floured surface, roll each piece into a 6-inch circle. Brush edge of circles with water. Spoon on desired filling as directed (see below). Fold top half of circle over filling to make a semicircle. Fold edge over; press edge down with tines of a fork to seal. Transfer calzones to prepared pans. Prick tops of each with a fork. Bake 15 to 17 minutes, until golden brown. Makes 8 calzones.

Zucchini Filling: Heat oil in a large skillet over medium heat. Add onions, salt and oregano. Cook 5 minutes, until onions are softened. Add zucchini and garlic. Cook 5 to 8 minutes more, until zucchini is just tender. Stir in red pepper flakes. Place a scant ½ cup of the filling in bottom half of each circle, leaving a ½-inch border. Top with ¼ cup of the cheese.

Provolone Filling: Combine oil and garlic in a small bowl. Brush center of each circle with oil mixture. Sprinkle each with 1 tablespoon of the bread crumbs. Place ½ cup of the cheese in bottom half of each circle, leaving a ½-inch border. Top each with 2 or 3 tomato slices. Lightly sprinkle with pepper.

Per serving for calzones with zucchini: 328 calories, 14 g total fat, 4 g saturated fat, 16 mg cholesterol, 864 mg sodium, 40 g carbohydrates, 13 g protein, 216 mg calcium, 5 g fiber

Per serving for calzones with provolone: 488 calories, 28 g total fat, 13 g saturated fat, 46 mg cholesterol, 1,034 mg sodium, 36 g carbohydrates, 22 g protein, 515 mg calcium, 3 g fiber

one-sided cooked salmon 🟢

Ladies' Home Journal food editor Jan Hazard enjoyed this entrée at a restaurant in New York City so much she decided to replicate it in her home kitchen. Jan's tip: You don't need to turn the fish. The fillets cook skin side down, so it gets nice and crispy.

Prep time: 5 minutes · Cooking time: 6 to 7 minutes

2	tablespoons flour
1	teaspoon salt, divided
¼	teaspoon freshly ground pepper

1¼ **pounds center-cut salmon fillet, cut crosswise into 4 pieces**

1 **tablespoon olive oil**

2 **tablespoons chopped fresh dill**

1. Combine flour, ½ teaspoon of the salt and the pepper on waxed paper. Dip each piece of salmon, skin side down, into flour mixture; shake off excess. Set aside on waxed paper. Sprinkle pieces evenly with the remaining ½ teaspoon salt; set aside.

2. Heat a heavy large skillet over high heat 1 minute. Reduce heat to medium-high; add oil and heat 1 minute more. Add salmon pieces, skin side down. Cover and cook 5 to 6 minutes, until cooked through. Sprinkle with dill. Makes 4 servings.

Per serving: 305 calories, 19 g total fat, 3.5 g saturated fat, 84 mg cholesterol, 666 mg sodium, 3 g carbohydrates, 29 g protein, 19 mg calcium, 0 g fiber

italian sausages with polenta (EASY)

Using the microwave can provide benefits beyond the obvious time-saving one. Ladies' Home Journal *associate food editor Carol Prager explains: "I'm constantly looking for the best ways to cook in my tiny apartment kitchen, so I often use the microwave. And I've found it's a great way to make a fabulous polenta." Pictured on page 164.*

Prep time: 5 minutes • Cooking time: 18 minutes
Microwave used

POLENTA:

1 **can (14½ oz.) chicken broth**

1 **cup yellow cornmeal**

2½ **cups milk**

¼ **teaspoon freshly ground pepper**

⅓ **cup freshly shredded Parmesan cheese**

■

8 **links Italian sausage (2 lbs.)**

½ **cup water**

1. *Make polenta:* Whisk broth and cornmeal in a large microwaveproof bowl. Whisk in milk and pepper. Microwave on HIGH 9 minutes. Whisk again; microwave 9 minutes more, until thickened.

2. Heat a 12-inch nonstick skillet over high heat 1 minute. Add sausages. Cook, turning often, until browned. Add water. Cover; cook sausages 5 minutes. Uncover; cook sausages, turning, until liquid evaporates and sausages are charred and cooked through. Whisk cheese into polenta. Divide among 4 shallow serving bowls. Top each serving with 2 sausages. Makes 4 servings.

Per serving: 805 calories, 51.5 g total fat, 20 g saturated fat, 157 mg cholesterol, 2,194 mg sodium, 37 g carbohydrates, 45 g protein, 334 mg calcium, 2 g fiber

chicken francese

The Crow's Nest, in Hackensack, New Jersey, serves this outstanding dish. It features tender chicken breasts with a light, lemony sauce delightfully spiked with white wine.

Prep time: 15 minutes • Cooking time: 12 to 15 minutes

2 **large eggs**

¼ **cup all-purpose flour**

2 **tablespoons vegetable oil**

4 **boneless, skinless chicken breast halves (4 to 5 oz. each)**

½ **teaspoon salt**

½ **cup chicken broth**

½ **cup white wine**

¼ **cup fresh lemon juice**

¼ **cup butter, cut up (no substitutes)**

1 **tablespoon chopped fresh parsley**

Freshly ground pepper, to taste

1. With a fork, beat eggs in a shallow dish. Spread flour in another shallow dish.

2. Heat oil in a large skillet over medium-high heat. Sprinkle chicken with salt. Dip each breast in flour, shake off excess, then dip in egg. Cook chicken 3 minutes each side, until cooked through. Transfer chicken to a plate; keep warm.

3. Discard oil from skillet. Add chicken broth, wine and lemon juice. Bring to boil. Boil 6 minutes, until mixture is reduced to ⅓ cup. Remove skillet from heat. Whisk butter into sauce, until slightly thickened. Stir in parsley and pepper. Serve with chicken. Makes 4 servings.

Per serving: 370 calories, 22.5 g total fat, 9.5 g saturated fat, 211 mg cholesterol, 651 mg sodium, 7 g carbohydrates, 34 g protein, 35 mg calcium, 0 g fiber

butterflied leg of lamb with herb crust

Todd English, award-winning chef and owner of the Olives and Figs restaurants in Boston, Massachusetts, is known for his bold and vibrant interpretations of Mediterranean dishes. He certainly puts his stamp on the classic lamb roast here, pairing it with a wonderful tapenade, tangy feta cheese and fresh herb bread crumbs. Tip: To make sure the leg of lamb cooks quickly and evenly, have the butcher bone and butterfly it so that it opens out to a uniform thickness. Pictured on page 166.

Prep time: 20 minutes plus marinating
Cooking time: 36 to 38 minutes

    1   boneless leg of lamb (3½ lbs.), butterflied,
        excess fat removed

MARINADE:

    3   tablespoons olive oil
    2   cloves garlic, minced
    2   teaspoons red pepper flakes
        Grated peel of 1 medium orange
    1   tablespoon fennel seeds, lightly crushed
    4   cardamom pods, lightly crushed
    1   tablespoon ginger

TAPENADE:

    2   tablespoons olive oil
    3   cloves garlic, chopped
    1½ cups pitted Moroccan dry-cured or kalamata
        olives
    2   tablespoons capers, drained
    2   anchovy fillets

HERB BREAD CRUMBS:

    2   tablespoons butter or margarine
    1   cup fresh white bread crumbs (about 2 slices)
    1   tablespoon chopped fresh rosemary or
        1 teaspoon dried rosemary
    2   tablespoons chopped fresh flat-leaf parsley

    1   cup feta cheese, crumbled
        Steamed asparagus and roasted potatoes
        (optional)

1. Arrange butterflied leg of lamb to lie flat on a cutting board. Make sure the meat is a uniform thickness. (If needed, use a meat mallet to pound thicker part of meat to make it uniform.)

2. *Make marinade:* Combine all ingredients for the marinade in a medium glass bowl. Add lamb to bowl. Rub marinade on meat to coat all sides. Cover bowl with plastic wrap. Marinate lamb in the refrigerator at least 2 hours. *(Can be made ahead. Refrigerate up to 12 hours.)*

3. *Make tapenade:* Combine oil and garlic in a small skillet. Cook and stir garlic over medium heat 1 minute, until fragrant. Add olives, capers and anchovies. Cook 3 to 4 minutes more, until anchovies begin to break apart and capers color slightly. Transfer olive mixture to food processor. Pulsing machine on and off several times, process mixture until all ingredients are combined, but still slightly chunky. Transfer tapenade to a small glass bowl. *(Can be made ahead. Cover with plastic wrap and refrigerate overnight. Bring to room temperature before using.)*

4. Remove lamb from the refrigerator 30 minutes before cooking. Arrange lamb to lie flat on the bottom of broiler pan.

5. *Make herb bread crumbs:* Meanwhile, melt butter in a large skillet over medium heat. Add bread crumbs and rosemary. Cook and stir 2 to 3 minutes, until bread crumbs are lightly browned. Remove skillet from heat; stir in parsley.

6. Heat broiler. Broil lamb 4 inches from heat source 10 to 12 minutes, until top of lamb is well browned. Reduce oven temperature to 400°F. Transfer broiler pan to center oven rack. Roast lamb 15 minutes. Remove lamb from oven.

7. Spread tapenade evenly over top of lamb. Sprinkle feta cheese over tapenade, then bread crumbs over feta cheese. Return lamb to oven and roast 7 to 8 minutes more, until meat registers 135°F. on instant-read thermometer when inserted into thickest portion of lamb (for medium-rare). Transfer lamb to a cutting board. Let stand 5 minutes before slicing. Thinly slice lamb. Arrange on a large serving platter. Serve with asparagus and potatoes, if desired. Makes 6 to 8 servings.

Per serving: 595 calories, 39 g total fat, 11 g saturated fat, 172 mg cholesterol, 1,588 mg sodium, 9 g carbohydrates, 52 g protein, 164 mg calcium, 1 g fiber

the perfect t-bone steak

If you're ready to sink your teeth into the juiciest, most succulent steak ever, then you've come to the right recipe. T-bone steak is prized for its mellow, beefy flavor, so once you have the right cut and grade (see box, right), you're all set. To create the ultimate steakhouse feast at home, we recommend serving T-bones with twice-baked potatoes and a tossed green salad.

Prep time: 30 minutes • Grilling time: 9 to 10 minutes

- **2   T-bone steaks, top choice or certified Black Angus (1¼ to 1½ lbs. each), cut 1½ inches thick**
- **2   teaspoons olive oil**
- **1   teaspoon kosher salt**
- **1   teaspoon freshly ground pepper**

1. Heat grill for direct grilling. For charcoal: Build a pile of briquettes on bottom grate. Ignite and burn briquettes 25 to 30 minutes, until coals are covered with a light coating of gray ash. Spread coals evenly across grate; cover with top cooking grate and heat grate 10 to 15 minutes. For gas: Heat all burners on high 10 to 15 minutes. Reduce heat to medium.

2. Brush each side of both steaks with ½ teaspoon of the oil. Combine salt and pepper in cup; sprinkle over both sides of each steak.

3. Arrange steaks in center of cooking grate; close lid and grill steaks over medium heat 5 minutes. Turn steaks; close lid and grill 4 to 5 minutes more, until instant-read thermometer inserted into thickest side of steak registers 130°F. Transfer steaks to 2 large plates; let stand 5 minutes (the temperature will increase to 135°F. for medium-rare). Makes 2 to 4 servings.

Per serving: 1,145 calories, 83 g total fat, 32 g saturated fat, 307 mg cholesterol, 963 mg sodium, 1 g carbohydrates, 93 g protein, 39 mg calcium, 0 g fiber

rigatoni with chicken and gorgonzola

Here's a luscious recipe, courtesy of Primavera restaurant at the Fairmont Hotel in Chicago, Illinois. An incredible sauce starts out innocently enough with skillet-cooked chicken breast slices and sautéed mushrooms; then heavy cream and a divine duo of gorgonzola and parmesan cheese make a most decadent finish. The sauce is tossed with rigatoni—but penne works fine, too.

Prep time: 15 minutes • Cooking time: 11 minutes

- ½ **pound boneless, skinless chicken breast, cut crosswise into ½-inch-thick slices**
- ½ **teaspoon salt, divided**
- ½ **teaspoon freshly ground pepper, divided**
- 1 **tablespoon olive oil**
- ¼ **pound shiitake mushrooms, sliced (2 cups)**
- 1 **cup heavy or whipping cream**
- ½ **cup (2 oz.) crumbled Gorgonzola cheese, divided**
- ⅓ **cup freshly grated Parmesan cheese**
- ½ **pound rigatoni or penne, cooked according to package directions**
- 2 **tablespoons chopped fresh parsley**

1. Sprinkle chicken with ¼ teaspoon each of the salt and pepper.

2. Heat oil in a 12-inch nonstick skillet over medium-high heat. Add chicken and cook, turning halfway through, 3 minutes, until edges are light brown. Add mushrooms. Cook, stirring, 2 to 4 minutes more, until mushrooms are softened and lightly golden and chicken is cooked through.

3. Stir in cream and cook about 3 minutes, until mixture is reduced by half. Stir in ¼ cup of the Gorgonzola and the Parmesan. Reduce heat to low; cook, stirring, 1 minute more, until cheeses melt. Stir in remaining ¼ teaspoon each salt and pepper.

4. Toss hot pasta with sauce; divide among 4 serving plates. Sprinkle top with remaining ¼ cup Gorgonzola and the parsley. Makes 4 servings.

Per serving: 605 calories, 34 g total fat, 19 g saturated fat, 133 mg cholesterol, 699 mg sodium, 46 g carbohydrates, 29 g protein, 245 mg calcium, 2 g fiber

crispy chicken tenders LOW FAT EASY

We all need fast meals for busy weeknight dinners, and Jane Yagoda Goodman, assistant food editor for Ladies' Home Journal, *is no exception. "Fried chicken is one of my family's all-time favorites, and these quick-cooking chicken tenders deliver the same great flavor and crunch as any takeout." Pictured on page 165.*

Prep time: 10 minutes plus standing
Cooking time: 8 to 12 minutes

- 1½ **pounds chicken tenders**
- ½ **teaspoon salt, divided**
- 1 **cup buttermilk**
- ⅛ **teaspoon red pepper sauce**
- 1¼ **cups all-purpose flour**
- ¼ **teaspoon freshly ground pepper**
- ¼ **teaspoon paprika**
- **Pinch cinnamon**
- 1 **cup vegetable oil**
- **Red pepper sauce or ketchup (optional)**

1. Heat oven to 300°F. Sprinkle chicken with ¼ teaspoon of the salt. Combine buttermilk and hot red pepper sauce in a large bowl. Add chicken; let stand 10 minutes.

2. Meanwhile, combine flour, the remaining ¼ teaspoon salt, the pepper, paprika and cinnamon in a large 1-gallon resealable plastic storage bag.

3. Remove chicken from buttermilk mixture, letting excess drip. Add half of the chicken to flour mixture, shaking to coat. Transfer chicken to a sheet of waxed paper. Repeat with remaining chicken.

4. Heat oil in a large skillet over medium-high heat 3 to 5 minutes, until oil is very hot. Cook chicken in batches 2 to 3 minutes per side, until golden brown and cooked through. Transfer chicken to a cookie sheet; keep warm in oven. Repeat.

5. Serve chicken with red pepper sauce or ketchup, if desired. Makes 4 servings.

Per serving: 435 calories, 13 g total fat, 2 g saturated fat, 100 mg cholesterol, 435 mg sodium, 31 g carbohydrates, 44 g protein, 6 mg calcium, 1 g fiber

the perfect burger

To do the basic burger one better, make it the absolute best it can be! We recommend choice-grade beef top round. Ask your butcher for the freshest available, and have it ground twice through a fine plate for the best burger texture. We added herb butter to the center of each patty for exceptionally velvety burgers. Tip: When shaping the patties, handle the meat as little as possible; too much handling toughens the meat. Pictured on page 162.

Prep time: 20 minutes plus chilling
Grilling time: 14 to 16 minutes

HERB BUTTER:

- ½ cup butter, softened (no substitutes)
- 2 tablespoons minced fresh tarragon
- 2 tablespoons minced fresh thyme
- 2 tablespoons finely chopped fresh flat-leaf parsley

- 2 pounds ground beef top round
- ½ teaspoon salt
- ½ teaspoon freshly ground pepper
- 4 crusty rolls or English muffins, split
- 4 lettuce leaves
- 8 tomato slices
- French fries or potato chips (optional)

1. *Make herb butter:* With a rubber spatula, beat all of the ingredients for the butter until well combined. Transfer butter to a sheet of plastic wrap. Roll butter into a 3×2-inch log and refrigerate 3 hours, until firm. *(Can be made ahead. Freeze up to 1 month.)* Cut chilled log crosswise into 8 equal slices. (Wrap 3 slices and refrigerate for another use.) Cut each slice into small pieces.

2. Divide beef into quarters. Gently shape each piece into a patty. Split 1 patty in half horizontally. Sprinkle pieces from 1 slice herb butter over split side of patty. Replace top half of patty, gently pinching edge to seal. Gently shape until 1 inch thick. Transfer to large plate. Repeat with remaining beef and herb butter. Chill patties in freezer 15 minutes.

3. Heat grill. Sprinkle salt and pepper over both sides of patties. Grill 7 to 8 minutes, until done (160°F.), turning once. (See tip, above.)

4. While burgers are grilling, spread the remaining slice of herb butter over cut sides of rolls. Grill rolls, cut side down, 1 to 2 minutes, until toasted.

5. Place lettuce leaves on bottom halves of rolls. Top with burgers, then tomato slices. Serve with french fries or chips, if desired. Makes 4 burgers.

Per burger: 755 calories, 42 g total fat, 18 g saturated fat, 197 mg cholesterol, 860 mg sodium, 32 g carbohydrates, 59 g protein, 78 mg calcium, 2 g fiber

linguine with artichokes

Here is one of our favorite ways to eat artichokes—sliced, drizzled with lemon and tossed with pancetta and onion in a wine broth with linguine. Pictured on page 165.

Prep time: 30 minutes • Cooking time: 18 to 20 minutes

- 2 **lemons, halved**
- 3 **large artichokes**
- 1 **tablespoon olive oil**
- 2 **ounces pancetta or 2 slices cooked bacon, chopped**
- 1 **cup chopped onions**
- 1 **tablespoon chopped garlic**
- ½ **teaspoon salt**
- 3 **tablespoons chopped fresh flat-leaf parsley, divided**
- 1 **cup chicken broth**
- ½ **cup white wine**
- 1 **pound linguine, cooked according to package directions**
- ½ **cup freshly shredded Parmesan cheese (3 oz.)**
- ¼ **teaspoon freshly ground pepper**

1. Fill a bowl with cold water. Squeeze juice from 2 lemon halves into bowl. For each artichoke, trim stem to 1 inch and peel. Bend back tough outer petals until they snap off near the base and a layer of tender yellow petals is exposed. Discard outer petals. Cut off top quarter of artichoke. With a knife, peel outer dark-green layer from base and stem. Cut artichoke in half from top to stem end. With sharp-edged spoon, scrape away the prickly inner purple petals and fuzzy center (choke); discard. Rub all sides of artichoke halves with remaining lemon halves. Place artichoke halves in water. (These steps prevent discoloration.) Repeat process with remaining artichokes. Place an artichoke half, cut side down, on a cutting board and thinly slice. Repeat with remaining artichoke halves. Squeeze juice from remaining lemon halves over artichoke slices.

2. Heat oil in a Dutch oven. Add pancetta; cook until pancetta begins to brown. Add onions, bacon (if using), garlic and salt. Cook until onions soften. Stir in artichoke slices and 2 tablespoons of the parsley. Add broth and wine. Bring to boil. Place a sheet of waxed paper directly on top of artichokes; then cover pan with lid. Simmer artichokes 15 minutes, until tender.

3. Toss hot pasta with artichokes and remaining parsley. Top with Parmesan cheese and pepper. Makes 4 servings.

Per serving: 680 calories, 16 g total fat, 6 g saturated fat, 23 mg cholesterol, 1,143 mg sodium, 102 g carbohydrates, 29 g protein, 338 mg calcium, 9 g fiber

pasta with bolognese sauce

This heavenly pasta comes from test kitchen associate Cynthia DePersio, who specializes in Italian food. She says, "This dish cooks up faster than the classic spaghetti and meatballs." Pictured on page 164.

Total prep and cooking time: 30 minutes
Microwave used

BOLOGNESE SAUCE:
- 1 **can (28 oz.) crushed tomatoes in puree**
- 3 **cans (8 oz. each) tomato sauce**
- ⅓ **cup water**
- ½ **teaspoon dried rosemary**
- ¼ **teaspoon red pepper flakes**
- ⅛ **teaspoon crushed fennel seed**
- 1 **tablespoon olive oil**
- ½ **cup chopped onion**
- ½ **pound sliced shiitake mushrooms, coarsely chopped**
- 1 **tablespoon chopped garlic**
- ½ **pound ground veal**
- ½ **pound ground pork**
- ½ **teaspoon salt**
- ¼ **teaspoon freshly ground pepper**
- ¾ **cup white wine**

- 1 **pound castellane or rigatoni pasta**
  Grated Romano or Parmesan cheese

1. Bring water for pasta to boil. Microwave tomatoes, tomato sauce, water, rosemary, red pepper flakes and fennel seed, covered, in a microwaveproof bowl on HIGH 15 minutes.

2. Heat oil in a 12-inch nonstick skillet. Add onion, mushrooms and garlic. Cook 8 minutes. Add veal

and pork; sprinkle with salt and pepper. Cook, breaking up meat, until no longer pink. Add wine. Gently boil 2 minutes. Stir in tomato mixture. Bring to boil. Cover and simmer 10 minutes.

3. Meanwhile, start to cook pasta according to package directions.

4. Drain pasta; return to pot. Toss pasta with 2 cups of the Bolognese Sauce; transfer to a bowl. Top with 1 cup of the sauce. Serve with the remaining sauce and cheese. Makes 4 servings.

Per serving: 815 calories, 21.5 g total fat, 7 g saturated fat, 87 mg cholesterol, 1,726 mg sodium, 115 g carbohydrates, 41 g protein, 149 mg calcium, 8 g fiber

curried vegetable stew with couscous EASY

Test kitchen assistant Alena Ramnauth, who grew up in Guyana, South America, says, "Vegetable curry was often eaten after a religious fast, but now it's simply one of my family's favorite dinners." Pictured on page 166.

Total prep and cooking time: 40 minutes

CURRY:
- 2 **tablespoons water**
- 1 **tablespoon cumin**
- 1 **teaspoon coriander**
- 1 **teaspoon curry powder**
- ¾ **teaspoon salt**
- ¼ **teaspoon allspice**
- ¼ **teaspoon cinnamon**
- ¼ **teaspoon freshly ground pepper**

- 3 **tablespoons olive oil**
- ½ **cup chopped onion**
- 1 **tablespoon chopped garlic**
- 1 **tablespoon chopped fresh cilantro**
- 1 **small head cauliflower, cut into florets**
- 2 **medium zucchini, diced**
- 1 **cup green beans, cut into ½-inch pieces**
- 1½ **cups water**
- 1 **cup canned chickpeas, drained and rinsed**
- 1 **cup diced fresh tomatoes**

Cooked couscous, fresh cilantro, sliced green onions and plain yogurt (optional)

1. *Make curry:* Whisk together all of the curry ingredients in a small bowl until smooth. Set aside.

2. Heat oil in a large skillet over medium heat. Add onion, garlic, cilantro and curry. Cook, stirring, 1 minute, until vegetables are just beginning to soften. Add cauliflower, zucchini and beans. Cook 2 minutes. Add water; bring mixture to boil. Cover; simmer 10 minutes, until vegetables are almost tender. Stir in chickpeas and tomatoes. Simmer 5 minutes more, until vegetables are tender. Serve with couscous, cilantro, green onions and yogurt, if desired. Makes 4 servings.

Per serving: 205 calories, 12 g total fat, 1.5 g saturated fat, 0 mg cholesterol, 540 mg sodium, 21 g carbohydrates, 7 g protein, 91 mg calcium, 6 g fiber

speedy sweet potatoes EASY

These yummy spuds are one of our favorite fast-and-good-for-you sides. The secret to cooking them up quickly is steaming the potatoes as opposed to baking them.

Prep time: 10 minutes • Cooking time: 15 minutes

- 1½ **pounds sweet potatoes, peeled and quartered**

GARLIC BUTTER:
- 1 **tablespoon butter or margarine**
- 1 **teaspoon minced garlic**
- ¼ **teaspoon salt**
- ¼ **teaspoon freshly ground pepper**

1. Arrange a steamer basket in a saucepan. Add enough water to reach just below the basket. Add potatoes, cover pan and bring water to boil. Reduce heat and cook potatoes 15 minutes, until tender.

2. *Make garlic butter:* Meanwhile, melt butter in a small skillet over low heat. Add garlic, salt and pepper. Cook 2 to 3 minutes, until garlic is fragrant. To serve, drizzle sweet potatoes with Garlic Butter; stir to evenly coat. Makes 4 servings.

Per serving: 155 calories, 3 g total fat, 2 g saturated fat, 8 mg cholesterol, 188 mg sodium, 30 g carbohydrates, 2 g protein, 30 mg calcium, 4 g fiber

beef tenderloin with mint mojo

Chef Douglas Rodriguez, who struts his flashy south-of-the-border cooking style at Chicama in New York City, shares this spectacular recipe. It features "mojo" (mo-HO), a combination of citrus juices, herbs, garlic and extra-virgin olive oil, commonly served as a condiment with grilled foods in Latin cooking. Rodriguez's mojo, however, substitutes mint jelly and vinegar for the citrus juices, and he serves it with charred cubes of juicy steak. How's that for invention?

Prep time: 30 minutes • Grilling time: 12 to 14 minutes

12 (4- to 5-inch) wooden skewers
MINT MOJO:
  ⅓ **cup olive oil, divided**
  ¾ **cup packed fresh mint leaves**
  2 **medium cloves garlic**
  ½ **teaspoon salt**
  ¼ **cup mint jelly**
  ¼ **cup red wine vinegar**
  ¼ **teaspoon freshly ground pepper**
     ■

1¼ **pounds boneless beef top tenderloin, cut into 1-inch chunks**
1½ **teaspoons kosher salt**
  ¼ **teaspoon freshly ground pepper**

1. ■ Soak the skewers in a shallow bowl of water 30 minutes. Drain; set aside.

2. ■ *Make mint mojo:* Meanwhile, drizzle 1 tablespoon of the oil over the mint leaves on a cutting board. Add garlic and salt; chop until mixture forms a paste. Transfer to a bowl; stir in the remaining oil, jelly, vinegar and pepper. *(Can be made ahead. Cover and refrigerate overnight.)*

3. ■ Heat grill. Toss beef with salt and pepper in a large bowl. Thread about 5 pieces of beef onto each skewer. Grill beef over medium heat 6 to 7 minutes each side for medium rare. Serve with Mint Mojo. Makes 12 skewers.

Per skewer: 170 calories, 12.5 g total fat, 3.5 g saturated fat, 27 mg cholesterol, 305 mg sodium, 6 g carbohydrates, 8 g protein, 28 mg calcium, 1 g fiber

grilled shrimp with chimichurri sauce

A fabulous twist on grilled shrimp with Chef Rodriguez's signature. "Chimichurri is almost like a pesto," he says. "It's a spicy condiment with lots of chopped fresh herbs that's usually paired with meat, but I love it with fish, too." Pictured on page 162.

Prep time: 30 minutes • Grilling time: 5 to 6 minutes

12 (4- to 5-inch) wooden skewers
CHIMICHURRI SAUCE:
  6 **cloves garlic**
  3 **fresh bay leaves, broken into pieces**
  2 **jalapeño chiles, seeded and coarsely chopped (see tip, page 15)**
  ½ **cup lightly packed fresh curly parsley leaves**
  ½ **cup lightly packed fresh flat-leaf parsley leaves**
  ¼ **cup lightly packed fresh oregano leaves**
  1 **teaspoon salt**
  ⅓ **cup extra-virgin olive oil**
  ¼ **cup distilled white vinegar**
     ■

  1 **pound (24) large shrimp, peeled and deveined**

1. ■ Soak the skewers in a shallow bowl of water 30 minutes. Drain; set aside.

2. ■ *Make chimichurri sauce:* Meanwhile, chop garlic, bay leaves, jalapeños, curly and flat-leaf parsley, oregano and salt on a cutting board until a coarse paste forms. Transfer to a bowl; stir in olive oil and vinegar. (If using a mortar and pestle, mince the parsley. Mash the garlic, bay leaves, jalapeño and salt until mixture forms a paste. Stir in parsley; then whisk in oil and vinegar.) *(Can be made ahead. Cover and refrigerate overnight.)* Makes ⅔ cup.

3. ■ Heat grill. Thread 2 shrimp on each skewer. Grill shrimp over medium heat 2½ to 3 minutes each side, until shrimp turn pink and are opaque. Serve with Chimichurri Sauce. Makes 12 skewers.

Per skewer: 95 calories, 7 g total fat, 1 g saturated fat, 47 mg cholesterol, 243 mg sodium, 2 g carbohydrates, 7 g protein, 40 mg calcium, 0 g fiber

panela-rum cured smoked salmon (EASY)

Here's another culinary contribution from Chef Douglas Rodriguez—and it may just be the moistest piece of fish you'll ever taste. The salmon gets its sweet-salty flavor from the marinade—a combination of "panela," a cooked form of pure unprocessed sugar cane (commonly available in Latin markets), rum, kosher salt, vanilla and spices. "The best part of the fish is the crunchy, crispy skin," Rodriguez declares, "because the sweetness of the marinade caramelizes the exterior of the salmon while it's grilling." Pictured on page 161.

Prep time: 30 minutes plus marinating
Grilling time: 8 to 11 minutes

MARINADE:

- 6   allspice berries
- 6   star anise
- 2   tablespoons coriander seeds
- 2   bay leaves
- 1½ cups dark rum
- ½   cup granulated sugar
- ½   cup grated panela, or ½ cup brown sugar plus 2 tablespoons molasses
- ½   cup brandy
- ⅓   cup kosher salt
- 1   vanilla bean, split
- 1   teaspoon chopped chipotle chile in adobo sauce

      Ice cubes
- 6   center-cut salmon fillets (6 oz. each), cut 1 inch thick
- 2   cups fruit wood chips

1. *Make marinade:* Heat allspice berries, star anise and coriander seeds in a small skillet over medium heat 2 minutes, until lightly toasted. Add the remaining marinade ingredients in a medium saucepan. Bring to boil; stirring occasionally. Boil 5 minutes, until salt and panela (or brown sugar) dissolve.

2. Remove marinade from heat. Add 5 or 6 ice cubes; cool completely. Pour marinade into a 13×9-inch baking dish. Add salmon, skin side up. Cover and marinate in the refrigerator 24 hours.

menu

fresh and simple

PANELA-RUM CURED SMOKED SALMON
left

GRILLED ARTICHOKES AND ASPARAGUS
page 113

PEACH-COCONUT ICE CREAM
page 215

3. Combine wood chips and enough cold water to cover in a bowl. Let stand 30 minutes. Remove salmon from marinade; pat dry with paper towels.

4. To barbecue: For gas: Punch holes with a knife in the bottom of a small foil pan. Drain wood chips. Place wood chips in the pan in a corner of the grill. Replace top cooking grate. Close lid and heat burners on high, about 10 minutes, until grill thermometer registers 500°F. to 550°F. Oil grill. Arrange salmon, skin side down. Grill over high heat 1 minute, until skin is lightly charred and crisp. Turn one burner off and move fillets off the heat. Reduce heat to medium on remaining burners. Close lid; grill salmon over indirect heat 7 to 10 minutes more, until fish is a rosy color in the center and flakes easily. For charcoal: Open all vents. Build a pile of 30 to 40 briquettes on one side of the grill. Ignite and burn briquettes 25 to 30 minutes, until coals are covered with a light coating of gray ash. Drain wood chips. Add chips to hot briquettes. Replace top grate. Oil grill. Arrange salmon, skin side down, on grill directly over coals. Grill 1 minute, until skin is lightly charred and crisp. Move fillets to opposite side of grill, off of the heat. Close lid; grill salmon, skin side down, over indirect heat 7 to 10 minutes more, until salmon is a rosy color in the center and flakes easily. Makes 6 servings.

Per serving: 300 calories, 17 g total fat, 3.5 g saturated fat, 92 mg cholesterol, 461 mg sodium, 3 g carbohydrates, 31 g protein, 25 mg calcium, 0 g fiber

barbecued beef brisket

Slow-smoked beef brisket is the most popular dish at Sonny Bryan's Smokehouse in Dallas, Texas. Crispy and crunchy on the outside, moist and tender inside, the flavor is rich with wood-smoke taste. The restaurant's veteran pit master Michael LeMaster shares his recipe and this tip. "If you're a first timer at fixing brisket, this simple test will tell you if it's ready," says LeMaster. "Insert a large fork straight down into the flat end of the brisket and lift it straight up; if the fork comes out easily and does not lift the meat, it's done." Pictured on page 163.

Prep time: 5 minutes plus standing
Grilling time: 9 to 10 hours

- 8 **cups hickory wood chips or about 60 hickory wood chunks**
- 1 **whole untrimmed beef brisket (10 to 12 lbs.)**
- 2 **tablespoons kosher salt (optional)**
- 2 **tablespoons freshly ground pepper**
  Sonny's Smokehouse Barbecue Sauce (see recipe, page 187)

1. Combine wood chips and enough cold water to cover in a large bowl. Let stand 30 minutes.

2. Pat beef brisket dry with paper towels. Rub salt (if using) and pepper over brisket.

3. To barbecue: For gas: Punch holes with a knife in the bottom of two small foil pans. Drain wood chips. Divide about 3 cups of the wood chips between pans. Place one pan in the front left-hand corner and the another one in the back right corner of the grill. Place a large 2-inch-deep disposable foil drip pan in center of bottom grate; fill halfway with water. Replace top cooking grate. Close lid and heat burners on low about 10 minutes. Place brisket, fat side up, in center of the cooking grate over the drip pan. Turn one burner off. (For triple burner grill, turn center burner off, as there should be no heat source underneath the drip pan.)
For charcoal: Close two of the three bottom vents. Build one pile of 45 to 50 briquettes over the opened vent. Ignite and burn 25 to 30 minutes, until coals are covered with a light coating of gray ash. Drain wood chips. Place a large 2-inch-deep disposable foil drip pan on opposite side of coals on

bottom grate. Fill pan halfway up with water (for steam inside kettle). Place 1 cup of chips over hot coals. Replace top grate. Place brisket, fat side up, over drip pan. Close lid with opening over meat.

4. Grill brisket 9 to 10 hours, turning occasionally and replenishing briquettes (if using), wood chips and water in drip pan as needed every 2 hours to maintain a temperature inside the grill between 225°F. and 250°F. The temperature in the grill can be controlled by adjusting top vent. The meat should be juicy and tender and pull apart easily.

5. Wrap brisket tightly in foil; let stand 30 minutes. To serve: Unwrap brisket; transfer to a large cutting board. Trim off top layer of fat. Thinly slice brisket against the grain. Serve with Sonny's Smokehouse Barbecue Sauce. Makes 12 servings.

Per serving: 505 calories, 26.5 g total fat, 9.5 g saturated fat, 194 mg cholesterol, 1,018 mg sodium, 1 g carbohydrates, 62 g protein, 17 mg calcium, 0 g fiber

barbecued pulled pork sandwich

Michael LeMaster was kind enough to provide this classic barbecue recipe done to perfection. The very best pork barbecue comes from the shoulder and is smoked until the skin is crisp and the meat is pull-apart tender. To finish it without burning, LeMaster wraps the pork in foil during the last 2 hours of grilling. Pictured on page 162.

Prep time: 5 minutes plus standing • Grilling time: 6 hours

- 4 **cups hickory wood chips or about 30 hickory wood chunks**
- 1 **(5 to 8 lbs.) boneless pork shoulder blade Boston roast (or Boston butt roast)**
- 2 **teaspoons kosher salt**
- ½ **teaspoon freshly ground pepper**
- 8 **soft potato or hamburger rolls**
  Sonny's Smokehouse Barbecue Sauce (see recipe, page 187)

1. Combine wood chips and enough cold water to cover in a large bowl. Let stand 30 minutes.

2. Pat pork roast dry with paper towels. Rub salt and pepper over roast.

3. To barbecue: For gas: Grill as directed for Barbecued Beef Brisket (see page, 186), except for gas place 3 cups of the chips in one small foil pan. Arrange pork in center of the cooking grate over the drip pan. Turn one burner off. (There should be no heat source underneath the drip pan.) Close lid; grill pork 4 hours. Add the remaining 1 cup of drained wood chips as needed. For charcoal: Replenish briquettes and drained wood chips as needed every 1 to 1½ hours to maintain a temperature inside the grill of about 225°F. to 250°F.

4. Wrap pork tightly in heavy-duty foil; grill 2 hours more, replenishing briquettes (for charcoal) and wood chips as needed, until pork is pull-apart tender. Remove pork roast from grill.

5. Let pork roast stand, loosely covered with foil, 30 minutes. Use two forks to gently separate the meat into long, thin shreds. Place 1 cup of the shredded pork on the bottom half of each roll. Drizzle pork with Sonny's Smokehouse Barbecue Sauce and top with roll halves. Makes 8 servings.

Per serving: 710 calories, 40 g total fat, 14 g saturated fat, 216 mg cholesterol, 673 mg sodium, 22 g carbohydrates, 62 g protein, 144 mg calcium, 1 g fiber

sonny's smokehouse barbecue sauce

This tangy sauce is served with all the barbecue meats at Sonny Bryan's Smokehouse in Dallas, Texas. Once you taste it, you'll soon understand why. Tip: The recipe can be easily doubled and frozen to keep on hand for serving with grilled chicken or burgers.

Prep time: 30 minutes • Cooking time: 30 minutes

- 4 **ancho chile peppers (2 oz.) (see tip, page 15)**
- 2 **cups water**
- 1 **cup ketchup**
- 1 **cup cider vinegar**
- ½ **cup Worcestershire sauce**
- 2 **tablespoons paprika**
- 2 **tablespoons dry mustard**

test kitchen tip

barbecue serve-alongs

When it comes to barbecue, the meat is usually the main event. Still, you want to have a few complementary dishes to round out the menu. Here are some suggestions:

A GOOD HOMEMADE POTATO SALAD: Try some of our new takes on this all-American favorite. The recipes on pages 80 and 107 call on convenient, ready-to-cook potatoes found in more and more produce sections.

CRISP GREEN SALADS: Complement hearty meats with cool salads. See tip, page 112, for some great ideas on combining some of the diverse greens now available.

BREADS: Don't forget some good soft breads for sopping up the sauce, such as biscuits, focaccia or a thick country-style bread.

- 1 **teaspoon freshly ground pepper**
- ½ **teaspoon cracked black pepper**
- ½ **lemon**
- ¼ **cup butter or margarine**

1. Toast anchos in a large skillet over medium heat, turning once, 4 to 5 minutes, until they are softened. Transfer to a saucepan; add water. Bring to boil. Reduce heat; simmer anchos 5 minutes. Remove from heat; let stand 10 minutes. Remove anchos, reserving water. Discard chile seeds and stems. Place anchos and reserved water in a blender; puree until smooth.

2. Transfer ancho mixture to a medium saucepan. Stir in ketchup, vinegar, Worcestershire sauce, paprika, mustard, ground pepper and cracked pepper. Squeeze juice from lemon half into mixture; add lemon half. Bring to boil. Reduce heat; gently boil 30 minutes. Remove and discard lemon half; stir in butter. Makes 4 cups.

Per tablespoon: 15 calories, 1 g total fat, 0.5 g saturated fat, 2 mg cholesterol, 79 mg sodium, 2 g carbohydrates, 0 g protein, 2 mg calcium, 0 g fiber

barbecue 101

When associate food editor Carol Prager made the decision to get serious about her barbecue know-how, she agreed to get drafted into barbecue boot camp. She reported to La Varenne Cooking School in White Sulphur Springs, West Virginia, where she got some serious training from commanding officer Steven Raichlen, author of The Barbecue Bible. *As Prager learned, it's easy to make barbecue, not war, if you follow a good battle plan. Here, the first two steps to getting it right:*

KNOW YOUR AMMO: "Barbecuing" is slow cooking over or adjacent to low heat, versus "grilling" where the food is placed directly over higher heat and cooks quickly. The cooking time and intensity of temperature needed for slow cooking vary depending on the type of barbecue unit you have, so take the time to learn how to control yours.

BATTLEFIELD CONDITIONS: Take the weather into consideration when you set out to barbecue. A piece of meat barbecued in summer will cook more rapidly than on a cold, blustery day. Keep the wind in mind, too. A well-sealed barbecue unit will slow-cook with only the vents providing airflow to maintain the fire. But if it's windy, some air will blow into the cooker and increase the temperature, so be prepared to adjust the vents.

chicken under a brick *EASY*

Reed Hearon, chef and owner of Rose Pistola in San Francisco (known for fine California cuisine with an Italian accent), creates exceptional dishes that are simple and fresh. As this recipe proves, Hearon certainly knows what it is to create perfectly cooked chicken. As he states, "It's all about crisp brown skin and juicy meat." That's why he grills the chicken pieces under a weight so they cook evenly without drying out. Pictured on page 163.

Prep time: 20 minutes • Grilling time: 25 to 40 minutes

4	cups fruit wood chips or 30 hickory chunks
2	whole chickens (3 to 3½ lbs. each), butterflied (see note, page 195)
2	tablespoons extra-virgin olive oil
2	teaspoons fresh rosemary
3	large cloves garlic, thinly sliced
1	teaspoon salt
¼	teaspoon freshly ground pepper
4	bricks covered in heavy-duty foil

1. Combine wood chips and enough cold water to cover in a large bowl. Let stand 30 minutes. Brush chicken with oil. Divide and press rosemary and garlic evenly on skin; sprinkle with salt and pepper.

2. To grill: For gas: Punch holes with a knife in the bottom of a small foil pan. Drain wood chips; place in pan in one corner of grill. Close lid and heat 10 minutes on high until grill registers 500°F. to 550°F. For charcoal: Ignite and burn 45 to 50 briquettes 25 to 30 minutes, until coals are covered with a light coating of gray ash. Drain chips; add to hot coals. Replace top cooking grate.

3. Arrange chicken halves, skin side down, on cooking grate; top each with a foil-covered brick. Close lid; reduce heat to medium for gas and grill chicken over medium heat 15 to 20 minutes. Turn chickens; replace bricks. Grill, covered, 10 to 20 minutes more, or until an instant-read thermometer inserted in leg registers 180°F. Makes 4 servings.

Per serving: 840 calories, 51 g total fat, 13.5 g saturated fat, 286 mg cholesterol, 850 mg sodium, 1 g carbohydrates, 89 g protein, 56 mg calcium, 0 g fiber

grilled portobella mushroom salad EASY

This refreshing salad headlining meaty portobellas is another popular dish at Reed Hearon's restaurant—but he says you can substitute other exotic mushrooms such as shiitake or cremini with equally delicious results. The mushrooms and onions quickly marinate in white wine and herbs, then are grilled just right and tossed warm with crisp salad greens. Pictured on page 163.

Prep time: 20 minutes plus marinating
Grilling time: 14 minutes

- 2 pounds portobella mushrooms
- 1 medium white onion

MARINADE:
- 1 cup white wine
- ¼ cup olive oil
- 2 cloves garlic, finely chopped
- 1 tablespoon fresh rosemary
- ¼ teaspoon salt

SALAD:
- 2 tablespoons olive oil
- 1½ teaspoons balsamic vinegar
- ¼ teaspoon salt
- ⅛ teaspoon freshly ground pepper
- 1 head (6 oz.) radicchio, separated into leaves, then torn into bite-size pieces
- 1 bunch (6 oz.) watercress, stems removed

1. Remove and discard stems from mushrooms. Turn mushrooms, top side down. With the side of a spoon, remove dark gills; discard gills.

2. Cut onion into quarters lengthwise, keeping root end intact.

3. *Make marinade:* Combine all of the marinade ingredients in a large bowl. Add mushrooms and onion. Marinate at room temperature 30 minutes. *(Can be made ahead. Marinate up to 3 hours.)*

4. Heat grill. Arrange mushrooms and onions on grill. Close lid and grill mushrooms over medium heat 10 minutes, onion 14 minutes, turning both occasionally, until mushrooms are tender and onion is tender and lightly charred. Slice mushrooms and onion crosswise in ½-inch strips.

5. *Make salad:* Whisk together oil, vinegar, salt and pepper in a large bowl. Add radicchio, watercress, warm mushrooms and onion. Gently toss to combine. Makes 4 servings.

Per serving: 225 calories, 14.5 g total fat, 2 g saturated fat, 0 mg cholesterol, 260 mg sodium, 17 g carbohydrates, 7 g protein, 88 mg calcium, 5 g fiber

---

test kitchen tip
barbecue 102

Appreciating that there was much more to the art of barbecuing than simply striking a match, associate food editor Carol Prager continued her course at Barbecue Boot Camp (see "Barbecue 101," left, for starters). After she learned the basics—such as how important it is to know your equipment and to keep Mother Nature in mind when cooking outdoors, the next step was to find out more about flavor. Read on:

CATCH THE FIRE There are some wonderful flavor enhancers available for the barbecue. Hickory and pecan produce a heavy smoke flavor. Fruit woods, such as apple or peach, have a mellow taste. Wood chips are best suited for gas grills, while chunks are optimal for charcoal grills. (Never use pine or other resinous softwoods.)

AVOID TEMPTATION: Don't trim the fat off the meat before you barbecue it! Leaving the fat on moistens and bastes the meat, producing the unique rich flavor and smooth texture of barbecue.

roast pork loin with apple-cider sauce EASY

This succulent roast comes from test kitchen associate Michele Peters, who features it on her menu when entertaining a small group of friends. Michele's tip on cooking it just right: "Boneless pork loin comes in a variety of sizes, so roasting times may vary. The best way to tell doneness is by using an instant-read thermometer."

Prep time: 40 minutes
Baking time: 58 to 65 minutes plus standing

- 1 **teaspoon salt**
- ½ **teaspoon dried thyme**
- ½ **teaspoon freshly ground pepper**
- 1 **tablespoon vegetable oil**
- 1 **boneless pork loin (3 lbs.), trimmed**
- 3 **medium onions, cut into 1-inch pieces**
- 3 **carrots, cut into 1-inch pieces**
- 3 **celery ribs, cut into 1-inch pieces**
- 1½ **cups apple cider**

APPLE-CIDER SAUCE:
- 1 **tablespoon butter or margarine**
- 2 **tablespoons minced shallots**
- 2 **Granny Smith apples, peeled, cored and cut into ¼-inch-thick slices**
- 1 **cup apple cider**
- 2 **teaspoons cider vinegar**
- 1 **tablespoon calvados (apple-flavored brandy) (optional)**
  Fresh thyme sprigs, for garnish (optional)

1. Heat oven to 400°F. Combine salt, thyme and pepper in a cup; rub over pork roast. Heat oil in a large skillet over medium-high heat. Add pork and cook 8 minutes, until well browned on all sides. Transfer roast to a platter; reserve pan drippings.

2. Add onions, carrots and celery to drippings in same skillet. Cook 10 minutes over medium-high heat, until vegetables are browned. Transfer vegetables to a 10×14-inch roasting pan and place pork roast on top.

3. Roast pork 48 to 55 minutes, until instant-read thermometer inserted in center of pork registers 160°F. Remove pork to a cutting board; cover loosely with foil and keep warm. Add apple cider to pan; return pan with vegetables to oven. Roast vegetables 10 minutes more. Strain drippings from pan through a sieve into a bowl, pressing vegetables with back of a spoon. Discard vegetables.

4. *Make apple-cider sauce:* Meanwhile, melt butter in a medium skillet over medium heat. Add shallots and cook 1 minute; add apples and cook 5 to 6 minutes, until tender. Transfer to a small bowl; set aside. Stir apple cider, strained drippings and vinegar into same skillet. Bring to boil; boil 6 to 8 minutes, until reduced by half. Return apple slices to skillet. Add calvados, if desired. Cook 2 minutes more, until heated through.

5. Serve with apple-cider sauce. Garnish with fresh thyme sprigs, if desired. Makes 6 servings.

Per serving: 455 calories, 16 g total fat, 6 g saturated fat, 138 mg cholesterol, 532 mg sodium, 16 g carbohydrates, 50 g protein, 75 mg calcium, 3 g fiber

spiced grill-pan lamb chops EASY

Here, perfection in a pan—another terrific no-fuss dish from associate food editor Carol Prager. She enjoys using a cast-iron grill pan to give the lamb chops a great outdoor taste any time of year.

Prep time: 15 minutes • Cooking time: 12 minutes per batch

DRY RUB:
- 1 **tablespoon cumin**
- 1 **teaspoon coriander**
- ½ **teaspoon salt**
- ¼ **teaspoon freshly ground pepper**

- 8 **bone-in loin lamb chops (2½ lbs.), cut 1½ inches thick, trimmed**
  Vegetable cooking spray

1. *Make dry rub:* Heat a small skillet over medium heat. Add cumin and coriander. Heat 1 to 2 minutes, until lightly toasted. Combine with salt and pepper in a cup. Rub spice mixture over both sides of chops.

2. Lightly coat a large cast-iron grill pan or heavy skillet with vegetable cooking spray. Heat pan over medium-high heat. Add 4 of the chops. Cook 6 minutes each side for medium-rare. Transfer to a plate; cover and keep warm. Repeat with the remaining 4 chops. Makes 4 servings.

Per serving: 328 calories, 16 g total fat, 6 g saturated fat, 139 mg cholesterol, 399 mg sodium, 1 g carbohydrates, 43 g protein, 45 mg calcium, 0 g fiber

the perfect pork chop EASY

See box, right, for our tips on creating the ultimate chop.

Prep time: 15 minutes plus brining
Cooking time: 10 to 12 minutes

BRINE:

 8 cups cold water, divided
 ¼ cup salt
 ¼ cup firmly packed brown sugar
 3 tablespoons dried thyme

 4 rib pork chops, cut 1 inch thick (about 2 lbs.)
 ½ teaspoon freshly ground pepper
 1 tablespoon olive oil

SAUCE:

 ¼ cup minced shallots or onion
 ½ cup white wine
 ½ cup reduced-sodium chicken broth
 ½ apple (Fuji, Gala or Golden Delicious), finely diced
 1 tablespoon honey Dijon mustard

1. *Make brine:* Combine 1 cup of the water, the salt and brown sugar in a large bowl. Stir to dissolve salt and sugar; let stand 5 minutes. Stir in the remaining 7 cups of water and the thyme. Add chops, pushing them down into brine. Cover; refrigerate 24 hours.

2. Remove chops from brine; discard brine. Rinse chops under cold running water. Pat dry with paper towels. Sprinkle both sides of chops with pepper.

3. Heat 12-inch skillet over high heat 2½ minutes, until very hot. Reduce heat to medium-high. Add oil and chops. Cook chops 2 minutes each side, until browned. Reduce heat to medium-low; cover

pork chop perfection

How to achieve the juiciest and most tender chops:

BUY ONLY THE BEST: Select "rib chops," which are cut from the rib end of the loin versus "center cut" loin chops. Look for the reddest chops available; they will be juicier and more moist than the paler chops. And ask the butcher to cut them an even 1 inch thick, thus avoiding uneven machine-cut chops.

MARINATE: We call for marinating the pork chops in a "brine" (water, salt, sugar and seasonings) to add extra moisture and flavor to the meat.

COOK CORRECTLY: Brown the chops first in a preheated skillet. This helps to seal in the juices. Then cover the skillet, reduce the heat and cook the chops until an instant-read thermometer inserted lengthwise in chop registers 145°F. to 155°F. (The chops will continue to cook while standing.)

skillet and cook chops 3 to 4 minutes more each side, until an instant-read thermometer inserted lengthwise in chop registers 145°F. to 155°F. Transfer chops to a serving platter and cover loosely with foil. (The chops will continue to cook while standing.)

4. *Make sauce:* Discard all but 1 tablespoon of the drippings from skillet. Add shallots and cook over medium heat 1 minute. Increase heat to high. Add wine. Bring to boil, stirring to scrape up any browned bits. Boil wine 1 to 2 minutes, until reduced by half. Add chicken broth, apple, mustard and any juices from chops on platter. Bring to boil. Boil 2 to 4 minutes, stirring frequently, until sauce thickens slightly and reduces to 1 cup. Pour sauce over chops. Serve immediately. Makes 4 servings.

Per serving: 405 calories, 29.5 g total fat, 10.5 g saturated fat, 94 mg cholesterol, 7 g carbohydrates, 25 g protein, 23 mg calcium, 1 g fiber

asparagus and morel tart with goat cheese

Serve this sophisticated appetizer, created by renowned Chef Todd English of Olives and Figs restaurants in Boston, Massachusetts, and your guests will feel like they're being treated to a four-star-restaurant specialty. Asparagus and creamy goat cheese are baked in the tart. Then a fabulous mushroom vinaigrette is sprinkled over the filling at the end.

Prep time: 1 hour plus standing • Baking time: 25 minutes

TART DOUGH:

1	cup plus 2 tablespoons all-purpose flour
1½	teaspoons sugar
¼	teaspoon salt
¼	pound cold unsalted butter, cut up (no substitutes)
¼	cup cold water

2	tablespoons olive oil
2	cups thinly sliced Spanish or sweet onions
1	tablespoon butter, cut up (no substitutes)
¼	teaspoon salt
⅛	teaspoon freshly ground pepper
1	pound fresh asparagus

MOREL VINAIGRETTE:

½	cup (.5 oz.) dried morel mushrooms
2	tablespoons butter (no substitutes)
2	shallots, minced
2½	tablespoons fresh lemon juice
1	tablespoon balsamic vinegar
1	tablespoon olive oil
¼	teaspoon salt
⅛	teaspoon freshly ground pepper

1	log (10 oz.) goat cheese

1. *Make tart dough:* Pulse flour, sugar and salt in a food processor to combine. Add butter and pulse until butter resembles small peas. Sprinkle water over butter-flour mixture, then pulse until coarse crumbs form. Gather dough, pressing together to form a disk. Wrap in plastic wrap and refrigerate 30 minutes. *(Can be made ahead. Refrigerate up to 2 days.)*

2. Meanwhile, heat oil in a large nonstick skillet over medium-high heat. Add onions. Cook 10 minutes, turning occasionally, until tender and golden brown. Remove from heat. Stir in butter, salt and pepper. Transfer to a bowl. Set aside.

3. Bring a large saucepan two-thirds full with water to boil. Trim bottoms of asparagus to make 6-inch spears. Add asparagus to boiling water. Cook 1 minute; drain in a colander.

4. Heat oven to 450°F.

5. *Make morel vinaigrette:* Place dried morels in a bowl. Add enough very hot water to cover; let stand 15 minutes, until softened. Drain, rinse well and pat dry with paper towel. Slice morels crosswise. Melt butter in the same skillet over medium heat. Add shallots and cook 2 minutes, until softened. Add morels. Cook 2 minutes, until tender. Transfer morel mixture to a small bowl, scraping pan with a rubber spatula. Cool 10 minutes. Stir in the remaining vinaigrette ingredients.

6. To assemble: On a lightly floured surface, roll tart dough into a 12-inch round, ⅛ inch thick; trim edges of circle. Transfer circle to a cookie sheet. To make a fluted edge, place finger on the edge of circle, pull dough over fingertip, then press to seal. (This will create a small air space in crust edge.) Spread onions evenly over circle. Arrange asparagus in a fan shape over onions. Crumble goat cheese into ½-inch pieces; sprinkle evenly over onions and asparagus.

7. Bake tart 25 minutes, until edge of crust is lightly browned. Remove tart from oven. Using a spoon, sprinkle Morel Vinaigrette evenly over filling. Slide tart off sheet onto a large serving plate. Serve warm. Makes 8 servings.

Per serving: 415 calories, 32 g total fat, 18 g saturated fat, 71 mg cholesterol, 457 mg sodium, 21 g carbohydrates, 11 g protein, 129 mg calcium, 2 g fiber

rum-and-pepper-painted grouper with a mango-habañero mojo

This exquisite fish dish comes from highly acclaimed Chef Norman Van Aken, proprietor of the award-winning restaurant Norman's, in Miami, Florida. Van Aken also authored Norman's New World Cuisine, *which celebrates a fusion of Latin, Caribbean, Asian and American flavors. Toasted peppercorns, cloves, soy sauce and white rum are among the ingredients called upon for the "paint," which is brushed over the grouper before cooking. The mango-habañero mojo provides a cunning contrast of hot and sweet, and the plantains are the perfect accompaniment.*

Prep time: 40 minutes • Cooking time: 13 minutes
Microwave used

RUM-AND-PEPPER PAINT:

- 2 teaspoons black peppercorns
- 4 whole cloves
- ¼ cup white rum
- ¼ cup soy sauce
- 2½ tablespoons sugar
- 1 tablespoon grated lemon peel
- 2 teaspoons fresh lemon juice

MANGO-HABAÑERO MOJO:

- 2 ripe mangoes, peeled, pitted and coarsely chopped
- ½ cup white wine
- 2 tablespoons fresh orange juice
- ½ to 1 habañero or Scotch bonnet chile, seeded and finely minced (see tip, page 15)

PANFRIED PLANTAINS:

- ½ teaspoon cumin seeds
- 1 teaspoon freshly ground pepper
- ¼ teaspoon salt
- ¼ teaspoon cinnamon
- 2 very ripe plantains, peeled and cut diagonally into ¼-inch-thick slices
- 2 tablespoons vegetable oil
-

- 4 black grouper, striped bass or red snapper fillets (8 oz. each)
- 1 tablespoon peanut or vegetable oil
- 4 lime wedges, for garnish (optional)

1. *Make rum-and-pepper paint:* Toast the peppercorns and cloves in a small skillet over medium-high heat 1 minute, just until spices begin to smoke. Cool. Transfer to a spice grinder and process until coarsely ground. Combine rum, soy, sugar, lemon peel and juice in a small heavy saucepan; add spices. Bring to boil. Reduce heat; simmer 10 to 12 minutes, until mixture is reduced to ¼ cup. Strain through a fine-mesh sieve into a small bowl; discard spices. Set aside.

2. *Make mango-habañero mojo:* Puree the mangoes, wine and orange juice in a blender. Strain through a fine mesh strainer into a microwaveproof bowl. Stir in chile. *(Can be made ahead. Cover and refrigerate up to 4 hours.)* To heat, microwave on HIGH 40 seconds. Stir and microwave 20 to 30 seconds more, just until heated through. Makes 2¼ cups.

3. *Make panfried plantains:* Toast cumin seeds in a small skillet over medium-high heat 1 minute, just until fragrant and slightly darkened. Cool. Transfer to a spice grinder and process to a powder. Transfer to a cup; stir in the pepper, salt and cinnamon. Arrange sliced plantains in a single layer on a sheet of waxed paper so that sides touch. Evenly sprinkle top side of plantain slices with spice mixture.

4. Heat vegetable oil in a 12-inch nonstick skillet over medium-high heat. Add plantains, spice-side down. Cook 1½ to 2½ minutes per side, until deep golden brown. Transfer to a plate lined with a double layer of paper towels; keep warm.

5. Heat oven to 450°F. Brush rum-and-pepper paint on side of fillets without skin. Heat peanut oil in a 12-inch nonstick, ovenproof skillet over medium-high heat 2 minutes. Add fish, coated side down. Cook 2 minutes, shaking pan occasionally to prevent sticking, until deep brown.

6. With a spatula, gently turn fillets. Transfer fish in skillet to oven. Bake fillets 7 to 9 minutes, until fish flakes easily in center. To serve, spoon about ½ cup mango-habañero mojo onto each of 4 plates. Top with fish. Serve with plantains. Garnish with lime wedges, if desired. Makes 4 servings.

Per serving: 590 calories, 16 g total fat, 3 g saturated fat, 181 mg cholesterol, 1,231 mg sodium, 57 g carbohydrates, 44 g protein, 66 mg calcium, 16 g fiber

rigatoni with roasted vegetables

An easy weeknight favorite from food editor Jan Hazard.

Prep time: 20 minutes • Baking time: 30 to 35 minutes
Microwave used

- 4 teaspoons plus 3 tablespoons olive oil, divided
- 1 bunch broccoli, trimmed, stalks peeled
- 1 pound carrots, cut into 1-inch slices
- 3 medium zucchini, cut into 1-inch slices
- 2 cups sliced red onions
- 1 large red bell pepper, cut into ½-inch-thick strips
- 1 tablespoon garlic-flavored oil
- 1 teaspoon salt
- ¼ teaspoon freshly ground pepper
- 1 pound rigatoni pasta
- 1 cup chicken broth
- ⅓ cup fresh mint leaves, chopped
- 1 teaspoon grated lemon peel

1. Adjust oven racks to middle and bottom third positions. Heat oven to 450°F. Brush two 15½×10½-inch jelly-roll pans with 2 teaspoons each of the olive oil.

2. Cut florets from broccoli stalks. Cut stalks in half lengthwise, then chop. Toss broccoli, carrots, zucchini, onions, bell pepper, 2 tablespoons of the olive oil, the garlic-flavored oil, salt and pepper in a large bowl until vegetables are well coated. Divide vegetables between prepared pans. Roast 15 minutes. Stir vegetables; switch pans on racks. Roast 15 to 20 minutes more, until onions are lightly browned and carrots are tender. Meanwhile, cook pasta according to package directions.

3. Heat broth in a 2-cup microwaveproof glass measure on HIGH 45 seconds. Combine the remaining 1 tablespoon olive oil, the mint and lemon peel in a large serving bowl. Drain pasta in a colander. Toss pasta and vegetables with broth and mint mixture. Serve immediately. Makes 6 servings.

Per serving: 480 calories, 14 g total fat, 2 g saturated fat, 0 mg cholesterol, 605 mg sodium, 75 g carbohydrates, 14 g protein, 93 mg calcium, 8 g fiber

spanish chicken with yellow rice

This recipe from test kitchen associate Cynthia DePersio turns ordinary chicken into a fabulous fix. It is a great dish when you don't have time to do a lot of grocery shopping. That's because it conveniently calls for lots of staple ingredients—olive oil, canned tomatoes, chicken broth, rice, spices and garlic. All you need to pick up are the chicken thighs, fresh veggies and wine. Cynthia's tip: To skin the chicken legs, grasp the skin with paper towels and pull it off the leg in one piece.

Prep time: 25 minutes • Cooking time: 50 to 55 minutes

- 6 whole chicken legs, skinned
- 1¼ teaspoons salt, divided
- ½ teaspoon freshly ground pepper, divided
- 1 tablespoon olive oil
- 2 cups chopped green bell pepper
- 2 cups chopped celery, with leaves
- 1 cup chopped onions
- 1 tablespoon chopped garlic
- 1 tablespoon cumin
- 1 can (16 oz.) whole tomatoes in juice
- 1 cup chicken broth
- 1 tablespoon flour
- 2 tablespoons white wine

YELLOW RICE:
- 4 cups water
- 2 cups long-grain rice
- ½ teaspoon salt
- ¼ teaspoon turmeric

1. Sprinkle chicken with ¼ teaspoon each of the salt and the pepper. Heat oil in a large Dutch oven over medium-high heat. Add 3 chicken legs. Cook 4 minutes each side, until browned. Transfer to a plate. Repeat with remaining chicken.

2. Add bell pepper, celery, onions and garlic to Dutch oven. Cook 5 minutes, stirring occasionally, until vegetables have softened. Add cumin. Cook 30 seconds.

3. Stir in tomatoes with juice, breaking up tomatoes with a spoon. Stir in broth, the remaining

1 teaspoon salt and ¼ teaspoon pepper. Return chicken to Dutch oven, stirring to cover with sauce. Bring to boil. Reduce heat to medium; cover and simmer 20 minutes. Uncover; simmer 20 minutes, until chicken is cooked through. Combine flour and wine in a small bowl. Stir into stew. Cook 5 minutes more, until thickened.

4. *Make yellow rice:* Meanwhile, bring water to boil in a medium saucepan. Stir in rice, salt and turmeric. Reduce heat; cover and simmer 20 minutes, until liquid is evaporated and rice is tender. Serve chicken with rice. Makes 6 servings.

Per serving: 434 calories, 7 g total fat, 1 g saturated fat, 78 mg cholesterol, 1,102 mg sodium, 62 g carbohydrates, 28 g protein, 84 mg calcium, 4 g fiber

chicken gremolata

Associate food editor Carol Prager likes this recipe because she can prepare it entirely on the stovetop. "I use a whole bird, split and flavored with gremolata—an Italian condiment of chopped parsley, lemon peel, nutmeg and garlic. I tuck the gremolata under the skin, then brown the bird breast side down under a weighted lid for the most incredible moistness."

Prep time: 15 minutes • Cooking time: 40 minutes

1	**teaspoon minced garlic**
	Salt
	Pepper
¼	**teaspoon freshly grated nutmeg**
3	**tablespoons chopped fresh parsley, divided**
1½	**teaspoons grated lemon peel, divided**
1	**small chicken (2 to 2½ lbs.), butterflied***

1. Combine garlic, ¼ teaspoon *each* salt and pepper and the nutmeg on a cutting board. With flat side of a large knife, mash mixture to form a paste. Mix with 2 tablespoons of the parsley and 1 teaspoon of the lemon peel in a small bowl. Combine the remaining 1 tablespoon of parsley and ½ teaspoon of lemon peel in a cup for garnish. Set aside.

2. Lift skin from chicken breast and legs. Spread lemon-garlic mixture evenly under skin. Sprinkle both sides of chicken with salt and pepper.

m e n u

food editor's speedy supper

RIGATONI WITH ROASTED VEGETABLES
page 194

CAESAR SALAD
page 36

PURCHASED ITALIAN BREAD

BUTTERSCOTCH PECAN TILES AND ICE CREAM
page 237

3. Heat a 12-inch nonstick skillet over medium-high heat. Arrange chicken, skin side down, and cover pan loosely with foil; then top with a pie plate that fits inside skillet and covers surface of chicken. Weigh down top of pie plate with a bacon press or a small cast-iron skillet. Reduce heat to medium; cook 20 minutes, until skin side is golden. Remove bacon press or cast-iron skillet, plate and foil; turn chicken. Cook, uncovered, 20 minutes more, until cooked through.

4. Transfer chicken to a cutting board and cut in half. Garnish with reserved parsley mixture. Makes 2 servings.

*Note: To butterfly chicken, use a large knife or poultry shears to cut chicken down the backbone. Turn chicken, breast side up, and push down the breastbone to flatten slightly.

Per serving: 435 calories, 24 g total fat, 7 g saturated fat, 157 mg cholesterol, 441 mg sodium, 2 g carbohydrates, 49 g protein, 44 mg calcium, 1 g fiber

bouillabaisse

This bouillabaisse comes from heralded New Orleans Chef Susan Spicer, who shares her superb rendition with us. She breaks from tradition by using freshly squeezed orange juice in the broth, which she says, "balances the acidity of the tomatoes, adding another flavor instead of just sweetening it." Just like in the classic version, Susan garnishes hers with rouille (roo-EE), a fiery garlic-chile sauce. Pictured on page 167.

Prep time: 40 minutes • Cooking time: 30 minutes

BOUILLABAISSE STOCK:

- 3 tablespoons olive oil
- 2 medium onions, chopped
- 1 medium fennel bulb, chopped
- 3 leeks, white part only, split lengthwise, rinsed well and chopped
- 1 tablespoon chopped garlic
- 1 quart fish stock or clam juice
- 1 scant teaspoon saffron threads
  Grated peel and juice of 2 oranges
- 2 cups diced tomatoes
- 2 tablespoons chopped fresh thyme
- 2 tablespoons Pernod (anise-flavored liqueur) (optional)
- ½ teaspoon salt
- ¼ teaspoon freshly ground pepper

ROUILLE:

- 1 red bell pepper
- 1 tablespoon fresh lemon juice
- 2 teaspoons red wine vinegar
- 1 teaspoon minced garlic
- ½ teaspoon salt
- ½ teaspoon red pepper flakes
- ½ teaspoon Asian chile paste (see tips, pages 16 and 17)
- ½ cup olive oil

- 1 tablespoon olive oil
- 1 pound fish fillets, such as snapper, red fish, drum, mahi mahi or grouper, cut into ½-inch dice
- 16 large shrimp, peeled and deveined
- 1 pound shucked oysters or scallops
- 1½ pounds mussels, scrubbed and debearded (see note, page 35)
  Croutons (optional)

1. *Make bouillabaisse stock:* Heat oil in a large Dutch oven over medium heat. Add onions, fennel, leeks and garlic. Cover and cook 10 to 12 minutes, until softened. Add stock, saffron and remaining stock ingredients. Bring to boil. Reduce heat and simmer 20 minutes. Set aside. *(Can be made ahead. Transfer to a large bowl. Cool. Cover and refrigerate overnight.)*

2. *Make rouille:* Meanwhile, heat broiler. Line a broiler pan with foil. Cut off ½ inch from top and bottom of bell pepper and cut lengthwise in half. Remove seeds and membrane. Broil bell pepper skin side up, 12 to 15 minutes, until skin is evenly charred. Cool 15 minutes; peel off skin and chop. Process pepper and remaining rouille ingredients except oil in food processor until smooth. With machine running, add oil though feed tube in a slow, steady stream. Set aside. *(Can be made ahead. Cover and refrigerate overnight.)* Makes ¾ cup.

3. Heat oil in a deep 12-inch skillet or Dutch oven over medium-high heat. Add fish fillets; cook 2 to 3 minutes, until skin is lightly crisp. Add bouillabaisse stock, shrimp, oysters and mussels. Bring mixture to boil. Reduce heat to medium; cover and cook 3 to 5 minutes, until mussels open. (Discard any unopened and empty shells.) Divide bouillabaisse among 8 large serving bowls. Serve with rouille and, if desired, croutons. Makes 8 servings.

Per serving: 400 calories, 23.5 g total fat, 3.5 g saturated fat, 90 mg cholesterol, 810 mg sodium, 22 g carbohydrates, 25 g protein, 142 mg calcium, 2 g fiber

the perfect crab cakes

What's the secret behind these golden cakes? A sprightly seasoned crumb mixture and more crabmeat than most recipes. To cook the cakes, we use a combination of oil and clarified butter, which has a higher smoke point that allows the cakes to cook to a golden-crisp without burning.

Prep time: 25 minutes plus chilling
Cooking time: 8 to 10 minutes • Microwave used

- 4 or 5 slices firm white bread, (such as Pepperidge Farm), crusts removed, torn into pieces

⅓ cup mayonnaise

2 tablespoons finely chopped shallots

2 tablespoons chopped fresh flat-leaf parsley

2 tablespoons fresh lemon juice

1 large egg, lightly beaten

1 teaspoon Dijon mustard

¼ teaspoon ground red pepper

1 pound lump or jumbo crabmeat, picked over

¼ cup butter (no substitutes)

4 tablespoons vegetable oil, divided

Lemon wedges (optional)

1. Pulse bread in a food processor until fine crumbs form. Set aside.

2. Combine mayonnaise, shallots, parsley, lemon juice, egg, mustard and red pepper in a medium bowl. Fold in crabmeat and 1 cup of the bread crumbs just until blended.

3. Line a large cookie sheet with waxed paper. Place the remaining 1 cup of bread crumbs on a large plate. Gently shape a rounded ⅓ cup of crab mixture into a 2¼-inch patty. Coat lightly with bread crumbs. Transfer crab cakes to prepared cookie sheet. Repeat with remaining crab mixture and crumbs. Refrigerate 4 hours.

4. Meanwhile, to clarify the butter, microwave butter on HIGH in a 1-cup glass measure covered with plastic wrap 1 to 1½ minutes, until melted. Let stand 2 minutes until milk solids settle to bottom. Skim off foam from top; discard. Pour clear, clarified butter into a cup. Set aside.

5. Heat oven to 250°F. Heat 1 tablespoon of the clarified butter and 2 tablespoons of the oil in a large skillet over medium heat. Add 4 of the crab cakes. Cook about 4 minutes, until golden. With a wide spatula, carefully turn cakes. Cook 4 minutes more. Transfer cakes to a cookie sheet; keep warm in oven. Wipe out skillet with a paper towel. Cook remaining cakes with the remaining butter and oil. Serve with lemon wedges, if desired. Makes 8 crab cakes.

Per crab cake: 280 calories, 22 g total fat, 6 g saturated fat, 104 mg cholesterol, 361 mg sodium, 7 g carbohydrates, 14 g protein, 82 mg calcium, 0 g fiber

---

test kitchen tip

food editors' quick desserts

Here are a few of our food editors' favorite ways to satisfy a sweet tooth in a hurry:

chocolate dive

Combine 1 package (6 oz.) semisweet chocolate chips, ⅓ cup heavy or whipping cream, 2 tablespoons light corn syrup and 1 tablespoon butter in a medium microwave-proof bowl. Microwave on HIGH 1 to 2 minutes, until chips are melted; stir until smooth. Transfer sauce to a serving bowl. Serve with assorted cut-up fruit for dipping. Makes 4 servings.

hot berry topping

Heat 2 tablespoons butter and 2 tablespoons sugar in a medium saucepan over medium heat until smooth. Add 1 bag (10 or 12 oz.) frozen mixed berries, partially thawed. Bring to boil. Cook about 2 minutes, just until berries are heated through. With a slotted spoon, transfer fruit to a serving bowl. Boil juices 1 minute, until thickened slightly. Stir into berries with 2 tablespoons almond-flavored liqueur. Serve with 1 pint vanilla ice cream. Makes 4 servings.

ricotta-chip filling

Process ¾ cup ricotta cheese, 1 package (3 oz.) cream cheese and 3 tablespoons confectioners' sugar in a food processor until smooth. Transfer to a medium bowl; stir in ¼ cup miniature chocolate chips. Assemble desserts using 12 Bordeaux cookies. For each, spread ¼ cup filling on 2 cookies, stack on top of each other and top with a plain cookie. Repeat with remaining filling and cookies. Dust tops with more confectioners' sugar. Makes 4 servings.

chocolate cups with rich chocolate mousse

This elegant chocolate dessert is magic. It comes from cookbook author Elaine Gonzalez, who deftly combines chocolate wizardry and simple, innovative techniques. "These chocolate mousse cups with chocolate scrolls and chocolate-dipped strawberries are deceptively easy," she insists. "Nearly everything can be made and assembled the day before." Pictured on page 166.

Prep time: 2 hours plus standing and chilling
Microwave used

CHOCOLATE BOWLS AND FILIGREE SCROLLS:
  20 ounces semisweet chocolate squares, divided
STRAWBERRY SAUCE:
    1 package (10 oz.) frozen strawberries in light syrup, thawed
    2 tablespoons raspberry-flavored liqueur
CHOCOLATE MOUSSE:
    9 ounces semisweet chocolate squares, coarsely chopped
   ⅓ cup lukewarm water
    3 cups heavy or whipping cream
    1 tablespoon vanilla extract
       Marbleized Strawberries (recipe follows)

1. *Make chocolate bowls:* Line 2 cookie sheets with waxed paper; secure with tape. Inflate eight 5-inch round talc-free balloons to measure 3¾ inches in diameter; twist and knot. Wipe balloons with damp paper towels and let dry.

2. To temper chocolate, coarsely chop 16 ounces of the chocolate. Transfer to a small microwaveproof bowl. Microwave chocolate on MEDIUM 2 minutes. Stir and microwave 1 minute, stirring every 10 seconds, until two-thirds of the chocolate is melted. Stir until smooth and chocolate registers less than 90°F. on an instant-read thermometer. If chocolate registers 90°F. or more, chop remaining chocolate into large chunks. Stir into the melted chocolate until the proper temperature is reached. Remove and reserve any extra chunks of chocolate.

3. Gently plunge each balloon 1½ inches into tempered chocolate. Jiggle over bowl to drain any excess chocolate. Arrange, dipped side down, on prepared cookie sheet. Repeat, arranging balloons 2 inches apart. Chill until chocolate is firm. Reserve the remaining tempered chocolate.

4. *Make filigree scrolls:* Draw a filigree scroll pattern (pictured on page 166) or use your imagination for a desired line drawing (butterfly, tulip, heart). To make piping the shapes easier, sketch drawing onto paper. Line 1 large cookie sheet with waxed paper.

5. Microwave the reserved tempered chocolate on MEDIUM 30 seconds. If temperature registers 90°F. or more, stir in the reserved chocolate chunks until proper temperature is reached. Spoon into pastry bag fitted with a ¹⁄₁₆-inch round tip. Place the paper pattern under sheet of waxed paper on cookie sheet. Pipe 8 scrolls or desired designs. Chill until firm. Carefully slide a thin metal spatula under chilled scrolls to loosen. Turn scrolls over. Pipe chocolate along the back. Chill until firm.

6. Pop each balloon. Gently pull popped balloons from chocolate cups. Chill until firm. *(Can be made ahead. Loosely cover chocolate cups and scrolls and refrigerate overnight.)*

7. *Make strawberry sauce:* Puree strawberries and liqueur in a food processor or blender. Strain through a sieve into a bowl. Set aside.

8. *Make chocolate mousse:* Microwave chocolate in a microwaveproof small bowl on MEDIUM 3 minutes; stir until smooth. Add water all at once, whisking until smooth. Cool 10 minutes, whisking occasionally.

9. Beat cream and vanilla at low speed, until cream starts to thicken. At medium-high speed, beat 30 seconds, until mixture is the consistency of thick cake batter. Add chocolate all at once. Beat until mousse is thick enough to hold its shape; spoon into a large pastry bag fitted with a ¾-inch star tip. Decoratively pipe mousse into chocolate cups. Add chocolate filigree scrolls. *(Can be made ahead. Chill up to 3 hours.)* Serve with Strawberry Sauce and Marbleized Strawberries. Makes 8 servings.

Per serving: 850 calories, 64 g total fat, 39 g saturated fat, 122 mg cholesterol, 46 mg sodium, 78 g carbohydrates, 6 g protein, 95 mg calcium, 6 g fiber

marbleized strawberries

The melted white and dark chocolate make a dazzling "marble" design on the fresh strawberries. And, while there's no denying these are a handsome complement to the Chocolate Cups with Rich Chocolate Mousse (see recipe, left), these indulgent treats are also perfectly delightful on their own. Serve them on an hors d'oeuvre buffet table or as an after-dinner dessert with freshly brewed espresso. For a romantic touch, pair these exquisite strawberries with chilled champagne.

Total prep time: 30 minutes plus chilling

- 11 **ounces white chocolate squares, melted (see tip, page 259)**
- 5 **ounces semisweet chocolate squares, melted (see tip, page 259)**
- 1 **quart large fresh strawberries, patted dry**

1. Line a cookie sheet with waxed paper. Pour white chocolate into a 9-inch glass pie plate. Pour semisweet chocolate into a bowl.

2. Drizzle parallel lines of semisweet chocolate, about ¾ inch apart, onto white chocolate. Set aside the remaining semisweet chocolate.

3. Holding strawberry stem end, dip strawberry into both of the chocolates in pie plate, pressing opposite sides of berry across dark and white lines to marbleize. Jiggle strawberry to drain off excess chocolate; arrange on sheet. Repeat, periodically drizzling more lines of semisweet chocolate across white chocolate. (If white chocolate starts to harden, microwave on MEDIUM for 30 seconds.)

4. Refrigerate marbleized strawberries until chocolate is firm, about 5 minutes. *(Can be made ahead. Loosely cover strawberries and let stand at room temperature up to 2 hours.)* Makes 28 strawberries.

Per strawberry: 90 calories, 5 g total fat, 3 g saturated fat, 0 mg cholesterol, 11 mg sodium, 12 g carbohydrates, 1 g protein, 28 mg calcium, 1 g fiber

molasses ginger cookies EASY

When food editor Jan Hazard attended Colora Women's College, she had a bake off with her t roommates to settle an ongoing dispute regarding who had the best gingersnap recipe. The consensus? Her roommate Linda Hansen's grandmother—Caroline Spenser Hansen—had the best and was nice enough to pass it along. Jan's tip: When grating the orange peel, be sure to use only the colored portion of the orange—the white membrane is bitter.

Prep time: 30 minutes
Baking time: 10 to 12 minutes per batch

- 2 **cups all-purpose flour**
- 2 **teaspoons baking soda**
- ½ **teaspoon salt**
- ½ **teaspoon ginger**
- ½ **teaspoon cinnamon**
- ¼ **teaspoon cloves**
- ½ **cup butter or margarine, softened**
- ¼ **cup vegetable shortening**
- 1¼ **cups sugar, divided**
- 1 **large egg**
- ¼ **cup light molasses**
- ½ **teaspoon grated orange peel**

1. Heat oven to 350°F. Whisk flour, baking soda, salt, ginger, cinnamon and cloves in a bowl.

2. Beat butter, shortening and 1 cup of the sugar in a mixer bowl on medium speed. Add egg, molasses and peel; then beat 5 minutes, until light and fluffy. Reduce speed to low and add dry ingredients just until combined.

3. Place the remaining ¼ cup of sugar in a pie plate. Shape dough into 1-inch balls; roll balls in sugar (dough will be sticky). Place balls 2 inches apart on ungreased cookie sheets. Bake 10 to 12 minutes. Transfer to wire racks; cool. *(Can be made ahead. Store in an airtight container and freeze up to 1 month.)* Makes 60 cookies.

Per cookie: 55 calories, 2.5 g total fat, 1 g saturated fat, 8 mg cholesterol, 80 mg sodium, 8 g carbohydrates, 1 g protein, 5 mg calcium, 3 g fiber

the perfect lemon bars (EASY)

When you want something sweet, but not too heavy or rich, this is the ultimate dessert. And for those who love lemon, prepare for an irresistible treat.

Prep time: 25 minutes plus cooling
Baking time: 35 to 43 minutes

CRUST:
- ½ cup butter, softened (no substitutes)
- ¼ cup granulated sugar
- 1¼ cups all-purpose flour

FILLING:
- ¾ cup granulated sugar
- 2 tablespoons all-purpose flour
- ¼ teaspoon baking powder
- Pinch salt
- 2 large eggs, lightly beaten
- ½ teaspoon grated lemon peel
- ¼ cup fresh lemon juice
- 1 tablespoon confectioners' sugar

1. ■ Heat oven to 350°F. Line a 9-inch square baking pan with foil, letting foil extend 2 inches over two sides of the pan.

2. ■ *Make crust:* With a wooden spoon, beat butter and sugar in a large bowl. Stir in flour, ½ cup at time, beating until well blended. (The dough should be crumbly, so be careful not to overbeat with the spoon. It helps to press the mixture against the sides of bowl to combine the ingredients.) Firmly press dough along the bottom and ¾ inch up the side of the prepared pan. Bake 20 to 25 minutes, until golden brown. Cool crust on a wire rack while making the filling.

3. ■ *Make filling:* Whisk together granulated sugar, flour, baking powder and salt in the same large bowl until combined. Whisk in eggs until blended. Add lemon peel and juice; whisk again until blended. Pour filling into cooled crust. Bake 15 to 18 minutes, just until filling is set. Cool completely on wire rack.

---

test kitchen tip

successful lemon bars

After testing and retesting this ever-popular classic, our test kitchen pros found these seven steps essential to lemon-bar perfection:

1. **LINE THE PAN** with foil for easy removal of the bars before cutting into squares.

2. **FIRMLY PRESS THE CRUST** into the pan, and press it ¾ inch up the sides so the filling doesn't run over the sides, which makes the crust soggy and the bars stick to the foil.

3. **FULLY PREBAKE** the buttery crust so it is baked through once the filling is added.

4. **USE FRESHLY SQUEEZED LEMON JUICE** and peel for the optimal lemon flavor.

5. **HAVE JUST THE RIGHT RATIO** of crust to lemon filling.

6. **USE THE RIGHT AMOUNT** of sugar and lemon juice in the filling for the perfect balance of sweet and tart.

7. **FOLLOW THE METHOD** of mixing the filling to achieve a creamy texture—it makes a difference. Whisk the beaten eggs into the dry ingredients; then whisk in the lemon juice and peel. And don't overwhisk the filling.

---

4. ■ To cut, use foil ends as a handle to lift the square out of pan. Dust top with confectioners' sugar. Cut into 16 bars. Makes 16 bars.

Per bar: 150 calories, 6.5 g total fat, 4 g saturated fat, 43 mg cholesterol, 86 mg sodium, 20 g carbohydrates, 2 g protein, 11 mg calcium, 0 g fiber

ORANGE
POUND CAKE
PG. 231

sweets for all seasons

PLUM KUCHEN
PG. 220

The most memorable delights are those we taste but a few times a year: a strawberry tart in spring, a fresh peach pie in August, a caramely Indian pudding on a crisp fall night. Here's where you'll find these recipes and more sweet ways to celebrate each season.

APPLE CRISP
PG. 226

easy recipes

can make

every day

MELON MEDLEY
PG. 217

PHYLLO CUPS
WITH ICE CREAM
AND ORANGE-
CARAMEL SAUCE
PG. 232

FRUIT SALAD WITH
STAR ANISE
PG. 209

an "I deserve dessert"
day

HONEY-BAKED
PEARS
PG. 226

CHERRY TART
PG. 221

where the
orchard
meets the oven

SUMMER-FRESH
PEACH PIE
PG. 218

BLUEBERRY
GRUNT
PG. 212

is a **very nice**

place to be

FOUR-BERRY PIE
PG. 214

CLASSIC
YELLOW
SHEET CAKE
PG. 230

APPLE TART
PG. 222

facing a
dessert dilemma?

LATTICE
FLOWER CAKE
PG. 230

BOSTON
CREAM PIE
PG. 240

BAKED APPLES
PG. 223

consider the **classics**

cookies
in 20 minutes?
(now **that's**
sweet!)

BUTTERSCOTCH-
PECAN TILES
PG. 237

PISTACHIO
CRESCENTS
PG. 237

strawberries in white zinfandel

This mix of berries, orange juice and Zinfandel makes an outstanding accompaniment to ice cream.

Prep time: 15 minutes plus chilling
Cooking time: 8 to 10 minutes

- 2 oranges
- 6 cups water, divided
- ½ cup white Zinfandel wine
- ¼ cup sugar
- 1 pint fresh strawberries, hulled and each berry cut into wedges
- 1 pint vanilla ice cream

1. Remove only the colored peel from 1 of the oranges. Cut peel into thin strips. Squeeze enough juice from oranges to equal ½ cup; set aside. Bring 2 cups of the water to boil in a small saucepan. Add peel and return to boil. Drain. Repeat process two more times with remaining water. Refrigerate peel. Bring orange juice, wine and sugar to simmer in a small saucepan. Cook 2 to 3 minutes, until sugar dissolves. Transfer to a bowl; stir in berries. Cover and refrigerate 1½ hours.

2. Divide berries among 4 serving glasses. Top each with a ½-cup scoop of ice cream and sprinkle with prepared orange peel. Makes 4 servings.

Per serving: 280 calories, 12.5 g total fat, 7.5 g saturated fat, 45 mg cholesterol, 44 mg sodium, 37 g carbohydrates, 3 g protein, 105 mg calcium, 2 g fiber

fruit salad with star anise

Summer fruit is wonderful unadorned, but if you want to make it extra special, try this easy dessert. The sugar syrup is flavored with wine and star anise (a star-shaped pod with a hint of licorice flavor). Pictured on page 203.

Prep time: 15 minutes plus chilling
Cooking time: 8 minutes

- ½ cup water
- ½ cup sugar
- 3 pods star anise*

- ½ cup white Zinfandel wine
- 6 cups assorted fresh fruit (combine at least three of the following: pineapple chunks, blueberries, raspberries, peeled and sliced pears, diced mango, quartered strawberries, cubed cantaloupe or honeydew melon)
- **Fresh mint sprigs, for garnish (optional)**

1. Bring water, sugar and star anise to boil in a small saucepan. Boil, stirring occasionally, until mixture is slightly thickened and syrupy, 8 to 10 minutes. Remove from heat; immediately stir in wine.

2. Combine desired fruits in a large bowl. Add syrup, tossing to coat. Refrigerate until cold, 2 hours. Discard star anise. Garnish with mint sprigs, if desired. Makes 6 servings.

*Note: Can be found in the spice aisle or ethnic sections of supermarkets, in Asian specialty stores or from Melissa's Specialty Foods, 800-588-0151.

Per serving: 155 calories, 0.5 g total fat, 0 g saturated fat, 0 mg cholesterol, 4 mg sodium, 36 g carbohydrates, 1 g protein, 20 mg calcium, 3 g fiber

---

test kitchen tip
good pickins

A few tidbits about berries...

STRAWBERRIES: Any size is sweet! Just be sure to pick them when they're plump, and choose bright red fruit with fresh green caps.

RASPBERRIES: Choose fuchsia-colored fruit with a soft, slightly downy appearance.

BLACKBERRIES: Look for big, juicy, glossy purple-black berries.

BLUEBERRIES: The whitish "bloom" means they're fresh.

WILD BLUEBERRIES: These are smaller than the regular berries, with more intense flavor.

fresh strawberry tart

This tart is brimming with gorgeous, juicy strawberries. If you don't plan to use the strawberries immediately, refrigerate them overnight in their container and loosely cover with plastic wrap. Then, for maximum fruit flavor, bring the berries back to room temperature before assembling the tart. If you don't have a rectangular tart pan, substitute a 9½-inch round tart pan with a removable bottom.

Prep time: 20 minutes plus chilling and freezing
Baking time: 28 minutes
Microwave used

PASTRY:
- 1¼   cups all-purpose flour
- ⅛   teaspoon salt
- ½   cup butter, cut up (no substitutes)
- 3   to 5 tablespoons ice water

FILLING:
- ¼   cup strawberry or seedless raspberry preserves
- 3   cups sliced fresh strawberries
  Confectioners' sugar

SWEETENED WHIPPED CREAM:
- 1   cup heavy or whipping cream
- 1   tablespoon confectioners' sugar
- 1   teaspoon vanilla extract

1. *Make pastry:* Combine flour and salt in a medium bowl. With a pastry blender or 2 knives, cut in butter until mixture resembles fine crumbs. Add ice water, 1 tablespoon at a time, tossing vigorously with a fork after each addition until pastry holds together. Shape pastry into a ball; flatten into a disk. Wrap in plastic wrap; refrigerate 1 hour or overnight.

2. On a lightly floured surface with a floured rolling pin, roll pastry into a 16×8-inch rectangle. Carefully transfer pastry to 13¾×4¼-inch rectangular tart pan with removable bottom. *(Or, roll pastry into a 13-inch circle and fit into a 9½-inch round tart pan with removable bottom.)* Trim pastry, leaving a 1-inch overhang. Fold overhang in and press against side of pan. Prick bottom of the pie shell with the tines of a fork at ½-inch intervals. Place in freezer until firm, about 20 minutes.

3. Heat oven to 425°F. Line frozen pastry with foil; fill the tart pan halfway with dried beans, uncooked rice or pie weights. Bake 12 minutes, until the pastry edge is set and lightly colored. Remove foil and beans *(reserve the beans, rice or weights for your next pastry)*; bake pastry 16 minutes or until deep golden. If pastry puffs up during baking, prick it again with a fork. Cool on a wire rack.

4. *Make filling:* Place preserves in a microwaveproof bowl; microwave on HIGH 45 seconds. Spread preserves over bottom of baked crust; fill with sliced strawberries. Sift confectioners' sugar generously over strawberries.

5. *Make sweetened whipped cream:* Beat cream and confectioners' sugar to soft peaks in a small mixer bowl. Beat in vanilla. Serve tart with whipped cream. Makes 8 servings.

Per serving: 330 calories, 23.5 g total fat, 14.5 g saturated fat, 74 mg cholesterol, 176 mg sodium, 27 g carbohydrates, 3 g protein, 38 mg calcium, 2 g fiber

strawberry-rhubarb bundles

The crust is actually phyllo dough. Wrap it around a fruity filling and bake into a melt-in-your-mouth pastry.

Prep time: 30 minutes • Baking time: 15 to 18 minutes

- 3   cups fresh or frozen sliced rhubarb
  Granulated sugar
- 2   tablespoons cornstarch
- 2   tablespoons orange-flavored liqueur
- 1   pint fresh strawberries, hulled and halved
  Vegetable cooking spray
- 24   sheets fresh or frozen (thawed) phyllo dough
- ½   cup butter or margarine, melted
  Confectioners' sugar
  Fresh mint sprigs, for garnish (optional)

1. *Make filling:* Place rhubarb and ¾ cup granulated sugar in a medium saucepan. Cook over medium-high heat, stirring, until rhubarb is tender, 10 to 12 minutes.

2. Stir cornstarch and liqueur in a cup until smooth. Add to rhubarb and cook over medium heat, 2 minutes longer, until thick. Stir in the strawberries; cool.

3. Heat oven to 400°F. Lightly coat a large cookie sheet with vegetable cooking spray.

4. Cut phyllo crosswise in half; stack and cover with a sheet of plastic wrap. Place 2 phyllo sheets on a work surface; brush with some of the butter. Sprinkle with ½ teaspoon granulated sugar. Arrange 2 more phyllo sheets crosswise over first; brush with butter and sprinkle with ½ teaspoon sugar. Repeat with 2 more phyllo sheets, butter and sugar.

5. Spoon ⅓ cup of the filling onto the center of phyllo sheets. Lift corners of phyllo upward and press in center to form a bundle. Carefully lift bundle and place on the prepared cookie sheet. Repeat to make 8 bundles. Bake 15 to 18 minutes, until golden. Cool slightly on cookie sheet.

6. *To serve:* Lift bundles with a metal spatula onto 8 dessert plates. Sprinkle bundles with confectioners' sugar. Garnish with mint sprigs, if desired. Makes 8 servings.

Per serving: 410 calories, 16 g total fat, 8.5 g saturated fat, 33 mg cholesterol, 402 mg sodium, 62 g carbohydrates, 5 g protein, 56 mg calcium, 3 g fiber

blackberry tarts

Filled with juicy fresh blackberries and sprinkled with confectioners' sugar, these individual desserts are elegant enough for any summer gathering.

Prep time: 35 minutes plus chilling
Baking time: 27 to 32 minutes

FILLING:
- **1 quart fresh blackberries**
- **1 cup granulated sugar**

PASTRY:
- **2 cups all-purpose flour**
- **¼ teaspoon salt**
- **½ cup cold butter or margarine, cut up**
- **¼ cup vegetable shortening**
- **5 to 7 tablespoons ice water**

Confectioners' sugar, for garnish (optional)

1. *Make filling:* Gently stir blackberries and granulated sugar in a Dutch oven to combine; bring to boil. Reduce heat; cook 12 to 15 minutes, until filling is reduced to 2½ cups. Transfer to a bowl. Refrigerate filling 1 hour.

2. *Make pastry:* Combine flour and salt in a bowl. With a pastry blender or 2 knives, cut in butter and shortening until mixture resembles coarse crumbs. Add ice water, 1 tablespoon at a time, tossing with a fork until pastry begins to hold together. Shape pastry into 2 balls. Flatten into disks and wrap in plastic wrap; refrigerate 30 minutes.

3. Heat oven to 450°F. Cover a large cookie sheet with foil.

4. On a floured surface, roll one disk into a 13×11-inch rectangle. Repeat rolling remaining disk. Cut three 4¼-inch circles from each rectangle; reserve trimmings. Fit circles into six nonstick 3½×1½-inch mini brioche molds.* Arrange molds on the prepared cookie sheet. For lattice, cut twenty-four 3½×½-inch strips from trimmings.

5. Drain blackberry filling in a colander placed in a large bowl. Reserve syrup. Fill each tart with a scant ¼ cup berry mixture. Arrange 4 strips in a lattice pattern over filling, pressing edges to side of pastry. Bake 12 minutes. Reduce oven temperature to 375°F; bake 15 to 20 minutes more, until pastry is golden and filling is bubbly. Transfer to a wire rack. With tip of a small knife, loosen crust around edges of pans. Cool. When cool enough to handle, unmold the tarts. Sift tops with confectioners' sugar. Serve with reserved blackberry syrup. Makes 6 servings.

*Note: Mini brioche molds are available in kitchenware stores or from Bridge Kitchenware, 800-274-3435 (in New York, call 212-838-1901).

Per serving: 535 calories, 25.5 g total fat, 12.5 g saturated fat, 44 mg cholesterol, 263 mg sodium, 74 g carbohydrates, 5 g protein, 42 mg calcium, 6 g fiber

blueberry grunt

To bring out the truest, bluest flavor, we thickened the blueberry juices with tapioca (versus flour or cornstarch) and added a spritz of lemon for a citrus boost. Tip: Be sure to use a deep baking dish to keep bubbling berry juices from boiling over the sides. Pictured on page 205.

Prep time: 15 minutes plus standing and cooling
Baking time: 55 to 60 minutes

  1 tablespoon butter or margarine, softened
FILLING:
  6 cups fresh blueberries
  ¾ cup sugar
  1 tablespoon instant tapioca
  1 teaspoon grated lemon peel
  2 teaspoons fresh lemon juice
  ½ teaspoon cinnamon
TOPPING:
  1¼ cups all-purpose flour
  ⅓ cup cornmeal
  ⅓ cup sugar
  2½ teaspoons baking powder
  ¼ teaspoon baking soda
  ¼ teaspoon salt
  ⅓ cup butter or margarine, cut up
  1⅓ cups buttermilk
  ■
  1 tablespoon sugar
     Pinch cinnamon
     Vanilla ice cream (optional)

1. Heat oven to 350°F. Generously butter a 2½-quart baking dish. Set aside.

2. *Make filling:* Combine berries and remaining filling ingredients in a large bowl. Let the mixture stand 15 minutes.

3. *Make topping:* Combine flour, cornmeal, sugar, baking powder, soda and salt in another large bowl. With a pastry blender or 2 knives, cut in butter until mixture resembles coarse crumbs. Stir in buttermilk with a rubber spatula just until blended.

4. Transfer filling to the prepared baking dish. Drop topping by tablespoons over blueberries. Sprinkle a mixture of sugar and cinnamon evenly over topping. Bake until topping is golden and filling is bubbly, 55 to 60 minutes. Cool on a wire rack 30 minutes. Serve with ice cream, if desired. Makes 8 servings.

Per serving: 375 calories, 11 g total fat, 6.5 g saturated fat, 29 mg cholesterol, 420 mg sodium, 67 g carbohydrates, 5 g protein, 147 mg calcium, 3 g fiber

three-berry bread pudding

Berry fans will love this down-home dessert—it's bursting with three berry varieties. If your market doesn't have all three varieties, however, you can use just one favorite.

Prep time: 15 minutes plus standing
Baking time: 50 minutes plus cooling

  12 slices white bread, crusts trimmed, divided
  5 tablespoons butter or margarine, softened
  1 cup blueberries, divided
  1 cup blackberries, divided
  1 cup raspberries, divided
  4 large eggs
  ⅔ cup granulated sugar
  3 cups milk
     Additional berries and confectioners' sugar, for garnish (optional)

1. Spread bread with butter. Place 6 slices of the bread, buttered side down, in a shallow 2-quart baking dish. Sprinkle ½ cup each of the blueberries, blackberries and raspberries on top. Top with remaining 6 slices bread, buttered side down, then remaining berries.

2. Whisk eggs with granulated sugar and milk in a large bowl. Pour over bread; press to moisten the bread. Let stand 30 minutes.

3. Heat oven to 350°F. Place baking dish in a larger pan. Pour enough boiling water into larger pan to reach 1 inch up side of baking dish. Bake 50 minutes or until a knife inserted in center comes out clean. Cool on a rack 45 minutes. Sprinkle with additional berries and confectioners' sugar, if desired. Makes 6 servings.

Per serving: 450 calories, 18 g total fat, 9 g saturated fat, 179 mg cholesterol, 477 mg sodium, 61 g carbohydrates, 13 g protein, 236 mg calcium, 4 g fiber

three-berry crumble EASY

Summer is prime berry-picking time in the Pacific Northwest. Marionberries are a rich, intensely flavored variety of blackberry from Oregon. Partnered with raspberries, blueberries and a toasted hazelnut topping, their unusual flavor transforms this classic dessert into something truly unique. Frozen marionberries are becoming more widely available at supermarkets, but if you can't find them, substitute fresh or frozen blackberries.

Prep time: 20 minutes • Baking time: 60 to 65 minutes

FILLING:

- 2 **cups whole frozen marionberries, not thawed, or 1 pint fresh blackberries**
- 1 **pint fresh blueberries**
- 1 **pint fresh raspberries**
- 1 **cup granulated sugar**
- 1 **teaspoon grated lemon peel**
- 2 **teaspoons fresh lemon juice**
- 1 **teaspoon cornstarch**

TOPPING:

- 1 **cup old-fashioned oats**
- 1 **cup toasted, skinned and chopped hazelnuts (see note, page 258)**
- 1 **cup firmly packed brown sugar**
- ½ **cup all-purpose flour**
- 1 **teaspoon cinnamon**
- ½ **cup butter, softened (no substitutes)**

   ▪

   Vanilla ice cream

test kitchen tip
crumble on call

Crumble and crisp toppings store well, so next time you're making one of these old-fashioned favorites, consider making a double batch of topping. You can freeze the extra portion for up to 1 month in a freezer bag or container. Then, when you're ready to make your next crumble dessert, simply let the mixture stand at room temperature 15 to 20 minutes, until the mixture can be crumbled. Continue as the recipe directs.

1. Adjust oven racks to center and lower thirds of oven. Place a large sheet of foil on lower rack. Heat oven to 375°F. Butter a shallow 2-quart baking dish.

2. *Make filling:* Combine berries, sugar and lemon peel in a large bowl. Stir lemon juice and cornstarch in a cup until smooth. Gently stir cornstarch mixture into berry mixture just until blended. Spoon filling into prepared dish.

3. *Make topping:* Combine oats, hazelnuts, brown sugar, flour and cinnamon in a medium bowl. With a pastry blender or 2 knives, cut in butter until mixture is crumbly and begins to stick together slightly. Sprinkle topping evenly over berries. Bake on center oven rack until filling begins to bubble around the sides and is hot in the center, 60 to 65 minutes. *(If topping browns too quickly, cover loosely with foil during the last 15 minutes of baking.)*

4. Cool crumble completely on a wire rack. Hot filling will be loose but will firm as it cools. *(Can be made ahead. Cover and refrigerate overnight. Bring to room temperature.)* Serve with vanilla ice cream. Makes 8 servings.

Per serving: 515 calories, 21.5 g total fat, 8 g saturated fat, 31 mg cholesterol, 131 mg sodium, 81 g carbohydrates, 5 g protein, 85 mg calcium, 6 g fiber

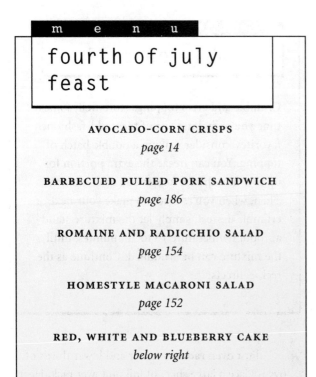

m e n u

fourth of july feast

AVOCADO-CORN CRISPS
page 14

BARBECUED PULLED PORK SANDWICH
page 186

ROMAINE AND RADICCHIO SALAD
page 154

HOMESTYLE MACARONI SALAD
page 152

RED, WHITE AND BLUEBERRY CAKE
below right

four-berry pie

What better way to celebrate the arrival of fresh strawberries, blueberries, blackberries and raspberries than by combining them into one very scrumptious one-crust pie. Pictured on page 205.

Prep time: 35 to 40 minutes plus chilling
Baking time: 15 minutes

PASTRY:
- 1 cup all-purpose flour
- 6 tablespoons cold butter, cut into small pieces
- ⅓ cup sour cream

FILLING:
- 2 cups fresh blueberries, divided
- 8 tablespoons water, divided
- ½ cup sugar plus 1 tablespoon sugar, divided
- 2 tablespoons cornstarch
- ½ teaspoon grated lemon peel
- 1 teaspoon fresh lemon juice
- Pinch salt
- 1 cup fresh raspberries
- 1 cup fresh blackberries
- 1 cup small strawberries, hulled and halved
- Small strawberries, blueberries or blackberries, for garnish (optional)
- Vanilla ice cream (optional)

1. *Make pastry:* Pulse flour and butter in a food processor until mixture is crumbly. Add sour cream; pulse until pastry begins to hold together. Shape pastry into a ball. Flatten into a disk and wrap in plastic wrap; refrigerate 1 hour.

2. *Make filling:* Combine 1 cup of the blueberries, 6 tablespoons of the water and ½ cup of the sugar in a saucepan. Cover and bring to boil. Uncover, reduce heat and simmer 3 minutes. Stir together remaining 2 tablespoons water and the cornstarch in a cup until smooth. Stir into fruit mixture. Add lemon peel, juice and salt. Simmer, stirring, 1 minute until mixture is thickened.

3. Pour filling into a large bowl. Fold in remaining 1 cup blueberries, the raspberries, blackberries and strawberries. Pour filling into a 9-inch pie plate; set aside to cool.

4. Roll pastry into a 12-inch circle; transfer to a cookie sheet. Using a 10-inch cake pan or lid as a guide, trim pastry into a 10½-inch circle. Tuck edge of circle and flute; cut pastry into 8 wedges. Refrigerate 30 minutes.

5. Heat oven to 400°F. Lightly brush pastry wedges with water; sprinkle with the remaining 1 tablespoon sugar. Bake 15 minutes, until golden. Cool on a wire rack. To serve, top berry mixture with pastry wedges. Garnish with strawberries, blueberries or blackberries and serve with ice cream, if desired. Makes 8 servings.

Per serving: 265 calories, 11 g total fat, 6.5 g saturated fat, 27 mg cholesterol, 113 mg sodium, 40 g carbohydrates, 3 g protein, 31 mg calcium, 3 g fiber

red, white and blueberry cake

A fabulous flag-waving finale, this sweet treat is a triple-tiered white cake with a luscious blueberry filling. Garnish the whipped cream frosting with strawberries.

Prep time: 40 minutes plus chilling
Baking time: 25 minutes

CAKE:
- 2¾ cups sifted cake flour (not self-rising)
- 2 teaspoons baking powder

¼ teaspoon salt

10 tablespoons butter or margarine, softened

1¾ cups granulated sugar

3 large eggs, at room temperature 20 to 30 minutes

1 teaspoon grated orange peel

1 teaspoon vanilla extract

1¼ cups milk

BLUEBERRY FILLING:

3 cups fresh blueberries, divided

⅔ cup granulated sugar

5 tablespoons water, divided

3 tablespoons cornstarch

1 tablespoon fresh lemon juice

TOPPING:

1 cup heavy or whipping cream

2 tablespoons confectioners' sugar

1 pint fresh strawberries, hulled and sliced

Fresh mint sprigs, for garnish (optional)

1. *Make cake:* Heat oven to 350°F. Grease three 8-inch round cake pans. Line bottoms with waxed paper; grease again and flour.

2. Combine flour, baking powder and salt in a medium bowl. Beat butter and granulated sugar in a large mixer bowl until light and fluffy. Add eggs, one at a time, beating 1 minute after each addition. Beat in orange peel and vanilla. At low speed, add milk to batter alternately with dry ingredients, beginning and ending with dry ingredients. Beat at medium speed 2 minutes. Pour into prepared pans.

3. Bake 25 minutes, until cakes pull away from sides of pans and spring back when lightly touched. Cool on wire racks 10 minutes. Remove from pans; peel off waxed paper and cool completely.

4. *Make blueberry filling:* Combine 2 cups of the blueberries, the granulated sugar and 2 tablespoons of the water in a large saucepan. Bring to full boil, stirring occasionally. Meanwhile, stir remaining 3 tablespoons water into cornstarch in a cup. Add to blueberry mixture, stirring constantly, and return to boil. Reduce heat to low and cook 2 minutes, stirring. Remove from heat;

stir in lemon juice and remaining 1 cup blueberries. Set pan in a large bowl of ice water, stirring occasionally, until cold, or transfer to a shallow container and refrigerate, uncovered, 1 hour.

5. Place 1 cake layer on a serving plate. Spread half of the blueberry mixture on top. Arrange second cake layer on top; spread with remaining blueberry mixture and top with third cake layer. Cover with plastic wrap and let stand 3 hours at room temperature to set (*or refrigerate up to 24 hours*).

6. *For topping:* Beat cream with confectioners' sugar in a mixer bowl to stiff peaks. Spread on top of cake. Top with strawberries and garnish with mint sprigs, if desired. Makes 12 servings.

Per serving: 470 calories, 19.5 g total fat, 11.5 g saturated fat, 110 mg cholesterol, 258 mg sodium, 70 g carbohydrates, 5 g protein, 103 mg calcium, 2 g fiber

peach-coconut ice cream

Rich, creamy and very peachy, the secret ingredient in this ice cream is the prepared cream of coconut. For best results, use perfectly ripe peaches.

Total prep time: 15 minutes plus chilling and freezing

4 cups peeled, sliced, very ripe peaches

¼ cup fresh lemon juice

1 can (15 oz.) cream of coconut

1 cup water

1. With a potato masher or fork, crush peaches with lemon juice in a large bowl. Blend cream of coconut and water in a blender until smooth; stir into peach mixture. Refrigerate 2 hours, until cold.

2. Freeze in an ice-cream maker according to manufacturer's instructions. Makes 5 cups.

Per ½ cup: 200 calories, 15 g total fat, 13 g saturated fat, 0 mg cholesterol, 2 mg sodium, 19 g carbohydrates, 3 g protein, 12 mg calcium, 4 g fiber

melon menagerie

Dozens of dazzling, juicy melons grow during the summer. Here are some varieties to consider at local farmers' markets:

WATERMELON: Depending on the variety, the rinds range in color from solid dark green to striped or mottled. Some are large and football-shaped while others are more basketball-shaped. The refreshing meat can be anywhere from deep pink to red to yellow. Many have flat, dark brown or black seeds, but seedless varieties also are available.

CANTALOUPE: This melon has a thick, raised "netting" which covers the round, straw-colored rind. The sweet flesh has a salmon-tinged color and a faint nutty scent. When buying them, press the blossom end slightly; ripe melons yield to gentle pressure and have a sweetly aromatic scent.

SHARLYN: This variety has a thin, orange rind beneath a faint netting. The luscious white flesh is a sweet mix of flowery honeydew and cantaloupe flavors.

JUAN CANARY: This melon has a football shape with a smooth, yellow skin. The flesh is pale white, fragrant and sweet.

GALIA: Look for a thin, light netting over a golden, cantaloupelike rind. The flesh is succulent, spicy sweet and a pale green color.

ORANGE-FLESHED HONEYDEW: These melons are smooth and rounded. The rind is a pale peach color, and the flesh is cantaloupe colored. They have a sweet honeydew taste and texture.

CASABA: This globe-shaped melon has one pointed end and a golden yellow rind with a ridged, wrinkled skin. The white-green flesh is juicy and crisp and has a melon-sweet flavor.

papaya sorbet

The creaminess of papaya brings the rich taste of ice cream to this low-fat dessert.

Total prep time: 10 minutes plus freezing

- **1 ripe papaya (1¼ lbs.), peeled and diced**
- **¼ cup plain low-fat yogurt**
- **½ cup light corn syrup**
- **1 teaspoon fresh lime juice**

1. Place papaya in a 9-inch square baking pan and place in freezer 1 hour.

2. Place frozen papaya in a food processor with yogurt, corn syrup and lime juice. Process until smooth. Freeze at least 1 hour. Makes 2 cups.

Per ½ cup: 160 calories, 0.5 g total fat, 0 g saturated fat, 1 mg cholesterol, 62 mg sodium, 41 g carbohydrates, 1 g protein, 52 mg calcium, 2 g fiber

trio of melon ices

Nothing could be easier than these summer refreshers—just dice the melon, freeze, then puree.

Prep time: 15 minutes plus chilling and freezing
Cooking time: 10 minutes

CANTALOUPE ICE:
- **3 cups cubed ripe cantaloupe**
- **⅓ cup sugar**
- **¼ cup water**
- **⅛ teaspoon grated lemon peel**
- **1 tablespoon fresh lemon juice**

1. Arrange cantaloupe pieces in a 13×9-inch baking dish; cover and freeze overnight.

2. Combine sugar and water in a small saucepan; cover and boil 2 to 3 minutes. Uncover and simmer 5 minutes. Transfer syrup to a glass measure; stir in lemon peel and lemon juice. Chill the mixture 45 minutes or overnight.

3. Puree frozen melon in a food processor. With machine running, gradually add syrup. Process melon mixture until completely smooth. Serve immediately. *(Can be made ahead; freeze up to 1 week.)* Makes 2 cups.

Per ½ cup: 100 calories, 0 g total fat, 0 g saturated fat, 0 mg cholesterol, 25 mg sodium, 26 g carbohydrates, 1 g protein, 16 mg calcium, 1 g fiber

HONEYDEW ICE: Prepare cantaloupe ice as directed, *except* substitute 3 cups cubed honeydew melon for cantaloupe and ⅛ teaspoon grated lime peel and 1 tablespoon lime juice for lemon peel and juice.

Per ½ cup: 105 calories, 0 g total fat, 0 g saturated fat, 0 mg cholesterol, 13 mg sodium, 27 g carbohydrates, 1 g protein, 8 mg calcium, 1 g fiber

WATERMELON ICE: Prepare cantaloupe ice as directed, *except* substitute 3 cups cubed watermelon, seeded, for the cantaloupe and 1 tablespoon Campari for the lemon peel and juice.

Per ½ cup: 100 calories, 0 g total fat, 0 g saturated fat, 0 mg cholesterol, 3 mg sodium, 25 g carbohydrates, 1 g protein, 7 mg calcium, 1 g fiber

melon medley

Today you can choose from a cornucopia of new melon varieties. A simple lime-and-sugar syrup drizzled on top makes their taste all the sweeter. Pictured on page 202.

Prep time: 25 minutes plus chilling • Cooking time: 2 minutes

- ¼ **cup sugar**
- ¼ **cup water**
- ½ **cantaloupe or orange-fleshed honeydew, peeled and cut into 4 wedges**
- 1½ **cups watermelon balls**
- 1 **cup diced honeydew or Galia melon**
- ½ **teaspoon grated lime peel**
- 1 **tablespoon fresh lime juice**
- 1 **tablespoon chopped crystallized ginger (optional)**

1. Combine sugar and water in a small saucepan. Bring to boil; reduce heat to medium-low and simmer 1 minute. Pour sugar syrup into a 1-cup glass measure; refrigerate 1 hour, or until cold. *(Can be made ahead. Cover; refrigerate up to 2 days.)*

2. Arrange cantaloupe wedges on 4 plates. Divide and top with watermelon balls and diced honeydew. Stir lime peel and juice into sugar syrup. Drizzle syrup over melons. Sprinkle with ginger, if desired. Makes 4 servings.

Per serving: 110 calories, 0.5 g total fat, 0 g saturated fat, 0 mg cholesterol, 12 mg sodium, 27 g carbohydrates, 1 g protein, 15 mg calcium, 1 g fiber

watermelon-tequila granita

A refreshing finish to a summertime meal.

Total prep time: 10 minutes plus cooling and freezing

- ½ **cup sugar**
- 4 **whole cardamom pods, crushed**
- ¼ **cup tequila**
- 2½ **pounds watermelon, rind and seeds removed**
- 2 **tablespoons fresh lime juice**
  Pinch salt

1. Combine 1 cup water, the sugar and cardamom in a medium saucepan; bring to boil. Stir well and boil 5 minutes. Transfer to a large bowl and stir in tequila. Cool. Meanwhile, cut watermelon into chunks. Puree watermelon in batches in a blender until smooth.

2. Remove cardamom from syrup. Line a fine mesh strainer with a double thickness of cheesecloth and set over bowl of syrup. Pour watermelon puree through strainer into syrup. Add lime juice and salt; stir well. Pour mixture into a 9-inch square baking pan. Cover pan with plastic wrap and freeze watermelon mixture 3 hours, until large ice crystals form. Stir ice crystals with a wooden spoon to break into large pieces. Freeze mixture 1 hour more, stirring after 30 minutes, until all the liquid is frozen. *(Can be made ahead. Transfer to an airtight container. Cover and freeze up to 1 week. Mash with a spoon before serving. Or, process 5 to 10 seconds in a food processor for a smooth-textured granita.)* Spoon into 6 serving bowls. Makes 6 servings.

Per serving: 120 calories, 0.5 g total fat, 0 g saturated fat, 0 mg cholesterol, 28 mg sodium, 24 g carbohydrates, 1 g protein, 10 mg calcium, 1 g fiber

pastry pitfalls

The term "easy as pie" doesn't necessarily ring true for everyone. While making a pie pastry is not difficult, a few problems may occur— fortunately, they're easily remedied.

SOGGY CRUST?
Cracks in the pastry can cause a soggy crust; before adding the fruit filling, be sure to patch cracks with pastry scraps. Also, make sure your oven temperature is correct; a too-low temperature will not bake the bottom crust properly.

EVEN BROWNING
Be sure to use a standard glass pie plate or a dull metal pie pan so the pastry browns evenly.

TOUGH PASTRY?
This could be due to any of a number of mistakes. Not mixing properly is one cause. Remember to cut in the shortening or butter until the mixture is well mixed—the texture of coarse crumbs. Using too much water to moisten the mixture can also result in a tough pastry, as can overmixing the flour mixture and water—you should toss them together just until the mixture is moistened. Another culprit: using too much flour when rolling out the pastry.

HARD TO ROLL?
If your pastry is too crumbly to roll easily, add more water—but just a teaspoon at a time. Make sure it's evenly moistened—however, don't overmix.

EXCESSIVE SHRINKAGE
You may have overmixed the flour and water mixture or stretched the pastry when transferring it to the pie plate.

summer-fresh peach pie

To prevent the edge of the pie from overbrowning, cover it with a metal pie ring or, if you don't have one, a piece of foil with the center removed. Pictured on page 204.

Prep time: 1 hour plus chilling and standing
Baking time: 75 to 85 minutes

PASTRY:
- 2¼ cups all-purpose flour
- ½ teaspoon salt
- ¼ teaspoon baking powder
- ½ cup cold butter, cut up (no substitutes)
- ⅓ cup cold vegetable shortening, cut up
- 1 tablespoon distilled white vinegar
- 5 to 6 tablespoons ice water

FILLING:
- 3 pounds fresh peaches
- ¾ cup sugar
- 2 tablespoons instant tapioca
- 1 tablespoon cornstarch
- Pinch salt
- 1 tablespoon fresh lemon juice
- ¼ teaspoon pure almond extract
- 2 tablespoons butter, cut up (no substitutes)

1. *Make pastry:* Combine flour, salt and baking powder in a large bowl. With a pastry blender or 2 knives, cut in butter and shortening until mixture resembles coarse crumbs (you'll find some small pieces of butter the size of a split pea). Combine vinegar and 1 tablespoon of the water in a small bowl. Drizzle over flour mixture, tossing with a fork. Drizzle in remaining water, 1 tablespoon at a time, tossing with a fork until pastry begins to hold together. Shape pastry into 2 balls, one slightly larger than the other. Flatten into disks and wrap in plastic wrap; refrigerate 1 hour. *(Can be made ahead. Refrigerate up to 2 days. Let stand at room temperature 10 minutes before rolling out.)*

2. On a lightly floured surface, roll larger pastry disk into a 14-inch circle. Fit into a 9-inch, deep dish pie plate; cover with plastic wrap and refrigerate. Roll remaining disk into a 13-inch circle. Place on a cookie sheet; cover and refrigerate.

3. ■ *Make filling:* Meanwhile, bring a medium saucepan of water to boil. Add peaches, one at a time, and let stand in boiling water 30 to 60 seconds. Using a slotted spoon, immediately transfer to a bowl of cold water and peel off skin of peach with a small, sharp knife.

4. ■ Combine sugar, tapioca, cornstarch and salt in a large bowl. Pit peaches and cut into ¾-inch slices; add to sugar mixture with lemon juice and almond extract. Stir gently until sugar mixture is moistened. Let stand 15 minutes.

5. ■ Arrange rack in lower third of oven. Slide a sheet of foil on the rack underneath the rack on which pie will bake.* Heat oven to 425°F. Add butter to filling and stir to combine. Pour filling into the pastry shell.

6. ■ Trim edge of pastry circle; cut circle with a fluted pastry wheel into eight 1½-inch-wide strips (the strips will be of varying lengths). Arrange 4 strips on top of filling, starting with the shorter strips, then the longer ones in the center and shorter ones at the opposite edge. Pull every other strip back; arrange another shorter strip on top in the opposite direction. Return pulled back strips to their former position. Repeat process with remaining 3 strips to weave a lattice pattern. Trim edge of pastry and strips and flute edge. Place pie in freezer 10 minutes.

7. ■ Bake pie 25 minutes. Cover edge of pastry with a metal pie ring or a piece of foil. Reduce oven temperature to 375°F. Bake 50 to 60 minutes more, until filling is bubbly in center. Remove pie ring from edge of crust; cool on a wire rack. Makes 8 servings.

*Note: If lower third of your oven is the bottom rack, slide a sheet of foil on the bottom of the oven. (For electric ovens, before heating the oven, lift the coil and place a sheet of aluminum foil under the coil.)

Per serving: 480 calories, 23.5 g total fat, 11 g saturated fat, 39 mg cholesterol, 336 mg sodium, 65 g carbohydrates, 5 g protein, 25 mg calcium, 3 g fiber

peach crumb cake

This cake's texture is similar to that of a pound cake. The surprise ingredient here is almond paste.

Prep time: 25 minutes • Baking time: 60 to 70 minutes

CRUMB TOPPING:
- ¼ cup all-purpose flour
- ¼ cup firmly packed brown sugar
- 2 tablespoons butter (no substitutes)

■

- 1½ cups all-purpose flour
- ½ teaspoon cream of tartar
- ½ teaspoon salt
- ¾ cup butter, softened (no substitutes)
- ⅓ cup almond paste, cut up
- 1 cup granulated sugar
- 4 large eggs, at room temperature 20 to 30 minutes
- 1 tablespoon fresh lemon juice
- 1 teaspoon vanilla extract
- 2 fresh peaches, peeled and cut into ½-inch slices
- ½ cup sliced natural almonds

1. ■ Heat oven to 350°F. Grease and flour a 9-inch springform pan.

2. ■ *Make crumb topping:* Combine flour and brown sugar; cut in butter with a pastry blender or a fork.

3. ■ Combine flour, cream of tartar and salt in a medium bowl. Beat butter and almond paste in a mixer bowl until creamy. Add sugar and continue beating until light and fluffy. Beat in eggs, one at a time, beating well after each addition. Beat in lemon juice and vanilla. Add dry ingredients to batter; beat 1 minute more. Spread into pan. Arrange peaches on top. Sprinkle with crumb topping, then nuts. Bake 60 to 70 minutes, until a toothpick inserted in center comes out clean. Cool on a wire rack. Run knife around edge of pan and release springform ring. *(Can be made ahead. Wrap and freeze up to 1 month. Thaw, wrapped, at room temperature 4 hours.)* Makes 12 servings.

Per serving: 375 calories, 21 g total fat, 10 g saturated fat, 109 mg cholesterol, 265 mg sodium, 43 g carbohydrates, 6 g protein, 48 mg calcium, 3 g fiber

plum kuchen

Kuchen ("cake" in German) is a classic fruit-filled yeast dough with sugar and spice. Our quick version is leavened with baking powder instead of yeast. Pictured on page 201.

Prep time: 12 minutes • Baking time: 48 to 50 minutes

TOPPING:

- ¼   **cup all-purpose flour**
- 1   **tablespoon firmly packed brown sugar**
- 1   **tablespoon butter or margarine, softened**

- 1½   **cups all-purpose flour**
- 1½   **teaspoons baking powder**
- ¼   **teaspoon cardamom**
- ¼   **teaspoon salt**
- ¾   **cup butter or margarine, softened**
- ¾   **cup granulated sugar**
- 3   **large eggs, at room temperature 20 to 30 minutes**
- ½   **pound ripe plums (2 medium or 1 large), pitted and sliced**
- **Whipped cream (optional)**

1. ▪ Heat oven to 350°F. Grease the bottom of a 9-inch springform pan. Line bottom with waxed paper; grease and flour paper and side of pan.

2. ▪ *Make topping:* Combine flour and sugar in a small bowl; with a pastry blender or 2 knives, cut in butter until mixture is crumbly.

3. ▪ Combine flour, baking powder, cardamom and salt in a bowl; set aside.

4. ▪ Beat butter in a large mixer bowl on high speed until creamy. Gradually beat in sugar until mixture is light and fluffy, 2 to 3 minutes. Add eggs, one at a time, beating well after each addition. Reduce speed to medium-low. Gradually beat in flour mixture just until blended. Spread batter evenly in prepared pan. Arrange plum slices, sides touching, around edge of pan in a circle. Arrange remaining slices in a smaller circle in the center. Sprinkle topping over top of cake. Bake 48 to 50 minutes, until top is golden and a toothpick inserted in center comes out clean. Run knife around edge of pan and release springform ring; cool on a wire rack, 15 minutes. Gently invert cake onto a flat plate; remove bottom of pan and waxed paper. Invert cake again onto a large serving plate and lift off top plate. Serve warm with whipped cream, if desired. Makes 8 servings.

Per serving: 390 calories, 21.5 g total fat, 12.5 g saturated fat, 130 mg cholesterol, 378 mg sodium, 45 g carbohydrates, 6 g protein, 72 mg calcium, 1 g fiber

nectarine kuchen

Top this quick coffee cake with luscious nectarines.

Prep time: 15 minutes • Baking time: 25 to 30 minutes

TOPPING:

- ¼   **cup sugar**
- 2   **tablespoons flour**
- **Pinch cinnamon**
- 2   **tablespoons butter or margarine, cut up**
- ¼   **cup coarsely chopped almonds**

- 1   **cup all-purpose flour**
- ½   **cup sugar**
- 1   **teaspoon baking powder**
- ¼   **teaspoon salt**
- 6   **tablespoons butter or margarine, cut up**
- 1   **large egg, lightly beaten**
- ⅓   **cup milk**
- 3   **nectarines, cut into eighths**

1. ▪ Heat oven to 425°F. Grease a 9-inch square baking pan.

2. ▪ *Make topping:* Combine sugar, flour and cinnamon in a small bowl; with a pastry blender or 2 knives, cut in butter until mixture is crumbly. Add almonds.

3. ▪ Combine flour, sugar, baking powder and salt in a bowl. With a pastry blender or 2 knives, cut in butter until mixture resembles coarse crumbs. Stir in egg and milk. Spread in the prepared pan. Arrange nectarines on top. Sprinkle with topping. Bake 25 to 30 minutes, until a toothpick inserted in center comes out clean. Cool on a wire rack, 10 minutes. Serve warm. Makes 9 servings.

Per serving: 265 calories, 13.5 g total fat, 7 g saturated fat, 53 mg cholesterol, 231 mg sodium, 34 g carbohydrates, 4 g protein, 57 mg calcium, 2 g fiber

cherry tart

Sweet Bing cherries baked in a luscious custard create an elegant dessert that's surprisingly easy to assemble: You don't need to roll out the pastry—just press it right into the tart pan. Pick up a cherry pitter to make quick work of the task (it also helps to retain their plump shape). Pictured on page 204.

Prep time: 30 minutes plus freezing
Baking time: 45 minutes

PASTRY:

1¼	cups all-purpose flour
¼	cup confectioners' sugar
½	cup butter, cut up (no substitutes)
1	large egg yolk
3	tablespoons toasted ground almonds, divided
1	teaspoon grated orange peel

1	pound fresh Bing cherries
1	tablespoon orange-flavored liqueur
1	teaspoon grated orange peel
6	tablespoons heavy or whipping cream
2	large eggs
⅓	cup granulated sugar
1	tablespoon flour
½	teaspoon vanilla extract
⅛	teaspoon almond extract

1. *Make pastry:* Pulse flour and confectioners' sugar in a food processor. Add butter; pulse 4 to 5 times, until mixture resembles coarse crumbs. Add egg yolk, 2 tablespoons of the almonds and the orange peel; pulse until mixture begins to come together. Mixture will be crumbly, but that's okay. Transfer pastry to a 9-inch tart pan with removable bottom. With lightly floured fingers, press evenly along the bottom and up the sides of pan. Place tart shell in freezer 20 minutes, until firm. *(Can be made ahead. Cover and refrigerate overnight.)*

2. Adjust oven rack to lowest position. Heat oven to 375°F. Bake tart shell until lightly golden, 18 minutes. Cool on a wire rack. Sprinkle crust with remaining 1 tablespoon almonds.

3. Meanwhile, pit cherries with a cherry pitter. Toss cherries, orange liqueur and orange peel in a medium bowl; let cherry mixture stand 15 minutes at room temperature.

4. Scatter cherries evenly over cooled crust. Pour any cherry juices on top. Whisk together cream, eggs, granulated sugar, flour, vanilla and almond extracts in a large bowl; pour mixture over cherries in cooled crust.

5. Bake tart until filling is set and golden brown, 45 minutes. Cool tart in pan on a wire rack, 10 minutes. Remove side of pan and serve warm or at room temperature. *(Can be made ahead. Cool tart completely. Cover and refrigerate overnight. Let stand at room temperature 30 minutes before serving.)* Makes 8 servings.

Per serving: 340 calories, 19.5 g total fat, 10.5 g saturated fat, 126 mg cholesterol, 139 mg sodium, 38 g carbohydrates, 5 g protein, 37 mg calcium, 2 g fiber

test kitchen tip
sweet as sugar

Come summertime, this flavored sugar syrup drizzled over fresh fruit or added to your favorite thirst-quencher will spell sweet refreshment:

Bring 1 cup each sugar and water to boil in a saucepan. Reduce heat and simmer 5 minutes. until the sugar dissolves. Add one of the following: ¼ cup chopped lemon; 1 vanilla bean, split; 3 cinnamon sticks; 3 star anise; or 2 cups fresh mint leaves. Chill, then strain. Store in a sealed container in the refrigerator up to 2 days.

meringue magic

Whether your dessert starts with a meringue crust or finishes with a meringue crown, here are a few steps for achieving meringue perfection:

LET EGG WHITES STAND at room temperature for 20 to 30 minutes before beating. This will help increase the volume of the beaten mixture.

BE SURE TO WAIT until soft peaks form—that is, the tips curl slightly—before gradually adding the sugar.

CONTINUE BEATING EGG WHITES until stiff peaks form and the sugar is completely dissolved. (To test, rub a bit of meringue between your fingers. It should feel smooth, not gritty.) If you underbeat the whites, the meringue may shrink as it bakes.

WHEN CUTTING a meringue-topped dessert, you can keep the meringue from clinging to the knife by dipping the knife in water, without drying, before making each cut.

angel pie

A meringue crust cradles the cream and berries in this sensational grand finale dessert.

Prep time: 40 minutes
Baking time: 1 hour plus standing

MERINGUE CRUST:

4	large egg whites, at room temperature 20 to 30 minutes
¼	teaspoon cream of tartar
⅛	teaspoon salt
1	cup superfine sugar, divided
1½	teaspoons raspberry brandy or ¼ teaspoon almond extract

LEMON FILLING:

2	large eggs
2	large egg yolks
⅔	cup granulated sugar
¼	cup fresh lemon juice

2	tablespoons butter or margarine, cut up
1	teaspoon grated lemon peel
½	cup heavy or whipping cream
	▪
2	cups cut-up fruit and berries

1. ▪ Heat oven to 225°F. Line a cookie sheet with foil or parchment. Draw an 8-inch circle on liner.

2. ▪ *Make meringue crust:* Beat egg whites, cream of tartar and salt in a mixer bowl at medium speed to soft peaks. Add superfine sugar, 2 tablespoons at a time, beating 30 seconds after each addition. Beat on high speed 1 minute. Fold in brandy.

3. ▪ Spoon meringue into a pastry bag fitted with a large star tip. Pipe in a spiral to fill in circle. Pipe 2 tiers of rosettes along edge for a rim (or spoon meringue into a circle, spooning sides upward). Bake 1 hour, until dry to the touch. Turn oven off; leave in oven 2 hours. Do not open oven door. Peel off liner; place crust on serving plate.

4. ▪ *Make filling:* Cook eggs, yolks, granulated sugar, lemon juice and butter in a double boiler over simmering water, stirring, until mixture thickens, 15 minutes. Remove from heat. Stir in peel. Set in a bowl of ice water, stirring, until cold.

5. ▪ Beat cream in a mixer bowl to stiff peaks. Whisk one-third of the whipped cream into lemon filling. Fold in remaining cream. Spoon into meringue shell. Arrange fruit on top. Makes 8 servings.

Per serving: 290 calories, 11.5 g total fat, 6 g saturated fat, 135 mg cholesterol, 119 mg sodium, 44 g carbohydrates, 5 g protein, 30 mg calcium, 1 g fiber

apple tart

The crisp bite of a glossy apple is a sure sign of fall, and what better way to showcase the fruit's natural sweetness than with this tart? The apples don't require much enhancement—we added only butter, sugar and apple brandy for a traditional fall flavor. Pictured on page 206.

Prep time: 40 minutes plus chilling
Baking time: 40 to 45 minutes

PASTRY:

1¼	cups all-purpose flour
2	tablespoons sugar

⅛ teaspoon salt

½ cup cold butter, cut up (no substitutes)

3 tablespoons ice water

1 teaspoon fresh lemon juice

    ■

½ cup sugar

6 tablespoons butter, cut up (no substitutes)

3 pounds Golden Delicious apples (about 8), peeled, cored and cut into ½-inch slices

4 tablespoons Calvados or brandy, divided

2 tablespoons fresh lemon juice

   Crème fraîche or whipped cream (optional)

1. *Make pastry:* Pulse flour, sugar and salt in a food processor. Add butter; pulse 4 to 5 times, until mixture resembles coarse crumbs. Add ice water and lemon juice; pulse until mixture just begins to come together. Shape pastry into a 6×4-inch rectangle; wrap in plastic wrap. Refrigerate 30 minutes or overnight. *(Can be made ahead. Freeze up to 2 weeks. Thaw in refrigerator overnight.)*

2. Meanwhile, melt sugar and butter in a large skillet over medium heat. Add apples, 2 tablespoons of the Calvados and the lemon juice. Cook apples, stirring gently, until light golden and tender, 8 to 10 minutes. Drain apples in a large strainer set over a bowl. Reserve juice. Transfer apples to a large plate and let stand until cool, 10 minutes.

3. Heat oven to 375°F. Divide pastry in half. On a lightly floured surface, roll each piece into a 12×4½-inch rectangle. Fold each rectangle gently in half; transfer to a large cookie sheet and unfold (rectangles should be 2 inches apart). Flute edges to form a rim. Refrigerate.

4. Coarsely chop 2 cups of the cooled apples; divide and sprinkle over each rectangle. Divide and arrange remaining apple slices over chopped apples, slightly overlapping in a single row. Bake until pastry and apples are golden, 40 to 45 minutes. Transfer tarts to a large wire rack and cool.

5. Bring reserved juice and the remaining 2 tablespoons Calvados to boil in a small saucepan over medium-high heat. Reduce mixture until it equals about ⅓ cup and is slightly thickened,

3 minutes. Spoon over apples. Transfer tarts to a large serving plate. Serve with crème fraîche, if desired. Makes 8 servings.

Per serving: 415 calories, 20.5 g total fat, 12.5 g saturated fat, 54 mg cholesterol, 242 mg sodium, 53 g carbohydrates, 3 g protein, 15 mg calcium, 3 g fiber

baked apples

You don't need anything fancy to make a delicious baked apple—just the freshest fruit available. Pictured on page 207.

Prep time: 10 minutes • Baking time: 40 to 45 minutes

¼ cup sugar

¼ teaspoon cinnamon

4 (7 oz. each) baking apples, cored (see tip, page 224)

4 teaspoons butter or margarine, cut up

½ cup apple juice

1. Heat oven to 375°F. Combine sugar and cinnamon in a small bowl.

2. Peel apples, leaving a 1-inch-wide band of peel around the center of each. Arrange apples in a 9-inch square baking dish. Fill each cavity with 1 teaspoon each butter and cinnamon-sugar. Sprinkle with remaining cinnamon-sugar.

3. Add apple juice to bottom of dish. Cover dish with foil and bake 25 minutes. Uncover and spoon the apple juice over apples; bake 15 to 20 minutes more, until tender.

4. Spoon apples and apple juice on each of 4 serving plates. Makes 4 servings.

Per serving: 220 calories, 4.5 g total fat, 2.5 g saturated fat, 10 mg cholesterol, 40 mg sodium, 48 g carbohydrates, 0 g protein, 20 mg calcium, 5 g fiber

a is for...

...apple, of course. Here's how to choose the best for your home-baked treats:

GOLDEN DELICIOUS, the variety we call for in many of our recipes, holds its shape and retains its flavor well when baked.

SUBSTITUTIONS? If you want to bake with a variety from your local orchard, seek out Granny Smith, Jonathan, McIntosh, Newton Pippin, Rome Beauty or Winesap apples.

SAVE THE RED DELICIOUS apple for eating out of hand—when baked, this lunchbox favorite can turn to mush.

apple baklava

Delicate, crisp layers of phyllo dough are layered with spicy sliced apples and a velvety caramel sauce. Ultra-thin phyllo dough dries out quickly, so keep it covered with a damp cloth or plastic wrap until you're ready to use it.

Prep time: 1 hour • Baking time: 10 minutes per batch

PHYLLO LAYERS:

- ½ cup walnuts or almonds
- ¼ cup granulated sugar
- 16 sheets phyllo dough
- ¼ cup butter or margarine, melted

APPLE FILLING:

- 2 tablespoons butter or margarine
- 2 pounds Golden Delicious apples, peeled, cored and cut into ¼-inch-thick slices (6 cups)
- 3 tablespoons firmly packed brown sugar
- ¾ teaspoon cinnamon
- ¼ teaspoon allspice
- ½ cup apple juice

CARAMEL SAUCE:

- ⅓ cup granulated sugar
- ⅓ cup heavy or whipping cream

Confectioners' sugar

1. Heat oven to 375°F. Grease 2 cookie sheets.

2. *Make phyllo layers:* Process nuts and granulated sugar in a food processor until finely ground. Stack phyllo sheets on a work surface. Starting at corner of phyllo and using an 8-inch-round cake pan as a guide, cut around pan with a sharp knife through all layers to make 16 circles. Repeat at opposite corner of phyllo stack, making a total of 32 circles. Discard trimmings. (Cover circles with a damp cloth.)

3. Place 1 phyllo circle at corner of a cookie sheet; brush lightly with some of the melted butter. Place another circle on top; brush with butter and sprinkle with 2 teaspoons of the ground nut mixture. Top with another circle. Continue brushing and layering for 8 layers. Assemble 3 more stacks of 8 phyllo circles each on cookie sheets, repeating the brushing and layering process. Bake 10 minutes, until golden. Transfer with spatula to a wire rack to cool.

4. *Make apple filling:* Melt butter in a large skillet over medium-high heat. Add apples, brown sugar, cinnamon and allspice. Cook, stirring, until apples begin to soften. Add apple juice. Reduce heat to medium; cover and simmer 5 minutes, stirring, until apples are tender. Remove cover; cook, stirring, until liquid is nearly evaporated and mixture thickens slightly.

5. *Make caramel sauce:* Melt sugar in a saucepan over medium heat until amber colored, 6 to 8 minutes. Remove from heat. Carefully stir in cream (mixture will bubble vigorously). Return to heat, stirring until mixture is smooth. Cool.

6. *To assemble:* Place 1 stack of phyllo on a platter; top with 1 cup of the apple filling. Drizzle with 2 tablespoons of the caramel sauce. Continue layering phyllo, filling and sauce, ending with phyllo. Sprinkle with confectioners' sugar. Makes 6 servings.

Per serving: 540 calories, 27 g total fat, 12 g saturated fat, 51 mg cholesterol, 377 mg sodium, 72 g carbohydrates, 6 g protein, 45 mg calcium, 5 g fiber

apple shortcake

This walnut-stuffed shortcake, filled with warm caramelized apples, compares to the best apple pie.

Prep time: 25 minutes • Baking time: 22 to 25 minutes

SHORTCAKES:

- 2 cups all-purpose flour
- ½ cup plus 1 tablespoon sugar, divided
- 2 teaspoons baking powder
- ¼ teaspoon salt
- ¼ teaspoon cinnamon
- 6 tablespoons butter or margarine, cut up
- ½ cup chopped walnuts
- ⅔ cup heavy or whipping cream, divided

- ¼ cup butter or margarine
- ¼ cup sugar
- 4 Golden Delicious apples, peeled, cored and cut into ½-inch-thick slices
- 1 tablespoon Calvados or apple-flavored brandy
- 2 pints vanilla ice cream
  Fresh mint sprigs, for garnish (optional)

1. Heat oven to 400°F. Line a large cookie sheet with parchment paper.

2. *Make shortcakes:* Combine flour, ½ cup of the sugar, the baking powder, salt and cinnamon in a bowl. With a pastry blender or 2 knives, cut in butter until crumbly. Stir in walnuts. Remove 1 tablespoon of the cream to a cup. Add remaining cream to dry ingredients, tossing with a fork to form a dough. On a floured surface, pat dough 1 inch thick. With a 3-inch round biscuit cutter, cut out 6 shortcakes. Transfer to prepared pan. Brush tops with reserved 1 tablespoon cream; sprinkle with remaining 1 tablespoon sugar. Bake 22 to 25 minutes, until tops are golden. Transfer to a wire rack; cool.

3. Melt butter and sugar in a 12-inch skillet over medium-high heat. Cook 2 minutes, until sugar is golden (if sugar doesn't dissolve, that's okay). Add apples and cook 4 to 5 minutes, until browned and tender. Add Calvados; boil 30 seconds.

4. Split shortcakes in half with a small knife; transfer bottoms to 6 serving plates. Divide 1½ cups of the apple mixture over bottoms of the

shortcakes, dividing evenly; cover with tops of shortcakes and top with remaining apple slices. Serve warm with ice cream. Garnish with mint sprigs, if desired. Makes 6 servings.

Per serving: 470 calories, 40.5 g total fat, 21.5 g saturated fat, 108 mg cholesterol, 501 mg sodium, 90 g carbohydrates, 8 g protein, 191 mg calcium, 4 g fiber

harvest apple cake

A sprinkling of confectioners' sugar lends a final touch to this low-fat dessert.

Prep time: 15 minutes plus standing
Baking time: 40 to 45 minutes

- 4 cups unpeeled, chopped Golden Delicious apples, divided
- 1 cup firmly packed brown sugar
- ¾ cup all-purpose flour
- ¾ cup whole wheat flour
- 1 teaspoon baking soda
- 1 teaspoon cinnamon
- ½ teaspoon salt
- ¼ teaspoon ginger
- ¼ teaspoon ground cloves
- ¼ cup vegetable oil
- 2 large eggs, lightly beaten
- 1 teaspoon vanilla extract
- 1 tablespoon confectioners' sugar

1. Combine 3 cups of the apples and the brown sugar in large bowl; let stand 45 minutes. Heat oven to 350°F. Grease and flour a 6-cup fluted tube pan.

2. Combine flours, soda, cinnamon, salt, ginger and cloves in a medium bowl. Combine oil, eggs and vanilla in a small bowl; stir into apple-sugar mixture. Stir in dry ingredients and remaining 1 cup apples until blended.

3. Pour into prepared pan. Bake 40 to 45 minutes, until a toothpick inserted in center of cake comes out clean. Cool in pan on a wire rack, 10 minutes; unmold cake and cool completely. Sprinkle with confectioners' sugar. Makes 12 servings.

Per serving: 200 calories, 5.5 g total fat, 1 g saturated fat, 35 mg cholesterol, 220 mg sodium, 35 g carbohydrates, 3 g protein, 29 mg calcium, 2 g fiber

m e n u

dinner for eight—at eight

BLACKENED SHRIMP WITH

TOMATO MAYONNAISE

page 28

GRAPEFRUIT AND ENDIVE SALAD

page 38 (double recipe)

BUTTERFLIED LEG OF LAMB

WITH HERB CRUST

page 178

STEAMED ASPARAGUS AND

ROASTED POTATOES

APRICOT SOUFFLÉS

page 227

apple crisp

Make the most of apple season with this easy crisp. Pictured on page 202.

Total prep and baking time: 1 hour

- ¼ **cup granulated sugar**
- 1 **teaspoon cinnamon**
  Pinch allspice
- 3 **pounds tart green apples, peeled**
- 1 **tablespoon fresh lemon juice**

OAT TOPPING:

- ¾ **cup all-purpose flour**
- ¾ **cup firmly packed brown sugar**
- 6 **tablespoons butter or margarine, cut up**
- ½ **cup oats, uncooked (not instant)**

1. Heat oven to 425°F. Butter a 9-inch square baking dish.

2. Combine granulated sugar, cinnamon and allspice in a bowl. Cut apples with an apple corer and slicer. Add apples and lemon juice to sugar mixture; toss. Spoon into prepared baking dish.

3. *Make oat topping:* Combine flour and brown sugar in a bowl. With a pastry blender or 2 knives, cut in butter until mixture resembles fine crumbs. Stir in oats. Sprinkle topping evenly over fruit to cover (it will be a generous layer).

4. Bake 15 minutes. Reduce oven temperature to 350°F. and bake 25 to 30 minutes more, until top is golden and fruit is bubbly. (If topping browns too quickly while baking, cover loosely with foil.) Cool crisp on a wire rack 5 minutes. Makes 6 servings.

Per serving: 440 calories, 13.5 g total fat, 7.5 g saturated fat, 33 mg cholesterol, 135 mg sodium, 81 g carbohydrates, 3 g protein, 46 mg calcium, 5 g fiber

honey-baked pears EASY

Bosc pears are the firmest variety of pears, which makes them ideal for baking. To speed the preparation, scoop out the core of each pear with a melon baller. Pictured on page 203.

Total prep and baking time: 45 minutes

- 3 **tablespoons butter or margarine, cut up**
- 4 **Bosc pears, quartered and seeded**
- ⅓ **cup honey**
- ¼ **cup fresh lemon juice**
- 2 **tablespoons sugar**
- ¼ **cup mascarpone cheese or sour cream**

1. Heat oven to 450°F. Place butter in a shallow 2-quart baking dish. Melt the butter in the oven, about 2 minutes.

2. Add pears to melted butter and toss. Pour honey and lemon juice over pears; sprinkle with sugar. Bake 35 minutes or until pears are tender. Serve warm with mascarpone. Makes 4 servings.

Per serving: 350 calories, 16 g total fat, 10 g saturated fat, 36 mg cholesterol, 97 mg sodium, 56 g carbohydrates, 2 g protein, 54 mg calcium, 4 g fiber

apricot soufflés LOW FAT

It's the puree of dried apricots, brandy, sugar and fresh lemon juice that makes these golden soufflés taste rich.

Prep time: 35 minutes plus chilling
Baking time: 25 to 30 minutes

- ¾ cup packed dried apricots
- 2 cups water
- 1 cup plus 2 tablespoons granulated sugar, divided
- 2 tablespoons fresh lemon juice
- 1 tablespoon brandy
  Pinch salt
- 1 tablespoon butter or margarine, melted
- 4 large egg whites, at room temperature 20 to 30 minutes
  Confectioners' sugar

1. Bring apricots and water to boil in a medium saucepan. Reduce heat to low; cover and simmer 20 minutes, until soft. Drain; puree in a food processor with ¾ cup of the granulated sugar, the lemon juice, brandy and salt. Transfer to a bowl. Refrigerate 45 minutes, stirring occasionally until mixture is cool.

2. Meanwhile, heat oven to 350°F. Brush the melted butter along bottom and sides of eight 6-ounce custard cups. Sprinkle with 2 tablespoons of the granulated sugar.

3. Beat egg whites in a large mixer bowl at medium speed to soft peaks; gradually add remaining ¼ cup granulated sugar and beat until stiff but not dry. Fold 1 cup of the beaten whites into apricot puree with a rubber spatula. Gently fold apricot mixture into remaining whites. Spoon into prepared cups, mounding mixture about ½ inch above rims.

4. Place soufflés in a roasting pan. Carefully pour enough hot water to reach one-third up sides of cups. Bake 25 to 30 minutes, until tops are browned. Carefully remove soufflés from pan. Sift confectioners' sugar over tops. Serve immediately. Makes 8 servings.

Per serving: 165 calories, 1.5 g total fat, 1 g saturated fat, 4 mg cholesterol, 65 mg sodium, 36 g carbohydrates, 2 g protein, 8 mg calcium, 1 g fiber

almond panna cotta with blueberry sauce LOW FAT EASY

Silky custards prepared with gelatin instead of eggs are chilled until firm, then unmolded onto a pool of luscious blueberry sauce.

Prep time: 10 minutes plus chilling
Cooking time: 5 minutes

PANNA COTTA:
- 1 envelope unflavored gelatin
- ¼ cup cold water
- 2⅓ cups milk
- ¼ cup sugar
- 2 tablespoons almond-flavored liqueur

BLUEBERRY SAUCE:
- 2 cups frozen blueberries
- 2 tablespoons sugar
- 1 tablespoon orange juice
- ½ teaspoon cornstarch
  Pinch salt
- ½ teaspoon vanilla extract

  Fresh lemon thyme, for garnish (optional)

1. *Make panna cotta:* Sprinkle gelatin over water in a small saucepan; let stand 3 minutes to soften. Heat gelatin over medium heat, stirring, until dissolved. Stir in milk and sugar; heat just until milk is hot and sugar is dissolved. Add liqueur and pour mixture into six 6-ounce custard cups or disposable plastic cups. Cover; refrigerate overnight.

2. *Make blueberry sauce:* Combine all sauce ingredients except vanilla in a medium saucepan. Bring to boil, stirring, and boil 2 to 3 minutes, until thickened. Stir in vanilla; transfer to a bowl. Cover and refrigerate overnight. Divide blueberry sauce among 6 stemmed cocktail glasses or dessert dishes. Run a small knife around edge of each panna cotta; unmold onto sauce. Garnish with lemon thyme, if desired. Makes 6 servings.

Per serving: 145 calories, 2 g total fat, 1 g saturated fat, 7 mg cholesterol, 75 mg sodium, 25 g carbohydrates, 4 g protein, 121 mg calcium, 1 g fiber

coffee-almond cake

This cake is great for parties, not just because it's delicious, but because it will feed a crowd. If you make the cake in advance and refrigerate it, let it stand at room temperature for at least an hour so the buttercream can soften. Press the almonds onto the sides just before serving.

Prep time: 1½ hours • Baking time: 22 to 23 minutes

CAKE:
- ½ cup whole blanched almonds
- ¾ cup cake flour (not self-rising)
- ½ teaspoon baking powder
- 1 cup sugar, divided
- ½ teaspoon salt, divided
- 8 large eggs, separated, at room temperature 20 to 30 minutes
- 2 tablespoons instant coffee powder
- ¼ cup unsalted butter, melted (no substitutes)

SUGARED ALMONDS:
- ¾ cup sliced natural almonds
- 3 tablespoons sugar
- 1 tablespoon water

COFFEE-BUTTERCREAM FROSTING:
- ⅔ cup sugar
- ¾ teaspoon cornstarch
- 2 tablespoons instant coffee powder
- 5 large egg yolks
- ⅓ cup milk, scalded
- 1½ teaspoons vanilla extract
- 1½ cups unsalted butter, softened (no substitutes)
- ■
- 2 ounces bittersweet chocolate squares, melted (see tip, page 259) and cooled slightly

1. ■ Heat oven to 350°F. Grease a 15½×10½×1-inch jelly-roll pan. Line with waxed paper. Grease and flour paper.

2. ■ *Make cake:* Spread almonds in a single layer on a cookie sheet and bake 8 to 10 minutes, until golden. Cool completely on a wire rack. Process cooled almonds, flour, baking powder, ¼ cup of the sugar and ¼ teaspoon of the salt in a food processor, until almonds are very finely ground. Set aside.

3. ■ Beat ¼ cup of the sugar, the egg yolks and coffee powder in a large mixer bowl on medium-high

speed, 5 minutes, scraping bowl occasionally, until thick and coffee is dissolved. Beat melted butter into batter in a thin, steady stream, until blended.

4. ■ Beat egg whites and remaining ¼ teaspoon salt in another large mixer bowl with clean beaters on medium-high speed to soft peaks. Gradually beat in remaining ½ cup sugar just to stiff peaks (do not overbeat). Fold a large spoonful of whites into yolk mixture. Fold in half of the almond mixture just until blended. Fold in half of the remaining whites just until blended. Repeat with remaining almond mixture and whites, folding just until no streaks of white remain.

5. ■ Pour batter into prepared pan, gently spreading batter evenly. Bake 22 to 23 minutes, until top springs back when pressed gently with fingertip. Immediately invert cake onto a large wire rack; remove pan and peel off waxed paper. Place another large wire rack over top; invert and cool completely.

6. ■ *Make sugared almonds:* Reduce oven temperature to 325°F. Grease a large cookie sheet. Toss sliced almonds, sugar and water in a medium bowl, until evenly coated. Spread on prepared sheet. Bake 12 to 15 minutes, until lightly browned. Immediately loosen almonds with a wide spatula. Cool completely on the cookie sheet. Break up almonds slightly to separate.

7. ■ *Make coffee-buttercream frosting:* Whisk sugar and cornstarch together in a heavy medium saucepan, until blended. Whisk in coffee powder and egg yolks until combined. Whisk in milk and vanilla. Cook over medium-low heat, stirring constantly with a heatproof rubber spatula, until thickened, about 2 minutes (do not boil). Pour custard into mixer bowl and beat on medium speed until slightly thickened and completely cool, about 5 minutes. Set bowl aside.

8. ■ Beat butter in another large mixer bowl on medium-high speed until light and fluffy, scraping bowl occasionally. With mixer on medium speed, gradually beat in custard mixture, scraping bowl occasionally, until blended and buttercream is light and fluffy.

9. ■ *To assemble,* transfer cake to a large cutting board. Cut lengthwise with a serrated knife into thirds. Transfer one layer to a serving platter. Spread top with ½ cup of the buttercream. Top with another cake layer and spread top with ½ cup of the buttercream. Top with remaining layer; spread sides, ends and top with remaining buttercream. Place melted chocolate in small plastic storage bag; snip a small hole in one corner. Drizzle chocolate over top of cake. (Can be made ahead. Refrigerate cake 1 hour. Then cover loosely with plastic wrap and refrigerate overnight.) Press sugared almonds onto ends and sides of cake. To serve, cut with a serrated knife into 16 slices. Makes 16 servings.

Per slice: 420 calories, 30.5 g total fat, 15 g saturated fat, 228 mg cholesterol, 128 mg sodium, 32 g carbohydrates, 7 g protein, 65 mg calcium, 1 g fiber

pear anise pie

Using different kinds of pears is essential for the flavor depth and juiciness. If you can find them, include fragrant Comice pears in the assortment.

Prep time: 40 minutes plus chilling and freezing
Baking time: 65 to 75 minutes

PASTRY:

  2   **cups all-purpose flour**
  ¼   **cup confectioners' sugar**
  ½   **teaspoon salt**
  ½   **cup cold butter, cut up (no substitutes)**
  ¼   **cup vegetable shortening**
  3   **tablespoons fresh lemon juice**
  1   **to 3 tablespoons ice water**

FILLING:

  ½   **cup granulated sugar**
  ¼   **cup all-purpose flour**
  ½   **teaspoon grated lemon peel**
  ¼   **teaspoon crushed aniseed**
  8   **cups assorted peeled, ripe pears, cut into 8 wedges each**

  1   **large egg white, lightly beaten**
  1   **tablespoon butter, cut up (no substitutes)**
  1   **tablespoon granulated sugar**
  ¼   **teaspoon grated lemon peel**

1. *Make pastry:* Combine flour, confectioners' sugar and salt in a large bowl. With a pastry blender or 2 knives, cut in butter and shortening until the mixture resembles fine crumbs. Add lemon juice, 1 tablespoon at a time, then water if necessary, tossing with a fork until moistened. Gently knead just until pastry holds together. Shape pastry into 2 balls, one slightly larger than the other. Flatten each into a disk. Wrap in plastic wrap and refrigerate 30 minutes.

2. Heat oven to 425°F.

3. *Make filling:* Combine ½ cup of the granulated sugar, the flour, ½ teaspoon of the lemon peel and the aniseed in a bowl. Add pears; toss to combine.

4. On a lightly floured surface, roll larger pastry disk into a 12-inch circle. Fit into a 9-inch pie plate and flute edges. Place in freezer for 10 minutes. Line pastry with foil and fill with dried beans or pie weights. Bake 10 minutes. Remove foil and beans. Brush pastry with some egg white and bake 5 minutes more.

5. Spoon pear mixture into pastry shell; dot with butter. Roll smaller pastry disk into a 9-inch circle and fit over fruit filling, tucking in edges. Cut vents. Brush top with egg white. Combine the 1 tablespoon sugar with the ¼ teaspoon lemon peel; sprinkle over top. Bake pie on a cookie sheet 15 minutes. Cover edges of pie with foil. Reduce oven temperature to 375°F. and bake 50 to 60 minutes more, until filling is bubbly in center. Cool on a wire rack 1 hour. Makes 8 servings.

Per serving: 460 calories, 21 g total fat, 10 g saturated fat, 37 mg cholesterol, 292 mg sodium, 67 g carbohydrates, 5 g protein, 28 mg calcium, 5 g fiber

---

test kitchen tip

pastry on call

Did you know you can prepare pastry ahead of time? That's good news for anyone who wants to get a jump start on the next pie or tart project!

Prepare pastry as directed in the recipe, but instead of rolling it out, flatten it into a disk. Freeze pastry in a freezer bag up to 2 months. To use, thaw pastry overnight in refrigerator. Then, continue as directed in the recipe.

classic yellow sheet cake 🏅

The yellow sheet cake is a classic for good reason, but sometimes the bakery-bought version is too sweet and sticky. Not this one! Not only did we cut down on the sugar used, our foolproof technique keeps this cake velvety without special cake flour or separating the eggs. Pictured on page 206.

Prep time: 20 minutes plus chilling
Baking time: 35 to 37 minutes

CAKE:
- 2¾ cups all-purpose flour
- 2 teaspoons baking powder
- ½ teaspoon salt
- 1 cup milk
- 1 teaspoon vanilla extract
- ¾ cup unsalted butter, softened (no substitutes)
- 1⅓ cups granulated sugar
- 4 large eggs, at room temperature 20 to 30 minutes

FROSTING:
- 4 ounces unsweetened chocolate squares, finely chopped
- ¼ cup unsalted butter (no substitutes)
- 1 cup heavy or whipping cream
- 3 cups confectioners' sugar
- ½ teaspoon vanilla extract
- 2 tablespoons sour cream

1. *Make cake:* Heat oven to 350°F. Grease a 13×9-inch baking pan with vegetable shortening. Sprinkle pan with flour, tapping out excess flour.

2. Sift together flour, baking powder and salt in a bowl. Combine milk and vanilla in a glass measure.

3. Beat butter in a large mixer bowl on medium speed until creamy, 1 minute. Gradually add granulated sugar. Continue to beat, scraping bowl occasionally with a rubber spatula, until mixture is very light and fluffy, 7 to 8 minutes. Add 3 of the eggs, one at a time, beating and scraping bowl 1 minute after each addition. Add remaining egg and beat 2 minutes. At low speed, beat in two-thirds of the flour mixture just until incorporated. Add milk mixture alternately with remaining flour mixture, ending with flour mixture, just until blended.

4. Spread batter into prepared pan. Bake cake until top is golden and a toothpick inserted in center comes out clean, 35 to 37 minutes. Cool cake in pan on a wire rack.

5. *Make frosting:* Melt chocolate, butter and cream in a saucepan over low heat; transfer to a large mixer bowl. Cool to room temperature, 15 minutes. Stir in confectioners' sugar and vanilla with a spoon, until smooth. Beat mixture until thickened but not stiff, 2 to 3 minutes. At low speed, beat in sour cream just until blended. Refrigerate until thick enough to spread, 1 hour. Makes 2½ cups.

6. Frost top of cooled cake. *(Can be made ahead. Cover pan loosely with plastic wrap and refrigerate up to 24 hours. Return to room temperature before serving.)* Makes 12 servings.

Per serving: 640 calories, 35 g total fat, 21 g saturated fat, 154 mg cholesterol, 368 mg sodium, 78 g carbohydrates, 12 g protein, 133 mg calcium, 2 g fiber

lattice flower cake

Decorate the chocolate-frosted yellow sheet cake with fondant cut into latticework, flowers and leaves. Pictured on page 206.

Prep time: about 1 hour

- 1 recipe Yellow Sheet Cake (see recipe, left)
- 1 recipe Frosting (see recipe, left)
  Cornstarch
- ½ of a box (24-oz.) pure white rolled fondant
  Yellow, orange, purple and green paste food colors
  ⅞- to 1½-inch assorted flower-shaped cutters
  1¼×¾-inch leaf-shaped cutter
- 75 orange, yellow and brown candy-coated chocolate bits

1. Line bottom and sides of a 13×9-inch pan with foil; grease and flour foil. Make cake and bake as directed; cool. Cover pan with a large wire rack or board. Invert cake; remove pan and peel off foil. Invert cake again onto a serving platter. Spread chilled frosting over top and sides of cake.

2. *Make lattice:* Sprinkle a work surface and rolling pin with cornstarch. Roll fondant into a 19×7-inch rectangle, ⅛ inch thick. (Save remaining fondant for another use. Wrap in plastic wrap and refrigerate up to 1 week.) With a scalloped pie cutter, trim one long side of the rectangle, and cut rectangle into ten ½-inch-wide strips. Arrange 5 strips in a diagonal pattern 2 inches apart over top and side of cake, pressing gently into frosting to adhere. Repeat with remaining 5 strips in a lattice pattern. Trim edge of strips with a knife.

3. *Make flowers:* Shape fondant scraps into a disk; divide into quarters. (Wrap one piece in plastic wrap and set aside for leaves.) Using a toothpick, tint remaining 3 pieces with yellow, orange and purple paste food colors; then knead until each color is blended. Working with one color at a time (wrap remaining colors in plastic wrap), roll fondant ⅛ inch thick. Cut out fondant flowers with assorted flower-shaped cutters. Transfer 2 or 3 cutouts to a clean sponge and gently press center with the narrow end of a chopstick to shape flower petals. Transfer flowers to a jelly-roll pan. (Makes about 75 flowers.)

4. *Make leaves:* Tint remaining fondant with green paste food color. Roll ⅛ inch thick. Cut out leaves with a leaf-shaped cutter. Gently pinch one end of each cut leaf; transfer to pan with flowers. *(Can be made ahead. Store flowers and leaves in an airtight container at room temperature up to 1 week.)*

5. With a small paintbrush dipped in water, attach flowers and leaves over lattice strips and candy-coated chocolate bits in center of each flower.

orange pound cake LOW FAT EASY

When you crave something special while on a diet, try this pound cake. Just stick to the recommended portion size for low-fat enjoyment. Pictured on page 201.

Prep time: 30 minutes • Baking time: 40 minutes

   Vegetable cooking spray
1½   **cups all-purpose flour**

½   **teaspoon salt**
¼   **teaspoon baking powder**
¼   **teaspoon baking soda**
1   **large orange**
1   **cup sugar**
½   **cup buttermilk, at room temperature 20 to 30 minutes**
½   **teaspoon vanilla extract**
¼   **cup butter (no substitutes)**
1   **large egg**
2   **large egg whites**

¼   **cup honey (optional)**

1. Heat oven to 350°F. Lightly coat a 9×5-inch loaf pan with vegetable cooking spray. Sift together flour, salt, baking powder and baking soda in a medium bowl; set aside.

2. With a vegetable peeler or a small, sharp knife, remove peel from orange; coarsely chop the peel. Cut orange in half and squeeze ¼ cup juice. Process sugar and peel in a food processor, pulsing until peel is finely chopped. Combine buttermilk, orange juice and vanilla in a glass measure.

3. Beat butter and orange-sugar mixture in a large mixer bowl on medium-high speed until combined. Beat in egg and egg whites, one at a time, beating well after each addition. At low speed, add dry ingredients alternately with buttermilk mixture, beginning and ending with dry ingredients.

4. Spoon batter into the prepared pan. Bake 40 minutes, until toothpick inserted in center comes out clean. Cool cake in pan 15 minutes; invert and remove pan. Cool on a wire rack, right side up. Cut into 12 slices. Serve each slice with 1 teaspoon honey, if desired. Makes 12 servings.

Per serving with 1 teaspoon honey: 190 calories, 4.5 g total fat, 2.5 g saturated fat, 29 mg cholesterol, 199 mg sodium, 34 g carbohydrates, 3 g protein, 25 mg calcium, 0 g fiber

phyllo cups with ice cream and orange-caramel sauce 🅴🅰🆂🆈

Pictured on page 202.

Total prep and baking time: 45 minutes

CARAMEL SAUCE:

- ½ cup sugar
- 2 tablespoons light corn syrup
- ½ teaspoon grated orange peel
- ⅓ cup fresh orange juice
- 2 teaspoons butter (no substitutes)
- 1 tablespoon Cointreau (orange-flavored liqueur)

PHYLLO CUPS:

- 1 teaspoon water
- 2 tablespoons sugar
- ¼ teaspoon cinnamon
- 3 large sheets phyllo dough
- 4 teaspoons butter, melted (no substitutes)
- 1 quart premium butter-pecan ice cream
- 4 oranges, peeled, pith removed and cut into sections

1. Heat oven to 350°F. Lightly butter 8 cups of a 12-cup, 2½-inch muffin pan; set aside.

2. *Make caramel sauce:* Heat sugar and corn syrup in a 2-quart saucepan over medium heat until golden around the edge. Stir mixture and cook until medium golden and sugar is completely dissolved. Remove from heat. With a long-handled spoon, carefully stir in remaining caramel sauce ingredients. (Mixture will be bubbly.) Cool slightly.

3. *Make phyllo cups:* Transfer 1 tablespoon of the caramel sauce to a cup; stir in water. Combine sugar and cinnamon in another cup. Arrange 1 phyllo sheet on a work surface; cover remaining phyllo with plastic wrap. Brush sheet lightly with some of the butter; then brush lightly with some caramel-water mixture. Sprinkle evenly with 2 teaspoons of the cinnamon-sugar. Top with another phyllo sheet, stacking evenly. Repeat process two more times with the remaining butter, caramel-water mixture and cinnamon-sugar. Cut rectangle into quarters.

Cut each quarter in half crosswise. Gently press 1 rectangle into 1 cup in prepared pan, allowing ends to stand up. Repeat. Bake 6 to 8 minutes, until golden. Cool phyllo cups in pan, 5 minutes. Gently lift out and transfer to wire racks; cool completely.

4. Fill each phyllo cup with ice cream; place on a serving dish and top with oranges and remaining caramel sauce. Makes 8 servings.

Per serving: 350 calories, 14 g total fat, 6.5 g saturated fat, 40 mg cholesterol, 279 mg sodium, 52 g carbohydrates, 5 g protein, 118 mg calcium, 3 g fiber

pecan layer cake 🅴🅰🆂🆈

Traditional Southern flavors—including bourbon and pecans—make this triple-layer cake a real Dixie delight.

Prep time: 1 hour plus cooling
Baking time: 20 to 25 minutes

CAKE:

- 2¾ cups all-purpose flour
- 2 teaspoons nutmeg
- 1½ teaspoons baking soda
- ½ teaspoon baking powder
- ½ teaspoon salt
- 1 cup butter or margarine, softened
- 2 cups granulated sugar
- 4 large eggs, separated
- 1 cup buttermilk
- ¼ cup bourbon
- 2 cups (8 oz.) chopped pecans, toasted

FROSTING:

- 3 cups heavy or whipping cream
- 5 tablespoons confectioners' sugar
- ⅓ cup bourbon

  Pecan halves, for garnish (optional)

1. Heat oven to 350°F. Grease three 9-inch round cake pans. Combine flour, nutmeg, baking soda, baking powder and salt in a medium bowl.

2. Beat butter and sugar in a mixer bowl at medium speed until creamy. Add egg yolks, one at a time, beating after each addition. At low speed beat in dry ingredients alternately with buttermilk and bourbon, beginning and ending with dry ingredients. Stir in nuts.

3. Beat egg whites in a clean mixer bowl with clean beaters until stiff, but not dry, peaks form. With rubber spatula, gently fold one-third of the egg whites into batter. Repeat process with remaining whites. Spread batter evenly among the prepared cake pans.

4. Bake 20 to 25 minutes, until a toothpick inserted in center comes out clean. Cool cakes in pans on wire racks 10 minutes; unmold and cool cakes completely on wire racks.

5. *Make frosting:* Beat all frosting ingredients together in a large mixer bowl until stiff.

6. Place 1 cake layer on a large platter; tuck 4 strips of waxed paper under cake. Spread top with 1 cup of the frosting; top with second cake layer and 1 cup of the frosting. Add third layer and spread top and sides with remaining frosting. Remove waxed-paper strips. *(Can be made ahead. Cover and refrigerate up to 24 hours. Let stand 45 minutes at room temperature before serving.)* Garnish with pecan halves, if desired. Makes 16 servings.

Per serving: 580 calories, 40.5 g total fat, 19.5 g saturated fat, 148 mg cholesterol, 377 mg sodium, 45 g carbohydrates, 6 g protein, 155 mg calcium, 2 g fiber

grand marnier soufflé

Serve this orange-flavored soufflé with whipped cream delicately flavored with orange liqueur.

Prep time: 25 minutes • Baking time: 40 minutes

SOUFFLÉ BASE:

- 3 tablespoons butter or margarine
- ⅓ cup all-purpose flour
- 1 cup milk
- 2 tablespoons granulated sugar
- 5 large egg yolks
- ⅓ cup Grand Marnier (orange-flavored liqueur)
- 1½ teaspoons grated orange peel

-

- ½ teaspoon grated orange peel
- 4 tablespoons granulated sugar, divided

- 8 large egg whites, at room temperature 20 to 30 minutes
- ¼ teaspoon salt

WHIPPED CREAM:

- 1 cup heavy or whipping cream
- 2 tablespoons confectioners' sugar
- 1 teaspoon Grand Marnier
- ½ teaspoon vanilla extract

1. *Make soufflé base:* Melt butter in a 3-quart saucepan over medium-low heat. Stir in flour; cook, stirring, 1 minute. Gradually whisk in milk; stir in granulated sugar. Cook, stirring frequently until sauce thickens and comes to boil; boil 1 minute. Remove the pan from heat.

2. Whisk egg yolks in a medium bowl. Gradually whisk in one-third of the hot milk mixture. Gradually pour yolk mixture into saucepan, whisking until blended. Return pan to low heat. Cook, stirring constantly, until mixture thickens and returns to a boil. Remove from heat. Vigorously whisk in Grand Marnier and orange peel until smooth. Remove from heat; pour into a medium bowl, scraping with a rubber spatula. Cover surface with plastic wrap; let cool 20 minutes. *(Can be made ahead. Refrigerate 2 hours or overnight.)*

3. Heat oven to 375°F. Adjust oven rack to bottom of oven. Grease a 2½-quart soufflé dish. Combine orange peel and 2 tablespoons of the granulated sugar in a cup. Coat dish with sugar mixture.

4. Beat egg whites and salt in a large mixer bowl on medium speed to soft peaks. At high speed, gradually beat in remaining 2 tablespoons granulated sugar; beat just to stiff peaks. (If soufflé base has been refrigerated, stir base to loosen.) Stir a large spoonful of beaten whites into the soufflé base. With rubber spatula, gently fold in remaining whites in two additions just until blended. (Do not overmix; it's okay if a few streaks of whites remain.) Pour mixture into prepared dish. Bake 40 minutes, until the soufflé puffs and the top is browned.

5. *Make whipped cream:* Meanwhile, beat all whipped cream ingredients in a small mixer bowl to soft peaks. Serve warm soufflé immediately with whipped cream. Makes 8 servings.

Per serving: 300 calories, 19.5 g total fat, 11 g saturated fat, 189 mg cholesterol, 205 mg sodium, 20 g carbohydrates, 7 g protein, 76 mg calcium, 0 g fiber

caramelized ☀ LOW FAT ☀ indian pudding

For a new take on New England's old-fashioned cornmeal-molasses pudding, we've prepared individual custards topped with caramel.

Prep time: 40 minutes plus chilling
Baking time: 35 minutes

- **2 teaspoons plus 2 tablespoons butter or margarine, divided**
- **1½ cups sugar, divided**
- **½ cup yellow cornmeal**
- **½ teaspoon ginger**
- **¼ teaspoon cinnamon**
- **4 cups milk, divided**
- **4 large eggs, lightly beaten**
- **⅓ cup light molasses**

1. Heat oven to 350°F. Melt 2 teaspoons of the butter. Brush ten 6-ounce custard cups with the melted butter. To caramelize the sugar, melt 1 cup of the sugar in a medium skillet over medium heat until deep amber in color, 10 minutes, stirring to dissolve lumps. Spoon 1 tablespoon of the caramelized sugar into each prepared custard cup.

2. Combine cornmeal, remaining ½ cup sugar, the ginger and cinnamon in a small bowl. Heat 3 cups of the milk in a large saucepan over medium heat until very hot. Slowly stir in cornmeal mixture. Reduce heat; cook, stirring constantly, 10 minutes, until mixture thickens. Stir in remaining 2 tablespoons butter. Cool 10 minutes.

3. Meanwhile, combine remaining 1 cup milk, the eggs and molasses in a medium bowl. Gradually add molasses mixture to cooled cornmeal mixture, whisking constantly. Pour into prepared custard cups. Place cups in a shallow baking dish and carefully pour boiling water halfway up sides of cups. Bake 35 minutes, until custard is set. Remove from water bath. Cool. *(Can be made ahead. Cover and refrigerate up to 2 days.)* To serve, cut around edge of custards; invert onto plates. Makes 10 servings.

Per serving: 275 calories, 7.5 g total fat, 4 g saturated fat, 101 mg cholesterol, 111 mg sodium, 47 g carbohydrates, 6 g protein, 153 mg calcium, 1 g fiber

caramel swirl cheesecake

If you've prepared and refrigerated the caramel sauce ahead of time, microwave on HIGH, 30 to 60 seconds, stirring halfway through, just until room temperature. The sauce should be about the same consistency as the cheesecake batter.

Prep time: 25 minutes plus chilling
Baking time: 60 to 70 minutes

CRUMB CRUST:
- **1 cup graham-cracker crumbs**
- **½ cup pecans, toasted and finely chopped**
- **3 tablespoons firmly packed brown sugar**
- **¼ cup butter or margarine, melted and cooled**

- **3 packages (8 oz. each) cream cheese, softened**
- **½ cup granulated sugar**
- **½ cup Caramel Sauce, at room temperature (see recipe, right)**
- **3 large eggs, at room temperature 20 to 30 minutes**
- **½ cup sour cream**

1. *Make crumb crust:* Heat oven to 350°F. Tightly cover the outside of a 9-inch springform pan with a double layer of heavy-duty foil. Combine all crumb crust ingredients in a medium bowl; toss until crumbs are evenly moistened. Press crumb mixture into bottom and 1 inch up sides of the prepared pan. Bake crust 10 minutes, or until lightly browned. Cool completely on a wire rack.

2. Beat cream cheese in a large mixer bowl at medium-high speed until light and fluffy, about 3 minutes. Beat in granulated sugar and ¼ cup of the Caramel Sauce until smooth. At low speed beat in eggs, one at a time, just until blended. Beat in sour cream. Pour half of the filling into crust; spread to cover bottom. Using a teaspoon, drizzle with half of the remaining caramel sauce. Spoon on remaining filling; spread evenly and drizzle with remaining caramel sauce. Run a table knife through filling to marbleize. Place springform pan in a large baking pan. *(Make sure there is at least 1 inch of space between springform and baking pan.)* Place on oven rack. Carefully pour enough very hot tap water into baking pan to reach 1 inch up side of springform pan. Bake 50 to 60 minutes, until filling is only slightly jiggly in center (it will firm as it cools).

3. Remove springform pan from water bath and place on a wire rack. Let stand 10 minutes. Remove foil from outside of pan. Run knife around inside edge of pan to release cheesecake (do not remove springform ring). Cool completely. Cover and refrigerate cheesecake overnight. *(Can be made ahead. Wrap well and refrigerate up to 2 days.)* Remove springform ring. Makes 12 servings.

Per serving: 445 calories, 34 g total fat, 19 g saturated fat, 141 mg cholesterol, 295 mg sodium, 28 g carbohydrates, 7 g protein, 72 mg calcium, 1 g fiber

caramel sauce

This recipe makes more sauce than needed in the Caramel Swirl Cheesecake, so refrigerate the remaining sauce, and serve it over ice cream for a luscious sundae.

Prep time: 5 minutes • Cooking time: 10 minutes

- 1 **cup sugar**
- ¼ **cup water**
- ½ **cup heavy or whipping cream**
- 6 **tablespoons unsalted butter, cut up (no substitutes)**
- 1 **teaspoon vanilla extract**
  Pinch salt

Bring sugar and water to boil in a 2-quart saucepan. Cook over medium-high heat, swirling pan occasionally, until syrup is a dark amber color, about 10 minutes. Immediately remove pan from heat. With a long-handled spoon, carefully stir in cream (mixture will bubble vigorously). Return to low heat; add butter. Stir until melted and sauce is smooth. Remove from heat; stir in vanilla and salt. *(Can be made ahead. Cool. Cover; refrigerate up to 2 days.)* Makes 1⅓ cups.

Per tablespoon: 85 calories, 5.5 g total fat, 3.5 g saturated fat, 17 mg cholesterol, 9 mg sodium, 10 g carbohydrates, 0 g protein, 5 mg calcium, 0 g fiber

vanilla-bean biscotti

These twice-baked cookies are wonderful served with fresh fruit or ice cream. Although the seeds from the vanilla bean add a special flavor, if a vanilla bean is not available, you can substitute 2 teaspoons vanilla extract.

Prep time: 20 minutes • Baking time: 60 to 65 minutes

- 1   vanilla bean, split
- 3   cups all-purpose flour
- 1   tablespoon baking powder
- ¼   teaspoon salt
- 3   large eggs
- ¾   cup sugar
- ½   cup butter or margarine, melted and cooled

1. Scrape seeds from vanilla bean with a knife.* Adjust oven racks to center and lower thirds of oven. Heat oven to 325°F. Grease a large cookie sheet.

2. Combine flour, baking powder and salt in a bowl; set aside. Beat eggs in a mixer bowl at medium-high speed, 1 minute. Gradually beat in sugar. At low speed, beat in butter and vanilla seeds. Beat in flour mixture just until blended.

3. Divide dough into thirds. On a lightly floured surface, roll each piece into a 14×1½-inch log. Arrange logs 2½ inches apart on prepared cookie sheet. Bake logs on the bottom oven rack 30 to 35 minutes, until firm. Cool on the cookie sheet on a wire rack, 15 minutes.

4. Reduce oven temperature to 275°F. Carefully transfer logs to a large cutting board. With a serrated knife, gently slice each log diagonally into ½-inch slices. Arrange slices, cut side down, 1 inch apart, on 2 large ungreased cookie sheets.

5. Bake slices 30 minutes, until pale golden, switching and rotating cookie sheets after 15 minutes. Cool biscotti slices on wire racks. Makes 4 dozen biscotti.

*Note: Place bean in a canister with granulated or confectioners' sugar to make vanilla sugar, if desired.

Per biscotti: 65 calories, 2.5 g total fat, 1.5 g saturated fat, 18 mg cholesterol, 66 mg sodium, 9 g carbohydrates, 1 g protein, 20 mg calcium, 0 g fiber

halloween cookies

Here are some sweet and spooky witches, ghosts, bats and spiders all made from easy-to-roll-out sugar cookie dough. Don't let decorating the cookies scare you! Our instructions won't leave you in the dark.

Prep time: 1 hour plus chilling and decorating
Baking time: 10 to 12 minutes per batch

- 3¼   cups all-purpose flour
- 1½   teaspoons baking powder
- ½   teaspoon salt
- 1   cup butter, softened (no substitutes)
- 1   cup granulated sugar
- 2   large eggs
- 1   tablespoon vanilla extract

DECORATIVE ICING:
- 1   box (1 lb.) confectioners' sugar
- 3   tablespoons meringue powder*
- 6   to 7 tablespoons cold water

   Orange, black, purple, yellow and green food paste colors

1. Lightly grease 2 large cookie sheets. Combine flour, baking powder and salt in a bowl; set aside.

2. Beat butter and granulated sugar in a mixer bowl on medium speed until light and fluffy. Beat in eggs, one at a time, until well blended. Beat in vanilla. At low speed, gradually beat in flour mixture, scraping bowl, just until blended. Divide dough into quarters; shape each piece into a thick disk. Wrap and refrigerate 2 hours or overnight.

3. Heat oven to 350°F. On a lightly floured surface with a floured rolling pin, roll 1 piece of dough to a generous ¼-inch-thickness. Cut out with 3½- to 5½-inch bat-, ghost-, witch- or spider-shaped cookie cutters. Transfer 1 inch apart onto prepared cookie sheets. Bake cookies 10 to 12 minutes, until edges are golden. Cool on wire racks. Repeat with remaining dough, rerolling scraps.

4. *Make icing:* Meanwhile, combine confectioners' sugar, meringue powder and 6 tablespoons of the water in a mixer bowl. Beat at medium speed until smooth. Increase speed to high and beat 5 minutes, until thick and smooth, adding up to 1 tablespoon more water for piping consistency.

5. Divide icing into bowls for separate colors. (Reserve a bowl of white icing.) To tint icing, dab a small amount of food color into each bowl of icing with a toothpick and stir until well blended, gradually adding additional dabs of food color, if necessary, for desired color.

6. Spoon 3 tablespoons of the white, orange, black, yellow-green and purple icing into each of 5 pastry bags fitted with a #2 plain tip. Thin remaining white, black, orange and yellow-green icing with a little water, until spreadable. Paint cookies with icing. Let dry 20 minutes. Pipe with reserved icing. Makes about 2 dozen cookies.

Note: Available from supermarkets, specialty baking stores or Wilton Enterprises, 800-794-5866.

Per cookie: 250 calories, 8.5 g total fat, 5 g saturated fat, 38 mg cholesterol, 166 mg sodium, 41 g carbohydrates, 3 g protein, 34 mg calcium, 0 g fiber

pistachio crescents

This nutty dough mixes up easily—then just shape and bake! Pictured on page 208.

Total prep and baking time: 20 minutes
Microwave used

2	tablespoons butter or margarine
⅓	cup granulated sugar
1	large egg
¼	teaspoon almond extract
¾	teaspoon baking powder
¾	cup all-purpose flour
2	tablespoons unsalted, shelled pistachio nuts, finely chopped
⅛	teaspoon salt
	Confectioners' sugar

1. Adjust oven rack to upper third of oven. Heat oven to 350°F. Grease a large cookie sheet.

2. Melt butter in a large microwaveproof bowl on HIGH 1 minute. Whisk in granulated sugar, egg and almond extract. Sprinkle baking powder over top; whisk to blend. Stir in flour, pistachios and salt. (Mixture will be sticky, but that's okay.)

3. Drop batter by level measuring tablespoonfuls onto waxed paper. With floured hands, lightly roll each into a 2-inch-long rope. Transfer to the cookie sheet, curving each cookie into a crescent shape. Bake 10 to 12 minutes, until bottoms are golden. Transfer to wire racks. Sprinkle with confectioners' sugar and cool. Makes 14 cookies.

Per cookie: 75 calories, 3 g total fat, 1.5 g saturated fat, 20 mg cholesterol, 69 mg sodium, 11 g carbohydrates, 1 g protein, 19 mg calcium, 0 g fiber

butterscotch-pecan tiles

These are terrific paired with ice cream. For perfect triangles, cut cookies before they cool completely. Pictured on page 208.

Total prep and baking time: 20 minutes
Microwave used

½	cup butter (no substitutes)
⅔	cup firmly packed brown sugar
1	large egg
1	teaspoon vanilla extract
¾	teaspoon baking powder
1⅓	cups all-purpose flour
¼	teaspoon salt
⅔	cup chopped pecans
	Dulce de leche or vanilla ice cream (optional)

1. Heat oven to 375°F. Grease a 15½×10½×1-inch jelly-roll pan.

2. Microwave butter and brown sugar in a microwaveproof bowl on HIGH 1 minute 45 seconds; stir until smooth. Stir in egg and vanilla. Sprinkle baking powder over top; stir in with flour and salt until blended.

3. Spread dough evenly to cover bottom of pan. Sprinkle top with pecans. Bake 11 to 12 minutes, until golden. Cool 5 minutes on a rack. Cut into 16 triangles. Serve with ice cream, if desired. Makes 16 cookies.

Per cookie: 160 calories, 9.5 g total fat, 4 g saturated fat, 29 mg cholesterol, 123 mg sodium, 18 g carbohydrates, 2 g protein, 27 mg calcium, 1 g fiber

lime soufflé

This is an easier, faster version of the standard soufflé—here, a cream cheese mixture is whirled in the blender, and beaten egg whites are folded into the mixture.

Prep time: 10 minutes • Baking time: 40 minutes

- ½ **cup plus 3 tablespoons granulated sugar, divided**
- 1 **package (8 oz.) cream cheese, softened**
- ¼ **teaspoon grated lime peel**
- ¼ **cup fresh lime juice**
- 4 **large egg yolks, at room temperature 20 to 30 minutes**
- 1 **tablespoon flour**
- 1 **tablespoon tequila**
- ⅛ **teaspoon salt**
- 6 **large egg whites, at room temperature 20 to 30 minutes**
- 1 **pint fresh strawberries, sliced**
  Confectioners' sugar

1. Heat oven to 375°F. Grease a 1-quart soufflé dish; coat sides and bottom with 1 tablespoon of the granulated sugar. Blend cream cheese, lime peel, lime juice, ½ cup of the granulated sugar, the egg yolks, flour, tequila and salt in a blender until smooth. Pour into a large bowl. Beat egg whites until stiff in a mixer bowl. Stir one-third of the whites into lime mixture; fold in remaining whites. Pour into prepared dish. Bake 40 minutes, or until set.

2. Meanwhile, combine strawberries and remaining 2 tablespoons granulated sugar in a medium bowl. Remove soufflé from oven; sprinkle with confectioners' sugar. Serve hot with strawberries. Makes 6 servings.

Per serving: 300 calories, 17 g total fat, 9.5 g saturated fat, 183 mg cholesterol, 221 mg sodium, 29 g carbohydrates, 9 g protein, 56 mg calcium, 1 g fiber

french lemon tart

Bursting with citrus flavor, this lemon tart is silky smooth and oh so sweet.

Prep time: 1 hour plus freezing and standing
Baking time: 28 to 32 minutes

PASTRY:
- 1¼ **cups all-purpose flour**
- ⅓ **cup confectioners' sugar**
- 1 **teaspoon grated lemon peel**
- ½ **cup cold butter, cut into ½-inch pieces (no substitutes)**
- 1 **large egg yolk, beaten**

FILLING:
- 1 **cup granulated sugar**
- 4 **large eggs**
- 2 **large egg yolks**
- ½ **cup fresh lemon juice**
- ½ **cup butter, cut into 8 pieces (no substitutes)**
- 1 **tablespoon grated lemon peel**

  Fresh mint sprigs and lemon peel, for garnish (optional)

1. *Make pastry:* Adjust oven rack to lower third of oven. Heat oven to 375°F. Process flour, confectioners' sugar and lemon peel in a food processor until blended. Add cold butter and process, pulsing, until mixture has the texture of fine meal. Drizzle beaten yolk over flour mixture, and pulse just until pastry begins to hold together. (If mixture is crumbly, that's okay.) Press pastry evenly along the bottom and side of a 9½-inch tart pan with removable bottom. Place pastry in freezer 10 minutes.

2. Bake pastry shell 18 to 20 minutes until golden. Cool in pan on a wire rack.

3. *Make filling:* Whisk together sugar, eggs and egg yolks in a 2- or 3-quart saucepan until blended; whisk in lemon juice and butter. Cook over medium-low heat, stirring constantly with a heatproof rubber spatula or wooden spoon, until mixture thickens (it should be the consistency of warm pudding) and temperature registers 160°F. on an instant-read thermometer, about 15 minutes. Strain filling through a fine sieve into a bowl, pressing with a spatula. Stir in grated lemon peel. Pour hot filling into cooled crust. Bake tart 10 to 12 minutes more, until filling is just set. (Do not overbake. If center of filling jiggles slightly, that's okay; it will set as it cools.) Cool completely on a wire rack, 1½ hours. Garnish with mint and lemon peel, if desired. Makes 12 servings.

Per serving: 305 calories, 18.5 g total fat, 10.5 g saturated fat, 165 mg cholesterol, 179 mg sodium, 31 g carbohydrates, 4 g protein, 22 mg calcium, 0 g fiber

coconut cream pie

White-chocolate whipped cream and toasted coconut top this pie that's indulgent, but worth it.

Prep time: 1½ hours plus freezing and chilling
Baking time: 28 to 34 minutes
Microwave used

PASTRY:
- 1⅓ cups all-purpose flour
- ¼ teaspoon salt
- ¼ cup cold butter, cut up (no substitutes)
- ⅓ cup vegetable shortening
- 3 to 4 tablespoons ice water

FILLING:
- 3 cups milk
- 1 package (7 oz.) shredded coconut, divided
- 1 vanilla bean, split lengthwise, or 2 teaspoons vanilla extract
- ½ cup sugar
- ¼ cup cornstarch
- ¼ teaspoon salt
- 5 large egg yolks
- 2 tablespoons butter

TOPPING:
- 1 cup heavy cream
- 2 ounces white chocolate squares, chopped
- ½ teaspoon vanilla extract

1. *Make pastry:* Combine flour and salt in a large bowl. Add butter and shortening; toss to coat with flour. Cut in butter and shortening until mixture is crumbly, but with some small pieces of butter remaining. Add ice water, 1 tablespoon at a time, over flour mixture, tossing with a fork, just until pastry begins to hold together. Shape pastry into a disk. Wrap and refrigerate 1 hour or overnight.

2. Adjust oven rack to lower third of oven. Heat oven to 425°F. On a floured surface, roll out pastry to a 13-inch circle. Fit pastry into a 9-inch pie plate, gently pressing pastry along bottom and side of pie plate. Trim edge and flute. Place in freezer 15 minutes.

3. Line pie shell with foil. Fill with dried beans or rice. Bake 12 to 14 minutes, until edge of crust is set and lightly colored. Remove foil and beans. Bake crust 10 to 12 minutes, until bottom and sides are golden brown. Cool completely on a wire rack.

4. *Make filling:* Heat milk, 1 cup of the coconut and the vanilla bean (if using) in a medium saucepan until hot. Remove pan from heat; cover and let stand 30 minutes. Strain milk mixture through a sieve set over a bowl, pressing on coconut to extract milk; discard coconut. Scrape seeds from vanilla bean, if using, into milk mixture. Discard pod. Whisk together sugar, cornstarch and salt in a 2-quart heavy-bottomed saucepan. Whisk in yolks until smooth. Gradually whisk in milk mixture. Bring mixture to boil, whisking constantly, over medium heat. Boil 1 minute, whisking gently. Remove from heat; add 1 cup coconut, the butter and vanilla extract, if using, stirring until butter melts. Pour filling into a medium bowl; place plastic wrap directly against surface and cool at room temperature, 30 minutes.

5. Meanwhile, reduce oven temperature to 325°F. Spread remaining coconut on a large cookie sheet. Bake 6 to 8 minutes, stirring once, until toasted; cool. Sprinkle crust with ⅓ cup of the toasted coconut. Pour filling into crust; spread evenly. Place plastic wrap loosely over pie; refrigerate 3 hours.

6. *Make topping:* Transfer 2 tablespoons of the cream to a small microwaveproof bowl. Add chocolate and microwave on HIGH 30 seconds. Stir until mixture is smooth (if chocolate does not melt completely, microwave 10 seconds more). Cool at room temperature 15 minutes. Beat remaining cream and the vanilla in a mixer bowl until thickened. Add chocolate mixture and beat just until stiff. Spread topping over filling. Sprinkle with toasted coconut. Makes 10 servings.

Per serving: 515 calories, 35.5 g total fat, 20.5 g saturated fat, 168 mg cholesterol, 290 mg sodium, 43 g carbohydrates, 7 g protein, 133 mg calcium, 2 g fiber

boston cream pie

Chefs speculate that this American classic, created at Boston's Parker House Hotel in the mid-1850s, was originally called a pie because it wasn't tall like most cakes. The custard filling benefits from the pure flavor of the vanilla bean, while coffee powder in the glaze intensifies its chocolate flavor. Pictured on page 207.

Prep time: 1 hour plus chilling and standing
Baking time: 35 to 40 minutes • Microwave used

CUSTARD:

- 1⅓ cups milk, divided
- 1 vanilla bean, split lengthwise, or 1 teaspoon vanilla extract
- ⅓ cup granulated sugar
- 2 tablespoons cornstarch
- 3 large egg yolks
- 2 tablespoons butter or margarine, cut up

CAKE:

- 2 cups cake flour (not self-rising)
- 2 teaspoons baking powder
- ¼ teaspoon salt
- ½ cup butter or margarine, softened
- 1 cup granulated sugar
- 2 large eggs, at room temperature 20 to 30 minutes
- ¾ cup milk, at room temperature 20 to 30 minutes
- 1 teaspoon vanilla extract

GLAZE:

- ¼ cup heavy or whipping cream
- 1 teaspoon instant coffee powder
- 4 ounces semisweet chocolate squares, finely chopped
- 1 tablespoon light corn syrup
- ¼ cup confectioners' sugar, sifted

1. *Make custard:* Combine 1 cup of the milk and the vanilla bean in a microwaveproof bowl. Microwave on HIGH 1 minute, until milk is hot. Whisk sugar and cornstarch in a 2-quart saucepan until blended. Whisk in remaining ⅓ cup milk and the egg yolks until smooth. Remove vanilla bean from milk and scrape seeds into mixture in saucepan. Discard pod. Gradually whisk in hot milk.

2. Cook custard over medium-low heat, whisking gently until it comes to a full boil. Reduce heat and boil for 1 minute, whisking gently. Remove from heat and stir (not whisk) in butter until melted. Strain custard through a sieve into a medium bowl. (Stir in vanilla extract, if using.) Cover surface directly with plastic wrap. Refrigerate 2 hours until cold. *(Can be made ahead. Refrigerate overnight. To proceed with recipe, stir custard until smooth.)*

3. *Make cake:* Heat oven to 350°F. Grease and flour a 9-inch springform pan. Whisk flour, baking powder and salt in a bowl until blended. Beat butter in a large mixer bowl, about 1 minute. Gradually beat in sugar; beat 4 to 5 minutes, until fluffy. At low speed, beat in eggs, one at a time, until well blended. Combine milk and vanilla in a glass measure. Alternately beat in flour mixture with milk mixture, beginning and ending with flour mixture, beating just until blended. Spread batter evenly into prepared pan.

4. Bake 35 to 40 minutes, or until a toothpick inserted in center of cake comes out clean. Cool cake in pan 10 minutes. Run a knife around side of pan and detach springform ring. Invert cake onto a wire rack. Remove pan bottom and invert cake again onto a rack. Cool. *(Can be made ahead. Wrap well and freeze up to 2 weeks. Thaw at room temperature 2 hours.)*

5. *Make glaze:* Bring cream and instant coffee to boil in a 1-quart saucepan. Remove pan from heat; add chocolate. Cover and let stand 1 minute. Whisk until chocolate melts. Add corn syrup and confectioners' sugar; whisk until smooth. (If there are any lumps of sugar remaining, let stand a few minutes and whisk again.) Let stand 10 minutes to cool until properly thickened.

6. Split cake in half horizontally with a long serrated knife. Remove top. Place bottom layer on a serving plate. Spoon chilled custard onto bottom layer and spread up to ½ inch from edge. Top with remaining cake layer, cut side down. Spoon glaze onto center of cake. Spread evenly on cake, letting some run down sides. Let stand until glaze firms up, about 30 minutes. Makes 12 servings.

Per serving: 380 calories, 18.5 g total fat, 10.5 g saturated fat, 127 mg cholesterol, 265 mg sodium, 50 g carbohydrates, 5 g protein, 117 mg calcium, 1 g fiber

PROFITEROLES
PG. 277

the
year in
chocolate

TRUFFLES
PG. 280

Sometimes (OK, lots of times) nothing but chocolate will do. However you like it— dark and bittersweet or light and creamy—we have your favorites here: cookies, cakes, tarts, pies, brownies, breads, puddings, sauces and, of course, hot chocolate.

BOURBON-CHOCOLATE
TIPSY CAKE
PG. 261

get **swept**

away...

CHOCOLATE
TURNOVERS
PG. 278

CHOCOLATE
PECAN TART
PG. 272

on a **wave** of
cocoa

CHOCOLATE-
HAZELNUT
ICE-CREAM
TORTE
PG. 266

BROWNIE-
ALMOND
TART
PG. 272

CHOCOLATE
TRUFFLE
TORTE
PG. 266

is there
anything
better than chocolate?

CHOCOLATE-
COATED PECANS
PG. 280

CHOCOLATE-
TEA BREAD
PUDDING
PG. 276

RICH HOT
CHOCOLATE
PG. 271

yes!
more chocolate!

MOCHA
ANGEL FOOD CAKE
PG. 262

a batch of
fresh
cookies

CHOCOLATE
CLOUDS
PG. 250

CHOCOLATE
CHOCOLATE
CHIPS
PG. 249

CHOCOLATE CHIP
PIZZA COOKIES
PG. 250

yields lots of
chocolate
kisses

CLASSIC
CHEESECAKE
BROWNIES
PG. 257

how about a little pb & c?

PEANUT BUTTER SILK PIE
PG. 274

PEANUT BUTTER-MILK CHOCOLATE BROWNIES
PG. 256

chocolate-cherry biscotti (EASY)

You'll adore these crisp finger cookies bejeweled with chunks of chocolate and candied cherries.

Prep time: 45 minutes plus decorating
Baking time: 1 hour

- **3 cups all-purpose flour**
- **1 tablespoon baking powder**
- **¼ teaspoon salt**
- **3 large eggs**
- **¾ cup sugar**
- **½ cup butter or margarine, melted and cooled**
- **1 tablespoon grated orange peel**
- **1 teaspoon vanilla extract**
- **6 ounces bittersweet or semisweet chocolate squares, cut into ¼-inch pieces**
- **1½ cups candied red cherries, halved**
- **4 ounces semisweet chocolate squares, melted (see tip, page 259) and cooled slightly**

1. Adjust oven racks to center and lower thirds of oven. Heat oven to 325°F. Grease a large cookie sheet. Combine flour, baking powder and salt in a bowl. Beat eggs in a large mixer bowl at medium-high speed, 1 minute. Gradually beat in sugar. At low speed, beat in butter, orange peel and vanilla. Beat in flour mixture just until blended. Stir in cut-up chocolate and cherries. Divide dough into thirds. On a lightly floured surface, roll each piece into a 14×1½-inch log. Arrange logs 2½ inches apart on the prepared cookie sheet. Bake on bottom oven rack 30 minutes, until firm. Cool on cookie sheet on a wire rack, 15 minutes.

2. Reduce oven temperature to 275°F. Carefully transfer logs to a cutting board. With a serrated knife, gently slice each log diagonally into ½-inch-thick slices. Arrange slices, cut side down, 1 inch apart on 2 large ungreased cookie sheets.

3. Bake 30 minutes, until cut sides feel dry to the touch, switching and rotating cookie sheets after 15 minutes. Transfer to wire racks to cool.

4. *To decorate:* Stack cookies, rounded side up and side by side, on a sheet of waxed paper. Spoon melted chocolate into a plastic storage bag; cut a very small hole in one corner. Drizzle chocolate over tops of cookies. Let stand until chocolate sets. Makes 6 dozen cookies.

Per biscotti: 75 calories, 3 g total fat, 1.5 g saturated fat, 13 mg cholesterol, 45 mg sodium, 11 g carbohydrates, 1 g protein, 15 mg calcium, 0 g fiber

chocolate (EASY) chocolate chips

Sprinkle toffee bits over these rich, chocolaty cookies while they're still warm for a doubly delicious treat. Pictured on page 247.

Total prep and baking time: 20 minutes
Microwave used

- **½ cup butter or margarine**
- **3 ounces unsweetened chocolate squares, broken in half**
- **1 cup sugar**
- **2 large eggs**
- **½ teaspoon vanilla extract**
- **¾ cup all-purpose flour**
- **⅓ cup unsweetened cocoa**
- **½ teaspoon baking soda**
- **¼ teaspoon salt**
- **1 cup semisweet chocolate chips**
- **2 tablespoons English toffee bits for baking**

1. Adjust oven racks to upper and lower thirds of oven. Heat oven to 350°F. Grease 2 large cookie sheets.

2. Microwave butter and chocolate in a microwaveproof bowl on HIGH 2 minutes 15 seconds; let stand 2 minutes. Stir until melted. Stir sugar into chocolate; beat in eggs and vanilla. Whisk together flour, cocoa, baking soda and salt in a bowl. Stir into chocolate mixture until blended. Stir in chips.

3. Drop batter by rounded measuring tablespoonfuls onto prepared cookie sheets. Bake 10 to 11 minutes, until tops look dry, not shiny. Transfer to wire racks. Immediately sprinkle with toffee bits. Cool. Makes 2½ dozen cookies.

Per cookie: 120 calories, 7 g total fat, 4 g saturated fat, 23 mg cholesterol, 82 mg sodium, 15 g carbohydrates, 1 g protein, 8 mg calcium, 1 g fiber

chocolate chip pizza cookies

These dessert "pizza pies" with white chocolate and candy topping will wow a crowd. Pictured on page 247.

Prep time: 30 minutes plus decorating
Baking time: 17 to 19 minutes per batch

2¼	cups all-purpose flour
1	teaspoon baking soda
½	teaspoon salt
1	cup butter or margarine, softened
1	cup firmly packed brown sugar
½	cup granulated sugar
2	teaspoons vanilla extract
2	large eggs
1¼	cups semisweet chocolate chips
1	cup quick-cooking oats
4	ounces white chocolate squares, melted (see tip, page 259)
¼	cup miniature M&M's baking bits

1. Heat oven to 350°F. Combine flour, baking soda and salt in a small bowl.

2. Beat butter, both sugars and vanilla in a mixer bowl on medium-high speed until light and creamy, 2 minutes. Beat in eggs, one at a time, beating well after each addition, until mixture is fluffy. At low speed, beat in flour mixture just until blended. Stir in chips and oats.

3. Divide dough into thirds. Place each piece of dough in the center of its own large, ungreased cookie sheet. Press each piece with floured fingers into a 6-inch circle. Bake 2 cookie sheets of dough 17 to 19 minutes, switching pans halfway through, until cookies are browned and set. Cool on cookie sheets, 5 minutes. With large spatula, transfer each cookie to a wire rack; cool completely. Repeat, baking remaining dough.

4. With a fork, drizzle half of the melted white chocolate over cookies; then divide and sprinkle baking bits over tops of cookies. Drizzle cookies with remaining white chocolate; let stand until chocolate sets. (Can be made ahead. Wrap well and freeze up to 1 month. Thaw at room temperature 2 hours before serving.) Cut each cookie into 8 wedges. Makes 24 wedges.

Per wedge: 265 calories, 13.5 g total fat, 8 g saturated fat, 42 mg cholesterol, 199 mg sodium, 31 g carbohydrates, 3 g protein, 23 mg calcium, 2 g fiber

chocolate clouds

With a crackly outside and a moist-and-chewy inside, these chocolate gems puff up beautifully when baked. Pictured on page 246.

Prep time: 50 minutes plus chilling
Baking time: 17 minutes per batch
Microwave used

3½	cups all-purpose flour
2	teaspoons baking powder
4	ounces unsweetened chocolate squares
1	cup butter or margarine
3	cups sugar
4	large eggs, at room temperature 20 to 30 minutes
1	teaspoon vanilla extract
1	teaspoon almond extract
2	cups chopped assorted nuts (walnuts, pecans and almonds)
1	package (6 oz.) semisweet chocolate chips

1. Combine flour and baking powder in a medium bowl. Microwave chocolate and butter in a medium microwaveproof bowl on HIGH 2 to 2½ minutes, until melted; stir until smooth. Transfer to a large mixer bowl; add sugar and beat on medium-high speed 1 minute, until combined. Add eggs, one at a time, beating well after each addition. Beat in extracts. At low speed, beat in flour mixture. Stir in nuts and chips. Cover and refrigerate 1 hour.

2. Heat oven to 350°F. Roll dough into 1¼-inch balls and arrange 1 inch apart on ungreased cookie sheets. Bake 17 minutes, until tops are cracked. Cool on wire racks. Makes about 4½ dozen cookies.

Per cookie: 160 calories, 9 g total fat, 4 g saturated fat, 25 mg cholesterol, 57 mg sodium, 19 g carbohydrates, 2 g protein, 18 mg calcium, 1 g fiber

monster mocha-chip cookies [EASY]

Want a new spin on thick, chewy, old-fashioned chocolate-chip cookies? Make them bigger, give them a shot of coffee and pack them with extra-large chips.

Prep time: 20 minutes plus chilling
Baking time: 16 to 18 minutes per batch

- 2½ cups all-purpose flour
- 1 teaspoon baking soda
- 1 teaspoon salt
- ½ cup butter or margarine, softened
- ¼ cup vegetable shortening
- 1½ cups sugar
- 2 tablespoons light corn syrup
- 1 teaspoon vanilla extract
- 2 large eggs
- 2 tablespoons instant espresso powder
- 1 tablespoon hot water
- 1 package (10 or 11½ oz.) megasize semisweet chocolate chips or large milk chocolate baking pieces
- 1 cup chopped pecans (optional)

1. Position rack in center of oven. Heat oven to 350°F. Grease a large cookie sheet. Combine flour, baking soda and salt in a small bowl.

2. Beat butter, shortening and sugar in a large mixer bowl at high speed until light and fluffy. Beat in corn syrup, vanilla and eggs. Dissolve espresso powder in the hot water; add to creamed mixture.

3. At low speed, beat in flour mixture just until blended. Stir in chips and nuts. Refrigerate 15 minutes.

4. Using a 2¼-inch ice-cream scoop or level ¼-cup measure, scoop dough onto prepared sheet, placing scoops 3 inches apart. Bake 16 to 18 minutes, until centers are set. Cool on wire racks. Repeat with remaining dough. *(Can be made ahead. Wrap well and freeze up to 1 month.)* Makes 18 cookies.

Per cookie: 300 calories, 13.5 g total fat, 7 g saturated fat, 38 mg cholesterol, 265 mg sodium, 42 g carbohydrates, 4 g protein, 8 mg calcium, 0 g fiber

chocolate-cinnamon meringues

Chocolate-flavored meringues? Yes indeed! Made with a pastry bag, a touch of cinnamon and a dip in melted chocolate, these elegant cookies are a special breed.

Prep time: 30 minutes plus cooling and decorating
Baking time: 1 hour 15 minutes

- 2 large egg whites, at room temperature 20 to 30 minutes
- ¼ teaspoon cream of tartar
- ⅛ teaspoon salt
- ½ cup sugar
- ½ teaspoon vanilla extract
- 3 tablespoons unsweetened cocoa
- ¼ teaspoon cinnamon

- 4 ounces semisweet chocolate squares, coarsely chopped

1. Heat oven to 225°F. Line 2 large cookie sheets with foil. Beat egg whites in a large mixer bowl at medium speed until foamy. Add cream of tartar and salt; continue to beat until soft peaks form. Gradually beat in sugar, 1 tablespoon at a time. Continue to beat until stiff. Beat in vanilla. With a rubber spatula, gently fold cocoa and cinnamon into beaten whites just until blended.

2. Spoon meringue into a large pastry bag fitted with a #47 (⅜-inch) large basket-weave tip. Pipe into 3-inch lengths onto prepared cookie sheets. Bake 1 hour 15 minutes. Turn off oven. *(Do not open oven door.)* Cool the cookies in the oven at least 1½ hours or overnight.

3. Melt chocolate in the top of a double boiler over simmering water. Carefully peel meringues from foil. Dip one tip of each meringue into melted chocolate. Transfer cookies to wire racks and let stand until chocolate sets. Makes 3½ dozen cookies.

Per cookie: 25 calories, 1 g total fat, 0.5 g saturated fat, 0 mg cholesterol, 10 mg sodium, 4 g carbohydrates, 0 g protein, 5 mg calcium, 0 g fiber

chocolate crinkles *EASY*

These pretty confections sport a super chocolate sensation with a touch of coffee flavor. They're even better the next day—if they last that long.

Prep time: 20 minutes plus chilling
Baking time: 10 to 12 minutes per batch

- ½ cup butter or margarine, cut up
- 4 ounces unsweetened chocolate squares, coarsely chopped
- 1 teaspoon instant coffee powder (optional)
- 2 cups all-purpose flour
- 2 teaspoons baking powder
- ½ teaspoon salt
- 2 cups granulated sugar
- 4 large eggs
- 1½ teaspoons vanilla extract
- 1 cup confectioners' sugar

1. Melt butter and chocolate with coffee powder (if using) in top of a double boiler over hot, not boiling, water until smooth. Remove from heat and set aside to cool slightly.

2. Combine flour, baking powder and salt in a medium bowl. Beat chocolate mixture and granulated sugar in a large mixer bowl at medium speed just until combined. Add eggs, one at a time, beating well after each addition. Beat in vanilla. At low speed, beat in flour mixture just until combined. Cover and refrigerate at least 2 hours, until dough is very firm.

3. Heat oven to 350°F. Grease 2 large cookie sheets. Place confectioners' sugar on a plate. Drop chilled dough by teaspoonfuls onto sugar and roll into balls. Place balls 2 inches apart on prepared cookie sheets. Bake 10 to 12 minutes, until the tops are just set *(do not overbake)*. Cool cookies on cookie sheets 1 minute; transfer to wire racks and cool completely. *(Can be made ahead. Store in an airtight container and freeze up to 3 months.)* Makes 5 dozen cookies.

Per cookie: 75 calories, 3 g total fat, 1.5 g saturated fat, 19 mg cholesterol, 54 mg sodium, 12 g carbohydrates, 1 g protein, 12 mg calcium, 0 g fiber

white-chocolate-chunk-cherry cookies *EASY*

Cocoa cookies studded with chunks of white chocolate, dried cherries and chopped pecans are a special treat. Use imported white chocolate bars if you have them, or substitute 1 cup white chocolate chips.

Prep time: 20 minutes plus cooling
Baking time: 8 to 10 minutes per batch

- 1 cup all-purpose flour
- ¼ cup unsweetened cocoa
- 1 teaspoon baking powder
- ¼ teaspoon salt
- ½ cup butter or margarine, softened
- 1 cup sugar
- 1 large egg
- ½ teaspoon vanilla extract
- 6 ounces white chocolate squares, coarsely chopped
- 1 cup chopped pecans
- ½ cup dried cherries or raisins

1. Heat oven to 350°F. Grease 2 large cookie sheets. Combine flour, cocoa, baking powder and salt in a medium bowl. Beat butter in a large mixer bowl at medium speed until smooth. Gradually beat in sugar until light and fluffy. Beat in egg and vanilla until blended. At low speed, beat in flour mixture just until combined. Stir in white chocolate, pecans and dried cherries.

2. Drop dough by heaping teaspoonfuls 2 inches apart onto prepared cookie sheets. Bake 8 to 10 minutes per batch, until tops are just firm. Transfer cookies to wire racks and cool completely. *(Can be made ahead. Store cookies in an airtight container and freeze up to 3 months.)* Makes about 5 dozen cookies.

Per cookie: 70 calories, 4 g total fat, 2 g saturated fat, 9 mg cholesterol, 37 mg sodium, 7 g carbohydrates, 1 g protein, 14 mg calcium, 0 g fiber

chocolate chunk cookies

Just like your favorite brownie, be sure not to overbake.

Prep time: 30 minutes plus cooling and decorating
Baking time: 8 to 8½ minutes per batch

1½	cups chopped walnuts
1½	cups chopped pecans
8	ounces semisweet chocolate squares, coarsely chopped
3	ounces unsweetened chocolate squares, coarsely chopped
½	cup unsalted butter, cut up (no substitutes)
⅔	cup all-purpose flour
½	teaspoon baking powder
¼	teaspoon salt
3	large eggs, at room temperature 20 to 30 minutes
1¼	cups sugar
2	teaspoons vanilla extract
1½	cups semisweet chocolate chips

4	ounces semisweet chocolate squares, coarsely chopped

1. Heat oven to 325°F. Spread walnuts and pecans on a baking sheet in a single layer. Bake 8 to 10 minutes, until lightly browned and fragrant. Cool. Leave oven on.

2. Melt the 8 ounces semisweet and 3 ounces unsweetened chocolate squares and butter in top of a double boiler over hot, not boiling, water until smooth. Remove from heat and set aside to cool.

3. Grease 2 large cookie sheets. Combine flour, baking powder and salt in a medium bowl. Beat the eggs and sugar in a large mixer bowl at medium-high speed for 10 minutes, until a ribbon forms when the beaters are lifted. Beat in the melted chocolate mixture and vanilla at medium speed. Stir in flour mixture just until combined (*do not overmix*). Stir in chocolate chips and toasted nuts.

4. Drop batter by teaspoonfuls 2 inches apart onto prepared cookie sheets. Bake 8 to 8½ minutes, until barely firm and tops are slightly cracked. Cool cookies on cookie sheets 2 minutes. Transfer to wire racks and cool completely.

5. Melt the 4 ounces chocolate squares in the top of a double boiler over hot, not boiling, water until smooth. Remove from heat and cool slightly. Drizzle melted chocolate over cooled cookies. Return cookies to wire racks; let stand until chocolate sets. (*Can be made ahead. Store in an airtight container and freeze up to 1 month.*) Makes 4 dozen cookies.

Per cookie: 165 calories, 12 g total fat, 4.5 g saturated fat, 19 mg cholesterol, 21 mg sodium, 13 g carbohydrates, 2 g protein, 13 mg calcium, 2 g fiber

test kitchen tip

from tree to recipe

This glossary explains how chocolate makes it from the plant to your table.

COCOA BEANS are what chocolate and cocoa are made from; the beans are found in the pods of the cocoa tree.

CHOCOLATE LIQUID, also known as chocolate liquor, comes from ground "nibs," which are the meat of the cocoa bean. Chocolate liquid is the basic ingredient of all cocoa and chocolate products.

COCOA BUTTER is vegetable fat extracted from chocolate liquid. It's used to add a smooth quality to foods, as well as flavor to some food products.

COCOA POWDER is what's left after cocoa butter has been removed from the chocolate liquid; also referred to as unsweetened cocoa.

SEMISWEET CHOCOLATE is a blend of chocolate liquid, sweetening, cocoa butter and sometimes flavorings. It is used primarily for baking.

MILK CHOCOLATE is a combination of chocolate liquid, cocoa butter, milk or cream, sweeteners and flavorings. It's the most popular variety for eating out of hand.

chocolate chip shortbread sticks (EASY)

Here's a yummy change of pace for those who love traditional chocolate-chip cookies. Chocolate-chip-laden dough is made in practically no time and then chilled. The refrigerated dough is then rolled into stick shapes before being baked. To complete the treat, the cookies are dipped in additional melted chocolate.

Prep time: 1 hour plus chilling and decorating
Baking time: 12 minutes per batch
Microwave used

1	cup butter, softened (no substitutes)
½	cup confectioners' sugar
1	teaspoon vanilla extract
2	cups all-purpose flour
½	cup miniature semisweet chocolate chips

GLAZE:

¾	cup miniature semisweet chocolate chips
2	teaspoons vegetable shortening

1 ▪ Beat butter, sugar and vanilla in a large mixer bowl at medium-high speed until light and fluffy. At low speed, gradually beat in flour just until blended. Stir in chips. Divide dough in half and flatten into disks. Wrap and refrigerate 2 hours or overnight, until firm.

2 ▪ Heat oven to 350°F. Grease 2 large cookie sheets. On a lightly floured smooth surface, roll rounded teaspoonfuls of dough into 2½-inch-long sticks. *(Keep remaining dough refrigerated.)* Arrange sticks, 2 inches apart, on prepared cookie sheets. Place in freezer 10 minutes.

3 ▪ Bake 12 minutes, until edges are golden. Let cookies cool on cookie sheets 2 minutes. Transfer to wire racks and cool completely. Repeat process with remaining dough.

4 ▪ *Make glaze:* Melt chips in a small microwave-proof bowl on HIGH 1 to 2 minutes; stir until smooth. Stir in shortening until melted. Dip both ends of cookies into chocolate; place on waxed paper. Let stand until chocolate sets, 30 minutes. Makes 4½ dozen cookies.

Per cookie: 80 calories, 5.5 g total fat, 3 g saturated fat, 10 mg cholesterol, 37 mg sodium, 8 g carbohydrates, 1 g protein, 2 mg calcium, 0 g fiber

chocolate-nut sugar crisps

To make the almonds adhere, sprinkle on the nuts while chocolate is still warm, then refrigerate just until it sets.

Prep time: 25 minutes plus freezing and decorating
Baking time: 8 to 9 minutes per batch
Microwave used

2½	cups all-purpose flour
3	tablespoons unsweetened cocoa
1½	teaspoons baking powder
½	teaspoon salt
1	cup butter, softened (no substitutes)
1½	cups sugar
1	large egg

GLAZE:

4	ounces semisweet chocolate squares
½	cup sliced natural almonds, chopped

1 ▪ Heat oven to 375°F. Grease 2 cookie sheets.

2 ▪ Combine flour, cocoa, baking powder and salt in a bowl. Beat butter and sugar in a mixer bowl until light and fluffy; beat in egg. Stir in flour mixture.

3 ▪ Divide dough in half; place in freezer 10 minutes. Shape dough into two 9-inch logs; wrap and place in freezer 1 hour, until firm. Cut logs into ¼-inch-thick slices. Bake on prepared cookie sheets 8 to 9 minutes, until edges are set. Cool on wire racks.

4 ▪ *Make glaze:* Melt chocolate in a small microwaveproof bowl on HIGH 1 to 2 minutes; stir until smooth. Spread on tops of cookies; sprinkle edges with nuts. Refrigerate until chocolate sets. Makes 6 dozen cookies.

Per cookie: 70 calories, 4 g total fat, 2 g saturated fat, 10 mg cholesterol, 53 mg sodium, 8 g carbohydrates, 1 g protein, 12 mg calcium, 0 g fiber

chocolate-toffee bars

Three glorious layers, each one more delectable than the next, are combined to create this bar cookie that often is mistaken for candy.

Prep time: 35 minutes plus cooling and chilling
Baking time: 28 to 35 minutes

CRUST:

1¾	**cups all-purpose flour**
¼	**cup sugar**
7	**tablespoons butter, cut up (no substitutes)**
1	**large egg**
1	**teaspoon water**
½	**teaspoon vanilla extract**

TOFFEE LAYER:

2	**cups chopped walnuts**
1	**cup sugar**
½	**cup heavy or whipping cream**
¾	**cup butter, cut into 12 pieces (no substitutes)**
4	**ounces semisweet chocolate squares, melted (see tip, page 259)**

1. Heat oven to 375°F. Line a 13×9-inch baking pan with foil.

2. *Make crust:* Process flour, sugar and butter in a food processor until coarse crumbs are formed. Add egg, water and vanilla and process, pulsing, until the dough begins to form a ball. Pat dough into prepared pan and bake 20 to 25 minutes, until golden. Cool completely in pan on a wire rack.

3. *Make toffee layer:* Reduce oven temperature to 350°F. Spread walnuts on a baking sheet in a single layer. Bake 8 to 10 minutes, until lightly browned and fragrant. Cool. Place sugar in a large heavy skillet and cook 8 to 10 minutes, swirling pan occasionally, until completely melted and syrup is a deep caramel color. With a long-handled spoon, quickly and carefully stir in the cream until smooth (mixture may bubble rapidly). Stir in butter, 3 pieces at a time, until melted. Stir in walnuts. Immediately pour mixture over the cooled crust. Spread evenly and let stand until toffee layer is completely cooled.

4. Spread melted chocolate evenly over the toffee layer. Refrigerate bars 1 hour, until chocolate sets. Cut into 2×1-inch bars. Makes 54 bars.

Per bar: 115 calories, 9 g total fat, 4 g saturated fat, 19 mg cholesterol, 46 mg sodium, 9 g carbohydrates, 1 g protein, 8 mg calcium, 1 g fiber

---

test kitchen tip

a bit about bars

These hints will help you make great bar cookies—bar none!

FOR BROWNIES THAT CALL FOR CREAM CHEESE (such as the Classic Cheesecake Brownies, page 257), soften the cheese by simply letting it stand at room temperature about 30 minutes. Or, place 8 ounces of cream cheese in a microwaveproof container and microwave, uncovered, on HIGH 30 to 60 seconds, or until softened.

DRESS UP THE PRESENTATION of bar cookies, if desired. For unfrosted bars, try topping with a powdered-sugar pattern. Simply lay waxed-paper strips across the top in a pattern, and sprinkle with powdered sugar. If desired, add a touch of spice or flavoring (such as espresso powder) called for in the recipe.

LINING THE PAN with foil before baking makes for easy removing, cutting and cleanup. Allow foil to slightly extend over edge of pan. Grease foil if the recipe calls for a greased pan. Spread dough evenly in the pan; bake and cool as directed. Use overhanging foil to lift out bars. Cut into desired shapes.

TO FREEZE BAR COOKIES, use the above tip for lining the pan with foil. Lift the bars out of the pan. Unless otherwise specified, place the uncut and unfrosted bars in freezer bags or airtight containers. Seal, label and freeze 6 to 8 months. Thaw cookies at room temperature about 30 minutes. Frost, if desired, and cut.

peanut butter-milk chocolate brownies EASY

The creamy peanut butter filling between layers of brownie may remind you of a favorite candy bar. Pictured on page 248.

Prep time: 10 minutes plus chilling
Baking time: 30 minutes
Microwave used

BROWNIE BATTER:

1½	ounces unsweetened chocolate squares, chopped
1	cup milk chocolate chips
½	cup butter or margarine, cut up
¾	cup sugar
2	large eggs
½	teaspoon vanilla extract
½	cup all-purpose flour
⅛	teaspoon salt

PEANUT BUTTER BATTER:

½	cup peanut butter
1	package (3 oz.) cream cheese, softened
¼	cup sugar
1	large egg
1	tablespoon flour
½	teaspoon vanilla extract

⅓	cup milk chocolate chips

1. ■ Heat oven to 350°F. Grease a 9-inch square baking pan.

2. ■ *Make brownie batter:* Combine unsweetened chocolate, the 1 cup chips and the butter in a microwaveproof bowl. Microwave on HIGH 1 to 1½ minutes; stir until smooth. Whisk in sugar, eggs and vanilla. Beat in flour and salt.

3. ■ *Make peanut butter batter:* Beat all peanut butter batter ingredients in a mixer bowl until smooth.

4. ■ Spread half of the brownie batter in the prepared pan. Drop peanut butter batter over brownie batter; spread evenly. Spread on remaining brownie batter. Bake 30 minutes, until a toothpick inserted in center comes out barely clean. Sprinkle top with the ⅓ cup milk chocolate chips. Let stand 3 minutes to soften chips; spread over top. Cool; refrigerate. Cut into 2½×2-inch bars. Makes 12 brownies.

Per brownie: 375 calories, 24.5 g total fat, 12 g saturated fat, 83 mg cholesterol, 207 mg sodium, 36 g carbohydrates, 7 g protein, 49 mg calcium, 1 g fiber

old-fashioned brownies EASY

Talk about simple! You don't even have to get out the mixer—just whisk the ingredients together.

Prep time: 10 minutes • Baking time: 30 to 32 minutes

¾	cup all-purpose flour
¾	cup unsweetened cocoa
¼	teaspoon salt
¾	cup butter or margarine, melted
1	teaspoon instant coffee powder
1½	cups sugar
3	large eggs
1½	teaspoons vanilla extract
½	pound walnuts, toasted and coarsely chopped

	Peppermint ice cream (optional)

1. ■ Heat oven to 350°F. Grease a 9-inch square baking pan. Combine flour, cocoa and salt in a medium bowl.

2. ■ Whisk butter and coffee powder together in another bowl. Add sugar, whisking to blend. Add eggs, one at a time, whisking well after each addition. Whisk in vanilla. Whisk in flour mixture just until blended. Stir in nuts.

3. ■ Pour batter into the prepared pan. Bake 30 to 32 minutes, until a toothpick inserted in center comes out barely clean. Cool in pan on a wire rack. Cut into 16 squares. Serve with peppermint ice cream, if desired. Makes 16 brownies.

Per brownie: 295 calories, 20 g total fat, 7 g saturated fat, 64 mg cholesterol, 142 mg sodium, 26 g carbohydrates, 5 g protein, 68 mg calcium, 1 g fiber

classic cheesecake brownies ⊛

Brownies swirled with a cream cheese batter are a bar-cookie favorite. Store them in the refrigerator. Pictured on page 247.

Prep time: 15 minutes • Baking time: 40 to 45 minutes
Microwave used

BROWNIE BATTER:

- ¾ cup all-purpose flour
- ½ teaspoon baking powder
- ¼ teaspoon salt
- 4 ounces semisweet chocolate squares, coarsely chopped
- ¼ cup butter or margarine
- 2 large eggs, lightly beaten
- ¾ cup sugar
- ½ teaspoon vanilla extract

CHEESECAKE BATTER:

- 1 package (8 oz.) cream cheese, softened
- 2 tablespoons sugar
- 1 large egg
- ½ teaspoon vanilla extract

1. Heat oven to 325°F. Line a 9-inch square baking pan with foil; lightly grease the foil.

2. *Make brownie batter:* Combine flour, baking powder and salt in a small bowl.

3. Combine chocolate and butter in a small microwaveproof bowl. Microwave on HIGH 1 minute, until melted; stir until smooth.

4. Whisk eggs, sugar, chocolate mixture and vanilla in a medium bowl. Stir in flour mixture just until blended. Reserve 1 cup of the batter; set aside. Spread remaining batter in the prepared pan.

5. *Make cheesecake batter:* Beat cream cheese in a small mixer bowl at medium speed until smooth. Beat in sugar, egg and vanilla. Spread over brownie batter in the prepared pan.

6. Drop reserved 1 cup brownie batter by tablespoonfuls over top of cheesecake batter. Run the tip of a knife back and forth through both batters to marbleize.

7. Bake 40 to 45 minutes, until top feels firm when gently pressed in center. Cool in pan on a wire rack. Invert pan onto rack; peel off foil. Invert brownie again onto a cutting board. Cut into 2½×2-inch bars. *(Can be made ahead. Cover and freeze up to 1 month.)* Makes 12 brownies.

Per brownie : 250 calories, 15 g total fat, 9 g saturated fat, 85 mg cholesterol, 178 mg sodium, 26 g carbohydrates, 4 g protein, 34 mg calcium, 1 g fiber

---

test kitchen tip

a doneness test for brownies

When it comes to brownies, testing for doneness can be a bit tricky. You can do a toothpick test; however, unlike when baking a cake, you don't want the toothpick to come out perfectly clean. Instead, unless specified otherwise, the brownies should be baked until the toothpick comes out "barely clean"—that is, with a few moist crumbs still clinging to the toothpick. This will ensure the gooey and moist texture so loved in these favorite bar cookies.

raspberry-hazelnut brownies

These sophisticated brownies boast a hazelnut shortbread crust, sweet raspberry jam, a bittersweet fudge filling and a shiny chocolate glaze.

Prep time: 1 hour plus cooling
Baking time: 38 to 45 minutes

CRUST:

1	cup butter or margarine, softened
¾	cup confectioners' sugar
1¾	cups all-purpose flour
1	cup hazelnuts, toasted, skinned and finely chopped*

FILLING:

1	jar (12 oz.) seedless raspberry preserves
1	cup butter or margarine
5	ounces unsweetened chocolate squares, coarsely chopped
3	large eggs, lightly beaten
2	cups granulated sugar
¼	teaspoon salt
1	teaspoon vanilla extract
1	cup all-purpose flour

6	ounces semisweet chocolate squares, melted and cooled (see tip, page 259)
½	pint fresh whole raspberries, for garnish (optional)

1. ■ Heat oven to 350°F.

2. ■ *Make crust:* Line a 15½×10½-inch jelly-roll pan with foil. Beat butter and confectioners' sugar in a large mixer bowl until light and fluffy. Add flour and hazelnuts, beating just until mixed. Spread dough evenly in the prepared pan. Bake 18 to 20 minutes, until top is lightly browned. Cool 30 minutes.

3. ■ *Make filling:* Spread crust evenly with raspberry preserves. Refrigerate until preserves are firm, about 20 minutes.

4. ■ Meanwhile, melt butter with unsweetened chocolate over low heat in a small saucepan. Beat eggs, granulated sugar and salt in a large mixer bowl until thick and fluffy. Beat in chocolate mixture and vanilla. Stir in flour. Pour chocolate filling over preserves. Bake 20 to 25 minutes, until a toothpick inserted in center of filling comes out barely clean. Cool in pan on a wire rack. *(Can be made ahead. Wrap well and freeze up to 1 month.)*

5. ■ Lift brownies out of pan by foil edges and peel off foil. Spread top evenly with melted chocolate. Garnish with fresh raspberries, if desired. Let stand until chocolate sets. Cut into 1-inch squares. Makes 12 dozen brownies.

*Note: To toast hazelnuts, arrange them in a single layer on a baking sheet. Bake at 350°F. until lightly browned and skins are crackly, 12 to 15 minutes. Wrap nuts in a clean kitchen towel and let stand 5 minutes. Rub nuts in the towel to remove skins; cool completely.

Per brownie: 70 calories, 4.5 g total fat, 2.5 g saturated fat, 12 mg cholesterol, 34 mg sodium, 8 g carbohydrates, 1 g protein, 4 mg calcium, 0 g fiber

saucepan brownies

In the years since Katherine Hepburn shared this easy brownie recipe with us, it has remained a favorite of both our staff and readers. We've made it even easier by melting the chocolate in the microwave.

Prep time: 10 minutes • Baking time: 40 minutes
Microwave used

1	cup chopped walnuts or pecans
3	ounces unsweetened chocolate squares, chopped
½	cup butter or margarine, cut up
1	cup sugar
2	large eggs
½	teaspoon vanilla extract
½	cup all-purpose flour
¼	teaspoon salt

1. ■ Heat oven to 350°F. Spread walnuts in an 8-inch square baking pan and bake 10 minutes, until toasted and fragrant. Cool walnuts completely in pan. Remove from pan and set aside.

2. ■ Reduce oven temperature to 325°F. Grease and flour the same baking pan; tap the pan to remove excess flour.

3. Combine chocolate and butter in a large microwaveproof bowl. Microwave on HIGH 1½ minutes, until melted. Stir in sugar, then eggs and vanilla; beat until well combined. Stir in flour and salt. Fold in walnuts. Spread batter into prepared pan. Bake 40 minutes, until a toothpick inserted in center of filling comes out barely clean. Cool completely in pan on a wire rack. Cut into 2-inch squares. *(Can be made ahead. Store in an airtight container and freeze up to 3 months.)* Makes 16 brownies.

Per brownie: 200 calories, 14.5 g total fat, 6 g saturated fat, 43 mg cholesterol, 107 mg sodium, 17 g carbohydrates, 3 g protein, 17 mg calcium, 1 g fiber

one-bowl chocolate cupcakes

These frosted cupcakes are perfect for birthdays and bake sales. Nothing could be simpler; just pour the liquid ingredients into the dry ones, beat and bake.

Prep time: 30 minutes plus cooling and decorating
Baking time: 18 to 20 minutes

- 1¼ **cups milk**
- 1 **teaspoon white vinegar**
- 1¾ **cups all-purpose flour**
- 1½ **cups sugar**
- ⅔ **cup unsweetened cocoa**
- 1 **teaspoon baking powder**
- ½ **teaspoon baking soda**
- ¼ **teaspoon salt**
- ¾ **cup butter or margarine, softened, cut up**
- 2 **large eggs**
- 1 **teaspoon vanilla extract**

FLUFFY WHITE FROSTING:

- 2 **large egg whites**
- 1½ **cups sugar**
- ¼ **teaspoon cream of tartar or 1 tablespoon light corn syrup**
- ⅓ **cup water**
- 1 **teaspoon vanilla extract**

    Unsweetened cocoa, for garnish (optional)

1. Heat oven to 350°F. Line twenty-four 2½-inch muffin-pan cups with paper liners. Combine milk and vinegar in a 1-cup measure. Let stand 5 minutes. Combine flour, sugar, cocoa, baking powder, baking soda and salt in a large mixer bowl. At low speed, beat in butter until mixture is crumbly. Add milk mixture, eggs and vanilla; beat at medium speed 3 minutes. Spoon about ¼ cup batter into each paper liner. Bake 18 to 20 minutes, until top springs back when lightly touched. Cool in pan on a wire rack 5 minutes. Remove from pan and cool completely.

2. *Make fluffy white frosting:* Combine egg whites, sugar, cream of tartar and water in top of a double boiler. Beat on high speed 1 minute with handheld mixer. Place over boiling water (water should not touch bottom of pan); beat on high speed 7 minutes. Remove pan from boiling water; add vanilla and beat on high 2 minutes more, until stiff enough to spread. Makes 2¾ cups.

3. Spread cupcakes with warm frosting. Sprinkle lightly with cocoa, if desired. Makes 24 cupcakes.

Per cupcake: 205 calories, 7 g total fat, 4 g saturated fat, 35 mg cholesterol, 146 mg sodium, 32 g carbohydrates, 3 g protein, 58 mg calcium, 0 g fiber

---

test kitchen tip

melting chocolate...

TO MELT IN THE MICROWAVE: Coarsely chop chocolate and place in a microwaveproof bowl or cup. Microwave on HIGH 1 minute; stir. Repeat in 30-second increments until melted. Keep in mind that chocolate pieces won't appear melted until they are stirred.

TO MELT ON THE STOVETOP: Coarsely chop chocolate. Make sure all utensils are dry. Melt chocolate in a heavy saucepan over low heat. (Or, place chocolate in the top of a double boiler over hot, not boiling, water.) Stir the chocolate frequently until it is completely melted.

cocoa bread

Laced with cocoa and baked to a mahogany brown, this bread is perfect any time of day. Because it's not too sweet, it's great toasted and topped with cream cheese or jam for breakfast.

Prep time: 30 minutes plus rising
Baking time: 50 minutes

2	cups milk
5½	cups all-purpose flour, divided
1	package active dry yeast
½	cup plus 1 tablespoon sugar, divided
2	large eggs, beaten
¼	cup butter or margarine, softened
½	cup unsweetened cocoa
½	teaspoon salt

1. Heat milk in a saucepan until small bubbles form around edge of pan; cool to 120°F. to 130°F.

2. Combine 3 cups of the flour, the yeast and 1 tablespoon of the sugar in a large bowl. Stir in milk and beat until smooth. Cover with a towel and place in a warm, draft-free place until double in bulk, about 1 hour.

3. Stir eggs and butter into dough, beating until smooth. Combine remaining 2½ cups all-purpose flour, remaining ½ cup sugar, the cocoa and salt in a medium bowl; stir into dough.

4. Turn dough onto a floured surface and knead 1 minute, adding only as much flour as necessary to keep dough from sticking. Place dough in a greased bowl, turning to grease top. Cover with a clean kitchen towel and let rise in a warm, draft-free place until doubled in bulk, about 1 hour. *(Can be made ahead. Cover with plastic wrap and refrigerate overnight.)*

5. Grease two 9×5-inch loaf pans. Divide dough in half, shape into loaves and place in prepared pans. Cover with a towel and let rise in a warm, draft-free place until doubled in bulk, about 1 hour (2 hours if dough has been refrigerated).

6. Heat oven to 350°F. Bake loaves 30 minutes. Cover tops loosely with foil, then bake 20 minutes more, until bottoms of breads sound hollow when removed from pans and lightly tapped. Cool on wire racks. Makes 2 loaves (32 servings).

Per serving: 115 calories, 2.5 g total fat, 1.5 g saturated fat, 19 mg cholesterol, 64 mg sodium, 20 g carbohydrates, 3 g protein, 39 mg calcium, 1 g fiber

our best devil's food cake

The secret ingredient in this recipe—coffee—adds depth of flavor and a dark, rich color.

Prep time: 40 minutes plus cooling
Baking time: 25 minutes

¾	cup milk
2	teaspoons instant coffee powder
¾	cup unsweetened cocoa
½	cup sour cream
1¼	cups all-purpose flour
1½	teaspoons baking soda
½	teaspoon baking powder
¼	teaspoon salt
1	cup butter, softened (no substitutes)
1½	cups granulated sugar
3	large eggs, at room temperature 20 to 30 minutes
2	teaspoons vanilla extract

CREAMY FUDGE FROSTING:

4	ounces unsweetened chocolate squares, coarsely chopped
1⅔	cups confectioners' sugar
¾	cup heavy or whipping cream
2	teaspoons vanilla extract
6	tablespoons butter, softened, cut up (no substitutes)

1. Heat oven to 350°F. Butter three 8-inch round cake pans. Line bottoms with waxed paper. Butter and flour paper; tap to remove excess flour.

2. Heat milk and coffee in a small saucepan over medium heat until small bubbles form around edge of pan. Remove from heat. Add cocoa and whisk until smooth. Whisk in sour cream. Cool.

3. Combine flour, baking soda, baking powder and salt in a medium bowl. Beat butter in a large mixer bowl at medium speed until light. Gradually beat in granulated sugar until light and fluffy. Beat in eggs, one at a time, beating well after each addition. Add vanilla. At low speed, gradually beat in flour mixture alternately with cocoa mixture, beginning and ending with flour mixture. Beat at medium speed 2 minutes. Pour batter into prepared pans.

4. Bake 25 minutes, or until tops spring back when lightly touched. Cool in pans on wire racks 10 minutes. Invert cakes onto racks. Carefully peel off paper. Cool completely, right side up.

5. *Make creamy fudge frosting:* Meanwhile, heat chocolate, confectioners' sugar and cream in a medium saucepan over medium heat, stirring constantly until smooth. Remove from heat; stir in vanilla. Transfer to a large mixer bowl and place in a larger bowl of ice water. Let stand, stirring occasionally, until cold and thick. Remove from ice bath. Gradually beat in butter at high speed; beat until frosting is fluffy and stiff enough to hold its shape.

6. Place 1 cake layer on a serving platter and spread with ¾ cup of the frosting. Top with second layer and another ¾ cup of the frosting. Top with third layer and spread top and sides with remaining frosting. Makes 12 servings.

Per serving: 570 calories, 37 g total fat, 22 g saturated fat, 139 mg cholesterol, 485 mg sodium, 57 g carbohydrates, 6 g protein, 129 mg calcium, 2 g fiber

bourbon-chocolate tipsy cake EASY

While this super-moist chocolate cake is sweet, it's not overwhelming. Plan to bake it at least a day ahead, as the flavor mellows with standing. Pictured on page 242.

Prep time: 25 minutes • Baking time: 70 to 75 minutes
Microwave used

- **2** cups all-purpose flour
- **1** teaspoon baking soda
- **½** teaspoon salt
- **1** tablespoon unsweetened cocoa

- **3** ounces unsweetened chocolate squares
- **2** ounces sweet baking chocolate
- **¼** cup instant coffee powder or espresso powder
- **2** tablespoons boiling water
- **½** cup plus 2 tablespoons bourbon, divided
- **1** cup unsalted butter, softened (no substitutes)
- **2** cups granulated sugar
- **3** large eggs
- **1½** teaspoons vanilla extract
- **1** tablespoon confectioners' sugar
  Fresh figs and sweetened whipped cream, for garnish (optional)

1. Heat oven to 325°F. Combine flour, baking soda and salt in a medium bowl. Butter a 12-cup fluted tube pan. Sift cocoa along bottom and sides of the pan to coat.

2. Combine unsweetened and sweet chocolates in a medium microwaveproof bowl. Microwave on HIGH 1½ minutes, until almost melted; stir until smooth. Cool slightly, 2 to 3 minutes.

3. Dissolve coffee powder in boiling water in a 2-cup glass measure; add enough cold water to equal 1½ cups. Stir in ½ cup of the bourbon.

4. Beat butter and granulated sugar in a large mixer bowl at medium-high speed until creamy. Beat in eggs, one at a time, beating well after each addition. Beat in melted chocolate and vanilla. At low speed, beat in flour mixture alternately with bourbon mixture, beginning and ending with flour mixture, just until blended. Pour batter into prepared pan.

5. Bake 70 to 75 minutes, until a toothpick inserted in center of cake comes out clean. Cool cake in pan on a wire rack 15 minutes. Invert onto rack, unmold and cool completely. Brush top and sides with remaining 2 tablespoons bourbon. *(Can be made ahead. Tightly wrap and store at room temperature up to 2 days.)*

6. *To serve:* Sift confectioners' sugar on top of cake. Serve with fresh figs and whipped cream, if desired. Makes 12 servings.

Per serving: 455 calories, 23 g total fat, 14 g saturated fat, 97 mg cholesterol, 223 mg sodium, 53 g carbohydrates, 5 g protein, 28 mg calcium, 2 g fiber

fudgy pudgy cake

Bake up three tender cake layers, spread a rich buttercream filling between each layer, then top with a chocolate-sour cream frosting. Heavenly bliss on a plate.

Prep time: 50 to 55 minutes plus chilling
Baking time: 20 to 25 minutes

- 2½ **cups sifted cake flour (not self-rising)**
- ½ **cup unsweetened cocoa**
- 2 **teaspoons baking soda**
- 1 **teaspoon baking powder**
- ¾ **teaspoon salt**
- 1 **box (16 oz.) brown sugar**
- ¾ **cup vegetable shortening**
- 3 **large eggs**
- 1½ **teaspoons vanilla extract**
- 1 **cup buttermilk**
- 1 **cup hot water**

BUTTERCREAM FILLING:

- 1 **cup milk**
- 2 **tablespoons cornstarch**
- ½ **cup butter or margarine, softened**
- ½ **cup vegetable shortening**
- 1 **cup granulated sugar**
- 1 **teaspoon vanilla extract**

CHOCOLATE-SOUR CREAM FROSTING:

- 16 **ounces milk chocolate, chopped**
- 12 **ounces semisweet chocolate squares, chopped**
- 2 **cups sour cream**
- 1 **teaspoon vanilla extract**
  Pinch salt

1. Heat oven to 350°F. Grease three 9-inch round cake pans. Line bottoms with waxed paper. Grease and flour paper; tap to remove excess flour.

2. Combine flour, cocoa, baking soda, baking powder and salt in a medium bowl. Gradually beat brown sugar into shortening in a mixer bowl until light and fluffy. Beat in eggs, one at a time, beating well after each addition. Add vanilla. At low speed, beat in flour mixture alternately with buttermilk,

beginning and ending with flour mixture, just until blended. Stir in hot water; beat at low speed just until blended. Pour batter into prepared pans.

3. Bake 20 to 25 minutes, until a toothpick inserted in center comes out clean. Cool in pans on wire racks 10 minutes. Invert cakes onto racks. Carefully peel off paper. Cool completely, right side up.

4. *Make buttercream filling:* Gradually whisk milk into cornstarch in a small saucepan until smooth. Cook over medium-low heat, whisking constantly, until mixture thickens and boils. Place saucepan in a large bowl of ice water, stirring occasionally, until cold. Beat butter and shortening in a mixer bowl until creamy. Beat in sugar until light and fluffy. Add cooled cornstarch mixture and vanilla; beat until creamy. Spread filling between layers. Refrigerate cake 30 minutes or until filling is firm.

5. *Make chocolate-sour cream frosting:* Heat milk chocolate and semisweet chocolate in a large saucepan over very low heat, stirring frequently, just until melted. Pour into a mixer bowl. At low speed, beat in sour cream, vanilla and salt until smooth. Let stand at room temperature until slightly thickened, about 1 hour. Spread over top and sides of cake. Makes 14 servings.

Per serving: 880 calories, 51.5 g total fat, 17.5 g saturated fat, 86 mg cholesterol, 513 mg sodium, 99 g carbohydrates, 10 g protein, 232 mg calcium, 3 g fiber

mocha angel food cake LOW FAT

Cold eggs are easier to separate; after separating the eggs, cover the mixer bowl of whites with plastic wrap. Egg whites that have been at room temperature for 20 to 30 minutes will produce a tall cake with a tender crumb. Pictured on page 245.

Prep time: 30 minutes · Baking time: 45 to 50 minutes

- 1½ **cups superfine sugar, divided**
- 1 **cup sifted cake flour (not self-rising)**
- ¼ **teaspoon salt**
- ½ **cup sifted unsweetened cocoa powder, preferably Dutch process**

½ cup warm brewed coffee

12 large egg whites, at room temperature 20 to 30 minutes

1½ teaspoons cream of tartar

■

Confectioners' sugar, fresh raspberries and strawberries, for garnish (optional)

1. Heat oven to 350°F. Sift 1 cup of the superfine sugar, the cake flour and salt three times into a bowl. Stir cocoa and coffee in a small bowl until smooth. Set aside.

2. Beat egg whites on medium-low speed in a large mixer bowl (preferably a standing mixer) until almost all the egg whites are foamy, 10 minutes (there will be a small amount of unbeaten whites at the bottom of the bowl). Add cream of tartar and increase speed to medium. When beaters begin to leave a ribbon pattern in whites, beat in the remaining ½ cup superfine sugar, 1 tablespoon at a time, until whites form soft peaks.

3. Sift half of the flour mixture over beaten whites. Gently fold in the flour mixture with a rubber spatula just until blended (flour does not have to be completely incorporated). Repeat with remaining half of flour mixture. Gently fold in cocoa mixture just until combined. Pour batter into an ungreased 10-inch tube pan. Gently run a long thin knife or metal spatula through the batter.

4. Bake 45 to 50 minutes, until top springs back and a wooden skewer inserted in center of cake comes out clean. Invert cake immediately onto the neck of a funnel or bottle. Let stand until completely cool, 1 hour. Run a sharp knife along the side of the pan and gently unmold. Then run knife along the bottom of pan and transfer cake to a large serving plate. Dust with confectioners' sugar and garnish with raspberries and strawberries, if desired. Makes 12 servings.

Per serving: 160 calories, 0.5 g total fat, 0 g saturated fat, 0 mg cholesterol, 104 mg sodium, 33 g carbohydrates, 5 g protein, 43 mg calcium, 0 g fiber

chocolate fudge cake

To achieve the perfect ultra-moist, dense texture, chill the cake overnight before serving.

Prep time: 25 minutes plus chilling
Baking time: 60 to 65 minutes

1 package (12 oz.) semisweet chocolate chips

5 tablespoons water

2 tablespoons instant coffee powder

1½ cups butter or margarine, softened

2 cups granulated sugar

6 large eggs, separated

1 cup all-purpose flour
  Confectioners' sugar

1. Heat oven to 350°F. Butter a 9-inch springform pan. Wrap the outside of the springform pan securely with heavy-duty foil.

2. Combine chocolate, water and coffee powder in a small saucepan and heat over very low heat, stirring occasionally, just until chocolate is melted. Cool to room temperature.

3. Beat butter in a mixer bowl until creamy. Beat in granulated sugar until light and fluffy, 5 minutes. Beat in egg yolks, one at a time, beating well after each addition. At low speed, gradually beat in flour. Stir in cooled chocolate mixture.

4. In a clean mixer bowl with clean beaters, beat egg whites until foamy. Gradually increase speed and beat until stiff but not dry. Fold into chocolate mixture. Pour into prepared pan.

5. Bake 60 to 65 minutes, until a toothpick inserted in cake about 1 inch from side comes out clean. (Top may crack.) Cool in pan on a wire rack. Cover and refrigerate overnight. Remove side of springform pan. Lightly sift confectioners' sugar over top of cake. Makes 14 to 16 servings.

Per serving: 445 calories, 28 g total fat, 16 g saturated fat, 138 mg cholesterol, 224 mg sodium, 40 g carbohydrates, 4 g protein, 18 mg calcium, 3 g fiber

classic german chocolate cake

This triple-layer cake originated in Texas and was named for Sam German, the man who developed the chocolate.

Prep time: 45 minutes plus cooling
Baking time: 30 to 35 minutes

1	bar (4 oz.) sweet baking chocolate, cut up
½	cup boiling water
¾	cup sour cream
¼	cup milk
2	cups all-purpose flour
1	teaspoon baking soda
½	teaspoon salt
1	cup butter or margarine, softened
1¾	cups sugar
4	large eggs, separated, at room temperature 20 to 30 minutes
1	teaspoon vanilla extract

FROSTING:

1	can (12 oz.) evaporated milk
1	cup sugar
¾	cup butter or margarine
1	teaspoon vanilla extract
4	large egg yolks, lightly beaten
1	package (7 oz.) shredded coconut
1½	cups pecans, toasted and finely chopped

1. Heat oven to 350°F. Butter three 9-inch round cake pans. Line bottoms with waxed paper. Butter and flour paper; tap to remove excess flour.

2. Stir chocolate and boiling water together in a small bowl until chocolate melts; cool. Stir sour cream and milk together in another small bowl. Combine flour, baking soda and salt in a medium bowl. Beat butter and sugar in a large mixer bowl until light and fluffy. Add egg yolks, one at a time, beating well after each addition. Gradually beat in melted chocolate and vanilla until smooth. At low speed, add flour mixture alternating with sour cream mixture, beginning and ending with the flour mixture.

3. Beat egg whites in a clean mixer bowl with clean beaters at medium-high speed until stiff but not dry. Gently fold into chocolate batter with a rubber spatula. Pour into prepared pans. Bake 30 to

35 minutes, until a toothpick inserted in center comes out clean. Cool in pans on wire racks 10 minutes. Invert cakes onto racks. Carefully peel off paper. Cool completely, right side up.

4. *Make frosting:* Heat 1 cup of the evaporated milk, the sugar, butter and vanilla in a large saucepan over medium-low heat until butter melts. Meanwhile, whisk together remaining evaporated milk and the egg yolks in a medium bowl; stir into saucepan with milk mixture. Cook, stirring, over medium heat until thickened, 8 to 10 minutes *(do not boil)*. Stir in coconut and pecans; transfer to a bowl and cool 15 minutes, stirring occasionally.

5. Place 1 cake layer on a serving platter and spread with one-quarter of the frosting. Top with second layer and spread with another one-quarter of the frosting. Top with third layer and spread top and sides with remaining frosting. Makes 16 servings.

Per serving: 610 calories, 41.5 g total fat, 20.5 g saturated fat, 175 mg cholesterol, 422 mg sodium, 55 g carbohydrates, 8 g protein, 108 mg calcium, 2 g fiber

fallen chocolate soufflé cake EASY

This flourless cake, which boasts a full pound of chocolate, owes its light texture to fluffy beaten eggs.

Prep time: 30 minutes plus chilling
Baking time: 25 to 30 minutes

8	ounces semisweet chocolate squares, coarsely chopped
8	ounces unsweetened chocolate squares, coarsely chopped
1	cup unsalted butter, cut up (no substitutes)
¼	cup orange- or coffee-flavored liqueur
9	large eggs, separated, at room temperature 20 to 30 minutes
¾	cup granulated sugar
	Confectioners' sugar
	Sweetened whipped cream and chocolate curls, for garnish (optional)

1. Heat oven to 350°F. Butter bottom of a 10-inch springform pan and line with parchment paper. Butter and flour paper and sides of pan. Melt chocolates and butter in top of a double boiler over simmering water. Cool to lukewarm. Stir in liqueur.

2. Beat egg yolks and granulated sugar in a large mixer bowl until pale and thick and a ribbon forms when beaters are lifted. Carefully fold in chocolate mixture using a rubber spatula. Using clean beaters, beat egg whites in a clean mixer bowl to soft peaks. Gently fold whites in three batches into chocolate mixture until blended. Pour into pan.

3. Bake 25 to 30 minutes, until cake is barely set in center. (Cake top will be cracked.) Cool on a wire rack. Cover and refrigerate cake at least 30 minutes or overnight. (If refrigerated overnight, let stand at room temperature 30 minutes before serving.)

4. Just before serving, run a small sharp knife around edge of pan; remove side of pan. Sprinkle top of cake with confectioners' sugar. Serve with whipped cream and chocolate curls, if desired. Makes 20 servings.

Per serving: 270 calories, 21.5 g total fat, 12.5 g saturated fat, 122 mg cholesterol, 30 mg sodium, 19 g carbohydrates, 5 g protein, 14 mg calcium, 2 g fiber

queen mother cake

This rich chocolate cake is fit for royalty, but you can make it at home and serve it at any occasion.

Prep time: 1 hour • Baking time: 45 to 50 minutes

- **6 ounces (1¼ cups) hazelnuts, toasted and skinned (see note, page 258)**
- **⅓ cup plus 2 tablespoons granulated sugar**
- **6 ounces semisweet chocolate squares, coarsely chopped**
- **2 ounces unsweetened chocolate squares, coarsely chopped**
- **½ cup heavy or whipping cream**
- **¾ cup unsalted butter, softened (no substitutes)**
- **⅓ cup firmly packed dark brown sugar**
- **Pinch salt**
- **6 large eggs, separated, at room temperature 20 to 30 minutes**
- **2 tablespoons hazelnut-flavored liqueur**

GLAZE:
- **3 ounces semisweet chocolate squares, coarsely chopped**

- **¼ cup unsalted butter, softened (no substitutes)**
- **1 tablespoon water**

  ▪

  Mint leaves and candied violets, for garnish (optional)

1. Heat oven to 350°F. Combine cooled hazelnuts and 1 tablespoon of the granulated sugar in a food processor; pulse until mixture is finely ground.

2. Heat semisweet chocolate, unsweetened chocolate and heavy cream in a small saucepan over low heat, stirring occasionally, until melted and smooth. Cool.

3. Butter a 9-inch springform pan. Line bottom with waxed paper. Butter and flour paper; tap to remove excess flour. Beat butter, ⅓ cup of the granulated sugar, the brown sugar and salt together in a large mixer bowl until light and fluffy. Beat in egg yolks, two at a time, beating well after each addition. Add cooled chocolate mixture and liqueur and beat just until blended. Stir in nut mixture.

4. Beat egg whites in a clean mixer bowl with clean beaters to soft peaks. Gradually beat in remaining 1 tablespoon granulated sugar; beat just until stiff. Gently fold egg whites into chocolate batter with a rubber spatula just until blended. Pour batter into prepared pan.

5. Bake 45 to 50 minutes, until center of cake is puffed and firm. Cool on a wire rack 20 minutes. Remove side of pan and invert cake onto rack. Remove bottom of pan, carefully peel off paper and cool completely.

6. *Make glaze:* Combine chocolate, butter and water in a small saucepan. Heat, stirring occasionally, over low heat until chocolate is melted and glaze is smooth.

7. Pour warm glaze over cake on rack, smoothing top and sides with a thin, metal spatula. Let stand at room temperature until glaze is firm, 2 hours or overnight. Garnish cake with mint leaves and candied violets, if desired. Makes 20 servings.

Per serving: 295 calories, 24.5 g total fat, 11.5 g saturated fat, 98 mg cholesterol, 161 mg sodium, 18 g carbohydrates, 5 g protein, 29 mg calcium, 2 g fiber

chocolate truffle torte 🅴🅰🆂🆈

It's hard to believe this silky torte is made without butter. The trick: We replaced some chocolate with cocoa and substituted evaporated skim milk for heavy cream. If you like, prepare the torte 1 or 2 days ahead and refrigerate. Serve at room temperature. Pictured on page 244.

Prep time: 20 minutes • Baking time: 30 minutes
Microwave used

> Vegetable cooking spray
> 3 ounces semisweet chocolate squares
> 1 ounce unsweetened chocolate square
> ⅓ cup unsweetened cocoa
> 1 cup sugar, divided
> ½ cup evaporated skim milk
> 2 large egg yolks
> ½ teaspoon vanilla extract
> 3 large egg whites, at room temperature 20 to 30 minutes
> 2 tablespoons flour

CHOCOLATE GLAZE:

> 2 ounces semisweet chocolate squares
> 2 tablespoons evaporated skim milk
> 1 teaspoon light corn syrup
> 1 teaspoon brandy (optional)
> ▪
> Fresh raspberries, for garnish (optional)

1. Heat oven to 350°F. Line bottom of an 8-inch springform pan or 8-inch cake pan with removable bottom with waxed paper or a nonstick bakeware liner.* Lightly coat bottom and sides of pan with vegetable cooking spray. Wrap outside of pan securely with heavy-duty foil.

2. Combine semisweet and unsweetened chocolates in a large microwaveproof bowl. Microwave on HIGH 1½ to 2 minutes; stir until smooth.

3. Combine cocoa and ¾ cup of the sugar in a small saucepan. Whisk in evaporated milk. Cook 2 minutes over medium heat, whisking constantly, until smooth. Stir cocoa mixture into melted chocolate until smooth; stir in yolks and vanilla.

4. Beat whites in a large mixer bowl at medium speed until foamy. Gradually beat in remaining ¼ cup sugar. Increase speed to high and beat just until stiff but not dry. With a rubber spatula, gently fold whites into chocolate mixture, one-third at a time. Fold in flour. Spread in the prepared pan. Place springform pan in a large baking pan. *(Make sure there is at least 1 inch of space between springform and baking pan.)* Place baking pan on oven rack. Carefully pour enough hot water into baking pan to reach 1 inch up side of springform pan. Bake 30 minutes. Remove springform pan from water; cool 10 minutes on wire rack. Discard foil. Remove side of pan and cool cake completely.

5. *Make chocolate glaze:* Melt chocolate in a medium microwaveproof bowl on HIGH 1½ to 2 minutes; stir until smooth. Stir in evaporated skim milk and corn syrup until well blended; add brandy, if desired. Pour glaze over top of cake, spreading over top and sides. Garnish with raspberries, if desired. Makes 8 servings.

*Note: Nonstick bakeware liners can be purchased at baking specialty shops, or by calling Wilton Enterprises, 800-794-5866. Ask for 8-inch parchment circles.

Per serving: 260 calories, 9.5 g total fat, 5 g saturated fat, 54 mg cholesterol, 47 mg sodium, 41 g carbohydrates, 6 g protein, 107 mg calcium, 2 g fiber

chocolate-hazelnut ice-cream torte

Prepared hazelnut spread (available in the supermarket in either the baking section or the peanut butter, jams and jellies aisle) is layered between chocolate sponge cake, along with toasted almonds and vanilla and coffee ice creams. Tip: Store the cake in the back of the freezer, where it's coldest. To serve, soften it in the refrigerator 15 to 20 minutes before cutting. Pictured on page 243.

Prep time: 50 minutes plus freezing
Baking time: 17 to 18 minutes
Microwave used

CHOCOLATE SPONGE CAKE:

> ½ cup all-purpose flour
> ½ cup unsweetened cocoa
> 2 tablespoons cornstarch
> ¼ teaspoon salt

3 large eggs
3 large egg yolks
⅔ cup granulated sugar

1 jar (13 oz.) hazelnut spread
⅔ cup blanched slivered almonds, toasted
2 pints premium vanilla ice cream
1 pint premium coffee ice cream

CHOCOLATE SAUCE:

1 package (6 oz.) semisweet chocolate chips
4 tablespoons butter or margarine
1 tablespoon light corn syrup
3 tablespoons heavy or whipping cream
1 tablespoon coffee-flavored liqueur

Confectioners' sugar
Fresh strawberries, for garnish (optional)

1. *Make chocolate sponge cake:* Heat oven to 350°F. Grease bottom of a 9-inch springform pan; line with foil. Sift flour, cocoa, cornstarch and salt in a medium bowl.

2. Beat eggs, egg yolks and granulated sugar in a large mixer bowl at high speed until doubled in volume and ribbon forms when beaters are lifted, 5 minutes. Gently fold flour mixture into beaten egg mixture with a rubber spatula until well blended. Spread evenly in prepared pan. Bake 17 to 18 minutes, until a toothpick inserted 2 inches from edge of pan comes out almost clean. *(Center will be slightly soft.)* Place cake pan on a wire rack; cover with a clean kitchen towel. Cool.

3. Uncover and run a knife around edge of cake; detach springform ring. Invert cake onto a flat plate. Remove bottom of pan; peel off foil. Reattach springform ring to bottom and line the inside of the springform pan with plastic wrap, allowing wrap to extend 5 inches over top rim.

4. Using a long, serrated knife, split cake horizontally in half. Invert top cake layer and gently press into bottom of prepared pan. Spread cake in pan with half (⅔ cup) of the hazelnut spread; sprinkle with ⅓ cup of the almonds. Place in freezer for 15 minutes. Spread remaining hazelnut spread on cut side of other half of cake. Sprinkle with remaining almonds. Refrigerate.

5. Meanwhile, refrigerate 1 pint of the vanilla ice cream 15 minutes to soften. Remove cake layer from freezer. Spread softened vanilla ice cream over top; freeze 30 minutes, until firm. Refrigerate coffee ice cream 15 minutes to soften; spread evenly over vanilla layer. Freeze 30 minutes, until firm.

6. Soften remaining pint of vanilla ice cream 15 minutes; spread over coffee layer. Invert refrigerated cake layer and press, nut side down, over ice cream. Cover top of pan with foil; freeze at least 3 hours, or until firm. *(Can be made ahead. Wrap well and freeze up to 1 week.)*

7. *Make chocolate sauce:* Combine all sauce ingredients in a small saucepan over medium-low heat, stirring occasionally, until chocolate and butter are melted and mixture is smooth. *(Can be made ahead. Transfer to a small microwaveproof bowl. Cover and refrigerate overnight. Uncover and microwave on HIGH 1 to 1½ minutes, until smooth.)*

8. Remove cake from freezer; uncover and detach springform ring. Peel off plastic wrap; remove bottom of pan and place cake on a serving plate. Run a small knife along side of cake to smooth ice cream. Refrigerate 10 to 15 minutes before serving. Sprinkle top with confectioners' sugar. Serve with chocolate sauce and garnish with strawberries, if desired. Makes 16 servings.

Per serving: 490 calories, 29.5 g total fat, 11.5 g saturated fat, 145 mg cholesterol, 149 mg sodium, 47 g carbohydrates, 8 g protein, 135 mg calcium, 2 g fiber

test kitchen tip

long live chocolate...

As long as basic conditions are met, solid chocolate can be stored and used for up to 1 year if it's wrapped well and kept in a cool (55°F. to 65°F.), dry place. Chocolate sometimes develops a pale gray discoloration known as "bloom," which is a result of the cocoa butter rising to the surface. This doesn't mean the chocolate is spoiled—the flavor and quality will not be significantly affected.

chocolate-almond terrine with raspberry puree

This gorgeous terrine is the perfect dessert for chocolate lovers, and all you need is a standard loaf pan to make it. The raspberry puree with almond liqueur is a light and refreshing counterpoint to the chocolate.

Total prep time: 40 minutes plus chilling and freezing

CHOCOLATE TERRINE:

- 3 large egg yolks
- 2 cups heavy or whipping cream, divided
- 2 boxes (8 oz. each) semisweet chocolate squares, coarsely chopped
- ½ cup light corn syrup
- ½ cup butter or margarine, cut up
- ¼ cup confectioners' sugar
- 1 teaspoon vanilla extract
- ¼ teaspoon almond extract

RASPBERRY PUREE:

- 1 bag (12 oz.) frozen raspberries, thawed
- 2 tablespoons granulated sugar
- ¼ cup light corn syrup
- 2 tablespoons almond-flavored liqueur

- 1 tablespoon unsweetened cocoa
- 1 teaspoon confectioners' sugar
  Fresh raspberries and mint leaves, for garnish (optional)

1. Line bottom and sides of an 8½×4½-inch loaf pan with plastic wrap.

2. *Make chocolate terrine:* Whisk egg yolks and ½ cup of the cream in a small bowl. Combine chocolate, corn syrup and butter in 3-quart saucepan. Cook over medium heat, stirring, until chocolate is melted. Stir in egg mixture and cook 3 minutes more, stirring constantly, until mixture is slightly thickened; transfer to a large bowl. Refrigerate chocolate mixture 20 minutes, stirring every 5 minutes, until cooled to room temperature.

3. At medium-high speed, beat remaining 1½ cups cream, the confectioners' sugar, vanilla and almond extracts in a mixer bowl to soft peaks. With a rubber spatula, fold into chocolate mixture until thoroughly combined. Pour into prepared pan; smooth top with a spatula. Cover and freeze overnight. *(Can be made ahead. Cover and freeze up to 2 weeks.)*

4. *Make raspberry puree:* Puree raspberries and sugar in a blender. Strain through a fine sieve into a bowl; discard the seeds. Stir in corn syrup and liqueur. *(Can be made ahead. Cover and refrigerate up to 3 days.)*

5. *To serve:* Combine cocoa and confectioners' sugar in a cup. Uncover top of terrine and place serving platter on top of pan. Holding bottom of platter and pan, invert terrine and remove pan. Carefully peel off plastic wrap. Smooth top and sides of terrine with a spatula; sift cocoa-sugar mixture evenly over top. Garnish with raspberries and mint leaves, if desired. Serve with raspberry puree. Makes 12 servings.

Per serving: 510 calories, 36.5 g total fat, 21.5 g saturated fat, 130 mg cholesterol, 124 mg sodium, 46 g carbohydrates, 5 g protein, 40 mg calcium, 3 g fiber

hazelnut-truffle cheesecake

Hazelnuts, sometimes called filberts, have a mild, sweet flavor and may be covered with a thin, brown skin.

Prep time: 50 minutes plus chilling
Baking time: 60 to 65 minutes

CRUST:

- ½ cup hazelnuts, toasted and skinned (see note, page 258)
- 2 tablespoons sugar
- ½ cup all-purpose flour
  Pinch salt
- ¼ cup cold unsalted butter, cut up (no substitutes)

FILLING:

- 3 packages (8 oz. each) cream cheese or Neufchâtel cheese, at room temperature
- 1¼ cups sugar
- 12 ounces bittersweet or semisweet chocolate squares, melted and cooled (see tip, page 259)

2 teaspoons vanilla extract

 Pinch salt

4 large eggs, at room temperature 20 to
 30 minutes

¾ cup heavy or whipping cream

2 tablespoons unsweetened cocoa

20 whole hazelnuts, toasted and skinned
 (see note, page 258)

2 ounces bittersweet or semisweet chocolate
 squares, melted (see tip, page 259)

1. Adjust oven rack to center of oven. Heat oven
to 350°F.

2. *Make crust:* Butter a 9-inch springform pan.
Combine cooled hazelnuts and 2 tablespoons sugar
in a food processor; pulse until finely ground. Add
flour and salt to nuts; pulse to blend. Add butter
and pulse until mixture resembles fine crumbs and
just begins to hold together. Pat crumbs evenly over
bottom of prepared pan. Bake 20 to 25 minutes,
until top is golden. Cool on a wire rack. Keep oven
on. Wrap the outside of the springform pan
securely with heavy-duty foil.

3. *Make filling:* Meanwhile, beat cream cheese in a
large mixer bowl at medium-high speed until light
and fluffy, 2 minutes. Gradually beat in sugar,
scraping sides of bowl with a rubber spatula, until
mixture is completely smooth, 3 minutes. Reduce
speed to medium. Beat in chocolate, vanilla and
salt. Add eggs, one at a time, beating just until
blended after each addition. Combine cream and
cocoa; stir into batter.

4. Pour filling over crust in springform pan and
place in a large roasting pan. *(Make sure there is at
least 1 inch of space between edge of springform and
roasting pan.)* Place roasting pan on oven rack.
Carefully pour enough hot water into roasting pan
to reach 1 inch up side of springform pan. Bake
60 to 65 minutes, until center is just set.

5. Remove springform pan from water. Cool
cheesecake completely on a wire rack. Discard foil.
Cover and refrigerate cheesecake overnight.

6. Just before serving, run a small, sharp knife
around edge of pan; remove side of pan. Dip each
whole hazelnut halfway into the 2 ounces melted
chocolate and arrange decoratively around edge of
cake. Drizzle or pipe remaining chocolate over cake.
Makes 20 servings.

Per serving: 380 calories, 28.5 g total fat, 15.5 g saturated fat,
99 mg cholesterol, 133 mg sodium, 29 g carbohydrates,
6 g protein, 58 mg calcium, 2 g fiber

test kitchen tip

champion cheesecakes

*A cheesecake is a guaranteed crowd-pleaser. Here
are our strategies for ensuring a rich, creamy,
smooth and crack-free beauty:*

FOR EASY MIXING, let your ingredients
stand at room temperature for 20 to
30 minutes before you begin.

AVOID LUMPY BATTER by making sure the
cheese and sugar are thoroughly blended
before adding any other ingredients. It is
difficult to smooth out lumps in the
cheesecake batter once it has been thinned.

DO NOT OVERBEAT THE BATTER,
especially after adding the eggs. This can cause
the cake to puff up, then fall or crack.

USE A WATERBATH. Cracks are caused by
fluctuations inside and outside of the oven.
Using the waterbath, as directed in our
cheesecake recipes, provides uniform heat. The
moist heat also helps ensure a rich, creamy
texture. Tip: Wrap the springform pan with
heavy-duty foil to make it watertight. To help
avoid spilling hot water into the cheesecake
batter, use a teapot or a large liquid measure
when adding the water to the roasting pan.

AVOID OVERBAKING, which can cause the
cheesecake to dry out and crack. Check the
cheesecake for doneness at the minimum
baking time. The center should be just set.
Never use a knife or toothpick test—while they
may work for a regular cake, these methods
can cause a cheesecake to crack.

triple layer cheesecake

Three delicious layers—one outstanding dessert.

Prep time: 45 minutes plus freezing and chilling
Baking time: 1½ hours

CRUST:
- ¾ cup (15 cookies) chocolate wafer crumbs
- 1 tablespoon butter or margarine, melted

FILLING:
- 4 packages (8 oz. each) cream cheese or Neufchâtel cheese, at room temperature
- 1¾ cups sugar
- 1 teaspoon vanilla extract
  Pinch salt
- 4 large eggs, at room temperature 20 to 30 minutes
- 1 teaspoon instant espresso powder dissolved in 1 tablespoon hot water
- 3 ounces unsweetened chocolate squares, melted and cooled (see tip, page 259)

1. *Make crust:* Heat oven to 350°F. Butter an 8-inch springform pan. Combine cookie crumbs and butter in a small bowl until crumbs are evenly moistened. Pat crumbs evenly over bottom of the prepared pan. Bake 10 minutes. Cool on a wire rack. Wrap the outside of the springform pan securely with heavy-duty foil.

2. *Make filling:* Meanwhile, beat cream cheese in a large mixer bowl at medium-high speed until light and fluffy, 2 minutes. Gradually beat in sugar, scraping sides of bowl, until mixture is completely smooth, 3 minutes. Reduce speed to medium; beat in vanilla and salt. Add eggs, one at a time, beating just until blended after each addition. Place 2 cups of the cream cheese filling in a medium bowl and fold in espresso mixture with a rubber spatula. Pour over crust in pan and freeze until firm, 1½ hours.

3. Meanwhile, place another 1¾ cups of the cream cheese filling in a medium bowl and fold in melted chocolate. *(Cover and refrigerate chocolate filling and remaining vanilla filling until ready to use.)* Carefully spread chocolate filling over chilled coffee layer and freeze 30 minutes.

4. Heat oven to 350°F. Spread remaining vanilla filling over chocolate layer. Place springform pan in a large roasting pan. *(Make sure there is at least 1 inch of space between edge of springform and roasting pan.)* Place roasting pan on oven rack. Carefully pour enough hot water into roasting pan to reach 1 inch up side of springform pan. Bake 1½ hours, or until center is just set. Remove springform pan from water. Cool cheesecake completely on a wire rack. Discard foil. Cover; refrigerate overnight. Just before serving, run a knife around edge of pan; remove side of pan. Makes 16 servings.

Per serving: 360 calories, 25.5 g total fat, 15.5 g saturated fat, 117 mg cholesterol, 234 mg sodium, 28 g carbohydrates, 7 g protein, 58 mg calcium, 1 g fiber

chocolate-caramel cheesecake

There's a good reason this cheesecake is featured on the cover—it's picture perfect and decadently delicious, too.

Prep time: 1 hour 15 minutes plus freezing and chilling
Baking time: 55 minutes

CRUST:
- ⅓ cup hazelnuts, toasted and skinned (see note, page 258)
- 1 tablespoon sugar
- ¾ cup (15 cookies) chocolate wafer crumbs
- 3 tablespoons butter or margarine, melted
- ¼ teaspoon espresso powder

- 1 cup sugar
- ⅓ cup water
- ½ cup heavy or whipping cream
- 3 packages (8 oz. each) cream cheese, at room temperature
- 3 large eggs, at room temperature 20 to 30 minutes
- 1 large yolk, at room temperature 20 to 30 minutes
- 2 teaspoons vanilla extract
- 6 ounces bittersweet or semisweet chocolate squares, melted and cooled (see tip, page 259)

1 teaspoon espresso powder dissolved in
1 teaspoon hot water

CARAMEL SAUCE:

1½ cups sugar

½ cup water

1 cup heavy or whipping cream

■

16 whole hazelnuts

1 ounce bittersweet or semisweet chocolate
square, melted (see tip, page 259)

1. *Make crust:* Heat oven to 350°F. Combine cooled hazelnuts and sugar in a food processor; pulse until finely ground. Add cookie crumbs, butter and espresso powder; pulse until evenly moistened. Press evenly over bottom of a 9-inch springform pan. Bake until firm to the touch, 8 to 10 minutes. Cool on a wire rack. Wrap outside of the springform pan securely with heavy-duty foil.

2. To make caramel mixture, combine sugar and water in a small saucepan. Cook over medium heat, stirring, until sugar dissolves. Increase heat to medium-high and cook mixture until it is golden amber in color. *(Do not stir after increasing the heat.)* Remove saucepan from heat and carefully stir in a little of the cream with a long-handled spoon (mixture will be bubbly). When bubbles subside, stir in remainder of the cream until smooth. Pour into a glass measure and let stand until cooled to room temperature.

3. Meanwhile, beat cream cheese in a large mixer bowl at medium speed (medium-high for handheld mixer) until light and fluffy, about 5 minutes. Gradually beat in caramel mixture. Add eggs and egg yolk, one at a time, beating well after each addition, scraping sides of bowl until blended. Beat in vanilla. Transfer 2½ cups of the cream cheese mixture to a small bowl and refrigerate. Beat chocolate and espresso mixture into remaining cheese mixture until smooth. Pour chocolate filling into cooled crust. Place in freezer 30 minutes.

4. Pour reserved caramel-cream cheese mixture over chocolate layer. Place springform pan in large roasting pan. *(Make sure there is at least 1 inch of space between edge of springform and roasting pan.)* Place roasting pan on oven rack. Carefully pour enough boiling water into roasting pan to reach halfway up side of springform pan. Bake

55 minutes, until center is just set. Remove from oven. Let cheesecake stand in water 30 minutes. Remove cheesecake from water; cool on a wire rack to room temperature. Cover; refrigerate 5 hours. *(Can be made ahead. Cover and refrigerate overnight.)*

5. *Make caramel sauce:* Combine sugar and water in a small saucepan. Cook over medium heat, stirring, until sugar dissolves. Increase heat to medium-high and cook mixture until it is golden amber in color. *(Do not stir after increasing heat.)* Remove saucepan from heat and carefully stir in a little of the cream with a long-handled spoon (mixture will be bubbly). When bubbles subside, stir in remainder of the cream until smooth. Pour into a bowl and let stand until cool. Remove side of springform pan. Dip each whole hazelnut halfway into melted chocolate; place on top of cheesecake. Serve cheesecake with sauce. Makes 16 servings.

Per serving: 495 calories, 34.5 g total fat, 19.5 g saturated fat, 137 mg cholesterol, 204 mg sodium, 44 g carbohydrates, 7 g protein, 67 mg calcium, 2 g fiber

rich hot chocolate

Prefer it sweeter? Add extra sugar. Pictured on page 245.

Total prep time: 10 minutes

1 ounce imported bittersweet chocolate

2 tablespoons Dutch process unsweetened cocoa

2 tablespoons sugar

1 pint half-and-half cream, divided
Whipped cream (optional)

Break chocolate into 1-inch pieces; set aside. Combine cocoa and sugar in a small saucepan. Gradually stir in 3 tablespoons of the cream to make a paste. Add chocolate pieces. Heat chocolate and cocoa paste over medium-low heat, stirring until melted. Whisk in remaining cream. Increase heat to medium-high; heat until hot and small bubbles appear around edge of pan. Top with whipped cream, if desired. Makes 2 servings.

Per serving: 445 calories, 33.5 g total fat, 20.5 g saturated fat, 89 mg cholesterol, 137 mg sodium, 33 g carbohydrates, 9 g protein, 265 mg calcium, 0 g fiber

brownie-almond tart

Heavy cream and corn syrup added to brownie batter create a satiny filling for this easy-to-make tart with a cookie crust. Serve in small slivers with berries. Pictured on page 243.

Prep time: 35 minutes plus chilling and standing
Baking time: 35 to 40 minutes
Microwave used

ALMOND CRUST:
  5 **tablespoons butter or margarine**
  ⅓ **cup confectioners' sugar**
  ⅔ **cup all-purpose flour**
  ¼ **cup ground, toasted almonds**

CHOCOLATE FILLING:
  2 **ounces unsweetened chocolate squares**
  ½ **cup butter or margarine, cut up**
  ½ **cup granulated sugar**
  3 **large eggs**
  ⅓ **cup heavy or whipping cream**
  ⅓ **cup light corn syrup**
  1 **tablespoon flour**
  1 **teaspoon vanilla extract**
  ¼ **teaspoon salt**

  1 **tablespoon confectioners' sugar**

CHOCOLATE DRIZZLE:
  1 **ounce semisweet chocolate square, chopped**
  1 **teaspoon butter or margarine**

     Fresh raspberries, for garnish (optional)

1. *Make almond crust:* Heat oven to 350°F. Beat butter in a large mixer bowl on medium speed until creamy; beat in confectioners' sugar. At low speed, beat in remaining crust ingredients until coarse crumbs form. Press into bottom of an 8-inch springform pan. Bake 20 minutes until lightly browned. Cool 10 minutes on a wire rack.

2. *Make chocolate filling:* Meanwhile, melt chocolate and butter in a medium microwaveproof

bowl on HIGH 1 to 1½ minutes; stir until smooth. Whisk in remaining filling ingredients.

3. Pour filling over almond crust. Bake 35 to 40 minutes, until a toothpick inserted in center comes out barely clean. Cool in pan on a wire rack. *(Can be made ahead. Cover and freeze up to 1 month.)* Run knife around edge; remove side of pan. Dust top of brownie with confectioners' sugar.

4. *Make chocolate drizzle:* Place chocolate and butter in a small microwaveproof bowl and microwave on HIGH 1 to 1½ minutes, until melted. Stir until smooth. Cool slightly.

5. Spoon melted chocolate into a plastic storage bag; cut a very small hole in one corner and drizzle over top of tart. Let stand until chocolate is set, about 30 minutes. Cut into 12 wedges. Serve with raspberries, if desired. Makes 12 servings.

Per serving: 310 calories, 22 g total fat, 12.5 g saturated fat, 99 mg cholesterol, 216 mg sodium, 28 g carbohydrates, 4 g protein, 26 mg calcium, 1 g fiber

chocolate pecan tart

This decadent tart ensures that chocolate lovers get their fill. But don't worry, the fabulous praline topping will satisfy classic pecan pie fans, too. Pictured on page 243.

Prep time: 20 minutes plus chilling
Baking time: 13 to 17 minutes

PASTRY:
  1¼ **cups all-purpose flour**
  ½   **cup plus 2 tablespoons confectioners' sugar**
  3   **tablespoons unsweetened cocoa**
      Pinch salt
  ½   **cup plus 2 tablespoons butter, cut up (no substitutes)**
  1   **large egg yolk**

FILLING:
  8 **ounces semisweet chocolate squares**
  1 **cup heavy or whipping cream**

PRALINE TOPPING:

- **1** cup granulated sugar
- **⅓** cup water
- **1⅓** cups pecan halves, toasted

1. *Make pastry:* Pulse flour, confectioners' sugar, cocoa and salt in a food processor to combine. Add butter and pulse until mixture resembles coarse crumbs. Add egg yolk, pulsing until mixture begins to hold together. Press pastry evenly along the bottom and side of a 9½-inch tart pan with removable bottom. Cover and refrigerate the pastry 40 minutes.

2. Heat oven to 375°F. Line pastry shell with foil and fill with dried beans or pie weights. Bake 8 minutes; remove foil and beans. Bake crust 5 to 9 minutes more, or until pastry is firm. Cool on a wire rack.

3. *Make filling:* Finely chop chocolate; transfer to a medium bowl. Bring cream to boil in a small saucepan over medium heat. Pour over chocolate. Let stand 5 minutes. Stir until smooth and all the chocolate is melted. Pour filling into cooled crust. Refrigerate tart until filling is firm, 2 hours. *(Can be made ahead. Cover loosely and refrigerate overnight. Let stand at room temperature 1 hour before serving.)*

4. *Make praline topping:* Grease a jelly-roll pan. Bring sugar and water to boil in a medium saucepan over medium heat. Increase heat to medium-high and continue to cook until syrup turns amber in color, 8 to 10 minutes. Remove from heat; when bubbles subside, stir in pecans. Immediately pour praline mixture into prepared pan. Let stand until cool, 45 minutes. Chop praline topping into small pieces. *(Can be made ahead. Store praline topping in an airtight container up to 1 week.)* Sprinkle praline topping over tart. Makes 10 servings.

Per serving: 560 calories, 37.5 g total fat, 18 g saturated fat, 85 mg cholesterol, 144 mg sodium, 58 g carbohydrates, 5 g protein, 38 mg calcium, 3 g fiber

---

test kitchen tip

chocolate chronicles

Ever wonder how cherished chocolate came to be? Here is the history of this sweet treasure:

BEAN ME UP: Chocolate is made from cacao beans, a.k.a. cocoa beans, which are found in the pods (or fruit) of the cocoa tree. According to Hershey Foods Corporation, the scientific name of this fruit is "Theobroma Cacao," which literally means "food of the gods."

CHEERS TO THE CHOCOLATE DRINK: The first chocolate was actually a chocolate drink, which can be traced back to the ancient Mayan and Aztec civilizations in Central America. Legend has it that this drink—made from roasted cocoa beans—was first consumed by Hernando Cortez in 1519. He later brought the cocoa beans back to Spain, where the chocolate drink was made with added sweeteners. Its popularity spread to France and England in the 1600s, and the first chocolate factory opened in Massachusetts in 1765.

MODERN CHOCOLATE: Milk chocolate wasn't invented until the next century when, in 1876, a Swiss candymaker named Daniel Peter added condensed milk to chocolate liquor. Much credit also goes to Milton Hershey, who founded the Hershey Chocolate Company in 1894; he is responsible for the mass production of a chocolate bar that working people could afford. Of course, now there are a multitude of chocolate manufacturers—and products—both throughout the United States and worldwide.

peanut butter silk pie 🥧

A reader asked us to obtain the recipe for this pie, which she had described as "the most scrumptious dessert ever." It comes from the Sea Cow Eatery in Edisto Beach, South Carolina, and the restaurant was kind enough to share it with our readers. While the eatery uses a homemade pastry crust, our version calls for a prepared chocolate cookie crumb crust to make this an entirely no-bake treat. Pictured on page 248.

Total prep time: 10 minutes plus chilling
Microwave used

FILLING:
- 1 package (8 oz.) cream cheese, softened
- 1 cup sugar
- 1 cup creamy peanut butter
- 1 tablespoon butter or margarine, melted
- 1 teaspoon vanilla extract
- 1 cup heavy or whipping cream, beaten until stiff

- 1 (9-inch) prepared chocolate cookie-crumb crust

TOPPING:
- 1 cup semisweet chocolate chips
- 3 tablespoons brewed coffee
- Chopped peanuts, for garnish (optional)

1. *Make filling:* Beat cream cheese, sugar, peanut butter, butter and vanilla in a large mixer bowl, until creamy. Gently fold in half of the beaten cream. Fold in remaining cream until blended. Spread filling in prepared crust; smooth top.

2. *Make topping:* Combine chips and coffee in a microwaveproof bowl. Cover with plastic wrap. Microwave on HIGH 1½ to 2 minutes; stir until smooth. Cool chocolate slightly. Pour over top of filling. Refrigerate pie 1 hour until chocolate is firm. Cover loosely and refrigerate overnight. Sprinkle with chopped peanuts, if desired. Makes 8 servings.

Per serving: 715 calories, 50 g total fat, 21 g saturated fat, 76 mg cholesterol, 362 mg sodium, 60 g carbohydrates, 14 g protein, 60 mg calcium, 2 g fiber

old-fashioned chocolate cream pie 🥧

A dark chocolate pudding in a crisp crust, topped off with sweetened whipped cream, takes you on a luscious trip down Memory Lane.

Total prep time: 20 minutes plus chilling

FILLING:
- 1 cup granulated sugar
- ¼ cup cornstarch
- ¼ teaspoon salt
- 2¾ cups milk
- 3 large egg yolks
- 3 ounces unsweetened chocolate squares, coarsely chopped
- 1 tablespoon butter or margarine
- 1 teaspoon vanilla extract

- 1 single 9-inch baked pastry crust

- 1 cup heavy or whipping cream
- 2 tablespoons confectioners' sugar

1. *Make filling:* Combine granulated sugar, cornstarch and salt in a large saucepan. Gradually whisk in milk until smooth. Bring to boil over medium-high heat, stirring constantly; boil 1 minute. Remove saucepan from heat.

2. Lightly beat egg yolks in a small bowl. Gradually whisk in 1 cup of the hot filling; return to same saucepan, whisking constantly. Return to boil and boil 1 minute more. Remove from heat; whisk in chocolate, butter and vanilla until completely smooth. Pour filling into baked pastry crust. Cool 15 minutes on a wire rack. Cover surface of filling with waxed paper or plastic wrap and refrigerate at least 3 hours.

3. Just before serving, beat cream and sugar in a large chilled mixer bowl to stiff peaks. Remove waxed paper from filling and spread whipped cream over pie. Makes 8 servings.

Per serving: 495 calories, 31 g total fat, 15 g saturated fat, 131 mg cholesterol, 213 mg sodium, 51 g carbohydrates, 7 g protein, 142 mg calcium, 2 g fiber

rich chocolate pudding

How did we manage to improve on this delicious all-time favorite? First, we used bittersweet chocolate to give the pudding an exceptionally intense flavor; next, we adjusted the mix of whole milk and heavy cream for a particularly satiny texture. Tip: Chill the pudding thoroughly before serving.

Prep time: 15 minutes plus chilling
Cooking time: 12 minutes

3½	ounces bittersweet chocolate squares or 1 bar (3.5 oz.) imported bittersweet chocolate
1	cup heavy or whipping cream
⅔	cup plus 1 tablespoon whole milk, divided
3	large egg yolks
⅓	cup granulated sugar
2¾	teaspoons cornstarch
1	tablespoon butter (no substitutes)
1	teaspoon vanilla extract
	Pinch salt

WHIPPED CREAM:

1	cup heavy or whipping cream
1	tablespoon confectioners' sugar

Chocolate shavings, for garnish (optional)

1. Coarsely chop chocolate; set aside. Heat cream and ⅔ cup of the milk in a medium saucepan over medium heat, 4 minutes, until small bubbles appear around edge of pan.

2. Meanwhile, whisk egg yolks and granulated sugar in a bowl. Stir remaining 1 tablespoon milk into cornstarch in a cup until smooth.

3. Gradually whisk half of the hot cream mixture into yolk mixture. Whisk egg mixture into hot cream in saucepan. Whisk in cornstarch-milk mixture. Bring to boil, stirring, over medium heat; boil 1 minute, until mixture is thick enough to coat the back of a spoon.

4. Remove pan from heat. Add chocolate, butter, vanilla and salt to hot cream mixture and stir until chocolate is melted and pudding is smooth. Strain pudding through a fine sieve into a bowl. Press a piece of plastic wrap directly on surface of pudding. Refrigerate until cold, 4 hours. *(Can be made ahead. Refrigerate overnight.)*

5. *Make whipped cream:* Place a large mixer bowl and beaters in freezer 10 minutes. Beat cream in bowl on medium-high speed 2 minutes, until thickened. Add confectioners' sugar and beat 1½ to 2 minutes more to soft peaks.

6. Divide and spoon pudding into 6 dessert cups or glasses. Serve pudding topped with whipped cream and garnish with chocolate shavings, if desired. Makes 6 servings.

Per serving without whipped cream: 330 calories, 26 g total fat, 15 g saturated fat, 170 mg cholesterol, 57 mg sodium, 24 g carbohydrates, 4 g protein, 81 mg calcium, 0 g fiber
Per serving with 2 tablespoons whipped cream: 385 calories, 31.5 g total fat, 18.5 g saturated fat, 190 mg cholesterol, 63 mg sodium, 25 g carbohydrates, 4 g protein, 91 mg calcium, 0 g fiber

---

test kitchen tip

pudding perfect

How can you make chocolate pudding the absolute best it can be?

Be sure to use bittersweet chocolate as called for in our recipe. This gives the pudding an intense chocolate flavor.

Stick with our well-worked balance of whole milk and heavy cream to achieve a truly satiny texture to the pudding.

Refrigerate at least 4 hours, avoiding the temptation to dig in as soon is it's cooked. The pudding will thicken significantly as it cools.

---

low-fat chocolate plunge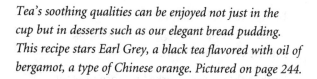

Everyone needs a chocolate treat now and again, even those trying to watch the waistline. Here's a tasty solution that couldn't be easier. A handful of ingredients are blended together and served with fresh fruit.

Total prep time: 10 minutes

- 1   tablespoon vegetable oil
- 3   tablespoons unsweetened cocoa
- ½   cup light corn syrup
- 1   teaspoon vanilla extract
-     Fresh fruit

Heat oil in a small saucepan over medium heat 20 seconds. Remove from heat; stir in cocoa until smooth. Stir in corn syrup and vanilla until blended. Serve with fresh fruit. Makes ⅔ cup.

Per tablespoon (without fruit): 65 calories, 1.5 g total fat, 0 g saturated fat, 0 mg cholesterol, 19 mg sodium, 13 g carbohydrates, 0 g protein, 18 mg calcium, 0 g fiber

chocolate-tea bread pudding

Tea's soothing qualities can be enjoyed not just in the cup but in desserts such as our elegant bread pudding. This recipe stars Earl Grey, a black tea flavored with oil of bergamot, a type of Chinese orange. Pictured on page 244.

Prep time: 50 minutes plus standing and chilling
Baking time: 45 to 50 minutes

TEA CUSTARD SAUCE:
- 1½ cups heavy or whipping cream
- 1   cup milk
- 4   Earl Grey tea bags
- 5   large egg yolks
- ½   cup sugar

BREAD PUDDING:
- 6   ounces bittersweet or semisweet chocolate squares, chopped
- 1   cup heavy or whipping cream
- 1   cup milk
- ½   cup sugar
-     Pinch salt
- 3   Earl Grey tea bags
- 4   large egg yolks, at room temperature 20 to 30 minutes
- 1   large egg, at room temperature 20 to 30 minutes
- 2   cups cubed Challah or other sweet egg bread, crusts removed

1. *Make tea custard sauce:* Heat cream and milk in a medium saucepan over medium-high heat, stirring, until mixture is very hot. Add tea bags. Remove pan from heat and let steep 10 minutes. Remove tea bags; gently squeeze liquid from each tea bag back into cream mixture. Discard tea bags.

2. Meanwhile, beat egg yolks and sugar in a large mixer bowl until thick and lemon-colored, about 3 to 4 minutes. Gradually beat in the cream-tea mixture. Return mixture to saucepan and cook over medium heat, stirring, until slightly thicker than heavy cream and temperature registers 170°F. on an instant-read thermometer, 3 to 4 minutes. Strain custard through a fine sieve set over a bowl. Cool 30 minutes. Cover and refrigerate until cold, 2 hours. *(Can be made ahead. Refrigerate up to 24 hours.)* Makes about 2⅔ cups sauce.

3. *Make chocolate-tea bread pudding:* Heat oven to 325°F. Place chocolate in a bowl. Heat cream, milk, sugar and salt in a small saucepan, stirring occasionally, until small bubbles appear around edge of pan and sugar dissolves. Remove pan from heat; add tea bags and let steep 10 minutes. Remove tea bags and gently squeeze liquid from each tea bag back into cream mixture. Discard tea bags. Pour mixture over chocolate; let stand 5 minutes. Stir until chocolate is completely melted.

4. Whisk egg yolks and egg into chocolate mixture until smooth, then stir in bread cubes; let mixture stand 15 minutes. Stir again and pour into a 1½-quart baking dish.

5. Place baking dish in a 13×9-inch roasting pan. *(Make sure there is at least 1 inch of space between edge of dish and roasting pan.)* Place roasting pan on center of oven rack. Carefully pour enough boiling water into roasting pan to reach halfway up side of baking dish. Bake 45 to 50 minutes, until top of pudding is firm to touch.

6. Remove baking dish from water bath; cool pudding 10 minutes. Serve warm with chilled tea custard sauce. Makes 8 servings.

Per serving: 390 calories, 27 g total fat, 15 g saturated fat, 221 mg cholesterol, 115 mg sodium, 35 g carbohydrates, 7 g protein, 104 mg calcium, 1 g fiber

profiteroles

Profiteroles (pruh-FIHT-uh-rohls) are miniature cream puffs filled with ice cream or custard. Our version is filled with a trio of ice-cream flavors—vanilla, coffee and the hottest new flavor, "dulce de leche." For the final touch, drizzle with homemade bittersweet chocolate sauce. C'est magnifique! Pictured on page 241.

Prep time: 45 minutes • Baking time: 30 minutes

CREAM PUFFS:

- 1   cup water
- ½   cup butter or margarine, cut into 8 pieces
- 1   cup all-purpose flour
- ⅛   teaspoon salt
- 4   large eggs, at room temperature 20 to 30 minutes
     Vegetable cooking spray

CHOCOLATE SAUCE:

- 4   ounces unsweetened chocolate squares, chopped
- 4   tablespoons butter or margarine
- 1   cup sugar
- 2   tablespoons light corn syrup
- 1   can (5 oz.) evaporated milk
- 1   teaspoon vanilla extract

- 8   small scoops *each* coffee, vanilla and dulce de leche ice creams

1. *Make cream puffs:* Combine water and butter in a 3-quart saucepan. Bring to boil over high heat. Add flour and salt; stir vigorously with a wooden spoon until dough comes together and is smooth. Remove pan from heat. Add eggs, one at a time, beating well after each addition, until dough is well blended and smooth.

2. Adjust oven racks to divide oven into thirds. Heat oven to 400°F. Lightly coat 2 large cookie sheets with vegetable cooking spray. Spoon 24 mounds of dough by rounded tablespoons 3 inches apart onto prepared cookie sheets.

3. Bake 15 minutes. Rotate cookie sheets and bake 15 minutes more, until well browned. Transfer cream puffs to wire racks; cool completely. *(Can be made ahead. Arrange baked puffs in a single layer in an airtight container. Freeze up to 2 weeks. To serve, heat oven to 350°F. Arrange puffs on a cookie sheet and bake 7 to 10 minutes until crisp. Cool.)*

4. *Make chocolate sauce:* Meanwhile, melt chocolate and butter in a 3-quart saucepan over low heat, stirring occasionally. Add sugar and corn syrup. Gradually stir in milk. Bring to simmer, stirring frequently. Cook 8 minutes, stirring, until sauce thickens slightly. Stir in vanilla and keep warm. *(Can be made ahead. Cool. Transfer to a large glass measure, cover and refrigerate up to 2 days. To reheat, microwave, covered with waxed paper, on HIGH 2 minutes, stirring after every 30 seconds, until heated through.)* Makes 1¾ cups sauce.

5. Cut cream puffs in half; remove any soft dough from inside. Place ice cream in bottoms and replace tops. Place one of each kind of puff (coffee, vanilla and dulce de leche) on 8 dessert plates. Drizzle with some of the chocolate sauce. Serve filled puffs immediately with remaining sauce. Makes 8 servings.

Per serving: 535 calories, 34 g total fat, 19.5 g saturated fat, 173 mg cholesterol, 300 mg sodium, 55 g carbohydrates, 9 g protein, 124 mg calcium, 0 g fiber

cappuccino soufflé

A dessert soufflé is always a showstopper. Espresso and a touch of cinnamon make this version extra special.

Prep time: 30 minutes plus chilling
Baking time: 35 to 40 minutes

- ½   cup plus 3 tablespoons granulated sugar, divided
- ½   cup all-purpose flour
- ⅛   teaspoon cinnamon
- ¾   cup milk, divided
- 4   large egg yolks
- ¼   cup brewed espresso or 2 tablespoons instant espresso powder dissolved in ¼ cup boiling water
- 2   teaspoons vanilla extract
- 5   large egg whites, at room temperature 20 to 30 minutes
- ⅛   teaspoon cream of tartar

CHOCOLATE SAUCE:

- 1   cup heavy or whipping cream
- 4   ounces semisweet chocolate squares, coarsely chopped

COGNAC WHIPPED CREAM:

- 1   cup heavy or whipping cream
- 2   tablespoons granulated sugar
- 1   tablespoon cognac

   Confectioners' sugar and grated semisweet chocolate, for garnish (optional)

1. Butter an 8-cup soufflé dish; coat bottom and sides with 2 tablespoons of the granulated sugar.

2. Combine flour, ½ cup of the granulated sugar and the cinnamon in a large saucepan. Add ¼ cup of the milk and whisk until smooth. Gradually whisk in remaining ½ cup milk; continue whisking until smooth. Cook over medium heat, stirring constantly, until very thick and smooth; cook 30 seconds more. Remove from heat and beat in egg yolks, one at a time. Beat in espresso and vanilla. Transfer to a large bowl; cover surface with plastic wrap and refrigerate 30 minutes, until cool.

3. Heat oven to 400°F. Beat egg whites in a large mixer bowl on medium speed until frothy. Add cream of tartar and continue to beat to soft peaks. Add remaining 1 tablespoon sugar and beat until

peaks are stiff but not dry. Gently fold one-quarter of the whites into the egg yolk base with a rubber spatula until blended. Fold in remaining whites. Gently pour into the prepared dish.

4. Place dish in oven and immediately reduce heat to 375°F. Bake 35 to 40 minutes, or until soufflé is puffed and top is lightly browned.

5. *Make chocolate sauce:* Heat cream in a small saucepan over medium-low heat until small bubbles form around edge of pan. Remove pan from heat. Add chocolate and stir until melted.

6. *Make cognac whipped cream:* Beat cream, sugar and cognac in a large mixer bowl to soft peaks.

7. Sprinkle top of soufflé with sifted confectioners' sugar and grated chocolate, if desired. Serve immediately with warm chocolate sauce and cognac whipped cream. Makes 6 servings.

Per serving: 585 calories, 40 g total fat, 23 g saturated fat, 254 mg cholesterol, 97 mg sodium, 49 g carbohydrates, 10 g protein, 108 mg calcium, 2 g fiber

chocolate turnovers

Flaky pie pastry rounds are stuffed with a bit of white and bittersweet chocolate. Pictured on page 242.

Prep time: 30 minutes plus freezing
Baking time: 16 to 20 minutes

- 1⅓   cups all-purpose flour
- 1   tablespoon sugar
- ¼   teaspoon salt
- 5   tablespoons vegetable shortening, cut up
- 4   tablespoons cold butter, cut up (no substitutes)
- 3   to 4 tablespoons ice water
- 1   large egg yolk
- 2   ounces bittersweet or semisweet chocolate squares, finely chopped
- 2   ounces premium white chocolate squares, finely chopped
- 4   teaspoons sugar, divided

1. For pastry, pulse flour, sugar and salt in a food processor. Add shortening and butter; pulse until mixture resembles coarse crumbs. Add water through feed tube, 1 tablespoon at a time, pulsing until mixture begins to hold together but still is crumbly. Shape pastry into a ball and flatten into a thick disk. Wrap and place in freezer, 15 minutes.

2. Meanwhile, adjust oven rack to lower third of oven. Heat oven to 425°F. Line a cookie sheet with parchment paper. Beat egg yolk and 1 tablespoon water in a cup. Set aside.

3. Divide pastry into 4 equal pieces. Working with 1 piece at a time (refrigerate remaining 3 pieces) on a lightly floured surface, roll pastry into a 6-inch circle. Sprinkle 1 heaping tablespoon each dark and white chocolate in center of circle, leaving a 1-inch border. Brush border with egg-water mixture. Fold pastry in half. Seal edges with fingertips. Trim with fluted pastry wheel. Transfer turnover with a spatula to the cookie sheet. Brush top with egg-water mixture; sprinkle with 1 teaspoon of the sugar. Refrigerate. Repeat with remaining pastry, chocolate and sugar. Bake turnovers 16 to 20 minutes, until golden brown. Serve immediately, while warm. Makes 4 turnovers.

Per turnover: 570 calories, 39 g total fat, 17 g saturated fat, 84 mg cholesterol, 278 mg sodium, 51 g carbohydrates, 7 g protein, 62 mg calcium, 1 g fiber

chocolate-coconut crunch

You'd be hard pressed to find a snack that's as fast, easy and tempting as this one. Stir the 3 ingredients together, drop onto a waxed-paper-lined plate and refrigerate for just a half hour.

Total prep time: 15 minutes plus chilling

- ½ **cup chopped toasted nuts**
- ¼ **cup toasted flaked coconut**
- 2 **ounces semisweet chocolate squares, melted (see tip, page 259)**

Stir nuts and coconut into melted chocolate; drop onto a plate lined with waxed paper and refrigerate 30 minutes until set. Makes 8 treats.

Per treat: 100 calories, 8.5 g total fat, 3 g saturated fat, 0 mg cholesterol, 11 mg sodium, 6 g carbohydrates, 1 g protein, 5 mg calcium, 1 g fiber

chocolate-peppermint pretzels

Here's a fun addition to your cookie jar.

Prep time: 30 minutes plus chilling and standing
Baking time: 8 to 9 minutes per batch
Microwave used

- 2½ **cups all-purpose flour**
- ½ **cup unsweetened cocoa**
- ¼ **teaspoon salt**
- ½ **cup butter or margarine, softened**
- ½ **cup vegetable shortening**
- 1 **cup confectioners' sugar**
- 1 **large egg**
- 1½ **teaspoons vanilla extract**

GLAZE:
- 2 **ounces unsweetened chocolate squares**
- 1 **tablespoon butter or margarine**
- 2 **cups confectioners' sugar, sifted**
- 4 **to 5 tablespoons water**
- ⅔ **cup crushed red and green peppermint candies**

1. Combine flour, cocoa and salt in a bowl. Beat butter, shortening, sugar, egg and vanilla in a large mixer bowl at medium-high speed until light and fluffy. At low speed, gradually beat in flour mixture just until blended. Refrigerate 15 minutes. Heat oven to 350°F. Grease 2 large cookie sheets. On a smooth surface, drop dough by level tablespoons. Roll each into a 9-inch-long rope. Twist into pretzel shapes. Place on prepared sheets. Bake 8 to 9 minutes, until firm. Transfer to wire racks to cool.

2. *Make glaze:* Melt chocolate and butter in a medium microwaveproof bowl on HIGH 1 to 2 minutes; stir until smooth. Whisk in sugar and 4 tablespoons of the water until smooth. (*Add remaining 1 tablespoon water, if necessary.*) Dip topside of pretzels into glaze, shaking off excess. Arrange glazed side up on waxed paper and immediately sprinkle with crushed candy. Let stand until glaze sets, 10 minutes. Makes 3½ dozen.

Per cookie: 130 calories, 6 g total fat, 2.5 g saturated fat, 12 mg cholesterol, 44 mg sodium, 18 g carbohydrates, 1 g protein, 15 mg calcium, 0 g fiber

chocolate chews

These mini bites of chocolate, marshmallows, nuts and cherries are highly irresistible and easy to make.

Total prep time: 20 minutes plus chilling

- **16 ounces semisweet chocolate squares**
- **21 large marshmallows, cut into halves**
- **½ cup walnuts or pecans, chopped**
- **8 candied red cherries, cut into halves**

1. Line an 8-inch square baking pan with foil; grease foil. Melt chocolate in top of a double boiler set over simmering water, stirring occasionally.

2. Scatter marshmallows in bottom of the prepared pan, then nuts and cherries. Pour melted chocolate on top, spreading evenly. Refrigerate until firm, 1 hour. Cut into 1-inch squares. Makes 64 squares.

Per square: 50 calories, 3 g total fat, 1.5 g saturated fat, 0 mg cholesterol, 2 mg sodium, 7 g carbohydrates, 1 g protein, 1 mg calcium, 1 g fiber

chocolate-coated pecans

Impress friends with these delectable nuts that look like they came from a fancy candy shop. Pictured on page 244.

Prep time: 15 minutes plus freezing
Baking time: 10 minutes

- **6 cups pecan halves**
- **12 ounces semisweet or bittersweet chocolate squares, melted (see tip, page 259)**
- **4 ounces white chocolate squares, melted (see tip, page 259) and cooled slightly**

1. Heat oven to 350°F. Line 2 jelly-roll pans with foil. Divide and spread pecans on prepared pans. Bake nuts 10 minutes, until golden and fragrant. Cool. Transfer pecans to a large bowl. Pour melted semisweet chocolate over pecans and stir well. (Leave foil on pans.) Divide and spread chocolate-coated nuts onto foil-lined pans.

2. Transfer melted white chocolate to a resealable plastic storage bag. Snip one corner from bag and

pipe decoratively over tops of nuts. Place pans in freezer until chocolate hardens, 5 minutes.

3. Remove pecans from pans; break into large pieces. Makes 9 cups. (*Can be made ahead. Store in airtight containers. Cover and refrigerate up to 1 week.*)

Per ½ cup: 365 calories, 32 g total fat, 6.5 g saturated fat, 0 mg cholesterol, 8 mg sodium, 22 g carbohydrates, 4 g protein, 32 mg calcium, 3 g fiber

truffles

These simple candies make great gifts or a perfect conclusion to a special dinner. Pictured on page 241.

Total prep time: 25 minutes plus standing and chilling

- **9 ounces semisweet chocolate squares, finely chopped**
- **½ cup heavy or whipping cream**
- **2 tablespoons Armagnac or brandy**
- **½ cup plus 2 tablespoons sifted unsweetened cocoa, divided**

1. Place chocolate in a large bowl. Heat cream in a small saucepan over medium heat, until cream just begins to come to boil. Pour hot cream over chocolate. Let stand 3 to 5 minutes. Stir until smooth. Stir in Armagnac.

2. Cool chocolate mixture to room temperature. Cover with plastic wrap and refrigerate until mixture holds its shape when rolled between hands, about 1 hour.

3. Line a jelly-roll pan with waxed paper; sprinkle top with 2 tablespoons of the cocoa. Place remaining ½ cup cocoa in a bowl. Measure 1 level tablespoon of the chocolate; roll into a 1-inch ball and arrange on the prepared pan. Repeat. Lightly toss 3 to 4 chocolate balls at a time with cocoa in bowl, until coated, shaking excess cocoa back into bowl. Return to prepared pan and refrigerate, 30 minutes. (*Can be made ahead. Transfer truffles to an airtight container. Cover and refrigerate up to 2 weeks. Let stand at room temperature 15 minutes before serving.*) Makes 24 truffles.

Per truffle: 75 calories, 5.5 g total fat, 3 g saturated fat, 7 mg cholesterol, 4 mg sodium, 8 g carbohydrates, 1 g protein, 9 mg calcium, 1 g fiber

BEST PARKER
HOUSE ROLLS
PG. 304

holiday
happenings

CRANBERRY-
PEAR SAUCE
PG. 299

TURKEY
WITH ROASTED
GARLIC GRAVY
PG. 294

Here's the best gift you can give your family and friends this holiday season: a magical feast that gets the people you love most around the table for lots of talking, sharing, laughter, and good cheer. Here's our gift to you: all the ideas you need to do just that.

POTATO-
PARSNIP
PUREE
PG. 301

stir and roast...
then **toast**

CLOCKWISE FROM
LEFT:
BEET MAYONNAISE
PG. 289
CHILE RANCH DIP
PG. 289
ALMOND PESTO
PG. 289

CHEESE
TARTLETS
PG. 290

BALSAMIC
ROASTED
CARROTS
PG. 300

another
glorious gathering

HOLIDAY BEEF
TENDERLOIN
PG. 291

SAUTEED
PEAS AND
CELERY
PG. 300

GINGER SPICED
SQUASH
PG. 303

joy to the
world

CRANBERRY
VINAIGRETTE
WITH SALAD
GREENS
PG. 293

BAKED HAM WITH
PEAR SAUCE
PG. 296

and **bless**
the cook!

SAVORY
MASHED
POTATOES
PG. 301

...with visions of sugar cookies

LINZER
COOKIES
PG. 317

SNOWMAN SUGAR
COOKIES
PG. 318

SABLÉS
PG. 315

POPPY
SEED
COOKIES
PG. 313

CHOCOLATE
ALMOND COOKIES
PG. 316

GINGER AND PINE
NUT BISCOTTI
PG. 312

BROWNIE
IN A JAR
PG. 315

BELGIAN
LACE
PG. 312

SHORTBREAD
DOVES
PG. 314

dancing through their heads

ZIMTSTERN
PG. 319

celebrate
best-loved
traditions

BUCHE DE
NOEL
PG. 310

SPICED
RUDOLPH
COOKIES
PG. 316

chile ranch dip

The roasted poblano chiles in this creamy dip impart a smoky flavor and just the right amount of heat. Pictured on page 282.

Prep time: 20 minutes plus standing
Broiling time: 12 to 15 minutes

- 2 poblano chiles (see tip, page 15)
- ⅔ cup buttermilk
- ½ cup mayonnaise
- ½ cup sour cream
- 1 tablespoon finely chopped onion, rinsed and drained
- 1 teaspoon fresh lime juice
- ½ teaspoon salt
  Assorted fresh vegetables (optional)

Heat broiler. Cut chiles in half lengthwise; remove seeds and discard. Arrange chiles, cut side down, on a foil-lined broiler pan. Broil 3 inches from heat 12 to 15 minutes, until skins are bubbly and evenly charred. Immediately wrap in foil. Let stand 15 minutes, until chiles are cool enough to handle. Use a small paring knife to gently remove blistered skin from chiles. Chop chiles; transfer to a medium bowl. Stir in remaining ingredients except assorted fresh vegetables. *(Can be made ahead. Refrigerate in an airtight container overnight.)* Serve with assorted vegetables, if desired. Makes 2 cups.

Per tablespoon: 35 calories, 3.5 g total fat, 1 g saturated fat, 4 mg cholesterol, 63 mg sodium, 1 g carbohydrates, 0 g protein, 12 mg calcium, 0 g fiber

almond pesto

Fresh parsley makes a great pesto, especially when paired with toasted almonds. For best results, let the nuts cool completely before grinding in the blender. Pictured on page 282.

Total prep time: 10 minutes

- ½ cup whole blanched almonds, toasted
- 1 cup fresh flat-leaf parsley leaves
- ½ cup olive oil

- 3 to 4 tablespoons water
- 2 tablespoons white wine vinegar
- ½ teaspoon salt
- ¼ teaspoon cumin
  Assorted fresh vegetables (optional)

Process almonds in a blender until finely ground. Add remaining ingredients except assorted fresh vegetables; process until smooth. *(Can be made ahead. Refrigerate in an airtight container overnight.)* Serve with assorted vegetables, if desired. Makes 1 cup.

Per tablespoon: 85 calories, 9 g total fat, 1 g saturated fat, 0 mg cholesterol, 74 mg sodium, 1 g carbohydrates, 1 g protein, 16 mg calcium, 1 g fiber

beet mayonnaise

Try this unique raspberry-red dip. The mellow sweetness of the beets will definitely win over your guests. Pictured on page 282.

Prep time: 15 minutes plus standing
Baking time: 45 to 60 minutes

- 2 medium beets (8 oz.), trimmed
- 2 tablespoons fresh lemon juice
- ¾ cup mayonnaise
- 1 teaspoon sugar
- ¼ teaspoon salt
  Assorted fresh vegetables (optional)

Heat oven to 400°F. Wrap beets in foil; roast 45 to 60 minutes, until tender. Let stand until beets are cool enough to handle; peel. Puree beets with lemon juice in a food processor until smooth. Transfer mixture to a medium bowl; stir in remaining ingredients except assorted fresh vegetables. *(Can be made ahead. Refrigerate in airtight container overnight.)* Serve with assorted vegetables, if desired. Makes 1¼ cups.

Per tablespoon: 65 calories, 6.5 g total fat, 1 g saturated fat, 5 mg cholesterol, 81 mg sodium, 1 g carbohydrates, 0 g protein, 3 mg calcium, 0 g fiber

cheese tartlets

Purchased mini phyllo pastry shells take the hassle out of these fancy-looking appetizers. The fresh basil leaves are blanched in boiling water to keep them bright green. Pictured on page 282.

Prep time: 20 minutes • Baking time: 10 to 12 minutes

- **2** teaspoons butter or margarine
- **3** tablespoons minced onion
- **½** teaspoon minced garlic
- **12** large fresh basil leaves
- **1** log (5.5 oz.) goat cheese, at room temperature
- **⅓** cup freshly grated Parmesan cheese
- **1** large egg, lightly beaten
- **2** tablespoons heavy or whipping cream
- **¼** teaspoon salt
- **⅛** teaspoon freshly ground pepper
- **2** packages (2 or 2.1 oz. each) frozen mini phyllo pastry shells*

1. Melt butter in a small nonstick skillet over medium heat. Add onion; cook 1 minute. Add garlic and cook 1 minute more, just until golden.

2. Heat oven to 350°F.

3. Drop basil leaves into a small saucepan with boiling water; immediately remove with a slotted spoon. Pat dry with paper towel; finely chop.

4. Process goat cheese, Parmesan, egg, cream, salt and pepper in a food processor until smooth. Transfer to a bowl; stir in onion mixture and basil.

5. Arrange phyllo shells on a large cookie sheet. Fill each with a scant tablespoon of the cheese filling. Bake 10 to 12 minutes, until puffed. Serve warm or at room temperature. *(Can be made ahead. Store tartlets in an airtight container and refrigerate overnight. Bring to room temperature. Reheat in 350°F. oven 12 minutes.)* Makes 30 tartlets.

*Note: Can be found in the freezer section of supermarkets.

Per tartlet: 55 calories, 3.5 g total fat, 1.5 g saturated fat, 14 mg cholesterol, 81 mg sodium, 3 g carbohydrates, 2 g protein, 31 mg calcium, 0 g fiber

she-crab soup

This classic cream soup from South Carolina is traditionally prepared in spring using the roe and meat from female crabs. We achieve a distinctive rosy blush by substituting paprika for the coral-colored roe. The soup is delicately flavored with sherry and fresh lemon peel, and will make an elegant starter course for a holiday dinner.

Prep time: 15 minutes • Cooking time: 55 to 60 minutes

- **¼** cup butter or margarine
- **1** cup finely chopped onions
- **½** cup finely chopped celery
- **1** shallot, finely chopped
- **¼** cup all-purpose flour
- **¾** teaspoon paprika
- **4** cups milk
- **2** cups half-and-half cream
- **1** teaspoon salt
- **1** teaspoon grated lemon peel
- **1** teaspoon Worcestershire sauce
- **½** teaspoon freshly ground pepper
  Pinch ground red pepper
- **1** pound fresh lump or jumbo crabmeat, picked over
- **¼** cup dry sherry
- **2** teaspoons chopped fresh parsley

1. Melt butter over medium heat in a Dutch oven. Add onions, celery and shallot and cook 5 minutes, until softened.

2. Add flour and paprika and cook 1 minute. Gradually stir in milk and cream until smooth. Add salt, lemon peel, Worcestershire and peppers. Bring to simmer. Reduce heat to low; cover and simmer 20 minutes. Stir in crabmeat and sherry. Cover and simmer 20 minutes more to blend flavors *(do not boil)*. Sprinkle with parsley. Makes 8 servings.

Per serving: 275 calories, 16 g total fat, 10 g saturated fat, 72 mg cholesterol, 927 mg sodium, 15 g carbohydrates, 17 g protein, 251 mg calcium, 1 g fiber

holiday beef tenderloin

A glorious holiday entrée in four easy steps. One: Make tomato jam. Two: Season the meat just right and sear it in a hot skillet to develop a caramelized, well-browned crust. Three: Roast the meat in a hot oven to the proper doneness (and that's easy when you use a meat thermometer!). And finally, let the roast stand before carving to allow the juices to redistribute and for the meat to achieve a firm texture. Our vibrant tomato jam is all you'll need to complete the dish. Pictured on page 283.

Prep time: 45 minutes
Baking time: 20 to 30 minutes plus standing

TOMATO JAM:

2	cans (28 oz. each) premium quality whole tomatoes in juice, drained
1	small onion, cut into 1-inch wedges
3	cloves garlic, peeled
¼	cup olive oil
¾	teaspoon kosher salt
½	teaspoon sugar
½	teaspoon grated orange peel

2½	pounds trimmed and tied center-cut beef tenderloin*
1	tablespoon olive oil
1	tablespoon kosher salt
1	teaspoon freshly ground pepper

1. *Make tomato jam:* Heat oven to 450°F. Arrange tomatoes, onion wedges and garlic on a jelly-roll pan; drizzle oil over vegetables. Roast 20 minutes, remove garlic; set aside. Roast 20 minutes more, until tomatoes start to brown on the bottom of the pan. Set aside to cool slightly. (Leave oven on to roast tenderloin.) Transfer tomatoes, onion and garlic to a cutting board; coarsely chop. Transfer to a serving bowl; stir in any accumulated tomato juices, salt, sugar and peel.

2. Rub entire tenderloin with oil; sprinkle all sides with the 1 tablespoon kosher salt and the pepper. Heat a 12-inch skillet over medium-high heat 2 minutes. Add tenderloin and sear 3 minutes each side, until browned. Transfer roast to bottom of a broiler pan.

3. Roast tenderloin until a meat thermometer inserted in center registers 130°F., 20 minutes. Let stand 10 minutes; temperature will continue to rise 10° to 15° for medium-rare.

4. To serve, slice beef into ½-inch-thick slices; serve with tomato jam. Makes 6 servings.

*Note: For whole tenderloin in cryovac: Remove cryovac from a 5-pound whole untrimmed tenderloin over a sink. Rinse tenderloin; pat dry with paper towels. Transfer tenderloin to a large cutting board. With a small, very sharp knife, remove the loose fat and membrane covering the meat, then cut and pull loose "the chain" (the side of meat that runs along the length of the tenderloin). Cut away the layer of connective tissue ("silver skin"). Cut both ends of tenderloin for an evenly sized 2½-pound roast. (Reserve trimming to add to your next stew.) Tie roast with 100-percent-cotton kitchen string at 1½ inch intervals.

Per serving: 480 calories, 28.5 g total fat, 8 g saturated fat, 118 mg cholesterol, 1,439 mg sodium, 14 g carbohydrates, 42 g protein, 93 mg calcium, 3 g fiber

test kitchen tip
raise a glass!

Below is a short and selective list of some of our favorite wines for holidays and entertaining. Need something more to celebrate? They're all priced under $15.

CHANDON BRUT FRESCO, ARGENTINA:
A festive bubbly that tastes much like French champagne—but at a fraction of the cost. (Around $13)

BARON HERZOG CHENIN BLANC, 1999:
With its hint of ripe-peach flavors, this refreshing Kosher white wine is a great choice for before-dinner sipping. (Around $6)

LE JA JA DE JAU SYRAH/GRENACHE ROUGE, VIN DE PAYS D'OC, FRANCE 1999:
A delicious bargain from the South of France, this bright and lively red wine goes well with turkey, pork or beef. (Around $7)

grilled turkey with apple chutney

Grilling is quite possibly the easiest and tastiest way to "roast" a whole turkey. Cooking indirectly over medium heat ensures an end result that is moist and tender.

Prep time: 20 minutes • Grilling time: 3 to 4 hours

- **1 whole turkey (12 to 14 lbs.), thawed if frozen**
- **1 tablespoon olive oil**
- **1 tablespoon coriander seed**
- **1 tablespoon paprika**
- **1½ teaspoons sugar**
- **1½ teaspoons salt**
- **1½ teaspoons mustard seed**
- **½ teaspoon dried marjoram**
- **Apple Chutney (see recipe, right) (optional)**

1. Remove neck and giblets from body and neck cavities; discard or save for another use. Rinse turkey and drain; pat dry with paper towels. Brush oil over skin. Combine remaining ingredients except apple chutney in a cup. Sprinkle over all sides of turkey.

2. Prepare grill for indirect grilling. For gas: Place a large 2-inch-deep disposable foil pan in center of bottom grate; fill halfway with water. Replace top cooking grate. Close lid and heat burners on medium about 10 minutes. Place turkey, breast side up, in center of grill over drip pan. Turn one burner off. (For a triple burner grill, turn center burner off, as there should be no heat source underneath the drip pan.) For charcoal: Open all vents. Build two equal piles of briquettes (about 30 to 50 total, depending on the size of your grill) opposite each other on bottom grate near the grate's edge. Ignite and burn 25 to 30 minutes, until coals are covered with a light coating of gray ash. Place a large 2-inch-deep disposable foil pan on center on bottom grate; fill halfway with water. Replace top cooking grate. Place turkey, breast side up, in center of grill over drip pan.

3. Cover and grill turkey 3 to 4 hours, replenishing briquettes (if using charcoal) to maintain a temperature inside grill of about 325°F. to 340°F. The temperature in the grill can be controlled by adjusting burner controls on gas or opening and closing vents on charcoal grill.

4. Start testing for doneness 30 minutes before end cooking times. Insert metal section of an instant-read thermometer at least 2 inches into the inner thigh of the bird. Let stand 15 to 20 seconds, until thermometer registers 180°F. If turkey needs more roasting, remove the thermometer, thoroughly washing the stem section in hot soapy water after each use. (Even if your turkey has a pop-up temperature device, the USDA recommends double-checking with another thermometer to be sure the turkey reaches 180°F. for safety and doneness.)

5. Transfer turkey to a serving platter; cover loosely with foil; let stand 20 minutes Carve turkey. Serve with apple chutney, if desired. Makes 12 servings.

Per 3-oz. serving: 180 calories, 8 g total fat, 2.5 g saturated fat, 71 mg cholesterol, 152 mg sodium, 0.5 g carbohydrates, 24 g protein, 25 mg calcium, 0 g fiber

apple chutney

Homemade chutney makes a great statement both on your menu and as a gift. This exceptionally delicious version calls for Golden Delicious and Granny Smith apples, in addition to cider, cranberries, raisins, mango and ginger.

Prep time: 20 minutes • Cooking time: 34 to 39 minutes

- **1 teaspoon grapeseed or vegetable oil**
- **1 cup diced onions**
- **1 tablespoon chopped garlic**
- **3 Golden Delicious apples, peeled, cored and diced**
- **2 Granny Smith apples, peeled, cored and diced**
- **1½ cups apple cider**
- **1 cup dried cranberries**
- **⅓ cup raisins**
- **1 mango, peeled, pitted and cut into 1-inch cubes**
- **1 cup firmly packed brown sugar**
- **1½ teaspoons minced fresh ginger**
- **1 teaspoon salt**
- **1 teaspoon cinnamon**

Heat oil in a 3-quart saucepan over medium-high heat. Add onions and cook 3 minutes, until softened. Add garlic and cook 1 minute. Add apples, cider, cranberries and raisins. Bring to boil. Reduce heat and cook at low boil 15 minutes. Add mango, brown sugar, ginger, salt and cinnamon. Bring to boil. Reduce heat and simmer 15 to 20 minutes more, until mixture is thick with chunks of apple still remaining. Cool. *(Can be made ahead. Cool. Transfer to an airtight container, or for gift giving, transfer to five 1-cup sterilized jars. Refrigerate up to 1 week.)* Makes 5 cups.

Per ¼-cup serving: 105 calories, 0.5 g total fat, 0 g saturated fat, 0 mg cholesterol, 122 mg sodium, 27 g carbohydrates, 0 g protein, 18 mg calcium, 1 g fiber

cranberry vinaigrette

Cranberry-orange juice and honey give the dressing a touch of sweetness. Toss it with salad greens or drizzle over sliced fresh fruit. Pictured on page 284.

Total prep and cooking time: 30 minutes

- 1 cup fresh or frozen cranberries
- 1 cup cranberry-orange juice
- 3 tablespoons olive oil, divided
- 2 tablespoons minced shallots or red onion
- 2 tablespoons red wine vinegar
- 2 tablespoons honey
- ¾ teaspoon salt
- ½ teaspoon freshly ground pepper
- Salad greens or sliced fresh fruit (optional)

1. Bring cranberries and juice to boil in a small saucepan. Boil 10 to 12 minutes, until reduced to 1 cup.

2. Meanwhile, heat 1 tablespoon of the oil in a small skillet over medium-low heat. Add shallots and cook 3 to 4 minutes, until softened.

3. Transfer cranberry mixture to a blender; puree with remaining 2 tablespoons oil, the shallots, vinegar, honey, salt and pepper until smooth. Transfer to a bowl and freeze 10 minutes until cold. Serve with salad greens, if desired. Makes 1⅓ cups.

Per tablespoon: 35 calories, 2 g total fat, 0 g saturated fat, 0 mg cholesterol, 83 mg sodium, 4 g carbohydrates, 0 g protein, 1 mg calcium, 0 g fiber

---

test kitchen tip
turkey 101

This year, LHJ's associate food editor Carol Prager went to Butterball University at the Butterball Headquarters in Downers Grove, Illinois. The course load was tough but rewarding. The class cooked a flock of nine turkeys in just one day! Carol came home with plenty of pointers on how every cook can pass Turkey 101 with flying colors.

first course: safety

KITCHEN-COUNTER THAWING: No! No! This is never a safe way to defrost. Don't be tempted to thaw turkey on a kitchen counter. Bacteria that cause food poisoning multiply rapidly at room temperature.

REFRIGERATOR THAWING: The best way to thaw a frozen turkey is in the refrigerator, so be sure to plan ahead. For every 4 pounds of turkey, allow at least 1 day of thawing. Thaw the turkey in the unopened wrapper, breast side up, on a tray or a jelly-roll pan. This prevents the uncooked juices from dripping on other foods.

COLD-WATER THAWING: If you're short on time, this is another safe way to defrost. Place the frozen turkey in its unopened wrapper, breast side down, in a sink or large bowl of cold water to cover. Change the water every 30 minutes to keep the surface cold. Minimum thawing time is 30 minutes per pound for a whole turkey. Thawed turkey can be refrigerated up to four days before cooking.

TURKEY 102: Be sure to read more about Carol's turkey training on pages 294 to 295.

turkey 102

Carol Prager, LHJ's Turkey U graduate (see tip, page 293), shares everything you need to know about stuffing and seasoning the bird.

the right stuff

USE ONLY COOKED INGREDIENTS in a stuffing. Combine the stuffing ingredients and spoon into the turkey cavity just before roasting, never the night before. It's okay to make the stuffing ahead and refrigerate it.

STUFF BOTH NECK AND BODY CAVITIES of completely thawed turkey (if frozen). Allow ¾ cup stuffing per pound of turkey. Spoon the stuffing into turkey loosely so there will be room for it to expand during roasting.

RETURN LEGS to original tucked position (if untucked for cleaning or stuffing). If legs are held with plastic, discard and tie with 100-percent-cotton kitchen string.

DO NOT STUFF a turkey if you plan to grill it because the turkey typically gets done faster than the stuffing.

seasoning & basting

SEASONING the bird and the cavity before cooking is not essential (but if making pan gravy, it's not a bad idea). Seasoning flavors the skin and drippings but doesn't penetrate meat.

DON'T BOTHER BASTING! Pouring juices over the skin while it roasts will not make the meat juicier. Basting liquid penetrates only ⅛ to ¼ inch beneath the skin, and most of the juice will run off into the pan. Plus, opening up the oven door periodically to baste the bird can lengthen the roasting time. Lightly coating the skin with oil or melted butter before roasting is sufficient to brighten the color of the bird and prevent the skin from drying out.

turkey with roasted garlic gravy EASY

It's easy to roast the perfect turkey using this recipe. And for those who think the gravy is the best part of the bird, our concoction with roasted garlic is the richest you'll ever taste. Best of all, the garlic roasts in the oven right next to the turkey, so you'll get a head start on the prep. Pictured on page 281.

Prep time: 20 minutes • Baking time: 3¾ to 4½ hours

> **Wild Rice Stuffing (see recipe, page 298)**
> 1 whole turkey (14 to 18 lbs.), thawed if frozen
> 2 tablespoons olive oil
> 2 teaspoons salt
> ½ teaspoon freshly ground pepper
>
> **ROASTED GARLIC GRAVY:**
> 1 head garlic
> 1 tablespoon flour
> 2 cups chicken broth, divided
> 1 tablespoon chopped fresh sage or
>   1½ teaspoons dried sage
> ¼ teaspoon salt
> ⅛ teaspoon freshly ground pepper

1. Prepare Wild Rice Stuffing as directed.

2. Heat oven to 325°F. Remove neck and giblets from body and neck cavities of turkey; discard or save for another use. Rinse turkey and drain; pat dry with paper towels. Lightly spoon stuffing into neck and body cavities. Pull the neck skin over the stuffing onto the back of turkey; fasten with small skewers or toothpicks.

3. Place stuffed turkey, breast side up, on a rack in a shallow roasting pan. Brush skin with oil and sprinkle with salt and pepper. Cover stuffing in cavity with a small piece of foil. Place turkey in oven and roast 3¾ to 4 hours.

4. When turkey skin is golden brown, about two-thirds done (2½ to 3 hours), loosely shield breast with foil to prevent overbrowning. Roast garlic at this point (see Roasted Garlic Gravy, step 8).

5. Start testing for doneness 30 minutes before end times. Insert metal section of an instant-read thermometer at least 2 inches into the inner thigh of the bird. Let stand 15 to 20 seconds, until thermometer reaches 180°F.

6. To test the stuffing doneness, insert the thermometer into the center part of stuffing and let stand 15 to 20 seconds, until the temperature is between 160°F and 165°F. If turkey needs more roasting, remove the thermometer before returning it to the oven, thoroughly washing the stem section in hot soapy water after each use. (Even if your turkey has a pop-up temperature device, the USDA recommends double-checking with another thermometer to be sure the turkey reaches 180°F. for safety and doneness.)

7. Remove turkey from oven; cover loosely with foil and let stand 20 minutes before carving.

8. *Make roasted garlic gravy:* Wrap garlic in foil and place next to turkey in oven. Roast garlic 1 hour, until soft. Remove from oven; set aside. When turkey is done, scrape drippings from roasting pan into a glass measure. Let stand 5 minutes, until fat rises to the top. Skim off fat, discard. Cut ½ inch off top of roasted garlic. Squeeze garlic pulp out of cloves into a small bowl. Stir flour and ¼ cup of the broth in another small bowl until smooth. Return drippings to pan. Bring to boil over medium heat; whisk in garlic and sage. Slowly whisk in flour mixture and the remaining 1¾ cups broth, whisking 2 to 3 minutes, until gravy thickens slightly. Season with salt and pepper. Makes 2¾ cups.

9. Use a spoon to remove stuffing from turkey; place in a serving bowl. Transfer turkey to a serving platter. Carve turkey. Serve with stuffing and gravy. Makes 10 to 14 servings.

Per 3-oz. serving and ¼ cup gravy (without rice stuffing): 195 calories, 9 g total fat, 2.5 g saturated fat, 70 mg cholesterol, 475 mg sodium, 2 g carbohydrates, 24 g protein, 31 mg calcium, 0 g fiber

check your thermometer

For testing meat and poultry for doneness, an instant-read thermometer is an essential kitchen tool. It's a good idea, however, to occasionally check your thermometer for accuracy. To do this, bring a pan of water to a boil. Insert the metal section of the thermometer at least 2 inches into the water. If the temperature reaches 212°F. (the temperature of boiling water), the thermometer is accurate. This test will not work, however, at high altitudes where water boils at a lower temperature.

baked ham with pear sauce EASY

Glorious baked ham has always been classic party food, but now it's better than ever. And now, you can ditch that carving set by selecting a pre-cut "spiral-cut" ham. It's so easy it practically serves itself. Our pick is a fully cooked, hardwood smoked (versus liquid smoked), bone-in shank portion ham with natural juices. The sliced meat is covered with cheesecloth and basted with pineapple juice, brandy, brown sugar and spices during baking so it's moist and succulent. Garnish each serving with a spoonful of pear sauce and you'll agree holiday dining doesn't get better than this. Pictured on page 285.

Prep time: 30 minutes plus standing
Baking time: 1 hour 20 minutes

1	fully cooked (5 to 7 lbs.) bone-in shank portion spiral-cut smoked ham
1	cup apple juice or cider
1	can (6 oz.) pineapple juice
¼	cup Calvados or apple brandy
2	tablespoons firmly packed brown sugar
10	allspice berries
10	black peppercorns
2	bay leaves

PEAR SAUCE:

1½	pounds Bosc pears, cut into 2-inch pieces
1½	pounds Bartlett pears, cut into 1-inch pieces
1	(1-inch) piece fresh ginger
3	tablespoons sugar
2	tablespoons cider vinegar
½	vanilla bean, split lengthwise

1. Adjust oven racks to center and lower third positions. Heat oven to 325°F. Rinse ham and pat dry with paper towels. Combine apple and pineapple juices, brandy, brown sugar, allspice, peppercorns and bay leaves in a small bowl. Arrange two 24×8-inch strips of cheesecloth across the bottom of a broiler pan. Place ham on its side in center of pan. Pour 1 cup of juice mixture over ham; bring up sides of cheesecloth and drape over ham to cover. Pour remaining juice mixture in bottom of broiler pan. Bake ham on center rack 1¼ hours, until an instant-read thermometer inserted in center of ham registers 135°F. Remove cheesecloth. Increase oven temperature to broil. Baste ham with pan drippings. Broil ham 4 inches from heat source 4 to 5 minutes more, until top is golden brown.

2. *Make pear sauce:* Meanwhile, arrange Bosc pears on a cookie sheet. After ham bakes 15 minutes, bake pears on lower oven rack 30 minutes. Turn and bake 30 minutes more, until golden brown.

3. Combine the remaining pear sauce ingredients in a medium saucepan. Bring to boil. Reduce heat and simmer 10 to 15 minutes, until Bartlett pears soften but still retain their shape. Remove from heat; cover and let stand 20 minutes. With a slotted spoon or tongs, remove vanilla bean; scrape seeds into pear mixture. (Discard pod.) Stir baked pears into saucepan. *(Can be made ahead. Cool. Refrigerate in an airtight container up to 3 days.)*

4. Transfer ham to a cutting board; let stand 15 minutes. Pour pan juices into a glass measure; discard bay leaves. Let stand 5 minutes. Skim fat from top. Serve ham with pan juices and pear sauce. Makes 12 servings.

Per 3-oz. serving: 240 calories, 6.5 g total fat, 2 g saturated fat, 50 mg cholesterol, 644 mg sodium, 27 g carbohydrates, 18 g protein, 19 mg calcium, 3 g fiber

chili corn pie

This main dish is easy as pie, thanks to frozen chili and deli corn muffins. It's perfect for busy nights around the holidays.

Prep time: 15 minutes
Baking time: 16 to 17 minutes plus standing
Microwave used

- **2 large corn muffins, crumbled (2¾ cups)**
- **1 large egg white, lightly beaten**
- **2 boxes (8¾ oz. each) frozen Stouffer's Chili with Beans**
- **1 cup coarsely shredded extra-sharp Cheddar cheese**
- **1 to 2 tablespoons chopped pickled jalapeño chiles**
- **2 tablespoons chopped fresh cilantro**
- **Sour cream, sliced green onions and fresh cilantro leaves, for garnish (optional)**
- **Tossed green salad (optional)**

1. Adjust oven racks to upper and lower third positions. Heat oven to 400°F.

2. Toss crumbled corn muffins with egg white in a medium bowl until crumbs are evenly moistened. Press crumbs along bottom and up side of a 9-inch pie plate, forming a crust with a ½-inch-thick edge. Bake crust on upper rack 10 to 11 minutes, until crisp and medium brown.

3. Meanwhile, microwave Stouffer's Chili with Beans according to package directions.

4. Fill crust with hot chili; then top with cheese. Sprinkle with chopped jalapeño. Bake pie 5 to 6 minutes more on lower rack, until hot and cheese has melted. Remove pie from oven and sprinkle with cilantro; let stand 5 minutes. Cut into wedges. Garnish with sour cream, green onions, cilantro leaves and serve with a green salad, if desired. Makes 4 to 6 servings.

Per serving: 385 calories, 17.5 g total fat, 8 g saturated fat, 75 mg cholesterol, 1,017 mg sodium, 39 g carbohydrates, 18 g protein, 237 mg calcium, 4 g fiber

ricotta soufflé pie

Looking for an easy lunch or brunch dish to serve to friends around the holidays? This recipe combines ricotta and Parmesan cheese with Stouffer's Spinach Soufflé to keep prep time minimal. It's all baked up in a flaky piecrust and makes a good choice for a light meal when you know more elaborate ones are coming!

Prep time: 12 minutes • Baking time: 32 to 34 minutes
Microwave used

- **1 package (12 oz.) Stouffer's frozen Spinach Soufflé**
- **1 container (15 oz.) ricotta cheese**
- **½ cup freshly grated Parmesan cheese**
- **¼ teaspoon salt**
- **¼ teaspoon nutmeg**
- **¼ teaspoon minced fresh garlic**
- **¼ teaspoon freshly ground pepper**
- **1 (9-inch) frozen deep-dish pie shell**

1. Adjust oven rack to lowest position. Place a cookie sheet on rack. Heat oven to 425°F.

2. Start to prepare Stouffer's frozen Spinach Soufflé according to package directions for the microwave *except* microwave only 5 minutes, until edges begin to puff and center is defrosted.

3. Combine soufflé, ricotta, Parmesan cheese, salt, nutmeg, garlic and pepper in a large bowl until well mixed. Pour into pie shell, spreading top evenly with a rubber spatula. Place pie on the cookie sheet and bake 32 to 34 minutes, until crust is brown and filling is puffed (center may not puff). Makes 6 servings.

Per serving: 350 calories, 22.5 g total fat, 11 g saturated fat, 103 mg cholesterol, 669 mg sodium, 20 g carbohydrates, 16 g protein, 307 mg calcium, 1 g fiber

vegetable strata

This savory dish is ideal for a holiday brunch buffet because it makes so many servings and it's do-ahead.

Prep time: 40 minutes plus chilling
Baking time: 75 to 80 minutes

- **2** tablespoons plus 1 teaspoon butter or margarine, divided
- ½ pounds white mushrooms, sliced
- ½ pound shiitake mushrooms, sliced
- **2** medium red bell peppers, cut into ¼-inch-thick strips
- **2** cups thinly sliced onions
- **1** teaspoon salt, divided
- **1** bag (10 oz.) fresh spinach, coarsely chopped
- **4** cups half-and-half cream
- **8** large eggs
- 1½ cups shredded Italian fontina cheese (6 oz.)
- ½ cup freshly grated Parmesan cheese
- ½ teaspoon dried thyme
- ¼ teaspoon ground red pepper
- **1** loaf (8 oz.) semolina bread, cut into ½-inch-thick slices, then quartered

1. Melt 2 tablespoons of the butter in a 12-inch skillet over medium-high heat. Add mushrooms, bell peppers, onions and ¼ teaspoon of the salt. Cook, stirring occasionally, 8 to 10 minutes, until mushrooms and onions are lightly browned. Transfer to a large bowl. Add the remaining 1 teaspoon butter and the spinach to same skillet. Cook, stirring, 2 to 3 minutes, until wilted and juices have evaporated. Transfer spinach to bowl with mushroom mixture.

2. Whisk together cream and eggs in another large bowl. Stir in cheeses, remaining ¾ teaspoon salt, the thyme and red pepper. Stir in bread and mushroom mixture. Pour mixture into a 13×9-inch baking dish. Cover with foil and refrigerate at least 4 hours or up to 24 hours.

3. Heat oven to 375°F. Bake strata 45 minutes. Uncover and bake 30 to 40 minutes more, until lightly browned and set in center. Makes 12 servings.

Per serving: 345 calories, 22 g total fat, 12 g saturated fat, 197 mg cholesterol, 628 mg sodium, 22 g carbohydrates, 170 g protein, 277 mg calcium, 4 g fiber

wild rice stuffing EASY

Wild rice is prized for its subtle, nutty taste, and when paired with smoky sausage and dried sweet cherries, it makes an excellent stuffing for turkey. It's equally delicious baked in a separate casserole and served as a side dish.

Prep time: 20 minutes
Cooking time: 45 to 50 minutes, plus standing
Baking time: 30 to 35 minute

- **1** cup wild rice
  Cold water
- **3** cups water
- **1** tablespoon olive oil
- **1** pound bulk pork sausage or fresh sweet Italian sausage links, casings removed
- **3** cups chopped onions
- **2** cups chopped fennel
- ½ pound cremini, shiitake or white mushrooms, quartered
- **1** bay leaf
- ¾ teaspoon salt
- ½ teaspoon freshly ground pepper
- ½ cup chopped fresh flat-leaf parsley
- ½ cup dried sweet cherries or cranberries
- ½ cup long-grain rice, cooked according to package directions
- **1** tablespoon butter, cut into quarters

1. Soak wild rice in enough cold water to cover in a large bowl, discard any grains that float to the top. Drain rice. Bring the 3 cups water and wild rice to boil in a medium saucepan over medium heat. Reduce heat; cover saucepan and simmer rice 45 to 50 minutes, until just tender but still has a slight crunch. Remove from heat; cool to room temperature.

2. Heat oil in a large skillet over medium heat. Add sausage and cook, breaking up with back of spoon, 5 to 8 minutes, until no longer pink. Stir in onions, fennel, mushrooms, bay leaf, salt and pepper. Cook 5 minutes, until vegetables soften slightly and sausage is thoroughly cooked. Stir in parsley and cherries; cook 2 minutes more. Remove bay leaf;

discard. Transfer mixture to a large bowl; stir in wild rice and cooked long-grain rice. *(Can be made ahead. Refrigerate in an airtight container overnight.)*

3. If using Wild Rice Stuffing to stuff turkey, proceed as directed for Turkey with Roasted Garlic Gravy, page 294.

4. To bake, heat oven to 325°F. Generously butter a 13×9-inch baking dish. Spoon stuffing into prepared dish. Dot top with the butter. Cover with foil and bake 30 to 35 minutes, until heated through. Makes 12 cups.

Per ½-cup serving: 145 calories, 8.5 g total fat, 3 g saturated fat, 14 mg cholesterol, 213 mg sodium, 13 g carbohydrates, 4 g protein, 17 mg calcium, 1 g fiber

cranberry-pear sauce

Perfect with the holiday bird, this savory sauce is ready in minutes or can be made up to 1 week ahead. Pictured on page 281.

Total prep and cooking time: 30 minutes

- 1 **tangerine or orange**
- 1 **bag (12 oz.) fresh or frozen cranberries**
- 1 **large pear, peeled, cored and diced**
- ¾ **cup sugar**
- ½ **cup ruby port**
- 2 **tablespoons crystallized ginger, chopped**

1. Grate the peel from tangerine and squeeze the juice into a bowl; reserve.

2. Combine tangerine juice and peel, cranberries, pear, sugar and port in a medium saucepan. Bring to boil. Reduce heat and gently boil 10 to 15 minutes, until sauce thickens and cranberries pop but still have some shape. Stir in ginger. Cool and refrigerate. *(Can be made ahead. Cover and refrigerate up to 1 week.)* Serve with turkey, chicken or pork. Makes about 3 cups.

Per ¼-cup serving: 100 calories, 0 g total fat, 0 g saturated fat, 0 mg cholesterol, 3 mg sodium, 23 g carbohydrates, 0 g protein, 8 mg calcium, 2 g fiber

---

m e n u

thanksgiving 2000

VEGETABLES WITH ASSORTED DIPS, INCLUDING CHILE RANCH, ALMOND PESTO, BEET MAYONNAISE
page 289

CHEESE TARTLETS
page 290

TURKEY WITH ROASTED GARLIC GRAVY
page 294
OR
GRILLED TURKEY WITH APPLE CHUTNEY
page 292

WILD RICE STUFFING
page 298

CRANBERRY-PEAR SAUCE
left

POTATO-PARSNIP PUREE
page 301

SAUTEED PEAS AND CELERY
page 300

BEST PARKER HOUSE ROLLS
page 304

PUMPKIN AND CARAMEL TIRAMISU
page 309

SWEET POTATO PIE
page 306

CHOCOLATE-PECAN TART
page 272

sauteed peas and celery (EASY)

A green vegetable is always a welcome addition to the holiday table, and this quick saute of peas, celery and red onion couldn't be easier. Pictured on page 283.

Prep time: 10 minutes • Cooking time: 15 minutes

- **1 tablespoon olive oil**
- **½ cup chopped red onion**
- **½ cup chopped celery**
- **2 boxes (10 oz. each) frozen peas, thawed**
- **¼ cup chopped celery leaves**
- **½ teaspoon salt**
- **¼ teaspoon freshly ground pepper**

Heat oil in a large skillet over medium heat. Add onion and cook 5 minutes, until softened. Stir in celery and cook 3 minutes, just until tender. Increase heat to medium-high; add peas. Cook 3 to 5 minutes more, until peas are heated through. Remove skillet from heat; stir in celery leaves, salt and pepper. Makes 8 servings.

Per serving: 75 calories, 2 g total fat, 0.5 g saturated fat, 0 mg cholesterol, 232 mg sodium, 11 g carbohydrates, 4 g protein, 24 mg calcium, 3 g fiber

balsamic roasted carrots (EASY)

Discover the wonderfully sweet flavor of balsamic vinegar. A simple pan roast with carrots and shallots is a great place to start. Pictured on page 283.

Prep time: 20 minutes • Baking time: 50 minutes

- **4 pounds carrots, cut diagonally into 2-inch pieces**
- **¼ pound shallots, cut into ½-inch-thick wedges**
- **3 tablespoons butter or margarine, divided**
- **⅓ cup balsamic vinegar**
- **2 tablespoons firmly packed brown sugar**
- **1 tablespoon light molasses**
- **½ teaspoon salt**

1. Heat oven to 450°F. Place carrots and shallots in a shallow 3-quart baking dish.

2. Melt 2 tablespoons of the butter in a large skillet over medium heat until lightly browned. Add vinegar, sugar and molasses. Bring to boil, stirring constantly, until reduced to ½ cup, 2 minutes.

3. Pour balsamic mixture over carrots and shallots; toss to coat. Roast 50 minutes, stirring once, until carrots are tender. Stir in remaining 1 tablespoon butter and the salt. *(Can be made ahead. Cover and refrigerate overnight. Let stand at room temperature 1 hour; then microwave, covered, on HIGH 5 to 6 minutes, stirring once.)* Makes 8 servings.

Per serving: 165 calories, 4.5 g total fat, 2.5 g saturated fat, 12 mg cholesterol, 273 mg sodium, 31 g carbohydrates, 3 g protein, 76 mg calcium, 7 g fiber

broccolini almondine (EASY)

Want a change of pace for the holidays? Try broccolini. This quick-cooking veggie tastes like a cross between broccoli and asparagus. Here it's steamed and combined with browned butter, orange peel and toasted almonds.

Total prep and cooking time: 30 minutes

- **2 pounds broccolini, trimmed (or broccoli, cut into 3-inch spears)**
- **5 tablespoons butter (no substitutes)**
- **¼ cup fresh orange juice**
- **1 teaspoon grated orange peel**
- **½ teaspoon salt**
- **⅓ cup sliced natural almonds, toasted**

Place a large steamer basket in a stockpot; add water to reach just under basket. Arrange broccolini in basket. Cover and bring to boil. Steam 5 to 7 minutes, until broccolini stems are tender. Melt butter in a large skillet over medium-high heat 3 to 4 minutes, until medium brown. Add orange juice and cook 10 seconds. Remove from heat; stir in orange peel and salt. Add broccolini and toss. Transfer to a platter and sprinkle with toasted almonds. Makes 6 servings.

Per serving: 185 calories, 12.5 g total fat, 6 g saturated fat, 26 mg cholesterol, 337 mg sodium, 13 g carbohydrates, 7 g protein, 129 mg calcium, 2 g fiber

potato-parsnip puree `EASY`

We don't normally use a food processor for mashing potatoes, but due to the proportion of parsnips to potatoes, this method works best. Pictured on page 282.

Prep time: 25 minutes • Cooking time: 25 minutes

- 1 **package (0.35 oz.) dried porcini mushrooms, rinsed well**
- 2½ **pounds parsnips, peeled and sliced**
- 1 **can (14½ oz.) chicken broth**
  Water
- 2½ **pounds Yukon Gold potatoes, peeled and cut into 1½-inch chunks**
- 8 **tablespoons butter or margarine, divided**
- 1½ **pounds leeks, trimmed, white part only, rinsed well and chopped**
- 1 **teaspoon salt, divided**

1. Pour ½ cup boiling water over dried porcini in a medium bowl; let stand 15 minutes. Drain, reserving ⅓ cup of liquid; mince porcini.

2. Meanwhile, bring parsnips, chicken broth and enough water to fill the broth can to boil in a stockpot. Reduce heat and cook at a low boil, 5 minutes. Add potatoes; cover and cook 20 minutes, until vegetables are tender. Drain vegetables in a colander set over a large bowl. Reserve 1¼ cups of the broth mixture. Add reserved porcini liquid to reserved broth mixture.

3. Melt 3 tablespoons of the butter in same stockpot. Add leeks and cook over medium heat, 7 minutes, until just starting to brown. Add porcini and ½ teaspoon of the salt. Cover and cook 3 minutes more, until tender.

4. Coarsely mash parsnip-potato mixture with a spoon. Transfer half of the mixture to a food processor. Add half of the broth mixture and half of the remaining butter. Process by pulsing 3 to 4 times, scraping bowl with a rubber spatula until smooth. Transfer mixture to pot with leek mixture. Repeat with remaining parsnip-potato mixture, broth mixture, butter and salt. If puree is not hot enough, heat in pot over medium heat, stirring, until heated through. *(Can be made ahead. Transfer to a microwaveproof bowl. Cool. Cover and*

refrigerate overnight. Reheat in microwave on HIGH 8 to 10 minutes, stirring every 2 to 3 minutes, until hot.) Makes 8 servings.

Per serving: 350 calories, 12.5 g total fat, 7.5 g saturated fat, 31 mg cholesterol, 659 mg sodium, 55 g carbohydrates, 5 g protein, 77 mg calcium, 10 g fiber

savory mashed potatoes `EASY`

Creamy Yukon Gold potatoes and a bacon, shallot and bread-crumb topping put ordinary potato dishes to shame. For the best texture, be sure the milk is hot when you're ready to mix it into the potatoes. Pictured on page 285.

Total prep and cooking time: 30 minutes

- 3 **pounds Yukon Gold potatoes, peeled and cut into 2-inch cubes**
- 4 **ounces pancetta (Italian bacon) or 5 thick-cut bacon slices, diced**
- 1 **tablespoon olive oil**
- ½ **cup minced shallots**
- 1 **cup fresh bread crumbs**
- 2 **tablespoons chopped fresh flat-leaf parsley**
- 6 **tablespoons butter or margarine, at room temperature**
- 1 **teaspoon salt**
- ¾ **cup very hot milk**

1. Bring potatoes and enough water to cover to boil in a stockpot. Cook 15 minutes, until tender.

2. Heat a large skillet 1 minute over medium-high heat. Add pancetta and cook until crisp. With a slotted spoon, transfer pancetta to a paper towel. Add oil and shallots to same skillet; cook 2 minutes. Add bread crumbs and cook 5 minutes more, until bread crumbs are golden, stirring often. Stir in parsley and pancetta.

3. Drain potatoes and return to same pot. Coarsely mash potatoes with butter and salt. Gradually beat in hot milk with a spoon. Transfer to a serving bowl; sprinkle top with ½ cup of the crumbs. Serve with the remaining crumbs. Makes 6 servings.

Per serving: 440 calories, 26.5 g total fat, 12 g saturated fat, 48 mg cholesterol, 705 mg sodium, 44 g carbohydrates, 8 g protein, 55 mg calcium, 4 g fiber

Homemade chicken stock adds a richness to recipes that canned stock lacks, but making a simmer-all-day stock is sometimes out of the question. Try this recipe, and in just minutes, canned broth tastes like homemade:

Combine 6 black peppercorns; 1 sprig fresh parsley; 1 clove garlic, crushed; ¼ bay leaf; and a pinch fennel seed in a tea infuser. Close lid; combine with 1 can (14½ oz.) chicken, beef or vegetable broth in a small saucepan. Bring to simmer; simmer 15 minutes. Remove infuser; use as desired. Makes 1⅓ cups.

tomato-cheese polenta

Here's a fast and festive side dish for your holiday table: instant polenta with sun-dried tomatoes, rich, creamy Italian fontina cheese and fresh rosemary. Splurge for the imported Italian fontina—it's worth it!

Total prep and cooking time: 30 minutes

- 5 teaspoons olive oil, divided
- 1 cup finely chopped onions
- 4 ounces sun-dried tomatoes in oil, finely chopped
- 3¼ cups chicken broth
- 1 cup heavy or whipping cream
- 1 teaspoon minced fresh rosemary
- ¼ teaspoon salt
- ¼ teaspoon freshly ground pepper
- 1½ cups instant polenta
- 4 ounces Italian fontina cheese, coarsely shredded

1. Heat 3 teaspoons of the oil in a large nonstick skillet over medium-high heat. Add onions and cook 4 to 5 minutes, until browned. Remove from heat and stir in sun-dried tomatoes.

2. Meanwhile, lightly oil a 13×9-inch baking pan. Set aside.

3. Combine broth, cream, rosemary, salt and pepper in a large saucepan. Gradually whisk polenta into broth mixture, bringing to boil. Cook, stirring, 5 minutes, until mixture is thick and pulls away from side of pan. Stir in cheese, the remaining 2 teaspoons olive oil and the onion mixture. Spread polenta evenly into prepared pan; let stand 5 minutes. Invert onto a cutting board; cut into 16 triangles. Makes 8 servings.

Per serving: 685 calories, 21.5 g total fat, 3 g saturated fat, 6 mg cholesterol, 1,518 mg sodium, 102 g carbohydrates, 21 g protein, 126 mg calcium, 5 g fiber

chestnut puree

The subtly sweet flavor of chestnuts in stuffing, side dishes and desserts is a mainstay of traditional holiday cooking. Our rich, creamy-smooth puree, scented with fresh fennel, is the perfect accompaniment to roast turkey, duck or goose. Tip: Cutting an "X" on the flat side of each chestnut prevents the shell from bursting during roasting. Chestnuts are highly perishable (they contain 50 percent water), so even unshelled nuts should be refrigerated (or frozen) to stay fresh.

Prep time: 1 hour • Baking time: 20 minutes
Cooking time: 30 minutes

- 1 pound fresh chestnuts
- 1 can (14½ oz.) chicken broth
- 1 small fennel bulb, trimmed, sliced
- ½ cup water
- 1 celery rib, sliced
- ¼ cup heavy or whipping cream
- 2 tablespoons butter or margarine
- ¼ teaspoon salt
- ⅛ teaspoon freshly ground pepper

1. Heat oven to 400°F. With a paring knife, cut an "X" in the flat side of each chestnut. Spread chestnuts on a jelly-roll pan. Roast 20 minutes, until peel curls back. Cool slightly. When cool enough to handle but still warm, remove outside peel and inside skin from chestnuts. If chestnuts don't peel easily, return to oven for 10 minutes.

2. Combine peeled chestnuts, chicken broth, fennel, water and celery in a large saucepan. Bring

to boil. Reduce heat; cover and simmer until chestnuts are tender, about 30 minutes. Drain vegetables in a sieve set over a medium bowl; reserve cooking liquid.

3. Place drained vegetables in a food processor. Process to puree. Add cream, butter, salt and pepper. Process until very smooth and creamy, adding the reserved cooking liquid if necessary. Reheat in a saucepan over low heat until hot. Makes 4 to 6 servings.

Per serving: 240 calories, 11 g total fat, 6 g saturated fat, 29 mg cholesterol, 555 mg sodium, 32 g carbohydrates, 3 g protein, 44 mg calcium, 7 g fiber

ginger spiced squash EASY

Use precut squash (from the produce aisle) to get this tasty dish to the table in record time. Pictured on page 284.

Total prep and cooking time: 30 minutes

- 3 tablespoons butter or margarine
- 2½ pounds peeled, cut-up butternut squash or 3¾ pounds whole butternut squash, peeled and cut into 1¼-inch chunks
- ½ cup chicken broth
- ¼ cup apricot preserves
- ½ teaspoon salt
- ½ teaspoon grated fresh ginger
- ½ teaspoon Asian chili garlic sauce*

1. Melt butter in a 12-inch nonstick skillet over medium heat. Add squash, spreading out in skillet. Add chicken broth and bring to boil. Reduce heat to medium; cover and simmer 16 to 18 minutes, until tender.

2. Gently stir in preserves, salt, ginger and chili sauce. Bring to boil and cook 1 to 2 minutes more. Transfer to a serving bowl. Makes 6 servings.

Note: Can be found in ethnic sections of supermarkets or in Asian speciality stores.

Per serving: 170 calories, 6 g total fat, 3.5 g saturated fat, 16 mg cholesterol, 353 mg sodium, 31 g carbohydrates, 2 g protein, 95 mg calcium, 4 g fiber

cranberry drop scones EASY

A perfect recipe for the holiday season, these scones feature both fresh and dried cranberries. Serve for breakfast or add to the Thanksgiving Day breadbasket. They're sure to become a family favorite.

Total prep and baking time: 30 minutes

- 2 cups all-purpose flour
- 6 tablespoons cold butter, cut up (no substitutes)
- ⅓ cup plus 1 tablespoon sugar, divided
- 2 teaspoons baking powder
- ¼ teaspoon salt
- ½ cup fresh or frozen cranberries, coarsely chopped
- ⅓ cup dried cranberries
- ½ cup milk
- 1 large egg

1. Heat oven to 425°F. Grease a large cookie sheet. Pulse flour, butter, ⅓ cup of the sugar, the baking powder and salt in a food processor until the texture of fine meal. Transfer to a large bowl. Stir in fresh and dried cranberries.

2. With a fork, beat milk and egg in a small bowl. Add to flour mixture; stir with fork until dry ingredients are moistened.

3. Drop dough by heaping tablespoonfuls, 2 inches apart, onto prepared sheet (there will be 12). Sprinkle with remaining 1 tablespoon sugar. Bake 12 to 14 minutes, until golden brown in spots. Remove to a wire rack to cool. Makes 12 scones.

Per scone: 180 calories, 7 g total fat, 4 g saturated fat, 35 mg cholesterol, 198 mg sodium, 26 g carbohydrates, 3 g protein, 64 mg calcium, 1 g fiber

from parker house to your house

Here's our take on this much-loved classic:

YEAST THRIVES on potatoes, so we added mashed potato to the dough, resulting in ultra-light, melt-in-your-mouth rolls.

WE'VE KEPT THE DISTINCTIVE SHAPE by making an off-center crease in each round before it's folded in half. Then we brushed the rolls with melted butter for extra flavor and baked them until puffed and golden brown.

PARKER HOUSE ROLLS, like all dinner rolls, taste best served warm. The good news: they freeze beautifully.

best parker house rolls

Pictured on page 281.

Prep time: 1 hour plus rising
Baking time: 18 to 20 minutes

1	medium all-purpose potato (5 oz.), peeled and cut into chunks
2	tablespoons plus 3 teaspoons sugar, divided
¼	cup warm water (105°F. to 115°F.)
1	package active dry yeast
10	tablespoons butter or margarine, softened, divided
¾	cup warm milk (105°F. to 115°F.)
1	large egg
1	teaspoon salt
3½	to 4¼ cups all-purpose flour

1. Bring potato and enough water to cover to boil in a small saucepan; cover pan and simmer 10 minutes, until tender. Drain potato and return to pan. With a potato masher, mash until smooth. Measure enough mashed potato to equal ½ cup; cool to room temperature.

2. Dissolve 1 teaspoon of the sugar in warm water in a large bowl. Sprinkle top of mixture with yeast and let stand 5 to 10 minutes, until yeast is bubbly.

3. Stir mashed potato into yeast mixture with remaining 2 tablespoons plus 2 teaspoons sugar, 6 tablespoons of the butter, the milk, egg and salt with a wooden spoon. Vigorously beat in 2 cups of the flour until smooth. Gradually stir in 1¼ cups more flour until blended and mixture forms soft, moist dough.

4. Grease a large bowl. On a lightly floured surface, knead dough 8 to 10 minutes, until smooth and elastic, adding enough of the remaining flour as necessary to prevent dough from sticking. Gather dough into a ball. Place dough in prepared bowl, turning to grease top. Cover bowl with plastic wrap and let dough rise in a warm, draft-free place until doubled in bulk, 1 to 1½ hours.

5. Meanwhile, melt the remaining 4 tablespoons butter. Grease a large cookie sheet.

6. Punch down dough; divide in half. On a lightly floured surface, roll each piece of dough to a ⅜-inch thickness (be sure dough is this measurement). Using a floured 2½- to 2¾-inch round cookie cutter, cut out circles. Gather scraps and set aside. Lightly brush circles with melted butter. With the handle of wooden spoon, firmly press an off-center crease in each circle. Fold each circle along crease with large half on top. Press folded edge firmly. Place rolls ¾ inch apart on prepared cookie sheet.

7. Repeat rolling, cutting and buttering with remaining half of dough. Gather scraps and lightly knead, then reroll. Lightly brush tops with butter. Cover with plastic wrap; let rise until almost doubled in bulk, about 45 minutes.

8. Meanwhile, heat oven to 375°F. Uncover rolls and bake 18 to 20 minutes, until golden brown. Immediately brush rolls with remaining butter. Transfer to a wire rack; cool slightly. Serve warm. (*Can be made ahead. Cool completely. Transfer rolls to an airtight container and freeze up to 2 weeks. Reheat in a 350°F. oven 8 minutes.*) Makes 24 rolls.

Per roll: 140 calories, 5.5 g total fat, 3 g saturated fat, 23 mg cholesterol, 153 mg sodium, 19 g carbohydrates, 3 g protein, 15 mg calcium, 1 g fiber

green onion corn bread ⊘

Bacon, green onions and Cheddar cheese make a festive corn bread for the holiday table.

Prep time: 15 minutes plus cooling
Baking time: 24 to 27 minutes

3	slices bacon, chopped
1¾	cups yellow cornmeal
¾	cup all-purpose flour
2	tablespoons sugar
1½	teaspoons baking powder
1	teaspoon salt
¾	teaspoon baking soda
¼	teaspoon ground red pepper
2	cups buttermilk
2	large eggs
½	cup sliced green onions
2	tablespoons butter or margarine, melted
1	cup whole kernel frozen corn, thawed and coarsely chopped
1	cup shredded extra-sharp Cheddar cheese

1. Heat oven to 425°F. Cook bacon in a 10-inch cast-iron skillet until crisp. With a slotted spoon, remove bacon to paper towels; drain. Reserve bacon drippings in skillet.

2. Combine cornmeal, flour, sugar, baking powder, salt, baking soda and red pepper in a large bowl. Whisk buttermilk, eggs, green onions and butter in a bowl until well combined. Stir buttermilk mixture into cornmeal mixture just until moistened. Stir in bacon, corn and cheese just until combined.

3. Heat drippings 1 minute over medium heat. Remove skillet from heat; carefully add batter and spread evenly. Bake 24 to 27 minutes, until toothpick inserted in center comes out clean. Cool on a wire rack 30 minutes. Run a knife around side of skillet and invert skillet onto rack. Remove pan. Invert corn bread again. *(Can be made ahead. Cool completely. Wrap well and freeze up to 2 weeks. Thaw at room temperature 4 hours. Reheat at 350°F. 20 minutes.)* Cut into wedges. Makes 12 servings.

Per serving: 215 calories, 7.5 g total fat, 4 g saturated fat, 54 mg cholesterol, 483 mg sodium, 28 g carbohydrates, 8 g protein, 156 mg calcium, 2 g fiber

pumpkin-pecan bread ⊘

A classic holiday quick bread, moist and spicy and studded with nuts—the best ever!

Prep time: 15 minutes • Baking time: 55 to 60 minutes

	Vegetable cooking spray
2	cups all-purpose flour
1½	teaspoons cinnamon
1	teaspoon baking powder
1	teaspoon baking soda
¾	teaspoon salt
½	teaspoon ginger
¼	teaspoon allspice
	Pinch freshly ground pepper
1	cup canned solid-pack pumpkin
1	cup sugar
½	cup skim milk
¼	cup vegetable oil
2	large eggs
½	cup chopped pecans, toasted

1. Heat oven to 350°F. Lightly coat a 9×5-inch loaf pan with vegetable cooking spray. Combine flour, cinnamon, baking powder, baking soda, salt, ginger, allspice and pepper in a medium bowl.

2. Whisk pumpkin, sugar, milk, oil and eggs in another bowl until well combined. Stir in dry ingredients just until blended; fold in nuts.

3. Pour batter into prepared pan. Bake 55 to 60 minutes, until toothpick inserted in center comes out clean. Cool in pan on a wire rack, 15 minutes. Unmold and cool. *(Can be made ahead. Cover and freeze up to 1 month. Let stand at room temperature 4 hours before serving.)* Makes 1 loaf (eighteen ½-inch-thick slices).

Per slice: 150 calories, 6 g total fat, 1 g saturated fat, 24 mg cholesterol, 201 mg sodium, 23 g carbohydrates, 3 g protein, 35 mg calcium, 1 g fiber

cranberry-pecan coffee cake

This moist coffee cake is layered with a dried cranberry, pecan and chocolate streusel, then drizzled with an orange-flavored glaze.

Prep time: 35 minutes
Baking time: 45 to 50 minutes

STREUSEL:

- ⅓ cup plus 1 tablespoon all-purpose flour
- ¼ cup firmly packed brown sugar
- 1 teaspoon cinnamon
- ¼ cup butter or margarine
- ⅔ cup chopped pecans
- ½ cup dried cranberries
- ⅓ cup miniature semisweet chocolate chips

- ⅔ cup sour cream
- 2 large eggs
- 1 large egg yolk
- 2 teaspoons vanilla extract
- 2 cups all-purpose flour
- ¾ teaspoon baking powder
- ½ teaspoon baking soda
- ¼ teaspoon salt
- 6 tablespoons butter or margarine, softened
- 1 cup granulated sugar

GLAZE:

- 5 tablespoons confectioners' sugar
- 2 teaspoons orange-flavored liqueur or orange juice
- 1 to 2 teaspoons water

1. ▪ Heat oven to 350°F. Grease a 9-inch springform pan; dust with flour and tap out excess.

2. ▪ *Make streusel:* Combine flour, brown sugar and cinnamon in medium bowl. With a pastry blender or 2 knives, cut in butter until mixture resembles coarse crumbs. Stir in pecans, cranberries and chocolate chips.

3. ▪ Whisk together sour cream, eggs, egg yolk and vanilla in a bowl. Combine flour, baking powder, baking soda and salt in another bowl. Beat butter in a large mixer bowl at medium-high speed until creamy. Add granulated sugar and beat until light

and fluffy. At low speed, alternately add flour mixture and sour cream mixture, beginning and ending with flour mixture just until blended.

4. ▪ Spread half the batter into the prepared pan. Sprinkle top evenly with half of streusel. Spoon large dollops of remaining batter over streusel; then lightly spread with spatula. Sprinkle top with remaining streusel. Bake 45 to 50 minutes, until top is lightly browned and toothpick inserted in center of cake comes out clean. Cool on a wire rack 5 minutes; remove side of pan and cool completely. *(Can be made ahead. Cover and freeze up to 1 month. Let stand at room temperature 3 hours before serving.)*

5. ▪ *Make glaze:* Combine confectioners' sugar and orange liqueur in a small bowl. Gradually add enough water to make a pourable consistency. Drizzle over cake. Makes 12 servings.

Per serving: 400 calories, 20 g total fat, 10 g saturated fat, 85 mg cholesterol, 249 mg sodium, 51 g carbohydrates, 5 g protein, 51 mg calcium, 2 g fiber

sweet potato pie

The holidays and pie go hand in hand, so it's hard to imagine not finding one of these on your holiday table.

Prep time: 45 minutes plus chilling
Baking time: 38 to 40 minutes

PASTRY:

- 1½ cups all-purpose flour
- ⅛ teaspoon salt
- 6 tablespoons butter or margarine, chilled and cut up
- 3 tablespoons vegetable shortening, chilled
- 3 to 4 tablespoons iced water

FILLING:

- 2 pounds sweet potatoes, peeled and quartered
- ½ cup firmly packed brown sugar
- ¼ cup granulated sugar
- 3 large eggs
- ½ teaspoon cinnamon
- ¼ teaspoon ginger
  Pinch nutmeg

- 1 cup heavy or whipping cream
- 1 tablespoon confectioners' sugar

1. *Make pastry:* Combine flour and salt in a bowl. With a pastry blender or 2 knives, cut in butter and shortening until mixture resembles coarse crumbs. With a fork, stir in water, 1 tablespoon at a time, until mixture begins to hold together. Shape pastry into a ball. Flatten into a disk. Wrap in plastic and refrigerate 30 minutes.

2. Adjust oven rack to lowest position. Heat oven to 400°F. On a lightly floured surface, roll pastry disk into a 12-inch circle. Fit into a 9-inch pie plate, trim edges and flute. Freeze pie shell 15 minutes. Line pastry with foil and fill with dried beans or pie weights. Bake 10 minutes. Remove foil and beans. Bake 8 minutes more, until crust is lightly golden. Cool crust on a wire rack.

3. *Make filling:* Reduce oven temperature to 375°F. Arrange a steamer basket in a saucepan. Add enough water to reach just under the basket. Add potatoes; cover and bring water to boil. Reduce heat; steam potatoes 20 to 25 minutes, until tender. Transfer to a large bowl. With a potato masher or wooden spoon, mash potatoes. Using a hand-held mixer, add the remaining filling ingredients, beating until well combined. Pour filling into warm crust. Bake 38 to 40 minutes, until filling is set. Cool on a wire rack.

4. Beat cream and confectioners' sugar in a bowl to stiff peaks. Serve sweetened whipped cream with warm or room temperature pie. Makes 8 servings.

Per serving: 500 calories, 26.5 g total fat, 14 g saturated fat, 144 mg cholesterol, 176 mg sodium, 59 g carbohydrates, 7 g protein, 66 mg calcium, 3 g fiber

holiday rice pudding EASY

Here's a classic comfort dessert for your holiday table. As an added bonus—it can be made ahead of time.

Prep time: 20 minutes plus cooling
Cooking time: 50 minutes

- 1 **quart milk**
- ½ **cup granulated sugar, divided**
- ½ **vanilla bean, split lengthwise**
- ½ **cup long-grain rice (not converted)**
- ½ **cup dried cranberries or blueberries**
- 3 **tablespoons pear brandy (eau-de-vie) or white rum, divided**
- 2 **large egg yolks**
- 1 **cup heavy or whipping cream, divided**
- ½ **teaspoon grated lemon peel**
- 2 **tablespoons confectioners' sugar**
- 2 **tablespoons diced candied orange peel Candied orange peel strips, for garnish (optional)**

1. Bring milk, ¼ cup of the granulated sugar and the vanilla bean just to boil in a large saucepan over medium-high heat; stir in rice. Reduce heat, cover and simmer 40 minutes, until rice is tender.

2. Meanwhile, stir together cranberries and 2 tablespoons of the pear brandy in a small bowl. Set aside.

3. Whisk yolks, ½ cup of the cream and the remaining ¼ cup granulated sugar in a medium bowl. Stir cream mixture into rice mixture. Bring to boil. Cook, stirring constantly, 2 minutes. Remove vanilla bean; discard. Transfer rice mixture to a large bowl; stir in lemon peel. Cool completely.

4. Drain cranberries; discard excess liquid. Beat the remaining ½ cup cream with confectioners' sugar in a mixer bowl until stiff. Fold cream, cranberries, candied orange peel and the remaining 1 tablespoon pear brandy into rice mixture.

5. To serve, transfer pudding to a serving bowl. Garnish with candied orange peel strips, if desired. (*Can be made ahead. Cover and refrigerate up to 24 hours.*) Makes 8 servings.

Per serving: 320 calories, 14.5 g total fat, 9 g saturated fat, 103 mg cholesterol, 76 mg sodium, 38 g carbohydrates, 6 g protein, 178 mg calcium, 1 g fiber

apple-cider spice cake (EASY)

Bundt cakes are every baker's dream. They're easy to make ahead, fancy enough for company or casual enough for snacking. So if you're craving a warm, comforting dessert that everyone will love, turn to this harvest cake with bourbon glaze and cider-glazed apples.

Prep time: 35 minutes • Baking time: 1 hour

- 3 cups all-purpose flour
- 2 teaspoons cinnamon
- 2 teaspoons ginger
- 1 teaspoon baking powder
- ½ teaspoon baking soda
- ½ teaspoon salt
- ½ teaspoon nutmeg
- ½ teaspoon allspice
- 1 cup butter or margarine, softened
- 1 cup firmly packed dark brown sugar
- 1 cup granulated sugar
- 5 large eggs, at room temperature 20 to 30 minutes
- ¾ cup apple cider

GLAZE:
- 1½ cups confectioners' sugar
- 4 teaspoons apple cider
- 4 teaspoons bourbon

CIDER-GLAZED APPLES:
- 4 tablespoons butter or margarine, divided
- 4 Golden Delicious apples, peeled, cored and sliced ½-inch thick, divided
- 2 Granny Smith apples, peeled, cored and sliced ½-inch thick, divided
- ⅔ cup apple cider, divided
- ½ cup golden raisins, divided

1. Heat oven to 325°F. Grease and flour a 12-cup bundt pan.

2. Combine flour, cinnamon, ginger, baking powder, baking soda, salt, nutmeg and allspice in a medium bowl; set aside. Beat butter in a large mixer bowl until creamy. Add brown and granulated sugars. Beat 3 minutes, until light and fluffy. Beat in eggs, one at a time, until well blended. At low speed, alternately beat in flour mixture with apple cider, beginning and ending with flour mixture, until blended. Spoon batter into prepared pan; spread evenly.

3. Bake 1 hour, or until a toothpick inserted in center of cake comes out clean. Cool cake in pan 20 minutes. Unmold onto a wire rack set over a sheet of waxed paper.

4. *Make glaze:* Sift confectioners' sugar into a small bowl. Whisk in cider and bourbon until smooth. Spoon over top of warm cake, spreading to cover top and letting some glaze run down sides. Let cool.

5. *Make cider-glazed apples:* Melt 2 tablespoons of the butter in a large skillet over medium-high heat. Add 2 of the Golden Delicious and 1 of the Granny Smith apples. Cook 6 to 8 minutes, until softened. Add ⅓ cup of the cider and ¼ cup of the raisins. Cook 1 to 2 minutes, until cider evaporates and apples are tender and glazed. Transfer to a bowl. Repeat with the remaining butter, apples, cider and raisins. Serve with cake. Makes 12 servings.

Per serving: 595 calories, 22.5 g total fat, 13 g saturated fat, 140 mg cholesterol, 421 mg sodium, 94 g carbohydrates, 6 g protein, 73 mg calcium, 3 g fiber

pumpkin and caramel tiramisu

*Try this festive holiday twist on an old Italian classic!
Tip: The dessert needs to refrigerate overnight. For its
fullest flavor, let the tiramisu stand at room temperature
1 hour before serving.*

Prep time: 20 minutes plus chilling
Cooking time: 15 minutes

CARAMEL:

3 tablespoons butter (no substitutes)

½ cup firmly packed brown sugar

½ cup pure maple syrup

¼ cup heavy or whipping cream

FILLING:

2 teaspoons cinnamon

1 teaspoon ginger

¼ teaspoon cloves

1 can (16 oz.) solid-pack pumpkin

½ cup granulated sugar

½ cup heavy or whipping cream

¼ teaspoon salt

1 package (7 oz.) Italian ladyfingers or
2 packages (3 oz. each) soft ladyfingers

TOPPING:

½ cup heavy or whipping cream

1 tablespoon confectioners' sugar

1 tablespoon bourbon

1 container (8¾ oz.) mascarpone, at room
temperature

¼ teaspoon freshly grated nutmeg

1. *Make caramel:* Melt butter in a medium
saucepan. Add the remaining caramel ingredients.
Bring to boil. Reduce heat; cook at a low boil
8 minutes, until syrupy. Cool 10 minutes.

2. *Make filling:* Meanwhile, toast cinnamon, ginger
and cloves in a medium saucepan over medium
heat 15 to 25 seconds, just until fragrant. Add
pumpkin and granulated sugar. Cook, stirring,
about 5 minutes more, until thick and slightly
darkened. Stir in cream and salt.

3. Arrange ladyfingers in a single layer in a
shallow dish. Pour caramel over ladyfingers;

turn each to coat well. Let stand 10 minutes,
turning occasionally.

4. *Make topping:* Beat cream in a mixer bowl on
medium-high speed until it starts to thicken. Add
confectioners' sugar and beat to soft peaks. Beat in
bourbon. Fold half of the whipped cream into the
mascarpone to lighten. Fold in the remaining half
of whipped cream. Set aside.

5. To assemble, arrange half of the soaked
ladyfingers in a single layer to cover the bottom of
a shallow 2-quart casserole dish, breaking 1 or
2 ladyfingers to fit, if necessary. Spread half of the
filling evenly over ladyfingers. Repeat with
remaining ladyfingers and filling. Evenly spread on
topping; sprinkle with nutmeg. Cover dish with
plastic wrap and refrigerate overnight. Let stand
at room temperature 1 hour before serving. Makes
8 servings.

Per serving: 575 calories, 32.5 g total fat, 20.5 g saturated fat,
88 mg cholesterol, 215 mg sodium, 67 g carbohydrates,
5 g protein, 152 mg calcium, 1 g fiber

---

test kitchen tip

a tale of tiramisu

*Once tasted, the all-at-once light, airy and rich
tiramisu won't last long on your dessert plate, but
the memory of its heavenly goodness will
most certainly remain. So what's its story?*

TIRAMISU literally means "carry me up,"
which makes sense if you've ever been
fortunate enough to enjoy good tiramisu.

THIS ITALIAN TREAT (also known as
"Italian Trifle" or "Tuscan Trifle") was
originally created in Siena, in Tuscany, where
it was created for Grand Duke Cosimo
de'Medici III. At the time it was called "Zuppa
Del Duca" (the "duke's soup"). The dessert
ultimately made its way to Treviso, in Italy's
Veneto region. Not surprisingly, one of the
things Treviso is best known for is its tiramisu!

buche de noel

Inspired by the classic French Christmas cake, our glorious hazelnut-chocolate "yule log" is an impressive sponge cake with satiny buttercream frosting. Pictured on page 288.

Prep time: 1 hour plus chilling and decorating
Baking time: 6 to 8 minutes

PRALINE:
- ⅓ cup granulated sugar
- ¼ teaspoon fresh lemon juice
- ¼ cup whole blanched almonds, toasted and coarsely chopped
- ¼ cup hazelnuts, toasted, skinned and coarsely chopped (see note, page 258)

CAKE:
- ½ cup cake flour (not self-rising)
- ⅛ teaspoon salt
- 3 large egg yolks, at room temperature 20 to 30 minutes
- 2 large eggs, at room temperature 20 to 30 minutes
- ¾ cup granulated sugar, divided
- 1 teaspoon vanilla extract
- 3 large egg whites, at room temperature 20 to 30 minutes
- 4 tablespoons confectioners' sugar, divided

BUTTERCREAM:
- ¼ cup water
- ½ cup granulated sugar
- 3 large egg whites, at room temperature 20 to 30 minutes
- ⅛ teaspoon salt
- 1½ cups unsalted butter, cut into small pieces, at room temperature (no substitutes)
- ¾ teaspoon vanilla extract
- 4 ounces semisweet chocolate squares, melted
- 2 ounces unsweetened chocolate squares, melted

CHOCOLATE-DIPPED HAZELNUTS:
- 12 whole hazelnuts, toasted and skinned (see note, page 258)
- 1 ounce semisweet chocolate square, melted
- 2 tablespoons praline
  Chocolate curls, white currants and Meringue Mushrooms (see recipe, page 311), for garnish (optional)

1. *Make praline:* Grease a cookie sheet; set aside. Combine sugar and lemon juice in a medium heavy saucepan. Cook over medium-low heat until sugar begins to melt (do not stir). Continue to cook 5 to 7 minutes more, stirring occasionally, until sugar completely melts and turns deep golden. Stir in nuts. Immediately pour praline onto prepared sheet. Cool completely, 45 minutes. Break praline into small chunks. Process in a food processor until finely ground. Makes ¾ cup. *(Can be made ahead. Store in an airtight container at room temperature up to 1 week.)*

2. *Make cake:* Heat oven to 425°F. Grease a 10½×15½×1-inch jelly-roll pan. Line bottom of pan with waxed paper. Grease and flour paper, tapping out excess.

3. Combine flour and salt in a bowl; set aside. Beat egg yolks and eggs in a large mixer bowl until thick and pale yellow, 4 to 5 minutes. Gradually beat in ½ cup of the sugar, 1 tablespoon at a time. Add vanilla. Beat until mixture holds a ribbon when beaters are lifted, 2 minutes more. Using clean beaters, beat egg whites in a clean mixer bowl on high speed until foamy, 1 minute. Gradually beat in the remaining ¼ cup sugar. Beat to soft peaks, 2 minutes. Gently fold whites into egg yolk mixture just to combine. Sift flour mixture over egg mixture. Gently fold flour into egg mixture just until combined. Do not stir. Evenly spread batter into prepared pan.

4. Bake cake 6 to 8 minutes, until edges come away from sides of pan and center of cake springs back when lightly touched with a fingertip. Sift 2 tablespoons of the confectioners' sugar over top. Immediately invert onto a clean kitchen towel. Remove pan and peel off waxed paper; sift the remaining 2 tablespoons confectioners' sugar over cake. Lifting from the long side, carefully roll hot cake up with towel. Completely cool cake in towel on a wire rack, 30 minutes.

5. *Make buttercream:* Combine water and sugar in a small saucepan. Whisk over medium-high heat to dissolve sugar; then cook until syrup registers 240°F. (soft ball stage) on a candy thermometer.

6. Meanwhile, beat egg whites in a large mixer bowl at high speed until foamy. Beat in salt. Beat to stiff peaks, 2 to 3 minutes. Gradually pour in boiling (240°F.) sugar syrup in a thin, steady stream. Beat 3 to 4 minutes, until mixture is thick, glossy and almost room temperature. At medium speed; beat in butter, a few pieces at a time, until blended. Add vanilla. (Buttercream may appear curdled during beating.) Continue to beat 2 to 3 minutes more, until buttercream is smooth, shiny and stiff.

7. Set aside 2 tablespoons of the praline for the chocolate dipped hazelnuts. Transfer 1½ cups of the buttercream to a bowl and stir in the remaining praline. Stir melted chocolates into the remaining buttercream. Set both aside.

8. To assemble, gently unroll cooled cake. Set aside ⅓ cup of the praline buttercream. Spread the remaining praline buttercream over top to edges of cake. Reroll cake (without towel) to within ½ inch of edges.

9. Spread log with ⅓ cup of the chocolate buttercream to form a very thin coat (do not coat ends of log). Spoon remaining chocolate buttercream into a pastry bag fitted with a #98 tip (French star semicircle). Pipe parallel lines of chocolate buttercream lengthwise along log to cover. Spoon the remaining praline buttercream into another pastry bag fitted with a ³⁄₁₆-inch round tip. Pipe praline buttercream in concentric circles to cover the ends of each log. (*Can be made ahead. Refrigerate until buttercream is firm, 1 hour; then cover loosely with plastic wrap and refrigerate overnight. Let stand at room temperature 2 hours before serving.*)

10. *Make chocolate-dipped hazelnuts:* Dip bottom half of each hazelnut into melted chocolate and then into the reserved 2 tablespoons praline. Refrigerate 10 minutes, until chocolate is firm.

11. Decorate with chocolate-dipped hazelnuts. Garnish cake with chocolate curls, currants and Meringue Mushrooms, if desired. Makes 12 servings.

Per serving: 520 calories, 37.5 g total fat, 19 g saturated fat, 151 mg cholesterol, 94 mg sodium, 44 g carbohydrates, 7 g protein, 44 mg calcium, 2 g fiber

meringue mushrooms

Prep time: 30 minutes plus standing
Baking time: 50 minutes

- **2** large egg whites, at room temperature 20 to 30 minutes
- **⅓** cup granulated sugar, divided
- **½** teaspoon almond extract
- **3** tablespoons confectioners' sugar
- **1** ounce semisweet chocolate square, melted
- **1** tablespoon unsweetened cocoa powder

1. Heat oven to 225°F. Line 2 large cookie sheets with parchment paper.

2. On high speed, beat egg whites in a mixer bowl with 1 tablespoon of the granulated sugar, until soft peaks form, 2 minutes. Gradually beat in remaining granulated sugar, 1 tablespoon at a time, until stiff peaks form, 2 to 3 minutes more. Beat in almond extract.

3. Sift confectioners' sugar over meringue; gently fold together just until combined.

4. Spoon meringue into a large pastry bag fitted with ½-inch round tip. For mushroom caps, keeping tip close to the parchment paper, hold bag vertically and pipe 36 mounds (each about 1¼ inches in diameter) onto lined cookie sheets. Smooth caps with a moist fingertip.

5. For mushroom stems, hold bag vertically and gently press 36 columns (each about ½ inch in diameter by 1¼ inches high) while slowly raising bag straight up. Cut stem from tip with a small knife.

6. Bake mushroom caps and stems until set and hardened, about 50 minutes. Do not allow meringues to brown. Turn oven off and let meringues cool and completely dry in oven, 2 hours or overnight.

7. To assemble, spread a thin layer of melted chocolate on underside of cap and attach stem. Repeat for remaining caps and stems. Let set 30 minutes, cap side down, in cool, dry place before turning upright. (*Can be made ahead. Store in airtight containers in a cool, dry place up to 2 days. Do not refrigerate.*) Dust tops with cocoa powder just before serving, if desired. Makes 36.

ginger and pine nut biscotti

Kathryn King's delectable assortment of comfort desserts is the star attraction at Aria, a restaurant in Atlanta, Georgia, where she is the pastry chef. These delicately spiced chocolate-dipped biscotti are a great example of her virtuosity with ingredients. Tip: The ends of the cookie logs bake faster than the center. To test for doneness, gently press the center with your fingertip—it should spring back when baked through. Pictured on page 286.

Prep time: 35 minutes plus decorating
Baking time: 38 to 40 minutes

    5½ cups all-purpose flour
     1 tablespoon plus 1½ teaspoons ginger
     ¾ teaspoon baking powder
     ½ teaspoon baking soda
     1 cup butter or margarine, softened
     2 cups sugar
     3 large eggs
     2 large egg yolks
     1 tablespoon grated orange peel
     1 cup pine nuts
    12 ounces semisweet chocolate squares, melted
        (see tip, page 259) and cooled

1. Adjust oven racks to center and lower third positions of oven. Heat oven to 350°F. Line 2 large cookie sheets with parchment paper or foil. Combine flour, ginger, baking powder and baking soda in a bowl.

2. Beat butter and sugar in a large mixer bowl until light and fluffy. Beat in eggs and egg yolks, one at a time, scraping bowl with a rubber spatula after each addition. At low speed, beat in flour mixture just until blended. Stir in orange peel and pine nuts.

3. Divide dough into quarters. On a lightly floured surface, roll each piece of dough into a 14×1½-inch log. Arrange 2 logs 5 inches apart on each prepared cookie sheet.

4. Bake 30 minutes, until logs crack on top and spring back when touched gently with a fingertip. Cool on cookie sheets on wire racks 15 minutes. Carefully transfer logs to a cutting board. With a serrated knife, gently slice each log diagonally into

½-inch-thick slices. Arrange slices, cut side down, 1 inch apart on ungreased cookie sheets. Bake 8 to 10 minutes more, until slices are toasted. Cool slices on wire racks.

5. *To decorate:* Brush off excess crumbs from slices and dip flat bottom side of each cookie in melted chocolate. Let stand 2 hours on racks, until chocolate has set. Makes 6½ dozen cookies.

Per biscotti: 110 calories, 5 g total fat, 2.5 g saturated fat, 20 mg cholesterol, 40 mg sodium, 15 g carbohydrates, 2 g protein, 8 mg calcium, 1 g fiber

belgian lace

Since 1993, Maureen Zammetti and her staff of 55 full- and part-time bakers have brought world-class breads, pastries and cookies to Wegmans, a chain of upscale supermarkets headquartered in Rochester, New York. Maureen is Bakery Manager and Trainer at the chain's Princeton, New Jersey, location. She loves this recipe because it's quick and easy without a lot of steps or ingredients. She chose pecans for this saucepan dough, but feel free to experiment with your favorite nuts. Pictured on page 287.

Prep time: 30 minutes plus decorating
Baking time: 8 to 9 minutes per batch

     1 cup sugar
     ¾ cup light corn syrup
     ½ cup butter, cut up (no substitutes)
    1¼ cups all-purpose flour
     2 cups chopped pecans
        Pinch nutmeg
     6 ounces semisweet chocolate squares, melted
        (see tip, page 259) and cooled
     6 ounces white chocolate squares, melted (see
        tip, page 259) and cooled

1. Heat oven to 350°F. Line 2 large cookie sheets with parchment paper or foil.

2. Bring sugar, corn syrup and butter just to boil in a small saucepan over medium-high heat. Remove from heat. Stir in the flour, pecans and nutmeg.

3. Drop the batter by rounded teaspoonfuls onto prepared cookie sheets (8 per sheet). Bake 8 to 9 minutes, until bubbly and golden. Cool cookies on cookie sheet 5 minutes, until firm; transfer to wire racks and cool completely. Repeat with remaining dough.

4. *To decorate:* Brush half of the flat side of each cookie with melted semisweet chocolate, then white chocolate. Decoratively swirl chocolates with tines of a fork. Transfer cookies to wire racks, chocolate side up. Let stand 1 hour, until chocolate sets. Makes 5 dozen cookies.

Per cookie: 100 calories, 5.5 g total fat, 2 g saturated fat, 4 mg cholesterol, 24 mg sodium, 13 g carbohydrates, 1 g protein, 9 mg calcium, 1 g fiber

angel thumbprints

Ask any loyal customer of the Macrina Bakery and Café in Seattle, Washington, and they'll tell you just how special this recipe is. These cookies are the most popular Christmas cookie at the café and are only available during the holidays. Head baker and owner Leslie Mackie got the recipe from her Norwegian great grandmother.

Prep time: 35 minutes plus chilling
Baking time: 17 minutes per batch

    4   cups all-purpose flour
    ¼   teaspoon salt
    1½ cups butter or margarine
    1   cup sugar
    3   large eggs
    1½ teaspoons vanilla extract
    1½ teaspoons almond extract
    3   cups toasted chopped pecans
    ⅔   cup apricot or raspberry preserves

1. Combine flour and salt in a bowl.

2. Beat butter and sugar in a large mixer bowl until light and fluffy. Beat in eggs, one at a time. Beat in vanilla and almond extracts. At low speed, gradually beat in flour mixture just until blended. Cover dough and refrigerate 1 hour.

3. Heat oven to 350°F. Spread pecans on a large plate. Shape dough into 1-inch balls and roll in pecans. Place balls 2 inches apart on ungreased cookie sheets. Press a ¾-inch-wide indentation in the center of each ball with thumb.

4. Bake 12 minutes. Press again with the back of a ¼ teaspoon measuring spoon and fill each indentation with ¼ teaspoon of the preserves. Bake 5 minutes more, until edges are golden. Transfer cookies to wire racks and cool completely. Makes 6½ dozen cookies.

Per cookie: 100 calories, 6.5 g total fat, 2.5 g saturated fat, 18 mg cholesterol, 47 mg sodium, 10 g carbohydrates, 1 g protein, 5 mg calcium, 1 g fiber

poppy seed cookies

At the Euro Pane Bakery in Pasadena, California, you'll find Sumi Chang, owner and baker, cheerfully greeting a long line of dedicated patrons. These simple slice-and-bake cookies are the customers' favorites. Pictured on page 286.

Prep time: 15 minutes plus chilling and decorating
Baking time: 9 to 10 minutes per batch

    2   cups all-purpose flour
    ½   teaspoon salt
    1   cup unsalted butter, softened (no substitutes)
    ½   cup sugar
    1   large egg yolk
    2   teaspoons vanilla extract
    1   teaspoon grated lemon peel
    1   tablespoon poppy seeds
        Decorative Icing (see recipe, page 318)

1. Combine flour and salt in a bowl. Beat butter and sugar in a large mixer bowl on medium speed until light and fluffy, 2 to 3 minutes. At low speed, beat in egg yolk, vanilla and lemon peel. Beat in flour mixture until combined; stir in poppy seeds.

2. Divide dough in half. Using a sheet of waxed paper and a ruler as a guide, shape each piece into a 8½×1¼-inch straight-edged rectangular shaped log; cover and refrigerate 2 hours or overnight. Heat oven to 350°F. Lightly grease 2 large cookie sheets. Unwrap logs; cut each into scant ¼-inch-thick slices. Place ½ inch apart on prepared sheets. Bake 9 to 10 minutes, until lightly browned on bottom. Cool on wire racks. Decorate as desired with Decorative Icing. Makes 6 dozen cookies.

Per cookie: 70 calories, 2.5 g total fat, 1.5 g saturated fat, 10 mg cholesterol, 18 mg sodium, 11 g carbohydrates, 1 g protein, 7 mg calcium, 0 g fiber

shortbread doves

Rebecca Rather's old-fashioned, down-home style is easily evident in these super-flaky shortbread cookies. The owner of Rather Sweet Bakery in Austin, Texas, says this recipe is one she has used "forever and ever," and she sells "tons" of them as special orders during the holidays. Tip: There's a good amount of butter in the recipe—Rebecca cautions to not overmix the dough. You want it to bake up melt-in-your-mouth tender. Pictured on page 287.

Prep time: 35 minutes plus chilling and decorating
Baking time: 12 minutes per batch

  4 cups all-purpose flour
  1 teaspoon baking powder
  ⅛ teaspoon salt
  2 cups butter, softened (no substitutes)
1½ cups confectioners' sugar
  1 tablespoon vanilla extract
  1 tablespoon grated lemon peel
    Decorative Icing (see recipe, page 318)

1. Combine flour, baking powder and salt in a bowl. Set aside.

2. Beat butter and confectioners' sugar in a large mixer bowl on medium speed 2 to 3 minutes. Beat in vanilla and lemon peel. At low speed, beat in flour mixture just until combined. Gather dough into a ball; divide in half and flatten into disks. Wrap and refrigerate 2 hours or overnight.

3. Heat oven to 350°F. Line 2 large cookie sheets with parchment paper. Roll 1 piece of dough between 2 sheets of waxed paper to a scant ¼-inch thickness. Place in freezer until firm, 15 minutes (keep remaining dough refrigerated). Uncover; cut out with a floured 4-inch dove-shaped cookie cutter. With a spatula, transfer cut-outs to prepared cookie sheets.

4. Bake 12 minutes, until golden brown at edges. Cool on cookie sheets 2 minutes. Transfer to wire racks and cool completely. Repeat with remaining dough, rerolling and cutting scraps. Decorate as desired. Makes about 4 dozen cookies.

Per cookie: 160 calories, 8 g total fat, 5 g saturated fat, 21 mg cholesterol, 96 mg sodium, 22 g carbohydrates, 1 g protein, 14 mg calcium, 0 g fiber

chocolate brownie cookies

This recipe is from Claudia Fleming, pastry chef at New York City's Gramercy Tavern and also this year's winner of the James Beard Outstanding Pastry Chef Award.

Prep time: 20 minutes plus standing and decorating
Baking time: 8 to 9 minutes per batch
Microwave used

  ¼ cup all-purpose flour
  ¼ teaspoon baking powder
  ⅛ teaspoon salt
  2 large eggs, at room temperature 20 to 30 minutes
  ⅔ cup granulated sugar
  1 teaspoon vanilla extract
  ½ teaspoon instant espresso powder dissolved in 1½ teaspoons water
  5 ounces bittersweet chocolate squares, chopped
  2 ounces unsweetened chocolate squares, chopped
  2 tablespoons butter or margarine
  ¾ cup miniature semisweet chocolate chips
    Confectioners' sugar (optional)

1. Heat oven to 375°F. Line 2 large cookie sheets with parchment paper or foil. Combine flour, baking powder and salt in a bowl. Beat eggs, granulated sugar, vanilla and dissolved espresso in a large mixer bowl until thick and tripled in volume, 5 minutes.

2. Meanwhile, combine chopped bittersweet and unsweetened chocolates with butter in a microwaveproof bowl. Microwave on MEDIUM (50 percent power) 1½ to 2 minutes; stir until chocolate is melted and mixture is smooth.

3. Gently fold chocolate mixture into egg mixture with a rubber spatula until partially combined (there will be streaks). Gently fold in flour mixture just until combined. Fold in chips. Let batter stand 15 to 20 minutes, until slightly thickened. Drop batter by heaping teaspoonfuls 1 inch apart onto prepared cookie sheets. Bake 8 to 9 minutes, until tops are puffed and cracked. Cool completely on cookie sheets. Dust the tops with confectioners' sugar, if desired. Makes about 3 dozen cookies.

Per cookie: 75 calories, 4 g total fat, 2.5 g saturated fat, 14 mg cholesterol, 22 mg sodium, 10 g carbohydrates, 1 g protein, 8 mg calcium, 0 g fiber

sablés

Our recipe for this classic French cookie—known for its delicate, crumbly texture—comes to us from Karl and Stephanie Boerner of Karl's Quality Bakery in Phoenix, Arizona. Sablés are usually flavored with citrus peel or nuts; however, Karl, the bakery's pastry chef, adds a holiday twist by stirring in colorful candied fruit. "Frost the cookies with the glaze while still warm," he advises, so it remains shiny and translucent. Pictured on page 286.

Prep time: 25 minutes plus chilling and decorating
Baking time: 9 to 10 minutes per batch

- **3 cups all-purpose flour**
- **½ teaspoon baking soda**
- **⅛ teaspoon salt**
- **1 cup butter, softened (no substitutes)**
- **1⅓ cups confectioners' sugar**
- **5 large egg yolks**
- **1 teaspoon vanilla extract**
- **1¼ cups finely diced candied fruit**

GLAZE:
- **1½ cups confectioners' sugar**
- **2 tablespoons hot water**

1. Combine flour, baking soda and salt in a bowl.

2. Beat butter and confectioners' sugar in a large mixer bowl until light and fluffy. At low speed, beat in egg yolks, 1 at a time, scraping bowl with a rubber spatula after each addition. Beat in vanilla. Gradually beat in flour mixture just until blended. Stir in candied fruit.

3. Divide dough into thirds. On a lightly floured surface, roll each piece of dough into a 9×1¼-inch log. Wrap each log in plastic wrap and refrigerate 3 hours or overnight.

4. Heat oven to 350°F. Cut thirty-two ¼-inch-thick slices from each log; arrange slices ½ inch apart on ungreased cookie sheets. Bake 9 to 10 minutes, until cookies are golden brown at edges.

5. *Make glaze:* Meanwhile, set a large wire rack over a sheet of waxed paper. Combine confectioners' sugar and water in a small bowl until smooth. Transfer cookies to the wire rack; brush tops of cookies with glaze while warm. Cool completely. Makes 8 dozen cookies.

Per cookie: 55 calories, 2 g total fat, 1 g saturated fat, 14 mg cholesterol, 35 mg sodium, 8 g carbohydrates, 1 g protein, 5 mg calcium, 0 g fiber

test kitchen tip
brownie in a jar

Here's a gift that's sure to win brownie points! Fill a decorative jar with a homemade brownie mix. Attach a gift tag that gives the baking instructions, below. Pictured on page 286.

MAKING BROWNIE MIX: Combine 1 cup flour and ½ teaspoon salt. Spoon mixture through a funnel into a 1-quart (4-cup) clean glass jar with lid, pushing mixture with a straw or fork handle. Repeat layering process with 6 tablespoons unsweetened cocoa, ¾ cup granulated sugar, ½ cup packed brown sugar, ¾ cup (additional) granulated sugar and 6 tablespoons more cocoa. Tap the jar to settle ingredients into layers. Add ½ cup chopped walnuts and ¼ cup *each* white and semisweet chocolate chips. Close lid on jar.

BAKING BROWNIES: Heat oven to 350°F. Grease a 9-inch square baking pan. Whisk brownie mix in a bowl. Stir in ½ cup melted butter; 3 large eggs, beaten and ½ teaspoon vanilla extract. Spread batter into the prepared pan. Bake 35 to 38 minutes, until a toothpick inserted in center has a few crumbs clinging to it. Cool on a wire rack. Makes 12 brownies.

clever cutters

Sources for a variety of fanciful cookie cutters:

VICTOR TRADING COMPANY offers more than 1,200 handmade cookie cutters, including reindeer and doves; many are reproductions of historic cutter designs. For a list, send $1 to: Victor Trading Company, 114 South Third Street/P.O. Box 43, Victor, CO 80860-0053. Also at www.VictorTradingCo.com.

COOKIECUTTERFACTORY.COM: Browse this website for more than 600 cookie cutters, including musical instrument shapes.

spiced rudolph cookies

These festive cookies have all the wonderful spices you think of at Christmastime. The recipes comes to us from BB and Spike Pearson, co-owners of Nonna's Bakery in Denver, Colorado. During the hectic holiday season, BB and Spike prepare 30 pounds of dough at a time, then roll, cut out and freeze the reindeer shapes to bake fresh every day. Nice and crisp, they're perfect for mailing to loved ones. Pictured on page 288.

Prep time: 1 hour plus chilling and decorating
Baking time: 10 to 12 minutes per batch

5¾ cups all-purpose flour
1 tablespoon ginger
2 teaspoons baking soda
½ teaspoon ground cloves
1 cup butter or margarine
1 cup firmly packed brown sugar
1 cup light molasses
2 teaspoons vinegar
2 large egg yolks
   Decorative Icing (see recipe, page 318)
   Red cinnamon candies

1. Combine flour, ginger, baking soda and cloves in a large bowl. Heat butter, brown sugar, molasses

and vinegar in a medium saucepan over medium heat until butter has melted and sugar dissolves. Remove from heat. Pour butter mixture into flour mixture and stir until well blended. Add the egg yolks and stir until smooth. Let stand 15 minutes.

2. Divide dough into quarters. While still warm, roll each piece of dough between 2 sheets of waxed paper until ⅛-inch thickness. Refrigerate on cookie sheets 1 hour or overnight.

3. Heat oven to 325°F. Lightly grease 2 large cookie sheets. Remove waxed paper and cut out dough with a floured 4-inch reindeer-shaped cookie cutter. Transfer cut-outs ½ inch apart to prepared cookie sheets. Bake 10 to 12 minutes, until crisp. Transfer to wire racks and cool completely. Repeat with remaining dough, rerolling and cutting scraps. Decorate as desired with icing and candies. Makes 6½ dozen cookies.

Per cookie: 100 calories, 2.5 g total fat, 1.5 g saturated fat, 12 mg cholesterol, 60 mg sodium, 19 g carbohydrates, 1 g protein, 17 mg calcium, 0 g fiber

chocolate almond cookies

Our recipe for these nutty chocolate bites, known as "Brun de Bale" in Switzerland, comes from Florence Quinn. She's Assistant Pastry Chef at Boulangerie Bay Bread in San Francisco, California. The cookies stand overnight to dry before baking, so they are crisp outside but soft and chewy in the center. Pictured on page 286.

Prep time: 35 minutes plus standing and decorating
Baking time: 5 minutes per batch

2 cups whole blanched almonds, toasted and ground
1⅓ cups plus 1 tablespoon granulated sugar
2 tablespoons flour
1 teaspoon cinnamon
¼ teaspoon salt
3½ ounces bittersweet or semisweet chocolate squares, melted (see tip, page 259)
2 large egg whites
GLAZE:
¾ cup confectioners' sugar
3 to 5 teaspoons water

¼ teaspoon vanilla extract

3 drops almond extract

■

Decorative Icing (see recipe, page 318)

1. Line 3 cookie sheets with parchment paper or foil. Combine almonds, sugar, flour, cinnamon and salt in a large bowl. Add melted chocolate and stir until well combined (mixture will be very dry).

2. Beat egg whites in a mixer bowl to firm peaks. Fold whites into chocolate-nut mixture with a rubber spatula just until blended (dough will be stiff). Divide dough in half; wrap 1 piece of dough in plastic wrap; set aside. Roll other dough half between 2 sheets of waxed paper until a scant ¼-inch thickness. Cut out with a 2-inch star-shaped cutter. Transfer cut-outs 1 inch apart to prepared cookie sheets. Repeat with remaining dough, rerolling and cutting scraps. Let stand, uncovered, 4 hours or overnight to dry.

3. Heat oven to 425°F. Bake cookies, 1 sheet at a time, 5 minutes, until cookies feel crisp on top. Transfer to wire racks and cool completely.

4. *Make glaze:* Combine all the glaze ingredients in a small bowl. Brush tops of cookies with glaze and let stand until glaze sets, about 20 minutes. Decorate as desired with icing. Transfer cookies to an airtight container and let stand overnight. Makes about 10½ dozen cookies.

Per cookie: 45 calories, 1.5 g total fat, 0.5 g saturated fat, 0 mg cholesterol, 6 mg sodium, 8 g carbohydrates, 1 g protein, 8 mg calcium, 0 g fiber

linzer cookies

When the customers at Ambrosia Patisserie in Barrington, Illinois, find this classic Viennese cookie in the case, it's a sweet reminder that the holiday season is close at hand! The recipe comes from Deborah and Richard Rivera, co-owners of the patisserie. Pictured on page 286.

Prep time: 1 hour plus standing and decorating
Baking time: 8 to 10 minutes per batch
Microwave used

2 cups all-purpose flour

¾ cup toasted, skinned hazelnuts (see note, page 258), ground

1 teaspoon cinnamon

½ teaspoon baking powder

⅛ teaspoon ground cloves

¾ cup butter, softened (no substitutes)

⅔ cup sugar

1 large egg

1 teaspoon grated lemon peel

⅓ cup white chocolate chips

⅓ cup semisweet chocolate chips

½ cup seedless raspberry jam

1. Heat oven to 375°F. Line 2 cookie sheets with parchment paper.

2. Combine flour, hazelnuts, cinnamon, baking powder and cloves in a large bowl. Beat butter and sugar in a mixer bowl until light and fluffy, about 3 minutes. Beat in egg and lemon peel. At low speed, beat in flour mixture just until combined.

3. Divide dough into thirds. Roll each piece of dough between 2 sheets of lightly floured waxed paper until ⅛-inch thickness. Refrigerate until firm, 10 minutes. Uncover and cut out with 3-inch horn-, saxophone- or cello-shaped cookie cutter. Transfer cut-outs to prepared cookie sheets. With a 1-inch round cookie cutter, cut out centers of half of the unbaked cookies. Reserve scraps. Bake cookies 8 to 10 minutes, just until golden brown on edges. Transfer cookies to wire racks to cool. Repeat process with remaining dough, rerolling and cutting scraps.

4. Microwave white chocolate chips in a small microwaveproof bowl on HIGH 1 minute 30 seconds. Microwave semisweet chocolate in another microwaveproof bowl on HIGH 1 minute. Let cool 5 minutes. Spoon into 2 small resealable plastic storage bags; cut a very small hole in 1 corner of each bag.

5. Decoratively pipe chocolates on top of each cookie with cut-out. Let stand 30 minutes, until chocolate sets. Spread ¾ teaspoon jam on top of each cookie without a cut-out. Top each jam cookie with a cut-out cookie. Makes about 1½ dozen.

Per cookie: 180 calories, 10 g total fat, 5 g saturated fat, 24 mg cholesterol, 77 mg sodium, 22 g carbohydrates, 2 g protein, 24 mg calcium, 1 g fiber

decorative icing

Rely on this simple icing for all your holiday and special-occasion sweet decorations:

COMBINE 1 box (1 lb.) confectioners' sugar, 3 tablespoons meringue powder* and 6 tablespoons cold water in a mixer bowl. Beat at medium speed until smooth. Increase speed to high and beat 5 minutes, until thick and smooth, adding up to 1 tablespoon more cold water, if necessary, until icing is a piping consistency.

TINT THE FROSTING, if desired. Paste food colors provide the most vibrant hues. Because they are concentrated, you won't need to use much. Divide the white icing into separate bowls for each color. Dab paste color into the icing with a toothpick. Mix with a spoon until well blended, gradually adding dabs of paste until desired color is attained.

Note: Meringue powder can be found in supermarkets, specialty baking stores and through baking mail-order sources.

snowman sugar cookies

These adorable snowmen are by far the most popular Christmas item at the Beaverton Bakery in Beaverton, Oregon. They're created in the hand-cut cookie department by owner and culinary artist, Carrie Ann Schubert, and her staff of six full-time decorators. Pictured on page 286.

Prep time: 35 minutes plus chilling and decorating
Baking time: 10 to 12 minutes per batch
Microwave used

- 3½ **cups all-purpose flour**
- ¼ **teaspoon salt**
- ⅔ **cup butter, softened (no substitutes)**
- ⅓ **cup vegetable shortening**
- ¾ **cup sugar**

- 1 **large egg**
- 1 **large egg yolk**
- 1 **teaspoon vanilla extract**
- 5 **ounces white chocolate squares, melted (see tip, page 259)**
- 4 **ounces semisweet chocolate squares, melted (see tip, page 259)**
- ½ **cup blue confectionery coating disks***
- ¼ **cup red confectionery coating disks***
- ¼ **cup green confectionery coating disks***
- ¼ **cup orange confectionery coating disks***
- ½ **teaspoon powdered blue food color****

1. Combine flour and salt in a small bowl; set aside.

2. Beat butter, shortening and sugar in a large mixer bowl on medium speed until light and fluffy, 2 to 3 minutes. At low speed, beat in egg and egg yolk, 1 at a time, until blended. Beat in vanilla. Beat in flour mixture just until combined. Gather dough into a ball; divide in half. Flatten each into a disk. Wrap and refrigerate 2 hours or overnight.

3. Heat oven to 350°F. Lightly grease 2 large cookie sheets.

4. On a lightly floured surface, roll 1 piece of dough to ⅛-inch thickness. (Keep remaining dough refrigerated.) Uncover and cut out with a 3- or 4-inch snowman-shaped cookie cutter. Transfer cut-outs with a spatula to prepared cookie sheets. Bake 10 to 12 minutes, until golden brown at edges. Transfer to wire racks and cool completely. Repeat with remaining dough, rerolling and cutting scraps.

5. With a small spatula, spread melted white chocolate to the edges of each cookie; let stand 1 hour until chocolate sets. Dip top of each cookie in semisweet chocolate for hat. Spoon remaining semisweet chocolate into a small, resealable plastic storage bag. Microwave blue, red, green and orange confectionery coating disks in 4 separate small microwaveproof bowls on LOW (30 percent power) 4 minutes for blue and 2½ minutes for other colors, until melted. Cool slightly.

6. Stir powdered blue food color into melted blue coating. Spoon each color into 4 small plastic storage bags. Snip 1 tiny corner of each bag and decoratively pipe cookies as desired. Let stand 1 hour until set. Makes 3½ dozen cookies.

Note: Can be found at Wilton Enterprises
(800) 794-5866.

**Note:* Can be found at New York Cake and Baking
Distributors (800) 942-2539.

Per cookie: 155 calories, 8.5 g total fat, 5 g saturated fat,
18 mg cholesterol, 54 mg sodium, 19 g carbohydrates,
2 g protein, 14 mg calcium, 0 g fiber

zimtstern

*You don't have to be German to become addicted to
Claudia Cooper's exceptional German cookies and
pastries. Born in Munich, Claudia had always dreamed
of coming to the United States as a top-notch pastry chef.
Zimtstern are classic cinnamon star cookies "and
considered a baking accomplishment among grandmother
circles back home," says Claudia, co-owner of the
Guglhupf Bakery & Patisserie in Durham, North
Carolina. The nut dough is a bit sticky, so make sure it's
thoroughly chilled before rolling and cutting it into shapes.
The dough is also very forgiving, so feel free to use as much
confectioners' sugar as necessary for easy handling.
Pictured on page 287.*

Prep time: 30 minutes plus chilling and decorating
Baking time: 12 to 13 minutes per batch

1⅓	**cups hazelnuts, toasted and skinned (see note, page 258)**
1	**cup whole blanched almonds, toasted**
1	**cup granulated sugar**
½	**cup packed almond paste**
½	**cup packed chopped candied lemon peel**
½	**cup packed chopped candied orange peel**
1	**tablespoon cinnamon**
¼	**teaspoon salt**
2	**large egg whites**
¼	**cup confectioners' sugar, for rolling dough**

MERINGUE TOPPING:

2	**large egg whites**
1	**box (1 lb.) confectioners' sugar, divided**

1. Process hazelnuts, almonds, granulated sugar,
almond paste, lemon and orange peels, cinnamon
and salt in a food processor until finely ground.
Add egg whites and process, pulsing until dough
begins to clump and come together, 30 seconds.
Transfer dough to a work surface and shape into a
rectangle; wrap in plastic wrap and refrigerate
4 hours. *(Can be made ahead. Refrigerate up to
4 days.)*

2. Heat oven to 300°F. Line 2 large cookie sheets
with parchment paper. Divide dough in half.
Between 2 sheets of waxed paper dusted with
confectioners' sugar, roll 1 piece of dough into a
12×8-inch rectangle. Cut rectangle crosswise into
twelve 1-inch-wide strips; then cut strips diagonally
at 1-inch intervals to form diamonds. Arrange
½ inch apart on prepared cookie sheets. Repeat
with remaining dough, rerolling and cutting scraps.

3. *Make meringue topping:* Beat egg whites and
3 cups of the confectioners' sugar in a mixer bowl
on low speed just until combined. At high speed,
beat meringue to soft peaks, 5 minutes. Beat in
remaining confectioners' sugar (about 1 cup) to
very stiff peaks, 2 to 3 minutes more.

4. Spoon a small amount of the meringue into
a pastry bag fitted with a ¼-inch star tip.
Decoratively pipe meringue over diamonds.
Bake 12 to 13 minutes, until dough is slightly firm
and meringue is hardened (just barely tinged with
color). Transfer cookies to wire racks; cool. Repeat
with remaining diamonds and meringue. Transfer
cookies to an airtight container and let stand
overnight. *(Can be made ahead. Store at room
temperature up to 1 month.)* Makes 12 dozen.

Per cookie: 45 calories, 1.5 g total fat, 0 g saturated fat,
0 mg cholesterol, 6 mg sodium, 7 g carbohydrates,
1 g protein, 7 mg calcium, 0 g fiber

test kitchen tip

cookies in store

Most of our cookies can be stored at room
temperature for just a few days before they lose
their fresh-baked flavor. For longer storage,
freezing is best. To freeze, place cookies
between sheets of waxed paper in airtight
freezer containers. Seal and label. Freeze
cookies up to 1 month. Thaw at room
temperature in a single layer about 15 minutes.

parmesan flats

Make a pretty gift package of these delicious crispy breads by wrapping them carefully in festively colored plastic food wrap. Then place them in a large holiday cookie tin alongside a can of purchased gourmet pâté for a scrumptious surprise.

Prep time: 20 minutes
Baking time: 9 to 11 minutes per batch

- 2½ to 3 cups all-purpose flour
- 1 cup whole wheat flour
- 1 package active dry yeast
- 2 teaspoons salt
- 1½ cups warm water (110°F. to 120°F.)
- 2 cups coarsely shredded Parmesan cheese, divided
- 1 teaspoon freshly ground pepper, divided
- ¼ teaspoon ground red pepper, divided
- 4 teaspoons sesame seeds, divided

1. Combine 2½ cups of the all-purpose flour, the whole wheat flour, yeast and salt in a bowl. Add warm water and stir vigorously until dough pulls away from side of the bowl.

2. Heat oven to 400°F. Grease 2 large cookie sheets. Knead dough until smooth and elastic, 8 to 10 minutes, adding just enough of the remaining ½ cup all-purpose flour to keep dough from sticking. Divide into 4 pieces.

3. Roll 1 piece of dough to a 20×9-inch rectangle. Cut rectangle into eight 9×2½-inch strips. Arrange strips on cookie sheets; sprinkle strips evenly with ½ cup of the Parmesan cheese, ¼ teaspoon of the pepper, pinch red pepper and 1 teaspoon of the sesame seeds.

4. Bake 9 to 11 minutes, until flats are golden brown (with some darker brown spots). Transfer to a wire rack and cool completely. Repeat process with remaining dough, cheese, seasonings and seeds. *(Can be made ahead. Store in an airtight container up to 1 week.)* Makes 32 flats.

Per flat: 80 calories, 2 g total fat, 1 g saturated fat, 4 mg cholesterol, 239 mg sodium, 12 g carbohydrates, 4 g protein, 76 mg calcium, 1 g fiber

asian-style vinegar

There may be many flavored vinegars on the market, but our homemade version truly dazzles the taste buds with its unique combination of rice vinegar, fresh ginger, chiles, coriander and cilantro. It makes a great salad dressing or marinade for chicken—as well as a memorable gift. Wrap the bottle in colorful tissue paper and attach a note that includes serving and storage suggestions.

Prep time: 15 minutes plus standing
Cooking time: 6 minutes

- 2 lemons
- 1 (6-inch) piece fresh ginger, peeled and sliced
- 2 green jalapeño or serrano chiles, halved lengthwise and seeded (see tip, page 15)
- 2 red jalapeño or serrano chiles, halved lengthwise and seeded (see tip, page 15)
- 4 teaspoons coriander seeds, toasted
- 4 cloves garlic, halved
- 8 large sprigs fresh cilantro
- 5 cups unseasoned Japanese rice vinegar or white wine vinegar

1. Cut long strips of lemon peel with a vegetable peeler.

2. With a chopstick or skewer, divide and insert lemon peel, ginger slices, green and red chiles, coriander seeds, garlic halves and cilantro sprigs into four 12-ounce clean glass bottles. Divide and slowly pour vinegar into bottles to fill.

3. Cover each bottle tightly with a nonmetallic lid (or cover each with plastic wrap and tightly seal a metal lid). Allow vinegar to stand in cool, dark place overnight. *(Can be made ahead. Store up to 1 month.)* Makes 4 (12 oz.) bottles.

Per tablespoon: 1 calorie, 0 g total fat, 0 g saturated fat, 0 mg cholesterol, 0 mg sodium, 0 g carbohydrates, 0 g protein, 1 mg calcium, 0 g fiber

nutrition information

To help you plan well-balanced meals, calorie and nutrient analyses appear at the end of each of our recipes.

how we analyze

- When a recipe gives a choice of ingredients, such as butter or margarine, we use the first ingredient mentioned when figuring the analysis.

- When the recipe gives a range in the amount of an ingredient, we average the two amounts. For example, if a recipe calls for ½ to 1 lb. of boneless beef top loin steak, we use ¾ pound when figuring the analysis.

- The analysis does not include optional ingredients.

- When there is a range in the amount of servings a recipe yields, the nutrition analysis is based on the average of the two numbers. For example, if a recipe serves 4 to 6, the analysis is based on 5 servings.

- When milk is a recipe ingredient, the analysis is calculated using 2-percent (reduced-fat) milk.

- Nutrition values are rounded to the nearest whole number, with the exception of calories, which are rounded to the nearest 5 calories, and total fat and saturated fat, which are rounded to the nearest .5 grams.

daily goal

The dietary guidelines below are nutrient levels suggested for moderately active adults. While there's no harm in occasionally going over or under these guidelines, maintaining a balanced diet can help you maintain good health.

	WOMEN	MEN
Calories	2,000	2,500
Total fat	60 g or less	70 g or less
Saturated fat	20 g or less	23 g or less
Cholesterol	300 mg or less	300 mg or less
Sodium	2,400 mg or less	2,400 mg or less
Carbohydrates	250 g or more	250 g or more
Protein	55 g to 90 g	55 g to 90 g
Calcium	1,000 mg	1,000 mg
Fiber	20 g to 35 g	20 g to 35 g

low-fat recipes

In planning a healthy diet, it's a good idea to try to keep the percentage of calories from fat to no more than 30 percent. To help you choose recipes that are low in fat, some of our recipes have been flagged with a low-fat symbol. This means that one serving of the recipe contains less than 3 grams of fat per 100 calories.

substitutions in a pinch

It's always best to use the exact ingredients a recipe calls for. But for those times when that's not possible, here are a few substitution ideas. Because they may affect the success of the recipe, use them only in a pinch.

BAKING POWDER
For 1 teaspoon: Use ½ teaspoon cream of tartar plus ¼ teaspoon baking soda

BOK CHOY
Use equal amount spinach, broccolini, or napa cabbage

BREADCRUMBS, PLAIN DRY
For 1 cup: Use ¾ cup cracker crumbs

BROTH, BEEF OR CHICKEN
For 1 cup: Use 1 bouillon cube or 1 teaspoon granules mixed with 1 cup boiling water

BUTTERMILK
For 1 cup: Use 1 tablespoon lemon juice or vinegar plus enough milk to make 1 cup (let stand 5 minutes before using); or 1 cup plain yogurt

CAKE FLOUR
For 1 cup: Use 1 cup minus 2 tablespoons all-purpose flour

CANADIAN BACON
Use equal amount smoked lean ham slices

CAPERS
Use equal amount chopped pitted green olives

CATFISH
Use equal amount of red snapper or sea trout

CHOCOLATE CHIPS
For 1 cup: Use 1 cup chopped semisweet chocolate squares

CONFECTIONERS' SUGAR
For 1 cup: Whirl 1 cup granulated sugar and 1 tablespoon cornstarch in a food processor until powdery

CORNSTARCH
For 1 tablespoon: Use 2 tablespoons all-purpose flour

CORN SYRUP
For 1 cup: Use 1 cup granulated sugar plus ¼ cup water

CURRANTS (DRIED)
Use equal amount dark seedless raisins

EGGS
For each whole egg, use 2 egg whites; 2 egg yolks; or ¼ cup frozen egg product, thawed

ESPRESSO POWDER
Use equal amount instant coffee crystals

FIVE-SPICE POWDER
Combine 4 teaspoons black peppercorns (preferably Szechuan), 1 tablespoon cinnamon, 2 teaspoons fennel seeds, 2 teaspoons anise or 6 star anise and ½ teaspoon cloves. Blend in a spice or coffee grinder until powdery. Measure amount needed.

FRUIT-FLAVORED LIQUEUR
Use equal amount fruit juice that has the same flavor of the liqueur called for

HERBS
To substitute dried herbs for fresh: For 1 tablespoon snipped fresh herb, use ½ to 1 teaspoon dried herb, crushed.
To substitute fresh herbs for dried herbs: Generally, triple the amount of dried herb called for. Add fresh herbs toward the end of cooking time; the exception is rosemary, which can withstand a long cooking time.

substitutions in a pinch

GARLIC
For 1 small clove: Use ⅛ teaspoon garlic powder

FRESH GINGER (GINGERROOT)
For 1 teaspoon grated fresh ginger (gingerroot): Use ¼ teaspoon ground ginger

GRAHAM CRACKER CRUMBS
Use equal amount vanilla wafer crumbs

GRUYÈRE CHEESE
Use equal amount Swiss cheese

HALF-AND-HALF OR LIGHT CREAM
For 1 cup: Use 1 tablespoon melted butter or margarine plus enough whole milk to make 1 cup

HAZELNUTS
Use equal amount blanched almonds

KALAMATA OLIVES
Use equal amount other brine-cured olives

LEMON JUICE
For 1 teaspoon: Use ½ teaspoon vinegar

LEMON OR ORANGE PEEL, GRATED
Use a few drops lemon or orange extract

LENTILS
Use equal amount green split peas; cook longer

MAPLE SYRUP
For 1 cup: Use 1 cup brown sugar syrup or dark corn syrup and a few drops maple extract

MASCARPONE CHEESE
Use equal amount whipped cream cheese

NUTMEG
Use equal amount mace

RIGATONI
Use equal amount penne, ziti or other tube-shaped pasta

ROMANO CHEESE
Use equal amount Parmesan cheese

SEMISWEET CHOCOLATE SQUARES
For each ounce: Use 3 tablespoons semisweet chocolate chips. Or use 1 ounce unsweetened chocolate plus 1 tablespoon sugar

SWEET BAKING CHOCOLATE SQUARES
(Also known as German chocolate). For 4 ounces: Use ¼ cup unsweetened cocoa plus ⅓ cup sugar and 3 tablespoons shortening

SUGAR (GRANULATED)
For 1 cup: Use one cup of firmly packed brown sugar or 2 cups confectioners' sugar

TERIYAKI SAUCE
For ¼ cup: Use ¼ cup soy sauce plus 1 tablespoon brown sugar

TOMATO SAUCE
For 2 cups: Use ¾ cup tomato paste plus 1 cup water

WATERCRESS
Use equal amount arugula or chicory

WORCESTERSHIRE SAUCE
Use equal amount steak sauce

YELLOW SUMMER SQUASH
Use equal amount zucchini

d-e

f-g

q-r

S

month-by-month index

january

february

march

april

may